# PETERSON'S

D1245712

# Guide ♂ College Visits

**HOW TO MAKE
THE MOST
OUT OF YOUR
CAMPUS VISITS**

**PETERSON'S**
Princeton, New Jersey

**About Peterson's**

Peterson's is the country's largest educational information/communications company, providing the academic, consumer, and professional communities with books, software, and online services in support of lifelong education access and career choice. Well-known references include Peterson's annual guides to private schools, summer programs, colleges and universities, graduate and professional programs, financial aid, international study, adult learning, and career guidance. Peterson's Web site at petersons.com is the only comprehensive—and most heavily traveled—education resource on the Internet. The site carries all of Peterson's fully searchable major databases and includes financial aid sources, test-prep help, job postings, direct inquiry and application features, and specially created Virtual Campuses for every accredited academic institution and summer program in the U.S. and Canada that offers in-depth narratives, announcements, and multimedia features.

Visit Peterson's Education Center on the Internet (World Wide Web) at
http://www.petersons.com

Copyright © 1998 by Peterson's

All rights reserved. No part of this book may be reproduced, stored in a retrieval system, or transmitted, in any form or by any means—electronic, mechanical, photocopying, recording, or otherwise—except for citations of data for scholarly or reference purposes with full acknowledgment of title, edition, and publisher and written notification to Peterson's prior to such use.

ISSN 1099-6540
ISBN 0-7689-0039-5

Printed in the United States of America

10 9 8 7 6 5 4 3 2 1

# Contents

# The College Visit: An Overview

**Dawn B. Sova, Ph.D.**

Dr. Sova currently teaches writing at Montclair State University. A former newspaper reporter and columnist, as well as the author of eight books and numerous magazine articles, she teaches creative and research writing, as well as scientific and technical writing, newswriting, and journalism. Her research on how to conduct a college visit was reinforced in practice by her recent experiences in visiting colleges with her son who is now an undergraduate at Cornell University.

# The Whats and Whys of College Visits

A campus visit is a key element in choosing the right college. No matter what anyone might tell you about a college and its surroundings, only you can determine what feels right for you. That's why, at the least, you should visit every school to which you apply.

Just like students, all colleges have unique personalities that can't be captured in catalogs or promotional videotapes. Even your best friend can't really be certain where you would be happiest studying and socializing for four years of your life. Choosing a college is a big decision that requires more than catalog shopping—and a lot more than secondhand information. Taking a test visit allows you to judge for yourself whether or not the campus layout, social atmosphere, student body, academic facilities, and campus dynamics fit your style. Just as important, visiting a variety of campuses permits you to compare schools and helps you to become more specific in assessing your individual needs. Campus visits also provide you with opportunities to evaluate different schools to determine how closely each matches your particular set of requirements. To be effective, however, the campus visit must be well timed and planned so that you can examine all aspects of the regular routine of campus life.

## What Different Visit Options Do Colleges Offer?

Colleges welcome your visits, and most see them as a source of excellent public relations. Because a college is, after all, a business, visits by even younger students and their friends are welcome by schools that want to make as many people as possible aware of the advantages they offer. Different times of the academic year are usually devoted to attracting students at different stages in their college search. This approach is reasonable because the high school sophomore, junior, or first-semester senior is still window shopping, but the second-semester senior has already sent out applications and will use the visit to make the final decision. Smart admissions counselors arrange different types of visits for each group, and they time these visits in order to make most effective their pitch for students.

Some colleges offer only guided tours of the campus and provide, essentially, only general knowledge that already appears in the college's catalog or on the college's Web site. Such visits are the least informative and may not be worth the effort if you live several hundred miles from the college and have no other reason for making the trip. If, however, this is the only option and you have a strong interest in the college, try to make the most of the prepackaged situation.

Other colleges offer full service to prospective students by personalizing the visit. During an initial telephone call or e-mail contact, counselors will ask a student about specific interests in sports and other activities or a tentative interest in a major, then contact the specific coach, adviser, or department head and arrange for a meeting when the student visits. They may also conduct a brief informal interview in which they assess the student and begin that student's file, even if that student has not yet applied. Keep this in mind when scheduling visits.

What other options might you find? While some colleges shy away from allowing prospective students to visit classes, others enthusiastically assign student guides to take visitors through a day of classes. The college arranges for permission from agreeable instructors.

You may also find that some colleges arrange for a student "angel" whom you can contact before you visit. Many questions come up, and you can save a lot of time by getting answers in advance. Of course, colleges choose their student "angels" carefully. They must know a lot about the college and they are expected to present a favorable impression. So don't expect to hear any dark secrets. Once again, even if this option is not offered by the college, ask the admissions counselor about contacting a student beforehand. You can cover a lot of territory by e-mail that will allow you to make the physical visits more valuable.

## What Goals Do Colleges Have for Campus Visits?

Colleges want to favorably impress student visitors and their parents. Even if most visitors decide against a given school because they find it unsuitable, good impressions are important when it comes to attracting other students who *may* be a good match.

Schools have clear goals for campus visits, and they do their best to control when and how visitors see what they have to offer. To do this, admissions officers frequently manipulate student callers into scheduling visits during specific weeks or weekends when special events are planned. Although such visits can be fun, because colleges go all out and use such events as another means of recruitment, you may be better off timing your visit during less lively periods on campus.

The campus visit is a good way to impress prospective students with what a school has to offer socially. Academic offerings are usually covered by print and Web sources, but a carefully timed visit period is the ideal way for a college to hide the fact that the campus becomes a ghost town on weekends or that students enjoy few social and cultural events on campus

and in the surrounding area. That's why admissions offices usually try to arrange visits during homecoming or carnival weekends. These events can be dazzling and may even convince you that the campus has a lively social life, but that is the danger to the prospective student. The excitement of a special weekend misleads visitors into seeing the social atmosphere as being much more active than it really is.

Overall, colleges hope to gain new students through campus visits, so they always try to create the most favorable impression possible. Their goal is to recruit, and they are not required to reveal the less favorable aspects of their institution. Certainly, a student's questions should be answered honestly, but don't expect campus representatives to volunteer negative information.

## What Can You Gain from a Campus Visit?

At the least, your campus visit should give you a good idea of the size and layout of a campus, and it will allow you to examine the condition of the buildings and grounds. You might find that the colorful and glossy pictures in the catalog are decades old and that the promised modern facilities are outdated. Others may not be bothered by classrooms that need paint or by dormitories and that are not clean, but either one may be a deciding factor for you.

During your visit, you might also consider the size of the campus. Large and sprawling grounds make a scenic photograph, but getting to class on time may be difficult if buildings are also widely spaced. Depending upon the time of the year, you can learn how hard getting around campus is during the winter months or how hot the classroom buildings and dormitories are in the early fall or late spring. Your visit will also allow you to examine where the dining halls are located in relation to the dormitories, a factor that can take on major importance during the winter months.

During the visit, make it a point to speak freely with current students and to attend classes so that you will have the chance to ask impromptu questions and learn how friendly people on campus really are. The canned answers of carefully selected tour guides offer little insight regarding the closeness or the alienation of students, a factor that varies widely from campus to campus.

Visiting different types of colleges while classes are in session will allow you to gain personal insight into the activities, social interaction, academic and residential facilities, and intellectual atmosphere of what might very well become your home for the next four years. Approach your task with careful forethought.

# Creating Your Visiting Strategy

Some students choose to visit colleges before they complete their applications; others wait until they have completed their applications and have a better idea of what they want from a college. Whichever route you take, you should not visit a campus without first identifying what you hope to accomplish with your visit and what information you hope to obtain—unless you can afford to waste the time.

Even if you schedule your visits after you mail your applications, you don't have to visit every college to which you apply. Many students simply can't afford the time involved and the expense of traveling great distances to see a college in which they are only moderately interested. That's why creating a visiting strategy is important.

## What Information Do You Wish to Obtain from a Visit?

Before arranging visits to several colleges, decide on the purpose of your visit and make a list of the information that you can obtain only through a visit. Before you do this, though, you have to do a little research. If the purpose of your visit is to select those colleges to which you will apply, then your research will be similar to the steps taken in choosing these colleges. Of course, some students simply "shotgun" their applications and hope that one will reach its mark, but that is very inefficient.

Because even those students who apply with care usually choose a range of schools with widely differing characteristics, the following questions are useful in identifying the information that you wish to obtain on a campus visit:

- Do you want to attend a small college or a large university?
- Do you want to attend school in a large city or small town?
- Are you interested in a public or private institution?
- Which geographical area is most attractive to you?
- Are special programs important?
- What cost range can you afford?
- How strong is your academic record?
- Are current friendships important or do you want to meet new people?
- How likely are you to be accepted by the college—and how likely are you to attend the college if you are accepted?

Once you have answered these questions, if you have not already done so, obtain catalogs from your high school guidance office or write or call the colleges, and visit their Web sites to learn more about them. University A may have sounded attractive in its promotional literature and when a friend described the social life there, but it may not offer the major in which you are interested. University B might offer your major and be desirable in many other ways, but the catalog declares that only a small percent of the students receive financial aid. University C may no longer appeal to you now that you have contacted current students and you have learned the truth about faculty-student relations.

Once you compile a list of schools that meet your criteria and learn all that you can from their catalogs, create a list of the questions that the catalogs and other contacts leave unanswered. The answers to these questions will compose the information that you should seek to obtain on a visit.

## How Can You Reach Beyond the Tour for Information?

Call the college admissions office as soon as you are ready to visit the campus, and ask for the types of arrangements offered to prospective students. Many colleges schedule regular campus tours for all prospective students during the high activity seasons, and they usually reserve structured overnight visits for only those people who have applied. Ask for details about the tour, including what it covers and how much opportunity you will have to interact with students and faculty members. Also ask if the admissions office has a list of students with whom you can correspond before making the visit.

If the college offers only a structured tour, you will have to do your own investigating to learn the answers to your questions.

Do you know students who have attended or who currently attend the college? Contact them and ask them if they will candidly answer your questions. Don't expect them to be entirely unbiased in their viewpoints, because most will judge the college on their own experiences, good or bad. Therefore, you should try to speak with several students and weigh their answers carefully.

Can you access the World Wide Web? Many college students have Web pages that you can access by simply calling up a search engine, such as AltaVista, Yahoo, Webcrawler, and others, and typing in the name of the college. The Web sites usually contain an e-mail address for contact. Some colleges also provide access to student e-mail directories through their Web sites. Most college URLs are simply http://www.collegename.edu. You might be shy about making a cold e-mail contact to ask about the college, but you will be surprised by the friendliness of the responses. Even disgruntled students will be happy to respond, if only to air their complaints to someone else. As with the in-person responses of students who attend the college, e-mail responses have to be carefully considered because some students will claim that the college is perfect in every way while others will contend that the school can do no right. You will have to use your judgment in sorting through them.

A third way in which you can reach beyond the tour for information is to locate newspaper or magazine articles that relate to the college. Such trade publications as the *Chronicle of Higher Education* report regularly on student- and faculty-related news at colleges across the nation. Large newspapers such as the *New York Times* carry stories of national interest related to the college. Some alumni magazines might be available on the Internet as will news of important issues at a given college.

These are only a few ways in which you may be able to obtain information that is not available through a structured campus tour. If you have enough time, you might call the campus newspaper office and ask to purchase several recent issues or even start a semester subscription. This will give you a feeling of the concerns and issues on the campus, but it can become expensive. You can also contact the school's local newspaper with the same request.

## How Can You Combine Visits to Several Schools?

Unless you have unlimited time and money, you will most likely try to visit several colleges on the same trip. The more distant the selections on your list, the more carefully you must plan to group together schools that are geographically close, as well as those that share common characteristics. The list that you compile after completing catalog research should come in handy now.

First list those schools that are geographically similar, a term that has widely different meanings for everyone.

- If you have limited your list to schools in the Northeastern United States, then your categories will be established by state.

- If your list contains schools on both the West and the East Coast, as well as in the South, then your list will be divided by national region.
- If you have selected only schools located within your state, then "geographically similar" refers to parts of your state.

After categorizing the colleges by location, rank them in order of preference, based on your earlier assessment of how likely a college is to accept you and the extent to which a college satisfies your requirements for a school. You might find that assigning a number to each level of satisfaction makes the process easier. Assign a "1" to schools that rank highest in meeting your requirements, a "2" to those that are moderately successful, and a "3" to those that are very low in meeting your requirements.

Does one geographical group contain schools rated "1"? If so, then consider making arrangements to visit that group first. If not, then look at a mix of "1s" and "2s," but put aside for now the schools designated with a "3." Why spend your travel time visiting a school that only moderately meets your requirements and holds any weak interest for you. If a distant region contains only one school, consider waiting to visit the school until you have been accepted and are seriously considering attending.

To minimize the possibility of confusing the characteristics of various schools when you return home, limit your visit to three campuses in one outing. Too many visits in a short amount of time will prevent you from viewing each school as a separate entity.

Once you have categorized the schools that you will visit, many other details have to be arranged.

- How will you travel to these schools? How much time do you have to make the visits?
- Can you afford to stay as long as will be needed to visit all of the colleges?

- Will admissions counselors arrange to have someone pick you up at the airport if you fly, or will you be responsible for getting to the campus?

As you answer these questions, you should also consider how many school absences you can afford. Remember that most campus visits take place during the regular academic year for colleges so that students can view the usual functioning of the college. That also means that you will have to miss school days, unless you are fortunate to be able to schedule visits when your high school is not open and the colleges are in session.

If time is limited and if resources allow, you should probably fly to the farthest school in the region, then rent a car to drive to the others. The difficulty with this plan is that many states do not allow people under the age of 21 to rent vehicles, so a parent may have to accompany you. That means taking yet another person's schedule into account. If the schools are all more than 200 miles from each other, you may have to think about regrouping your choices, extending your travel time, or delaying trips to only one school at a time. Once again, using your list will be helpful.

Identify the distance from your home of each school in the geographical categories, then identify the distance of each school from the others in each group.

- What is the farthest you will have to travel to reach the school in each group that is most distant from your home?
- How long will that trip take?
- How long will the trips between the schools within each group take?
- How much time do you have?

Combining visits to several schools is easier when your choices are within driving distance. Even then, however, you have to plan carefully. Make a good estimate of the time that you will need and plan your trip *before* you call the college admissions offices for appointments.

Make an initial call to the admissions office or consult the college Web sites to review their calendars and to obtain a clear idea of their tour and interview schedules.

- Which weeks can you visit and which weeks are not permitted?
- Which weeks are you available when the college classes are in session?
- When are tours encouraged and when are they canceled?

You might find that the second week in May is perfect in *your* schedule for a visit, but many colleges will not schedule tours then because students will be taking their final exams. Similarly, you might try to schedule a visit at a time that is convenient for you but would take place when the college is on spring break and no tours are scheduled.

Once you have a reasonable schedule worked out and have taken into account the traveling times and distances, call the colleges of your choice to set up appointments. Be aware of your time limitations and do not schedule appointments too closely together. Allow yourself travel time between colleges to avoid the embarrassment of a missed appointment. When visiting several colleges within a short space of time, if the colleges' schedules permit, save for last the school that you want most to be accepted by. In this way, you will build up experience in asking questions and gathering information. You will also build up confidence in answering questions in the interviews, even the informal interviews, that are often part of the tour package.

# Scheduling the Visit

Call the admissions office as soon as you have determined when you will be able to make the campus visit. You may feel that calling several months in advance will allow you substantial choice in arranging an appointment; however, it may not because timing is critical and availability depends upon the time of the year.

Even careful attention to the time of year may not be enough to guarantee that you will be able to schedule an appointment at the time of your choice. Colleges report that their busiest season for campus visits is the fall, when high school seniors are making their application decisions. With many college applications for regular admissions due by January 15, the requests for campus visits decrease from that date through early April, when acceptances and rejections are mailed. This less busy period might *seem* to be the ideal time for juniors and younger high school students to schedule their visits, but admissions officers caution that students should always check with each college they intend to visit. Many colleges either severely curtail or completely suspend campus tours from January through April in order to devote their energies to evaluating the hundreds and even thousands of applications they receive.

## What Questions Should You Ask the Admissions Counselors?

Once you have created a list of colleges that you wish to visit, write a letter, make a telephone call, or send an e-mail request to the admissions offices of each college for complete information regarding campus visits. Ask for an itinerary of the tour and compare what it offers with the list of questions that you compiled while researching the colleges.

If many of your questions remain unanswered by a standard tour, don't be shy in contacting the admissions offices another time and asking if you can arrange modifications or a special extension to the tour. Explain that you are serious about wanting to really learn as much about College A (and B, C, D, and E) as you can while you are on campus. Identify the areas that you would like to personalize and ask directly if admissions will provide you with someone to take you places that are not included on the standard tour.

Even if the catalogs and promotional literature do not mention such options, admissions counselors report that they do try to personalize campus visits for prospective students, when time allows. That means scheduling your visit during the less busy periods of the school year. Admissions counselors also suggest that you ask to receive a detailed map of the campus so that you can specify which facilities you wish to add to a tour.

Ask the admissions counselor to explain the full extent of the arrangements that are offered to students. Be sure to mention any special accommodations that you will need while you are on campus, and ask if the campus can meet those needs.

- Do you have special physical accessibility needs?
- Are you visually or hearing impaired and would you like to have a student with similar needs accompany you on the tour?
- Do you have special dietary needs, either religious or health-related?
- Have you a chronic health problem of which the college should be made aware if you stay overnight?

Also ask the admissions counselor if you will be able to meet students who share your special needs and interests and if you can schedule a visit during the time that specific activities of interest will occur.

To be thorough in setting up your campus visit, make a list of all the areas that you want to cover during your visit *before* you call for an appointment.

- Do you want to visit the library?
- Do you care to see the computer laboratories?
- Are you interested in the physical training facilities?

Admissions counselors also prefer that students have a clear idea of when they will be free to visit, so that they can discuss definite dates. Make a list of several dates that are convenient and offer them as possibilities when you speak with an admissions counselor.

If you call in the early fall, you may find that many of your selected dates are already taken, but remain firm in offering several choices, nonetheless. Do not just accept an appointment for a guided tour. Instead, ask if the college offers overnight stays or stays of several days in the dormitories. If it does, arrange to spend this time on campus, and ask if you can be matched with a student who has already completed at least one semester. In this way, you are more likely to receive knowledgeable answers to your questions and the student will have attended the school for enough time to form a solid impression of the academic and social life. You will learn a lot about the campus and how you fit in both academically and socially during the time in the dormitory and when eating meals with students.

Should you also ask to visit classes? Of course. Sitting through several classes can give you a feeling for average class size, teacher-student ratio, the physical condition of classrooms, difficulty in covering the campus between classes, and the nature of the classroom atmosphere in random courses. Although such behavior may be rare, a professor who exhibits hostility toward students in the presence of guests, especially prospective students, might be sending out a strong message about the relationship between students and faculty members on that campus.

The key to a successful campus visit is to be an educated consumer. Learn as much as you can *before* you call admissions office, so that you can focus your time on asking counselors the important questions that will make the campus tour valuable to you.

## Whom Else Should You Contact on Campus?

Camp tours are usually informative, but they are targeted for the general student consumer and cannot possibly cover all of the areas in which you may have questions. Don't feel that your campus visit has to be arranged and guided only by the admissions office. This is only the first step, and the usually required interview, however informal, will start your file with a college, but its arrangements do not have to be the last word regarding how you see the campus.

After you have completed your arrangements for the campus tour and verified your date and time for the interview, begin to make more specific arrangements. You can contact other people who will give you an even more accurate look at what being a student at College A *really* entails. Making additional arrangements will cost you more time and money, but you will definitely save money in the long run if you take a thorough look at the schools before committing to attend one. After calling admissions offices and arranging the initial tours for each college, decide what you would like to see and whom you would like to meet at each campus. The admissions counselors will review your file when you apply or if you have already applied, but other aspects of the college should also influence your acceptance.

In addition to making additional contacts to bolster your knowledge, use the campus visit to cultivate initial relationships with people in your future major or in extracurricular activities in which you plan to participate. Although admissions offices do not encourage such contact, they don't discourage it either. You should take steps toward additional contact when visiting any college in which you have a strong interest.

- Would you like to take a look at the music department?
- Do you intend to try out for the cheerleading squad?
- Are you interested in joining the debate team?
- Have you always wanted to major in Slavic languages but do not know anyone who has?
- Do you want to play a particular sport at the college level?

Part of the reason for extending the campus visit beyond what the admissions office offers is informational.

- A student who plans to major in music will want to schedule a visit when department recitals are being given.
- The member of a high school debate team might wish to visit the campus when the college is hosting a debate tournament in order to meet debaters at all levels.
- A student who is deeply involved in cheerleading competitions in high school will want to see the quality of the campus cheerleaders and speak with the adviser to explore the chances of making the squad.
- The student who wishes to major in a subject area that high school friends and teachers find unusual will find support for that desire by talking to professors and students majoring in that area.
- A student who hopes to go out for a specific team sport should see the current team in action and even attend practices, in addition to meeting the coach.

What are your reasons? You have many valid reasons for making specific contacts outside of the admissions office, and most of the people whom you contact will welcome your sincerity in wanting to learn more about the college and particularly about their areas of interest and expertise. Be realistic, however, and decide which of the colleges you will visit in this more thorough manner in which will simply receive the cursory experience of the preplanned campus tour. Unless you have unlimited time and money, you will not be able to visit more than two or three schools in this way. Choose the colleges in which you have the greatest interest and which you would attend if they accepted you.

To locate the names of professors, consult the college catalog or check the faculty directory on the college Web site. Some, but not all, colleges that list a student directory with e-mail addresses also group students by department. If you are interested in meeting with people in your proposed major, call the department office and ask if someone would meet with you on the day that you have an appointment for the campus tour. Be businesslike in your approach and honestly inform people of the reason for your visit and of your specific time restraints. If you do speak by phone or correspond via e-mail with faculty members, ask if you can meet with students in your proposed major area. You will be surprised to learn how eager many people are to encourage students to enter their areas of interest. You will find a much warmer welcome then you expect.

Connecting with advisers and members of activities can be more difficult because their names do not usually appear in the college catalog or on the official Web sites. If you are persistent, you can obtain the information that you need, although you will probably have to make several calls to the college to do so. Locating the names of coaches and members of athletic teams might prove the easiest, because you will probably only need to call the athletic office for information.

For other activities, your first call should be to the office that oversees student activities and organizations. Refer to the catalog and locate the pages, usually in the front and near the statements of policy and costs, that relate the extracurricular activities offered by the college. The body responsible for coordinating those activities might be identified. If it is, call that office and tell them whom you wish to contact. If, however, no office is listed, then you will have to use your ingenuity and charm. Call the general college number and ask to be connected with the Office of the Dean of Students. One connected, identify yourself as a *prospective* student and explain that you want to get in touch with the adviser of the debate team, the director of the school band, the adviser of the cheerleading squad, or anyone else who sponsors an activity in which you have an interest. Why emphasize that you are a prospective rather than a current student? While college staff members might deny it, current students are often taken for granted but *prospective* students are courted.

## When Is the Best Time to Visit?

Several considerations are important in deciding the best time for *you* to visit colleges. Before contacting admissions offices, identify where you are in the college search process. This determines your purpose for making a campus visit and the time frame in which you should visit.

- Will your visits be used to window-shop and compile a list of colleges to *consider*?
- Are you visiting campuses to decide to which schools in an already compiled list you *will* apply?
- Have you already sent out applications, and are you now assessing which colleges you might like to attend if they accept you?
- Have you already received your acceptances, and are you visiting colleges to decide which college you will attend?

Colleges are familiar with the varied reasons that students have for making campus visits, and admissions offices often vary the nature of the

campus visits offered according to the time of the year and the status of the student visitors. Students who are just browsing and compiling their lists of colleges to apply to have less urgent reasons to visit than do students who have already been accepted and who want to use the visit as a means of determining where they will spend the next four years of their lives.

From April 1 to early May—from when the acceptances are sent out to the dates that most colleges require registration deposits—many colleges reserve most of their campus visit appointments for high school seniors who have been accepted. Most students do not wait until they have been accepted before taking their first look at a college, but those who do are offered substantially different visit options. Eager to convince accepted students to enroll, colleges usually offer planned pre-admission weekends or weeks, during which high school seniors are treated to a flurry of activities and meetings aimed at convincing them to attend. Unless you are a second-semester high school senior who has already been accepted by several colleges, you will probably have to forego a visit during April.

If you are in the early steps of the application process, plan to visit during the spring of your junior year or the fall or early winter of your senior year. The campus arrangements will be less elaborate than if you visit after receiving acceptances, but you will be able to take a more leisurely look at each school that interests you. Students who save their campus visits until after the applications are sent out and who wish to avoid the April rush are limited to a less desirable time frame. Visiting any campus during the months from January through March, except those located in temperate zones, can be a depressing, if enlightening, experience. The low sunlight, possibility of snow and ice, lack of foliage, and sometimes bitter winds do reveal the worst weather conditions of a campus, and they also make the visit less appealing.

Plan your campus visit well in advance so that you can have your choice of appointments. The best time to make a first visit to a college is in the early fall, a time when most campuses are filled with busy students involved in numerous activities. Because many colleges begin classes in mid- to late-August, you may be able to visit before your high school year begins. If this is not possible, review the high school academic calendar to determine if other days are available for visits to colleges that are not too distant. Compare your calendar with the college academic calendars to avoid a visit when students are on break and only the admissions office is operating. The best and most valuable visits occur when a college campus is at the height of its academic and social activity.

The time of year that you visit is not the only important factor. Consider which day of the week you will arrive and when you will visit one or several colleges. Early in the week is best, because many campus offices close early on Fridays and the enthusiasm levels are usually lower by then. Few admissions offices schedule tours on weekends, aside from a few at mainly commuter colleges where weekend classes are common.

Schedule a solo campus visit for Monday, and plan to arrive in the area on Sunday evening in order to give yourself time to organize your thoughts. If you have planned to visit several campuses on the same trip, make all of the appointments for Monday, Tuesday, and Wednesday, if you can, even if you plan to stay in the area for a week. You can always revisit a campus informally after the initial tour when you will be relaxed because the official tours and interviews are over.

When is the best time to visit? That depends on you and your family and what information you hope to obtain from your visit. You can always make a second visit to a college and learn more about it if you feel that the first visit occurred too early in your search.

# How to Visit a Campus

The campus visit should not be a passive activity for you and your parents, and you will have to take the initiative and use all of your senses to gather information beyond that provided in the official tour. You will see many important indicators during your visit that will tell you more about the true character of a college and its students than the tour guide will reveal. Know what to look for and how to assess the importance of such indicators.

## What Should You Ask and What Should You Look For?

Your first stop on a campus visit is the admissions office, where you will probably have to wait to meet with a counselor and undergo the interview. Colleges usually plan to greet visitors later than the appointed time in order to give them the opportunity to review some of the campus information that is liberally scattered throughout the admissions waiting room. Take advantage of the time to become even more familiar with the college by arriving 15 to 30 minutes before your appointment to observe the behavior of staff members and to browse through the yearbooks and student newspapers that will be available.

If you prepare in advance, you will have already reviewed the college catalog and map of the campus. These materials familiarize you with the academic offerings and the physical layout of the campus, but the true character of the college and its students emerges in other ways.

Begin your investigation with the admissions office staff. As a student's first official contact with the college, they should make every effort to welcome prospective students and to project a friendly image.

- How do they treat you and other prospective students who are waiting? Are they friendly and willing to speak with you, or do they try their hardest to avoid eye contact and conversation?
- Are they friendly with each other and with students who enter the office, or are they curt and unwilling to help?
- Does the waiting room have a friendly feeling or is it cold and sterile?

If the admissions staff members seem indifferent to *prospective* students, there is little reason to believe that they will be warm and welcoming to current students. View such behavior as a warning to watch very carefully the interaction of others with you during the tour. An indifferent or unfriendly reception in the admissions office may be simply the first of many signs that attending this college will not be a pleasant experience.

Look through several yearbooks and see the types of activities that are actually photographed, as opposed to the activities that colleges promise in their promotional literature. Some questions are impossible to answer if the college is very large, but for small and moderately sized colleges the yearbook is a good indicator of campus activity.

- Has the number of clubs and organizations increased or decreased in the past five years?
- Do the same students appear repeatedly in activities?
- Do sororities and fraternities dominate campus activities?

- Are participants limited to one sex or one ethnic group or are the participants diverse?
- Are all activities limited to the campus, or are students involved in activities in the community?

Use what you observe in the yearbooks as a means of forming a more complete understanding of the college, but don't base your entire impression on just one facet. If time permits, look through several copies of the school newspaper, which should reflect the major concerns and interests of the students. The paper is also a good way to learn about the campus social life.

- Does the paper contain a mix of national and local news?
- What products or services are advertised?
- How assertive are the editorials?
- With what topics are the columnists concerned?
- Are movies and concerts that meet your tastes advertised or reviewed?
- What types of ads appear in the classified section?

The newspaper should be a public forum for students, and, as such, should reflect the character of the campus and of the student body. A paper that deals only with seemingly safe and well-edited topics on the editorial page and in regular feature columns might indicate administrative censorship. A lack of ads for restaurants might indicate either a lack of good places to eat or that area restaurants do not welcome student business. A limited mention of movies, concerts, or other entertainment might reveal a severely limited campus social life. Even if ads and reviews are included, you can also learn a lot about how such activities reflect your tastes.

You will have only a limited amount of time to ask questions during your initial meeting with the admissions counselor, for very few schools include a formal interview in the initial campus visit or tour. Instead, this brief meeting is often just a social nicety that allows the admissions office to begin a file for the student and to record some initial impressions. Save your questions for the tour guide and for campus members that you meet along the way.

## How Can You Assess the True Character of a College and Its Students?

Colleges do not train their tour guides to deceive prospective students, but they do caution guides to avoid unflattering topics and campus sites. Does this mean that you are condemned to see only a sugarcoated version of life on a particular college campus? Not at all, especially not if you are observant.

Most organized campus visits include such campus facilities as dormitories, dining halls, libraries, student activity and recreation centers, and the health and student services centers. Some may only be pointed out, while you will walk through others. Either way, you will find that many signs of the true character of the college emerge if you are observant.

Bulletin boards in dormitories and student centers contain a wealth of information about campus activities, student concerns, and campus groups. Read the posters, notices, and messages to learn what *really* interests students. Unlike ads in the school newspaper, posters put up by students advertise both on- and off- campus events, so they will give you an idea of what is also available in the surrounding community.

Review the notices, which may cover either campuswide events or events that concern only small groups of students. The catalog may not mention a performance group, but an individual dormitory with its own small theater may offer regular productions. Poetry readings, jam sessions, writers' groups, and other activities may be announced and show diversity of student interests on that campus.

Even the brief bulletin board messages offering objects for sale and noting objects that people want to purchase reveal a lot about a campus. Are most of the items computer related? Or do the messages specify compact discs, audio equipment, or musical instruments? Are offers to barter goods or services posted? Don't ignore the "ride wanted" messages. Students who want to share rides home during a break may specify widely diverse geographical locations. If so, then you know that the student body is not limited to only the immediate area or one locale. Other messages can also enhance your knowledge of the true character of the campus and its students.

As you walk through various buildings, examine their condition carefully.

- Is the paint peeling, and do the exteriors look worn?
- Are the exteriors and interiors of the building clean?
- Do they look well maintained?
- Is the equipment in the classrooms up-to-date or outdated?

Pay particular attention to the dormitories, especially to factors that might affect your safety. Observe the appearance of the structure, and ask about the security measures in and around the dormitories.

- Are the dormitories noisy or quiet?
- Do they seem crowded?
- How good is the lighting around each dormitory?
- Are the dormitories spread throughout the campus or are they clustered in one main area?
- Who has access to the dormitories in addition to students?
- How secure are the means by which students enter and leave the dormitory?

While you are on the subject of dormitory safety, you should also ask about campus safety. Don't expect that the guide will rattle off a list of crimes that have been committed in the past year. To obtain that information, access the recent year of issues of the *Chronicle of Higher Education* and locate its yearly report on campus

crime. Also ask the guide about safety measures that the campus police take and those that students have initiated.

- Can students request escorts to their residences late at night?
- Do campus shuttle buses run at frequent intervals all night?
- Are "blue-light" telephones liberally placed throughout the campus for students to use to call for help?
- Do the campus police patrol the campus regularly?

If the guide does not answer your questions satisfactorily, wait until after the tour to contact the campus police or traffic office for answers.

Campus tours usually just point out the health services center without taking the time to walk through. Even if you don't see the inside of the building, you should take a close look at the location of the health services center and ask the guide questions about services.

- How far is the health center from the dormitories?
- Is a doctor always on call?
- Does the campus transport sick students from their dormitories or must they walk?
- What are the operating hours of the health center?
- Does the health center refer students to the town hospital?

If the guide can't answer your questions, visit the health center later and ask someone there.

Most campus tours seem to take pride in showing students their activities centers, which may contain snack bars, game rooms, workout facilities, and other means of entertainment. Should you scrutinize this building as carefully as the rest? Of course. Outdated and poorly maintained activity equipment contributes to your total impression of the college. You should also ask about the hours, availability, and cost (no, the activities are usually *not* free) of using the bowling alleys, pool tables, air hockey tables, and other items.

As you walk through campus with the tour, also look carefully at the appearance of the students who pass. The way in which both men and women groom themselves, the way they dress, and even their physical bearing communicate a lot more than any guidebook can. If everyone seems to conform to the same look, you might feel that you would be uncomfortable at the college, however nonconformist that look might be. On the other hand, you might not feel comfortable on a campus that stresses diversity of dress and behavior, and your observations now can save you discomfort later.

- Does every student seem to wear a sorority or fraternity t-shirt or jacket?
- Is everyone of your sex sporting the latest fad haircut?
- Do all of the men or the women seem to be wearing expensive designer clothes?
- Do most of the students seem to be working hard to look outrageous in regard to clothing and hair color?
- Would you feel uncomfortable in a room full of these students?

Is appearance important to you? If it is, then you should consider very seriously if you answer *yes* to any of the above questions. You don't have to be the same as everyone else on campus, but standing out too rigorously may make you unhappy.

As you observe the physical appearance of the students, also listen to their conversations as you pass them? What are they talking about? How are they speaking? Are their voices and accents all the same, or do you hear diversity in their speech? Are you offended by their language? Think how you will feel if surrounded by the same speech habits and patterns for four years.

## Where Should You Visit on Your Own?

Your campus visit is not over when the tour ends because you will probably have many questions yet to be answered and many places to still be seen. Where you go depends upon the extent to which the organized tour covers the campus. Your tour should take you to view residential halls, health and student services centers, the gymnasium or field house, dining halls, the library, and recreational centers. If any of the facilities on this list have been omitted, visit them on your own and ask questions of the students and staff members you meet. In addition, you should step off campus and gain an impression of the surrounding community. You will probably become bored with life on campus and spend at least some time off campus. Make certain that you know what the surrounding area is like.

The campus tour leaves little time to ask impromptu questions of current students, but you can do so after the tour. Eat lunch in one of the dining halls. Most will allow visitors to pay cash to experience a typical student meal. Food may not be important to you now while you are living at home and can simply take anything you want from the refrigerator at any time, but it will be when you are away at college with a meal ticket to feed you.

- How clean is the dining hall? Consider serving tables, floors, and seating.
- What is the quality of the food?
- How big are the portions?
- How much variety do students have at each meal?
- How healthy are the food choices?

While you are eating, try to strike up a conversation with students and tell them that you are considering attending their college. Their reactions and advice can be eye-opening. Ask them questions about the academic atmosphere and the professors.

- Are the classes large or small?
- Do the majority of the professors only lecture or are tutorials and seminars common?
- Is the emphasis of the faculty career oriented or abstract?

- Do they find the teaching methods innovative and stimulating or boring and dull?
- Is the academic atmosphere pressured, lax, or somewhere in between?
- Which are the strong majors? the weak majors?
- Is the emphasis on grades or social life or a mix of both at the college?
- How hard do students have to work to receive high grades?

Current students can also give you the inside line on the true nature of the college social life. You may gain some idea through looking in the yearbook, in the newspaper, and on the bulletin boards, but students will reveal the true highs and lows of campus life. Ask them about drug use, partying, dating rituals, drinking, and anything else that may affect your life as a student.

- Which are the most popular club activities?
- What do students do on weekends? Do most go home?
- How frequently do concerts occur on campus? Ask them to name groups that have recently performed.
- How can you become involved in specific activities (name them)?
- How strictly are campus rules enforced and how severe are penalties?
- What counseling services are available?
- Are academic tutoring services available?
- Do they feel that the faculty really cares about students, especially freshmen?

You will receive the most valuable information from current students, but you will only be able to speak with them after the tour is over. And you might have to risk rejection as you try to initiate conversations with students who might not want to reveal how they feel about the campus. Still, the value of this information in making the right decision is worth the chance.

If you have the time, you should also visit the library to see just how accessible research materials are and to observe the physical layout.

The catalog usually specifies the days and hours of operation, as well as the number of volumes contained in the library and the number of periodicals to which it subscribes. A library also requires accessibility, good lighting, an adequate number of study carrels, and lounge areas for students. Many colleges have created 24-hour study lounges for students who find the residence halls too noisy for studying, although most colleges claim that they designate areas of the residences as "quiet study" areas. You may not be interested in any of this information, but when you are a student you will have to make frequent use of the campus library so you should know what is available. You should at least ask how extensive their holdings are in your proposed major area. If they have virtually nothing, you will have to spend a lot of time ordering items via interlibrary loan or making copies, which can become expensive. The ready answer of students that they will obtain their information from the Internet is unpleasantly countered by professors who demand journal articles with documentation.

Make a point of at least driving through the community surrounding the college, because you will be spending time there shopping, dining, working in a part-time job, or attending events. Even the largest and best-stocked campus will not meet all of your social and personal needs. If you can spare the time, stop in several stores to see if they welcome college students.

- Is the surrounding community suburban, urban, or rural?
- Does the community offer stores of interest, such as bookstores, craft shops, boutiques?
- Do the businesses employ college students?
- Does the community have a movie or stage theater?
- Are there several types of interesting restaurants?
- Do there seem to be any clubs that court a college clientele?

- Is the center of activity easy to walk to, or do you need a car or other transportation?

You might feel that a day is not enough to answer all of your questions, but even answering some questions will provide you with a stronger basis for choosing a college. Many students visit a college campus several times before making their decision, as you also should. Keep in mind that for the rest of your life you will be associated with the college that you attend. You will spend four years of your life at this college. The effort of spending several days to obtain the information to make your decision is worthwhile.

# Assessing It All

You should wait until you have visited most of your college choices before trying to make any major decisions whether to eliminate colleges or apply to them. Certain aspects of one college might make you uncomfortable, but you may view these aspects as normal in comparison with your observations from other colleges. Methodically organize the information that you require and keep it available for ready reference as you investigate additional colleges.

## How Should You Organize the Information Obtained?

Create separate files for each college visit and place all of the information that you obtain and all of your notes in these files. Identify each file with the name of the college, the location, and the ranking that you have given it, from "1" to "3." Your information will be more valuable if you develop priority lists before you begin your campus visits, then complete them with information that you gather from each college.

Which aspects should you list? Even if you do not address all of the same issues during each campus visit, create a uniform list to which you can refer after each visit. List the major categories of student body, academic life, social life, dining halls, recreation facilities, residences, library, and surrounding community, then create subcategories within each.

Don't expect to address all of the subcategories in each visit, but use them as guides that you might address in return visits. Suggested divisions follow:

### STUDENT BODY
- Grooming
- Clothing styles
- Interaction with strangers
- Interaction with other students
- Extracurricular interests
- Political awareness

### ACADEMIC LIFE
- Condition of classroom buildings
- Class size/faculty-student ratio
- Faculty attitudes
- Teaching styles
- Grade pressures

### SOCIAL LIFE
- Level of fraternity/social activity
- Party habits
- Drug and alcohol use
- Dating problems

### DINING HALLS
- Cleanliness of the facilities
- Abundance of food served
- Variety of food choices
- Crowdedness of dining rooms
- Friendliness of servers

### RECREATION FACILITIES
- Student activity centers
- Workout rooms/fitness centers
- Intramural sports
- Movies/theater productions
- Clubs and activities

### RESIDENCES
- Condition of buildings
- Distance of residences from dining facilities
- Distance of residences from classroom buildings and library
- External security measures
- Internal safety features

- Noise levels
- Level of privacy

## LIBRARY
- Range of facilities
- Availability of materials
- Number of volumes
- Number of periodical subscriptions
- Student lounges
- Days and hours of operation

## SURROUNDING COMMUNITY
- Distance to commercial center
- Number and types of restaurants
- Number and types of stores
- Attitude of town residents to college students
- Theaters

The notes that you make for each category should be as complete as possible and made during the visit or as soon afterward as possible. You might feel that you will remember everything that you have seen and heard, but the impressions from the colleges will begin to confuse you if you wait too long. Your answers are important, but they should be compared with your responses to other colleges and not used in isolation. Looking at the reported faculty attitudes of four colleges will mean more than simply assessing the responses made after only one visit, and the same is true of all other categories. Reviewing all of the responses allows you to put your reactions into perspective and to logically assess the importance of any one category.

## Which Colleges Should You Visit Again?

You will eliminate some of the colleges that you visit as soon as you compare them with the other colleges, because they will not compete in areas that are important to you. Don't be surprised, however, if you find that three or more colleges still seem attractive and that you need another visit to make your decision.

Should you make a second visit to every college that still interests you? More important, do you feel that you *need* to make another visit to a college in order to make the right decision? If so, then you should visit the campus again, if only to fill in information that you did not obtain during the first trip. You should also make a second visit to colleges where you were unable to see all of the facilities that interest you or if you were unable to speak freely with students.

Your initial campus visit can convince you that a college is completely wrong for you and, if that happens, cross if off your list. If, however, you remain undecided, take the time to view the areas that leave you unsure of your choice.

# Following Up

Your connection with a college does not end when you return home, no matter what your impression might be. Whether or not you wish to attend the school, you should take the time to follow up.

### What Is Post-Visit Etiquette?

Use the same good manners in dealing with the colleges that you use in personal social situations. Whether or not you feel that the admissions office provided you with a complete tour and sufficient information, and whether or not you have decided against attending a college, write a letter to thank people specifically for taking the time to meet with you. Beyond common courtesy, this also leaves the college officials with a positive view of you and the letter will most likely be placed in your file. Will it make the difference between being accepted or rejected? No one can say. Still, to take the time to acknowledge the effort, however minimal, of the college to organize a campus tour and to provide other information is a show of courtesy that cannot hurt your chances. Communicate with and thank students with whom you spoke, because your first months of school will be significantly less lonely should you attend that college if you cultivate friendships in advance.

Write to the admissions office to thank counselors for their time, even if your experience was less than pleasant. You may have contact with them in the future and there is no reason not to leave them with a good impression.

### What Should You Plan for a Return Visit?

Return visits should be made if you are undecided about either choosing or eliminating a college from consideration or if you feel that you did not obtain enough needed information during the initial visit. Once again, contact the admissions office and write directly to the counselor with whom you spoke on your first visit. Explain that having visited other colleges you now have made College A one of your final choices and state that you want to take a more in-depth look at the college. Ask if you can stay in one of the dormitories for several nights and attend several days of classes. At this time, ask any questions that were not answered in the first visit.

Before you make the return visit, review your priority lists and write down all of the areas that need further investigation. This is also a good time to contact students with whom you spoke or communicated by e-mail and arrange to spend additional time together, perhaps at campus social events.

On your return to the campus, you will feel more comfortable exploring on your own. Use this time wisely to answer remaining questions so that you can choose the college that is right for you.

# How to Use This Guide

The following section provides information on the profiles, including eligibility criterion, research procedures, and using and understanding the profiles, and a brief description about the TripMaker™ CD-ROM.

# About the Profiles

*Peterson's Guide to College Visits* provides students and parents with the most comprehensive, up-to-date guide to visiting college and university campuses: schedules, types of visits available, visit policies, and sights that visitors should make a point to see whether on or off campus. A special edition of Rand McNally's TripMaker™ CD-ROM provides point-to-point maps, route planning, driving instructions, and information about lodging, restaurants, and local sights between any location in the U.S. and any college or university in the U.S.

## Which Schools Are Profiled?

The essential criterion for inclusion in this publication is that a college be a baccalaureate degree–granting institution accredited by an accrediting body recognized by either the U.S. Department of Education or the Council for Higher Education Accreditation.

Because Peterson's aim is to produce a guide that can be easily packed, carried, and used on a trip, coverage has been limited.

Colleges do not universally record the number of visitors, and the data definitions vary from school to school. So, data from which to make valid comparisons among schools does not exist. In place of this missing data, Peterson's has developed a formula to quantify the attractiveness of a college as a visit target. The formula that we have used is the product of the college's number of applicants multiplied by the percentage of out-of-state students at that college.

Why this particular formula? First, a correlation between the number of applicants to a college and the number of its visitors is apparent. However, we believe that this factor requires a bit of modification because of the common practice among applicants of sending applications to the colleges they "really" want to go to and to one or more "safe colleges" with entrance requirements that may be easier for the applicant to meet or with lower tuition rates. Such a safe college typically is a local public college or university, and we assume that a family's interest in visiting these colleges is weaker than in visiting a college that may be more focal in a student's aspirations. Our belief is that a disproportionate number of students from beyond a college's state borders indicates that the college has an intrinsic appeal based on factors other than geography. So we factored in the percentage of out-of-state students at a college. Despite this, every first-tier state university, as well as a many second-level ones, were among the almost 750 colleges that we surveyed through Peterson's College Visits Survey in February and March 1998.

The information for the 487 colleges profiled in *Peterson's Guide to College Visits* was obtained from the colleges themselves. Those colleges that completed our survey are profiled. Any college that is not in this guide but likely has a combined number of applicants and percentage of out-of-state students to place them among the top 750 colleges in the U.S. should send the name and address of the proper person to contact to complete our College Visits questionnaire to the Research Analyst, College Visits, Peterson's, 202 Carnegie Center, P.O. Box 2123, Princeton, NJ 08543-2123; telephone: 609-243-9111 Ext. 448; fax: 609-520-1360; e-mail: danm@petersons.com. If the college does indeed meet our criterion, we will be certain that the designated individual receives our survey mailing.

The profiles are organized alphabetically by state. If you prefer to locate a school by its name, an alphabetical index of school names appears at the back of the book.

## How to Use the Profiles

The college profiles in this guide can be put to several uses.

### Contacting Colleges Prior to a Visit

The first paragraph in each profile contains the college's visit contact. If provided by the college, this paragraph contains the name of the individual in charge of visits, his or her title, mailing address, telephone number, fax number, e-mail address, Web site address, and visit location, usually the building on campus from which a campus visit begins.

### Selecting Colleges to Visit

Under the heading Quick Facts, you will find the factors that are often basic in a prospective student's consideration of a school.

- the institution's total enrollment
- the number of undergraduate students enrolled
- the entrance difficulty designated by the college; there are five categories: *most difficult*—more than 75 percent of entering students are in the top 10 percent of their high school class, more than 75 percent score more than 1310 on the SAT or more than 29 on the ACT, 40 percent or more of applicants are denied; *very difficult*—more than 50 percent are in the top 10 of their high school class, more than 50 percent score more than 1230 on the SAT or more than 26 on the ACT, 15 to 40 percent of applicants are denied; *moderately difficult*—more than 75 percent are in the top 50 percent of their high school class, more than 75 percent score more than 1010 on the SAT or more than 18 on the ACT, 5 to 15 percent of applicants are denied; *minimally difficult*—most students are not in the top 50 percent of their high school class,

score somewhat below 1010 on the SAT or below 19 on the ACT, 5 percent or fewer of applicants are denied; *noncompetitive*—virtually all applicants accepted regardless of high school rank or test scores

- percentage of students in the entering class with SAT verbal and mathematics scores above 500 or ACT scores above 18
- basic undergraduate tuition and fees (if resident tuition differs, this is noted)
- average undergraduate room and board expenses or room only expense
- application deadline

Under General, you will find the following essential descriptive information regarding the school.

- whether the institution is state-supported, independent, religiously affiliated
- whether its functional definition is as a two-year college, four-year college, upper-level institution, five-year college, comprehensive institution, or university (offers more than two doctoral programs)
- if it is part of a larger system
- what type of degrees are awarded—associate, bachelor, master's, or doctoral
- founding date
- size and setting of the campus (urban, suburban, small town, rural)
- the number of undergraduate faculty members, the number of full- and part-time members, and the student–undergraduate faculty ratio
- the most popular major or majors—limited to a maximum of three

While all of these are elements that often enter into a prospective student's consideration of colleges, we recommend that if you seriously are seeking to select a list of colleges for a student's consideration, you look at one of the large general college reference guides, such as *Peterson's Guide to Four-Year Colleges*, that provides a more comprehensive list of colleges and fuller descriptive information in each profile.

## Planning When and When Not to Visit

In the Campus Visits section, a College Calendar (for 1998–99) tells you when regular classes are in session, when the school is on break, when final exams are scheduled, when the admissions office is closed, and when special campus days, such as commencement or homecoming, occur. If you want to get a good picture of what a campus is really like, visiting it when it is in regular session is advised. On the other hand, final exam periods or special campus days usually are such distractions to staff and students that visits are better scheduled during other times.

## Planning Kinds of Visits

A quick reference chart lists the kinds of visit opportunities that are available—campus tour, information session, admission interview, classroom visit, faculty meetings, and overnight visits; whether appointments are required, recommended, recommended but not required, or not needed; and if the specific opportunity is open to all in a party, restricted to applicants and parents, restricted to applicants, restricted to admitted applicants and parents, or restricted to admitted applicants. Absence of one of these lines means that the college either has responded that the opportunity is not offered or has not provided the information.

Specific details for information sessions, interviews, campus tours, and overnight visits follow the chart. Under Information Sessions are shown the normal days, times, and length of these sessions. Interviews lists the days and times interviews are available and the length of these interviews. Campus Tours indicates who leads the tours, the normal days and times of the tours, if appointments are needed to schedule interviews on special days, and the average length of these sessions. Class Visits indicates how classes to be visited are identified, whether

the prospective students may choose a subject area of interest, whether visited classrooms are predetermined, or if visits are randomly assigned to accommodate the visit schedule. Overnight Visits lists whether a student may stay in a residence hall, whether he or she has an assigned student host, and what time of year overnight visits are available. Video indicates if a video tour of the campus is available to prospective students and whether or not a fee is charged for this.

## Sights to See on a Visit

The Campus Facilities section lists special campus features or institutional facilities that prospective students and their families are encouraged to see during their visit. These are organized into four categories: science, arts, athletic, and those of special interest. Local Attractions indicates other attractions in the vicinity that campus visitors may be interested in taking some time to see.

# Planning Travel to a College

The Rand McNally TripMaker™ Peterson's Edition CD-ROM allows you to reproduce and print maps and itineraries on your computer to make your automobile travel planning easier. The program can locate any address in the U.S. on a map and select a route that you can modify—either the most direct, the most scenic, or the one that makes specific stops or side trips that you select—to any college location in the United States, regardless of whether it is profiled in this publication, and can give you the approximate mileage and time needed to complete the trip. TripMaker™ can provide eating and lodging sites along the route. The TripMaker™ CD-ROM can continue to serve your trip-planning needs long after your campus visit adventures are done.

# College and University Profiles

The profiles are listed alphabetically by state and contain basic information about the institutions, including contact information and quick facts about enrollment, entrance difficulty, SAT and ACT scores, tuition, room and board, and application deadlines. Also provided in the profiles is information about features such as the college calendar, information sessions, interviews, campus tours, class visits, overnight visits, campus facilities, and local attractions.

# ALABAMA

## ALABAMA AGRICULTURAL AND MECHANICAL UNIVERSITY
**Normal, Alabama**

**Contact:** Mr. Antonio Boyle, Director, Office of Admissions, PO Box 908, Normal, AL 35762. *Phone:* 256-851-5245 or toll-free 800-553-0816. *Fax:* 256-851-5249. *E-mail:* aboyle@asnaam.aamu.edu *Web site:* http://www.aamu.edu/ *Visit location:* Admissions Office, Patton Hall 111, PO Box 908.

### QUICK FACTS
Enrollment: 5,094; UG: 3,745. Entrance: minimally difficult. SAT>500: N/R; ACT>18: 41%. Resident tuition and fees: $2168. Nonresident tuition and fees: $4100. Room and board: $2678. Application deadline: rolling.

### GENERAL
State-supported, university, coed. Awards bachelor's, master's, and doctoral degrees. Founded 1875. Setting: 2,001-acre suburban campus. Undergraduate faculty: 347 (306 full-time, 41 part-time); student-faculty ratio is 12:1. Most popular recent majors: elementary education, biology, business statistics.

### CAMPUS VISITS
**College Calendar 1998–99:** *Regular classes:* Aug. 31–Dec. 4; Jan. 11–Apr. 30. *Breaks:* Nov. 24–30; Mar. 29–Apr. 5. *Final exams:* Dec. 7–11; May 3–7.

### VISIT OPPORTUNITIES

|  | Appointments? | Who? |
| --- | --- | --- |
| **Campus Tour** | required | open to all |
| **Information Session** | recommended, not required | open to all |
| **Admission Interview** | recommended, not required | open to all |
| **Classroom Visit** | required | open to all |
| **Faculty Meeting** | required | open to all |
| **Overnight Visit** | required | open to all |

**Information Sessions:** M–F 8:00 am–5:00 pm.

**Interviews:** M–F; 120 minutes.

**Campus Tours:** Conducted by students and admission reps. M–F 9:00 am–3:00 pm; annual fall visit day; special weekend groups; 120 minutes.

**Class Visits:** Classroom visits are determined by the visit schedule.

**Overnight Visits:** During the regular academic year and over the summer, prospective applicants may spend an evening in a residence hall.

### CAMPUS FACILITIES
**Science:** Physics Laboratories, Agriculture Laboratories and Greenhouses.

**Arts:** Music Department, Art Department.

**Athletic:** Stadium, Fieldhouse.

**Of Special Interest:** Appointment Required: State Black Archives in Wilson Hall.

### LOCAL ATTRACTIONS
Space and Rocket Center; Twickenham Historic District; Botanical Gardens.

## AUBURN UNIVERSITY
**Auburn, Alabama**

**Contact:** Admissions Office, 202 Martin Hall, Auburn University, AL 36849-5145. *Phone:* 334-844-4080 or toll-free 800-AUBURN9 (in-state). *Fax:* 334-844-6436. *E-mail:* admissions@groupwise1.duc.auburn.edu *Web site:* http://www.auburn.edu/ *Visit location:* Admissions Office, Mary Martin Hall, 202 Martin Hall.

### QUICK FACTS
Enrollment: 21,447; UG: 18,171. Entrance: moderately difficult. SAT>500: 83% V, 84% M; ACT>18: 98%. Resident tuition and fees: $2610. Nonresident tuition and fees: $7830. Room only: $1905. Application deadline: 9/1.

### GENERAL
State-supported, university, coed. Awards bachelor's, master's, doctoral, and first professional degrees and post-master's certificates. Founded 1856. Setting: 1,875-acre small-town campus. Undergraduate faculty: 1,262 (1,145 full-time, 117 part-time); student-faculty ratio is 16:1. Most popular recent majors: psychology, business administration, civil engineering.

### CAMPUS VISITS
**College Calendar 1998–99:** *Regular classes:* Sept. 22–Dec. 4; Jan. 5–Mar. 11; Mar. 29–June 2. *Final exams:* Dec. 7–11; Mar. 13–18; June 4–9. *Special campus days:* A-Day, Apr. 23; Homecoming, Nov. 7.

## VISIT OPPORTUNITIES

| | Appointments? | Who? |
|---|---|---|
| **Campus Tour** | recommended | open to all |
| **Information Session** | recommended | open to all |
| **Classroom Visit** | required | |
| **Faculty Meeting** | required | |

**Information Sessions:** M–F 8:00 am–4:00 pm; 30 minutes.

**Campus Tours:** Conducted by students. M–F 8:00 am–4:00 pm; 45 minutes.

**Class Visits:** Classroom visits are determined by the visit schedule.

## CAMPUS FACILITIES

**Arts:** Art Gallery—Foy Union.

**Athletic:** Athletic Complex Museum.

**Of Special Interest:** University Chapel.

## LOCAL ATTRACTIONS

Chewacla State Park; Kiesal Park Nature Trails; Tiger Trail of Auburn—Walk of Fame Downtown commemorating greatest athletes, coaches, and Auburn administrators.

# SAMFORD UNIVERSITY

Birmingham, Alabama

**Contact:** Dean of Admission and Financial Aid, 800 Lakeshore Drive, Birmingham, AL 35229-0002. *Phone:* 205-870-2871 or toll-free 800-888-7218. *Fax:* 205-870-2171. *E-mail:* ppkimpey@samford.edu *Web site:* http://www.samford.edu/ *Visit location:* Office of Admission, Samford Hall, 800 Lakeshore Drive.

## QUICK FACTS

Enrollment: 4,446; UG: 2,880. Entrance: moderately difficult. SAT>500: 81% V, 78% M; ACT>18: 98%. Tuition and fees: $9432. Room and board: $4396. Application deadline: rolling.

## GENERAL

Independent Baptist, university, coed. Awards associate, bachelor's, master's, doctoral, and first professional degrees. Founded 1841. Setting: 280-acre suburban campus. Undergraduate faculty: 399 (234 full-time, 165 part-time); student-faculty ratio is 14:1. Most popular recent majors: liberal arts and studies, business administration.

## CAMPUS VISITS

**College Calendar 1998–99:** *Regular classes:* Aug. 24–Dec. 4; Jan. 27–May 12. *Final exams:* Dec. 7–10; May 14–19.

## VISIT OPPORTUNITIES

| | Appointments? | Who? |
|---|---|---|
| **Campus Tour** | recommended, not required | open to all |
| **Information Session** | recommended | open to all |
| **Admission Interview** | required | open to all |
| **Classroom Visit** | required | open to all |
| **Faculty Meeting** | required | open to all |
| **Overnight Visit** | required | open to all |

**Information Sessions:** Sat.; 45 minutes.

**Interviews:** M–F; 45 minutes.

**Campus Tours:** Conducted by students. M–F, Sat.; 60 minutes.

**Class Visits:** Prospective students may attend a class in their area of interest.

**Overnight Visits:** During the regular academic year, prospective applicants may spend an evening in a residence hall with a student host.

## CAMPUS FACILITIES

**Of Special Interest:** Harwell G. Davis Library.

## LOCAL ATTRACTIONS

Birmingham's Southside, The Civil Rights Institute, Riverside Galleria.

# TROY STATE UNIVERSITY

Troy, Alabama

**Contact:** Jim Hutto, Dean of Enrollment Management, Troy State University, Troy, AL 36082. *Phone:* 334-670-3179 or toll-free 800-551-9716 (in-state). *Fax:* 334-670-3733. *E-mail:* jhutto@trojan.troyst.edu *Web site:* http://www.troyst.edu/ *Visit location:* Admissions, Adams Administration Building, Room 134.

## QUICK FACTS

Enrollment: 6,468; UG: 5,293. Entrance: moderately difficult. SAT>500: N/R; ACT>18: N/R. Resident tuition and fees: $2250. Nonresident tuition and fees: $4305. Room and board: $3480. Application deadline: rolling.

*Troy State University (continued)*

## GENERAL
State-supported, comprehensive, coed. Part of Troy State University System. Awards associate, bachelor's, and master's degrees. Founded 1887. Setting: 500-acre small-town campus. Most popular recent majors: education, business administration, nursing.

## CAMPUS VISITS
**College Calendar 1998–99:** *Regular classes:* Sept. 14–Nov. 18; Jan. 6–Mar. 11; Mar. 31–Apr. 26; June 9–Aug. 3. *Breaks:* Nov. 25–Jan. 3; Mar. 20–28. *Final exams:* Nov. 20–24; Mar. 15–17; May 28–June 1; Aug. 3. *Special campus days:* Commencement, Mar. 19, June 4; Homecoming, Oct. 24.

## VISIT OPPORTUNITIES

|  | Appointments? | Who? |
| --- | --- | --- |
| **Campus Tour** | recommended | applicants and parents |
| **Information Session** | recommended | |
| **Admission Interview** | | applicants and parents |
| **Classroom Visit** | required | |
| **Faculty Meeting** | required | applicants and parents |

**Information Sessions:** M–F, select Sat. at 10:00 am; 30 minutes.

**Interviews:** M–F, select Sat.; 30 minutes.

**Campus Tours:** Conducted by students. M–F, select Sat. at 10:00 am; 45 minutes.

**Class Visits:** Prospective students may attend a class in their area of interest.

## CAMPUS FACILITIES
**Science:** Science Facilities.

**Arts:** Gallery, Theater, New Music Hall of Fame.

**Athletic:** Field House, Natatorium, Recreational Facilities.

**Of Special Interest:** Dormitories, student center.

## LOCAL ATTRACTIONS
Pike Pioneer Museum.

# ARIZONA

## ARIZONA STATE UNIVERSITY
**Tempe, Arizona**

**Contact:** Undergraduate Admissions, PO Box 870112, Tempe, AZ 85287-0112. *Phone:* 602-965-7788. *Fax:* 602-965-3610. *E-mail:* ugradadm@asuvm.inre.asu.edu *Web site:* http://www.asu.edu/ *Visit location:* Undergraduate Admissions, Student Services Building.

## QUICK FACTS
Enrollment: 43,295; UG: 32,537. Entrance: moderately difficult. SAT>500: 72% V, 73% M; ACT>18: 91%. Resident tuition and fees: $2059. Nonresident tuition and fees: $8711. Room and board: $4500. Application deadline: rolling.

## GENERAL
State-supported, university, coed. Awards bachelor's, master's, doctoral, and first professional degrees and post-master's certificates. Founded 1885. Setting: 814-acre suburban campus with easy access to Phoenix. Undergraduate faculty: 1,972 (1,744 full-time, 228 part-time); student-faculty ratio is 17:1. Most popular recent majors: elementary education, psychology.

## CAMPUS VISITS
**College Calendar 1998–99:** *Regular classes:* Aug. 24–Dec. 9; Jan. 19–May 5. *Breaks:* Dec. 18–Jan. 17; Mar. 14–20. *Final exams:* Dec. 11–17; May 7–13. *Special campus days:* Commencement, Dec. 18, May 14; Family Weekend, Oct. 9–11; Homecoming, Nov. 7.

## VISIT OPPORTUNITIES

|  | Appointments? | Who? |
| --- | --- | --- |
| **Campus Tour** | not required | open to all |
| **Information Session** | not required | open to all |
| **Admission Interview** | required | open to all |
| **Classroom Visit** | required | open to all |
| **Faculty Meeting** | required | open to all |

**Information Sessions:** M–F, select Sat.; call to verify times and dates or access our Web site; 60 minutes.

**Interviews:** M–F; unavailable 12:00 pm to 1:00 pm and Mon. 3:00 pm to 5:00 pm; 30 minutes.

**Campus Tours:** Conducted by students. M–F at 10:30 am, 2:00 pm; select Sat. at 11:00 am; during summer M–F at 9:00 am; call ahead to verify times and dates or access our Web site; 60 minutes.

**Class Visits:** Prospective students may attend a class in their area of interest.

**Video:** Free on request.

## CAMPUS FACILITIES

**Science:** Appointment Required: Planetarium, Greenhouse.

**Arts:** Nelson Fine Arts Center, Museum and Playhouse; Appointment Required: Grady Gammage Memorial Auditorium.

**Athletic:** Appointment Required: Sun Devil Stadium.

**Of Special Interest:** Computing Commons Building, Student Recreation Center, Memorial Union.

## LOCAL ATTRACTIONS

Downtown Mill Avenue, Tempe, AZ; Old Town Scottsdale, Scottsdale, AZ.

# EMBRY-RIDDLE AERONAUTICAL UNIVERSITY

**Prescott, Arizona**

**Contact:** Bill Thompson, Assistant Director of Admissions, 3200 North Willow Creek Road, Prescott, AZ 86301. *Phone:* toll-free 800-888-3728. *Fax:* 520-708-6606. *E-mail:* thompsb@pr.erau.edu *Web site:* http://www.pr.erau.edu/ *Visit location:* Office of Admissions/Visitor Center, 3200 Willow Creek Road.

## QUICK FACTS

Enrollment: 1,499; UG: 1,499. Entrance: moderately difficult. SAT>500: 77% V, 87% M; ACT>18: 96%. Tuition and fees: $9920. Room and board: $4950. Application deadline: rolling.

## GENERAL

Independent, 4-year, coed. Part of Embry-Riddle Aeronautical University. Awards bachelor's degrees. Founded 1978. Setting: 547-acre small-town campus. Faculty: 83 (57 full-time, 26 part-time); student-faculty ratio is 17:1. Most popular recent majors: aircraft pilot (professional), aerospace engineering, aviation/airway science.

## CAMPUS VISITS

**College Calendar 1998–99:** *Regular classes:* Sept. 1–Dec. 8; Jan. 7–Apr. 20. *Breaks:* Nov. 25–28; Mar.

15–19. *Final exams:* Dec. 10–15; Apr. 22–27. *Admission office closed:* Nov. 25–27, Dec. 24–Jan. 4. *Special campus days:* Alumni Weekend/20th Anniversary Celebration, Oct. 2–3; Commencement, Dec. 19, May 1.

## VISIT OPPORTUNITIES

| | Appointments? | Who? |
|---|---|---|
| **Campus Tour** | recommended, not required | open to all |
| **Information Session** | recommended | open to all |
| **Admission Interview** | recommended, not required | open to all |
| **Classroom Visit** | recommended | open to all |
| **Faculty Meeting** | recommended | open to all |
| **Overnight Visit** | | applicants only |

**Interviews:** M–F at 9:00 am, 11:00 am, 1:00 pm; select Sat. at 10:00 am; 45 minutes.

**Campus Tours:** Conducted by students. M–F at 9:00 am, 11:00 am, 1:00 pm; select Sat. at 10:00 am; 120 minutes.

**Class Visits:** Classroom visits are determined by the visit schedule.

**Overnight Visits:** During the regular academic year.

## CAMPUS FACILITIES

**Science:** Wind Tunnels For Aerospace Engineering.

**Of Special Interest:** Appointment Required: Flight Line with Simulators, Aircraft Crash Investigation Lab and Safety Center.

## LOCAL ATTRACTIONS

Prescott Area: County Historic Court, Grand Canyon.

# NORTHERN ARIZONA UNIVERSITY

**Flagstaff, Arizona**

**Contact:** Tour Coordinator, PO Box 4084, Flagstaff, AZ 86011-4084. *Phone:* toll-free 800-345-1987 (in-state), 888-MORE-NAU (out-of-state). *Fax:* 520-523-6023. *Web site:* http://www.nau.edu/ *Visit location:* Undergraduate Admissions, North Union, PO Box 4084.

*Northern Arizona University (continued)*

## QUICK FACTS

Enrollment: 19,618; UG: 14,058. Entrance: moderately difficult. SAT>500: 62% V, 63% M; ACT>18: N/R. Resident tuition and fees: $2080. Nonresident tuition and fees: $7826. Room and board: $3500. Application deadline: 7/15.

## GENERAL

State-supported, university, coed. Awards bachelor's, master's, and doctoral degrees. Founded 1899. Setting: 730-acre small-town campus. Undergraduate faculty: 935 (659 full-time, 276 part-time); student-faculty ratio is 22:1. Most popular recent majors: business administration, education, psychology.

## CAMPUS VISITS

**College Calendar 1998–99:** *Regular classes:* Aug. 24–Dec. 11; Jan. 11–May 7. *Breaks:* Mar. 7–13; Nov. 26–27. *Final exams:* Dec. 7–10; May 3–6. *Special campus days:* Fall Commencement, Dec. 12; Homecoming, Sept. 26; On Campus Information Day, Oct. 10, Nov. 14, Apr. 17, Feb. 26; Parents Weekend, Oct. 10; Spring Commencement, May 8.

### VISIT OPPORTUNITIES

|  | Appointments? | Who? |
|---|---|---|
| **Campus Tour** | recommended, not required | open to all |
| **Information Session** | not required | open to all |
| **Classroom Visit** | required | open to all |

**Information Sessions:** M–F at 12:30 pm; 30 minutes.

**Campus Tours:** Conducted by students. M–F at 10:30 am, 1:15 pm; Sat. at 10:30 am; 120 minutes.

**Class Visits:** Prospective students may attend a class in their area of interest.

**Video:** Free on request.

## CAMPUS FACILITIES

**Science:** Appointment Required: Observatory.

**Arts:** Old Main Art Gallery.

**Athletic:** J. Lawrence Walk-up Sky Dome, Wall Aquatic Center, Recreation Center.

**Of Special Interest:** Residence Halls, Student Union, Library.

## LOCAL ATTRACTIONS

The Grand Canyon, Lowell Observatory.

# THE UNIVERSITY OF ARIZONA
## Tucson, Arizona

**Contact:** University of Arizona Campus Tours, PO Box 210040, Nugent Building, Tucson, AZ 85721. *Phone:* 520-621-3641. *Fax:* 520-621-9799. *E-mail:* visitua@arizona.edu *Web site:* http://www.arizona.edu/ *Visit location:* Office of Admissions and New Student Enrollment, Robert L. Nugent Building, 1212 East University Boulevard.

## QUICK FACTS

Enrollment: 32,889; UG: 24,769. Entrance: moderately difficult. SAT>500: 72% V, 71% M; ACT>18: 90%. Resident tuition and fees: $2058. Nonresident tuition and fees: $8710. Room and board: $4930. Application deadline: 4/1.

## GENERAL

State-supported, university, coed. Awards bachelor's, master's, doctoral, and first professional degrees. Founded 1885. Setting: 351-acre urban campus. Undergraduate faculty: 1,551 (1,448 full-time, 103 part-time); student-faculty ratio is 18:1. Most popular recent majors: psychology, political science, finance.

## CAMPUS VISITS

**College Calendar 1998–99:** *Regular classes:* Aug. 24–Dec. 9; Jan. 13–May 5. *Final exams:* Dec. 11–18; May 7–14. *Admission office closed:* Dec. 24–Jan. 4. *Special campus days:* Family weekend, Oct. 9–11; Homecoming, Nov. 6–8; Spring Commencement, May 15; Spring Fling, Apr. 1–4; Winter Commencement, Dec. 19.

### VISIT OPPORTUNITIES

|  | Appointments? | Who? |
|---|---|---|
| **Campus Tour** | recommended | open to all |
| **Admission Interview** | recommended | open to all |
| **Classroom Visit** | required | open to all |
| **Faculty Meeting** | required | open to all |

**Interviews:** M–F; unavailable during university holidays; 30 minutes.

**Campus Tours:** Conducted by students. M–F at 10:00 am, 2:00 pm; Sat. at 10:00 am; unavailable during university holidays, may be available during Christmas break; call to verify availability and times; 90 minutes.

**Class Visits:** Certain predetermined classrooms are open to visitors.

**Video:** Available, fee charged.

## CAMPUS FACILITIES

**Science:** Flandrau Science Center.

**Arts:** University of Arizona Museum of Art, Center for Creative Photography.

**Athletic:** Student Recreation Center.

# ARKANSAS

## ARKANSAS STATE UNIVERSITY
### Jonesboro, Arkansas

**Contact:** Vicki Walker, Administrative Assistant, PO Box 1630, State University, AR 72467. *Phone:* toll-free 800-382-3030 (in-state), 800-643-0080 (out-of-state). *Fax:* 870-972-3843. *E-mail:* admissions@chickasaw.astate.edu *Web site:* http://www.astate.edu/ *Visit location:* Admissions Office, Chickasaw Student Services Center, 106 North Caraway Road.

### QUICK FACTS
Enrollment: 10,012; UG: 8,983. Entrance: moderately difficult. SAT>500: N/R; ACT>18: 86%. Resident tuition and fees: $2280. Nonresident tuition and fees: $5370. Room and board: $2840. Application deadline: 8/12.

### GENERAL
State-supported, comprehensive, coed. Awards associate, bachelor's, master's, and doctoral degrees and post-master's certificates. Founded 1909. Setting: 900-acre small-town campus with easy access to Memphis. Undergraduate faculty: 513 (435 full-time, 78 part-time); student-faculty ratio is 18:1. Most popular recent majors: accounting, early childhood education, business administration.

### CAMPUS VISITS
**College Calendar 1998–99:** *Regular classes:* Aug. 19–Dec. 8; Jan. 7–Apr. 28. *Breaks:* Nov. 25–29; Mar. 15–21; Dec. 17–Jan. 6. *Final exams:* Dec. 10–16; Apr. 30–May 6. *Admission office closed:* Dec. 24–Jan. 3. *Special campus days:* Convocation of Scholars, Apr. 19–23; Fall Commencement, Dec. 18; Homecoming, Oct. 3; Spring Commencement, May 7; Summer Commencement, Aug. 6.

## VISIT OPPORTUNITIES

| | Appointments? | Who? |
|---|---|---|
| **Campus Tour** | recommended, not required | open to all |
| **Information Session** | not required | open to all |

**Information Sessions:** M–F 8:00 am–5:00 pm; 30 minutes.

**Campus Tours:** Conducted by students and admission reps. M–F at 10:30 am, 2:00 pm.

**Video:** Free on request.

### CAMPUS FACILITIES
**Science:** Laboratory Science Building, Computer Lab; Appointment Required: Greenhouse, ASU Farm.

**Arts:** Performing Arts Complex, Museum, Library, Delta Studies Center.

**Athletic:** Health and Physical Education Complex; Appointment Required: Convocation Center, Indian Stadium.

**Of Special Interest:** KASU Radio Station, ASU Television Studio.

### LOCAL ATTRACTIONS
Craighead Forrest Park; Ernest Hemingway Museum and Conference Center; Crowley's Ridge Scenic Parkway.

## HARDING UNIVERSITY
### Searcy, Arkansas

**Contact:** Mr. Mike Williams, Assistant Vice President of Admissions and Financial Aid, Box 12255, Searcy, AR 72149. *Phone:* toll-free 800-477-4407. *Fax:* 501-279-4865. *E-mail:* admissions@harding.edu *Web site:* http://www.harding.edu/ *Visit location:* Admissions Office, American Heritage, 900 East Center.

### QUICK FACTS
Enrollment: 3,754; UG: 3,573. Entrance: very difficult. SAT>500: N/R; ACT>18: 91%. Tuition and fees: $7712. Room and board: $3986. Application deadline: 7/1.

### GENERAL
Independent, comprehensive, coed, Church of Christ. Awards bachelor's and master's degrees. Founded 1924. Setting: 200-acre small-town campus with easy access to Little Rock. Undergraduate faculty: 262

*Harding University (continued)*

(208 full-time, 54 part-time); student-faculty ratio is 17:1. Most popular recent majors: business administration, elementary education, mass communications.

## CAMPUS VISITS

**College Calendar 1998–99:** *Regular classes:* Aug. 25–Dec. 11; Jan. 13–May 7. *Breaks:* Nov. 22–28; Mar. 14–20. *Final exams:* Dec. 14–18; May 10–14. *Admission office closed:* Dec. 21–25. *Special campus days:* Fall Festival, Oct. 16–17; Homecoming, Nov. 6–7; Spring Spirit, Apr. 9–10.

## VISIT OPPORTUNITIES

|  | Appointments? |
|---|---|
| **Campus Tour** | recommended |
| **Information Session** | recommended |
| **Admission Interview** | recommended |
| **Classroom Visit** | recommended |
| **Faculty Meeting** | recommended |
| **Overnight Visit** | recommended |

**Information Sessions:** M–Sat., select Sun.; by appointment; 45 minutes.

**Interviews:** M–Sat., select Sun.; 30 minutes.

**Campus Tours:** Conducted by students and admission reps. M–Sat., select Sun.; by appointment; 60 minutes.

**Class Visits:** Prospective students may attend a class in their area of interest.

**Overnight Visits:** During the regular academic year and over the summer, prospective applicants may spend an evening in a residence hall with a student host.

**Video:** Free on request.

## CAMPUS FACILITIES

**Science:** Pryor Science Center.

**Arts:** Stephens Art Center, Reynolds Center for Music and Communications.

**Athletic:** Rhodes Memorial Fieldhouse, Ganus Athletic Center.

**Of Special Interest:** Mainteer Bible and World Missions Center, Brackett Library.

# OUACHITA BAPTIST UNIVERSITY
## Arkadelphia, Arkansas

**Contact:** Mr. Randy Garner, Director Admissions Counseling, Ouachita Baptist University, Box 3776, Arkadelphia, AR 71923. *Phone:* 870-245-5110 or toll-free 800-342-5628 (in-state). *Fax:* 870-245-5500. *E-mail:* gardnerr@alpha.obu.edu *Web site:* http://www.obu.edu/ *Visit location:* Admissions Counseling, Cone Bottoms Hall, Room 100, Ouachita Street.

## QUICK FACTS

Enrollment: 1,619; UG: 1,619. Entrance: moderately difficult. SAT>500: 62% V, 64% M; ACT>18: 93%. Tuition and fees: $8090. Room and board: $3040. Application deadline: 8/15.

## GENERAL

Independent Baptist, 4-year, coed. Awards associate and bachelor's degrees. Founded 1886. Setting: 60-acre small-town campus with easy access to Little Rock. Faculty: 150 (108 full-time, 42 part-time); student-faculty ratio is 12:1. Most popular recent majors: education, business administration, religious studies.

## CAMPUS VISITS

**College Calendar 1998–99:** *Regular classes:* Aug. 26–Dec. 18; Jan. 13–May 14. *Breaks:* Mar. 22–28. *Final exams:* Dec. 14–18; May 10–14. *Special campus days:* Commencement, May 15; Homecoming, Oct. 23; Tiger Tunes, Oct. 21–23.

## VISIT OPPORTUNITIES

|  | Appointments? | Who? |
|---|---|---|
| **Campus Tour** | recommended, not required | open to all |
| **Information Session** | recommended, not required | open to all |
| **Admission Interview** | recommended, not required | open to all |
| **Classroom Visit** | recommended | open to all |
| **Faculty Meeting** | recommended | open to all |
| **Overnight Visit** | recommended | open to all |

**Information Sessions:** M–F 8:00 am–5:00 pm; Sat. by appointment; 60 minutes.

**Interviews:** M–F, select Sat.; 30 minutes.

**Campus Tours:** Conducted by students and admission reps. M–F 8:00 am–5:00 pm; Sat. by appointment; 30 minutes.

**Class Visits:** Prospective students may attend a class in their area of interest.

**Overnight Visits:** During the regular academic year, prospective applicants may spend an evening in a residence hall with a student host.

**Video:** Free on request.

### CAMPUS FACILITIES

**Science:** Jones Science Complex.

**Arts:** Jones Center for Performing Arts.

**Athletic:** Sturgis Athletic Complex, Heflin Tennis Center.

**Of Special Interest:** Riley-Hickingbotham Library, Anthony and Maddox Dorms.

### LOCAL ATTRACTIONS

Lake DeGray State Park.

# CALIFORNIA

## ART CENTER COLLEGE OF DESIGN

**Pasadena, California**

**Contact:** Admissions Office, 1700 Lida Street, Pasadena, CA 91103. *Phone:* 626-396-2373. *Fax:* 626-795-0578. *E-mail:* admissions@artcenter.edu *Web site:* http://www.artcenter.edu/ *Visit location:* Admissions Office, Main Campus, 1700 Lida Street.

### QUICK FACTS

Enrollment: 1,433; UG: 1,334. Entrance: very difficult. SAT>500: N/R; ACT>18: N/R. Tuition and fees: $17,180. Room and board: N/Avail. Application deadline: rolling.

### GENERAL

Independent, comprehensive, coed. Awards bachelor's and master's degrees. Founded 1930. Setting: 175-acre suburban campus with easy access to Los Angeles. Undergraduate faculty: 385 (57 full-time, 328 part-time); student-faculty ratio is 5:1. Most popular recent majors: graphic design/commercial art/illustration, industrial design, photography.

### CAMPUS VISITS

**College Calendar 1998–99:** *Regular classes:* Sept. 12–Dec. 19; Jan. 16–Apr. 24. *Breaks:* Dec. 21–Jan. 15; Apr. 26–May 14. *Admission office closed:* Martin Luther King, Jr., Day, Jan. 18.

### VISIT OPPORTUNITIES

|                       | Appointments? | Who?        |
|-----------------------|---------------|-------------|
| **Campus Tour**       | required      | open to all |
| **Information Session** | required    | open to all |
| **Admission Interview** | required    | open to all |

**Information Sessions:** M–F; unavailable during holidays and semester breaks; 10 minutes.

**Interviews:** M–F; unavailable holidays; 45 minutes.

**Campus Tours:** Conducted by students and docents. Mon., Tue., Wed., Thu. at 2:00 pm; Fri. at 10:30 am; unavailable during holidays and semester breaks; 60 minutes.

**Video:** Free on request.

### CAMPUS FACILITIES

**Arts:** Student Gallery, Alyce de Roulet Williamson Gallery, Sculpture Garden.

## BIOLA UNIVERSITY

**La Mirada, California**

**Contact:** Laura Sizelove, Coordinator of Student Services and Campus Visitation, 13800 Biola Avenue, La Mirada, CA 90639-0001. *Phone:* 562-903-4752 or toll-free 800-652-4652. *Fax:* 562-903-4709. *Web site:* http://www.biola.edu/ *Visit location:* Admissions Office, Metzger Hall, 13800 Biola Avenue.

### QUICK FACTS

Enrollment: 3,257; UG: 2,153. Entrance: moderately difficult. SAT>500: 71% V, 69% M; ACT>18: N/R. Tuition and fees: $14,286. Room and board: $4902. Application deadline: 6/1.

### GENERAL

Independent interdenominational, university, coed. Awards bachelor's, master's, and doctoral degrees. Founded 1908. Setting: 95-acre suburban campus with easy access to Los Angeles. Undergraduate faculty: 269 (143 full-time, 126 part-time); student-faculty ratio is 17:1. Most popular recent majors: business administration, mass communications, psychology.

*Biola University (continued)*

## CAMPUS VISITS

**College Calendar 1998–99:** *Regular classes:* Aug. 27–Dec. 18; Jan. 4–22; Feb. 1–May 28. *Breaks:* Apr. 2–11. *Final exams:* Dec. 14–18; May 24–28. *Special campus days:* Celebrate the Son, Dec. 11–12; Christmas Tree Lighting, Dec. 4; Commencement, May 29; University Day, Dec. 3–4.

## VISIT OPPORTUNITIES

|  | Appointments? | Who? |
|---|---|---|
| **Campus Tour** | recommended | open to all |
| **Information Session** | recommended | open to all |
| **Admission Interview** | recommended | open to all |
| **Classroom Visit** | recommended | open to all |
| **Faculty Meeting** | required | open to all |
| **Overnight Visit** | required | open to all |

**Information Sessions:** M–F, select Sat.; call for schedule; 30 minutes.

**Interviews:** M–F, select Sat.; 30 minutes.

**Campus Tours:** Conducted by students and admission reps. M–F, select Sat.; call for schedule; 60 minutes.

**Class Visits:** Classroom visits are determined by the visit schedule.

**Overnight Visits:** During the regular academic year, prospective applicants may spend an evening in a residence hall with a student host.

**Video:** Free on request.

## CAMPUS FACILITIES

**Science:** Appointment Required: Cell Biology Lab, Chemistry Lab, Biology Lab, Physics Lab.

**Arts:** Appointment Required: Ceramics Studio, Art Gallery, Music Building, Film Studio.

**Athletic:** Track, Baseball Diamond; Appointment Required: Gym, Training Facilities.

**Of Special Interest:** Student Union Building, Cafeteria, Student Book Store.

## LOCAL ATTRACTIONS

Disneyland, Knotts Berry Farm, Huntington and Newport Beaches.

# CALIFORNIA INSTITUTE OF TECHNOLOGY
**Pasadena, California**

**Contact:** Visitor's Center/Public Relations, 315 South Hill Avenue, Pasadena, CA 91106. *Phone:* 626-395-6327 or toll-free 800-568-8324. *Fax:* 626-577-0636. *Web site:* http://www.caltech.edu/ *Visit location:* Visitor's Center/Public Relations, 315 South Hill Avenue.

## QUICK FACTS

Enrollment: 1,925; UG: 904. Entrance: most difficult. SAT>500: 100% V, 100% M; ACT>18: N/App. Tuition and fees: $18,816. Room and board: $5700. Application deadline: 1/1.

## GENERAL

Independent, university, coed. Awards bachelor's, master's, and doctoral degrees. Founded 1891. Setting: 124-acre suburban campus with easy access to Los Angeles. Undergraduate faculty: 353 (315 full-time, 38 part-time); student-faculty ratio is 3:1. Most popular recent majors: engineering, physics, biology.

## CAMPUS VISITS

**College Calendar 1998–99:** *Regular classes:* Sept. 28–Dec. 4; Jan. 4–Mar. 10; Mar. 30–June 4. *Breaks:* Nov. 26–29; Mar. 19–29; Dec. 13–Jan. 3. *Final exams:* Dec. 9–11; Mar. 15–17; June 9–11. *Special campus days:* Commencement, June 11.

**Class Visits:** Prospective students may attend a class in their area of interest.

## CAMPUS FACILITIES

**Science:** Synchrotron Lab, Graduate Aeronautical Laboratories.

**Arts:** Baxter Hall of the Humanities and Social Sciences.

**Athletic:** Braun Athletic Center, Brown Gymnasium.

**Of Special Interest:** The Athenaeum, the Olive Walk, Millikan Library.

## LOCAL ATTRACTIONS

Huntington Library and Gardens; Norton Simon Museum of Art; Gamble House Museum; Old Town Pasadena; Rose Bowl and Tournament of Roses Museum; Los Angeles.

# CALIFORNIA STATE POLYTECHNIC UNIVERSITY, POMONA

Pomona, California

**Contact:** Visitor Center, 3801 West Temple, Pomona, CA 91768. *Phone:* 909-869-3529. *E-mail:* tours@csupomona.edu *Web site:* http://www.csupomona.edu/ *Visit location:* Visitor Center, University Union, 3801 West Temple.

## QUICK FACTS

Enrollment: 17,025; UG: 14,852. Entrance: moderately difficult. SAT>500: 41% V, 62% M; ACT>18: N/R. Resident tuition and fees: $1923. Nonresident tuition and fees: $9467. Room and board: $5300. Application deadline: rolling.

## GENERAL

State-supported, comprehensive, coed. Part of California State University System. Awards bachelor's and master's degrees. Founded 1938. Setting: 1,400-acre urban campus with easy access to Los Angeles. Undergraduate faculty: 972 (559 full-time, 413 part-time); student-faculty ratio is 19:1. Most popular recent majors: information sciences/systems, electrical/electronics engineering, business marketing and marketing management.

## CAMPUS VISITS

**College Calendar 1998–99:** *Regular classes:* Sept. 24–Dec. 4; Jan. 4–Mar. 12; Mar. 29–June 4; June 21–Aug. 27. *Breaks:* Nov. 26–29; Mar. 20–28; June 12–20; Dec. 12–Jan. 3. *Final exams:* Dec. 7–11; Mar. 15–19; June 7–11; Aug. 30–Sept. 2. *Admission office closed:* Dec. 25–Jan. 4; Fri. mid-Jun. to early Sept. *Special campus days:* Admission Day; Commencement; Founders' Day, Nov. 12.

### VISIT OPPORTUNITIES

| | Appointments? | Who? |
|---|---|---|
| **Campus Tour** | required | applicants and parents |
| **Admission Interview** | required | applicants and parents |
| **Classroom Visit** | required | applicants and parents |
| **Faculty Meeting** | required | applicants and parents |

**Interviews:** Call 909-869-3210 for appointment; 60 minutes.

**Campus Tours:** Conducted by students. M–F; select Sat. at 1:30 pm; available during summer Mon.–Thu.; call for times; 90 minutes.

**Class Visits:** Prospective students may attend a class in their area of interest.

**Video:** Free on request.

### CAMPUS FACILITIES

**Science:** Appointment Required: Geography Information Systems.

**Arts:** Appointment Required: Keith and Janet Kellogg Art Gallery, Motor Development Clinic, Music, "The Post".

**Of Special Interest:** Farm Fresh Store, Computing Commons; Appointment Required: Center for Regenerative Studies, W.K. Kellogg Arabian Horse Center.

# CALIFORNIA STATE UNIVERSITY, HAYWARD

Hayward, California

**Contact:** Joe Mazares, Office Manager, 25800 Carlos Bee Boulevard—LM55, Hayward, CA 94542. *Phone:* 510-885-3982. *Fax:* 510-885-4751. *E-mail:* adminfo@csuhayward.edu *Web site:* http://www.csuhayward.edu/ *Visit location:* Recruitment and Pre-admission Advising, Warren Hall-LM55, 25800 Carlos Bee Boulevard.

## QUICK FACTS

Enrollment: 12,863; UG: 9,905. Entrance: moderately difficult. SAT>500: N/R; ACT>18: N/R. Resident tuition and fees: $1827. Nonresident tuition and fees: $9207. Room only: $3230. Application deadline: 9/9.

## GENERAL

State-supported, comprehensive, coed. Part of California State University System. Awards bachelor's and master's degrees. Founded 1957. Setting: 343-acre suburban campus with easy access to San Francisco and San Jose. Undergraduate faculty: 695 (368 full-time, 327 part-time). Most popular recent majors: business administration, liberal arts and studies, computer science.

## CAMPUS VISITS

**College Calendar 1998–99:** *Regular classes:* Sept. 24–Dec. 4; Jan. 5–Mar. 12; Mar. 29–June 4; June

*California State University, Hayward (continued)*

21–Aug. 27. *Breaks:* Nov. 26–29; Jan. 16–18; May 29–31; July 3–5. *Final exams:* Dec. 7–11; Mar. 22–26; June 7–11; Aug. 30–Sept. 3. *Special campus days:* Commencement, June 12; Hayward Admit-A-Thon (Admission On-the-Spot), Nov. 14; Jazz Festival: April '99; Moon Dazzle: An Astro Musical Adventure; Spring Preview Day.

## VISIT OPPORTUNITIES

|  | Appointments? | Who? |
|---|---|---|
| **Campus Tour** | recommended | open to all |
| **Information Session** | recommended, not required | open to all |
| **Faculty Meeting** | required | admitted applicants and parents |

**Information Sessions:** T–F 9:00 am–12:00 pm, 1:00–4:00 pm; afternoons require an appointment; 20 minutes.

**Campus Tours:** Conducted by students. Fri. at 2:00 pm; school group tours available upon request; out of state visitors may make special arrangements; 45 minutes.

## CAMPUS FACILITIES
**Science:** School of Science Lab Facilities, Math/Computer Science Computer Lab, Statistics Computer Lab; Telecommunications Computer Lab; Appointment Required: Electron Microscope Lab; Nursing Skills Lab, Museum of Entomology.

**Arts:** Art Gallery, Multimedia Studios; Appointment Required: Theatre and Dance Studies, Instructional Media Center.

**Athletic:** Gymnasium, Sports fields, two Olympic-sized swimming pools; 12 tennis courts.

**Of Special Interest:** Library complex, Computer labs, University Union, Early Childhood Education Center, Distance Learning Facility; Appointment Required: Student apartments.

## LOCAL ATTRACTIONS
San Francisco Bay Area Attractions; Contra Costa Campus.

# CALIFORNIA STATE UNIVERSITY, LOS ANGELES
Los Angeles, California

**Contact:** Mr. George Bachmann, Associate Director, Admissions and University Outreach, 5151 State University Drive, Los Angeles, CA 90032. *Phone:* 213-343-3131. *Fax:* 213-343-3888. *E-mail:* gbachma@cslanet.calstatela.edu *Visit location:* Admissions and University Outreach, Student Affairs 101, 5151 State University Drive.

## QUICK FACTS
Enrollment: 19,160; UG: 13,742. Entrance: moderately difficult. SAT>500: N/App; ACT>18: N/App. Resident tuition and fees: $1757. Nonresident tuition and fees: $9418. Room only: $2915. Application deadline: 6/15.

## GENERAL
State-supported, comprehensive, coed. Part of California State University System. Awards bachelor's and master's degrees. Founded 1947. Setting: 173-acre urban campus. Undergraduate faculty: 1,123 (481 full-time, 642 part-time); student-faculty ratio is 19:1. Most popular recent majors: child care/development, accounting, psychology.

## CAMPUS VISITS
**College Calendar 1998–99:** *Regular classes:* June 22–Sept. 6; Sept. 24–Dec. 13; Jan. 4–Mar. 21; Mar. 29–June 13. *Breaks:* Sept. 6–23; Dec. 13–Jan. 3; Mar. 21–28; June 13–20. *Final exams:* Aug. 31–Sept. 5; Dec. 7–12; Mar. 15–20; June 7–12. *Special campus days:* Commencement.

## VISIT OPPORTUNITIES

|  | Appointments? | Who? |
|---|---|---|
| **Campus Tour** | recommended | open to all |
| **Admission Interview** | required | open to all |
| **Classroom Visit** | required | open to all |
| **Faculty Meeting** | required | open to all |
| **Overnight Visit** | required | open to all |

**Campus Tours:** Conducted by students. M–F.
**Video:** Free on request.

## CAMPUS FACILITIES
**Of Special Interest:** John K. Kennedy Memorial Library.

# CLAREMONT MCKENNA COLLEGE
Claremont, California

**Contact:** Admission Office, 890 Columbia Avenue, Claremont, CA 91711. *Phone:* 909-621-8088. *E-mail:*

admission@mckenna.edu *Web site:* http://www.mckenna.edu/ *Visit location:* Admission Office, 890 Columbia Avenue.

## QUICK FACTS
Enrollment: 979; UG: 979. Entrance: very difficult. SAT>500: 99% V, 100% M; ACT>18: N/R. Tuition and fees: $19,020. Room and board: $6720. Application deadline: 1/15.

## GENERAL
Independent, 4-year, coed. Part of The Claremont Colleges Consortium. Awards bachelor's degrees. Founded 1946. Setting: 50-acre small-town campus with easy access to Los Angeles. Faculty: 130 (112 full-time, 18 part-time); student-faculty ratio is 9:1. Most popular recent majors: economics, political science, psychology.

## CAMPUS VISITS
**College Calendar 1998–99:** *Regular classes:* Sept. 1–Dec. 11; Jan. 19–May 7. *Breaks:* Oct. 16–21; Mar. 12–22; Dec. 11–Jan. 18. *Final exams:* Dec. 14–19; May 10–15. *Special campus days:* Commencement, May 16.

## VISIT OPPORTUNITIES

|  | Appointments? | Who? |
|---|---|---|
| **Campus Tour** | recommended, not required | open to all |
| **Information Session** | recommended, not required | open to all |
| **Admission Interview** | required | open to all |
| **Classroom Visit** | required | open to all |
| **Faculty Meeting** | required | open to all |
| **Overnight Visit** | required | open to all |

**Information Sessions:** M–F at 9:00 am, 1:30 pm; Sat. at 9:00 am; 60 minutes.

**Interviews:** M–F, Sat.; no senior interviews after Jan. 15.

**Campus Tours:** Conducted by students. M–F at 10:00 am, 2:30 pm; Sat. at 10:00 am, 11:00 am; 60 minutes.

**Class Visits:** Certain predetermined classrooms are open to visitors.

**Overnight Visits:** During the regular academic year, prospective applicants may spend an evening in a residence hall with a student host.

## CAMPUS FACILITIES
**Science:** Appointment Required: Keck Science Center.

**Arts:** Scripps Campus.

**Athletic:** Aquatics Center, Tennis Courts/Rubber Track; Appointment Required: Ducey Gymnasium.

**Of Special Interest:** Appointment Required: Athenaeum, Research Institutes.

# HARVEY MUDD COLLEGE
**Claremont, California**

**Contact:** Admission Office, 301 East 12th Street, Claremont, CA 91711-5990. *Phone:* 909-621-8011. *Fax:* 909-621-8360. *E-mail:* admission@hmc.edu *Web site:* http://www.hmc.edu/ *Visit location:* Admission Office, Kingston Hall, 301 East 12th Street.

## QUICK FACTS
Enrollment: 657; UG: 652. Entrance: most difficult. SAT>500: 100% V, 100% M; ACT>18: N/App. Tuition and fees: $20,325. Room and board: $7521. Application deadline: 1/15.

## GENERAL
Independent, comprehensive, coed. Part of The Claremont Colleges Consortium. Awards bachelor's and master's degrees. Founded 1955. Setting: 33-acre suburban campus with easy access to Los Angeles. Undergraduate faculty: 87 (76 full-time, 11 part-time); student-faculty ratio is 8:1. Most popular recent majors: engineering, computer science, chemistry.

## CAMPUS VISITS
**College Calendar 1998–99:** *Regular classes:* Sept. 1–Dec. 11; Jan. 19–May 5. *Breaks:* Oct. 16–21; Mar. 12–22; Nov. 25–30. *Final exams:* Dec. 14–19; May 10–15. *Special campus days:* Commencement, May 16; Student Presentations, Apr. 26–28.

## VISIT OPPORTUNITIES

|  | Appointments? | Who? |
|---|---|---|
| **Campus Tour** | required | open to all |
| **Admission Interview** | required | open to all |
| **Classroom Visit** | recommended | open to all |
| **Faculty Meeting** | required | open to all |
| **Overnight Visit** | required | open to all |

*Harvey Mudd College (continued)*

**Interviews:** M–F; Sat. interviews available in fall; no interviews scheduled Feb. and Mar.; 30 minutes.

**Campus Tours:** Conducted by students. M–F at 11:00 am, 1:30 pm, 3:00 pm; Sat. at 11:00 am during fall; summer schedule: M–F at 10:00 am, 2:00 pm; 60 minutes.

**Class Visits:** Prospective students may attend a class in their area of interest.

**Overnight Visits:** During the regular academic year, prospective applicants may spend an evening in a residence hall with a student host.

## CAMPUS FACILITIES
**Science:** F.W. Olin Science Center, W.M. Keck Laboratories, Parsons Engineering Building, Jacobs Science Center.

**Arts:** Lang Art Building and Florence Rand Lang Studios, Millard Sheets Art Center, Bridges Hall of Music and Thatcher Music Building, Seaver Theatre and the Greek Theater, Dance Studio.

**Athletic:** Ducey Gymnasium, Linde Activities Center, Aquatics Center.

**Of Special Interest:** Joseph B. Platt Campus Center, Honnold/Mudd Library and Earl W. Huntley Bookstore, McAlister Religious Center, Office of Black Student Affairs, Chicano Student Affairs Center, Asian American Resource Center, International Place.

## LOCAL ATTRACTIONS
The Village Restaurants and Shops; San Gabriel Mountain Resorts (hiking and skiing); Rancho Santa Ana Botanic Garden.

# LOYOLA MARYMOUNT UNIVERSITY
## Los Angeles, California

**Contact:** Office of Admissions, 7900 Loyola Boulevard, Los Angeles, CA 90045-8350. *Phone:* toll-free 800-LMU-INFO. *Fax:* 310-338-2797. *E-mail:* admissions@lmumail.lmu.edu *Web site:* http://www.lmu.edu/ *Visit location:* Undergraduate Admissions, Leaney Center, 7900 Loyola Boulevard.

## QUICK FACTS
Enrollment: 6,721; UG: 4,113. Entrance: moderately difficult. SAT>500: 75% V, 77% M; ACT>18: N/R. Tuition and fees: $16,495. Room and board: $6736. Application deadline: 2/1.

## GENERAL
Independent Roman Catholic, comprehensive, coed. Awards bachelor's, master's, and first professional degrees. Founded 1911. Setting: 128-acre suburban campus. Undergraduate faculty: 518 (264 full-time, 254 part-time); student-faculty ratio is 14:1. Most popular recent majors: business administration, mass communications, psychology.

## CAMPUS VISITS
**College Calendar 1998–99:** *Regular classes:* Aug. 31–Dec. 10; Jan. 11–Apr. 30. *Breaks:* Oct. 22–26; Mar. 1–8. *Final exams:* Dec. 14–18; May 3–7. *Admission office closed:* Dec. 24–Jan. 1, Mar. 1–8, Apr. 2. *Special campus days:* Open House, Nov. 8.

## VISIT OPPORTUNITIES

|  | Appointments? | Who? |
|---|---|---|
| **Campus Tour** | recommended | open to all |
| **Information Session** | recommended | open to all |
| **Admission Interview** | required | open to all |
| **Classroom Visit** | required | admitted applicants only |
| **Faculty Meeting** | required | admitted applicants only |
| **Overnight Visit** | required | admitted applicants only |

**Information Sessions:** M–F; scheduled after tour; 15 minutes.

**Interviews:** M–F; 30 minutes.

**Campus Tours:** Conducted by students. M–F at 10:00 am, 1:00 pm; Sat. at 11:00 am; 70 minutes.

**Class Visits:** Classroom visits are determined by the visit schedule.

**Overnight Visits:** During the regular academic year, prospective applicants may spend an evening in a residence hall with a student host.

**Video:** Free on request.

## CAMPUS FACILITIES
**Science:** Appointment Required: Engineering, Civil, Electrical, Mechanical, Science Labs, Physics, Chemistry, Genetics, Biochemistry and Biology.

**Arts:** Appointment Required: Burns Fine Arts Center, Art Gallery.

**Athletic:** Alumni Gymnasium; Appointment Required: Page Stadium, Gersten Pavilion.

**Of Special Interest:** Hilton Business Center, Von Der Ahe Library.

## LOCAL ATTRACTIONS

Getty Museum, Hollywood, Santa Monica, Beaches, Universal Studios, Disneyland, Dorothy Chandler Pavilion, Schubert Theater, Music Center and the Great Western Forum.

# OCCIDENTAL COLLEGE
## Los Angeles, California

**Contact:** William D. Tingley, Dean of Admission and Financial Aid, Occidental College, Office of Admission, Los Angeles, CA 90041. *Phone:* toll-free 800-825-5262. *Fax:* 213-341-4875. *E-mail:* admission@oxy.edu *Web site:* http://www.oxy.edu/ *Visit location:* Admission Office, 1600 Campus Road.

## QUICK FACTS

Enrollment: 1,548; UG: 1,520. Entrance: very difficult. SAT>500: 85% V, 87% M; ACT>18: N/R. Tuition and fees: $19,957. Room and board: $5890. Application deadline: 1/15.

## GENERAL

Independent, comprehensive, coed. Awards bachelor's and master's degrees. Founded 1887. Setting: 136-acre urban campus. Undergraduate faculty: 188 (139 full-time, 49 part-time); student-faculty ratio is 11:1. Most popular recent majors: psychology, comparative literature, biology.

## CAMPUS VISITS

**College Calendar 1998–99:** *Regular classes:* Aug. 31–Dec. 8; Jan. 19–Apr. 30. *Final exams:* Dec. 10–16; May 4–10. *Special campus days:* Commencement, May 16.

## VISIT OPPORTUNITIES

| | Appointments? | Who? |
|---|---|---|
| **Campus Tour** | not required | applicants and parents |
| **Information Session** | not required | |
| **Admission Interview** | required | |
| **Classroom Visit** | | open to all |
| **Faculty Meeting** | | open to all |

| | Appointments? | Who? |
|---|---|---|
| **Overnight Visit** | required | |

**Information Sessions:** M–F, select Sat.; call for available schedule; 45 minutes.

**Interviews:** M–F, select Sat.; 45 minutes.

**Campus Tours:** Conducted by students. M–F, select Sat.; call for available schedule; 45 minutes.

**Class Visits:** Prospective students may attend a class in their area of interest.

**Overnight Visits:** During the regular academic year, prospective applicants may spend an evening in a residence hall with a student host.

## CAMPUS FACILITIES

**Arts:** Mullin Family Art Studio, Keck Theatre.

## LOCAL ATTRACTIONS

Old Town Pasadena.

# PEPPERDINE UNIVERSITY
## Malibu, California

**Contact:** Admissions Office, 24255 Pacific Coast Highway, Malibu, CA 90263. *Phone:* 310-456-4392. *Fax:* 310-456-4861. *E-mail:* admission-seaver@pepperdine.edu *Web site:* http://www.pepperdine.edu/ *Visit location:* Office of Admission, 24255 Pacific Coast Highway.

## QUICK FACTS

Enrollment: 7,804; UG: 3,320. Entrance: very difficult. SAT>500: 94% V, 95% M; ACT>18: N/R. Tuition and fees: $21,170. Room and board: $6980. Application deadline: 1/15.

## GENERAL

Independent, university, coed, Church of Christ. Awards bachelor's, master's, doctoral, and first professional degrees (the university is organized into four colleges: Seaver, the School of Law, the School of Business and Management, and the Graduate School of Education and Psychology. Seaver College is the undergraduate, residential, liberal arts school of the University and is committed to providing education of outstanding academic quality with particular attention to Christian values). Founded 1937. Setting: 830-acre small-town campus with easy access to Los Angeles. Undergraduate faculty: 310

*Pepperdine University (continued)*

(168 full-time, 142 part-time); student-faculty ratio is 13:1. Most popular recent majors: business administration, communications, international relations.

## CAMPUS VISITS

**College Calendar 1998–99:** *Regular classes:* Aug. 24–Dec. 9; Jan. 6–Apr. 22. *Breaks:* Dec. 10–Jan. 5; Mar. 3–7. *Final exams:* Dec. 3–9; Apr. 15–21. *Admission office closed:* Dec. 24–Jan. 1.

## VISIT OPPORTUNITIES

| | Appointments? | Who? |
|---|---|---|
| **Campus Tour** | recommended, not required | open to all |
| **Information Session** | required | open to all |
| **Admission Interview** | required | applicants only |
| **Classroom Visit** | required | open to all |
| **Faculty Meeting** | required | open to all |
| **Overnight Visit** | required | applicants only |

**Information Sessions:** M–F 9:00 am–3:00 pm; Sept.–Nov. available at sites around the country; 45 minutes.

**Interviews:** M–F; out-of-state interviews available; 45 minutes.

**Campus Tours:** Conducted by students. M–F 9:00 am–4:00 pm; 45 minutes.

**Class Visits:** Prospective students may attend a class in their area of interest, classroom visits are determined by the visit schedule.

**Overnight Visits:** During the regular academic year, prospective applicants may spend an evening in a residence hall with a student host.

**Video:** Free on request.

## CAMPUS FACILITIES

**Arts:** Smother's theater, Frederick R. Weisman Museum, Lindhurst theater, Raitt Recital Hall.

**Athletic:** Eddy D. Field Baseball Stadium, Firestone Fieldhouse, Ralphs-Straus Tennis Center.

**Of Special Interest:** Cultural Arts Center, Equestrian Center.

# SAINT MARY'S COLLEGE OF CALIFORNIA
**Moraga, California**

**Contact:** Jeanne Olin, Visit Coordinator, PO Box 4800, Moraga, CA 94575. *Phone:* toll-free 800-800-4SMC. *Fax:* 925-376-7193. *E-mail:* smcadmit@stmarys-ca.edu *Web site:* http://www.stmarys-ca.edu/ *Visit location:* Admissions, Filippi Hall—2nd Floor, PO Box 4800.

## QUICK FACTS

Enrollment: 4,238; UG: 2,998. Entrance: moderately difficult. SAT>500: 79% V, 79% M; ACT>18: 88%. Tuition and fees: $15,998. Room and board: $7119. Application deadline: 2/1.

## GENERAL

Independent Roman Catholic, comprehensive, coed. Awards bachelor's and master's degrees. Founded 1863. Setting: 440-acre suburban campus with easy access to San Francisco. Undergraduate faculty: 162 (150 full-time, 12 part-time); student-faculty ratio is 14:1. Most popular recent majors: business administration, psychology, mass communications.

## CAMPUS VISITS

**College Calendar 1998–99:** *Regular classes:* Sept. 1–Dec. 4; Jan. 4–29; Feb. 9–May 14. *Breaks:* Dec. 11–Jan. 3; Jan. 30–Feb. 7; Mar. 27–Apr. 5. *Final exams:* Dec. 5–10; May 15–20. *Admission office closed:* Good Friday, Apr. 2. *Special campus days:* All School Colloquium, Jan. 13; Commencement, May 22; Mid-session Holiday, Oct. 16.

## VISIT OPPORTUNITIES

| | Appointments? | Who? |
|---|---|---|
| **Campus Tour** | recommended | applicants and parents |
| **Admission Interview** | recommended | |
| **Classroom Visit** | required | |
| **Overnight Visit** | required | applicants only |

**Interviews:** M–F, select Sat.; 30 minutes.

**Campus Tours:** Conducted by students. M–F at 9:00 am, 11:00 am, 1:00 pm, 3:00 pm; select Sat. at 10:00 am; 60 minutes.

**Class Visits:** Prospective students may attend a class in their area of interest.

**Overnight Visits:** During the regular academic year, prospective applicants may spend an evening in a residence hall with a student host.

### CAMPUS FACILITIES
**Science:** Sichel Hall, Galileo Hall.
**Arts:** Hearst Art Gallery.
**Athletic:** McKeon Pavilion, Power Plant.
**Of Special Interest:** Garavonta Hall, Chapel.

## SAN DIEGO STATE UNIVERSITY
San Diego, California

**Contact:** Ambassadors Office, Student Resource Center, San Diego State University, San Diego, CA 92182-7440. *Phone:* 619-594-6868 (VMS). *Fax:* 619-594-1045. *E-mail:* ambassad@mail.sdsu.edu *Web site:* http://www.sdsu.edu/ *Visit location:* Student Resource Center, Student Services Building, Room 1602, 5500 Campanile Drive.

### QUICK FACTS
Enrollment: 29,898; UG: 24,448. Entrance: moderately difficult. SAT>500: 43% V, 50% M; ACT>18: 69%. Resident tuition and fees: $1854. Nonresident tuition and fees: $9480. Room and board: $6730. Application deadline: 11/15.

### GENERAL
State-supported, university, coed. Part of California State University System. Awards bachelor's, master's, and doctoral degrees. Founded 1897. Setting: 300-acre urban campus. Undergraduate faculty: 2,264 (886 full-time, 1,378 part-time); student-faculty ratio is 13:1. Most popular recent majors: business administration, psychology, biology.

### CAMPUS VISITS
**College Calendar 1998–99:** *Regular classes:* Aug. 31–Dec. 11; Jan. 25–May 13. *Breaks:* Nov. 26–28; Mar. 29–Apr. 3. *Final exams:* Dec. 12–19; May 14–21. *Special campus days:* Commencement, May 22–23; Family Weekend, Sept. 25–26; Homecoming; Open House.

### VISIT OPPORTUNITIES

|  | Appointments? | Who? |
| --- | --- | --- |
| **Campus Tour** | not required | open to all |
| **Information Session** | required |  |
| **Classroom Visit** | required |  |

**Information Sessions:** Call Student Outreach Services 619-594-6336 for availability and special arrangements; 30 minutes.
**Campus Tours:** Conducted by students. M–F at 9:00 am, 10:00 am, 11:00 am, 12:00 pm, 1:00 pm, 2:00 pm; Sat. at 11:00 am; abbreviated schedule during summer and school breaks; 50 minutes.
**Class Visits:** Classroom visits are determined by the visit schedule.
**Video:** Free on request.

### CAMPUS FACILITIES
**Science:** Astronomy Lab, Wind Tunnel.
**Arts:** University Art Gallery, Special Collections displayed in Love Library.
**Athletic:** Cox Avenue, Aztec Recreation Center, Tony Gwynn Stadium.
**Of Special Interest:** Residence Halls, Aztec Center (student union).

### LOCAL ATTRACTIONS
San Diego Zoo, Wild Animal Park, Sea World, Old Town, Gaslamp Quarter, Beaches, Coronado.

## SAN FRANCISCO STATE UNIVERSITY
San Francisco, California

**Contact:** Student Outreach Services, 1600 Holloway Avenue, San Francisco, CA 94132. *Phone:* 415-338-2355. *Fax:* 415-338-0903. *E-mail:* outreach@sfsu.edu *Web site:* http://www.sfsu.edu/ *Visit location:* Student Outreach Services, Centennial Square, San Francisco State University, 1600 Holloway Avenue.

### QUICK FACTS
Enrollment: 27,420; UG: 21,049. Entrance: moderately difficult. SAT>500: 42% V, 47% M; ACT>18: 65%. Resident tuition and fees: $1982. Nonresident tuition and fees: $7886. Room and board: $5935. Application deadline: 11/30.

### GENERAL
State-supported, comprehensive, coed. Part of California State University System. Awards bachelor's and master's degrees. Founded 1899. Setting: 90-acre urban campus. Undergraduate faculty: 1,557 (785 full-time, 772 part-time); student-faculty ratio is 21:1. Most popular recent majors: accounting, liberal arts and studies, business administration.

*San Francisco State University (continued)*

## CAMPUS VISITS

**College Calendar 1998–99:** *Regular classes:* Aug. 26–Dec. 11; Jan. 27–May 19. *Breaks:* Dec. 21–Jan. 26. *Final exams:* Dec. 12–18; May 21–28. *Special campus days:* Commencement, May 29.

## VISIT OPPORTUNITIES

| | Appointments? | Who? |
|---|---|---|
| **Campus Tour** | not required | open to all |
| **Information Session** | required | |

**Information Sessions:** By appointment only.
**Campus Tours:** Conducted by students. M–F; call for schedule; 50 minutes.

## CAMPUS FACILITIES

**Of Special Interest:** J. Paul Leonard Library.

# SCRIPPS COLLEGE

**Claremont, California**

**Contact:** Office of Admission, 1030 Columbia Avenue, Claremont, CA 91711. *Phone:* toll-free 800-770-1333. *Fax:* 909-621-8323. *E-mail:* admofc@ad.scrippscol.edu *Web site:* http://www.ScrippsCol.edu/ *Visit location:* Office of Admission, Balch Hall, 1030 Columbia Avenue.

## QUICK FACTS

**Enrollment:** 713; UG: 713. **Entrance:** very difficult. SAT>500: 97% V, 96% M; ACT>18: 100%. Tuition and fees: $19,480. Room and board: $7750. Application deadline: 2/1.

## GENERAL

Independent, 4-year, women only. Part of The Claremont Colleges Consortium. Awards bachelor's degrees. Founded 1926. Setting: 30-acre suburban campus with easy access to Los Angeles. Faculty: 79 (52 full-time, 27 part-time); student-faculty ratio is 11:1. Most popular recent majors: psychology, biology, international relations.

## CAMPUS VISITS

**College Calendar 1998–99:** *Regular classes:* Sept. 1–Dec. 11; Jan. 19–May 7. *Breaks:* Oct. 17–20; Mar. 13–21; Nov. 25–29. *Final exams:* Dec. 14–19; May 10–15. *Special campus days:* Commencement, May 16.

## VISIT OPPORTUNITIES

| | Appointments? | Who? |
|---|---|---|
| **Campus Tour** | required | open to all |
| **Admission Interview** | required | open to all |
| **Classroom Visit** | required | open to all |
| **Faculty Meeting** | required | open to all |
| **Overnight Visit** | required | open to all |

**Interviews:** M–F; Sat. morning in Oct. and Nov.; 30 minutes.
**Campus Tours:** Conducted by students. M–F at 10:00 am, 12:00 pm, 3:00 pm; select Sat.; during breaks and summer at 10:00 am, 2:00 pm; Sat. at 10:00 am during Oct. and Nov.; 60 minutes.
**Class Visits:** Prospective students may attend a class in their area of interest.
**Overnight Visits:** During the regular academic year, prospective applicants may spend an evening in a residence hall with a student host.

## CAMPUS FACILITIES

**Science:** Appointment Required: W.M. Keck Science Center.
**Arts:** Appointment Required: Millard Sheets Art Center, Ruth Chandler Williamson Gallery.
**Athletic:** Appointment Required: Ducey Athletic Center.

# STANFORD UNIVERSITY

**Stanford, California**

**Contact:** Stanford Visitor Information, Press Courtyard, Santa Teresa Street, Stanford, CA 94305-2250. *Phone:* 650-723-2560. *Fax:* 650-725-6232. *E-mail:* visinfo@sherlock.stanford.edu *Web site:* http://www.stanford.edu/ *Visit location:* Undergraduate Admission, Old Union 232.

## QUICK FACTS

**Enrollment:** 15,796; UG: 6,427. **Entrance:** most difficult. SAT>500: 99% V, 99% M; ACT>18: N/R. Tuition and fees: $21,389. Room and board: $7560. Application deadline: 12/15.

## GENERAL

Independent, university, coed. Awards bachelor's, master's, doctoral, and first professional degrees. Founded 1891. Setting: 8,180-acre suburban campus with easy access to San Francisco. Undergraduate faculty: 1,534; student-faculty ratio is 10:1. Most popular recent majors: engineering, economics.

## CAMPUS VISITS
**College Calendar 1998–99:** *Regular classes:* Sept. 23–Dec. 6; Jan. 5–Mar. 14; Mar. 30–June 3. *Breaks:* Dec. 12–Jan. 4; Mar. 20–29; June 10–Sept. 21; Nov. 26–29. *Final exams:* Dec. 7–11; Mar. 15–19; June 4–9. *Admission office closed:* first Tue. morning of each month. *Special campus days:* Commencement, June 13; School holiday, Jan. 18, Feb. 15, May 31.

## VISIT OPPORTUNITIES

| | Appointments? | Who? |
| --- | --- | --- |
| **Campus Tour** | not required | open to all |
| **Information Session** | | open to all |
| **Classroom Visit** | not required | open to all |
| **Overnight Visit** | | admitted applicants only |

**Information Sessions:** M–F at 2:00 pm; M–F at 2:00 pm Jun. 1 through Dec. 15 with 9:30 am also available Jul. 1 to Aug. 31; no sessions Dec. 15 to May 31; call for availability during high school spring break period; 50 minutes.
**Campus Tours:** Conducted by students. M–F at 11:00 am, 3:15 pm; daily except Dec.; 60 minutes.
**Class Visits:** Prospective students may attend a class in their area of interest.
**Overnight Visits:** During the regular academic year, prospective applicants may spend an evening in a residence hall with a student host.
**Video:** Free on request.

## CAMPUS FACILITIES
**Science:** Appointment Required: Stanford Linear Accelerator.
**Arts:** Rodin Sculpture Garden, New Guinea Sculpture Garden, Stanford Art Gallery, Stanford Art Museum (open spring 1999).
**Athletic:** Rosenberg Athletic Hall of Fame.
**Of Special Interest:** Hoover Tower Observation Platform, Memorial Church.

# UNIVERSITY OF CALIFORNIA, BERKELEY
**Berkeley, California**

**Contact:** Visitor Services, University of California, Berkeley, 101 University Hall, #4206, Berkeley, CA 94720-4206. *Phone:* 510-642-5215. *Fax:* 510-642-3423. *Web site:* http://www.berkeley.edu/ *Visit location:* Visitor Services, University Hall, 2200 University Avenue.

## QUICK FACTS
Entrance: very difficult. SAT>500: N/App; ACT>18: N/App. Resident tuition and fees: $4355. Nonresident tuition and fees: $13,289. Room and board: $7657. Application deadline: 11/30.

## GENERAL
State-supported, university, coed. Part of University of California System. Awards bachelor's, master's, doctoral, and first professional degrees. Founded 1868. Setting: 1,232-acre urban campus with easy access to San Francisco. Undergraduate faculty: 1,787; student-faculty ratio is 17:1. Most popular recent majors: molecular biology, English, psychology.

## CAMPUS VISITS
**College Calendar 1998–99:** *Regular classes:* Aug. 24–Dec. 5; Jan. 19–May 10. *Breaks:* Dec. 17–Jan. 18. *Final exams:* Dec. 9–17; May 14–22. *Admission office closed:* Nov. 27, Dec. 5–Jan. 19, Mar. 22–26, May 10–22. *Special campus days:* Cal Day; Homecoming Reunion and Parents Weekend, Sept. 25–27; Welcome Week, Aug. 17–21.

## VISIT OPPORTUNITIES

| | Appointments? | Who? |
| --- | --- | --- |
| **Campus Tour** | not required | open to all |
| **Information Session** | not required | open to all |
| **Classroom Visit** | not required | open to all |
| **Faculty Meeting** | required | applicants and parents |
| **Overnight Visit** | required | applicants only |

**Information Sessions:** M–F 11:30 am–12:00 pm; 30 minutes.

**Campus Tours:** Conducted by students. M–F 10:00–11:30 am; summer tours Sat. at 10:00 am, Sun. at 1:00 pm; self-guided tours Sat. at 10:00 am and 1:00 pm, Sun. at 1:00 pm; group tours available with two weeks notice; 90 minutes.

**Class Visits:** Certain predetermined classrooms are open to visitors.

*University of California, Berkeley (continued)*

**Overnight Visits:** During the regular academic year, prospective applicants may spend an evening in a residence hall with a student host.

### CAMPUS FACILITIES
**Science:** Valley Life Sciences Building, Lawrence Hall of Science, Phoebe Hearst Museum of Anthropology.

**Arts:** University Art Museum and Pacific Film Archive, Zellerback Performing Arts Center.

**Athletic:** Recreational Sports Facility.

**Of Special Interest:** Campanile-Lidi Tree Top, Doe Library, Bancroft Library, UC Botanical Garden.

### LOCAL ATTRACTIONS
San Francisco Bay Area; Point Reyes National Seashore; the vineyards of Napa and Sonoma Counties.

# UNIVERSITY OF CALIFORNIA, LOS ANGELES
**Los Angeles, California**

**Contact:** Campus Tours, 1147 Murphy Hall, Box 951436, Los Angeles, CA 90095-1436. *Phone:* 310-825-8764. *Fax:* 310-206-1206. *E-mail:* ugadm@saonet. ucla.edu *Web site:* http://www.ucla.edu/ *Visit location:* 405 Hilgard Avenue.

### QUICK FACTS
Enrollment: 35,557; UG: 23,924. Entrance: very difficult. SAT>500: 91% V, 95% M; ACT>18: 97%. Resident tuition and fees: $4050. Nonresident tuition and fees: $13,034. Room and board: $6490. Application deadline: 11/30.

### GENERAL
State-supported, university, coed. Part of University of California System. Awards bachelor's, master's, doctoral, and first professional degrees. Founded 1919. Setting: 419-acre urban campus. Undergraduate faculty: 3,276; student-faculty ratio is 19:1. Most popular recent majors: biology, psychology, economics.

### CAMPUS VISITS
**College Calendar 1998–99:** *Regular classes:* Oct. 1–Dec. 11; Jan. 11–Mar. 19; Apr. 5–June 11. *Final exams:* Dec. 12–18; Mar. 20–26; June 12–18. *Admission office closed:* Nov. 27, Dec. 24, Dec. 31, Mar. 29.

### VISIT OPPORTUNITIES

| | Appointments? | Who? |
|---|---|---|
| **Campus Tour** | required | open to all |
| **Information Session** | not required | open to all |
| **Classroom Visit** | not required | open to all |
| **Faculty Meeting** | | open to all |

**Information Sessions:** M–F 9:00 am–5:00 pm.

**Campus Tours:** Conducted by students. M–F at 10:15 am, 2:15 pm; Sat. at 10:15 am; call for schedule during holidays and breaks; during final exams one tour daily at 12:15 pm; 120 minutes.

**Class Visits:** Certain predetermined classrooms are open to visitors.

### CAMPUS FACILITIES
**Science:** Laserama.

**Arts:** Fowler Museum of Cultural History, Franklin Murphy Sculpture Garden, UCLA at the Armand Hammer.

**Athletic:** Morgan Center Athletic Hall of Fame, Wooden Center, Sunset Canyon Recreational Center.

**Of Special Interest:** Appointment Required: Hannah Carter Japanese Garden.

### LOCAL ATTRACTIONS
J. Paul Getty Museum; 3rd Street Promenade, Santa Monica.

# UNIVERSITY OF SAN FRANCISCO
**San Francisco, California**

**Contact:** Office of Admission, 2130 Fulton Street, San Francisco, CA 94117. *Phone:* 415-422-6563 or toll-free 800-CALL USF (out-of-state). *Fax:* 415-422-2217. *Web site:* http://www.usfca.edu/ *Visit location:* Office of Admission, Campion Hall, Room B-10, 2130 Fulton Street.

### QUICK FACTS
Enrollment: 7,814; UG: 4,534. Entrance: moderately difficult. SAT>500: 67% V, 70% M; ACT>18: 91%. Tuition and fees: $15,950. Room and board: $7260. Application deadline: 2/1.

## GENERAL

Independent Roman Catholic (Jesuit), university, coed. Awards bachelor's, master's, doctoral, and first professional degrees. Founded 1855. Setting: 55-acre urban campus. Undergraduate faculty: 770 (295 full-time, 475 part-time); student-faculty ratio is 15:1. Most popular recent majors: nursing, mass communications, psychology.

## CAMPUS VISITS

**College Calendar 1998–99:** *Regular classes:* Aug. 27–Dec. 9; Jan. 21–May 11. *Breaks:* Mar. 15–19. *Final exams:* Dec. 12–18; May 13–19. *Special campus days:* Fall Commencement, Dec. 18; Spring Commencement, May 21–22.

## VISIT OPPORTUNITIES

|  | Appointments? | Who? |
| --- | --- | --- |
| **Campus Tour** | recommended | open to all |
| **Information Session** | recommended | open to all |
| **Admission Interview** | required | applicants and parents |
| **Classroom Visit** | required | open to all |
| **Faculty Meeting** | required | open to all |
| **Overnight Visit** | required | open to all |

**Information Sessions:** M–F at 10:00 am, 2:00 pm; reservations required for select Sat. in spring and fall at 10:00 am.

**Interviews:** M–F.

**Campus Tours:** Conducted by students. M–F; follows information session; 90 minutes.

**Class Visits:** Classroom visits are determined by the visit schedule.

**Overnight Visits:** During the regular academic year, prospective applicants may spend an evening in a residence hall with a student host.

**Video:** Free on request.

## CAMPUS FACILITIES

**Science:** Harney Science Center.

**Arts:** Gill Theatre, Gershwin Theatre, Donohue Rare Book Room.

**Athletic:** Koret Health and Recreation Center, War Memorial Gymnasium.

**Of Special Interest:** Center for the Pacific Rim, KUSF—Radio Station 90.3 FM.

## LOCAL ATTRACTIONS

Downtown San Francisco; Pacific Ocean; Fisherman's Wharf; Pier 39; Golden Gate Bridge and Park.

# UNIVERSITY OF SOUTHERN CALIFORNIA
## Los Angeles, California

**Contact:** Admission Office, University Park Campus, Los Angeles, CA 90089-0911. *Phone:* 213-740-6616. *Fax:* 213-740-9076. *E-mail:* visitusc@usc.edu *Web site:* http://www.usc.edu/ *Visit location:* Admission Center, Trojan Hall Room 101, University Park Campus.

## QUICK FACTS

Enrollment: 27,663; UG: 14,751. Entrance: very difficult. SAT>500: 90% V, 95% M; ACT>18: N/App. Tuition and fees: $20,480. Room and board: $6748. Application deadline: 1/31.

## GENERAL

Independent, university, coed. Awards bachelor's, master's, doctoral, and first professional degrees and post-master's certificates. Founded 1880. Setting: 155-acre urban campus. Undergraduate faculty: 3,508 (2,532 full-time, 976 part-time); student-faculty ratio is 14:1. Most popular recent majors: business administration, mass communications, political science.

## CAMPUS VISITS

**College Calendar 1998–99:** *Regular classes:* Sept. 2–Dec. 11; Jan. 13–May 3. *Breaks:* Dec. 22–Jan. 12. *Final exams:* Dec. 14–21; May 6–13. *Admission office closed:* university holidays. *Special campus days:* Academic Honors, Mar. 9; Commencement, May 14; Homecoming, Oct. 31.

## VISIT OPPORTUNITIES

|  | Appointments? | Who? |
| --- | --- | --- |
| **Campus Tour** | required | open to all |
| **Information Session** | required | open to all |
| **Admission Interview** | required | applicants only |
| **Classroom Visit** |  | admitted applicants only |
| **Faculty Meeting** |  | admitted applicants only |

*University of Southern California (continued)*

## VISIT OPPORTUNITIES—*continued*

| | Appointments? | Who? |
|---|---|---|
| **Overnight Visit** | | admitted applicants only |

**Information Sessions:** Mon. at 9:00 am, 1:00 pm; Wed. at 9:00 am, 1:00 pm; Fri. at 9:00 am, 12:00 pm; 50 minutes.

**Interviews:** M–F; Sat. by invitation; 30 minutes.

**Campus Tours:** Conducted by students. M–F, select Sat. 10:00 am–3:00 pm; 50 minutes.

**Overnight Visits:** During the regular academic year, prospective applicants may spend an evening in a residence hall with a student host.

## CAMPUS FACILITIES

**Science:** Seeley G. Mudd Science, Lecture and Laboratory Facilities; Appointment Required: Hedco Neurosciences Building, IMSC Demonstration Lab.

**Arts:** Fisher Gallery; Appointment Required: Cinema Television Complex.

**Athletic:** Heritage Hall, McDonalds Olympic Swim Stadium; Appointment Required: Lyon Recreation Facility.

**Of Special Interest:** Leavey Library, Taper Hall Language Laboratories.

## LOCAL ATTRACTIONS

Exposition Park Museums, Shrine Auditorium.

# UNIVERSITY OF THE PACIFIC
**Stockton, California**

**Contact:** Office of Admissions, University of the Pacific, 3601 Pacific Avenue, Stockton, CA 95211. *Phone:* toll-free 800-959-2867. *Fax:* 209-946-2413. *E-mail:* admissions@uop.edu *Web site:* http://www.uop.edu/ *Visit location:* Office of Admissions, Knoles Hall, 3601 Pacific Avenue.

## QUICK FACTS

Enrollment: 5,584; UG: 2,761. Entrance: moderately difficult. SAT>500: 70% V, 78% M; ACT>18: N/R. Tuition and fees: $19,365. Room and board: $5770. Application deadline: 2/15.

## GENERAL

Independent, university, coed. Awards bachelor's, master's, doctoral, and first professional degrees. Founded 1851. Setting: 175-acre suburban campus with easy access to Sacramento. Undergraduate faculty: 592 (375 full-time, 217 part-time). Most popular recent majors: liberal arts and studies, pharmacy, business administration.

## CAMPUS VISITS

**College Calendar 1998–99:** *Regular classes:* Aug. 25–Dec. 11; Jan. 19–May 4. *Breaks:* Dec. 21–Jan. 15; Mar. 15–19. *Final exams:* Dec. 14–18; May 6–12. *Special campus days:* Commencement, May 15–16; Thanksgiving vacation, Nov. 25–27.

## VISIT OPPORTUNITIES

| | Appointments? | Who? |
|---|---|---|
| **Campus Tour** | recommended | open to all |
| **Admission Interview** | recommended | open to all |
| **Classroom Visit** | required | open to all |
| **Faculty Meeting** | required | open to all |
| **Overnight Visit** | required | open to all |

**Interviews:** M–F, select Sat.; Sat. by appointment only; two weeks notice recommended; 50 minutes.

**Campus Tours:** Conducted by students. M–F at 11:00 am, 2:00 pm; select Sat. at 11:00 am, 1:30 pm; Sun. at 1:30 pm; call to verify availability of Sat. and Sun. tours; 60 minutes.

**Class Visits:** Classroom visits are determined by the visit schedule.

**Overnight Visits:** During the regular academic year, prospective applicants may spend an evening in a residence hall with a student host.

## CAMPUS FACILITIES

**Of Special Interest:** Holt Memorial Library.

# COLORADO

# ADAMS STATE COLLEGE
**Alamosa, Colorado**

**Contact:** Gary C. Pierson, Director of Admission, 208 Edgemont Boulevard, Alamosa, CO 81102. *Phone:* 719-587-7712 or toll-free 800-824-6494. *Fax:* 719-587-7522. *E-mail:* ascadmit@adams.edu *Web site:*

http://www.adams.edu/ *Visit location:* Office of Admissions, Richardson Hall, 208 Edgemont Boulevard.

## QUICK FACTS

Enrollment: 2,331; UG: 2,039. Entrance: moderately difficult. SAT>500: N/R; ACT>18: 75%. Resident tuition and fees: $1956. Nonresident tuition and fees: $5890. Room and board: $4424. Application deadline: 8/1.

## GENERAL

State-supported, comprehensive, coed. Part of State Colleges in Colorado. Awards associate, bachelor's, and master's degrees. Founded 1921. Setting: 90-acre small-town campus. Undergraduate faculty: 151 (100 full-time, 51 part-time); student-faculty ratio is 18:1. Most popular recent majors: biology, business administration, education.

## CAMPUS VISITS

**College Calendar 1998–99:** *Regular classes:* Aug. 25–Dec. 14; Jan. 12–May 3. *Breaks:* Nov. 25–29; Mar. 15–19; Dec. 19–Jan. 10. *Final exams:* Dec. 15–17; May 4–7. *Admission office closed:* Dec. 23–Jan. 4. *Special campus days:* Fall Commencement, Dec. 18; Fall Recess, Oct. 29–30; Homecoming, Oct. 17; Open House, Nov. 14, Feb. 20; Snow Day, Feb. 19; Spring Commencement, May 8.

## VISIT OPPORTUNITIES

|  | Appointments? | Who? |
|---|---|---|
| **Campus Tour** | recommended, not required | open to all |
| **Information Session** | not required | open to all |
| **Admission Interview** | not required | open to all |
| **Classroom Visit** | required | open to all |
| **Faculty Meeting** | recommended | open to all |
| **Overnight Visit** | required | |

**Information Sessions:** M–F; Sat. by appointment only; 30 minutes.

**Interviews:** M–F; Sat. visit/interviews by appointment only; 30 minutes.

**Campus Tours:** Conducted by students. M–F at 11:00 am, 2:00 pm; Sat. by appointment only; 60 minutes.

**Class Visits:** Classroom visits are determined by the visit schedule.

**Overnight Visits:** During the regular academic year and over the summer, prospective applicants may spend an evening in a residence hall.

## CAMPUS FACILITIES

**Science:** Science, Mathematics, and Technology Center; Appointment Required: planetarium.

**Athletic:** Rex Activity Center—Student Recreation Center.

**Of Special Interest:** Appointment Required: Luther Bean Museum.

## LOCAL ATTRACTIONS

Great Sand Dunes National Monument; SLV Alligator Farm.

# THE COLORADO COLLEGE
**Colorado Springs, Colorado**

**Contact:** Mrs. Gerry Schmitt, 14 East Cache La Poudre, Colorado Springs, CO 80903. *Phone:* toll-free 800-542-7214. *Fax:* 719-389-6816. *Web site:* http://www.cc.colorado.edu/ *Visit location:* Admission Office, Cutler Hall, 912 North Cascade.

## QUICK FACTS

Enrollment: 2,024; UG: 1,999. Entrance: very difficult. SAT>500: 95% V, 98% M; ACT>18: 100%. Tuition and fees: $19,980. Room and board: $5100. Application deadline: 1/15.

## GENERAL

Independent, comprehensive, coed. Awards bachelor's and master's degrees (master's degree in education only). Founded 1874. Setting: 90-acre suburban campus with easy access to Denver. Undergraduate faculty: 187 (167 full-time, 20 part-time); student-faculty ratio is 11:1. Most popular recent majors: English, biology, economics.

## CAMPUS VISITS

**College Calendar 1998–99:** *Regular classes:* Aug. 31–Dec. 18; Jan. 18–May 12. *Breaks:* Dec. 18–Jan. 4; Mar. 10–22. *Admission office closed:* Thanksgiving, Nov. 26–29; spring break, Mar. 11–21; winter break, Dec. 19–Jan. 4. *Special campus days:* Commencement, May 17; Homecoming and Parent's Weekend, Oct. 9–11.

## VISIT OPPORTUNITIES

|  | Appointments? | Who? |
|---|---|---|
| **Campus Tour** | recommended, not required | open to all |

*The Colorado College (continued)*

## VISIT OPPORTUNITIES—*continued*

|  | Appointments? | Who? |
|---|---|---|
| **Information Session** | recommended, not required | open to all |
| **Admission Interview** | required | |
| **Classroom Visit** | required | open to all |
| **Faculty Meeting** | recommended | open to all |
| **Overnight Visit** | required | open to all |

**Information Sessions:** M–F at 11:00 am, 2:30 pm; Sat. at 10:00 am during academic year; Wed. and afternoons not available during Jan., Feb., and Mar.; 60 minutes.

**Interviews:** Private appointments with staff representative available.

**Campus Tours:** Conducted by students. M–F at 1:15 pm; Sat. during academic year at 11:00 am; 75 minutes.

**Class Visits:** Prospective students choose three areas of interest; visit based upon availability.

**Overnight Visits:** During the regular academic year, prospective applicants may spend an evening in a residence hall with a student host.

**Video:** Available, fee charged.

## CAMPUS FACILITIES
**Science:** Olin Hall, Barres Science Center.
**Arts:** Packard Hall.
**Athletic:** El Pomar Sports Center.

## LOCAL ATTRACTIONS
Gardens of the Gods; Olympic Training Center; Pikes Peak.

# COLORADO SCHOOL OF MINES
**Golden, Colorado**

**Contact:** Admissions Office, 1811 Elm Street, Golden, CO 80401. *Phone:* 303-273-3220 or toll-free 800-446-9488 (out-of-state). *Fax:* 303-273-3509. *E-mail:* admit@mines.edu *Web site:* http://www.mines. edu/ *Visit location:* Undergraduate Admissions Office, Weaver Towers, Suite 14E, 1811 Elm Street.

## QUICK FACTS
Enrollment: 3,199; UG: 2,405. Entrance: very difficult. SAT>500: 90% V, 98% M; ACT>18: N/R.

Resident tuition and fees: $5013. Nonresident tuition and fees: $14,475. Room and board: $4730. Application deadline: 6/1.

## GENERAL
State-supported, university, coed. Awards bachelor's, master's, and doctoral degrees. Founded 1874. Setting: 373-acre small-town campus with easy access to Denver. Undergraduate faculty: 290 (200 full-time, 90 part-time); student-faculty ratio is 16:1. Most popular recent majors: engineering, chemical engineering, computer science.

## CAMPUS VISITS
**College Calendar 1998–99:** *Regular classes:* Aug. 26–Dec. 10; Jan. 6–Apr. 29. *Breaks:* Nov. 26–29; Mar. 13–21; Dec. 18–Jan. 3. *Final exams:* Dec. 14–17; May 3–6. *Special campus days:* Commencement, Dec. 18, May 7.

## VISIT OPPORTUNITIES

|  | Appointments? | Who? |
|---|---|---|
| **Campus Tour** | required | applicants and parents |
| **Information Session** | required | |
| **Admission Interview** | required | applicants and parents |
| **Classroom Visit** | required | applicants and parents |
| **Faculty Meeting** | required | applicants and parents |

**Information Sessions:** Included with tour and interview.

**Interviews:** M–F 9:00 am–4:00 pm; 60 minutes.

**Campus Tours:** Conducted by students. M–F 9:00 am–4:00 pm; 60 minutes.

**Class Visits:** Classroom visits are determined by the visit schedule.

## CAMPUS FACILITIES
**Science:** Coolbaugh Hall, Hill Hall; Appointment Required: Alderson Hall.
**Athletic:** Appointment Required: Steinhauer Field House.

# COLORADO STATE UNIVERSITY
**Fort Collins, Colorado**

**Contact:** Office of Admissions, Spruce Hall, Fort Collins, CO 80523-0015. *Phone:* 970-491-6909. *Web site:* http://www.colostate.edu/ *Visit location:* Office of Admissions, Spruce Hall.

## QUICK FACTS

Enrollment: 22,344; UG: 18,451. Entrance: moderately difficult. SAT>500: 78% V, 81% M; ACT>18: 99%. Resident tuition and fees: $3083. Nonresident tuition and fees: $10,305. Room and board: $5050. Application deadline: 7/1.

## GENERAL

State-supported, university, coed. Part of Colorado State University System. Awards bachelor's, master's, doctoral, and first professional degrees. Founded 1870. Setting: 666-acre urban campus with easy access to Denver. Undergraduate faculty: 939 (all full-time); student-faculty ratio is 20:1. Most popular recent majors: business administration, liberal arts and studies, exercise sciences.

## CAMPUS VISITS

**College Calendar 1998–99:** *Regular classes:* Aug. 24–Dec. 11; Jan. 19–May 7. *Breaks:* Nov. 21–30; Mar. 6–15. *Final exams:* Dec. 14–18; May 10–14. *Admission office closed:* Nov. 27, Dec. 23–24, Jan. 18. *Special campus days:* Commencement, Dec. 18–19, May 14–15; Homecoming, Oct. 10; Parents Weekend, Oct. 23–25.

## VISIT OPPORTUNITIES

| | Appointments? | Who? |
| --- | --- | --- |
| **Campus Tour** | not required | open to all |
| **Information Session** | not required | open to all |
| **Admission Interview** | not required | applicants and parents |
| **Classroom Visit** | required | applicants and parents |
| **Faculty Meeting** | required | applicants and parents |
| **Overnight Visit** | required | |

**Information Sessions:** M–F at 9:30 am, 1:30 pm; 30 minutes.

**Interviews:** M–F 9:00 am–4:00 pm; 20 minutes.

**Campus Tours:** Conducted by students. M–F at 10:00 am, 2:00 pm; 75 minutes.

**Class Visits:** Classroom visits are available during Showcase Visit Days.

**Video:** Available, fee charged.

## CAMPUS FACILITIES

**Science:** Appointment Required: Veterinary Teaching Hospital, Biochemistry, Biology.

**Arts:** Curfman Art Gallery, Duhesa Lounge, Hatton Art Gallery.

**Athletic:** Moby Gym; Appointment Required: Recreation Facility.

**Of Special Interest:** Lory Student Center, Colorado State University Bookstore, Morgan Library.

## LOCAL ATTRACTIONS

Old Town Square; Lory State Park; Rocky Mountain National Park and Horsetooth Reservoir.

# FORT LEWIS COLLEGE
**Durango, Colorado**

**Contact:** Mr. Harlan Steinle, Vice President, 1000 Rim Drive, Durango, CO 81301. *Phone:* 970-247-7184. *Fax:* 970-247-7179. *E-mail:* steinle_h@fortlewis. edu *Web site:* http://www.fortlewis.edu/ *Visit location:* Admission Office, Admission Building, 1000 Rim Drive.

## QUICK FACTS

Enrollment: 4,247; UG: 4,247. Entrance: moderately difficult. SAT>500: N/R; ACT>18: N/R. Resident tuition and fees: $2084. Nonresident tuition and fees: $8150. Room and board: $4236. Application deadline: 6/15.

## GENERAL

State-supported, 4-year, coed. Part of Colorado State University System. Awards associate and bachelor's degrees. Founded 1911. Setting: 350-acre small-town campus. Faculty: 250 (175 full-time, 75 part-time); student-faculty ratio is 20:1. Most popular recent majors: business administration, humanities, English.

## CAMPUS VISITS

**College Calendar 1998–99:** *Regular classes:* Aug. 28–Dec. 18; Jan. 11–Apr. 30. *Breaks:* Nov. 23–27; Mar. 9–13. *Final exams:* Dec. 14–18; Apr. 27–30.

## VISIT OPPORTUNITIES

| | Appointments? | Who? |
| --- | --- | --- |
| **Campus Tour** | recommended | open to all |
| **Information Session** | recommended | open to all |
| **Admission Interview** | required | open to all |
| **Classroom Visit** | required | open to all |
| **Faculty Meeting** | required | open to all |

*Fort Lewis College (continued)*

**Information Sessions:** M–F, Sat.; 30 minutes.

**Interviews:** M–F, select Sat.; 30 minutes.

**Campus Tours:** Conducted by students and admission reps. M–F, Sat.; 120 minutes.

**Class Visits:** Prospective students may attend a class in their area of interest.

**Video:** Available, fee charged.

## CAMPUS FACILITIES

**Science:** Bennot Hall—Science Wing.

**Arts:** New Art Building, Concert Hall, Southwest Center.

**Athletic:** Gymnasium, athletic fields; Appointment Required: swimming pool.

## LOCAL ATTRACTIONS

Mesa Verde; Purgatory Ski Area; Southern Ute Reservation; Navajo Lake; Valleceto Lake; narrow gauge tram.

# UNIVERSITY OF COLORADO AT BOULDER

**Boulder, Colorado**

**Contact:** Office of Admissions, Campus Box 30, Boulder, CO 80309. *Phone:* 303-492-6301. *Fax:* 303-492-7115. *E-mail:* apply@colorado.edu *Web site:* http://www.colorado.edu/ *Visit location:* University Memorial Center-Reception Desk, UMC, Euclid and Broadway.

## QUICK FACTS

Enrollment: 24,943; UG: 20,271. Entrance: moderately difficult. SAT>500: 86% V, 90% M; ACT>18: 98%. Resident tuition and fees: $2939. Nonresident tuition and fees: $14,983. Room and board: $4566. Application deadline: 2/15.

## GENERAL

State-supported, university, coed. Part of University of Colorado System. Awards bachelor's, master's, doctoral, and first professional degrees. Founded 1876. Setting: 600-acre suburban campus with easy access to Denver. Undergraduate faculty: 1,522 (1,217 full-time, 305 part-time); student-faculty ratio is 14:1. Most popular recent majors: psychology, biology, English.

## CAMPUS VISITS

**College Calendar 1998–99:** *Regular classes:* Aug. 24–Dec. 9; Jan. 11–May 3. *Breaks:* Dec. 19–Jan. 10; May 13–Aug. 22. *Final exams:* Dec. 11–18; May 6–12. *Admission office closed:* Mar. 26. *Special campus days:* CU Sampler; CU Student for a Day; Engineering Open House, Oct. 31; Homecoming, Sept. 26; Parents Weekend, Oct. 16–18; Spring Commencement, May 14; Winter Commencement, Dec. 19.

## VISIT OPPORTUNITIES

|  | Appointments? | Who? |
| --- | --- | --- |
| **Campus Tour** | recommended | applicants and parents |
| **Information Session** | recommended | |
| **Admission Interview** | recommended | |
| **Classroom Visit** | required | |
| **Faculty Meeting** | required | |
| **Overnight Visit** | | applicants only |

**Information Sessions:** M–F at 9:30 am, 1:30 pm; Sat. at 10:30 am; unavailable campus holidays, Sat. during May, and week following graduation; 60 minutes.

**Interviews:** M–F; 30 minutes.

**Campus Tours:** Conducted by students. M–F at 10:30 am, 2:30 pm; Sat. at 11:30 am; unavailable during spring break, week following graduation, Sat. in May, and campus holidays; 75 minutes.

**Class Visits:** Certain predetermined classrooms are open to visitors.

**Overnight Visits:** During the regular academic year, prospective applicants may spend an evening in a residence hall with a student host.

**Video:** Available, fee charged.

## CAMPUS FACILITIES

**Science:** Appointment Required: Engineering—Integrated Teaching and Learning Lab.

**Athletic:** Student Recreation Center.

**Of Special Interest:** Appointment Required: Planetarium.

## LOCAL ATTRACTIONS

"The Hill," Pearl Street Mall, Chautauqua Park, Flat Irons.

# UNIVERSITY OF DENVER
Denver, Colorado

**Contact:** Jean Sanderson, Coordinator of Prospective Student Office, 2199 South University Boulevard, Denver, CO 80208. *Phone:* toll-free 800-525-9495 (out-of-state). *Fax:* 303-871-3301. *E-mail:* admi34@du.edu *Web site:* http://www.du.edu/ *Visit location:* Office of Undergraduate Admission, University Hall, 2199 South University Boulevard.

## QUICK FACTS
Enrollment: 8,565; UG: 3,425. Entrance: moderately difficult. SAT>500: 73% V, 80% M; ACT>18: 97%. Tuition and fees: $17,886. Room and board: $5743. Application deadline: rolling.

## GENERAL
Independent, university, coed. Awards bachelor's, master's, doctoral, and first professional degrees. Founded 1864. Setting: 125-acre suburban campus. Undergraduate faculty: 423 (403 full-time, 20 part-time); student-faculty ratio is 13:1. Most popular recent majors: biology, communications, business marketing and marketing management.

## CAMPUS VISITS
**College Calendar 1998–99:** *Regular classes:* Sept. 14–Nov. 20; Jan. 4–Mar. 12; Mar. 24–May 28. *Breaks:* Nov. 28–Jan. 4; Mar. 18–23. *Final exams:* Nov. 23–24; Mar. 15–17; June 1–3. *Admission office closed:* Dec. 24. *Special campus days:* Commencement, June 5; Summer Commencement, Aug. 13.

## VISIT OPPORTUNITIES

| | Appointments? | Who? |
| --- | --- | --- |
| **Campus Tour** | recommended, not required | open to all |
| **Information Session** | recommended, not required | open to all |
| **Admission Interview** | recommended | open to all |
| **Classroom Visit** | recommended | open to all |
| **Faculty Meeting** | recommended | open to all |
| **Overnight Visit** | recommended | open to all |

**Information Sessions:** M–F at 10:00 am, 2:00 pm; Sat. at 10:00 am; 60 minutes.
**Interviews:** M–F; Sat. 9:00 am–12:00 pm; 60 minutes.
**Campus Tours:** Conducted by students. M–F at 11:00 am, 3:00 pm; Sat. at 11:00 am; 60 minutes.

**Class Visits:** Prospective students may attend a class in their area of interest.
**Overnight Visits:** During the regular academic year, prospective applicants may spend an evening in a residence hall with a student host.
**Video:** Free on request.

## CAMPUS FACILITIES
**Science:** Olin Hall of Science, Seeley Mudd Building, Knudson Hall.
**Arts:** Shwayder Art Building, School of Art and Art History Gallery.
**Athletic:** Daniel Ritchie Wellness Center, Joy Burns Arena.
**Of Special Interest:** Lamont School of Music, Career Placement Office, Counseling Services, Penrose Library.

## LOCAL ATTRACTIONS
Cherry Creek Shopping area, the Capitol and downtown Denver, Red Rocks.

# UNIVERSITY OF NORTHERN COLORADO
Greeley, Colorado

**Contact:** Colleen Denzin, Visitors Center Coordinator, University of Northern Colorado, Greeley, CO 80639. *Phone:* 970-351-2097. *Fax:* 970-351-2984. *Web site:* http://www.univnorthco.edu/ *Visit location:* Visitors Center, Carter Hall, Room 3006, 17th Street and 9th Avenue.

## QUICK FACTS
Enrollment: 10,943; UG: 8,736. Entrance: moderately difficult. SAT>500: 59% V, 60% M; ACT>18: 91%. Resident tuition and fees: $2578. Nonresident tuition and fees: $9346. Room and board: $4420. Application deadline: rolling.

## GENERAL
State-supported, university, coed. Awards bachelor's, master's, and doctoral degrees. Founded 1890. Setting: 240-acre suburban campus with easy access to Denver. Undergraduate faculty: 576 (408 full-time, 168 part-time); student-faculty ratio is 21:1. Most popular recent majors: business administration, physical education, social sciences.

## CAMPUS VISITS
**College Calendar 1998–99:** *Regular classes:* Aug. 26–Dec. 4; Jan. 12–Apr. 30. *Breaks:* Dec. 14–Jan. 12;

*University of Northern Colorado (continued)*

Mar. 15–19. *Final exams:* Dec. 7–11; May 3–7. *Admission office closed:* Nov. 27, Dec. 23, Dec. 24. *Special campus days:* Commencement, May 8; Homecoming, Oct. 10; Preview Days.

## VISIT OPPORTUNITIES

|  | Appointments? | Who? |
| --- | --- | --- |
| **Campus Tour** | required | open to all |
| **Information Session** | required | open to all |
| **Admission Interview** | required | open to all |
| **Classroom Visit** | required | open to all |
| **Faculty Meeting** | required | open to all |
| **Overnight Visit** | required | open to all |

**Information Sessions:** M–F; 30 minutes.

**Interviews:** M–F; 30 minutes.

**Campus Tours:** Conducted by students. M–F; Sat. by arrangement; 90 minutes.

**Class Visits:** Prospective students may attend a class in their area of interest.

**Overnight Visits:** During the regular academic year, prospective applicants may spend an evening in a residence hall with a student host.

**Video:** Free on request.

## CAMPUS FACILITIES

**Science:** Math and Science Teaching Center, Undergraduate Research Laboratories, Mathematics Learning Center.

**Arts:** Mariani Art Gallery, Music Technology Center, Music Library, Helen Langworthy Theatre.

**Athletic:** Recreation Center, Nottingham Field, Butler-Hancock Gymnasium.

**Of Special Interest:** Gunter Hall—Health and Human Sciences, Kepner Hall—Business, University Center, James A. Michener Library.

## LOCAL ATTRACTIONS

Greeley Stampede; Denver Broncos Training Camp; Rocky Mountain National Park.

# WESTERN STATE COLLEGE OF COLORADO

**Gunnison, Colorado**

**Contact:** Ms. Sara Axelson, Director of Admissions, 600 North Adams Street, Gunnison, CO 81231.

*Phone:* 970-943-2119 or toll-free 800-876-5309. *Fax:* 970-943-2212. *E-mail:* saxelson@western.edu *Web site:* http://www.western.edu/ *Visit location:* Admissions Office, Taylor Hall-Room 204, 600 North Adams Street.

## QUICK FACTS

Enrollment: 2,492; UG: 2,492. Entrance: moderately difficult. SAT>500: 52% V, 44% M; ACT>18: N/R. Resident tuition and fees: $2152. Nonresident tuition and fees: $7332. Room and board: $4790. Application deadline: rolling.

## GENERAL

State-supported, 4-year, coed. Part of State Colleges in Colorado. Awards bachelor's degrees. Founded 1901. Setting: 381-acre small-town campus. Faculty: 143 (101 full-time, 42 part-time); student-faculty ratio is 20:1. Most popular recent majors: business administration, exercise sciences, sociology.

## CAMPUS VISITS

**College Calendar 1998–99:** *Regular classes:* Aug. 24–Dec. 18; Jan. 11–May 7. *Breaks:* Nov. 25–27; Mar. 20–28. *Final exams:* Dec. 14–18; May 3–7.

## VISIT OPPORTUNITIES

|  | Appointments? | Who? |
| --- | --- | --- |
| **Campus Tour** | recommended | open to all |
| **Information Session** | required | open to all |
| **Admission Interview** | recommended | open to all |
| **Classroom Visit** | required | open to all |
| **Faculty Meeting** |  | open to all |

**Information Sessions:** Call for schedule; 20 minutes.

**Interviews:** M–F; 30 minutes.

**Campus Tours:** Conducted by students. M–F at 10:00 am, 2:00 pm; 60 minutes.

**Class Visits:** Classroom visits are determined by the visit schedule.

**Video:** Free on request.

## CAMPUS FACILITIES

**Arts:** Art Gallery.

**Athletic:** Training Facility, Locker Rooms, Athletic Training Center, Climbing Wall.

# CONNECTICUT

## CONNECTICUT COLLEGE
### New London, Connecticut

**Contact:** Laureen Ambot, Scheduling Coordinator, 270 Mohegan Avenue, New London, CT 06320. *Phone:* 860-439-2200. *Fax:* 860-439-4301. *E-mail:* admit@cooncoll.edu *Web site:* http://www.camel.conncoll.edu/ *Visit location:* Office of Admission, Horizon Admission Building, 270 Mohegan Avenue.

### QUICK FACTS
Enrollment: 1,720; UG: 1,671. Entrance: very difficult. SAT>500: 98% V, 97% M; ACT>18: 100%. Comprehensive fee: $28,475. Room and board: N/App. Application deadline: 1/15.

### GENERAL
Independent, comprehensive, coed. Awards bachelor's and master's degrees. Founded 1911. Setting: 702-acre suburban campus. Undergraduate faculty: 174 (147 full-time, 27 part-time); student-faculty ratio is 11:1. Most popular recent majors: psychology, English, biology.

### CAMPUS VISITS
**College Calendar 1998–99:** *Regular classes:* Sept. 3–Dec. 15; Jan. 25–May 14. *Breaks:* Oct. 8–12; Mar. 12–29; Nov. 24–30. *Final exams:* Dec. 16–23; May 16–24.

### VISIT OPPORTUNITIES

|  | Appointments? | Who? |
|---|---|---|
| **Campus Tour** | not required | open to all |
| **Information Session** | not required | open to all |
| **Admission Interview** | required | open to all |
| **Classroom Visit** | not required | open to all |
| **Faculty Meeting** | required | open to all |
| **Overnight Visit** | required | open to all |

**Information Sessions:** M–F at 11:30 am, 1:30 pm; Sat. mid-Sept. to mid-Dec. at 10:30 am; 60 minutes.
**Interviews:** M–F; Sat. mid-Sept. to mid-Dec.; 30 minutes.
**Campus Tours:** Conducted by students. M–F 9:30 am–3:30 pm; Sat. mid-Sept. to mid-Dec. at 9:30 am to 1:30 pm; 60 minutes.

**Class Visits:** Prospective students may attend a class in their area of interest.
**Overnight Visits:** During the regular academic year, prospective applicants may spend an evening in a residence hall with a student host.

### CAMPUS FACILITIES
**Science:** F.W. Olin Science Center, Hale Laboratory, New London Hall.
**Arts:** Cummings Arts Center, Lyman Allyn Art Museum, Palmer Auditorium.
**Athletic:** Luce Field House, Dayton Arena, Gordon Natatorium.
**Of Special Interest:** College Center at Crozier Williams, Shain Library, Unity House, Arboretum.

### LOCAL ATTRACTIONS
Downtown New London; Mystic, CT; Harkness and Rocky Neck State Parks.

## FAIRFIELD UNIVERSITY
### Fairfield, Connecticut

**Contact:** Admission Office, North Benson Road, Fairfield, CT 06430. *Phone:* 203-254-4100. *Fax:* 203-254-4199. *E-mail:* admis@fair1.fairfield.edu *Web site:* http://www.fairfield.edu/ *Visit location:* Office of Admission, Bellarmine Hall, North Benson Road.

### QUICK FACTS
Enrollment: 4,508; UG: 3,598. Entrance: moderately difficult. SAT>500: 85% V, 85% M; ACT>18: N/R. Tuition and fees: $18,310. Room and board: $7024. Application deadline: 2/1.

### GENERAL
Independent Roman Catholic (Jesuit), comprehensive, coed. Awards bachelor's and master's degrees and post-master's certificates. Founded 1942. Setting: 200-acre suburban campus with easy access to New York City. Undergraduate faculty: 384 (203 full-time, 181 part-time); student-faculty ratio is 13:1. Most popular recent majors: English, psychology, nursing.

### CAMPUS VISITS
**College Calendar 1998–99:** *Regular classes:* Sept. 9–Dec. 11; Jan. 20–May 4. *Breaks:* Dec. 22–Jan. 19; Mar. 8–12. *Final exams:* Dec. 12–21; May 6–14. *Admission office closed:* Christmas to New Year's week; Fri. afternoons in summer. *Special campus days:*

*Fairfield University (continued)*

Homecoming, Sept. 26; Preview Day, Sept. 27; School of Business Open House, Oct. 19; Sciences and Nursing Day.

## VISIT OPPORTUNITIES

| | Appointments? | Who? |
|---|---|---|
| **Campus Tour** | not required | open to all |
| **Information Session** | recommended | |
| **Admission Interview** | required | open to all |
| **Classroom Visit** | required | open to all |
| **Faculty Meeting** | required | applicants only |
| **Overnight Visit** | required | admitted applicants only |

**Information Sessions:** Call for available summer schedule; 40 minutes.

**Interviews:** M–F, select Sat.; unavailable Feb. 1–Apr. 1; 30 minutes.

**Campus Tours:** Conducted by students. M–F, select Sat. at 10:45 am, 11:45 am, 1:15 pm, 2:30 pm, 3:30 pm; during summer Mon.–Thu. at 11:00 am, 2:00 pm and Fri. at 11:00 am; 75 minutes.

**Class Visits:** Classroom visits are determined by the visit schedule.

**Overnight Visits:** During the regular academic year, prospective applicants may spend an evening in a residence hall with a student host.

**Video:** Free on request.

## CAMPUS FACILITIES

**Science:** Appointment Required: Bannow Science Center, School of Nursing.

**Arts:** Quick Center for the Arts; Appointment Required: Pepsico Theatre, Mutrux Gallery.

**Athletic:** Alumni Hall and Recreational Complex; Appointment Required: Athletic Center.

## LOCAL ATTRACTIONS

Town of Fairfield; Fairfield Beach.

# QUINNIPIAC COLLEGE

**Hamden, Connecticut**

**Contact:** Admissions Office, 275 Mount Carmel Avenue, Hamden, CT 06518. *Phone:* toll-free 800-462-1944 (out-of-state). *Fax:* 203-281-8906. *E-mail:* admissions@quinnipiac.edu *Web site:* http://www.quinnipiac.edu/ *Visit location:* Undergraduate Admissions, Library Building, 275 Mount Carmel Avenue.

## QUICK FACTS

Enrollment: 5,282; UG: 3,908. Entrance: moderately difficult. SAT>500: 68% V, 72% M; ACT>18: 91%. Tuition and fees: $14,880. Room and board: $7190. Application deadline: 2/15.

## GENERAL

Independent, comprehensive, coed. Awards bachelor's, master's, and first professional degrees. Founded 1929. Setting: 200-acre suburban campus with easy access to Hartford. Undergraduate faculty: 390 (245 full-time, 145 part-time); student-faculty ratio is 15:1. Most popular recent majors: physical therapy, accounting, occupational therapy.

## CAMPUS VISITS

**College Calendar 1998–99:** *Regular classes:* Aug. 31–Dec. 12; Jan. 19–May 1. *Breaks:* Nov. 23–29; Mar. 8–13. *Final exams:* Dec. 14–19; May 3–8. *Admission office closed:* Dec. 25–Jan. 1; school breaks, during reading period. *Special campus days:* Graduate Commencement, May 9; Homecoming, Oct. 9–11; Parents Weekend, Sept. 26–27; Spring Weekend, Apr. 23–24; Undergraduate Commencement, May 16.

## VISIT OPPORTUNITIES

| | Appointments? | Who? |
|---|---|---|
| **Campus Tour** | | open to all |
| **Information Session** | | open to all |
| **Admission Interview** | required | open to all |
| **Classroom Visit** | required | open to all |
| **Faculty Meeting** | required | admitted applicants only |
| **Overnight Visit** | required | admitted applicants only |

**Information Sessions:** M–F, select Sat.; 45 minutes.

**Interviews:** M–F; 45 minutes.

**Campus Tours:** Conducted by students. M–F, select Sat.; tours are available during fall, spring and summer sessions; 60 minutes.

**Overnight Visits:** During the regular academic year, prospective applicants may spend an evening in a residence hall with a student host.

**Video:** Free on request.

## CAMPUS FACILITIES
**Science:** Nursing Critical Care Lab, Physical Therapy and Occupational Therapy Labs, Echlin Health Science Center.

**Arts:** Buckman Theater, News Technology Center.

**Athletic:** Recreation Center, Lighted tennis courts, Fitness Center.

**Of Special Interest:** Ed McMahon Center for Mass Communications, Residence Halls, School of Law, Arnold Bernhard Library.

## LOCAL ATTRACTIONS
Sleeping Giant State Park.

# SACRED HEART UNIVERSITY
**Fairfield, Connecticut**

**Contact:** Admissions Office, 5151 Park Avenue, Fairfield, CT 06432-1000. *Phone:* 203-371-7880. *Fax:* 203-365-7607. *E-mail:* enroll@sacredheart.edu *Visit location:* Admissions Office, Campus Center, 5151 Park Avenue.

## QUICK FACTS
Enrollment: 5,900; UG: 2,300. Entrance: moderately difficult. SAT>500: 67% V, 58% M; ACT>18: N/R. Tuition and fees: $13,475. Room and board: $6570. Application deadline: 4/15.

## GENERAL
Independent Roman Catholic, comprehensive, coed. Awards associate, bachelor's, and master's degrees (also offers part-time program with significant enrollment not reflected in profile). Founded 1963. Setting: 56-acre suburban campus with easy access to New York City. Undergraduate faculty: 349 (129 full-time, 220 part-time); student-faculty ratio is 14:1. Most popular recent majors: business administration, mass communications, psychology.

## CAMPUS VISITS
**College Calendar 1998–99:** *Regular classes:* Sept. 8–Dec. 14; Jan. 19–May 10. *Breaks:* Nov. 25–29; Mar. 7–14; Mar. 31–Apr. 6. *Final exams:* Dec. 15–19; May 11–18. *Special campus days:* Commencement, May 22–23; Open House, Sept. 19, Nov. 14.

## VISIT OPPORTUNITIES

|  | Appointments? | Who? |
|---|---|---|
| **Campus Tour** | required | open to all |
| **Information Session** | required | open to all |
| **Admission Interview** | required | open to all |
| **Classroom Visit** | required | open to all |
| **Faculty Meeting** | required | open to all |
| **Overnight Visit** | required | open to all |

**Information Sessions:** M–F, Sat.; 60 minutes.

**Interviews:** M–F, Sat.; 60 minutes.

**Campus Tours:** Conducted by students. M–F, Sat.; 60 minutes.

**Class Visits:** Prospective students may attend a class in their area of interest.

**Overnight Visits:** During the regular academic year, prospective applicants may spend an evening in a residence hall with a student host.

## CAMPUS FACILITIES
**Science:** New Classrooms, New Laboratories; Appointment Required: Physical Therapy/Occupational Therapy Clinic, Nursing Laboratory.

**Arts:** Gallery of Contemporary Art.

**Athletic:** William H. Pitt Health and Recreation Center, Football Field/Multipurpose Field, Tennis Courts.

# TRINITY COLLEGE
**Hartford, Connecticut**

**Contact:** Admissions Office, Trinity College, Hartford, CT 06106. *Phone:* 860-297-2180. *Fax:* 860-297-2287. *E-mail:* admissions.office@trincoll.edu *Web site:* http://www.trincoll.edu/ *Visit location:* Admissions Office, Downes Memorial, Summit Street.

## QUICK FACTS
Enrollment: 2,161; UG: 1,990. Entrance: very difficult. SAT>500: 98% V, 95% M; ACT>18: 100%. Tuition and fees: $22,470. Room and board: $6320. Application deadline: 1/15.

## GENERAL
Independent, comprehensive, coed. Awards bachelor's and master's degrees. Founded 1823. Setting: 100-acre urban campus. Undergraduate faculty: 306

*Trinity College (continued)*

(180 full-time, 126 part-time); student-faculty ratio is 10:1. Most popular recent majors: English, political science, economics.

## CAMPUS VISITS

**College Calendar 1998–99:** *Regular classes:* Sept. 2–Dec. 11; Jan. 19–May 3. *Breaks:* Oct. 10–19; Mar. 27–Apr. 4; Feb. 20–28. *Final exams:* Dec. 14–18; May 6–13. *Admission office closed:* Fri. afternoons from mid-May to mid-Aug. *Special campus days:* Commencement, May 23; Homecoming, Nov. 6–8; Parents Weekend, Sept. 25–27; Reunion Weekend, June 4–7.

## VISIT OPPORTUNITIES

|  | Appointments? | Who? |
| --- | --- | --- |
| **Campus Tour** | not required | open to all |
| **Information Session** | not required | open to all |
| **Admission Interview** | required | open to all |
| **Classroom Visit** | recommended, not required | open to all |
| **Faculty Meeting** | required | open to all |
| **Overnight Visit** | required | open to all |

**Information Sessions:** M–F at 10:30 am, 2:30 pm; select Sat. at 9:30 am, 11:30 am; Sat. (Oct. through mid-Dec.); Fri. afternoons unavailable in summer; 60 minutes.
**Interviews:** M–F (Jun. through mid-Mar.); Sat. from Sept. to mid-Dec.; 30 minutes.
**Campus Tours:** Conducted by students. M–F at 9:30 am, 11:30 am, 1:30 pm, 2:30 pm, 3:30 pm; Sat. (Oct. to mid-Dec.) at 9:30 am, 10:30 am, 11:30 am, and 12:00 pm; Sat. (mid-May to mid-Aug.) at 9:30 am and 11:30 am; Fri. afternoons unavailable mid-May to mid-Aug.; 60 minutes.
**Class Visits:** Prospective students may attend a class in their area of interest.
**Overnight Visits:** During the regular academic year, prospective applicants may spend an evening in a residence hall with a student host.

## CAMPUS FACILITIES

**Science:** Life Sciences Center, Botany Lab, Greenhouse, Mathematics, Computing, and Engineering Center.
**Arts:** Austin Arts Center, Studio Arts Building.
**Athletic:** Ferris Athletic Center and Playing Fields.
**Of Special Interest:** Dining Halls, Chapel, Library.

## LOCAL ATTRACTIONS

Wadsworth Athenaeum; Mark Twain House; Harriet Beecher Stowe House; State Capitol; Bushnell Park.

# UNIVERSITY OF BRIDGEPORT
**Bridgeport, Connecticut**

**Contact:** Mr. Joseph Marrone, Director of Undergraduate Admissions, 126 Park Avenue, Bridgeport, CT 06601. *Phone:* toll-free 800-EXCEL-UB (in-state), 800-243-9496 (out-of-state). *Fax:* 203-576-4941. *E-mail:* admit@cse.bridgeport.edu *Web site:* http://www.bridgeport.edu/ *Visit location:* Office of Admissions, Wahlstrom Library, 126 Park Avenue.

## QUICK FACTS

Enrollment: 2,427; UG: 1,098. Entrance: moderately difficult. SAT>500: 43% V, 52% M; ACT>18: N/App. Tuition and fees: $13,644. Room and board: $6810. Application deadline: 4/1.

## GENERAL

Independent, comprehensive, coed. Awards associate, bachelor's, master's, doctoral, and first professional degrees and post-master's certificates. Founded 1927. Setting: 86-acre urban campus with easy access to New York City. Undergraduate faculty: 266 (88 full-time, 178 part-time); student-faculty ratio is 10:1. Most popular recent majors: liberal arts and studies, dental hygiene, business administration.

## CAMPUS VISITS

**College Calendar 1998–99:** *Regular classes:* Aug. 31–Dec. 11; Jan. 25–May 7. *Breaks:* Oct. 10–13; Mar. 13–21; Dec. 18–Jan. 25. *Final exams:* Dec. 14–18; May 10–14. *Special campus days:* Campus Visit Day, Oct. 3, Jan. 9, Mar. 6, Nov. 7, June 5, May 1; Commencement, May 16; Guidance Counselor Luncheon, Oct. 9; New Student Orientation, Jan. 21–24; Scholars Brunch, Apr. 18; Undergraduate Open House, Oct. 18, Feb. 15.

## VISIT OPPORTUNITIES

|  | Appointments? | Who? |
| --- | --- | --- |
| **Campus Tour** | recommended | open to all |
| **Information Session** | recommended | open to all |
| **Admission Interview** | recommended | open to all |
| **Classroom Visit** | required | open to all |
| **Faculty Meeting** | required | open to all |

## VISIT OPPORTUNITIES—*continued*

| | Appointments? | Who? |
|---|---|---|
| **Overnight Visit** | recommended | open to all |

**Information Sessions:** Wed.; first Sat. of each month; includes meeting with Admission Counselor, Financial Aid, Faculty, lunch and tour; 120 minutes.

**Interviews:** M–F; 60 minutes.

**Campus Tours:** Conducted by students and admission reps. Wed.; first Sat. of each month; special arrangements may be made for students traveling from foreign countries or distant states; 90 minutes.

**Class Visits:** Prospective students may attend a class in their area of interest, classroom visits are determined by the visit schedule.

**Overnight Visits:** During the regular academic year, prospective applicants may spend an evening in a residence hall with a student host.

**Video:** Available.

## CAMPUS FACILITIES

**Science:** Dana Hall of Science, Fones School of Dental Hygiene, College of Chiropractic, Technology Building.

**Arts:** University Gallery, Arnold Bernhard Center, Bruel Hall, Rennell Hall.

**Athletic:** Harvey Hubbell Gymnasium, Wheeler Recreation Center.

**Of Special Interest:** John J. Cox Student Center, Wahlstrom Library.

## LOCAL ATTRACTIONS

P.T. Barnum Museum, Seaside Park, Discovery Museum, Beardsley Park and Zoo, Captain's Cove, and Bridgeport Bluefish Baseball.

# UNIVERSITY OF CONNECTICUT
## Storrs, Connecticut

**Contact:** Office of Orientation Services, 2131 Hillside Road, U-88X, Storrs, CT 06269-3088. *Phone:* 860-486-4866. *Fax:* 860-486-0233. *E-mail:* beahusky@uconnvm.uconn.edu *Web site:* http://www.uconn.edu/ *Visit location:* Department of Admissions and Orientation Services, Undergraduate Admissions Building, 2131 Hillside Road.

## QUICK FACTS

Enrollment: 17,694; UG: 10,926. Entrance: moderately difficult. SAT>500: 79% V, 80% M; ACT>18: N/R. Resident tuition and fees: $5242. Nonresident tuition and fees: $13,760. Room and board: $5462. Application deadline: 3/1.

## GENERAL

State-supported, university, coed. Awards associate, bachelor's, master's, doctoral, and first professional degrees. Founded 1881. Setting: 4,212-acre rural campus. Undergraduate faculty: 1,071 (1,040 full-time, 31 part-time); student-faculty ratio is 14:1. Most popular recent majors: psychology, individual/family development.

## CAMPUS VISITS

**College Calendar 1998–99:** *Regular classes:* Sept. 2–Dec. 14; Jan. 20–May 4. *Breaks:* Dec. 24–Jan. 20; Mar. 13–21; Nov. 26–29. *Final exams:* Dec. 16–23; May 7–14. *Special campus days:* Family Weekend, Sept. 19–20; Graduate Commencement, May 16; Homecoming, Oct. 23–25; Undergraduate Commencement, May 15; Winter Weekend, Feb. 5–7.

## VISIT OPPORTUNITIES

| | Appointments? | Who? |
|---|---|---|
| **Campus Tour** | required | open to all |
| **Information Session** | required | open to all |
| **Admission Interview** | required | open to all |
| **Faculty Meeting** | required | open to all |
| **Overnight Visit** | required | admitted applicants only |

**Information Sessions:** M–F and select Sun. during fall and spring semesters; part of campus tour, not scheduled separately; 60 minutes.

**Interviews:** M–F; 30 minutes.

**Campus Tours:** Conducted by students. M–F and select Sun. during fall and spring semesters; 60 minutes.

**Overnight Visits:** During the regular academic year, prospective applicants may spend an evening in a residence hall with a student host.

## CAMPUS FACILITIES

**Science:** Greenhouses.

**Arts:** Appointment Required: Art Department, Drama Department, Music Department.

*University of Connecticut (continued)*

**Of Special Interest:** Appointment Required: School of Engineering facilities, School of Nursing facilities.

## LOCAL ATTRACTIONS
University of Connecticut's Dairy Bar; State Museum of Natural History; Benton Museum of Art.

# UNIVERSITY OF HARTFORD
**West Hartford, Connecticut**

**Contact:** University of Hartford Office of Admission and Student Financial Assistance, 200 Bloomfield Avenue, West Hartford, CT 06117-1599. *Phone:* toll-free 800-947-4303. *Fax:* 860-768-4961. *E-mail:* admission@uhavar.hartford.edu *Web site:* http://www.hartford.edu/ *Visit location:* Office of Admission and Student Financial Assistance, Bates House, 200 Bloomfield Avenue.

## QUICK FACTS
Enrollment: 6,704; UG: 5,002. Entrance: moderately difficult. SAT>500: 66% V, 63% M; ACT>18: 84%. Tuition and fees: $18,224. Room and board: $7200. Application deadline: rolling.

## GENERAL
Independent, comprehensive, coed. Awards associate, bachelor's, master's, and doctoral degrees. Founded 1877. Setting: 320-acre suburban campus with easy access to Hartford. Undergraduate faculty: 737 (307 full-time, 430 part-time); student-faculty ratio is 13:1.

## CAMPUS VISITS
**College Calendar 1998–99:** *Regular classes:* Sept. 1–Dec. 14; Jan. 19–May 3. *Breaks:* Oct. 8–11; Mar. 13–22. *Final exams:* Dec. 15–21; May 5–12. *Special campus days:* Commencement, May 16; Homecoming, Oct. 2–4.

## VISIT OPPORTUNITIES

|  | Appointments? | Who? |
|---|---|---|
| **Campus Tour** | recommended | open to all |
| **Information Session** | recommended | open to all |
| **Admission Interview** | recommended, not required | open to all |
| **Classroom Visit** | required | open to all |
| **Faculty Meeting** | required |  |
| **Overnight Visit** | required | open to all |

**Information Sessions:** M–F 8:30 am–4:30 pm; Sat. at 12:00 pm, 1:00 pm; 30 minutes.

**Interviews:** M–F; 60 minutes.

**Campus Tours:** Conducted by students. Mon., Wed., Fri. at 9:30 am, 10:30 am, 11:30 am, 12:30 pm, 1:30 pm, 2:30 pm; Thu. at 10:00 am, 11:30 am, 12:30 pm, 1:30 pm; Sat. at 11:00 am, 12:00 pm; 90 minutes.

**Class Visits:** Prospective students may attend a class in their area of interest.

**Overnight Visits:** During the regular academic year, prospective applicants may spend an evening in a residence hall with a student host.

**Video:** Free on request.

## CAMPUS FACILITIES
**Arts:** The Joseloff Gallery, Student Exhibition Gallery, Taub Hall.

**Athletic:** University of Hartford Sports Center.

**Of Special Interest:** Museum of American Political Life.

## LOCAL ATTRACTIONS
Mark Twain House, Wadsworth Athenaeum, Basketball Hall of Fame.

# YALE UNIVERSITY
**New Haven, Connecticut**

**Contact:** Mr. Richard H. Shaw Jr., Dean of Admissions, PO Box 208234, New Haven, CT 06520. *Phone:* 263-432-9300. *Fax:* 203-432-9370. *E-mail:* undergraduate.admissions@yale.edu *Web site:* http://www.yale.edu/ *Visit location:* Admissions Office, 38 Hillhouse Avenue.

## QUICK FACTS
Enrollment: 10,979; UG: 5,355. Entrance: most difficult. SAT>500: N/R; ACT>18: N/R. Tuition and fees: $23,100. Room and board: $6850. Application deadline: 12/31.

## GENERAL
Independent, university, coed. Awards bachelor's, master's, doctoral, and first professional degrees. Founded 1701. Setting: 200-acre urban campus with easy access to New York City. Undergraduate faculty: 2,986. Most popular recent majors: biology, history, economics.

## CAMPUS VISITS
**College Calendar 1998–99:** *Regular classes:* Sept. 2–Dec. 7; Jan. 11–Apr. 23. *Breaks:* Nov. 20–30; Mar.

5–22. *Final exams:* Dec. 13–21; May 3–11. *Admission office closed:* between Christmas and New Year's holiday. *Special campus days:* Baccalaureate Day, May 23; University Commencement, May 24; Yale–Princeton football—last home game, Nov. 14.

## VISIT OPPORTUNITIES

|                       | Appointments?     |
| --------------------- | ----------------- |
| **Campus Tour**       | not required      |
| **Information Session** | not required    |
| **Admission Interview** | required        |
| **Classroom Visit**   | not required      |
| **Faculty Meeting**   | required          |
| **Overnight Visit**   | required          |

**Information Sessions:** M–F, select Sat.; also available with admissions officers around the country at local venues, in the fall; call for seasonal schedule; 75 minutes.

**Interviews:** M–F; available Jul.– Nov.; 30 minutes.

**Campus Tours:** Conducted by students. M–F, select Sat.; select Sun. available; call for schedule; 60 minutes.

**Class Visits:** Prospective students may attend a class in their area of interest, recommended list of courses available in the admissions office.

**Overnight Visits:** During the regular academic year, prospective applicants may spend an evening in a residence hall with a student host.

## CAMPUS FACILITIES

**Science:** Peabody Museum of Natural History, Klein Biology Tower, Bass Center/Gibbs Lab, Sterling Chemistry and Physics Laboratories.

**Arts:** University Art Gallery, Center for British Art, Art and Architecture Building, Repertory Theatre, Yale Drama.

**Athletic:** Payne Whitney Gymnasium, Yale Field/the Yale Bowl, Ingalls Hockey Rink, Intramural Fields.

**Of Special Interest:** Sterling Memorial Library, Yale Collection of Musical Instruments, Beinecke Rare Book and Manuscript Library.

## LOCAL ATTRACTIONS

Yale's Old Campus located on New Haven's Historic Town Green, the New Haven City Hall and the Amistad Memorial.

# DISTRICT OF COLUMBIA

## AMERICAN UNIVERSITY
### Washington, District of Columbia

**Contact:** Enrollment Services, 4400 Massachusetts Avenue, NW, Washington, DC 20016-8001. *Phone:* 202-885-6000. *Fax:* 202-885-1025. *E-mail:* afa@american.edu *Web site:* http://www.american.edu/ *Visit location:* Office of Admissions, Hamilton Building, 4400 Massachusetts Avenue, NW.

### QUICK FACTS
Enrollment: 10,337; UG: 5,054. Entrance: moderately difficult. SAT>500: 93% V, 89% M; ACT>18: N/R. Tuition and fees: $18,555. Room and board: $7250. Application deadline: 2/1.

### GENERAL
Independent Methodist, university, coed. Awards associate, bachelor's, master's, doctoral, and first professional degrees. Founded 1893. Setting: 77-acre suburban campus. Undergraduate faculty: 1,002 (546 full-time, 456 part-time); student-faculty ratio is 14:1. Most popular recent majors: international relations, mass communications, political science.

### CAMPUS VISITS
**College Calendar 1998–99:** *Regular classes:* Aug. 31–Dec. 9; Jan. 19–May 3. *Breaks:* Dec. 19–Jan. 19; Mar. 14–21. *Final exams:* Dec. 12–18; May 6–12. *Admission office closed:* Dec. 21–Jan. 2. *Special campus days:* Admissions Open House, Aug. 14, Oct. 12, Nov. 6; Artemis Ward Week (Spirit Week); Homecoming; Parents Weekend; Spring Commencement, May 16; Winter Commencement, Jan. 31.

### VISIT OPPORTUNITIES

|                         | Appointments?              | Who?        |
| ----------------------- | -------------------------- | ----------- |
| **Campus Tour**         | recommended, not required  | open to all |
| **Information Session** | recommended, not required  | open to all |
| **Admission Interview** | required                   | open to all |
| **Classroom Visit**     | required                   | open to all |
| **Faculty Meeting**     | required                   | open to all |
| **Overnight Visit**     | required                   | open to all |

*American University (continued)*

**Information Sessions:** M–F at 11:00 am, 2:00 pm; Sat. at 10:30 am and 12:30 pm during academic year after tour; 60 minutes.

**Interviews:** M–F; Sat. during academic year, call for schedule; unavailable during Apr.; 30 minutes.

**Campus Tours:** Conducted by students. M–F at 10:00 am, 1:00 pm, 3:00 pm; Sat. at 9:30 am and 11:30 am during academic year; 60 minutes.

**Class Visits:** Prospective students may attend a class in their area of interest, certain predetermined classrooms are open to visitors, classroom visits are determined by the visit schedule.

**Overnight Visits:** During the regular academic year, prospective applicants may spend an evening in a residence hall with a student host.

## CAMPUS FACILITIES

**Arts:** Appointment Required: Performing Arts, Fine Arts.

**Athletic:** Sports Center and athletic fields.

**Of Special Interest:** Mary Graydon Center, The Main Quad, The Library.

## LOCAL ATTRACTIONS

Washington, DC.

# THE CATHOLIC UNIVERSITY OF AMERICA

**Washington, District of Columbia**

**Contact:** Office of Admissions, 102 McMahon Hall, Washington, DC 20064. *Phone:* toll-free 800-673-2772 (out-of-state). *Fax:* 202-319-6533. *E-mail:* cua-admissions@cua.edu *Web site:* http://www.cua.edu/ *Visit location:* Office of Admissions, McMahon Hall, 620 Michigan Avenue.

## QUICK FACTS

Enrollment: 5,529; UG: 2,229. Entrance: moderately difficult. SAT>500: 86% V, 82% M; ACT>18: 98%. Tuition and fees: $17,110. Room and board: $7036. Application deadline: 2/15.

## GENERAL

Independent, university, coed, Roman Catholic Church. Awards bachelor's, master's, doctoral, and first professional degrees and post-master's certificates. Founded 1887. Setting: 144-acre urban campus. Undergraduate faculty: 648 (360 full-time, 288

part-time); student-faculty ratio is 10:1. Most popular recent majors: architecture, engineering, political science.

## CAMPUS VISITS

**College Calendar 1998–99:** *Regular classes:* Aug. 31–Dec. 11; Jan. 11–Apr. 30. *Breaks:* Mar. 1–8. *Final exams:* Dec. 14–19; May 4–8. *Admission office closed:* Holy Thursday, Good Friday, Easter Monday, Apr. 1–6. *Special campus days:* Open House.

## VISIT OPPORTUNITIES

|  | Appointments? | Who? |
|---|---|---|
| **Campus Tour** | recommended | open to all |
| **Information Session** | recommended | open to all |
| **Classroom Visit** |  | admitted applicants only |
| **Faculty Meeting** |  | admitted applicants only |

**Information Sessions:** Mon., Wed., Fri. at 10:30 am, 2:00 pm; Sat. at 10:30 am; unavailable Christmas and Easter weeks; 45 minutes.

**Campus Tours:** Conducted by students. Mon., Wed., Fri. at 10:30 am, 2:00 pm; Sat. at 10:30 am; 45 minutes.

**Class Visits:** Classroom visits are determined by the visit schedule.

**Video:** Free on request.

## CAMPUS FACILITIES

**Arts:** Architecture building.

**Athletic:** DuFour Athletic Center.

**Of Special Interest:** Computer labs, bookstore; Appointment Required: Residence Halls.

## LOCAL ATTRACTIONS

Union Station; The Basilica of the National Shrine of the Immaculate Conception.

# THE CORCORAN SCHOOL OF ART

**Washington, District of Columbia**

**Contact:** Office of Admissions, 500 17th Street, NW, Washington, DC 20006. *Phone:* 202-639-1814. *Fax:* 202-639-1830. *E-mail:* admofc@aol.com *Web site:*

http://www.corcoran.edu/ *Visit location:* Main Office, The Corcoran School of Art, New York Avenue.

## QUICK FACTS
Enrollment: 363; UG: 363. Entrance: moderately difficult. SAT>500: N/R; ACT>18: N/R. Tuition and fees: $12,800. Room and board: N/Avail. Application deadline: rolling.

## GENERAL
Independent, 4-year, coed. Awards bachelor's degrees. Founded 1890. Setting: 7-acre urban campus. Faculty: 113 (58 full-time, 55 part-time). Most popular recent majors: art, graphic design/commercial art/illustration, photography.

## CAMPUS VISITS
**College Calendar 1998–99:** *Regular classes:* Sept. 8–Dec. 20; Jan. 19–May 10. *Breaks:* Dec. 21–Jan. 18; Mar. 8–14. *Final exams:* Nov. 26–29. *Admission office closed:* all Tue. *Special campus days:* Commencement, May 15.

## VISIT OPPORTUNITIES

| | Appointments? | Who? |
|---|---|---|
| **Campus Tour** | required | open to all |
| **Information Session** | required | open to all |
| **Admission Interview** | required | open to all |
| **Classroom Visit** | required | open to all |

**Information Sessions:** Mon., Wed., Thu., Fri. 10:00 am–3:00 pm; Tue., Sat., and after 3:00 pm by special arrangement; 30 minutes.

**Interviews:** Mon., Wed., Thu., Fri. 10:00 am–3:00 pm; Tue., Sat., and after 3:00 pm by special arrangement; 45 minutes.

**Campus Tours:** Conducted by students and admission reps. Mon., Wed., Thu., Fri. 10:00 am–3:00 pm; Tue., Sat., and after 3:00 pm by special arrangement; 45 minutes.

**Class Visits:** Certain predetermined classrooms are open to visitors.

## CAMPUS FACILITIES
**Arts:** The Corcoran Museum of Art.

## LOCAL ATTRACTIONS
Washington DC, National Monuments; Smithsonian Institutions.

# GALLAUDET UNIVERSITY
**Washington, District of Columbia**

**Contact:** Gallaudet University, 800 Florida Avenue, NE, Washington, DC 20002. *Phone:* 202-651-5050 or toll-free 800-995-0550 (out-of-state). *Fax:* 202-651-5704. *E-mail:* publicrel@gallua.gallaudet.edu *Web site:* http://www.gallaudet.edu/ *Visit location:* Gallaudet University, Visitors Center, 800 Florida Avenue, NE.

## QUICK FACTS
Enrollment: 1,697; UG: 1,251. Entrance: moderately difficult. SAT>500: N/App; ACT>18: N/App. Tuition and fees: $6283. Room and board: $6709. Application deadline: 5/15.

## GENERAL
Independent, university, coed. Awards bachelor's, master's, and doctoral degrees (all undergraduate programs open primarily to hearing-impaired). Founded 1864. Setting: 99-acre urban campus. Undergraduate faculty: 297 (242 full-time, 55 part-time). Most popular recent majors: psychology, business administration, biology.

## CAMPUS VISITS
**College Calendar 1998–99:** *Regular classes:* Aug. 31–Dec. 11; Jan. 19–May 3. *Breaks:* Nov. 25–29; Mar. 15–21. *Final exams:* Dec. 15–18; May 5–8. *Admission office closed:* Dec. 24–Jan. 5. *Special campus days:* Commencement, May 14; Home Coming, Oct. 17; New Signers Program, July 23–Aug. 21; New Students Orientation, Aug. 24–28; Open House, Oct. 16, Nov. 13; Spring Open House.

## VISIT OPPORTUNITIES

| | Appointments? | Who? |
|---|---|---|
| **Campus Tour** | required | open to all |
| **Information Session** | required | open to all |
| **Admission Interview** | required | open to all |
| **Classroom Visit** | required | open to all |
| **Faculty Meeting** | required | open to all |
| **Overnight Visit** | required | open to all |

**Information Sessions:** M–F; 30 minutes.

**Interviews:** M–F; 60 minutes.

**Campus Tours:** Conducted by students. M–F; 60 minutes.

**Class Visits:** Prospective students may attend a class in their area of interest.

*Gallaudet University (continued)*

**Overnight Visits:** During the regular academic year and over the summer, prospective applicants may spend an evening in a residence hall.

**Video:** Free on request.

## CAMPUS FACILITIES
**Of Special Interest:** Merrill Learning Center.

# GEORGETOWN UNIVERSITY
**Washington, District of Columbia**

**Contact:** Office of Undergraduate Admissions, Georgetown University, Washington, DC 20057. *Phone:* 202-687-3600. *Fax:* 202-687-5084. *Web site:* http://www.georgetown.edu/ *Visit location:* Office of Undergraduate Admissions, White Gravenor, Room 103, Georgetown University.

## QUICK FACTS
Enrollment: 12,238; UG: 5,883. Entrance: most difficult. SAT>500: 97% V, 98% M; ACT>18: 99%. Tuition and fees: $21,405. Room and board: $8091. Application deadline: 1/10.

## GENERAL
Independent Roman Catholic (Jesuit), university, coed. Awards bachelor's, master's, doctoral, and first professional degrees. Founded 1789. Setting: 110-acre urban campus. Undergraduate faculty: 1,683 (1,174 full-time, 509 part-time); student-faculty ratio is 11:1. Most popular recent majors: international relations, finance, political science.

## CAMPUS VISITS
**College Calendar 1998–99:** *Regular classes:* Sept. 2–Dec. 9; Jan. 13–Dec. 9. *Breaks:* Nov. 25–30; Mar. 5–15; Mar. 31–Apr. 6. *Final exams:* Dec. 14–22; May 10–19. *Special campus days:* Commencement Weekend, May 29–30.

## VISIT OPPORTUNITIES

| | Appointments? | Who? |
|---|---|---|
| **Campus Tour** | recommended | |
| **Information Session** | recommended | |
| **Classroom Visit** | not required | |
| **Faculty Meeting** | required | |

| | Appointments? | Who? |
|---|---|---|
| **Overnight Visit** | | admitted applicants only |

**Information Sessions:** Call for schedule; 45 minutes.

**Campus Tours:** Conducted by students. Conducted at conclusion of information session; 60 minutes.

**Class Visits:** Certain predetermined classrooms are open to visitors.

## CAMPUS FACILITIES
**Of Special Interest:** Lauinger Library.

# THE GEORGE WASHINGTON UNIVERSITY
**Washington, District of Columbia**

**Contact:** Visitor Center, 2121 I Street, NW, Suite 201, Washington, DC 20052. *Phone:* toll-free 800-447-3765. *Fax:* 202-994-7163. *E-mail:* gwadm@gwis2.circ.gwu.edu *Web site:* http://www.gwu.edu/index.html *Visit location:* Visitor Center, Academic Center, 801 22nd Street, NW.

## QUICK FACTS
Enrollment: 18,584; UG: 7,058. Entrance: very difficult. SAT>500: 94% V, 96% M; ACT>18: 99%. Tuition and fees: $21,360. Room and board: $7325. Application deadline: 2/1.

## GENERAL
Independent, university, coed. Awards associate, bachelor's, master's, doctoral, and first professional degrees and post-master's certificates. Founded 1821. Setting: 36-acre urban campus. Undergraduate faculty: 2,214 (1,428 full-time, 786 part-time); student-faculty ratio is 14:1. Most popular recent majors: international relations, biology, psychology.

## CAMPUS VISITS
**College Calendar 1998–99:** *Regular classes:* Aug. 24–Dec. 9; Jan. 11–Apr. 28. *Final exams:* Dec. 14–21; May 3–11. *Admission office closed:* day after Thanksgiving (includes Visitor's Center), Nov. 27. *Special campus days:* Commencement, May 16; Open House, Oct. 10, Nov. 8; Reading Days (no tours), Dec. 10–11, Apr. 29–30.

## VISIT OPPORTUNITIES

| | Appointments? | Who? |
|---|---|---|
| **Campus Tour** | recommended, not required | open to all |
| **Information Session** | recommended, not required | open to all |
| **Admission Interview** | required | open to all |
| **Classroom Visit** | required | open to all |
| **Faculty Meeting** | required | open to all |
| **Overnight Visit** | required | applicants only |

**Information Sessions:** M–F at 10:00 am, 2:00 pm; select Sat. at 10:00 am, 1:00 pm; available Sat. during months of Aug. through Nov. (until Thanksgiving) and late Jan. through Apr.; 60 minutes.

**Interviews:** M–F; we strongly recommend students attend an information session and tour before scheduling an interview. Off-campus interviews are available; 40 minutes.

**Campus Tours:** Conducted by students. M–F at 11:00 am, 3:00 pm; select Sat. at 11:00 am, 2:00 pm; available Sat. during months of Aug. through Nov. (until Thanksgiving) and late Jan. through Apr.; no tours during exam periods and winter break. Call 202-625-4682 or 800-682-4636 to arrange tour of Mount Vernon Residential College; 60 minutes.

**Class Visits:** Prospective students may attend a class in their area of interest.

**Overnight Visits:** During the regular academic year, prospective applicants may spend an evening in a residence hall with a student host.

**Video:** Free on request.

## CAMPUS FACILITIES
**Science:** Corcoran Hall, Bell Hall.

**Arts:** Music Department; Appointment Required: Smith Hall of Art, Theatre Department.

**Athletic:** Smith Center.

**Of Special Interest:** Marvin Center, Thurston Hall, Gelman Library.

## LOCAL ATTRACTIONS
Washington, DC national and historic sites.

# FLORIDA

## BARRY UNIVERSITY
**Miami Shores, Florida**

**Contact:** Adriana Cronin, Admission Counselor/ Visitation Coordinator, 11300 Northeast Second Avenue, Miami Shores, FL 33161-6695. *Phone:* 305-899-3113 or toll-free 800-695-2279. *Fax:* 305-899-2971. *E-mail:* cronin@jeanne.barry.edu *Web site:* http://www.barry.edu/ *Visit location:* Division of Enrollment Services, Kelley House, 11300 Northeast Second Avenue.

### QUICK FACTS
Enrollment: 6,829; UG: 4,615. Entrance: moderately difficult. SAT>500: 49% V, 45% M; ACT>18: 70%. Tuition and fees: $13,550. Room and board: $5850. Application deadline: rolling.

### GENERAL
Independent Roman Catholic, comprehensive, coed. Awards bachelor's, master's, doctoral, and first professional degrees and post-master's and first professional certificates. Founded 1940. Setting: 122-acre suburban campus with easy access to Miami. Undergraduate faculty: 552 (248 full-time, 304 part-time); student-faculty ratio is 11:1. Most popular recent majors: nursing, education, biology.

### CAMPUS VISITS
**College Calendar 1998–99:** *Regular classes:* Sept. 2–Dec. 11; Jan. 11–Apr. 29. *Breaks:* Dec. 19–Jan. 10. *Final exams:* Dec. 14–18; Apr. 30–May 6. *Admission office closed:* Christmas, Dec. 24–25; Good Friday, Apr. 2; Martin Luther King, Jr., Jan. 18; New Year's, Dec. 31–Jan. 1; Thanksgiving, Nov. 26–27. *Special campus days:* Commencement, May 8; Festival of Nations; Founder's Week; Homecoming; International Assistant Program, Aug. 29; Labor Day Pool Party, Sept. 7; Spring Dance; Winter Semi-formal.

## VISIT OPPORTUNITIES

| | Appointments? | Who? |
|---|---|---|
| **Campus Tour** | recommended, not required | open to all |
| **Information Session** | required | open to all |
| **Admission Interview** | recommended, not required | open to all |
| **Classroom Visit** | required | open to all |

*Barry University (continued)*

## VISIT OPPORTUNITIES—*continued*

|  | **Appointments?** | **Who?** |
|---|---|---|
| **Faculty Meeting** | required | open to all |

**Information Sessions:** M–F; Sat. by appointment.

**Interviews:** M–F; Sat. by appointment; 30 minutes.

**Campus Tours:** Conducted by students and admission reps. M–F at 10:00 am, 1:00 pm, 3:00 pm; expanded Sat. tours by appointment; 45 minutes.

**Class Visits:** Prospective students may attend a class in their area of interest.

## CAMPUS FACILITIES

**Science:** Appointment Required: labs with instrumentation.

**Arts:** Appointment Required: David Brinkley Television Studio, Photography Labs (color, black/white, computer imaging), Ceramics Studio, Music Studio.

**Athletic:** Health and Sports Center; Appointment Required: State of the Art Training Facilities.

**Of Special Interest:** Appointment Required: The Learning Center and Center for Advanced Learning, Academic Computer Center, School of Education— Classroom of Tomorrow.

## LOCAL ATTRACTIONS

Los Olas Boulevard; South Beach; Bayside; Coconut Grove; Everglades National Park; Miami City Ballet; New World Symphony; Vizcaya; Metro Zoo; Parrot Jungle; Museum of Contemporary Art; Bass Museum; Jackie Gleason Theatre; Broward Performing Arts Center.

# BETHUNE-COOKMAN COLLEGE

**Daytona Beach, Florida**

**Contact:** Mr. William Byrd, Assistant Vice President– Enrollment, 640 Dr Mary McLeod Bethune Blvd, Daytona Beach, FL 32114-3099. *Phone:* 904-255-1401 Ext. 358 or toll-free 800-448-0228. *Fax:* 904-257-5338. *Web site:* http://www.bethune.cookman.edu/ *Visit location:* Admissions Office, 640 Dr. Mary McLead Belhune Boulevard.

## QUICK FACTS

Enrollment: 2,523; UG: 2,523. Entrance: minimally difficult. SAT>500: 35% V, 16% M; ACT>18: 20%.

Tuition and fees: $8047. Room and board: $4984. Application deadline: 7/30.

## GENERAL

Independent Methodist, 4-year, coed. Awards bachelor's degrees. Founded 1904. Setting: 60-acre urban campus with easy access to Orlando. Faculty: 214 (130 full-time, 84 part-time); student-faculty ratio is 17:1. Most popular recent majors: business administration, elementary education, criminal justice/law enforcement administration.

## CAMPUS VISITS

**College Calendar 1998–99:** *Regular classes:* Aug. 26–Dec. 6; Jan. 11–Apr. 26. *Breaks:* Dec. 11–Jan. 3. *Final exams:* Dec. 8–10; Apr. 28–30. *Special campus days:* Baccalaureate, Apr. 25; CLAST Registration Deadline, Sept. 4; Commencement, Apr. 26; Founders Day, Oct. 5; Homecoming, Oct. 3.

## VISIT OPPORTUNITIES

|  | **Appointments?** |
|---|---|
| **Campus Tour** | required |
| **Information Session** | recommended |
| **Admission Interview** | recommended |
| **Classroom Visit** | required |
| **Faculty Meeting** | recommended |
| **Overnight Visit** | required |

**Information Sessions:** M–F; call for special arrangements; 60 minutes.

**Interviews:** M–F; call for special arrangements; 30 minutes.

**Campus Tours:** Conducted by students. M–F; call for special arrangements; 60 minutes.

**Class Visits:** Classroom visits are determined by the visit schedule.

**Overnight Visits:** During the regular academic year and over the summer, prospective applicants may spend an evening in a residence hall with a student host.

**Video:** Free on request.

## CAMPUS FACILITIES

**Of Special Interest:** Carl S. Swisher Library.

## LOCAL ATTRACTIONS

Daytona Beach Speedway, Daytona's Beaches, downtown Daytona.

# ECKERD COLLEGE
## St. Petersburg, Florida

**Contact:** Gerri Eley, Receptionist, 4200 54th Avenue South, St. Petersburg, FL 33711. *Phone:* 813-864-8331 or toll-free 800-456-9009. *Fax:* 813-866-2304. *E-mail:* admissions@eckerd.edu *Web site:* http://www.eckerd.edu/ *Visit location:* Admissions Office, Franklin Templeton Hall, 4200 54th Avenue South.

### QUICK FACTS
Enrollment: 1,443; UG: 1,443. Entrance: moderately difficult. SAT>500: 85% V, 84% M; ACT>18: 97%. Tuition and fees: $17,130. Room and board: $4660. Application deadline: rolling.

### GENERAL
Independent Presbyterian, 4-year, coed. Awards bachelor's degrees. Founded 1958. Setting: 267-acre suburban campus with easy access to Tampa. Faculty: 124 (96 full-time, 28 part-time); student-faculty ratio is 14:1. Most popular recent majors: marine biology, international business, business administration.

### CAMPUS VISITS
**College Calendar 1998–99:** *Regular classes:* Aug. 7–28; Aug. 31–Dec. 4; Feb. 2–May 7. *Breaks:* Oct. 5–6; Mar. 20–29; Nov. 26–27. *Final exams:* Aug. 27–28; Dec. 7–11; May 10–14.

### VISIT OPPORTUNITIES

|  | Appointments? | Who? |
|---|---|---|
| **Campus Tour** | required | open to all |
| **Information Session** | required | open to all |
| **Admission Interview** | required | open to all |
| **Classroom Visit** | required | open to all |
| **Faculty Meeting** | required | open to all |
| **Overnight Visit** | required | open to all |

**Information Sessions:** M–F; offered during fall for large number of visitors; 60 minutes.

**Interviews:** M–F; Sat. mornings Sept. through May; 45 minutes.

**Campus Tours:** Conducted by students. M–F, Sat.; 60 minutes.

**Class Visits:** Prospective students may attend a class in their area of interest.

**Overnight Visits:** During the regular academic year, prospective applicants may spend an evening in a residence hall with a student host.

### CAMPUS FACILITIES
**Science:** Appointment Required: Galbraith Marine Science Lab, Marine Mammal Necropsy Lab.

**Arts:** Appointment Required: Theater, Computer Graphics Lab, Art Gallery.

**Athletic:** Appointment Required: Gymnasium, Playing Fields, Waterfront Program.

**Of Special Interest:** Appointment Required: Chapel, Campus Center.

### LOCAL ATTRACTIONS
Dali Museum; International Museum; The Pier; Tropicana Field; Ft. De Soto Park; St. Petersburg Beach, Busch Gardens, Tampa Aquarium.

# FLAGLER COLLEGE
## St. Augustine, Florida

**Contact:** Mona Evans, Secretary to the Director of Admissions, PO Box 1027, St. Augustine, FL 32085. *Phone:* toll-free 800-304-4208. *Fax:* 904-826-0094. *E-mail:* admiss@flagler.edu *Web site:* http://www.flagler.edu/ *Visit location:* Admissions Office, Wiley Hall, 6 Valencia Street.

### QUICK FACTS
Enrollment: 1,655; UG: 1,655. Entrance: moderately difficult. SAT>500: 82% V, 70% M; ACT>18: 98%. Tuition and fees: $5950. Room and board: $3680. Application deadline: 3/1.

### GENERAL
Independent, 4-year, coed. Awards bachelor's degrees. Founded 1968. Setting: 36-acre small-town campus with easy access to Jacksonville. Faculty: 137 (52 full-time, 85 part-time); student-faculty ratio is 21:1. Most popular recent majors: elementary education, business administration, mass communications.

### CAMPUS VISITS
**College Calendar 1998–99:** *Regular classes:* Sept. 2–Dec. 4; Jan. 13–Apr. 16. *Breaks:* Nov. 26–29; Mar. 18–21. *Final exams:* Dec. 7–10; Apr. 19–22. *Special campus days:* Convocation, Oct. 1; Fall Commencement, Dec. 12; Fall Visitation Day for Seniors, Sept. 26; Homecoming/Alumni Weekend, Feb. 26–28; Parent's Weekend, Nov. 6–8; Spring Commencement, Apr. 24; Spring Visitation Day for Juniors, Mar. 6.

*Flagler College (continued)*

## VISIT OPPORTUNITIES

| | Appointments? | Who? |
|---|---|---|
| **Campus Tour** | required | open to all |
| **Admission Interview** | required | open to all |
| **Classroom Visit** | required | open to all |
| **Faculty Meeting** | required | open to all |
| **Overnight Visit** | required | open to all |

**Interviews:** M–F, select Sat.; 45 minutes.

**Campus Tours:** Conducted by students. M–F, select Sat.; 45 minutes.

**Class Visits:** Classroom visits are determined by the visit schedule.

**Overnight Visits:** During the regular academic year, prospective applicants may spend an evening in a residence hall with a student host.

**Video:** Free on request.

## CAMPUS FACILITIES

**Of Special Interest:** William L. Proctor Library.

## LOCAL ATTRACTIONS

St. Augustine and its beaches.

# FLORIDA AGRICULTURAL AND MECHANICAL UNIVERSITY

**Tallahassee, Florida**

**Contact:** Rosell Caswell, Director of Student Affairs, William Gray Core Unit, Florida A & M University, Tallahassee, FL 32307. *Phone:* 850-599-3869. *Fax:* 850-599-3850. *Web site:* http://www.famu.edu/ *Visit location:* New Student Orientation, William Gray Core Unit, Florida A & M University.

## QUICK FACTS

Enrollment: 10,587; UG: 9,361. Entrance: moderately difficult. SAT>500: N/R; ACT>18: N/R. Resident tuition and fees: $2105. Nonresident tuition and fees: $8022. Room and board: $3198. Application deadline: 5/1.

## GENERAL

State-supported, university, coed. Part of State University System of Florida. Awards associate, bachelor's, master's, doctoral, and first professional degrees. Founded 1887. Setting: 419-acre urban campus. Undergraduate faculty: 727 (723 full-time, 4 part-time); student-faculty ratio is 16:1. Most popular recent majors: education, pharmacy, business administration.

## CAMPUS VISITS

**College Calendar 1998–99:** *Regular classes:* Aug. 24–Dec. 4; Jan. 6–Apr. 23. *Breaks:* Mar. 8–12. *Final exams:* Dec. 7–11; Apr. 26–30.

## VISIT OPPORTUNITIES

| | Appointments? | Who? |
|---|---|---|
| **Campus Tour** | required | open to all |
| **Information Session** | required | open to all |
| **Classroom Visit** | not required | open to all |
| **Faculty Meeting** | required | open to all |

**Information Sessions:** M–F 9:00 am–4:00 pm; Sat. by special arrangement; 90 minutes.

**Campus Tours:** Conducted by orientation staff. M–F 9:00 am–4:00 pm; Sat. by special arrangement; 120 minutes.

**Class Visits:** Prospective students may attend a class in their area of interest.

## CAMPUS FACILITIES

**Of Special Interest:** Coleman Memorial Library.

# FLORIDA ATLANTIC UNIVERSITY

**Boca Raton, Florida**

**Contact:** Office of Admissions, 777 Glades Road, PO Box 3091, Boca Raton, FL 33431-0991. *Phone:* 561-297-3040 or toll-free 800-299-4FAU. *Fax:* 561-297-2758. *Web site:* http://www.fau.edu/ *Visit location:* Office of Admissions, Administration Building, 777 Glades Road, PO Box 3091.

## QUICK FACTS

Enrollment: 17,124; UG: 13,589. Entrance: moderately difficult. SAT>500: 65% V, 65% M; ACT>18: N/R. Resident tuition and fees: $2022. Nonresident tuition and fees: $7940. Room and board: $4680. Application deadline: rolling.

## GENERAL

State-supported, university, coed. Part of State University System of Florida. Awards associate, bachelor's, master's, and doctoral degrees. Founded 1961. Setting: 850-acre suburban campus with easy access to Miami. Undergraduate faculty: 1,169 (743 full-time, 426 part-time); student-faculty ratio is 15:1. Most popular recent majors: elementary education, biology, accounting.

## CAMPUS VISITS

**College Calendar 1998–99:** *Regular classes:* Aug. 24–Dec. 11; Jan. 11–Apr. 30. *Breaks:* Mar. 8–13. *Final exams:* Dec. 4–10; Apr. 23–29. *Special campus days:* Commencement Fall, Dec. 11; Commencement Spring, Apr. 30; Homecoming; Open House.

## VISIT OPPORTUNITIES

|  | Appointments? |
| --- | --- |
| **Campus Tour** | not required |
| **Information Session** | required |
| **Admission Interview** | required |
| **Classroom Visit** | required |
| **Faculty Meeting** | required |
| **Overnight Visit** | required |

**Information Sessions:** M–F; available upon request; 60 minutes.

**Interviews:** M–F; contact admissions counselor, 561-297-2720, to schedule appointment; 20 minutes.

**Campus Tours:** Conducted by students. M–F at 10:00 am; Mon., Wed., Fri. at 2:00 pm; tours available first Sat. of the month and Sept.–May at 10:00 am; 60 minutes.

**Class Visits:** Prospective students may attend a class in their area of interest.

**Overnight Visits:** During the regular academic year.

**Video:** Free on request.

## CAMPUS FACILITIES

**Science:** Appointment Required: Laboratories, Gumbo Limbo Nature Center, Robotics Lab.

**Arts:** Appointment Required: Art Gallery, Art Studios, Theatre Department.

**Athletic:** Olympic Pool, Baseball/Soccer/Cross-Country Fields, Gymnasium.

**Of Special Interest:** Appointment Required: Ocean Engineering Area.

## LOCAL ATTRACTIONS

Mizner Park, Town Center Mall, Sawgrass Mills Mall, Beach, Recreation facilities.

# FLORIDA INTERNATIONAL UNIVERSITY
**Miami, Florida**

**Contact:** Office of Admissions, University Park, PC 140, Miami, FL 33199. *Phone:* 305-348-2363. *Fax:* 305-348-3648. *Web site:* http://www.fiu.edu/ *Visit location:* Office of Admission, Charles Perry Building (PC) 140, 10700 SW 8th Street.

## QUICK FACTS

Enrollment: 27,042; UG: 21,166. Entrance: moderately difficult. SAT>500: 85% V, 86% M; ACT>18: 99%. Resident tuition and fees: $2035. Nonresident tuition and fees: $7951. Room and board: $7378. Application deadline: rolling.

## GENERAL

State-supported, university, coed. Part of State University System of Florida. Awards bachelor's, master's, and doctoral degrees. Founded 1965. Setting: 573-acre urban campus. Undergraduate faculty: 1,241 (831 full-time, 410 part-time); student-faculty ratio is 14:1. Most popular recent majors: psychology, biology, accounting.

## CAMPUS VISITS

**College Calendar 1998–99:** *Regular classes:* Aug. 24–Dec. 4; Jan. 5–Apr. 16. *Breaks:* Nov. 25–30; Mar. 22–27. *Final exams:* Dec. 5–11; Apr. 17–23. *Special campus days:* Commencement, Dec. 13, Apr. 25.

## VISIT OPPORTUNITIES

|  | Appointments? | Who? |
| --- | --- | --- |
| **Campus Tour** | required | open to all |
| **Information Session** | required | open to all |
| **Admission Interview** | not required | open to all |
| **Classroom Visit** | required | open to all |
| **Faculty Meeting** | required | open to all |

**Information Sessions:** Wed. at 9:30 am; Mon. at 9:30 am; Fri. at 3:00 pm; call to confirm schedule; 45 minutes.

**Interviews:** M–F; 45 minutes.

**Campus Tours:** Conducted by students and admission reps. Mon. at 9:30 am; Wed. at 9:30 am; Fri. at 3:00 pm; call to confirm schedule.

**Class Visits:** Classroom visits are determined by the visit schedule.

*Florida International University (continued)*

### CAMPUS FACILITIES

**Science:** National Oceanographic and Atmospheric Administration (NOAA).

**Arts:** The Art Museum, The Wertheim Center for the Performing Arts.

**Athletic:** Golden Panther Arena, Baseball, football, and soccer fields, State of the art gymnasium.

**Of Special Interest:** Panther residence hall.

### LOCAL ATTRACTIONS

Miami Beach–Art Deco District, the historical Museum of South Florida, Vizcaya Coconut Grove, the Wolfsonian Museum, Everglades National Park, Metro Zoo, Parrot Jungle, the Florida Keys, Miami Seaquarium.

# FLORIDA SOUTHERN COLLEGE
## Lakeland, Florida

**Contact:** Admissions Office, 11 Lake Hollingsworth Drive, Lakeland, FL 33801-5698. *Phone:* toll-free 800-274-4131. *Fax:* 941-680-4120. *E-mail:* fscadm@ flsouthern.edu *Web site:* http://www.flsouthern.edu/ *Visit location:* Admissions Office, Thad Buckner Building.

### QUICK FACTS

Enrollment: 1,775; UG: 1,775. Entrance: moderately difficult. SAT>500: 69% V, 68% M; ACT>18: 91%. Tuition and fees: $10,604. Room and board: $5430. Application deadline: 8/1.

### GENERAL

Independent, comprehensive, coed, United Methodist Church. Awards bachelor's and master's degrees. Founded 1885. Setting: 100-acre suburban campus with easy access to Tampa and Orlando. Undergraduate faculty: 150 (96 full-time, 54 part-time); student-faculty ratio is 17:1. Most popular recent majors: business administration, education, biology.

### CAMPUS VISITS

**College Calendar 1998–99:** *Regular classes:* Sept. 10–Dec. 11; Jan. 14–Apr. 23. *Breaks:* Nov. 25–30; Mar. 5–15. *Final exams:* Dec. 12–17; Apr. 24–29. *Special campus days:* Baccalaureate and Commencement, May 2; Mid-Year Commencement, Dec. 18.

### VISIT OPPORTUNITIES

| | Appointments? |
|---|---|
| **Campus Tour** | recommended |
| **Admission Interview** | recommended |
| **Classroom Visit** | required |
| **Faculty Meeting** | required |
| **Overnight Visit** | required |

**Interviews:** M–F; Sat. appointments between 10:00 am and 2:00 pm; 60 minutes.

**Campus Tours:** Conducted by students and admission reps. M–F, Sat. 9:00 am–4:00 pm; 75 minutes.

**Class Visits:** Prospective students may attend a class in their area of interest.

**Overnight Visits:** During the regular academic year, prospective applicants may spend an evening in a residence hall with a student host.

**Video:** Free on request.

### CAMPUS FACILITIES

**Science:** Polk Science Center, Citrus Institute.

**Arts:** Melvin Art Gallery, Branscomb Auditorium, Buckner Theatre, L.N. Pipkin Bandshell.

**Athletic:** Jenkins Field House, Henley Field/Joker Marchant Stadium, Nina B. Hollis Wellness Center.

**Of Special Interest:** Annie Pfeiffer Chapel (11 Frank Lloyd Wright Building), Hindu Garden of Meditation, Rose Garden.

### LOCAL ATTRACTIONS

Disney World, Tampa Bay area.

# LYNN UNIVERSITY
## Boca Raton, Florida

**Contact:** Office of Admission, 3601 North Military Trail, Boca Raton, FL 33431-5598. *Phone:* toll-free 800-544-8035 (out-of-state). *Fax:* 651-241-3552. *E-mail:* admission@lynn.edu *Web site:* http://www.lynn. edu/ *Visit location:* Office of Admission, Schmidt Building, 3601 North Military Trail.

### QUICK FACTS

Enrollment: 1,782; UG: 1,638. Entrance: minimally difficult. SAT>500: 23% V, 24% M; ACT>18: N/R. Tuition and fees: $17,200. Room and board: $6250. Application deadline: 8/15.

## GENERAL

Independent, comprehensive, coed. Awards associate, bachelor's, master's, and doctoral degrees. Founded 1962. Setting: 123-acre suburban campus with easy access to Fort Lauderdale. Undergraduate faculty: 168 (63 full-time, 105 part-time). Most popular recent majors: hotel and restaurant management, international business, business administration.

## CAMPUS VISITS

**College Calendar 1998–99:** *Regular classes:* Sept. 8–Dec. 16; Jan. 11–Apr. 30. *Breaks:* Nov. 25–Dec. 29. *Final exams:* Dec. 17–22; May 3–6. *Special campus days:* Commencement, May 8; Families Weekend, Mar. 26–28; Homecoming Weekend, Feb. 12–14; Honors Convocation, Oct. 29, Mar. 26; Orientation for International Students, Sept. 6–7, Jan. 9–10.

## VISIT OPPORTUNITIES

| | Appointments? | Who? |
|---|---|---|
| **Campus Tour** | recommended | open to all |
| **Information Session** | recommended | open to all |
| **Admission Interview** | recommended | open to all |
| **Classroom Visit** | required | open to all |
| **Faculty Meeting** | required | open to all |

**Information Sessions:** Call for available time and schedule.

**Interviews:** M–F, Sat.; call for available times and schedule; 30 minutes.

**Campus Tours:** Conducted by students. M–F, Sat.; 45 minutes.

**Class Visits:** Prospective students may attend a class in their area of interest.

## CAMPUS FACILITIES

**Science:** Science Lab, Computer Labs.

**Arts:** The Lois and Anne Green Center for the Expressive Arts.

**Athletic:** De Hoernle Sports and Cultural Center, Fitness Center, McCusker Sports Complex.

**Of Special Interest:** De Hoernle International Center, Lynn Library, University Bookstore.

## LOCAL ATTRACTIONS

Atlantic Ocean; Mizner Park; Town Center Mall; historic Boca Raton Resort and Club; outdoor recreation facilities: golf, tennis, polo, surfing, and more.

# RINGLING SCHOOL OF ART AND DESIGN

**Sarasota, Florida**

**Contact:** James; H. Dean, Dean of Admissions, 2700 North Tamiami Trail, Sarasota, FL 34234. *Phone:* toll-free 800-255-7695. *Fax:* 941-359-7517. *E-mail:* admissions@rsad.edu *Web site:* http://www.rsad.edu/ *Visit location:* Admissions Office, Keating Center, 2700 North Tamiami Trail.

## QUICK FACTS

Enrollment: 850; UG: 850. Entrance: moderately difficult. SAT>500: N/App; ACT>18: N/App. Tuition and fees: $13,250. Room and board: $6692. Application deadline: rolling.

## GENERAL

Independent, 4-year, coed. Awards bachelor's degrees. Founded 1931. Setting: 35-acre urban campus with easy access to Tampa–St. Petersburg. Faculty: 98; student-faculty ratio is 13:1. Most popular recent major: graphic design/commercial art/illustration.

## CAMPUS VISITS

**College Calendar 1998–99:** *Regular classes:* Aug. 19–Dec. 9; Jan. 6–May 4. *Breaks:* Mar. 6–14. *Admission office closed:* Dec. 19–Jan. 3, Jan. 18. *Special campus days:* Commencement, May 8.

## VISIT OPPORTUNITIES

| | Appointments? | Who? |
|---|---|---|
| **Campus Tour** | recommended | open to all |
| **Information Session** | recommended | open to all |
| **Admission Interview** | recommended | open to all |
| **Classroom Visit** | required | open to all |
| **Faculty Meeting** | required | open to all |

**Information Sessions:** M–F 8:30 am–4:30 pm; appointments available year-round; call for break and summer schedules; 60 minutes.

**Interviews:** M–F; appointments available year-round; 60 minutes.

**Campus Tours:** Conducted by admission reps. M–F 8:30 am–4:30 pm; appointments available year-round; call for break and summer schedules; 60 minutes.

**Class Visits:** Prospective students may attend a class in their area of interest, certain predetermined classrooms are open to visitors.

*Ringling School of Art and Design (continued)*

**CAMPUS FACILITIES**
**Arts:** Selby Gallery.

**LOCAL ATTRACTIONS**
Ringling Museum; St. Armand's Circle.

# ROLLINS COLLEGE
## Winter Park, Florida

**Contact:** Libby Dennis, Visitor Liaison, 1000 Holt Avenue-2720, Winter Park, FL 32789. *Phone:* 407-646-1573. *Fax:* 407-646-1502. *E-mail:* admission@rollins.edu *Web site:* http://www.rollins.edu/ *Visit location:* Office of Admission, Carnegie, 1000 Holt Avenue.

**QUICK FACTS**
Enrollment: 2,166; UG: 1,480. Entrance: very difficult. SAT>500: 82% V, 85% M; ACT>18: 83%. Tuition and fees: $20,010. Room and board: $6340. Application deadline: 2/15.

**GENERAL**
Independent, comprehensive, coed. Awards bachelor's and master's degrees. Founded 1885. Setting: 67-acre suburban campus with easy access to Orlando. Undergraduate faculty: 255 (156 full-time, 99 part-time); student-faculty ratio is 12:1. Most popular recent majors: psychology, economics, English.

**CAMPUS VISITS**
**College Calendar 1998–99:** *Regular classes:* Aug. 26–Dec. 8; Jan. 20–May 4. *Breaks:* Oct. 15–18; Mar. 6–14; Dec. 16–Jan. 19. *Final exams:* Dec. 10–15; May 6–11. *Admission office closed:* Nov. 27, Dec. 24, Dec. 31. *Special campus days:* Alumni Weekend, Mar. 13–14; Bach Festival, Feb. 26–28; Parents Weekend; Prospective Student Open Houses.

**VISIT OPPORTUNITIES**

| | Appointments? | Who? |
|---|---|---|
| **Campus Tour** | recommended, not required | open to all |
| **Information Session** | recommended | open to all |
| **Admission Interview** | recommended | open to all |
| **Classroom Visit** | required | open to all |
| **Faculty Meeting** | required | open to all |

| | Appointments? | Who? |
|---|---|---|
| **Overnight Visit** | required | admitted applicants only |

**Information Sessions:** M–F at 10:00 am, 12:00 pm, 1:00 pm, 3:00 pm; Sat. at 9:00 am, 10:00 am, 12:00 pm; Sat. (May–Aug.); 60 minutes.

**Interviews:** M–F, select Sat.; 45 minutes.

**Campus Tours:** Conducted by students. M–F at 11:00 am, 2:00 pm; May–Aug. at 11:00 am; 55 minutes.

**Class Visits:** Prospective students may attend a class in their area of interest, classroom visits are determined by the visit schedule.

**Overnight Visits:** During the regular academic year, prospective applicants may spend an evening in a residence hall with a student host.

**CAMPUS FACILITIES**
**Science:** Bush Science Center, Hauck Greenhouse, Student Resource Center (Mills Building), Rollins Computing Laboratory.

**Arts:** Cornell Fine Arts Museum, Knowles Memorial Chapel; Appointment Required: Annie Russell Theatre and Fred Stone Theatre, Keene Hall, Dance Studio.

**Athletic:** Enyart Alumni Field House, Bert M. Martin Tennis Complex and J. Tiedke Tennis Complex, Alfond Stadium/Harper-Shepherd Field (baseball), Sandspur Field (soccer), Alfond Swimming Pool.

**Of Special Interest:** Olin Library, Walk of Fame, Cornell Campus Center, Olin Information and Technology Center.

**LOCAL ATTRACTIONS**
Alfond Boathouse; U.T. Bradley Boathouse.

# ST. THOMAS UNIVERSITY
## Miami, Florida

**Contact:** Constance Willems, Assistant Director of Admissions, 16400 Northwest 32nd Avenue, Miami, FL 33054. *Phone:* 305-628-6546 or toll-free 800-367-9006 (in-state), 800-367-9010 (out-of-state). *Fax:* 305-628-6591. *E-mail:* cwillems@stu.edu *Web site:*

http://www.stu.edu/ *Visit location:* Office of Admissions, Kennedy Hall, Room 103, 16400 Northwest 32nd Avenue.

## QUICK FACTS

Enrollment: 2,203; UG: 1,102. Entrance: moderately difficult. SAT>500: N/R; ACT>18: N/R. Tuition and fees: $11,840. Room and board: $4000. Application deadline: rolling.

## GENERAL

Independent Roman Catholic, comprehensive, coed. Awards bachelor's, master's, and first professional degrees. Founded 1961. Setting: 140-acre suburban campus. Undergraduate faculty: 132 (72 full-time, 60 part-time); student-faculty ratio is 15:1. Most popular recent majors: elementary education, business administration, psychology.

## CAMPUS VISITS

**College Calendar 1998–99:** *Regular classes:* Aug. 24–Dec. 2; Jan. 11–Apr. 28. *Breaks:* Nov. 25–29; Mar. 1–7. *Final exams:* Dec. 5–11; May 1–7. *Special campus days:* Commencement, May 15.

## VISIT OPPORTUNITIES

|  | Appointments? | Who? |
|---|---|---|
| **Campus Tour** | recommended, not required | open to all |
| **Information Session** | required | |
| **Admission Interview** | required | |
| **Classroom Visit** | required | |
| **Faculty Meeting** | required | applicants and parents |
| **Overnight Visit** | required | admitted applicants only |

**Information Sessions:** By appointment; 20 minutes.

**Interviews:** M–F, select Sat.; Scholarship Competition Sat. at 9:00 am–1:00 pm; call for dates in Nov., Feb., May; 20 minutes.

**Campus Tours:** Conducted by students. M–F, select Sat.; 45 minutes.

**Class Visits:** Prospective students may attend a class in their area of interest.

**Overnight Visits:** During the regular academic year, prospective applicants may spend an evening in a residence hall with a student host.

## CAMPUS FACILITIES

**Science:** Lab rooms.

**Arts:** Library art exhibits, library computer labs, library resource center.

**Athletic:** Training facilities, pool, fields.

## LOCAL ATTRACTIONS

Miami—Bayside, Coconut Grove, South Beach, Ft. Lauderdale, and the Florida Keys.

# SCHILLER INTERNATIONAL UNIVERSITY
**Dunedin, Florida**

**Contact:** Muriel Jault, Admissions Representative, 453 Edgewater Drive, Dunedin, FL 34698. *Phone:* 813-736-5082 or toll-free 800-336-4133. *Fax:* 813-734-0359. *E-mail:* siuadmis@aol.com *Visit location:* Admissions Office, 453 Edgewater Drive.

## QUICK FACTS

Enrollment: 248; UG: 177. Entrance: noncompetitive. SAT>500: N/App; ACT>18: N/App. Tuition and fees: $11,750. Room and board: $4700. Application deadline: rolling.

## GENERAL

Independent, comprehensive, coed. Part of Schiller International University. Awards associate, bachelor's, and master's degrees. Founded 1991. Undergraduate faculty: 34 (6 full-time, 28 part-time). Most popular recent majors: international business, hotel and restaurant management, travel-tourism management.

## CAMPUS VISITS

**College Calendar 1998–99:** *Regular classes:* Aug. 27–Dec. 18; Jan. 14–May 14. *Breaks:* Oct. 23–Nov. 2; Mar. 22–Apr. 6. *Final exams:* Dec. 14–18; May 10–14.

## VISIT OPPORTUNITIES

|  | Appointments? | Who? |
|---|---|---|
| **Campus Tour** | recommended | applicants and parents |
| **Information Session** | recommended | |
| **Admission Interview** | recommended | |
| **Classroom Visit** | required | |
| **Faculty Meeting** | required | applicants and parents |

*Schiller International University (continued)*

**Information Sessions:** M–F, select Sat. 9:00 am–5:00 pm, 6:00–8:00 pm; appointment required 6:00 pm–8:00 pm; 30 minutes.

**Interviews:** M–F, select Sat.; appointment required Sat. and after 5:00 pm; 45 minutes.

**Campus Tours:** Conducted by admission reps. M–F, Sat.; 15 minutes.

**Class Visits:** Prospective students may attend a class in their area of interest.

# UNIVERSITY OF CENTRAL FLORIDA
## Orlando, Florida

**Contact:** Undergraduate Admissions, PO Box 160111, Orlando, FL 32816. *Phone:* 407-823-3000. *Fax:* 407-823-3419. *E-mail:* admissio@pegasus.cc.ucf.edu *Web site:* http://www.ucf.edu/ *Visit location:* Undergraduate Admissions, Administration Building, 4000 Central Florida Parkway.

### QUICK FACTS
Enrollment: 27,806; UG: 22,850. Entrance: moderately difficult. SAT>500: 81% V, 84% M; ACT>18: 100%. Resident tuition and fees: $2025. Nonresident tuition and fees: $7941. Room and board: $4370. Application deadline: 7/15.

### GENERAL
State-supported, university, coed. Part of State University System of Florida. Awards associate, bachelor's, master's, and doctoral degrees. Founded 1963. Setting: 1,445-acre suburban campus. Undergraduate faculty: 714 full-time; student-faculty ratio is 16:1. Most popular recent majors: psychology, elementary education, liberal arts and studies.

### CAMPUS VISITS
**College Calendar 1998–99:** *Regular classes:* Aug. 20–Dec. 5; Jan. 6–Apr. 26. *Breaks:* Mar. 15–20. *Final exams:* Dec. 7–12; Apr. 27–May 3. *Special campus days:* Activities Expo, Aug. 6; Commencement, Dec. 19, May 8; Family Weekend, Oct. 9–11; Homecoming, Nov. 8–14.

### VISIT OPPORTUNITIES

|  | Appointments? | Who? |
| --- | --- | --- |
| **Campus Tour** | not required | open to all |

### VISIT OPPORTUNITIES—*continued*

|  | Appointments? | Who? |
| --- | --- | --- |
| **Information Session** | not required | open to all |
| **Admission Interview** | recommended | open to all |
| **Classroom Visit** | required | open to all |
| **Faculty Meeting** | required | open to all |

**Information Sessions:** M–F at 12:00 pm, 3:00 pm; unavailable holidays; 45 minutes.

**Interviews:** M–F; unavailable holidays; 45 minutes.

**Campus Tours:** Conducted by students. M–F at 11:00 am, 2:00 pm; unavailable holidays; 60 minutes.

**Class Visits:** Prospective students may attend a class in their area of interest.

### CAMPUS FACILITIES
**Science:** Appointment Required: Center for Research and Education in Optics and Lasers (CREDL).

**Arts:** Visual Arts Building Gallery.

**Athletic:** Wayne Densch Athletic Center, UCF Arena.

**Of Special Interest:** UCF Student Union, UCF Arboretum, University Library.

### LOCAL ATTRACTIONS
Orlando; Universal Studios; Sea World; Kennedy Space Center; Beaches; Disney World.

# UNIVERSITY OF FLORIDA
## Gainesville, Florida

**Contact:** Admission Office, 201 Criser Hall, Gainesville, FL 32611. *Phone:* 352-392-1365. *Web site:* http://www.ufl.edu/ *Visit location:* Admission Office, 201 Criser Hall.

### QUICK FACTS
Enrollment: 40,278; UG: 30,100. Entrance: very difficult. SAT>500: 93% V, 97% M; ACT>18: N/R. Resident tuition and fees: $1930. Nonresident tuition and fees: $7570. Room and board: $4610. Application deadline: 1/30.

### GENERAL
State-supported, university, coed. Part of State University System of Florida. Awards associate, bachelor's, master's, doctoral, and first professional degrees. Founded 1853. Setting: 2,000-acre suburban campus with easy access to Jacksonville. Undergradu-

ate faculty: 1,633 (all full-time); student-faculty ratio is 17:1. Most popular recent majors: psychology, finance, English.

## CAMPUS VISITS
**College Calendar 1998–99:** *Regular classes:* Aug. 24–Dec. 9; Jan. 5–Apr. 21; May 10–16; June 28–Aug. 4. *Breaks:* Mar. 6–19. *Final exams:* Dec. 14–18; Apr. 26–30; May 17–18; Aug. 5–6. *Special campus days:* Homecoming, Oct. 10.

## VISIT OPPORTUNITIES

|  | Appointments? | Who? |
|---|---|---|
| **Campus Tour** | recommended, not required | open to all |
| **Information Session** | recommended, not required | open to all |

**Information Sessions:** M–F at 10:00 am, 2:00 pm; 30 minutes.
**Campus Tours:** Conducted by students. M–F; 60 minutes.

## CAMPUS FACILITIES
**Science:** Microkelvin Lab, Nuclear reactor.
**Arts:** Harn Museum, Florida Museum of Natural Science.
**Of Special Interest:** Lake Alice—Wildlife Sanctuary on Campus.

# UNIVERSITY OF MIAMI
## Coral Gables, Florida

**Contact:** Marc Camille, Associate Director of Admission, PO Box 248025, Coral Gables, FL 3124-4616. *Phone:* 305-284-4324. *Fax:* 305-284-2507. *E-mail:* admission@miami.edu *Web site:* http://www.miami.edu/ *Visit location:* Office of Admission, Bowman Foster Ashe Administration Building (Room 132), 1250 Memorial Drive.

## QUICK FACTS
Enrollment: 13,211; UG: 7,955. Entrance: moderately difficult. SAT>500: 82% V, 84% M; ACT>18: 83%. Tuition and fees: $19,512. Room and board: $7352. Application deadline: 3/1.

## GENERAL
Independent, university, coed. Awards bachelor's, master's, doctoral, and first professional degrees.

Founded 1925. Setting: 260-acre suburban campus with easy access to Miami. Undergraduate faculty: 2,351 (1,856 full-time, 495 part-time); student-faculty ratio is 13:1. Most popular recent majors: psychology, biology, business marketing and marketing management.

## CAMPUS VISITS
**College Calendar 1998–99:** *Regular classes:* Aug. 26–Dec. 4; Jan. 8–Apr. 30. *Breaks:* Oct. 16–18; Mar. 13–21. *Final exams:* Dec. 9–16; May 5–13. *Special campus days:* Commencement, May 14.

## VISIT OPPORTUNITIES

|  | Appointments? | Who? |
|---|---|---|
| **Campus Tour** | not required | open to all |
| **Information Session** | not required | open to all |
| **Classroom Visit** | required | open to all |
| **Faculty Meeting** | required | open to all |

**Information Sessions:** M–F at 12:00 pm; Sat. at 11:00 am; Sat. unavailable during summer; 60 minutes.
**Campus Tours:** Conducted by students. M–F at 11:00 am, 1:00 pm, 3:00 pm; Sat. at 10:00 am; Sat. unavailable during summer; 60 minutes.
**Class Visits:** Prospective students may attend a class in their area of interest.
**Video:** Free on request.

## CAMPUS FACILITIES
**Science:** Cox Science Center, Unger Building, Mac Arthur Building; Appointment Required: Rosenstiel School of Marine and Atmospheric Science.
**Arts:** Lowe Art Museum; Appointment Required: Gusman Concert Hall, Jerry Herman Ring Theatre.
**Athletic:** George Smathers Wellness Center, University Center Swimming Pool, Scriff Tennis Stadium.
**Of Special Interest:** Richter Library.

# THE UNIVERSITY OF TAMPA
## Tampa, Florida

**Contact:** Admissions Office, 401 West Kennedy Boulevard, Tampa, FL 33606-1490. *Phone:* 813-253-6211 or toll-free 800-733-4773. *Fax:* 813-254-4955. *E-mail:* admissions@alpha.utampa.edu *Web site:* http://www.utampa.edu/ *Visit location:* Admissions Office, Plant Hall, 401 West Kennedy Boulevard.

*The University of Tampa (continued)*

## QUICK FACTS

Enrollment: 2,854; UG: 2,292. Entrance: moderately difficult. SAT>500: 65% V, 62% M; ACT>18: 94%. Tuition and fees: $14,652. Room and board: $4780. Application deadline: rolling.

## GENERAL

Independent, comprehensive, coed. Awards associate, bachelor's, and master's degrees. Founded 1931. Setting: 70-acre urban campus with easy access to Orlando. Undergraduate faculty: 220 (115 full-time, 105 part-time); student-faculty ratio is 15:1. Most popular recent majors: mass communications, nursing, business administration.

## CAMPUS VISITS

**College Calendar 1998–99:** *Regular classes:* Aug. 31–Dec. 11; Jan. 19–May 3. *Breaks:* Nov. 25–29; Mar. 6–14. *Final exams:* Dec. 14–17; May 4–7. *Special campus days:* Family Weekend, Oct. 2–3; Homecoming, Oct. 23; Spring Commencement, May 8; Winter Commencement, Dec. 19.

---

## VISIT OPPORTUNITIES

| | Appointments? | Who? |
|---|---|---|
| **Campus Tour** | recommended, not required | open to all |
| **Information Session** | recommended | open to all |
| **Admission Interview** | recommended | open to all |
| **Classroom Visit** | required | applicants only |
| **Faculty Meeting** | required | applicants and parents |
| **Overnight Visit** | required | admitted applicants only |

---

**Information Sessions:** Call for schedule.

**Interviews:** M–F; Sat. 9:00 am–12:00 pm; 30 minutes.

**Campus Tours:** Conducted by students. M–F; Sat. at 11:00 am during academic year; 60 minutes.

**Class Visits:** Prospective students may attend a class in their area of interest.

**Overnight Visits:** During the regular academic year, prospective applicants may spend an evening in a residence hall with a student host.

## CAMPUS FACILITIES

**Science:** Appointment Required: Science—Biology or Chemistry.

**Arts:** Appointment Required: Scarfone Art Gallery, Art Studios, Auditions or Art Portfolio Reviews, Theatre, Music Building, practice rooms.

**Athletic:** McNiff Fitness Center; Appointment Required: Martinez Athletic Building.

**Of Special Interest:** Henry B. Plant Museum, Communication Studios, ROTC Unit.

## LOCAL ATTRACTIONS

Busch Gardens; Clearwater Beaches; Florida Aquarium; Dali Museum; Disney Attractions; Universal Studios; Sea World.

# GEORGIA

## AGNES SCOTT COLLEGE
**Decatur, Georgia**

---

**Contact:** Kay Connelly, Coordinator of Campus Visits, 141 East College Avenue, Decatur, GA 30030. *Phone:* 404-638-6285 or toll-free 800-868-8602. *Fax:* 404-638-6414. *E-mail:* kconelly@agnesscott.edu *Web site:* http://www.agnesscott.edu/ *Visit location:* Office of Admission, Rebekah Scott Hall, 141 East College Avenue.

## QUICK FACTS

Enrollment: 737; UG: 716. Entrance: very difficult. SAT>500: 94% V, 84% M; ACT>18: 100%. Tuition and fees: $14,960. Room and board: $6230. Application deadline: 3/1.

## GENERAL

Independent, comprehensive, women only, Presbyterian Church (U.S.A.). Awards bachelor's and master's degrees. Founded 1889. Setting: 100-acre urban campus with easy access to Atlanta. Undergraduate faculty: 95 (67 full-time, 28 part-time); student-faculty ratio is 9:1. Most popular recent majors: English, psychology, biology.

## CAMPUS VISITS

**College Calendar 1998–99:** *Regular classes:* Aug. 28–Dec. 9; Jan. 21–May 4. *Breaks:* Dec. 18–Jan. 20. *Final exams:* Dec. 12–17; May 7–12. *Admission office closed:* Dec. 24–25; Fall Break, Oct. 16; Martin Luther King Jr. Day, Jan. 18. *Special campus days:* Commencement, May 15; Great Scott, Sept. 26, Apr. 17, Nov. 14; Summer Snapshot (admission), July 17; Writers' Festival, Mar. 27.

## VISIT OPPORTUNITIES

|  | Appointments? | Who? |
| --- | --- | --- |
| **Campus Tour** | recommended, not required | open to all |
| **Information Session** | recommended | open to all |
| **Admission Interview** | recommended | applicants and parents |
| **Classroom Visit** | required | open to all |
| **Faculty Meeting** | required | applicants and parents |
| **Overnight Visit** | required | applicants only |

**Information Sessions:** M–F; 30 minutes.

**Interviews:** M–F; Sat. and Sun. by special arrangement; 30 minutes.

**Campus Tours:** Conducted by students. M–F at 10:00 am, 2:00 pm; scheduled appointments available; 60 minutes.

**Class Visits:** Prospective students may attend a class in their area of interest.

**Overnight Visits:** During the regular academic year, prospective applicants may spend an evening in a residence hall with a student host.

## CAMPUS FACILITIES

**Science:** Campbell Science Hall; Appointment Required: Bradley Observatory.

**Arts:** Dalton Gallery.

**Athletic:** Woodruff Physical Activities Building, Gellerstedt Track and Field; Appointment Required: Swimming Facility.

## LOCAL ATTRACTIONS

City of Decatur, Martin Luther King, Jr. Center, World of Coca-Cola Museum, CNN Center, Carter Presidential Center, Underground Atlanta.

# BERRY COLLEGE
**Mount Berry, Georgia**

**Contact:** Office of Admissions, PO Box 490159, Mount Berry, GA 30149-0159. *Phone:* 706-236-2215 or toll-free 800-237-7942. *Fax:* 706-290-2178. *E-mail:* admissions@berry.edu *Web site:* http://www.berry.

edu/ *Visit location:* Admissions Office, North Recitation Hall—Ford Buildings.

## QUICK FACTS

Enrollment: 2,070; UG: 1,875. Entrance: moderately difficult. SAT>500: 94% V, 90% M; ACT>18: 100%. Tuition and fees: $10,210. Room and board: $4536. Application deadline: rolling.

## GENERAL

Independent, comprehensive, coed. Awards bachelor's and master's degrees. Founded 1902. Setting: 28,000-acre small-town campus with easy access to Atlanta. Undergraduate faculty: 126 (108 full-time, 18 part-time); student-faculty ratio is 15:1. Most popular recent majors: early childhood education, psychology, communications.

## CAMPUS VISITS

**College Calendar 1998–99:** *Regular classes:* Aug. 24–Dec. 4; Jan. 11–Apr. 23. *Breaks:* Oct. 10–13; Mar. 15–19; Nov. 25–27. *Final exams:* Dec. 7–11; Apr. 26–30. *Special campus days:* Fall Commencement, Dec. 12; Homecoming; Mountain Day Weekend, Oct. 2–4; Spring Commencement, May 1.

## VISIT OPPORTUNITIES

|  | Appointments? | Who? |
| --- | --- | --- |
| **Campus Tour** | required | applicants and parents |
| **Information Session** | required |  |
| **Admission Interview** | required | applicants and parents |
| **Classroom Visit** | required |  |
| **Faculty Meeting** | required | applicants and parents |

**Information Sessions:** M–F 8:30 am–3:30 pm; Sat. 9:00–11:30 am; 45 minutes.

**Interviews:** M–F, Sat.; 45 minutes.

**Campus Tours:** Conducted by students. M–F 8:30 am–3:30 pm; Sat. 9:00–11:30 am; 45 minutes.

**Class Visits:** Prospective students may attend a class in their area of interest.

**Overnight Visits:** During the regular academic year, prospective applicants may spend an evening in a residence hall with a student host.

**Video:** Free on request.

*Berry College (continued)*

### CAMPUS FACILITIES
**Of Special Interest:** Oak Hill and Martha Berry Museum.

# COVENANT COLLEGE
## Lookout Mountain, Georgia

**Contact:** Lora Erickson, Admissions Coordinator, Covenant College, 14049 Scenic Highway, Lookout Mountain, GA 30750. *Phone:* 706-820-2398 or toll-free 800-926-8362. *Fax:* 706-820-0893. *E-mail:* lerickson@covenant.edu *Web site:* http://www.covenant. edu/ *Visit location:* Admissions Office, Probasco Visitor's Center, 14049 Scenic Highway.

### QUICK FACTS
Enrollment: 945; UG: 884. Entrance: moderately difficult. SAT>500: 86% V, 80% M; ACT>18: 100%. Tuition and fees: $12,900. Room and board: $4120. Application deadline: rolling.

### GENERAL
Independent, comprehensive, coed, Presbyterian Church in America. Awards associate, bachelor's, and master's degrees (master's degree in education only). Founded 1955. Setting: 250-acre suburban campus. Undergraduate faculty: 60 (45 full-time, 15 part-time); student-faculty ratio is 15:1. Most popular recent majors: elementary education, business administration, history.

### CAMPUS VISITS
**College Calendar 1998–99:** *Regular classes:* Aug. 28–Dec. 11; Jan. 5–Apr. 30. *Breaks:* Oct. 17–21; Mar. 6–15. *Final exams:* Dec. 12; May 3–6. *Admission office closed:* Good Friday, Apr. 2.

### VISIT OPPORTUNITIES

|  | Appointments? |
|---|---|
| **Campus Tour** | required |
| **Information Session** | recommended |
| **Admission Interview** | required |
| **Classroom Visit** | required |
| **Faculty Meeting** | required |
| **Overnight Visit** | required |

**Information Sessions:** M–F 10:00 am–3:00 pm; other times by appointment; 60 minutes.

**Interviews:** M–F, select Sat.; 45 minutes.
**Campus Tours:** Conducted by students and admission reps. M–F, Sat. 9:00 am–6:00 pm; Sun. afternoon by appointment.
**Class Visits:** Classroom visits are determined by the visit schedule.
**Overnight Visits:** During the regular academic year, prospective applicants may spend an evening in a residence hall with a student host.
**Video:** Free on request.

### CAMPUS FACILITIES
**Science:** Mills Hall.
**Arts:** McLellan Fine Arts Building, Sanderson Hall.
**Athletic:** Barnes Athletic Center.
**Of Special Interest:** Kresge Library.

### LOCAL ATTRACTIONS
Tennessee Aquarium; Rock City.

# EMMANUEL COLLEGE
## Franklin Springs, Georgia

**Contact:** Mary-Helen Menken, Administrative Assistant, PO Box 129, Franklin Springs, GA 30639. *Phone:* toll-free 800-860-8800 (in-state). *Fax:* 706-245-4424. *E-mail:* mhmenken@emmanuel-college.edu *Web site:* http://www.emmanuel-college.edu/ *Visit location:* Admissions Office, Spring Street.

### QUICK FACTS
Enrollment: 810; UG: 810. Entrance: minimally difficult. SAT>500: N/R; ACT>18: N/R. Tuition and fees: $6060. Room and board: $3420. Application deadline: 8/1.

### GENERAL
Independent, 4-year, coed, Pentecostal Holiness Church. Awards associate and bachelor's degrees. Founded 1919. Setting: 90-acre rural campus with easy access to Atlanta. Faculty: 62 (44 full-time, 18 part-time); student-faculty ratio is 15:1. Most popular recent majors: biblical studies, early childhood education, business administration.

### CAMPUS VISITS
**College Calendar 1998–99:** *Regular classes:* Aug. 20–Dec. 4; Jan. 7–Apr. 26. *Breaks:* Oct. 16–19; Mar. 6–14. *Final exams:* Dec. 7–10; Apr. 27–30. *Special campus days:* Commencement, May 2; Fall Preview Weekend.

## VISIT OPPORTUNITIES

| | Appointments? | Who? |
|---|---|---|
| **Campus Tour** | not required | open to all |
| **Information Session** | recommended | open to all |
| **Classroom Visit** | not required | open to all |
| **Faculty Meeting** | required | open to all |
| **Overnight Visit** | required | open to all |

**Information Sessions:** M–F; 30 minutes.

**Campus Tours:** Conducted by admission reps. M–F, Sat.; 60 minutes.

**Class Visits:** Prospective students may attend a class in their area of interest.

**Overnight Visits:** During the regular academic year, prospective applicants may spend an evening in a residence hall with a student host.

**Video:** Free on request.

### CAMPUS FACILITIES

**Science:** Wellons Science Resources Center.

**Athletic:** Student Activity Center.

**Of Special Interest:** Swails Convocation Center.

# EMORY UNIVERSITY
## Atlanta, Georgia

**Contact:** Mr. Daniel C. Walls, Dean of Admission, 200 Boisfeuillet Jones Center, Atlanta, GA 30322. *Phone:* toll-free 800-727-6036. *Fax:* 404-727-4303. *E-mail:* admiss@learnlink.emory.edu *Web site:* http://www.emory.edu/ *Visit location:* Office of Admission, Boisfeuillet Jones Center.

### QUICK FACTS

Enrollment: 11,109; UG: 5,996. Entrance: most difficult. SAT>500: 98% V, 100% M; ACT>18: 100%. Tuition and fees: $21,120. Room and board: $6800. Application deadline: 1/15.

### GENERAL

Independent Methodist, university, coed. Awards bachelor's, master's, doctoral, and first professional degrees (enrollment figures include Emory University, Oxford College; application data for main campus only). Founded 1836. Setting: 631-acre suburban campus. Undergraduate faculty: 2,486 (2,061 full-time, 425 part-time); student-faculty ratio is 10:1. Most popular recent majors: psychology, biology, political science.

## CAMPUS VISITS

**College Calendar 1998–99:** *Regular classes:* Aug. 27–Dec. 8; Jan. 13–Apr. 26. *Breaks:* Oct. 12–13; Mar. 8–12. *Final exams:* Dec. 10–16; Apr. 29–May 5. *Special campus days:* Alumni Weekend, Sept. 25–27; Commencement, May 10; Dooley's Week, Oct. 26–31.

## VISIT OPPORTUNITIES

| | Appointments? | Who? |
|---|---|---|
| **Campus Tour** | required | open to all |
| **Information Session** | required | open to all |
| **Classroom Visit** | not required | open to all |
| **Faculty Meeting** | recommended | open to all |
| **Overnight Visit** | required | applicants only |

**Information Sessions:** M–F, select Sat.; 60 minutes.

**Campus Tours:** Conducted by students. M–F, select Sat.; call for available times; 60 minutes.

**Class Visits:** Prospective students may attend a class in their area of interest.

**Overnight Visits:** During the regular academic year, prospective applicants may spend an evening in a residence hall with a student host.

**Video:** Free on request.

### CAMPUS FACILITIES

**Science:** O. Wayne Rollins Research Center, Atwood Chemistry Building; Appointment Required: Centers for Disease Control (CDC), Yerkes Primate Center.

**Arts:** Mary Gray Monroe Theater, Burlington Road Building (Performing Arts Studio), Michael C. Carlos Museum, Studio Arts Building.

**Athletic:** Woodruff Physical Education Center, Chappell Park.

**Of Special Interest:** Lullwater Park, Carter Center of Emory University.

### LOCAL ATTRACTIONS

CNN Center, Coca Cola Museum, Olympic Centennial Park, Virginia-Highlands, Buckhead, Stone Mountain, Martin Luther King, Jr. Center, Turner Field.

# GEORGIA SOUTHERN UNIVERSITY
## Statesboro, Georgia

**Contact:** Dr. W. Dale Wasson, Director, PO Box 8024, Statesboro, GA 30460-8024. *Phone:* 912-681-

*Georgia Southern University (continued)*

5532. *Web site:* http://www.gasou.edu/ *Visit location:* Admissions Office, Rosenwald Building, Sweetheart Circle, PO Box 8024.

## QUICK FACTS
Enrollment: 13,962; UG: 12,245. Entrance: moderately difficult. SAT>500: 43% V, 37% M; ACT>18: N/App. Resident tuition and fees: $2256. Nonresident tuition and fees: $6717. Room and board: $3465. Application deadline: 7/1.

## GENERAL
State-supported, comprehensive, coed. Part of University System of Georgia. Awards bachelor's, master's, and doctoral degrees. Founded 1906. Setting: 601-acre small-town campus. Undergraduate faculty: 935 (734 full-time, 201 part-time); student-faculty ratio is 20:1. Most popular recent majors: early childhood education, business marketing and marketing management, finance.

## CAMPUS VISITS
**College Calendar 1998–99:** *Regular classes:* Aug. 21–Dec. 11; Jan. 6–Apr. 28. *Breaks:* Oct. 8–12; Mar. 15–19; Nov. 25–30. *Final exams:* Dec. 14–17; Apr. 30–May 6. *Special campus days:* Graduation, May 8–9; Homecoming, Oct. 17; Parent's Day, Oct. 31.

## VISIT OPPORTUNITIES

| | Appointments? | Who? |
|---|---|---|
| **Campus Tour** | recommended | open to all |
| **Information Session** | recommended, not required | open to all |
| **Faculty Meeting** | required | |

**Information Sessions:** M–F at 11:00 am, 3:00 pm; select Sat. at 10:00 am; 45 minutes.

**Campus Tours:** Conducted by students. M–F at 10:00 am, 2:00 pm; select Sat. at 11:00 am; 60 minutes.

**Video:** Free on request.

## CAMPUS FACILITIES
**Science:** National Tick Collection; Appointment Required: Planetarium.

**Arts:** Museum.

**Athletic:** Hanner Fieldhouse, Recreational Activity Center.

**Of Special Interest:** Wildlife Center-Raptor Center, Botanical gardens.

# SAVANNAH COLLEGE OF ART AND DESIGN
### Savannah, Georgia

**Contact:** Anna Crowley, Admission Event Coordinator, 342 Bull Street, Savannah, GA 31401. *Phone:* 912-238-2483 or toll-free 800-869-SCAD. *Fax:* 912-238-2498. *E-mail:* acrowley@scad.edu *Web site:* http://www.scad.edu/ *Visit location:* Greeter's Desk, Poetter Hall, 342 Bull Street.

## QUICK FACTS
Enrollment: 3,437; UG: 2,920. Entrance: moderately difficult. SAT>500: 61% V, 51% M; ACT>18: N/R. Tuition and fees: $13,500. Room and board: $6375. Application deadline: rolling.

## GENERAL
Independent, comprehensive, coed. Awards bachelor's and master's degrees. Founded 1978. Undergraduate faculty: 195 (156 full-time, 39 part-time); student-faculty ratio is 15:1. Most popular recent majors: graphic design/commercial art/illustration, computer graphics, architecture.

## CAMPUS VISITS
**College Calendar 1998–99:** *Regular classes:* Sept. 16–Nov. 24; Jan. 4–Mar. 11; Mar. 22–May 27. *Breaks:* Nov. 25–Jan. 4; Mar. 12–22. *Admission office closed:* Mar. 17; Commencement, May 29. *Special campus days:* Commencement, May 29; Fall Orientation, Sept. 11–15; Saturday Special Open House.

## VISIT OPPORTUNITIES

| | Appointments? | Who? |
|---|---|---|
| **Campus Tour** | required | open to all |
| **Admission Interview** | required | open to all |
| **Classroom Visit** | required | open to all |
| **Faculty Meeting** | required | open to all |

**Interviews:** M–F, select Sat.; 30 minutes.

**Campus Tours:** Conducted by admission reps. M–F at 9:30 am, 2:30 pm; select Sat.; 90 minutes.

**Class Visits:** Prospective students may attend a class in their area of interest, classroom visits are determined by the visit schedule.

**CAMPUS FACILITIES**

**Arts:** Appointment Required: Metals and Jewelry, Graduate Painting Studios, Furniture Design Studio, Industrial Design Studio.

**Athletic:** Appointment Required: Fitness Center.

**Of Special Interest:** Appointment Required: Residence Hall room.

**LOCAL ATTRACTIONS**

City Market, River Street, Mrs. Wilkes Board House (restaurant), local shopping facilities, local churches.

# UNIVERSITY OF GEORGIA
## Athens, Georgia

**Contact:** Visitors Center, River Road and College Station Avenue, Athens, GA 30602. *Phone:* 706-542-0842. *Fax:* 706-542-5151. *Web site:* http://www.uga.edu/ *Visit location:* Visitors Center, The Four Towers Building, River Road and College Station Avenue.

**QUICK FACTS**

Enrollment: 29,440; UG: 22,983. Entrance: moderately difficult. SAT>500: 93% V, 92% M; ACT>18: N/R. Resident tuition and fees: $2838. Nonresident tuition and fees: $8790. Room and board: $4323. Application deadline: 2/1.

**GENERAL**

State-supported, university, coed. Part of University System of Georgia. Awards associate, bachelor's, master's, doctoral, and first professional degrees. Founded 1785. Setting: 1,289-acre suburban campus with easy access to Atlanta. Undergraduate faculty: 3,075 (2,841 full-time, 234 part-time). Most popular recent majors: English, accounting, political science.

**CAMPUS VISITS**

**College Calendar 1998–99:** *Regular classes:* Aug. 24–Dec. 10; Jan. 7–Apr. 29. *Breaks:* Nov. 25–29; Mar. 6–14. *Final exams:* Dec. 14–18; May 3–7. *Special campus days:* Commencement, May 8; Homecoming, Oct. 17.

**VISIT OPPORTUNITIES**

| | Appointments? | Who? |
|---|---|---|
| **Campus Tour** | required | open to all |
| **Information Session** | | open to all |

**Information Sessions:** M–F at 10:30 am, 2:30 pm; 60 minutes.

**Campus Tours:** Conducted by students. M–F at 9:00 am, 1:15 pm, 3:15 pm; Sat. at 10:30 am, 2:30 pm; Sun. at 2:30 pm; 60 minutes.

**CAMPUS FACILITIES**

**Arts:** Georgia Museum of Art.

**Athletic:** Butts-Mehre Athletic Center, Ramsey Student Activities Center.

# VALDOSTA STATE UNIVERSITY
## Valdosta, Georgia

**Contact:** Mr. Walter Peacock, Director of Admissions, 1500 North Patterson Street, Valdosta, GA 31698. *Phone:* toll-free 800-618-1878. *Fax:* 912-333-5482. *Web site:* http://www.valdosta.edu/ *Visit location:* Admissions Office, Admissions House, 1500 North Patterson Street.

**QUICK FACTS**

Enrollment: 9,779; UG: 8,524. Entrance: moderately difficult. SAT>500: 42% V, 32% M; ACT>18: 50%. Resident tuition and fees: $1974. Nonresident tuition and fees: $6435. Room and board: $3465. Application deadline: rolling.

**GENERAL**

State-supported, university, coed. Part of University System of Georgia. Awards associate, bachelor's, master's, and doctoral degrees. Founded 1906. Setting: 168-acre small-town campus with easy access to Jacksonville. Undergraduate faculty: 472 (392 full-time, 80 part-time); student-faculty ratio is 23:1. Most popular recent majors: biology, business administration, early childhood education.

**CAMPUS VISITS**

**College Calendar 1998–99:** *Regular classes:* Aug. 19–Dec. 9; Jan. 11–May 3. *Breaks:* Nov. 23–27; Mar. 29–Apr. 2; Dec. 17–Jan. 6. *Final exams:* Dec. 11–16; May 5–10. *Admission office closed:* Aug. 15–19, Jan. 7–11, May 31–June 2. *Special campus days:* Fall Graduation, Dec. 17; Homecoming, Oct. 9–11; Spring Graduation, May 11; Summer Graduation, Aug. 1.

*Valdosta State University (continued)*

## VISIT OPPORTUNITIES

| | Appointments? | Who? |
|---|---|---|
| **Campus Tour** | required | applicants and parents |
| **Information Session** | recommended | |
| **Classroom Visit** | required | |
| **Faculty Meeting** | required | applicants and parents |
| **Overnight Visit** | required | |

**Information Sessions:** M–F at 10:30 am, 2:00 pm; select Sat. at 10:30 am; tours and information sessions are combined; 120 minutes.

**Campus Tours:** Conducted by students and admission reps. M–F 10:30 am–2:00 pm; select Sat. at 10:30 am; 120 minutes.

**Class Visits:** Classroom visits are determined by the visit schedule.

**Overnight Visits:** During the regular academic year, prospective applicants may spend an evening in a residence hall.

## CAMPUS FACILITIES

**Science:** Science Classes/Labs; Appointment Required: Planetarium, Herbarium.

**Arts:** Sawyer Theater, Whitehead Auditorium; Appointment Required: Art Gallery–Art Studios, Telecommunications–TV Studio.

**Athletic:** Physical Education Complex; Appointment Required: Gymnasium.

**Of Special Interest:** Dining Facilities, Student Centers and Library; Appointment Required: Residence Halls.

## LOCAL ATTRACTIONS

Cresent Center; Lake Park Outlet Mall; Wild Adventures Amusement Park; Okefonokee Swamp Park; Spirit of Suwannee Park.

# IDAHO

## BOISE STATE UNIVERSITY
Boise, Idaho

**Contact:** Beth Winslow, Campus Tour Coordinator, 1910 University Drive, Boise, ID 83725. *Phone:* toll-free 800-824-7017 Ext. 1820, 800-632-6586 (in-state). *Fax:* 208-385-4253. *E-mail:* bsuinfo@bsu. idbsu.edu *Web site:* http://www.idbsu.edu/ *Visit location:* New Student Information Center, Student Union Building, 1910 University Drive.

## QUICK FACTS
Enrollment: 14,125; UG: 11,979. Entrance: minimally difficult. SAT>500: 50% V, 49% M; ACT>18: 80%. Resident tuition and fees: $2294. Nonresident tuition and fees: $8174. Room and board: $3264. Application deadline: 7/23.

## GENERAL
State-supported, comprehensive, coed. Part of Idaho System of Higher Education. Awards associate, bachelor's, master's, and doctoral degrees. Founded 1932. Setting: 130-acre urban campus. Undergraduate faculty: 860 (503 full-time, 357 part-time); student-faculty ratio is 17:1. Most popular recent majors: elementary education, accounting, business marketing and marketing management.

## CAMPUS VISITS
**College Calendar 1998–99:** *Regular classes:* Aug. 24–Dec. 11; Jan. 19–May 7. *Breaks:* Dec. 18–Jan. 18; Mar. 22–25. *Final exams:* Dec. 14–17; May 10–14. *Special campus days:* Commencement, May 15; Discover BSU, Oct. 17; Homecoming, Oct. 17.

## VISIT OPPORTUNITIES

| | Appointments? | Who? |
|---|---|---|
| **Campus Tour** | required | open to all |
| **Information Session** | recommended | open to all |
| **Admission Interview** | required | open to all |
| **Classroom Visit** | required | open to all |
| **Faculty Meeting** | required | open to all |
| **Overnight Visit** | required | open to all |

**Information Sessions:** Wed. at 1:00 pm; Thu. at 4:00 pm; 60 minutes.

**Interviews:** M–F, select Sat.; 30 minutes.

**Campus Tours:** Conducted by students. M–F at 1:30 pm; tour added during spring semester daily M–F at 10:30 am; 60 minutes.

**Overnight Visits:** During the regular academic year, prospective applicants may spend an evening in a residence hall with a student host.

**Video:** Free on request.

## CAMPUS FACILITIES
**Science:** Raptor Biology.
**Arts:** Appointment Required: Morrison Center.
**Athletic:** Appointment Required: Bronco Stadium.
**Of Special Interest:** Library.

## LOCAL ATTRACTIONS
Bogus Basin Ski Resort; Lucky Peak; World Birds of Prey Center; Art/Historical Museums.

## NORTHWEST NAZARENE COLLEGE
**Nampa, Idaho**

**Contact:** Stacey Henrickson, Campus Visit/Events Coordinator, 623 Holly Street, Nampa, ID 83686. *Phone:* toll-free 800-NNC-4-YOU. *Fax:* 208-467-8522. *E-mail:* sahenrickson@exodus.nnc.edu *Web site:* http://www.nnc.edu/ *Visit location:* Admission and Financial Aid, Administration Building, 623 Holly Street.

## QUICK FACTS
Enrollment: 1,708; UG: 1,050. Entrance: moderately difficult. SAT>500: N/R; ACT>18: 86%. Tuition and fees: $12,456. Room and board: $3519. Application deadline: 9/19.

## GENERAL
Independent, comprehensive, coed, Church of the Nazarene. Awards bachelor's and master's degrees. Founded 1913. Setting: 85-acre small-town campus. Undergraduate faculty: 96 (76 full-time, 20 part-time); student-faculty ratio is 13:1. Most popular recent majors: elementary education, business administration, social sciences.

## CAMPUS VISITS
**College Calendar 1998–99:** *Regular classes:* Sept. 22–Dec. 4; Jan. 4–Mar. 12; Mar. 29–June 4. *Breaks:* Dec. 11–Jan. 4; Mar. 19–28. *Final exams:* Dec. 7–10; Mar. 15–18; June 7–10. *Special campus days:* Commencement, June 11–12; Homecoming, Nov. 25–28.

## VISIT OPPORTUNITIES

|  | Appointments? | Who? |
|---|---|---|
| **Campus Tour** | recommended | open to all |
| **Information Session** | recommended | open to all |
| **Admission Interview** | recommended | open to all |

VISIT OPPORTUNITIES—*continued*

|  | Appointments? | Who? |
|---|---|---|
| **Classroom Visit** | recommended | open to all |
| **Faculty Meeting** | required | open to all |
| **Overnight Visit** | required | open to all |

**Interviews:** M–F; 30 minutes.
**Campus Tours:** Conducted by students and admission reps. M–F; 60 minutes.
**Class Visits:** Classroom visits are determined by the visit schedule.
**Overnight Visits:** During the regular academic year, prospective applicants may spend an evening in a residence hall with a student host.

## CAMPUS FACILITIES
**Arts:** Brandt Center for Fine Arts.
**Athletic:** Montgomery Fieldhouse.
**Of Special Interest:** Gilbert Ford Dorm.

# ILLINOIS

## AUGUSTANA COLLEGE
**Rock Island, Illinois**

**Contact:** Martin R. Sauer, Director of Admissions, 639 38th Street, Rock Island, IL 61201. *Phone:* toll-free 800-798-8100 Ext. 7341. *Fax:* 309-794-7174. *E-mail:* admissions@augustana.edu *Web site:* http://www.augustana.edu/ *Visit location:* Office of Admissions, Seminary Hall, 639 38th Street.

## QUICK FACTS
Enrollment: 2,249; UG: 2,249. Entrance: moderately difficult. SAT>500: N/R; ACT>18: 99%. Tuition and fees: $15,300. Room and board: $4689. Application deadline: 4/1.

## GENERAL
Independent, 4-year, coed, Evangelical Lutheran Church in America. Awards bachelor's degrees. Founded 1860. Setting: 115-acre suburban campus. Faculty: 191 (145 full-time, 46 part-time); student-faculty ratio is 13:1. Most popular recent majors: biology, business administration, English.

*Augustana College (continued)*

## CAMPUS VISITS

**College Calendar 1998–99:** *Regular classes:* Sept.
8–Nov. 13; Nov. 30–Feb. 19; Mar. 8–May 14. *Breaks:*
Nov. 20–29; Feb. 26–Mar. 7. *Final exams:* Nov.
16–19; Feb. 22–25; May 17–20. *Admission office closed:*
Mar. 3–6. *Special campus days:* Commencement, May
23; Family Weekend, Oct. 16–18; Homecoming, Oct.
30–Nov. 1.

## VISIT OPPORTUNITIES

|  | Appointments? | Who? |
|---|---|---|
| **Campus Tour** | recommended | open to all |
| **Information Session** | recommended | open to all |
| **Admission Interview** | required | open to all |
| **Classroom Visit** | required | open to all |
| **Faculty Meeting** | required | open to all |
| **Overnight Visit** | required | applicants only |

**Information Sessions:** M–F 8:00 am–4:30 pm; select
Sat. 9:00 am–1:00 pm.

**Interviews:** M–F.

**Campus Tours:** Conducted by students. M–F 8:00
am–4:30 pm; select Sat. 9:00 am–1:00 pm.

**Class Visits:** Prospective students may attend a class
in their area of interest.

**Overnight Visits:** During the regular academic year,
prospective applicants may spend an evening in a
residence hall with a student host.

**Video:** Free on request.

## CAMPUS FACILITIES

**Science:** Augustana Science Center, Olin Educational Technology Center, Fryxell Geology Museum.

**Arts:** Studio's, Augustana Art Gallery.

**Athletic:** Carver Physical Education Center, Pepsico
Recreation Center.

**Of Special Interest:** Library, Residence Halls.

# BRADLEY UNIVERSITY
## Peoria, Illinois

**Contact:** JoAnn Homann, Visit Specialist, Visitors
Center, Bradley University, Peoria, IL 61625. *Phone:*
toll-free 800-447-6460. *Fax:* 309-677-2797. *E-mail:*
admissions@bradley.edu *Web site:* http://www.bradley.
edu/ *Visit location:* Admissions Office, Visitors Center,
Bradley University.

## QUICK FACTS

Enrollment: 5,840; UG: 4,895. Entrance: moderately
difficult. SAT>500: 77% V, 81% M; ACT>18: 96%.
Tuition and fees: $12,690. Room and board: $4690.
Application deadline: rolling.

## GENERAL

Independent, comprehensive, coed. Awards bachelor's and master's degrees. Founded 1897. Setting:
65-acre urban campus. Undergraduate faculty: 475
(311 full-time, 164 part-time); student-faculty ratio is
14:1. Most popular recent majors: communications,
psychology, accounting.

## CAMPUS VISITS

**College Calendar 1998–99:** *Regular classes:* Sept.
1–Dec. 10; Feb. 1–May 5. *Final exams:* Dec. 10–17;
May 6–13. *Admission office closed:* Dec. 20–Jan. 2.
*Special campus days:* Fall Break, Oct. 10–13; Homecoming, Oct. 1–3; Spring Break, Mar. 13–21.

## VISIT OPPORTUNITIES

|  | Appointments? | Who? |
|---|---|---|
| **Campus Tour** | recommended | open to all |
| **Information Session** | required | open to all |
| **Admission Interview** | required | open to all |
| **Classroom Visit** | required | open to all |
| **Faculty Meeting** | required | open to all |
| **Overnight Visit** | required | applicants only |

**Information Sessions:** M–F, select Sat.; 45 minutes.

**Interviews:** M–F, select Sat.; 20 minutes.

**Campus Tours:** Conducted by students. M–F, select
Sat.; 55 minutes.

**Class Visits:** Classroom visits are determined by the
visit schedule.

**Overnight Visits:** During the regular academic year,
prospective applicants may spend an evening in a
residence hall with a student host.

## CAMPUS FACILITIES

**Of Special Interest:** Appointment Required: Global
Communications Center.

## LOCAL ATTRACTIONS

Peoria Riverfront includes Illinois Antique Center, Riverboat, Technical Center, restaurant in restored Train Station and Marina.

# ILLINOIS INSTITUTE OF TECHNOLOGY
## Chicago, Illinois

**Contact:** Paula Black, Visit Coordinator, Office of Admission, 10 West 33rd Street, Chicago, IL 60616. *Phone:* 312-567-3909 or toll-free 800-448-2329 (out-of-state). *Fax:* 312-567-6939. *E-mail:* admission@vax1. ais.iit.edu *Web site:* http://www.iit.edu/ *Visit location:* Office of Undergraduate Admission, Perlstein Hall 101, 10 West 33rd Street.

## QUICK FACTS

Enrollment: 5,929; UG: 1,677. Entrance: very difficult. SAT>500: 92% V, 100% M; ACT>18: 100%. Tuition and fees: $16,620. Room and board: $4940. Application deadline: rolling.

## GENERAL

Independent, university, coed. Awards bachelor's, master's, doctoral, and first professional degrees. Founded 1890. Setting: 120-acre urban campus. Undergraduate faculty: 535 (295 full-time, 240 part-time); student-faculty ratio is 11:1. Most popular recent majors: electrical/electronics engineering, mechanical engineering, architecture.

## CAMPUS VISITS

**College Calendar 1998–99:** *Regular classes:* Aug. 24–Dec. 5; Jan. 19–May 8. *Breaks:* Mar. 15–20. *Final exams:* Dec. 7–12; May 10–15. *Admission office closed:* Christmas and New Years week. *Special campus days:* Fall Open House, Oct. 31; Summer Open House, July 11.

## VISIT OPPORTUNITIES

| | Appointments? | Who? |
|---|---|---|
| **Campus Tour** | not required | open to all |
| **Information Session** | not required | open to all |
| **Admission Interview** | required | open to all |
| **Classroom Visit** | recommended | open to all |
| **Faculty Meeting** | required | open to all |

VISIT OPPORTUNITIES—*continued*

| | Appointments? | Who? |
|---|---|---|
| **Overnight Visit** | required | admitted applicants only |

**Information Sessions:** M–F 8:30 am–5:00 pm; Sat. 9:00 am–12:00 pm; 30 minutes.

**Interviews:** M–F, select Sat.; 30 minutes.

**Campus Tours:** Conducted by students. M–F, select Sat. at 12:00 pm; 60 minutes.

**Class Visits:** Prospective students may attend a class in their area of interest, certain predetermined classrooms are open to visitors, classroom visits are determined by the visit schedule.

## CAMPUS FACILITIES

**Of Special Interest:** Paul V. Galvin Library.

# ILLINOIS WESLEYAN UNIVERSITY
## Bloomington, Illinois

**Contact:** Mr. James R. Ruoti, Dean of Admission, PO Box 2900, Bloomington, IL 61702-2900. *Phone:* toll-free 800-332-2498. *Fax:* 309-556-3411. *E-mail:* iwuadmit@titan.iwu.edu *Web site:* http://www.iwu. edu/ *Visit location:* Admission Office, Holmes Hall—Room 103, 1312 North Park Street.

## QUICK FACTS

Enrollment: 2,016; UG: 2,016. Entrance: very difficult. SAT>500: 95% V, 96% M; ACT>18: 100%. Tuition and fees: $18,376. Room and board: $4824. Application deadline: rolling.

## GENERAL

Independent, 4-year, coed. Awards bachelor's degrees. Founded 1850. Setting: 70-acre suburban campus. Faculty: 165 (140 full-time, 25 part-time); student-faculty ratio is 13:1. Most popular recent majors: business administration, biology, English.

## CAMPUS VISITS

**College Calendar 1998–99:** *Regular classes:* Aug. 31–Dec. 10; Jan. 6–Apr. 20; May 5–25. *Breaks:* Nov. 24–30; Mar. 12–22. *Final exams:* Dec. 14–18; Apr. 23–28; May 26. *Special campus days:* Commencement, May 2; Homecoming, Oct. 10; Open House, Oct. 12, Feb. 20.

*Illinois Wesleyan University (continued)*

## VISIT OPPORTUNITIES

|  | Appointments? | Who? |
|---|---|---|
| **Campus Tour** | required | open to all |
| **Admission Interview** | required | open to all |
| **Classroom Visit** | required | open to all |
| **Faculty Meeting** | required | open to all |
| **Overnight Visit** | required | applicants only |

**Interviews:** M–F 9:00 am–4:00 pm; Sat. 9:00 am–12:00 pm; M–F Jun. 1 through Aug.15 from 9:00 am to 2:00 pm; 60 minutes.

**Campus Tours:** Conducted by students. M–F 9:00 am–4:00 pm; Sat. 9:00 am–12:00 pm; M–F Jun. 1–Aug. 15 from 9:00 am–3:00 pm; 60 minutes.

**Class Visits:** Prospective students may attend a class in their area of interest.

**Overnight Visits:** During the regular academic year, prospective applicants may spend an evening in a residence hall with a student host.

**Video:** Free on request.

### CAMPUS FACILITIES
**Science:** Center for Natural Science.

**Arts:** School of Art, School of Music, School of Theatre Arts.

**Athletic:** Shirk Athletic/Wellness Center.

**Of Special Interest:** Residence Hall.

# KNOX COLLEGE
### Galesburg, Illinois

**Contact:** Kim Schrader, Campus Visit Coordinator, Knox College Box K-148, Galesburg, IL 61401. *Phone:* toll-free 800-678-KNOX. *Fax:* 309-341-7070. *E-mail:* kschrade@knox.edu *Web site:* http://www.knox.edu/ *Visit location:* Office of Admission, Center for Fine Arts, Knox College 2 East South Street.

### QUICK FACTS
Enrollment: 1,149; UG: 1,149. Entrance: very difficult. SAT>500: 89% V, 94% M; ACT>18: 99%. Tuition and fees: $19,074. Room and board: $5076. Application deadline: 2/15.

### GENERAL
Independent, 4-year, coed. Awards bachelor's degrees. Founded 1837. Setting: 75-acre small-town campus with easy access to Peoria. Faculty: 115 (94 full-time, 21 part-time); student-faculty ratio is 12:1. Most popular recent majors: biology, creative writing, psychology.

### CAMPUS VISITS
**College Calendar 1998–99:** *Regular classes:* Sept. 10–Nov. 18; Jan. 3–Mar. 9; Mar. 21–May 26. *Breaks:* Nov. 24–Jan. 2; Mar. 14–20. *Final exams:* Nov. 19–23; Mar. 10–13; May 27–31. *Admission office closed:* Christmas, Dec. 24–25; Thanksgiving, Nov. 26–27. *Special campus days:* Commencement, June 5; Homecoming, Oct. 16–18.

## VISIT OPPORTUNITIES

|  | Appointments? | Who? |
|---|---|---|
| **Campus Tour** | recommended | open to all |
| **Admission Interview** | recommended | open to all |
| **Classroom Visit** | required | open to all |
| **Faculty Meeting** | required | open to all |
| **Overnight Visit** | required | open to all |

**Interviews:** M–F; Sat. during the academic term; 60 minutes.

**Campus Tours:** Conducted by students. M–F at 9:20 am, 10:40 am, 1:20 pm, 2:40 pm; Sat. during academic term at 10:00 am, 11:00 am; 60 minutes.

**Class Visits:** Prospective students may attend a class in their area of interest.

**Overnight Visits:** During the regular academic year, prospective applicants may spend an evening in a residence hall with a student host.

### CAMPUS FACILITIES
**Science:** Green Oaks Biological Field Station.

**Arts:** Harbach and Studio Theatre, Kresge Recital Hall, Art Studios.

**Athletic:** Fieldhouse complex.

**Of Special Interest:** Old Main—Lincoln Douglas Debate site.

### LOCAL ATTRACTIONS
Carl Sandburg Birthplace; Seminary Street Shops; Central Congregational Church.

# LAKE FOREST COLLEGE
**Lake Forest, Illinois**

**Contact:** Renee Wruck Bischoff, Senior Assistant Director of Admissions, 555 North Sheridan Road, Lake Forest, IL 60045. *Phone:* toll-free 800-828-4751. *Fax:* 847-735-6271. *E-mail:* admissions@lfc.edu *Web site:* http://www.lfc.edu/ *Visit location:* Admissions Office, Patterson Lodge, 555 North Sheridan Road.

## QUICK FACTS
Enrollment: 1,173; UG: 1,154. Entrance: very difficult. SAT>500: 84% V, 78% M; ACT>18: 98%. Tuition and fees: $19,560. Room and board: $4550. Application deadline: 3/1.

## GENERAL
Independent, comprehensive, coed. Awards bachelor's and master's degrees. Founded 1857. Setting: 110-acre suburban campus with easy access to Chicago. Undergraduate faculty: 118 (76 full-time, 42 part-time); student-faculty ratio is 11:1. Most popular recent majors: psychology, English, business economics.

## CAMPUS VISITS
**College Calendar 1998–99:** *Regular classes:* Aug. 27–Dec. 8; Jan. 12–Apr. 27. *Breaks:* Oct. 17–20; Mar. 6–14; Nov. 26–29. *Final exams:* Dec. 11–16; Mar. 1–May 5. *Special campus days:* Athletic Open House, Dec. 6; Commencement, May 8; Fall Campus Visit Day, Oct. 12, Nov. 11; Family Weekend; Homecoming; Multicultural Visit Weekend, Jan. 17–18; Preview Program for Admitted Students, Apr. 18–19.

## VISIT OPPORTUNITIES

| | Appointments? | Who? |
|---|---|---|
| **Campus Tour** | recommended, not required | open to all |
| **Information Session** | not required | open to all |
| **Admission Interview** | recommended | open to all |
| **Classroom Visit** | required | open to all |
| **Faculty Meeting** | recommended | open to all |
| **Overnight Visit** | required | open to all |

**Information Sessions:** Call for available schedule; 30 minutes.

**Interviews:** M–F 8:30 am–4:30 pm; Sat. 9:00 am–12:00 pm; unavailable Easter, Passover, Hanukkah, Christmas, Thanksgiving, New Year's Day, Memorial Day weekend, Fourth of July; 45 minutes.

**Campus Tours:** Conducted by students. Sat. at 9:00 am, 10:00 am, 11:00 am, 12:00 pm; M–F 9:00 am–4:00 pm; appointment required during school breaks; abbreviated during final exam periods; 60 minutes.

**Class Visits:** Prospective students may attend a class in their area of interest.

**Overnight Visits:** During the regular academic year, prospective applicants may spend an evening in a residence hall with a student host.

## CAMPUS FACILITIES
**Science:** Science classrooms, science labs.
**Arts:** Studio Spaces, Art Department Building.
**Athletic:** Hockey Rink, Sports Center.
**Of Special Interest:** Computer lab, library, music department.

## LOCAL ATTRACTIONS
Chicago area; Six Flags Great America; Ravinia.

# LOYOLA UNIVERSITY CHICAGO
**Chicago, Illinois**

**Contact:** Ms. Lori Kingen, Visit Coordinator, 6525 N. Sheridan Road CC116, Chicago, IL 60626. *Phone:* toll-free 800-262-2373. *Fax:* 773-508-8926. *E-mail:* lkingen@luc.edu *Web site:* http://www.luc.edu/ *Visit location:* Undergraduate Admission Office, Crown Center, 6525 North Sheridan Road.

## QUICK FACTS
Enrollment: 13,090; UG: 7,006. Entrance: moderately difficult. SAT>500: 84% V, 82% M; ACT>18: 97%. Tuition and fees: $16,054. Room and board: $6380. Application deadline: 4/1.

## GENERAL
Independent Roman Catholic (Jesuit), university, coed. Awards bachelor's, master's, doctoral, and first professional degrees (also offers adult part-time program with significant enrollment not reflected in profile). Founded 1870. Setting: 105-acre urban campus. Undergraduate faculty: 961 (536 full-time, 425 part-time); student-faculty ratio is 13:1. Most popular recent majors: psychology, biology, nursing.

## CAMPUS VISITS
**College Calendar 1998–99:** *Regular classes:* Aug. 31–Dec. 8; Jan. 18–May 1. *Breaks:* Oct. 19–21; Mar. 8–14; Dec. 19–Jan. 18. *Final exams:* Dec. 11–18; May 5–12. *Admission office closed:* Christmas, Dec. 24–25;

*Loyola University Chicago (continued)*

Thanksgiving, Nov. 26–27. *Special campus days:* Commencement, Jan. 16, May 15.

## VISIT OPPORTUNITIES

|  | Appointments? | Who? |
|---|---|---|
| **Campus Tour** | required | applicants and parents |
| **Information Session** | required | |
| **Classroom Visit** | required | open to all |
| **Faculty Meeting** | required | applicants and parents |
| **Overnight Visit** | required | |

**Information Sessions:** M–F 9:00 am–4:00 pm; Sat. 10:00 am–2:00 pm; individual and group sessions available; 50 minutes.

**Campus Tours:** Conducted by students. M–F, Sat.; 60 minutes.

**Class Visits:** Certain predetermined classrooms are open to visitors, will consider student's request for a particular class.

**Overnight Visits:** During the regular academic year, prospective applicants may spend an evening in a residence hall with a student host.

**Video:** Free on request.

## CAMPUS FACILITIES

**Arts:** Fine Arts Gallery.

**Athletic:** Joseph J. Gentile Center, Recreational Sports Center.

**Of Special Interest:** Martin D'Arcy Renaissance and Baroque Museum.

# MOODY BIBLE INSTITUTE

**Chicago, Illinois**

**Contact:** Unity Olivencia, Campus Visit Coordinator, 820 North LaSalle Boulevard, Chicago, IL 60610. *Phone:* 312-329-2153 or toll-free 800-967-4MBI. *Fax:* 312-329-8987. *E-mail:* uolivenc@moody.edu *Web site:* http://www.moody.edu/ *Visit location:* Admissions Office, Crowell Hall, 820 North LaSalle Boulevard.

## QUICK FACTS

Enrollment: 1,383; UG: 1,305. Entrance: moderately difficult. SAT>500: N/App; ACT>18: N/App. Tuition and fees: $830. Room and board: $4480. Application deadline: 3/1.

## GENERAL

Independent nondenominational, comprehensive, coed. Awards bachelor's and master's degrees. Founded 1886. Setting: 25-acre urban campus. Undergraduate faculty: 144 (94 full-time, 50 part-time); student-faculty ratio is 18:1. Most popular recent major: biblical studies.

## CAMPUS VISITS

**College Calendar 1998–99:** *Regular classes:* Aug. 24–Dec. 10; Jan. 11–May 7. *Breaks:* Mar. 13–28. *Final exams:* Dec. 14–17; May 11–14. *Special campus days:* Commencement; Day of Prayer, Mar. 3; Founders Week Conference, Feb. 1–6; Homecoming; Spiritual Enrichment Week, Nov. 26–29; Student Missions Conference, Oct. 13–16.

## VISIT OPPORTUNITIES

|  | Appointments? | Who? |
|---|---|---|
| **Campus Tour** | required | open to all |
| **Information Session** | | open to all |
| **Classroom Visit** | required | open to all |
| **Faculty Meeting** | required | open to all |
| **Overnight Visit** | required | open to all |

**Information Sessions:** M–F at 9:15 am, 2:15 pm; 40 minutes.

**Campus Tours:** Conducted by students and admission reps. Mon. at 10:00 am; T–F at 12:00 pm; 60 minutes.

**Class Visits:** Certain predetermined classrooms are open to visitors.

**Overnight Visits:** During the regular academic year, prospective applicants may spend an evening in a residence hall with a student host.

**Video:** Free on request.

## CAMPUS FACILITIES

**Athletic:** Appointment Required: Solheim Center.

**Of Special Interest:** Moody Memorial Museum; Appointment Required: Torrey Gray Auditorium, Sweeting Center.

## LOCAL ATTRACTIONS

Downtown Chicago; Lake Michigan; The Magnificent Mile.

# NORTHERN ILLINOIS UNIVERSITY
De Kalb, Illinois

**Contact:** Director Of Admissions, Office of Admission, Northern Illinois University, Williston Hall, DeKalb, IL 60115-2857. *Phone:* 815-753-8301 or toll-free 800-892-3050 (in-state). *Fax:* 815-753-1783. *E-mail:* admissions-info@niu.edu *Web site:* http://www.niu.edu/ *Visit location:* Office of Admission, Williston Hall, Northern Illinois University.

## QUICK FACTS

Enrollment: 22,054; UG: 15,827. Entrance: moderately difficult. SAT>500: N/R; ACT>18: 92%. Resident tuition and fees: $3837. Nonresident tuition and fees: $9741. Room and board: $4000. Application deadline: 8/1.

## GENERAL

State-supported, university, coed. Awards bachelor's, master's, doctoral, and first professional degrees. Founded 1895. Setting: 589-acre small-town campus with easy access to Chicago. Undergraduate faculty: 1,203 (1,020 full-time, 183 part-time); student-faculty ratio is 17:1. Most popular recent majors: mass communications, education, accounting.

## CAMPUS VISITS

**College Calendar 1998–99:** *Regular classes:* Aug. 24–Dec. 12; Jan. 11–May 7. *Final exams:* Dec. 7–12; May 4–7. *Special campus days:* Fall Commencement, Dec. 13; Spring Commencement, May 8.

### VISIT OPPORTUNITIES

|  | Appointments? | Who? |
|---|---|---|
| **Campus Tour** | not required | open to all |
| **Admission Interview** | not required | open to all |
| **Classroom Visit** | required | |
| **Faculty Meeting** | required | applicants and parents |
| **Overnight Visit** | required | |

**Interviews:** M–F 8:30 am–4:30 pm; select Sat. Sept. through May 10:00 am–2:00 pm; 60 minutes.

**Campus Tours:** Conducted by students. M–F at 11:30 am, 2:00 pm; select Sat.; select Sat. Sept. through May at 12:00 pm; 60 minutes.

**Overnight Visits:** During the regular academic year, prospective applicants may spend an evening in a residence hall with a student host.

**Video:** Free on request.

## CAMPUS FACILITIES

**Science:** Appointment Required: Faraday Hall, Faraday Hall—West, Davis Hall, Montgomery Hall.

**Arts:** Appointment Required: Jack Arends Hall, Altgeld Hall Art Museum, Stevens Building Anthropology Museum, Jack Olson Gallery.

**Athletic:** Student Recreation Center; Appointment Required: Chick Evans Field House, Huskie Stadium.

**Of Special Interest:** Holmes Student Center; Appointment Required: Engineering Building, Residence Halls.

## LOCAL ATTRACTIONS

Ellwood House; Stagecoach Players; Egyptian Theatre; Corn Festival; Sycamore Pumpkin Festival.

# NORTHWESTERN UNIVERSITY
Evanston, Illinois

**Contact:** Office of Undergraduate Admission, 1801 Hinman Avenue, Evanston, IL 60202. *Phone:* 847-491-7271. *Fax:* 847-467-1317. *E-mail:* ug-admission@nwu.edu *Web site:* http://www.nwu.edu/ *Visit location:* Office of Undergraduate Admissions, PO Box 3060, 1801 Hinman Avenue.

## QUICK FACTS

Enrollment: 15,436; UG: 7,619. Entrance: most difficult. SAT>500: 99% V, 100% M; ACT>18: 100%. Tuition and fees: $22,458. Room and board: $6675. Application deadline: 1/1.

## GENERAL

Independent, university, coed. Awards bachelor's, master's, doctoral, and first professional degrees. Founded 1851. Setting: 231-acre suburban campus with easy access to Chicago. Undergraduate faculty: 2,649 (2,123 full-time, 526 part-time); student-faculty ratio is 9:1. Most popular recent majors: economics, political science, engineering.

*Northwestern University (continued)*

## CAMPUS VISITS

**College Calendar 1998–99:** *Regular classes:* Sept. 23–Dec. 5; Jan. 4–Mar. 13; Mar. 29–June 5. *Breaks:* Dec. 12–Jan. 3; Mar. 20–28. *Final exams:* Dec. 7–11; Mar. 15–19; June 7–11.

## VISIT OPPORTUNITIES

|  | Appointments? | Who? |
|---|---|---|
| **Campus Tour** | not required | open to all |
| **Information Session** | not required | open to all |
| **Admission Interview** | required | applicants only |
| **Classroom Visit** | not required | open to all |
| **Faculty Meeting** | recommended | applicants and parents |
| **Overnight Visit** | required |  |

**Information Sessions:** M–F at 1:15 pm; also available M–F Sept. through Dec. at 11:00 am, Jun. 23 through Aug. at 9:15 am; Sat. only available Oct. through Apr. at 11:45 am; 45 minutes.

**Interviews:** M–F; available Sat. Oct. through May; 45 minutes.

**Campus Tours:** Conducted by students. M–F at 2:00 pm; M-F during summer Jun. 23 through Aug. 31 at 10:00 am and 2:00 pm; available on Sat. Oct. 1 through Apr. 30 at 12:30 pm.

**Class Visits:** Certain predetermined classrooms are open to visitors.

**Overnight Visits:** During the regular academic year, prospective applicants may spend an evening in a residence hall with a student host.

**Video:** Available, fee charged.

## CAMPUS FACILITIES

**Science:** Appointment Required: Technological Institute, Hogan Hall, Frances Searle Building.

**Arts:** Pick-Staiger Concert Hall, Mary and Leigh Block Gallery; Appointment Required: Theatre Interpretation Building, Marjorie Ward Marshall Dance Center.

**Athletic:** Henry Crown Sports Pavilion; Appointment Required: Ryan Field, McGaw Hall.

**Of Special Interest:** Louis Hall (Studio Building), Norris University Center.

## LOCAL ATTRACTIONS

City of Chicago.

# OLIVET NAZARENE UNIVERSITY

**Kankakee, Illinois**

**Contact:** Campus Visit Coordinator, Box 6005, Kankakee, IL 60901. *Phone:* toll-free 800-648-1463. *Fax:* 815-935-4998. *E-mail:* swolff@olivet.edu *Web site:* http://www.olivet.edu/ *Visit location:* Admissions Office, Burke Administration Building, 240 East Marsile Street.

## QUICK FACTS

Enrollment: 2,285; UG: 1,874. Entrance: moderately difficult. SAT>500: N/App; ACT>18: 84%. Tuition and fees: $10,838. Room and board: $4560. Application deadline: 8/1.

## GENERAL

Independent, comprehensive, coed, Church of the Nazarene. Awards bachelor's and master's degrees. Founded 1907. Setting: 168-acre small-town campus with easy access to Chicago. Undergraduate faculty: 145 (100 full-time, 45 part-time); student-faculty ratio is 17:1. Most popular recent majors: elementary education, nursing, psychology.

## CAMPUS VISITS

**College Calendar 1998–99:** *Regular classes:* Aug. 26–Dec. 10; Jan. 12–Apr. 30. *Breaks:* Oct. 9–14; Feb. 18–22; Nov. 24–30; Apr. 2–6. *Final exams:* Dec. 11–16; May 3–6. *Special campus days:* Commencement, May 8; Fall Revival, Sept. 20–23; Homecoming, Nov. 6–8; Red Carpet Days, Oct. 1–2; Winter Revival, Feb. 7–10.

## VISIT OPPORTUNITIES

|  | Appointments? | Who? |
|---|---|---|
| **Campus Tour** | required | open to all |
| **Admission Interview** | required | open to all |
| **Classroom Visit** | required | open to all |
| **Faculty Meeting** | required | open to all |
| **Overnight Visit** | required | open to all |

**Interviews:** M–F; select Sat.; 35 minutes.

**Campus Tours:** Conducted by students. M–F, select Sat.; 60 minutes.

**Class Visits:** Prospective students may attend a class in their area of interest, classroom visits are determined by the visit schedule.

**Overnight Visits:** During the regular academic year, prospective applicants may spend an evening in a residence hall with a student host.

## CAMPUS FACILITIES

**Science:** Museum, Labs.

**Arts:** Display Area, Auditorium, Practice Rooms.

**Athletic:** McHie Arena; Appointment Required: Fitness Center and racquetball courts.

**Of Special Interest:** Ludwig Center (Student Center); Appointment Required: WONU Radio Station.

# QUINCY UNIVERSITY
## Quincy, Illinois

**Contact:** Mr. Jeff Van Camp, Director of Admissions, 1800 College Avenue, Quincy, IL 62301. *Phone:* toll-free 800-688-4295. *Fax:* 217-228-5479. *E-mail:* admissions@quincy.edu *Web site:* http://www.quincy.edu/ *Visit location:* Office of Admissions, Francis Hall, 1800 College Avenue.

## QUICK FACTS

Enrollment: 1,122; UG: 1,024. Entrance: moderately difficult. SAT>500: 59% V, 75% M; ACT>18: 89%. Tuition and fees: $12,410. Room and board: $4420. Application deadline: rolling.

## GENERAL

Independent Roman Catholic, comprehensive, coed. Awards associate, bachelor's, and master's degrees. Founded 1860. Setting: 75-acre small-town campus. Undergraduate faculty: 96 (54 full-time, 42 part-time); student-faculty ratio is 12:1. Most popular recent majors: elementary education, mass communications, psychology.

## CAMPUS VISITS

**College Calendar 1998–99:** *Regular classes:* Aug. 25–Dec. 11; Jan. 12–May 7. *Breaks:* Nov. 25–30; Mar. 27–Apr. 5. *Final exams:* Dec. 14–17; May 10–13.

## VISIT OPPORTUNITIES

|  | Appointments? | Who? |
|---|---|---|
| **Campus Tour** | recommended, not required | open to all |
| **Information Session** | recommended, not required | open to all |
| **Admission Interview** | recommended, not required | open to all |
| **Classroom Visit** | recommended | open to all |
| **Faculty Meeting** | recommended | open to all |

|  | Appointments? | Who? |
|---|---|---|
| **Overnight Visit** | required | open to all |

**Information Sessions:** M–F 9:00 am–4:00 pm; Sat. 9:00 am–12:00 pm; 30 minutes.

**Interviews:** M–F, select Sat.; unavailable on Sat. during open houses or group visits; 30 minutes.

**Campus Tours:** Conducted by students. Sat. 9:00 am–4:00 pm; M–F; unavailable on Sat. during open houses or group visits; 90 minutes.

**Class Visits:** Prospective students may attend a class in their area of interest, classroom visits are determined by the visit schedule.

**Overnight Visits:** During the regular academic year, prospective applicants may spend an evening in a residence hall with a student host.

**Video:** Free on request.

## CAMPUS FACILITIES

**Science:** Appointment Required: North Campus (Math and Science facility).

**Arts:** Appointment Required: Solano Hall–Music.

**Athletic:** Memorial Gymnasium.

**Of Special Interest:** Student Center, Brenner Library; Appointment Required: Francis Hall.

# SOUTHERN ILLINOIS UNIVERSITY AT CARBONDALE
## Carbondale, Illinois

**Contact:** Visit Coordinator, Southern Illinois University, Carbondale, IL 62901-4710. *Phone:* 618-536-4405. *Fax:* 618-453-3250. *E-mail:* admrec@siu.edu *Web site:* http://www.siu.edu/cwis *Visit location:* Admission Reception Center, Woody Hall, Southern Illinois University.

## QUICK FACTS

Enrollment: 21,864; UG: 17,773. Entrance: moderately difficult. SAT>500: N/R; ACT>18: 98%. Resident tuition and fees: $3420. Nonresident tuition and fees: $8820. Room and board: $3649. Application deadline: rolling.

## GENERAL

State-supported, university, coed. Part of Southern Illinois University. Awards associate, bachelor's, master's, doctoral, and first professional degrees.

*Southern Illinois University at Carbondale (continued)*

Founded 1869. Setting: 1,128-acre small-town campus. Undergraduate faculty: 1,057 (903 full-time, 154 part-time); student-faculty ratio is 18:1. Most popular recent majors: trade and industrial education, industrial technology, aviation management.

### CAMPUS VISITS

**College Calendar 1998–99:** *Regular classes:* Aug. 24–Dec. 11; Jan. 19–May 7. *Breaks:* Oct. 29–Nov. 1; Mar. 13–21; Nov. 21–29. *Final exams:* Dec. 15–18; May 10–14. *Special campus days:* Fall commencement, Dec. 19; Family weekend, Sept. 19; Homecoming, Oct. 17; Spring commencement, May 14–15.

### VISIT OPPORTUNITIES

|  | Appointments? |
|---|---|
| **Campus Tour** | recommended |
| **Information Session** | recommended |
| **Admission Interview** | required |
| **Classroom Visit** | required |
| **Faculty Meeting** | required |

**Information Sessions:** M–F 9:00 am–3:00 pm; call for Sat. schedules; 60 minutes.
**Campus Tours:** Conducted by students. M–F, select Sat. at 10:00 am, 12:00 pm, 2:00 pm; 60 minutes.
**Class Visits:** Prospective students indicate their desire to visit a classroom when they make their visit appointment.
**Video:** Available, fee charged.

### CAMPUS FACILITIES

**Science:** Appointment Required: College of Science.
**Arts:** University Museum, Mclead Theater, Shryock Auditorium.
**Athletic:** Student Recreation Center, Intercollegiate sports events.
**Of Special Interest:** Morris Library, Student Center, College of Mass Communication and Media Arts.

### LOCAL ATTRACTIONS

Giant City State Park, Shawnee National Forest.

# SOUTHERN ILLINOIS UNIVERSITY AT EDWARDSVILLE
### Edwardsville, Illinois

**Contact:** Admission Counseling, Box 1600, Edwardsville, IL 62026. *Phone:* 618-692-3705 or toll-free 800-447-SIUE (in-state). *Fax:* 618-692-5013. *E-mail:* admis@siue.edu *Web site:* http://www.siue.edu/ *Visit location:* Admission Counseling, Peck Hall, Room 1307, Box 1600.

### QUICK FACTS

Enrollment: 11,007; UG: 8,507. Entrance: moderately difficult. SAT>500: N/R; ACT>18: 84%. Resident tuition and fees: $2665. Nonresident tuition and fees: $6826. Room and board: $4066. Application deadline: 8/4.

### GENERAL

State-supported, comprehensive, coed. Part of Southern Illinois University. Awards bachelor's, master's, and first professional degrees. Founded 1957. Setting: 2,660-acre suburban campus with easy access to St. Louis. Undergraduate faculty: 771 (557 full-time, 214 part-time); student-faculty ratio is 15:1. Most popular recent majors: nursing, business administration, elementary education.

### CAMPUS VISITS

**College Calendar 1998–99:** *Regular classes:* Aug. 24–Dec. 11; Jan. 11–Apr. 30. *Final exams:* Dec. 14–18; May 3–7. *Special campus days:* Homecoming; Preview SIUE, campuswide open house, Oct. 12; Spring Commencement, May 8.

### VISIT OPPORTUNITIES

|  | Appointments? | Who? |
|---|---|---|
| **Campus Tour** | recommended | applicants and parents |
| **Information Session** | recommended, not required | |
| **Classroom Visit** | required | open to all |
| **Faculty Meeting** | required | open to all |

**Information Sessions:** Tue. 8:00 am–4:30 pm; Wed. 8:00 am–4:30 pm; Fri. 8:00 am–4:30 pm; Mon. 8:00 am–6:30 pm; Sat. 9:00 am–12:00 pm; Thu. 8:00 am–6:30 pm; call for special appointment time.

**Campus Tours:** Conducted by students. M–F at 10:30 am, 2:30 pm; Sat. at 10:30 am; during summer M–Sat. at 10:30 am; 60 minutes.

**Class Visits:** Prospective students may attend a class in their area of interest, students make classroom visit arrangements through Admission Counseling.

**Video:** Free on request.

## CAMPUS FACILITIES
**Science:** Arboretum Trail; Appointment Required: Greenhouse.

**Arts:** Art and Design Building Gallery, Museum Gallery in University Center, University Theater; Appointment Required: WSIE (radio station).

**Athletic:** Vadalabene Center, Student Fitness Center, Track and Field Stadium.

**Of Special Interest:** Appointment Required: Residence Halls, on-campus Apartment Complex.

## LOCAL ATTRACTIONS
St. Louis, MO.

# UNIVERSITY OF ILLINOIS AT URBANA–CHAMPAIGN
**Urbana, Illinois**

**Contact:** Campus Visitors Center, 919 West Illinois Street, Levis Faculty Center, Urbana, IL 61801. *Phone:* 217-333-0824. *Fax:* 217-244-8416. *E-mail:* visits@oar.uiuc.edu *Web site:* http://www.uiuc.edu/ *Visit location:* Campus Visitors Center, Levis Faculty Center, Room 104, 919 West Illinois Street.

## QUICK FACTS
Enrollment: 35,545; UG: 26,391. Entrance: very difficult. SAT>500: 90% V, 96% M; ACT>18: 99%. Resident tuition and fees: $4120. Nonresident tuition and fees: $10,736. Room and board: $5078. Application deadline: 1/1.

## GENERAL
State-supported, university, coed. Part of University of Illinois System. Awards bachelor's, master's, doctoral, and first professional degrees. Founded 1867. Setting: 1,470-acre small-town campus. Undergraduate faculty: 1,896 (1,846 full-time, 50 part-time); student-faculty ratio is 16:1. Most popular recent majors: biology, electrical/electronics engineering, psychology.

## CAMPUS VISITS
**College Calendar 1998–99:** *Regular classes:* Aug. 26–Dec. 11; Jan. 19–May 5. *Breaks:* Nov. 24–29; Mar. 13–21. *Final exams:* Dec. 14–19; May 7–14. *Admission office closed:* Mar. 19. *Special campus days:* ACES Open House, Mar. 5–6; Commencement, May 16; Dads Weekend, Sept. 18–20; Engineering Open House, Mar. 5–6; Homecoming, Oct. 16–17; Moms Weekend, Apr. 16–18; Veterinary Medicine Open House, Apr. 10.

## VISIT OPPORTUNITIES

|  | **Appointments?** | **Who?** |
|---|---|---|
| **Campus Tour** | recommended, not required | open to all |
| **Information Session** | recommended, not required | open to all |
| **Admission Interview** | | open to all |
| **Classroom Visit** | not required | open to all |
| **Faculty Meeting** | required | open to all |

**Information Sessions:** M–F at 10:00 am, 1:00 pm; Sat. at 10:00 am during the academic year when classes are in session; 60 minutes.

**Interviews:** M–F; 30 minutes.

**Campus Tours:** Conducted by students. M–F at 11:00 am, 2:00 pm; Sat. at 11:00 am during the academic year when classes are in session; 75 minutes.

**Class Visits:** Certain predetermined classrooms are open to visitors.

## CAMPUS FACILITIES
**Science:** Beckman Institute; Appointment Required: Grainger Engineering Library.

**Arts:** Appointment Required: Krannert Art Museum, Krannert Center for the Performing Arts, John P. Sousa Museum, World Heritage Museum (closed summers).

**Athletic:** Appointment Required: Assembly Hall, Memorial Stadium, IMPE.

## LOCAL ATTRACTIONS
Allerton Park at Monticello, IL; Lake of the Woods Park at Mahomet, IL.

# WESTERN ILLINOIS UNIVERSITY
**Macomb, Illinois**

**Contact:** Admissions Reception Staff, 1 University Circle-Sherman Hall 115, Macomb, IL 61455. *Phone:* 309-298-3140. *Fax:* 309-298-3111. *Web site:* http://www.wiu.edu/ *Visit location:* Admissions Reception Center, Sherman Hall 115, 1 University Circle.

## QUICK FACTS
Enrollment: 12,200; UG: 9,703. Entrance: moderately difficult. SAT>500: N/R; ACT>18: 89%.

*Western Illinois University (continued)*

Resident tuition and fees: $3037. Nonresident tuition and fees: $7276. Room and board: $3838. Application deadline: 8/10.

## GENERAL

State-supported, comprehensive, coed. Awards bachelor's and master's degrees. Founded 1899. Setting: 1,050-acre small-town campus. Undergraduate faculty: 644 (605 full-time, 39 part-time); student-faculty ratio is 15:1. Most popular recent majors: criminal justice/law enforcement administration, liberal arts and studies, elementary education.

## CAMPUS VISITS

**College Calendar 1998–99:** *Regular classes:* Aug. 24–Dec. 18; Jan. 18–May 14. *Breaks:* Nov. 23–27; Mar. 15–19. *Final exams:* Dec. 14–18; May 10–14.

## VISIT OPPORTUNITIES

|                      | Appointments? | Who?       |
|----------------------|---------------|------------|
| **Campus Tour**      | recommended   | open to all |
| **Information Session** | required   | open to all |
| **Faculty Meeting**  | required      | open to all |

**Information Sessions:** M–F 8:00 am–4:30 pm; Sat. 10:00 am–2:30 pm; 30 minutes.

**Campus Tours:** Conducted by students. M–F, Sat. at 11:00 am, 2:00 pm; available when school is in session; 75 minutes.

## CAMPUS FACILITIES

**Athletic:** Student Recreation Center.

**Of Special Interest:** Library, Residence Halls, University Union.

## LOCAL ATTRACTIONS

The community of Macomb.

# WHEATON COLLEGE
**Wheaton, Illinois**

**Contact:** Milli Bishop, Campus Visit Coordinator, 501 East College Avenue, Wheaton, IL 60187. *Phone:* 630-752-5600 or toll-free 800-222-2419 (out-of-state). *Fax:* 630-752-5285. *Web site:* http://www.wheaton.edu/ *Visit location:* Admissions Office, Student Services Building, 418 Chase Street.

## QUICK FACTS

Enrollment: 2,680; UG: 2,276. Entrance: very difficult. SAT>500: 100% V, 97% M; ACT>18: 100%. Tuition and fees: $13,780. Room and board: $4740. Application deadline: 1/15.

## GENERAL

Independent nondenominational, comprehensive, coed. Awards bachelor's, master's, and doctoral degrees. Founded 1860. Setting: 80-acre suburban campus with easy access to Chicago. Undergraduate faculty: 286 (174 full-time, 112 part-time); student-faculty ratio is 15:1. Most popular recent majors: literature, biblical studies, music.

## CAMPUS VISITS

**College Calendar 1998–99:** *Regular classes:* Aug. 26–Dec. 11; Jan. 11–Apr. 30. *Breaks:* Oct. 17–20; Mar. 6–13; Nov. 25–29. *Final exams:* Dec. 14–17; May 3–6. *Admission office closed:* Dec. 21–25. *Special campus days:* Campus Visit Day, Sept. 21, Oct. 12, Nov. 16, Apr. 19, Mar. 22; Commencement, May 8; Family Weekend, Oct. 23; Good Friday, Apr. 2; Homecoming, Oct. 2; Martin Luther King, Jr. Day, Jan. 18; President's Day, Feb. 15.

## VISIT OPPORTUNITIES

|                         | Appointments? | Who?                        |
|-------------------------|---------------|-----------------------------|
| **Campus Tour**         | not required  | open to all                 |
| **Information Session** | recommended   | open to all                 |
| **Admission Interview** | required      | admitted applicants only    |
| **Classroom Visit**     | not required  | open to all                 |
| **Faculty Meeting**     | required      | applicants and parents      |
| **Overnight Visit**     | required      | open to all                 |

**Information Sessions:** M–F at 9:15 am, 1:15 pm, 3:00 pm; only one daily session during Jan. and Feb.; please call for available schedule; 60 minutes.

**Interviews:** M–F, select Sat.; unavailable on Campus Visit days; 30 minutes.

**Campus Tours:** Conducted by students and admission reps. M–F at 9:15 am, 1:30 pm, 3:15 pm; Sat. at 11:30 am; one tour daily during school breaks; 60 minutes.

**Class Visits:** Prospective students may attend a class in their area of interest.

**Overnight Visits:** During the regular academic year, prospective applicants may spend an evening in a residence hall.

## CAMPUS FACILITIES
**Science:** Appointment Required: Archaeology Museum.

## LOCAL ATTRACTIONS
Billy Graham Museum; Wade Collection (English literature).

# INDIANA

## ANDERSON UNIVERSITY
### Anderson, Indiana

**Contact:** Cassaundra Day, Event Coordinator, 1100 East Fifth Street, Anderson, IN 46012. *Phone:* toll-free 800-421-3014 (in-state), 800-428-6414 (out-of-state). *Fax:* 765-641-4091. *E-mail:* cassday@ anderson.edu *Web site:* http://www.anderson.edu/ *Visit location:* Welcome Center, Decker Hall, 1100 East Fifth Street.

### QUICK FACTS
Enrollment: 2,155; UG: 1,919. Entrance: moderately difficult. SAT>500: 66% V, 72% M; ACT>18: 94%. Tuition and fees: $13,360. Room and board: $4330. Application deadline: 8/25.

### GENERAL
Independent, comprehensive, coed, Church of God. Awards associate, bachelor's, master's, doctoral, and first professional degrees. Founded 1917. Setting: 100-acre suburban campus with easy access to Indianapolis. Undergraduate faculty: 204 (135 full-time, 69 part-time); student-faculty ratio is 13:1. Most popular recent majors: elementary education, social work, business administration.

### CAMPUS VISITS
**College Calendar 1998–99:** *Regular classes:* Aug. 31–Dec. 11; Jan. 13–Apr. 30. *Breaks:* Dec. 18–Jan. 12. *Final exams:* Dec. 14–17; May 3–6. *Admission office closed:* Dec. 24–Jan. 3, Oct. 9, Nov. 26–27. *Special campus days:* Candles and Carols, Dec. 4; Celebration, Apr. 9–10; Commencement, May 8; Homecoming, Oct. 2–3; Scholars Banquet, Feb. 20; Symposium on Public Policy, Nov. 20–21.
**Class Visits:** Prospective students may attend a class in their area of interest.

**Overnight Visits:** During the regular academic year, prospective applicants may spend an evening in a residence hall with a student host.
**Video:** Free on request.

## CAMPUS FACILITIES
**Science:** Appointment Required: biology, chemistry, and physics labs, nursing labs.
**Arts:** Studios for sculpture, hot glass, ceramics, Reardon Auditorium, "Helios" Glass Sculpture, "Eternal Flame"; Appointment Required: Art Gallery.
**Athletic:** Football, baseball, and softball complex; Appointment Required: athletic training area.
**Of Special Interest:** Appointment Required: Bible Museum, Church of God Archives, Hymnology Collection.

## LOCAL ATTRACTIONS
Paramount Theatre; Fine Arts Center; Indiana Factory Outlet Mall; city of Indianapolis.

## BUTLER UNIVERSITY
### Indianapolis, Indiana

**Contact:** Larry Williamson, Campus Visit Coordinator, 4600 Sunset Avenue, Indianapolis, IN 46208. *Phone:* toll-free 888-940-8100. *Fax:* 317-940-8175. *E-mail:* lmwilli1@butler.edu *Web site:* http://www. butler.edu/ *Visit location:* Office of Admission, Robertson Hall.

### QUICK FACTS
Enrollment: 3,893; UG: 3,099. Entrance: moderately difficult. SAT>500: 86% V, 86% M; ACT>18: 99%. Tuition and fees: $15,690. Room and board: $5430. Application deadline: 8/15.

### GENERAL
Independent, comprehensive, coed. Awards associate, bachelor's, and master's degrees (also offers 6-year undergraduate doctor of pharmacy degree). Founded 1855. Setting: 290-acre urban campus. Undergraduate faculty: 403 (228 full-time, 175 part-time); student-faculty ratio is 11:1. Most popular recent majors: pharmacy, elementary education, secondary education.

### CAMPUS VISITS
**College Calendar 1998–99:** *Regular classes:* Aug. 27–Dec. 11; Jan. 11–Apr. 23. *Breaks:* Mar. 8–12; Nov.

*Butler University (continued)*

23–27. *Final exams:* Dec. 14–19; Apr. 24–May 4. *Special campus days:* Commencement, May 8.

## VISIT OPPORTUNITIES

| | Appointments? | Who? |
|---|---|---|
| **Campus Tour** | recommended | applicants and parents |
| **Information Session** | recommended | |
| **Admission Interview** | recommended | applicants and parents |
| **Classroom Visit** | required | |
| **Faculty Meeting** | required | applicants and parents |
| **Overnight Visit** | | admitted applicants only |

**Information Sessions:** M–F; Sat. during the academic year only; 60 minutes.

**Interviews:** M–F; Sat. during the academic year only; 60 minutes.

**Campus Tours:** Conducted by students. M–F at 10:00 am, 1:00 pm, 3:00 pm; Sat. during the academic year at 10:00 am, 11:00 am; 60 minutes.

**Class Visits:** Prospective students may attend a class in their area of interest.

**Overnight Visits:** During the regular academic year, prospective applicants may spend an evening in a residence hall with a student host.

## CAMPUS FACILITIES

**Science:** Holcomb Observatory.

**Arts:** Clowes Memorial Hall.

**Athletic:** Hinkle Field House.

## LOCAL ATTRACTIONS

Indianapolis Art Museum, The Children's Museum, Indianapolis Zoo, Circle Centre Mall, the RCA Dome.

# DEPAUW UNIVERSITY
## Greencastle, Indiana

**Contact:** Office of Admissions, 101 East Seminary Street, Greencastle, IN 46135. *Phone:* toll-free 800-447-2495. *Fax:* 765-658-4007. *E-mail:* admission@depauw.edu *Web site:* http://www.depauw.edu/ *Visit location:* Office of Admission, 101 East Seminary Street.

## QUICK FACTS

Enrollment: 2,283; UG: 2,283. Entrance: moderately difficult. SAT>500: 87% V, 85% M; ACT>18: 99%. Tuition and fees: $17,050. Room and board: $5616. Application deadline: 2/15.

## GENERAL

Independent, 4-year, coed, United Methodist Church. Awards bachelor's degrees. Founded 1837. Setting: 175-acre small-town campus with easy access to Indianapolis. Faculty: 217 (162 full-time, 55 part-time); student-faculty ratio is 12:1. Most popular recent majors: mass communications, economics, English composition.

## CAMPUS VISITS

**College Calendar 1998–99:** *Regular classes:* Aug. 27–Dec. 11; Jan. 4–29; Feb. 1–May 13. *Breaks:* Oct. 15–18; Mar. 20–28; Nov. 21–29. *Final exams:* Dec. 14–17; May 15–19. *Special campus days:* Alumni Weekend, June 4–6; Commencement, May 22; Homecoming, Oct. 9–10; Little 5 Race, Apr. 17; Little Sibs' Weekend, Feb. 26–28; Parent's Weekend, Oct. 2–4; Preview Days.

## VISIT OPPORTUNITIES

| | Appointments? | Who? |
|---|---|---|
| **Campus Tour** | recommended, not required | open to all |
| **Information Session** | required | open to all |
| **Admission Interview** | required | open to all |
| **Classroom Visit** | required | open to all |
| **Faculty Meeting** | required | open to all |
| **Overnight Visit** | required | open to all |

**Information Sessions:** M–F at 1:00 pm; 60 minutes.

**Interviews:** M–F, Sat.; 45 minutes.

**Campus Tours:** Conducted by students. M–F at 9:00 am, 10:00 am, 11:00 am, 1:00 pm, 2:00 pm, 3:00 pm; Sat. at 9:00 am, 10:00 am, 11:00 am, 12:00 pm; 50 minutes.

**Class Visits:** Prospective students may attend a class in their area of interest, classroom visits are determined by the visit schedule.

**Overnight Visits:** During the regular academic year, prospective applicants may spend an evening in a residence hall with a student host.

## CAMPUS FACILITIES
**Science:** F.W. Olin Biological Sciences Building.
**Arts:** Performing Arts Center.
**Athletic:** Lilly Physical Education and Recreation Center.
**Of Special Interest:** The Center for Contemporary Media, East College.

# EARLHAM COLLEGE
## Richmond, Indiana

**Contact:** Cindy Parshall, Visit Coordinator/Assistant Dean of Admissions, 801 National Road West-Earlham College, Richmond, IN 47374. *Phone:* toll-free 800-327-5426 Ext. 1591, 800-327-5426. *Fax:* 765-983-1560. *E-mail:* parshci@earlham.edu *Web site:* http://www.earlham.edu/ *Visit location:* Admissions Office, 801 National Road West.

## QUICK FACTS
Enrollment: 1,025; UG: 1,025. Entrance: moderately difficult. SAT>500: 89% V, 85% M; ACT>18: 98%. Tuition and fees: $18,618. Room and board: $4544. Application deadline: 2/15.

## GENERAL
Independent, 4-year, coed, Society of Friends. Awards bachelor's degrees. Founded 1847. Setting: 800-acre small-town campus with easy access to Cincinnati, Indianapolis, and Dayton. Faculty: 132 (108 full-time, 24 part-time); student-faculty ratio is 11:1. Most popular recent majors: biology, English, psychology.

## CAMPUS VISITS
**College Calendar 1998–99:** *Regular classes:* Aug. 27–Dec. 11; Jan. 14–Apr. 30. *Breaks:* Oct. 15–17; Mar. 13–22. *Final exams:* Dec. 15–17; May 4–6. *Admission office closed:* Thanksgiving, Nov. 25–27. *Special campus days:* Commencement, May 9; Homecoming, Oct. 23–24.

## VISIT OPPORTUNITIES

| | Appointments? | Who? |
|---|---|---|
| **Campus Tour** | recommended | open to all |
| **Information Session** | recommended | open to all |
| **Admission Interview** | required | open to all |
| **Classroom Visit** | required | open to all |
| **Faculty Meeting** | required | open to all |

**VISIT OPPORTUNITIES—***continued*

| | Appointments? | Who? |
|---|---|---|
| **Overnight Visit** | required | open to all |

**Information Sessions:** M–F, Sat.; 60 minutes.
**Interviews:** M–F, Sat.; Sat. mornings during academic year; 60 minutes.
**Campus Tours:** Conducted by students. M–F, Sat.; Sat. mornings during academic year; 60 minutes.
**Class Visits:** Prospective students may attend a class in their area of interest.
**Overnight Visits:** During the regular academic year, prospective applicants may spend an evening in a residence hall with a student host.
**Video:** Available, fee charged.

## CAMPUS FACILITIES
**Arts:** Ceramics Room; Appointment Required: Wilkinson Theatre, Leeds Gallery.
**Of Special Interest:** Lilly Library; Appointment Required: Joseph Moore Museum, Conner Prairie Living Museum.

## LOCAL ATTRACTIONS
Hayes Arboretum; Cope Environmental Center.

# INDIANA STATE UNIVERSITY
## Terre Haute, Indiana

**Contact:** Student to Student - Office of Admissions, Tirey Hall, Terre Haute, IN 47809. *Phone:* 812-237-4968 or toll-free 800-742-0891. *Fax:* 812-237-8023. *E-mail:* admsts@amber.indstate.edu *Web site:* http://www.isu.indstate.edu/ *Visit location:* Office of Admissions, Tirey Hall.

## QUICK FACTS
Enrollment: 10,784; UG: 9,180. Entrance: moderately difficult. SAT>500: 40% V, 40% M; ACT>18: 69%. Resident tuition and fees: $3196. Nonresident tuition and fees: $7916. Room and board: $4143. Application deadline: 8/15.

## GENERAL
State-supported, university, coed. Awards associate, bachelor's, master's, and doctoral degrees. Founded 1865. Setting: 91-acre suburban campus with easy access to Indianapolis. Undergraduate faculty: 706 (563 full-time, 143 part-time); student-faculty ratio is

*Indiana State University (continued)*

15:1. Most popular recent majors: elementary education, criminology, nursing.

## CAMPUS VISITS

**College Calendar 1998–99:** *Regular classes:* Aug. 26–Dec. 11; Jan. 11–Apr. 30. *Breaks:* Oct. 9; Mar. 15–19; Nov. 25–27. *Final exams:* Dec. 14–18; May 3–7. *Admission office closed:* Nov. 26–27, Dec. 24–Jan. 1. *Special campus days:* Commencement, Dec. 19, May 8; Orientation, Aug. 24–25.

## VISIT OPPORTUNITIES

|  | Appointments? | Who? |
|---|---|---|
| **Campus Tour** | recommended | open to all |
| **Admission Interview** | not required | open to all |
| **Classroom Visit** | required | open to all |
| **Faculty Meeting** | required | open to all |
| **Overnight Visit** | required | open to all |

**Interviews:** M–F, select Sat.; 40 minutes.

**Campus Tours:** Conducted by students. M–F at 10:00 am, 12:00 pm, 1:00 pm, 2:00 pm; Sat. at 11:00 am; 60 minutes.

**Class Visits:** Prospective students may attend a class in their area of interest.

**Overnight Visits:** During the regular academic year, prospective applicants may spend an evening in a residence hall with a student host.

## CAMPUS FACILITIES

**Arts:** Center for Performing and Fine Arts.

**Athletic:** Health and Human Performance Building.

**Of Special Interest:** Technology Center, Cunningham Memorial Library, Hulman Memorial Student Union.

# INDIANA UNIVERSITY BLOOMINGTON

**Bloomington, Indiana**

**Contact:** Scheduling Director, 300 North Jordan Avenue, Bloomington, IN 47405. *Phone:* 812-855-0661. *Fax:* 812-855-5102. *E-mail:* iuadmit@indiana.edu *Web site:* http://www.indiana.edu/ *Visit location:* Office of Admissions, 300 North Jordan Avenue.

## QUICK FACTS

Enrollment: 33,650; UG: 25,852. Entrance: moderately difficult. SAT>500: N/R; ACT>18: N/R. Resident tuition and fees: $3929. Nonresident tuition and fees: $11,853. Room and board: $4900. Application deadline: 2/15.

## GENERAL

State-supported, university, coed. Part of Indiana University System. Awards associate, bachelor's, master's, doctoral, and first professional degrees. Founded 1820. Setting: 1,878-acre small-town campus with easy access to Indianapolis. Undergraduate faculty: 1,635 (1,430 full-time, 205 part-time); student-faculty ratio is 17:1.

## CAMPUS VISITS

**College Calendar 1998–99:** *Regular classes:* Aug. 31–Dec. 12; Jan. 11–May 1. *Breaks:* Dec. 19–Jan. 10. *Final exams:* Dec. 14–18; May 3–7. *Special campus days:* Commencement, May 8; Founder's Day, Mar. 1; Homecoming, Oct. 17; Parents Weekend, Oct. 31.

## VISIT OPPORTUNITIES

|  | Appointments? |
|---|---|
| **Campus Tour** | recommended |
| **Information Session** | required |
| **Admission Interview** | required |
| **Classroom Visit** | not required |
| **Faculty Meeting** | required |
| **Overnight Visit** | required |

**Information Sessions:** Mon.; Fri.; additional dates and times available; call for schedule; 60 minutes.

**Interviews:** M–F; Sat. mornings during academic year; 45 minutes.

**Campus Tours:** Conducted by students. M–F, select Sat. at 10:30 am, 1:30 pm, 2:30 pm; daily residence hall tours also available separately; 75 minutes.

**Class Visits:** Classrooms open to visitors are predetermined with daily lists of available classes.

**Overnight Visits:** During the regular academic year, prospective applicants may spend an evening in a residence hall with a student host.

**Video:** Free on request.

## CAMPUS FACILITIES

**Science:** Jordan Hall, Chemistry Building, Kirkwood Observatory; Appointment Required: Cyclotron.

**Arts:** Art Museum, Lilly Library—Rare Books, Mathers Museum of World Cultures; Appointment Required: Musical Arts Center.

**Athletic:** Assembly Hall, Student Recreational Sports Center, Wildemuth Intramural/Recreation Center.

**Of Special Interest:** Well House, Indiana Memorial, Carmichael Center—Visitors Center/Shopping, Arboretum.

## LOCAL ATTRACTIONS

Lake Monroe, Brown County State Park, Hoosier Nationally Forest, Ski World, Courthouse Square/Kirkwood Ave., Monroe County Historical Museum, Farmers Market, Oliver Winery, Tibetan Cultural Center, Waldron Performing Arts Center.

# PURDUE UNIVERSITY
## West Lafayette, Indiana

**Contact:** Office of Admissions, 1080 Schleman Hall, West Lafayette, IN 47907. *Phone:* 765-494-1776. *Fax:* 765-494-0544. *E-mail:* adms@adms.purdue.edu *Web site:* http://www.purdue.edu/ *Visit location:* Office of Admissions, Schleman Hall, Room 109, 1080 Schleman Hall.

## QUICK FACTS

Enrollment: 35,200; UG: 28,607. Entrance: moderately difficult. SAT>500: 68% V, 78% M; ACT>18: 96%. Resident tuition and fees: $3368. Nonresident tuition and fees: $11,200. Room and board: $4800. Application deadline: rolling.

## GENERAL

State-supported, university, coed. Part of Purdue University System. Awards associate, bachelor's, master's, doctoral, and first professional degrees. Founded 1869. Setting: 1,579-acre suburban campus with easy access to Indianapolis. Undergraduate faculty: 2,233 (2,002 full-time, 231 part-time); student-faculty ratio is 14:1. Most popular recent majors: electrical/electronics engineering, communications, civil engineering.

## CAMPUS VISITS

**College Calendar 1998–99:** *Regular classes:* Aug. 24–Dec. 11; Jan. 11–Apr. 30. *Breaks:* Oct. 10–13; Mar. 15–21; Nov. 25–29. *Final exams:* Dec. 14–19; May 3–8. *Special campus days:* Fall Preview Days (open house); Introducing Purdue (sophomores and juniors).

| | Appointments? | Who? |
|---|---|---|
| **Campus Tour** | recommended | |
| **Admission Interview** | not required | applicants and parents |
| **Classroom Visit** | recommended | |
| **Faculty Meeting** | recommended | |

**Interviews:** M–F; Sat. Sept.–May; 30 minutes.

**Campus Tours:** Conducted by students. M–F at 9:30 am, 1:30 pm, 2:30 pm; Sat. Sept. through Apr. only at 9:30 am; 90 minutes.

**Class Visits:** Prospective students may attend a class in their area of interest.

**Video:** Free on request.

## CAMPUS FACILITIES

**Science:** Purdue Engineering Mall, Knoy Hall of Technology.

**Arts:** Elliott Hall of Music, Slayter.

**Athletic:** Mackey Arena, Ross-Ade Stadium, Co-Recreational Gymnasium.

**Of Special Interest:** Purdue Memorial Union, residence halls.

# ROSE-HULMAN INSTITUTE OF TECHNOLOGY
## Terre Haute, Indiana

**Contact:** Jane Staley, Campus Visit Coordinator, 5500 Wabash Avenue, Terre Haute, IN 47803. *Phone:* 812-877-8214 or toll-free 800-248-7448 (in-state). *Fax:* 812-877-8941. *E-mail:* jane.staley@rose-hulman.edu *Web site:* http://www.Rose-Hulman.edu/ *Visit location:* Admissions Office, Moench Hall, 5500 Wabash Avenue.

## QUICK FACTS

Enrollment: 1,757; UG: 1,554. Entrance: very difficult. SAT>500: 99% V, 100% M; ACT>18: 100%. Tuition and fees: $18,105. Room and board: $5300. Application deadline: rolling.

## GENERAL

Independent, comprehensive, coed. Awards bachelor's and master's degrees. Founded 1874. Setting: 130-acre rural campus with easy access to Indianapolis. Undergraduate faculty: 130 (125 full-time, 5 part-time); student-faculty ratio is 11:1. Most popular

*Rose-Hulman Institute of Technology (continued)*

recent majors: mechanical engineering, electrical/ electronics engineering, chemical engineering.

## CAMPUS VISITS

**College Calendar 1998–99:** *Regular classes:* Sept. 3–Nov. 13; Nov. 30–Feb. 19; Mar. 8–May 21. *Breaks:* Oct. 15–18; Dec. 18–Jan. 3; Apr. 2–11; Nov. 20–29; Feb. 26–Mar. 7. *Final exams:* Nov. 16–19; Feb. 22–25; May 24–27. *Special campus days:* Commencement, May 29; Dad's Day, Oct. 17; Family Weekend; Homecoming, Sept. 25–26; Mom's Night, Feb. 13.

## VISIT OPPORTUNITIES

|                       | Appointments? | Who?                        |
| --------------------- | ------------- | --------------------------- |
| **Campus Tour**       | required      | open to all                 |
| **Information Session** | recommended | admitted applicants only    |
| **Admission Interview** | required    |                             |
| **Classroom Visit**   |               | open to all                 |
| **Faculty Meeting**   |               | open to all                 |
| **Overnight Visit**   | required      |                             |

**Information Sessions:** Sun. in Jan. and Feb. for admitted students and their families in select cities; 120 minutes.

**Interviews:** M–F; campus visits are scheduled on an individual basis M–F at 8:30 am or 1:30 pm (EST). The visit includes an interview, campus tour, and meetings with financial aid, faculty, and coaching staff if needed. Classroom visits are possible at the 8:30 am appointment only. Large group (60-80 students) visit programs are typically held one Fri. or Mon. per month from Aug.–Apr. These programs generally begin at 1:00 pm and conclude at 4:30 pm. Classroom visits or individual interviews are not permitted on these days; 30 minutes.

**Campus Tours:** Conducted by students and admission reps. M–F; campus tours are given as part of the scheduled visit appointment; 60 minutes.

**Class Visits:** Certain predetermined classrooms are open to visitors.

**Overnight Visits:** During the regular academic year, prospective applicants may spend an evening in a residence hall with a student host.

## CAMPUS FACILITIES

**Of Special Interest:** Logan Library.

# SAINT JOSEPH'S COLLEGE
**Rensselaer, Indiana**

**Contact:** Welcome Center, PO Box 890, Rensselaer, IN 47978. *Phone:* toll-free 800-447-8781 (out-of-state). *Fax:* 219-866-6122. *E-mail:* admissions@saintjoe. edu *Web site:* http://www.saintjoe.edu/ *Visit location:* Office of Admissions-Welcome Center, Schwietermann Hall.

## QUICK FACTS

Enrollment: 903; UG: 902. Entrance: moderately difficult. SAT>500: 60% V, 60% M; ACT>18: 95%. Tuition and fees: $12,950. Room and board: $4780. Application deadline: rolling.

## GENERAL

Independent Roman Catholic, comprehensive, coed. Awards associate, bachelor's, and master's degrees. Founded 1889. Setting: 340-acre small-town campus with easy access to Chicago. Undergraduate faculty: 85 (60 full-time, 25 part-time); student-faculty ratio is 15:1. Most popular recent majors: business administration, elementary education, psychology.

## CAMPUS VISITS

**College Calendar 1998–99:** *Regular classes:* Aug. 24–Dec. 11; Jan. 11–Apr. 30. *Breaks:* Oct. 9–12; Mar. 5–15; Nov. 20–30; Apr. 2–6. *Final exams:* Dec. 14–17; May 3–6. *Special campus days:* Commencement, May 9; Discover Days, Oct. 17, Feb. 15, Mar. 27, Nov. 14; Homecoming, Oct. 2–3; Little 500; Parents Weekend, Nov. 6–7; Snowcoming.

## VISIT OPPORTUNITIES

|                         | Appointments? | Who?                        |
| ----------------------- | ------------- | --------------------------- |
| **Campus Tour**         | required      | applicants and parents      |
| **Information Session** | required      |                             |
| **Admission Interview** | required      |                             |
| **Classroom Visit**     | required      | applicants and parents      |
| **Faculty Meeting**     | required      | applicants and parents      |
| **Overnight Visit**     | required      | admitted applicants only    |

**Information Sessions:** M–F at 9:00 am, 1:30 pm; Sat. at 9:30 am available Sept. through May; tours included with session; 150 minutes.

**Interviews:** M–F, Sat.; 30 minutes.

**Campus Tours:** Conducted by students. Held with information sessions; 75 minutes.

**Class Visits:** Prospective students may attend a class in their area of interest, certain predetermined classrooms are open to visitors, classroom visits are determined by the visit schedule.

**Overnight Visits:** During the regular academic year, prospective applicants may spend an evening in a residence hall with a student host.

## CAMPUS FACILITIES

**Science:** Arts and Science Center (East—West Wing); Appointment Required: Core Science Lab.

**Arts:** Banet Core Education Center, Arts and Science Center (North—South Wing); Appointment Required: WPUM-FM 90.5, WPUM TV-6 Studio.

**Athletic:** Joseph L. Minielli Memorial Soccer Field, Gil Hodges Memorial Baseball Field/Rueth-Fitzgibbon Baseball Facility, Alumni Football Field, Richard F. Scharf Alumni Fieldhouse, Hanson Recreation Center.

**Of Special Interest:** Chapel, Grotto, Halleck Student Center, Robinson Memorial Library.

## LOCAL ATTRACTIONS

Downtown Rensselaer, Jasper County Courthouse.

# SAINT MARY'S COLLEGE
**Notre Dame, Indiana**

**Contact:** Mrs. Bobbi Wiseman, Campus Visit Coordinator, Admission Office, Notre Dame, IN 46556. *Phone:* toll-free 800-551-7621. *Fax:* 219-284-4716. *E-mail:* bwiseman@saintmarys.edu *Web site:* http://www.saintmarys.edu/ *Visit location:* Admission Office, 122 Le Mans Hall, Saint Mary's College.

## QUICK FACTS

Enrollment: 1,287; UG: 1,287. Entrance: moderately difficult. SAT>500: 77% V, 76% M; ACT>18: 100%. Tuition and fees: $15,652. Room and board: $5197. Application deadline: 3/1.

## GENERAL

Independent Roman Catholic, 4-year, women only. Awards bachelor's degrees. Founded 1844. Setting: 275-acre suburban campus. Faculty: 176 (110 full-time, 66 part-time); student-faculty ratio is 11:1. Most popular recent majors: business administration, mass communications, nursing.

## CAMPUS VISITS

**College Calendar 1998–99:** *Regular classes:* Aug. 25–Dec. 11; Jan. 12–Apr. 30. *Breaks:* Oct. 17–25; Mar. 6–14. *Final exams:* Dec. 14–18; May 3–7. *Special campus days:* Fall Day on Campus for prospective students, Sept. 20; Spring Day on Campus for prospective students, Apr. 18.

## VISIT OPPORTUNITIES

|  | Appointments? | Who? |
|---|---|---|
| **Campus Tour** | recommended | open to all |
| **Information Session** | recommended | open to all |
| **Admission Interview** | required | open to all |
| **Classroom Visit** | required | open to all |
| **Faculty Meeting** | required | open to all |
| **Overnight Visit** | required | open to all |

**Interviews:** M–F, Sat.; Sat. interviews during the academic year.; 60 minutes.

**Campus Tours:** Conducted by students. M–F at 10:00 am, 1:00 pm, 3:00 pm; Sat. at 10:00 am; Sat. tours during academic year; 60 minutes.

**Class Visits:** Prospective students may attend a class in their area of interest.

**Overnight Visits:** During the regular academic year, prospective applicants may spend an evening in a residence hall with a student host.

**Video:** Free on request.

## CAMPUS FACILITIES

**Science:** Science Hall, Havican Hall.

**Arts:** Moreau Center for the Arts.

**Athletic:** Angela Athletic Facility.

**Of Special Interest:** Residence Halls: Le Mans, Regina, McCandless and Holy Cross, Cushwa-Leighton Library, Haggar College Center, Noble Family Dining Hall.

## LOCAL ATTRACTIONS

University of Notre Dame, Collegiate Football Hall of Fame, East Race Waterway, Northern Indiana Center for History, Studebaker National Museum.

# TAYLOR UNIVERSITY
**Upland, Indiana**

**Contact:** Jan Hagar, Visit Coordinator, 236 West Reade Avenue, Upland, IN 46989-1001. *Phone:*

*Taylor University (continued)*

toll-free 800-882-3456. *Fax:* 765-998-4952. *E-mail:* jnhagar@tayloru.edu *Web site:* http://www.tayloru.edu/ *Visit location:* Admissions Office, Helena Memorial Hall, 256 West Reade Avenue.

## QUICK FACTS

Enrollment: 1,864; UG: 1,864. Entrance: very difficult. SAT>500: 88% V, 88% M; ACT>18: 96%. Tuition and fees: $13,484. Room and board: $4410. Application deadline: rolling.

## GENERAL

Independent interdenominational, 4-year, coed. Awards associate and bachelor's degrees. Founded 1846. Setting: 250-acre rural campus with easy access to Indianapolis. Faculty: 137 (105 full-time, 32 part-time); student-faculty ratio is 18:1. Most popular recent majors: business administration, elementary education, psychology.

## CAMPUS VISITS

**College Calendar 1998–99:** *Regular classes:* Sept. 1–Dec. 11; Jan. 4–26; Feb. 1–May 14. *Breaks:* Oct. 23–26; Mar. 26–Apr. 6. *Final exams:* Dec. 14–17; Jan. 27; May 17–20. *Special campus days:* Commencement, May 22; Homecoming, Oct. 30–Nov. 1; Martin Luther King, Jr. Day, Jan. 18; Parents Weekend, Oct. 9–11; Relational Enrichment Week, Mar. 8–12; Spiritual Renewal Week, Sept. 14–18, Feb. 8–12; World Opportunities Week (missions focus week), Nov. 2–6.

### VISIT OPPORTUNITIES

| | Appointments? | Who? |
|---|---|---|
| **Campus Tour** | recommended | open to all |
| **Information Session** | recommended | open to all |
| **Admission Interview** | recommended | open to all |
| **Classroom Visit** | required | open to all |
| **Faculty Meeting** | required | open to all |
| **Overnight Visit** | required | open to all |

**Information Sessions:** M–F at 9:00 am; Sat. at 9:30 am; call for available Sat.; 30 minutes.

**Interviews:** M–F; Sat. 8:00 am–1:00 pm; call for available Sat.; 30 minutes.

**Campus Tours:** Conducted by students. M–F at 11:00 am, 2:00 pm; Sat. at 10:00 am; call for available Sat.; 60 minutes.

**Class Visits:** Prospective students may attend a class in their area of interest.

**Overnight Visits:** During the regular academic year, prospective applicants may spend an evening in a residence hall with a student host.

## CAMPUS FACILITIES

**Science:** Randall Environmental Studies Center, Computer Science Facilities.

**Arts:** Mitchell Theater.

**Of Special Interest:** Samuel Morris Sculptures.

# UNIVERSITY OF EVANSVILLE
## Evansville, Indiana

**Contact:** Visit Coordinator, 1800 Lincoln Avenue, Evansville, IN 47722. *Phone:* toll-free 800-423-8633 Ext. 2468, 800-992-5877 (in-state). *Fax:* 812-474-4076. *E-mail:* admission@evansville.edu *Web site:* http://www.evansville.edu/ *Visit location:* Office of Admission, Olmsted Building, 1800 LIncoln Avenue.

## QUICK FACTS

Enrollment: 2,811; UG: 2,774. Entrance: moderately difficult. SAT>500: 82% V, 84% M; ACT>18: 100%. Tuition and fees: $13,880. Room and board: $4900. Application deadline: 2/15.

## GENERAL

Independent, comprehensive, coed, United Methodist Church. Awards associate, bachelor's, and master's degrees. Founded 1854. Setting: 75-acre suburban campus. Undergraduate faculty: 193 (184 full-time, 9 part-time); student-faculty ratio is 13:1. Most popular recent majors: accounting, electrical/electronics engineering, elementary education.

## CAMPUS VISITS

**College Calendar 1998–99:** *Regular classes:* Aug. 26–Dec. 8; Jan. 11–Apr. 27. *Breaks:* Oct. 10–13; Mar. 6–14; Nov. 25–29; Apr. 2–4. *Final exams:* Dec. 10–16; Apr. 29–May 5. *Admission office closed:* Christmas, Dec. 23–Jan. 3; Easter, Apr. 2–4; Thanksgiving, Nov. 26–29.

### VISIT OPPORTUNITIES

| | Appointments? | Who? |
|---|---|---|
| **Campus Tour** | recommended | open to all |
| **Information Session** | required | open to all |
| **Admission Interview** | recommended | open to all |

VISIT OPPORTUNITIES—*continued*

| | Appointments? | Who? |
|---|---|---|
| Classroom Visit | required | open to all |
| Faculty Meeting | required | open to all |
| Overnight Visit | required | applicants only |

**Information Sessions:** M–F 8:00 am–5:00 pm; available only when classes in session; 30 minutes.

**Interviews:** M–F, Sat.; not available on holiday weekends; 30 minutes.

**Campus Tours:** Conducted by students. M–F 8:00 am–5:00 pm; Sat. 9:00 am–12:00 pm; not available on holiday weekends; 60 minutes.

**Class Visits:** Prospective students may attend a class in their area of interest.

**Overnight Visits:** During the regular academic year, prospective applicants may spend an evening in a residence hall with a student host.

**Video:** Free on request.

## CAMPUS FACILITIES
**Science:** Koch Building.
**Arts:** Shanklin Theatre, Fine Arts Building.
**Athletic:** Carson Center.

## LOCAL ATTRACTIONS
Historic Evansville; Rosse Field.

# UNIVERSITY OF INDIANAPOLIS
## Indianapolis, Indiana

**Contact:** Marylynne Winslow, Campus Visit Coordinator, 1400 East Hanna Avenue, Indianapolis, IN 46227-3697. *Phone:* 317-788-3441 or toll-free 800-232-8634. *Fax:* 317-788-3300. *E-mail:* winslow@uindy. edu *Web site:* http://www.uindy.edu/ *Visit location:* Office of Admissions, Esch Hall, 1400 East Hanna Avenue.

## QUICK FACTS
Enrollment: 3,656; UG: 2,691. Entrance: moderately difficult. SAT>500: 53% V, 57% M; ACT>18: N/R. Tuition and fees: $12,990. Room and board: $4550. Application deadline: 8/15.

## GENERAL
Independent, comprehensive, coed, United Methodist Church. Awards associate, bachelor's, master's,

and doctoral degrees. Founded 1902. Setting: 60-acre suburban campus. Undergraduate faculty: 321 (136 full-time, 185 part-time); student-faculty ratio is 11:1. Most popular recent majors: nursing, physical therapy assistant, business administration.

## CAMPUS VISITS
**College Calendar 1998–99:** *Regular classes:* Aug. 31–Dec. 19; Jan. 11–Apr. 30. *Breaks:* Apr. 8–14. *Final exams:* Dec. 14–18; Apr. 24–29. *Admission office closed:* Brown County Day, Oct. 21; Good Friday, Apr. 2. *Special campus days:* High School Day, Oct. 17.

## VISIT OPPORTUNITIES

| | Appointments? | Who? |
|---|---|---|
| Campus Tour | required | applicants and parents |
| Information Session | required | |
| Admission Interview | required | applicants and parents |
| Classroom Visit | required | |
| Faculty Meeting | required | applicants and parents |
| Overnight Visit | required | |

**Interviews:** M–F, Sat.; 45 minutes.

**Campus Tours:** Conducted by students. M–F 8:00 am–4:00 pm; Sat. 10:00 am–12:00 pm; high school students are encouraged to visit Mon.–Fri.; 60 minutes.

**Class Visits:** Prospective students may attend a class in their area of interest, classroom visits are determined by the visit schedule.

**Overnight Visits:** During the regular academic year, prospective applicants may spend an evening in a residence hall with a student host.

**Video:** Free on request.

## CAMPUS FACILITIES
**Of Special Interest:** Krannert Memorial Library.

# UNIVERSITY OF NOTRE DAME
## Notre Dame, Indiana

**Contact:** Office of Undergraduate Admissions, 1 Grace Hall, Notre Dame, IN 46556. *Phone:* 219-631-7505. *Fax:* 219-631-8865. *Web site:* http://www.nd. edu/ *Visit location:* Office of Undergraduate Admissions, 1 Grace Hall.

*University of Notre Dame (continued)*

### QUICK FACTS
Enrollment: 10,266; UG: 7,829. Entrance: most difficult. SAT>500: 97% V, 99% M; ACT>18: N/R. Tuition and fees: $19,947. Room and board: $5060. Application deadline: 1/9.

### GENERAL
Independent Roman Catholic, university, coed. Awards bachelor's, master's, doctoral, and first professional degrees. Founded 1842. Setting: 1,250-acre suburban campus. Undergraduate faculty: 944 (698 full-time, 246 part-time); student-faculty ratio is 12:1. Most popular recent majors: accounting, political science, finance.

### CAMPUS VISITS
**College Calendar 1998–99:** *Regular classes:* Aug. 25–Dec. 9; Jan. 12–Apr. 28. *Breaks:* Oct. 17–25; Mar. 6–14; Dec. 19–Jan. 10. *Final exams:* Dec. 14–18; May 3–7. *Special campus days:* Commencement, May 14–16.

### VISIT OPPORTUNITIES

|  | Appointments? | Who? |
|---|---|---|
| **Campus Tour** | required | open to all |
| **Information Session** | required | open to all |
| **Admission Interview** | required | admitted applicants and parents |
| **Classroom Visit** |  | admitted applicants and parents |
| **Faculty Meeting** | required | open to all |
| **Overnight Visit** | required | open to all |

**Information Sessions:** Select Sat. at 9:00 am, 10:15 am; M–F at 10:00 am, 2:00 pm; unavailable during Mar. and on Sat. during summer; 40 minutes.

**Interviews:** M–F, select Sat.

**Campus Tours:** Conducted by students. M–F at 11:00 am, 3:00 pm; select Sat. at 10:00 am, 11:15 am; 75 minutes.

**Class Visits:** Certain predetermined classrooms are open to visitors.

**Overnight Visits:** During the regular academic year, prospective applicants may spend an evening in a residence hall with a student host.

**Video:** Free on request.

### CAMPUS FACILITIES
**Of Special Interest:** University Libraries of Notre Dame.

# VALPARAISO UNIVERSITY
### Valparaiso, Indiana

**Contact:** Office of Admissions, Kretzmann Hall, Valparaiso, IN 46383. *Phone:* toll-free 888-GO-VALPO (out-of-state). *Fax:* 219-464-6898. *E-mail:* undergrad_admissions@valpo.edu *Web site:* http://www. valpo.edu/ *Visit location:* Office of Admissions, Kretzmann Hall, Valparaiso University.

### QUICK FACTS
Enrollment: 3,391; UG: 2,675. Entrance: moderately difficult. SAT>500: 79% V, 81% M; ACT>18: 97%. Tuition and fees: $15,060. Room and board: $3930. Application deadline: rolling.

### GENERAL
Independent, comprehensive, coed, Lutheran Church. Awards associate, bachelor's, master's, and first professional degrees. Founded 1859. Setting: 310-acre small-town campus with easy access to Chicago. Undergraduate faculty: 356 (242 full-time, 114 part-time); student-faculty ratio is 14:1. Most popular recent majors: nursing, business administration, elementary education.

### CAMPUS VISITS
**College Calendar 1998–99:** *Regular classes:* Aug. 25–Dec. 11; Jan. 6–May 4. *Breaks:* Oct. 8–11; Feb. 27–Mar. 14; Nov. 21–29. *Final exams:* Dec. 14–18; May 6–11. *Admission office closed:* Nov. 25–27, Dec. 24–25, Dec. 31–Jan. 1, Apr. 2. *Special campus days:* Commencement, May 16; Homecoming, Oct. 17; Martin Luther King, Jr. Day, Jan. 18; Parent's Day, Nov. 14.

### VISIT OPPORTUNITIES

|  | Appointments? | Who? |
|---|---|---|
| **Campus Tour** | recommended, not required | open to all |
| **Admission Interview** | recommended | open to all |
| **Classroom Visit** | required | open to all |
| **Faculty Meeting** | required | open to all |
| **Overnight Visit** | required | open to all |

**Interviews:** M–F; select Sat. 8:00 am–12:00 pm; 30 minutes.

**Campus Tours:** Conducted by students. M–F at 9:00 am, 10:15 am, 1:00 pm, 3:00 pm; Mon. and Fri. added tours at 12:00 pm; Sat. during academic year at 9:00 am, 10:00 am, 10:30 am; 60 minutes.

**Class Visits:** Prospective students may attend a class in their area of interest.

**Overnight Visits:** During the regular academic year, prospective applicants may spend an evening in a residence hall with a student host.

## CAMPUS FACILITIES

**Science:** Neils Science Center, Schnabel Hall Computer Center.

**Arts:** Braver Museum of Art, Valparaiso University Center for the Arts.

**Athletic:** Athletic Recreation Center.

**Of Special Interest:** Chapel of the Resurrection.

## LOCAL ATTRACTIONS

Lake Michigan Indiana Dunes State Park.

# IOWA

# CENTRAL COLLEGE

**Pella, Iowa**

**Contact:** Phyllis VanderPol, Campus Visit Coordinator, 812 University, Pella, IA 50219. *Phone:* toll-free 800-458-5503. *Fax:* 515-628-5316. *E-mail:* vanderpolp@central.edu *Web site:* http://www.central.edu/ *Visit location:* Office of Admission, Central Hall, 812 University.

## QUICK FACTS

Enrollment: 1,098; UG: 1,098. Entrance: moderately difficult. SAT>500: 77% V, 68% M; ACT>18: 97%. Tuition and fees: $12,802. Room and board: $4350. Application deadline: rolling.

## GENERAL

Independent, 4-year, coed, Reformed Church in America. Awards bachelor's degrees. Founded 1853. Setting: 133-acre small-town campus with easy access to Des Moines. Faculty: 127 (82 full-time, 45 part-time); student-faculty ratio is 11:1. Most popular recent majors: business administration, elementary education, general studies.

## CAMPUS VISITS

**College Calendar 1998–99:** *Regular classes:* Aug. 25–Dec. 11; Jan. 18–May 7. *Breaks:* Dec. 18–Jan. 18. *Final exams:* Dec. 14–17; May 10–13. *Admission office closed:* Dec. 24–Jan. 5. *Special campus days:* Family Weekend, Sept. 18–20; Homecoming, Oct. 2–4; Spring Break, Mar. 26–Apr. 6.

## VISIT OPPORTUNITIES

|  | Appointments? | Who? |
| --- | --- | --- |
| **Campus Tour** | not required | open to all |
| **Information Session** | recommended, not required | open to all |
| **Admission Interview** | not required | open to all |
| **Classroom Visit** | recommended | open to all |
| **Faculty Meeting** | recommended | open to all |
| **Overnight Visit** | required | open to all |

**Information Sessions:** M–F 8:00 am–4:00 pm; Sat. Sept. through May 9:00 am–12:00 pm; 30 minutes.

**Interviews:** M–F, Sat.; 30 minutes.

**Campus Tours:** Conducted by students. M–F, Sat.; 15 minutes.

**Class Visits:** Prospective students may attend a class in their area of interest.

**Overnight Visits:** During the regular academic year, prospective applicants may spend an evening in a residence hall with a student host.

**Video:** Free on request.

## CAMPUS FACILITIES

**Science:** Vermeer Science Center.

**Arts:** Kruidenier Theatre, Mills Art Gallery.

**Athletic:** Ron Schipper Fitness Center, H.S. Kuyper Fieldhouse, P.H. Kuyper Gymnasium.

**Of Special Interest:** Collegiate Honor Houses, Central Market, Maytag Student Center.

## LOCAL ATTRACTIONS

Dutch bakeries, Red Rock Lake, Bos Landen golf course, historic downtown.

# COE COLLEGE

**Cedar Rapids, Iowa**

**Contact:** Mr. Dennis Trotter, Vice President for Admission and Financial Aid, 1220 First Avenue NE, Cedar Rapids, IA 52402. *Phone:* toll-free 800-332-

*Coe College (continued)*

8404. *Fax:* 319-399-8816. *E-mail:* admission@coe.edu *Web site:* http://www.coe.edu/ *Visit location:* Office of Admission, Gage Memorial Union, 1220 First Avenue, NE.

## QUICK FACTS
Enrollment: 1,318; UG: 1,253. Entrance: moderately difficult. SAT>500: 83% V, 83% M; ACT>18: 98%. Tuition and fees: $16,320. Room and board: $4570. Application deadline: 3/1.

## GENERAL
Independent, comprehensive, coed, Presbyterian Church. Awards bachelor's and master's degrees. Founded 1851. Setting: 55-acre urban campus. Undergraduate faculty: 122 (80 full-time, 42 part-time); student-faculty ratio is 12:1. Most popular recent majors: business administration, psychology, biology.

## CAMPUS VISITS
**College Calendar 1998–99:** *Regular classes:* Aug. 31–Dec. 11; Jan. 4–27; Feb. 3–May 12. *Breaks:* Oct. 29–Nov. 2; Jan. 27–Feb. 3; Mar. 19–29; Dec. 19–Jan. 4. *Final exams:* Dec. 14–18; May 14–19. *Special campus days:* Commencement, May 23; Family Weekend, Oct. 10; Homecoming, Oct. 24.

## VISIT OPPORTUNITIES

|  | Appointments? | Who? |
| --- | --- | --- |
| **Campus Tour** | recommended | open to all |
| **Admission Interview** | recommended | open to all |
| **Classroom Visit** | required | open to all |
| **Faculty Meeting** | required | open to all |
| **Overnight Visit** | required | open to all |

**Interviews:** M–F, select Sat.; available Sat. during academic year; 30 minutes.

**Campus Tours:** Conducted by students. M–F; Sat. during academic year; 60 minutes.

**Class Visits:** Prospective students may attend a class in their area of interest, classroom visits area assigned to accommodate student's and professor's schedules.

**Overnight Visits:** During the regular academic year, prospective applicants may spend an evening in a residence hall with a student host.

## CAMPUS FACILITIES
**Arts:** Dows Theater, Sinclair Theater, Dows Art Studios.

**Athletic:** Clark Raquet Center.

**Of Special Interest:** Perrine Gallery in Stuart Memorial Library.

# DORDT COLLEGE
**Sioux Center, Iowa**

**Contact:** Garry Zonnefeld, Admissions Counselor, 498 4th Avenue, NE, Sioux Center, IA 51250. *Phone:* 712-722-6080 or toll-free 800-343-6738. *Fax:* 712-722-1967. *E-mail:* garry@dordt.edu *Web site:* http://www.dordt.edu/ *Visit location:* Admissions, Admissions/Art, Dordt College, 498 4th Avenue, NE.

## QUICK FACTS
Enrollment: 1,283; UG: 1,283. Entrance: moderately difficult. SAT>500: 79% V, 65% M; ACT>18: 94%. Tuition and fees: $11,450. Room and board: $3030. Application deadline: 8/1.

## GENERAL
Independent Christian Reformed, comprehensive, coed. Awards associate, bachelor's, and master's degrees. Founded 1955. Setting: 65-acre small-town campus. Undergraduate faculty: 95 (75 full-time, 20 part-time); student-faculty ratio is 15:1. Most popular recent majors: education, business administration, engineering.

## CAMPUS VISITS
**College Calendar 1998–99:** *Regular classes:* Aug. 27–Dec. 10; Jan. 12–May 2. *Breaks:* Dec. 17–Jan. 12. *Final exams:* Dec. 11–16; May 3–6.

## VISIT OPPORTUNITIES

|  | Appointments? | Who? |
| --- | --- | --- |
| **Campus Tour** | required | applicants and parents |
| **Information Session** | required |  |
| **Admission Interview** | required | applicants and parents |
| **Classroom Visit** | required |  |
| **Faculty Meeting** | required | applicants and parents |
| **Overnight Visit** | required |  |

**Information Sessions:** M–F 8:00 am–5:00 pm; 60 minutes.

**Campus Tours:** Conducted by admission reps. M–F 8:00 am–5:00 pm; Sat. 9:00 am–12:00 pm; 90 minutes.

**Class Visits:** Prospective students may attend a class in their area of interest.

**Overnight Visits:** During the regular academic year, prospective applicants may spend an evening in a residence hall with a student host.

**Video:** Free on request.

### CAMPUS FACILITIES

**Athletic:** New recreational complex.

# DRAKE UNIVERSITY
## Des Moines, Iowa

**Contact:** Campus Visit Coordinator, 2507 University Avenue, Des Moines, IA 50310. *Phone:* toll-free 800-44-DRAKE. *Fax:* 515-271-2831. *E-mail:* admitinfo@acad.drake.edu *Web site:* http://www.drake. edu/ *Visit location:* Office of Admission, Cole Hall, 27th and University.

### QUICK FACTS

Enrollment: 5,144; UG: 3,368. Entrance: moderately difficult. SAT>500: 83% V, 81% M; ACT>18: 99%. Tuition and fees: $15,200. Room and board: $4970. Application deadline: rolling.

### GENERAL

Independent, university, coed. Awards bachelor's, master's, doctoral, and first professional degrees. Founded 1881. Setting: 120-acre suburban campus. Undergraduate faculty: 269 (all full-time); student-faculty ratio is 12:1. Most popular recent majors: pharmacy, advertising, business marketing and marketing management.

### CAMPUS VISITS

**College Calendar 1998–99:** *Regular classes:* Aug. 24–Dec. 10; Jan. 19–May 6. *Breaks:* Oct. 19–21; Nov. 25–30. *Final exams:* Dec. 14–18; May 10–14. *Admission office closed:* Nov. 27, Dec. 24, Dec. 28–Jan. 4. *Special campus days:* Open House, Oct. 12, Nov. 9; Open House for Admitted Applicants, Mar. 15, Apr. 12.

### VISIT OPPORTUNITIES

| | Appointments? | Who? |
| --- | --- | --- |
| **Campus Tour** | recommended, not required | open to all |
| **Admission Interview** | recommended, not required | open to all |
| **Classroom Visit** | required | open to all |
| **Faculty Meeting** | required | open to all |
| **Overnight Visit** | required | applicants only |

**Interviews:** M–F 9:00 am–4:00 pm; select Sat. at 9:00 am–1:00 pm during Oct. to Apr.; 60 minutes.

**Campus Tours:** Conducted by students. M–F at 9:00 am, 10:00 am, 11:00 am, 12:00 pm, 1:00 pm, 2:00 pm; Sat. at 9:00 am, 10:00 am, 11:00 am, 12:00 pm; two week advance reservation encouraged; 60 minutes.

**Class Visits:** Prospective students may attend a class in their area of interest, certain predetermined classrooms are open to visitors, classroom visits are determined by the visit schedule.

**Overnight Visits:** During the regular academic year, prospective applicants may spend an evening in a residence hall with a student host.

**Video:** Free on request.

### CAMPUS FACILITIES

**Science:** Pharmacy and Science Hall, Olin Hall, Harvey Ingam Hall, Fitch Hall.

**Arts:** Fine Arts Center, Sheslow Auditorium, Anderson Gallery, Graphic Design Studio.

**Athletic:** Knapp Center, Bell Center, Tennis Complex.

**Of Special Interest:** Olmsted Student Union, Residence Halls, Opperman Law Library.

### LOCAL ATTRACTIONS

Iowa Capitol; Des Moines Art Center; Des Moines Botanical Center; Adventureland Amusement Park; Valley Junction Historical District; Living History Farms, The Science Center of Iowa.

# GRACELAND COLLEGE
## Lamoni, Iowa

**Contact:** Daphne A. Morrison, Coordinator of Publications and On-Campus Programs, 700 College Avenue, Lamoni, IA 50140. *Phone:* 515-784-5116 or toll-free 800-346-9208. *Fax:* 515-784-5480. *E-mail:*

*Graceland College (continued)*

admissions@graceland.edu *Web site:* http://www.graceland.edu/ *Visit location:* Admissions Office, Higdon Administration Building, 700 College Avenue.

## QUICK FACTS

Entrance: moderately difficult. SAT>500: 54% V, 56% M; ACT>18: N/R. Tuition and fees: $10,860. Room and board: $3620. Application deadline: 5/1.

## GENERAL

Independent Reorganized Latter Day Saints, comprehensive, coed. Awards bachelor's and master's degrees. Founded 1895. Setting: 169-acre small-town campus. Undergraduate faculty: 95 (85 full-time, 10 part-time); student-faculty ratio is 15:1. Most popular recent majors: nursing, business administration, education.

## CAMPUS VISITS

**College Calendar 1998–99:** *Regular classes:* Sept. 2–Dec. 11; Jan. 4–21; Jan. 25–May 7. *Breaks:* Nov. 24–29; Mar. 26–Apr. 5; Dec. 18–Jan. 3. *Final exams:* Dec. 14–17; May 10–13. *Admission office closed:* Christmas, Dec. 25–Jan. 3; Good Friday, Apr. 2. *Special campus days:* Commencement, May 16; Homecoming, Oct. 2–4; New Student Arrival, Aug. 29.

## VISIT OPPORTUNITIES

|  | Appointments? | Who? |
| --- | --- | --- |
| **Campus Tour** | recommended | open to all |
| **Information Session** | recommended | open to all |
| **Classroom Visit** | recommended | open to all |
| **Faculty Meeting** | recommended | open to all |
| **Overnight Visit** | recommended | open to all |

**Information Sessions:** M–F 8:00 am–5:00 pm; weekend appointments available; 45 minutes.

**Campus Tours:** Conducted by students and admission reps. M–F 8:00 am–5:00 pm; weekend appointments available; 60 minutes.

**Class Visits:** Prospective students may attend a class in their area of interest.

**Overnight Visits:** During the regular academic year, prospective applicants may spend an evening in a residence hall with a student host.

**Video:** Free on request.

## CAMPUS FACILITIES

**Science:** Appointment Required: Platz-Mortimore Science Hall Observatory.

**Arts:** Appointment Required: The Shaw Center for the Performing Arts.

**Athletic:** Appointment Required: Eugene E. Closson Field House/Bruce Jenner Sports Complex.

**Of Special Interest:** Historic Higdon Administration Building.

## LOCAL ATTRACTIONS

Liberty Hall; Antique shops.

# IOWA STATE UNIVERSITY OF SCIENCE AND TECHNOLOGY
**Ames, Iowa**

**Contact:** Office of Campus Visits, 100 Alumni Hall, Iowa State University, Ames, IA 50011. *Phone:* toll-free 800-262-3810. *Fax:* 515-294-2592. *E-mail:* admissions@iastate.edu *Web site:* http://www.iastate.edu/ *Visit location:* Office of Campus Visits/Admissions, Alumni Hall, 100 Alumni Hall.

## QUICK FACTS

Enrollment: 25,384; UG: 20,717. Entrance: moderately difficult. SAT>500: 75% V, 86% M; ACT>18: 97%. Resident tuition and fees: $2766. Nonresident tuition and fees: $8808. Room and board: $3647. Application deadline: 8/21.

## GENERAL

State-supported, university, coed. Awards bachelor's, master's, doctoral, and first professional degrees. Founded 1858. Setting: 1,788-acre suburban campus. Undergraduate faculty: 1,561 (1,360 full-time, 201 part-time); student-faculty ratio is 13:1. Most popular recent majors: elementary education, mechanical engineering, civil engineering.

## CAMPUS VISITS

**College Calendar 1998–99:** *Regular classes:* Aug. 24–Dec. 11; Jan. 11–Apr. 30. *Breaks:* Nov. 23–27; Mar. 15–19; Dec. 21–Jan. 8. *Final exams:* Dec. 14–18; May 3–7. *Admission office closed:* Sept. 7, Nov. 26–28, Dec. 24–26, Jan. 2, May 31, July 3, July 5. *Special campus days:* Commencement, May 8, Dec. 19; Family Weekend, Sept. 25–27; Homecoming, Oct. 10.

## VISIT OPPORTUNITIES

| | Appointments? | Who? |
|---|---|---|
| Campus Tour | recommended, not required | open to all |
| Information Session | recommended, not required | open to all |
| Classroom Visit | required | admitted applicants and parents |
| Faculty Meeting | required | open to all |

**Information Sessions:** M–F at 9:15 am, 10:15 am, 3:15 pm; Sat. at 9:15 am; 45 minutes.

**Campus Tours:** Conducted by students. M–F at 10:00 am, 2:10 pm; Sat. at 10:00 am; separate residence hall tour daily and Sat.; 60 minutes.

**Class Visits:** Classroom visits are determined by the visit schedule.

## CAMPUS FACILITIES

**Science:** Durham Computation Center; Appointment Required: College of Veterinary Medicine.

**Arts:** Grant Wood Murals in Parks Library, Brunnier Art Museum, Farm House Museum, Art on Campus Program; Appointment Required: Gallery 181, College of Design.

**Athletic:** Lied Recreation Center.

**Of Special Interest:** Residence Halls, Reiman Gardens, Memorial Union.

# LORAS COLLEGE
## Dubuque, Iowa

**Contact:** Tina Lape, Visit Coordinator, 1450 Alta Vista, Dubuque, IA 52001. *Phone:* toll-free 800-24-LORAS. *Fax:* 319-588-7964. *E-mail:* tlape@loras.edu *Web site:* http://www.loras.edu/ *Visit location:* Admissions Office, Keane Hall, 1450 Alta Vista.

## QUICK FACTS

Enrollment: 1,776; UG: 1,695. Entrance: moderately difficult. SAT>500: 76% V, 80% M; ACT>18: 94%. Tuition and fees: $13,750. Room and board: $5005. Application deadline: rolling.

## GENERAL

Independent Roman Catholic, comprehensive, coed. Awards associate, bachelor's, and master's degrees. Founded 1839. Setting: 60-acre suburban campus. Undergraduate faculty: 136 (111 full-time, 25 part-

time); student-faculty ratio is 13:1. Most popular recent majors: business administration, social sciences, education.

## CAMPUS VISITS

**College Calendar 1998–99:** *Regular classes:* Aug. 25–Dec. 11; Jan. 19–May 7. *Breaks:* Nov. 25–29; Feb. 27–Mar. 7; Dec. 18–Jan. 18; Apr. 1–5. *Final exams:* Dec. 14–17; May 10–13. *Admission office closed:* Tri college Free Day, Oct. 23. *Special campus days:* Graduation, May 16; Homecoming, Oct. 16–18; Tri college Free Day, Oct. 23.

## VISIT OPPORTUNITIES

| | Appointments? | Who? |
|---|---|---|
| Campus Tour | recommended, not required | open to all |
| Information Session | recommended, not required | open to all |
| Admission Interview | recommended, not required | open to all |
| Classroom Visit | required | open to all |
| Faculty Meeting | required | open to all |
| Overnight Visit | required | open to all |

**Information Sessions:** M–F 9:00 am–3:00 pm; Sat.; call to arrange specific athletic or academic meetings; 15 minutes.

**Interviews:** M–F 9:00 am–3:00 pm; Sat. 10:00 am–1:00 pm; 30 minutes.

**Campus Tours:** Conducted by students. M–F 9:00 am–3:00 pm; Sat. 10:00 am–1:00 pm; 60 minutes.

**Class Visits:** Prospective students may attend a class in their area of interest.

**Overnight Visits:** During the regular academic year, prospective applicants may spend an evening in a residence hall with a student host.

## CAMPUS FACILITIES

**Of Special Interest:** Wahlert Memorial Library.

# LUTHER COLLEGE
## Decorah, Iowa

**Contact:** Admissions Office, 700 College Drive, Decorah, IA 52101. *Phone:* toll-free 800-458-8437. *Fax:* 319-387-2159. *E-mail:* admissions@luther.edu

*Luther College (continued)*

*Web site:* http://www.luther.edu/luther.htm *Visit location:* Admissions Office, Centennial Union, 700 College Drive.

## QUICK FACTS

Enrollment: 2,400; UG: 2,400. Entrance: moderately difficult. SAT>500: 91% V, 91% M; ACT>18: 99%. Tuition and fees: $15,630. Room and board: $3700. Application deadline: 6/1.

## GENERAL

Independent, 4-year, coed, Evangelical Lutheran Church in America. Awards bachelor's degrees. Founded 1861. Setting: 800-acre small-town campus. Faculty: 224 (175 full-time, 49 part-time); student-faculty ratio is 13:1. Most popular recent majors: biology, business administration, elementary education.

## CAMPUS VISITS

**College Calendar 1998–99:** *Regular classes:* Sept. 2–Dec. 11; Jan. 5–28; Feb. 3–May 13. *Breaks:* Oct. 24–28; Jan. 29–Feb. 3; Mar. 27–Apr. 5; Dec. 19–Jan. 5. *Final exams:* Dec. 15–18; May 15–19. *Admission office closed:* Nov. 27, Dec. 24; Good Friday, Apr. 2. *Special campus days:* Commencement, May 23; Homecoming, Oct. 16–18; Juletide/Messiah, Dec. 4–6; Parents Weekend, Sept. 25–27.

### VISIT OPPORTUNITIES

|  | Appointments? | Who? |
|---|---|---|
| **Campus Tour** | recommended | open to all |
| **Information Session** |  | open to all |
| **Admission Interview** | recommended | open to all |
| **Classroom Visit** | required | open to all |
| **Faculty Meeting** | required | open to all |
| **Overnight Visit** | required | open to all |

**Information Sessions:** Held during large group visit events, Parents Weekend and Homecoming; 45 minutes.

**Interviews:** M–F, select Sat.; 30 minutes.

**Campus Tours:** Conducted by students. Fri. at 9:00 am, 10:30 am, 11:30 am, 12:30 pm, 1:30 pm, 2:30 pm; Tue., Thu. at 10:30 am, 11:30 am, 1:30 pm; Mon. at 9:00 am, 10:30 am, 11:30 am, 12:30 pm, 1:30 pm, 2:30 pm; Wed. at 10:30 am, 11:30 am, 1:30 pm; Sat. at 10:00 am, 11:00 am, 12:00 pm, 1:00 pm; 60 minutes.

**Class Visits:** Prospective students may attend a class in their area of interest, classroom visits are determined by the visit schedule.

**Overnight Visits:** During the regular academic year, prospective applicants may spend an evening in a residence hall with a student host.

**Video:** Free on request.

## CAMPUS FACILITIES

**Of Special Interest:** Preus Library.

# NORTHWESTERN COLLEGE
## Orange City, Iowa

**Contact:** Lori McDonald, Visitation Coordinator, 101 Seventh Street, SW, Orange City, IA 51041. *Phone:* 712-737-7142 or toll-free 800-747-4757 (in-state). *Fax:* 712-737-7164. *E-mail:* ronald@nwciowa.edu *Web site:* http://www.nwciowa.edu/ *Visit location:* Admissions Office, Zwemer Hall.

## QUICK FACTS

Enrollment: 1,140; UG: 1,140. Entrance: moderately difficult. SAT>500: 81% V, 81% M; ACT>18: 95%. Tuition and fees: $11,300. Room and board: $3300. Application deadline: rolling.

## GENERAL

Independent, 4-year, coed, Reformed Church in America. Awards associate and bachelor's degrees. Founded 1882. Setting: 45-acre rural campus. Faculty: 105 (64 full-time, 41 part-time); student-faculty ratio is 16:1. Most popular recent majors: business administration, elementary education, biology.

## CAMPUS VISITS

**College Calendar 1998–99:** *Regular classes:* Aug. 25–Oct. 14; Oct. 21–Dec. 11; Jan. 5–Feb. 24; Mar. 10–Apr. 30. *Breaks:* Oct. 19–20; Dec. 18–Jan. 4; Mar. 1–9. *Final exams:* Oct. 15–16; Dec. 14–17; Feb. 25–26; May 3–6. *Special campus days:* Commencement, May 8; Homecoming, Oct. 2–4; Parent's Weekend, Oct. 30–Nov. 1.

### VISIT OPPORTUNITIES

|  | Appointments? | Who? |
|---|---|---|
| **Campus Tour** | recommended | applicants and parents |
| **Information Session** | recommended |  |

## VISIT OPPORTUNITIES—*continued*

| | Appointments? | Who? |
| --- | --- | --- |
| **Admission Interview** | recommended | applicants and parents |
| **Classroom Visit** | recommended | applicants and parents |
| **Faculty Meeting** | recommended | applicants and parents |
| **Overnight Visit** | required | |

**Information Sessions:** M–F; Sat. mornings; 25 minutes.

**Interviews:** M–F; Sat. mornings; 45 minutes.

**Campus Tours:** Conducted by students. M–F; Sat. mornings; 75 minutes.

**Class Visits:** Classroom visits are determined by the visit schedule.

**Overnight Visits:** During the regular academic year, prospective applicants may spend an evening in a residence hall with a student host.

## CAMPUS FACILITIES

**Science:** Classroom building and laboratories.

**Athletic:** Bultman Athletic Center.

**Of Special Interest:** Chapel, Student Center; Appointment Required: Residence Halls.

# ST. AMBROSE UNIVERSITY

Davenport, Iowa

**Contact:** Tiffaney McCannon, 518 West Locust Street, Davenport, IA 52803. *Phone:* toll-free 800-383-2627. *E-mail:* tmccanon@saunix.sau.edu *Visit location:* Admissions Office, St. Ambrose Hall, 518 West Locust Street.

## QUICK FACTS

Enrollment: 2,740; UG: 1,934. Entrance: moderately difficult. SAT>500: N/R; ACT>18: 97%. Tuition and fees: $12,850. Room and board: $4810. Application deadline: rolling.

## GENERAL

Independent Roman Catholic, comprehensive, coed. Awards bachelor's and master's degrees. Founded 1882. Setting: 11-acre urban campus. Undergraduate faculty: 210 (126 full-time, 84 part-time); student-faculty ratio is 16:1. Most popular recent majors: business administration, biology, mass communications.

## CAMPUS VISITS

**College Calendar 1998–99:** *Regular classes:* Aug. 24–Dec. 4; Jan. 18–Apr. 29. *Breaks:* Oct. 9–16; Mar. 8–15. *Final exams:* Dec. 5–10; May 1–9.

## VISIT OPPORTUNITIES

| | Appointments? |
| --- | --- |
| **Campus Tour** | not required |
| **Information Session** | required |
| **Admission Interview** | required |
| **Classroom Visit** | required |
| **Faculty Meeting** | required |
| **Overnight Visit** | required |

**Information Sessions:** M–F 9:00 am–4:00 pm; select Sat. 9:00 am–12:00 pm; 60 minutes.

**Interviews:** M–F, select Sat.; 60 minutes.

**Campus Tours:** Conducted by students. M–F 9:00 am–5:00 pm; select Sat. 9:00 am–12:00 pm; 60 minutes.

**Class Visits:** Prospective students may attend a class in their area of interest.

**Overnight Visits:** During the regular academic year, prospective applicants may spend an evening in a residence hall with a student host.

**Video:** Free on request.

## CAMPUS FACILITIES

**Arts:** Theatre; Appointment Required: Catish Gallery.

**Of Special Interest:** Radio/TV Stations; Appointment Required: Observatory, Children's Campus.

## LOCAL ATTRACTIONS

North Park Mall, President River Boat, Le Claire Levee.

# THE UNIVERSITY OF IOWA

Iowa City, Iowa

**Contact:** Admissions Visitor Center Reservation Staff, 100 Bowman House, Iowa City, IA 52242. *Phone:* toll-free 800-553-IOWA. *Fax:* 319-335-3637. *E-mail:* admissions@uiowa.edu *Web site:* http://www.

*The University of Iowa (continued)*

uiowa.edu/ *Visit location:* Admissions Visitor Center, Bowman House, 230 North Clinton Street.

## QUICK FACTS
Enrollment: 28,409; UG: 18,913. Entrance: moderately difficult. SAT>500: 83% V, 86% M; ACT>18: 98%. Resident tuition and fees: $2760. Nonresident tuition and fees: $9616. Room and board: $4046. Application deadline: 5/15.

## GENERAL
State-supported, university, coed. Awards bachelor's, master's, doctoral, and first professional degrees. Founded 1847. Setting: 1,900-acre small-town campus. Undergraduate faculty: 1,712 (1,647 full-time, 65 part-time); student-faculty ratio is 16:1. Most popular recent majors: psychology, English, finance.

## CAMPUS VISITS
**College Calendar 1998–99:** *Regular classes:* Aug. 24–Dec. 11; Jan. 19–May 7. *Breaks:* Nov. 24–30; Mar. 12–22. *Final exams:* Dec. 14–18; May 10–14.

## VISIT OPPORTUNITIES

|  | Appointments? | Who? |
|---|---|---|
| **Campus Tour** | recommended | open to all |
| **Information Session** | recommended | open to all |
| **Admission Interview** | recommended | open to all |
| **Classroom Visit** | not required | open to all |
| **Faculty Meeting** | required | open to all |

**Information Sessions:** Sat. at 9:30 am; M–F at 10:30 am, 3:30 pm; 60 minutes.

**Interviews:** M–F; 40 minutes.

**Campus Tours:** Conducted by students. M–F at 10:30 am, 11:30 am, 2:30 pm; Sat. at 10:30 am.

**Class Visits:** Certain predetermined classrooms are open to visitors.

## CAMPUS FACILITIES
**Of Special Interest:** Main Library.

## LOCAL ATTRACTIONS
Downtown Iowa City.

# UNIVERSITY OF NORTHERN IOWA
## Cedar Falls, Iowa

**Contact:** Admissions Office, 1222 West 27th Street, Cedar Falls, IA 50614-0018. *Phone:* toll-free 800-772-2037. *Fax:* 319-273-2885. *E-mail:* debra.sturm@uni.edu *Web site:* http://www.uni.edu/ *Visit location:* Admissions, Gilchrist Hall, 120 Gilchrist Hall.

## QUICK FACTS
Enrollment: 13,503; UG: 11,767. Entrance: moderately difficult. SAT>500: N/R; ACT>18: 96%. Resident tuition and fees: $2752. Nonresident tuition and fees: $7136. Room and board: $3452. Application deadline: rolling.

## GENERAL
State-supported, comprehensive, coed. Part of Iowa State Board of Regents. Awards bachelor's, master's, and doctoral degrees. Founded 1876. Setting: 940-acre small-town campus. Undergraduate faculty: 820 (636 full-time, 184 part-time); student-faculty ratio is 17:1. Most popular recent majors: elementary education, accounting, biology.

## CAMPUS VISITS
**College Calendar 1998–99:** *Regular classes:* Aug. 24–Dec. 18; Jan. 11–May 7. *Breaks:* Nov. 24–30; Mar. 12–22. *Final exams:* Dec. 14–18; May 3–7. *Special campus days:* Fall Commencement, Dec. 19; Family Weekend, Oct. 3; Homecoming, Oct. 17; Spring Commencement, May 8.

## VISIT OPPORTUNITIES

|  | Appointments? | Who? |
|---|---|---|
| **Campus Tour** | required | open to all |
| **Information Session** | required | open to all |
| **Admission Interview** | required | open to all |
| **Faculty Meeting** | required | open to all |

**Information Sessions:** Select Sat. at 10:00 am, 11:00 am; call for preview days schedule; 60 minutes.

**Interviews:** M–F; 60 minutes.

**Campus Tours:** Conducted by students. M–F 9:00 am–2:00 pm; select Sat. at 10:00 am, 11:00 am; times limited during academic breaks; 60 minutes.

## CAMPUS FACILITIES
**Science:** McCollum Science Hall.

**Arts:** Strayer-Wood Theatre.

**Athletic:** University of Northern Iowa Dome, Wellness and Recreation Center.

**Of Special Interest:** Residence Halls, Rod Library, Maucker University Union.

# KANSAS

## BENEDICTINE COLLEGE
### Atchison, Kansas

**Contact:** Kathy Kinney, Coordinator of Campus Visits, 1020 North 2nd Street, Atchison, KS 66002. *Phone:* toll-free 800-467-5340. *Fax:* 913-367-5462. *E-mail:* kkinney@raven.benedictine.edu *Web site:* http://www.benedictine.edu/ *Visit location:* Admission Office, Administration Building, 1020 North 2nd Street.

### QUICK FACTS
Enrollment: 827; UG: 784. Entrance: moderately difficult. SAT>500: 43% V, 50% M; ACT>18: 93%. Tuition and fees: $11,750. Room and board: $4620. Application deadline: 8/15.

### GENERAL
Independent Roman Catholic, comprehensive, coed. Awards associate, bachelor's, and master's degrees. Founded 1859. Setting: 225-acre small-town campus with easy access to Kansas City. Undergraduate faculty: 74 (48 full-time, 26 part-time); student-faculty ratio is 12:1. Most popular recent majors: business administration, elementary education, biology.

### CAMPUS VISITS
**College Calendar 1998–99:** *Regular classes:* Aug. 25–Dec. 8; Jan. 12–May 4. *Breaks:* Oct. 16–18; Mar. 6–14; Nov. 25–29; Apr. 1–5. *Final exams:* Dec. 10–15; May 6–11. *Admission office closed:* Nov. 26–27, Dec. 24–25, Dec. 31–Jan. 1, Apr. 2, May 31. *Special campus days:* Commencement, May 15; Discovery Week, Apr. 13–15; Homecoming, Oct. 23–25; Parents Weekend, Oct. 2–4.

### VISIT OPPORTUNITIES

|  | Appointments? | Who? |
| --- | --- | --- |
| **Campus Tour** | not required | open to all |
| **Admission Interview** | not required | open to all |
| **Classroom Visit** | recommended | open to all |

**VISIT OPPORTUNITIES**—*continued*

|  | Appointments? | Who? |
| --- | --- | --- |
| **Faculty Meeting** | recommended | open to all |
| **Overnight Visit** | required | open to all |

**Interviews:** Sat. 9:00 am–12:00 pm; M–F; 30 minutes.

**Campus Tours:** Conducted by students. M–F 9:00 am–5:00 pm; Sat. 9:00 am–12:00 pm; 60 minutes.

**Class Visits:** Prospective students may attend a class in their area of interest, classroom visits are determined by the visit schedule.

**Overnight Visits:** During the regular academic year, prospective applicants may spend an evening in a residence hall with a student host.

### CAMPUS FACILITIES
**Science:** Westerman Hall; Appointment Required: Benedictine Bottoms Wildlife Preservation.

**Arts:** Mabee Theatre; Appointment Required: O'Malley-McAllister Auditorium.

**Athletic:** Ralph Nolan Gymnasium, tennis court, Stadium and Outdoor Sports Complex.

**Of Special Interest:** St. Benedict's Abbey Church, Cray Center for Entrepreneurship, Benedictine College Library.

### LOCAL ATTRACTIONS
Amelia Earhart Birthplace, Amelia Earhart Earthworks; Santa Fe Depot and Museum; Evah Cray Historical Home.

## KANSAS STATE UNIVERSITY
### Manhattan, Kansas

**Contact:** Susan Hansen, Assistant Director, New Student Services, New Student Services, 1 Anderson Hall, Manhattan, KS 66506. *Phone:* toll-free 800-432-8270 (in-state). *Fax:* 785-532-6108. *E-mail:* kstate@ksu.edu *Web site:* http://www.ksu.edu/ *Visit location:* Admissions Office, Anderson Hall, Room 119.

### QUICK FACTS
Enrollment: 20,196; UG: 16,826. Entrance: noncompetitive. SAT>500: N/App; ACT>18: 91%. Resident tuition and fees: $2467. Nonresident tuition and fees: $8772. Room and board: $3640. Application deadline: rolling.

*Kansas State University (continued)*

## GENERAL

State-supported, university, coed. Awards associate, bachelor's, master's, doctoral, and first professional degrees. Founded 1863. Setting: 668-acre suburban campus. Undergraduate faculty: 1,389 (1,204 full-time, 185 part-time); student-faculty ratio is 15:1. Most popular recent majors: journalism, animal sciences, elementary education.

## CAMPUS VISITS

**College Calendar 1998–99:** *Regular classes:* Aug. 24–Dec. 11; Jan. 14–May 7. *Breaks:* Dec. 21–Jan. 14. *Final exams:* Dec. 14–18; May 10–14. *Special campus days:* All University Open House, Apr. 10; Family Weekend, Sept. 25–27; Homecoming, Oct. 24.

## VISIT OPPORTUNITIES

| | Appointments? | Who? |
|---|---|---|
| **Campus Tour** | recommended, not required | open to all |
| **Information Session** | recommended, not required | open to all |
| **Admission Interview** | recommended | applicants and parents |
| **Faculty Meeting** | recommended | open to all |
| **Overnight Visit** | | open to all |

**Information Sessions:** M–F 9:00 am–4:30 pm; closed 12:00 pm to 1:00 pm; 30 minutes.

**Interviews:** M–F.

**Campus Tours:** Conducted by students. M–F at 11:30 am, 1:30 pm, 3:30 pm; 60 minutes.

**Overnight Visits:** During the regular academic year and over the summer, prospective applicants may spend an evening in a residence hall.

**Video:** Free on request.

## CAMPUS FACILITIES

**Science:** Appointment Required: College of Veterinary Medicine, Animal Science Facilities.

**Arts:** McCain Auditorium, K-State Student Union Art Gallery; Appointment Required: Beach Museum of Art.

**Athletic:** Chester E. Peters Recreation Complex; Appointment Required: Bramlage Coliseum, Wagner Field (Football Stadium).

**Of Special Interest:** Appointment Required: Dole Educational Communications Center, College of Technology and Aviation.

# WICHITA STATE UNIVERSITY
**Wichita, Kansas**

**Contact:** Jennifer Champman, Associate Director, Admissions, 1845 North Fairmount, Wichita, KS 67260-0124. *Phone:* 316-978-3085 or toll-free 800-362-2594. *Fax:* 316-978-3174. *E-mail:* chapman@twsuvm.twsu.edu *Web site:* http://www.twsu.edu/ *Visit location:* Admissions, Jardine Hall, Room 111, 1845 North Fairmount.

## QUICK FACTS

Enrollment: 13,205; UG: 10,142. Entrance: noncompetitive. SAT>500: N/R; ACT>18: N/R. Resident tuition and fees: $1986. Nonresident tuition and fees: $6914. Room and board: $3760. Application deadline: rolling.

## GENERAL

State-supported, university, coed. Awards associate, bachelor's, master's, and doctoral degrees and post-master's certificates. Founded 1895. Setting: 335-acre urban campus. Undergraduate faculty: 758 (445 full-time, 313 part-time); student-faculty ratio is 15:1. Most popular recent major: business administration.

## CAMPUS VISITS

**College Calendar 1998–99:** *Regular classes:* Aug. 24–Dec. 10; Jan. 15–May 7. *Breaks:* Nov. 25–29; Mar. 22–28. *Final exams:* Dec. 12–18; May 8–14. *Admission office closed:* Dec. 23–Jan. 1, Nov. 26–27, Sept. 7. *Special campus days:* Open House, Apr. 10.

## VISIT OPPORTUNITIES

| | Appointments? | Who? |
|---|---|---|
| **Campus Tour** | recommended | open to all |
| **Information Session** | recommended | open to all |
| **Admission Interview** | recommended, not required | open to all |
| **Classroom Visit** | recommended | open to all |
| **Faculty Meeting** | recommended | open to all |
| **Overnight Visit** | recommended | open to all |

**Information Sessions:** Mon.; Thu.; Fri.; walk-ins are welcome; 30 minutes.

**Interviews:** M–F; Mon. 5:00–7:00 pm; Tue. 5:00–7:00 pm; select Sat. Shocker Showcase programs; call to schedule appointments; 30 minutes.

**Campus Tours:** Conducted by students and admission reps. Mon. at 10:30 am, 1:30 pm; Thu. at 10:30 am, 1:30 pm; Fri. at 10:30 am, 1:30 pm; 60 minutes.

**Class Visits:** Prospective students may attend a class in their area of interest.

**Overnight Visits:** During the regular academic year, prospective applicants may spend an evening in a residence hall.

**Video:** Free on request.

## CAMPUS FACILITIES

**Science:** Beech Wind Tunnel, National Institute of Aviation Research.

**Arts:** Appointment Required: Ulrich Museum.

**Athletic:** Appointment Required: Baseball and Soft-ball facilities.

**Of Special Interest:** Elliott School of Communications; Appointment Required: Martin H. Bush Sculpture Collection.

# KENTUCKY

## ASBURY COLLEGE
### Wilmore, Kentucky

**Contact:** Annette Boring, Visit Coordinator, 1 Macklem Drive, Wilmore, KY 40390. *Phone:* 606-858-3511 Ext. 2142 or toll-free 800-888-1818. *Fax:* 606-858-3921. *E-mail:* admissions@asbury.edu *Web site:* http://www.asbury.edu/ *Visit location:* Admissions, Hager Administration Building, 1 Macklem Drive.

### QUICK FACTS
Enrollment: 1,225; UG: 1,225. Entrance: moderately difficult. SAT>500: 79% V, 64% M; ACT>18: 98%. Tuition and fees: $12,020. Room and board: $3390. Application deadline: rolling.

### GENERAL
Independent nondenominational, 4-year, coed. Awards bachelor's degrees. Founded 1890. Setting: 400-acre small-town campus with easy access to Lexington. Faculty: 118 (85 full-time, 33 part-time); student-faculty ratio is 14:1.

### CAMPUS VISITS
**College Calendar 1998–99:** *Regular classes:* Aug. 25–Dec. 11; Jan. 11–Apr. 30. *Breaks:* Oct. 23–27; Mar. 15–22. *Final exams:* Dec. 14–17; May 3–6.

## VISIT OPPORTUNITIES

| | Appointments? | Who? |
|---|---|---|
| **Campus Tour** | required | open to all |
| **Information Session** | required | open to all |
| **Admission Interview** | required | open to all |
| **Classroom Visit** | required | open to all |
| **Faculty Meeting** | required | applicants and parents |
| **Overnight Visit** | required | open to all |

**Information Sessions:** M–F 8:00 am–5:00 pm; select Sat. 9:00 am–12:00 pm; 50 minutes.

**Interviews:** M–F, select Sat.; 50 minutes.

**Campus Tours:** Conducted by students. M–F 8:00 am–5:00 pm; select Sat. 9:00 am–12:00 pm; 50 minutes.

**Class Visits:** Certain predetermined classrooms are open to visitors.

**Overnight Visits:** During the regular academic year, prospective applicants may spend an evening in a residence hall with a student host.

**Video:** Free on request.

### CAMPUS FACILITIES

**Science:** Computer Science facility.

**Arts:** Appointment Required: Gallery, Photography Lab, Studio.

**Athletic:** Luce Athletic Center, Outdoor facilities/soccer, baseball, softball, archery.

**Of Special Interest:** Hughes Auditorium, Men's/Women's Resident Halls.

### LOCAL ATTRACTIONS
Horsemanship Program—farm; Challenge Course.

## BEREA COLLEGE
### Berea, Kentucky

**Contact:** Kif Skidmore, Admissions Counselor, CPO 2344 Berea College, Berea, KY 40404. *Phone:* toll-free 800-326-5948. *Fax:* 606-986-7476. *E-mail:* admissions@berea.edu *Web site:* http://www.berea.edu/ *Visit location:* Office of Admissions, Edwards, CPO 2344.

### QUICK FACTS
Enrollment: 1,418; UG: 1,418. Entrance: moderately difficult. SAT>500: 74% V, 61% M; ACT>18: 96%.

*Berea College (continued)*

Tuition and fees: $195. Room and board: $3330. Application deadline: 4/15.

## GENERAL

Independent, 4-year, coed. Awards bachelor's degrees. Founded 1855. Setting: 140-acre small-town campus. Faculty: 140 (118 full-time, 22 part-time); student-faculty ratio is 12:1. Most popular recent majors: business administration, child care/development, nursing.

## CAMPUS VISITS

**College Calendar 1998–99:** *Regular classes:* Sept. 3–Dec. 10; Jan. 4–29; Mar. 4–May 13. *Breaks:* Dec. 17–Jan. 4; Jan. 29–Feb. 3; May 20–June 7; Mar. 19–29. *Final exams:* Dec. 14–17; Jan. 29; May 17–20. *Admission office closed:* Nov. 26–29, Dec. 24–26, Jan. 1, Apr. 2. *Special campus days:* Homecoming, Nov. 20–22; Labor Day, Apr. 27; Mountain Day, Oct. 7.

### VISIT OPPORTUNITIES

| | Appointments? | Who? |
|---|---|---|
| **Campus Tour** | recommended | open to all |
| **Information Session** | required | open to all |
| **Admission Interview** | required | open to all |
| **Classroom Visit** | required | open to all |
| **Faculty Meeting** | required | open to all |
| **Overnight Visit** | required | open to all |

**Information Sessions:** M–F, Sat.; 60 minutes.

**Interviews:** M–F, Sat.; unavailable during school breaks and school conferences; 60 minutes.

**Campus Tours:** Conducted by students. M–F; Sat. by appointment; 55 minutes.

**Class Visits:** Classroom visits are determined by the visit schedule.

**Overnight Visits:** During the regular academic year, prospective applicants may spend an evening in a residence hall with a student host.

## CAMPUS FACILITIES

**Science:** Martin Hall Science Building; Appointment Required: Planetarium, Agriculture and Natural Resources Farm.

**Arts:** Log House Craft Gallery.

**Athletic:** Seabury Athletic Complex.

## LOCAL ATTRACTIONS

Local arts and crafts, antique stores; racetrack; Boone Tavern Hotel.

# CENTRE COLLEGE
### Danville, Kentucky

**Contact:** Lucy Kirkpatrick, Visit Coordinator, 600 West Walnut Street, Danville, KY 40422. *Phone:* toll-free 800-423-6236. *Fax:* 606-238-5373. *E-mail:* kirk@centre.edu *Web site:* http://www.centre.edu/ *Visit location:* Admission Office, Hosky House, 600 West Walnut Street.

## QUICK FACTS

Enrollment: 998; UG: 998. Entrance: very difficult. SAT>500: 95% V, 94% M; ACT>18: 100%. Tuition and fees: $14,600. Room and board: $4800. Application deadline: 3/1.

## GENERAL

Independent, 4-year, coed. Awards bachelor's degrees. Founded 1819. Setting: 100-acre small-town campus. Faculty: 101 (88 full-time, 13 part-time); student-faculty ratio is 11:1. Most popular recent major: English.

## CAMPUS VISITS

**College Calendar 1998–99:** *Regular classes:* Sept. 3–Dec. 3; Jan. 4–Feb. 9; Feb. 18–May 19. *Breaks:* Oct. 10–13; Apr. 3–10; Nov. 25–29. *Final exams:* Dec. 5–12; Feb. 10; May 21–26. *Special campus days:* Commencement, May 30; Family Weekend, Oct. 2–3; Homecoming, Oct. 23–24.

### VISIT OPPORTUNITIES

| | Appointments? | Who? |
|---|---|---|
| **Campus Tour** | recommended | open to all |
| **Admission Interview** | recommended | open to all |
| **Classroom Visit** | recommended | open to all |
| **Faculty Meeting** | recommended | open to all |
| **Overnight Visit** | required | open to all |

**Interviews:** M–F; select Sat. 8:30 am–12:00 pm; 45 minutes.

**Campus Tours:** Conducted by students. M–F at 10:00 am, 1:00 pm, 3:00 pm; select Sat. at 10:00 am; 75 minutes.

**Class Visits:** Prospective students may attend a class in their area of interest.

**Overnight Visits:** During the regular academic year, prospective applicants may spend an evening in a residence hall with a student host.

**Video:** Free on request.

### CAMPUS FACILITIES
**Science:** Olin Hall.

**Arts:** Norton Center for the Arts, Visual Arts Center.

**Athletic:** Sutcliffe Hall.

**Of Special Interest:** Old Centre (built in 1820), Combs Center (Student Center-Warehouse).

### LOCAL ATTRACTIONS
Shaker Village, Perryville Battlefield.

## CUMBERLAND COLLEGE
**Williamsburg, Kentucky**

**Contact:** Shelleigh Moses, Campus Visit Coordinator, 6178 College Station Drive, Williamsburg, KY 40769. *Phone:* toll-free 800-343-1609. *Fax:* 606-539-4303. *E-mail:* smoses@cc.cumber.edu *Web site:* http://www.cc.cumber.edu/ *Visit location:* Office of Admissions and Alumni Services, Norman Perkins House, 816 Walnut Street.

### QUICK FACTS
Enrollment: 1,528; UG: 1,428. Entrance: moderately difficult. SAT>500: 49% V, 49% M; ACT>18: 84%. Tuition and fees: $8430. Room and board: $3776. Application deadline: rolling.

### GENERAL
Independent Kentucky Baptist, comprehensive, coed. Awards bachelor's and master's degrees. Founded 1889. Setting: 30-acre rural campus with easy access to Knoxville. Undergraduate faculty: 91 (87 full-time, 4 part-time); student-faculty ratio is 17:1. Most popular recent majors: biology, psychology, education.

### CAMPUS VISITS
**College Calendar 1998–99:** *Regular classes:* Aug. 24–Dec. 11; Jan. 13–May 5. *Breaks:* Oct. 15–18; Mar. 15–19. *Final exams:* Dec. 12–18; May 6–12. *Special campus days:* Campus Day, Sept. 12, Nov. 7; Commencement, May 15; Homecoming, Nov. 13–14; Quest, Nov. 20–21.

### VISIT OPPORTUNITIES

| | Appointments? | Who? |
|---|---|---|
| **Campus Tour** | recommended | open to all |
| **Information Session** | recommended | open to all |
| **Admission Interview** | required | admitted applicants only |
| **Classroom Visit** | required | open to all |
| **Faculty Meeting** | required | open to all |
| **Overnight Visit** | required | open to all |

**Information Sessions:** M–F 9:00 am–3:00 pm; select Sat. 9:00 am–12:00 pm; 60 minutes.

**Interviews:** Select Mon.–Sat.; 30 minutes.

**Campus Tours:** Conducted by students. M–F 9:00 am–3:00 pm; select Sat. 9:00 am–12:00 pm; 60 minutes.

**Class Visits:** Prospective students may attend a class in their area of interest.

**Overnight Visits:** During the regular academic year, prospective applicants may spend an evening in a residence hall with a student host.

**Video:** Free on request.

### CAMPUS FACILITIES
**Athletic:** Rollins Center.

**Of Special Interest:** Distance Learning Lab.

### LOCAL ATTRACTIONS
Cumberland Falls National State Park.

## EASTERN KENTUCKY UNIVERSITY
**Richmond, Kentucky**

**Contact:** Director of Admissions, 203 Jones Building, Eastern Kentucky University, Richmond, KY 40475-3101. *Phone:* 606-622-2106 or toll-free 800-262-7493 (in-state). *Web site:* http://www.eku.edu *Visit location:* Admissions, 203 Jones Building, Eastern Kentucky University.

### QUICK FACTS
Enrollment: 15,424; UG: 13,424. Entrance: noncompetitive. SAT>500: N/R; ACT>18: 73%. Resident tuition and fees: $2060. Nonresident tuition and fees: $5660. Room and board: $3240. Application deadline: rolling.

*Eastern Kentucky University (continued)*

## GENERAL
State-supported, comprehensive, coed. Part of Kentucky Council on Higher Education. Awards associate, bachelor's, and master's degrees. Founded 1906. Setting: 500-acre small-town campus with easy access to Lexington. Undergraduate faculty: 966 (628 full-time, 338 part-time); student-faculty ratio is 23:1. Most popular recent major: nursing.

## CAMPUS VISITS
**College Calendar 1998–99:** *Regular classes:* Aug. 24–Dec. 12; Jan. 11–May 1. *Breaks:* Nov. 24–30; Mar. 14–22. *Final exams:* Dec. 14–19; May 3–8.

## VISIT OPPORTUNITIES

|  | Appointments? | Who? |
|---|---|---|
| **Campus Tour** | required | applicants and parents |
| **Information Session** | recommended | |
| **Admission Interview** | recommended | |
| **Classroom Visit** | required | |
| **Faculty Meeting** | required | |
| **Overnight Visit** | required | |

**Information Sessions:** M–F; 60 minutes.

**Interviews:** M–F.

**Campus Tours:** Conducted by students and admission reps. Mon., Tue., Wed., Thu. at 10:30 am, 2:30 pm; campus tours available one Sat. in fall, one Sat. in spring.

**Class Visits:** Students may arrange clasroom visit with department.

**Overnight Visits:** During the summer, prospective applicants may spend an evening in a residence hall.

## CAMPUS FACILITIES
**Science:** Arnim D. Hummel Planetarium.

**Arts:** Campbell Fine Arts Gallery.

**Athletic:** Roy Kidd Stadium, Fitness Center, indoor tennis courts, swimming pools.

**Of Special Interest:** Student Center, Residence Hall and Lobby, Meditation Chapel, Stratton Law Enforcement Center, Lilly Cornett Woods.

# MURRAY STATE UNIVERSITY
**Murray, Kentucky**

**Contact:** School Relations Office, PO Box 9, Murray, KY 42071. *Phone:* toll-free 800-272-4MSU Ext. 1. *Fax:* 502-762-3050. *E-mail:* paul.radke@murraystate.edu *Web site:* http://www.murraystate.edu/ *Visit location:* School Relations Office, Sparks Hall, 15th and Main Streets.

## QUICK FACTS
Enrollment: 8,811; UG: 7,210. Entrance: moderately difficult. SAT>500: N/App; ACT>18: N/R. Resident tuition and fees: $2300. Nonresident tuition and fees: $6140. Room and board: $3560. Application deadline: rolling.

## GENERAL
State-supported, comprehensive, coed. Part of Kentucky Council on Higher Education. Awards associate, bachelor's, and master's degrees. Founded 1922. Setting: 238-acre small-town campus. Undergraduate faculty: 384 (356 full-time, 28 part-time); student-faculty ratio is 16:1. Most popular recent major: business administration.

## CAMPUS VISITS
**College Calendar 1998–99:** *Regular classes:* Aug. 24–Dec. 9; Jan. 11–Apr. 30. *Breaks:* Mar. 7–13. *Final exams:* Dec. 11–17; May 3–7. *Admission office closed:* Nov. 25–27, Dec. 24–Jan. 3, Mar. 10–12. *Special campus days:* Fall Senior Days, Oct. 31, Nov. 21; Homecoming, Oct. 3.

## VISIT OPPORTUNITIES

|  | Appointments? | Who? |
|---|---|---|
| **Campus Tour** | recommended, not required | open to all |
| **Information Session** | recommended, not required | open to all |
| **Admission Interview** | recommended, not required | open to all |
| **Classroom Visit** | required | open to all |
| **Faculty Meeting** | recommended, not required | open to all |
| **Overnight Visit** | required | open to all |

**Information Sessions:** M–F 8:00 am–4:30 pm; Sat. 9:00 am–12:00 pm; 30 minutes.

**Interviews:** M–F, select Sat.; 30 minutes.

**Campus Tours:** Conducted by students. M–F 8:00 am–4:30 pm; Sat. 9:00 am–12:00 pm; 60 minutes.

**Class Visits:** Prospective students may attend a class in their area of interest.

**Overnight Visits:** During the regular academic year, prospective applicants may spend an evening in a residence hall.

**Video:** Free on request.

## CAMPUS FACILITIES

**Science:** Appointment Required: Hancock Biological Station, Equine Center.

**Arts:** Clara M. Eagle Art Gallery.

**Athletic:** Regional Special Event Center, Stewart Stadium.

**Of Special Interest:** Weather West Kentucky Museum, National Scouting Museum.

## LOCAL ATTRACTIONS

Land Between the Lakes (LBL) Nature and Recreational Area.

# NORTHERN KENTUCKY UNIVERSITY

### Highland Heights, Kentucky

**Contact:** Louie B Nunn Drive, Highland Heights, KY 41099. *Phone:* 606-572-5100 or toll-free 800-637-9948. *Web site:* http://www.nku.edu/ *Visit location:* Office of Admissions, Lucas Administrative Center, Nunn Drive.

## QUICK FACTS

Enrollment: 11,309; UG: 10,148. Entrance: noncompetitive. SAT>500: N/App; ACT>18: 73%. Resident tuition and fees: $2120. Nonresident tuition and fees: $5720. Room and board: $3439. Application deadline: rolling.

## GENERAL

State-supported, comprehensive, coed. Awards associate, bachelor's, master's, and first professional degrees and post-master's certificates. Founded 1968. Setting: 300-acre suburban campus with easy access to Cincinnati. Undergraduate faculty: 750 (373 full-time, 377 part-time); student-faculty ratio is 17:1. Most popular recent majors: education, nursing, psychology.

## CAMPUS VISITS

**College Calendar 1998–99:** *Regular classes:* Aug. 26–Dec. 12; Jan. 11–May 3. *Breaks:* Dec. 20–Jan. 11; Mar. 15–19. *Final exams:* Dec. 14–19; May 5–11. *Admission office closed:* Dec. 24–Jan. 4.

## VISIT OPPORTUNITIES

| | Appointments? | Who? |
|---|---|---|
| **Campus Tour** | required | open to all |
| **Information Session** | required | open to all |
| **Admission Interview** | required | open to all |
| **Classroom Visit** | required | open to all |
| **Faculty Meeting** | required | open to all |

**Information Sessions:** Mon., Wed., Fri. at 1:00 pm; select Sat. at 12:00 pm; 60 minutes.

**Interviews:** Scheduled upon request; 30 minutes.

**Campus Tours:** Conducted by students and admission reps. Mon., Wed., Fri. at 12:00 pm; Sat. at 11:00 am; 60 minutes.

**Class Visits:** Prospective students may attend a class in their area of interest.

## CAMPUS FACILITIES

**Arts:** Art Gallery.

**Athletic:** Campus Recreation Center.

**Of Special Interest:** Library, Computer Labs.

# SULLIVAN COLLEGE

### Louisville, Kentucky

**Contact:** Greg Cawthon, Director of Admissions, 3101 Bardstown Road, Louisville, KY 40205. *Phone:* 502-456-6505 or toll-free 800-844-1354 (in-state). *Fax:* 502-454-4880. *Visit location:* Admissions Department, 3101 Bardstown Road.

## QUICK FACTS

Enrollment: 2,481; UG: 2,426. Entrance: minimally difficult. SAT>500: N/R; ACT>18: N/R. Tuition and fees: $8904. Room only: $2700. Application deadline: rolling.

## GENERAL

Proprietary, comprehensive, coed. Awards associate, bachelor's, and master's degrees (master's degree in business administration only). Founded 1864. Setting: 10-acre suburban campus. Undergraduate faculty: 88 (40 full-time, 48 part-time); student-faculty ratio is 20:1. Most popular recent majors: business administration, culinary arts, paralegal/legal assistant.

## CAMPUS VISITS

**College Calendar 1998–99:** *Regular classes:* Sept. 28–Dec. 17; Jan. 4–Mar. 19; Mar. 29–June 11; June

*Sullivan College (continued)*

28–Sept. 10. *Breaks:* Nov. 20–29; Mar. 20–28; June 12–27; Sept. 11–26; Dec. 18–Jan. 3. *Final exams:* Dec. 7–18; Mar. 8–19; June 1–11; Aug. 30–Sept. 10. *Special campus days:* Commencement.

## VISIT OPPORTUNITIES

| | Appointments? | Who? |
|---|---|---|
| **Campus Tour** | required | open to all |
| **Information Session** | required | |
| **Admission Interview** | required | open to all |
| **Classroom Visit** | required | applicants and parents |
| **Overnight Visit** | required | applicants only |

**Information Sessions:** M–F 8:00 am–8:00 pm; Sat. 9:00 am–2:00 pm; 45 minutes.

**Interviews:** M–F, Sat.; 30 minutes.

**Campus Tours:** Conducted by admission reps. M–F 8:00 am–8:00 pm; Sat. 9:00 am–2:00 pm; 30 minutes.

**Class Visits:** Prospective students may attend a class in their area of interest.

**Overnight Visits:** During the regular academic year.

**Video:** Free on request.

## CAMPUS FACILITIES

**Of Special Interest:** Appointment Required: Student Housing, Winston's—on campus gourmet restaurant.

## LOCAL ATTRACTIONS

Churchill Downs—Home of the Kentucky Derby; J.B Speed Art Museum; Louisville Slugger Bat Museum.

# THOMAS MORE COLLEGE

**Crestview Hills, Kentucky**

**Contact:** Beth Maley, Visit Coordinator, 333 Thomas More Parkway, Crestview Hills, KY 41017. *Phone:* 606-344-3332 or toll-free 800-825-4557. *Fax:* 606-344-3638. *E-mail:* beth.maley@thomasmore.edu *Web site:* http://www.thomasmore.edu/ *Visit location:* Admissions, Administration Building, 333 Thomas More Parkway.

## QUICK FACTS

Enrollment: 1,402; UG: 1,324. Entrance: moderately difficult. SAT>500: N/R; ACT>18: 94%. Tuition and fees: $11,250. Room and board: $4500. Application deadline: 8/15.

## GENERAL

Independent Roman Catholic, comprehensive, coed. Awards associate, bachelor's, and master's degrees. Founded 1921. Setting: 100-acre suburban campus with easy access to Cincinnati. Undergraduate faculty: 174 (76 full-time, 98 part-time); student-faculty ratio is 12:1. Most popular recent majors: business administration, biology, information sciences/systems.

## CAMPUS VISITS

**College Calendar 1998–99:** *Regular classes:* Aug. 26–Dec. 5; Jan. 11–Apr. 30. *Breaks:* Oct. 16–19; Mar. 8–13; Nov. 25–29; Apr. 1–5. *Final exams:* Dec. 7–12; May 1–6. *Admission office closed:* Oct. 16, Nov. 25–29, Dec. 8, Jan. 1–3; Christmas, Dec. 24–31; Labor Day, Sept. 7.

## VISIT OPPORTUNITIES

| | Appointments? | Who? |
|---|---|---|
| **Campus Tour** | recommended, not required | open to all |
| **Information Session** | recommended, not required | open to all |
| **Admission Interview** | recommended, not required | open to all |
| **Classroom Visit** | recommended, not required | open to all |
| **Faculty Meeting** | recommended, not required | open to all |
| **Overnight Visit** | required | applicants only |

**Information Sessions:** Select Sat. at 10:00 am, 12:00 pm; available Sept. through Apr.; 120 minutes.

**Interviews:** M–F; 30 minutes.

**Campus Tours:** Conducted by students. M–F, select Sat. at 10:30 am, 12:30 pm, 2:00 pm; 60 minutes.

**Class Visits:** Prospective students may attend a class in their area of interest.

**Overnight Visits:** During the regular academic year, prospective applicants may spend an evening in a residence hall with a student host.

**Video:** Free on request.

## CAMPUS FACILITIES

**Science:** Appointment Required: Biology Field Station.
**Arts:** Theatre, Art Studio.
**Athletic:** Connor Athletic Center.

## LOCAL ATTRACTIONS

Cincinnati Reds Baseball and Bengals Football teams; Covington Landing; Sawyer Point; Downtown Cincinnati.

# UNIVERSITY OF KENTUCKY
## Lexington, Kentucky

**Contact:** Visitors Center, University of Kentucky Student Center, Lexington, KY 40506-0026. *Phone:* 606-257-3595 or toll-free 800-432-0967 (in-state). *E-mail:* ukvc@pop.uky.edu *Web site:* http://www.uky. edu/ *Visit location:* University of Kentucky Visitors Center, Student Center, Euclid Avenue.

## QUICK FACTS

Enrollment: 23,157; UG: 16,625. Entrance: moderately difficult. SAT>500: N/R; ACT>18: N/R. Resident tuition and fees: $2736. Nonresident tuition and fees: $7536. Room and board: $3388. Application deadline: 6/1.

## GENERAL

State-supported, university, coed. Awards bachelor's, master's, doctoral, and first professional degrees. Founded 1865. Setting: 682-acre urban campus with easy access to Cincinnati and Louisville. Undergraduate faculty: 2,237 (1,802 full-time, 435 part-time); student-faculty ratio is 16:1. Most popular recent majors: psychology, accounting, business marketing and marketing management.

## CAMPUS VISITS

**College Calendar 1998–99:** *Regular classes:* Aug. 26–Dec. 18; Jan. 13–May 7. *Breaks:* Nov. 26–30; Mar. 15–20. *Final exams:* Dec. 14–18; May 3–7.

## VISIT OPPORTUNITIES

| | Appointments? | Who? |
|---|---|---|
| **Campus Tour** | recommended, not required | open to all |
| **Information Session** | recommended, not required | open to all |
| **Classroom Visit** | recommended | open to all |

VISIT OPPORTUNITIES— *continued*

| | Appointments? | Who? |
|---|---|---|
| **Faculty Meeting** | recommended | open to all |

**Information Sessions:** M–F 9:00 am–4:30 pm; Sat. 10:00 am–1:00 pm; unavailable May–Aug.; 45 minutes.

**Campus Tours:** Conducted by students. M–F, Sat.; 60 minutes.

**Class Visits:** Prospective students may attend a class in their area of interest.

## CAMPUS FACILITIES

**Science:** Gluck Equine Research Facility, Agricultural Science Center, Mining and Minerals Research Facility.

**Arts:** Singletary Center for the Arts (Performing), Fine Arts Complex (Studio).

**Athletic:** Nutter Center, Seaton Center, Boone Tennis Center, Lancaster Aquatics Center.

## LOCAL ATTRACTIONS

Kentucky Horse Park, Keeneland Race Track.

# UNIVERSITY OF LOUISVILLE
## Louisville, Kentucky

**Contact:** Admissions Office, University of Louisville, 2301 South Third Street, Louisville, KY 40292. *Phone:* toll-free 800-334-8635 (out-of-state). *Fax:* 502-852-6526. *E-mail:* admitme@ulkyvm.louisville. edu *Web site:* http://www.louisville.edu/ *Visit location:* Information Center, University of Louisville.

## QUICK FACTS

Enrollment: 18,666; UG: 12,931. Entrance: moderately difficult. SAT>500: N/R; ACT>18: 80%. Resident tuition and fees: $2630. Nonresident tuition and fees: $7430. Room and board: $4982. Application deadline: rolling.

## GENERAL

State-supported, university, coed. Awards associate, bachelor's, master's, doctoral, and first professional degrees. Founded 1798. Setting: 169-acre urban campus. Undergraduate faculty: 1,798 (1,279 full-time, 519 part-time); student-faculty ratio is 15:1. Most popular recent majors: psychology, accounting.

*University of Louisville (continued)*

## CAMPUS VISITS
**College Calendar 1998–99:** *Regular classes:* Aug. 24–Dec. 7; Jan. 11–Apr. 26. *Breaks:* Dec. 16–Jan. 10. *Final exams:* Dec. 9–15; Apr. 28–May 5. *Special campus days:* Commencement, May 8; Homecoming, Oct. 24.

## VISIT OPPORTUNITIES

|  | Appointments? | Who? |
|---|---|---|
| **Campus Tour** | recommended | open to all |
| **Information Session** | required | open to all |
| **Admission Interview** | recommended, not required | open to all |
| **Classroom Visit** | required | open to all |
| **Faculty Meeting** | required | open to all |
| **Overnight Visit** | required | open to all |

**Information Sessions:** Mon.; Fri.; 60 minutes.

**Interviews:** M–F, select Sat.; 45 minutes.

**Campus Tours:** Conducted by students. M–F at 9:00 am, 1:00 pm, 3:30 pm; third Sat. of each month at 10:00 am; 60 minutes.

**Class Visits:** Prospective students may attend a class in their area of interest, certain predetermined classrooms are open to visitors.

**Overnight Visits:** During the regular academic year and over the summer, prospective applicants may spend an evening in a residence hall.

## CAMPUS FACILITIES
**Science:** Appointment Required: Health Science Campus, Engineering.

**Of Special Interest:** Student Activities Center, Grawemeyer Hall, Library.

## LOCAL ATTRACTIONS
Churchill Downs; Louisville Slugger Baseball Museum; Belle of Louisville; Louisville Zoo; Kentucky Kingdom Amusement Park; Kentucky Center for the Arts, Louisville Stoneware.

# LOUISIANA

## GRAMBLING STATE UNIVERSITY
**Grambling, Louisiana**

**Contact:** Shirley Kidd, Admissions Counselor/Recruiter, PO Box 864, Grambling, LA 71245. *Phone:* 318-274-3284. *Fax:* 318-274-3292. *Visit location:* Office of Admissions/Recruitment, Long-Jones Hall, Room 252, Main Street.

## QUICK FACTS
Entrance: noncompetitive. SAT>500: N/R; ACT>18: N/R. Resident tuition and fees: $2088. Nonresident tuition and fees: $4238. Room and board: $2636. Application deadline: 7/15.

## GENERAL
State-supported, comprehensive, coed. Awards associate, bachelor's, master's, and doctoral degrees. Founded 1901. Setting: 340-acre small-town campus. Undergraduate faculty: 224 (221 full-time, 3 part-time). Most popular recent majors: criminal justice/law enforcement administration, business administration, information sciences/systems.

## CAMPUS VISITS
**College Calendar 1998–99:** *Regular classes:* Aug. 24–Dec. 9; Jan. 19–May 18. *Breaks:* Dec. 15–Jan. 19; May 18–June 9. *Final exams:* Dec. 10–15; May 13–18. *Admission office closed:* Mardi Gras Holiday. *Special campus days:* Fall Commencement, Dec. 18; Homecoming, Nov. 7; Spring Commencement, May 23.

## VISIT OPPORTUNITIES

|  | Appointments? | Who? |
|---|---|---|
| **Campus Tour** | recommended | applicants and parents |
| **Information Session** | recommended |  |
| **Admission Interview** | recommended |  |
| **Faculty Meeting** | recommended |  |

**Information Sessions:** M–F; 45 minutes.

**Interviews:** M–F.

**Campus Tours:** Conducted by students and admission reps. M–F; 60 minutes.

## CAMPUS FACILITIES
**Science:** Appointment Required: Computer Science Department.

**Arts:** Student/Faculty Art Gallery.

**Athletic:** Appointment Required: Eddie Robinson Football Stadium.

**Of Special Interest:** Appointment Required: Marching Band Auditions, Choir Auditions, Air Force and Army ROTC Programs.

# LOUISIANA STATE UNIVERSITY AND AGRICULTURAL AND MECHANICAL COLLEGE

**Baton Rouge, Louisiana**

**Contact:** Dr. Lisa B. Harris, Dean of Undergraduate Admissions, Plesant Hall Room 64, Baton Rouge, LA 70803. *Phone:* 504-388-6652. *Fax:* 504-388-4433. *E-mail:* lsuadmit@lsu.edu *Web site:* http://www.lsu.edu/ *Visit location:* Office of Undergraduate Admissions—Tour Division, Plesant Hall.

## QUICK FACTS

Enrollment: 26,568; UG: 21,216. Entrance: moderately difficult. SAT>500: N/R; ACT>18: 94%. Resident tuition and fees: $2711. Nonresident tuition and fees: $6311. Room and board: $3772. Application deadline: 6/1.

## GENERAL

State-supported, university, coed. Part of Louisiana State University System. Awards bachelor's, master's, doctoral, and first professional degrees and post-master's certificates. Founded 1860. Setting: 2,000-acre urban campus with easy access to New Orleans. Undergraduate faculty: 1,316 (1,218 full-time, 98 part-time); student-faculty ratio is 23:1. Most popular recent majors: liberal arts and studies, psychology, accounting.

## CAMPUS VISITS

**College Calendar 1998–99:** *Regular classes:* Aug. 20–Dec. 5; Jan. 7–May 1. *Breaks:* Oct. 28–Nov. 1; Mar. 29–Apr. 3. *Final exams:* Dec. 7–12; May 3–8. *Admission office closed:* Christmas Break, Dec. 24–Jan. 1; Mardi Gras, Feb. 16. *Special campus days:* Tiger Day and Homecoming, Sept. 26.

## VISIT OPPORTUNITIES

|  | Appointments? | Who? |
|---|---|---|
| **Campus Tour** | recommended | open to all |
| **Information Session** | recommended | open to all |
| **Admission Interview** | not required | open to all |
| **Classroom Visit** | required | open to all |
| **Faculty Meeting** | required | open to all |

**Information Sessions:** M–F at 10:00 am; unavailable during university holidays; 60 minutes.

**Interviews:** M–F.

**Campus Tours:** Conducted by students. M–F at 11:00 am; unavailable during university holidays; 60 minutes.

**Class Visits:** Prospective students may attend a class in their area of interest, classroom visits are determined by the visit schedule.

**Video:** Available, fee charged.

## CAMPUS FACILITIES

**Science:** PaleoKew; Appointment Required: Forensic Anthropology Lab, Pennington Biomedical Research Facility.

**Arts:** LSU Museum, Museum of Natural History, LSU Union Art Gallery; Appointment Required: Hill Memorial Library.

**Athletic:** Athletic Hall of Fame, Mike the Tiger (Royal Bengal Tiger) cage.

**Of Special Interest:** Textile and Costume Gallery, Lod Cook Alumni Center; Appointment Required: LSU Rural Life Museum.

## LOCAL ATTRACTIONS

Louisiana State Capitol, Governmental Complex (Governor's Mansion); Old State Capitol Museum, numerous Antebellum homes; USS Kidd (Battleship), LASC Museum.

# LOYOLA UNIVERSITY NEW ORLEANS

**New Orleans, Louisiana**

**Contact:** Office of Admissions, 6363 St. Charles Avenue., Box 18, New Orleans, LA 70118. *Phone:* toll-free 800-4-LOYOLA. *Fax:* 504-865-3383. *E-mail:* admit@loyno.edu *Web site:* http://www.loyno.edu/ *Visit location:* Office of Admissions, Marquette Hall, Room 315, 6363 St. Charles Avenue.

## QUICK FACTS

Enrollment: 5,042; UG: 3,343. Entrance: moderately difficult. SAT>500: 93% V, 81% M; ACT>18: 100%. Tuition and fees: $13,354. Room and board: $5830. Application deadline: rolling.

## GENERAL

Independent Roman Catholic (Jesuit), comprehensive, coed. Awards bachelor's, master's, and first professional degrees. Founded 1912. Setting: 26-acre urban campus. Undergraduate faculty: 390 (273 full-time, 117 part-time); student-faculty ratio is 12:1. Most popular recent majors: communications, psychology, accounting.

*Loyola University New Orleans (continued)*

## CAMPUS VISITS

**College Calendar 1998–99:** *Regular classes:* Aug. 31–Dec. 9; Jan. 11–May 3. *Breaks:* Nov. 25–30; Feb. 15–18; Mar. 29–Apr. 5. *Final exams:* Dec. 11–17; May 5–11. *Admission office closed:* Loyola Day, Oct. 12; Mardi Gras Holidays, Feb. 15–17. *Special campus days:* Graduation, Dec. 20, May 16–17; New Student Orientation, Aug. 26–29; President's Open House, Feb. 15–17; The Mardi Gras, Feb. 15–17.

## VISIT OPPORTUNITIES

| | Appointments? | Who? |
|---|---|---|
| **Campus Tour** | not required | open to all |
| **Information Session** | not required | open to all |
| **Admission Interview** | recommended | open to all |
| **Classroom Visit** | required | open to all |
| **Faculty Meeting** | required | open to all |
| **Overnight Visit** | required | open to all |

**Information Sessions:** Follows campus tour.

**Interviews:** M–F, select Sat.; call for schedule; 30 minutes.

**Campus Tours:** Conducted by students. M–F at 11:30 am, 3:30 pm; 60 minutes.

**Class Visits:** Prospective students may attend a class in their area of interest, classroom visits are determined by the visit schedule.

**Overnight Visits:** During the regular academic year, prospective applicants may spend an evening in a residence hall with a student host.

## CAMPUS FACILITIES

**Science:** Appointment Required: Biology Labs, Chemistry Labs.

**Arts:** Appointment Required: Visual Arts Department.

**Athletic:** Appointment Required: Recreational Sports Complex.

**Of Special Interest:** Appointment Required: Office of Academic Enrichment, Computer Labs, Residence Halls.

## LOCAL ATTRACTIONS

New Orleans, Audubon Zoo, Aquarium of the Americas, Jackson Square, local restaurants.

# SOUTHERN UNIVERSITY AND AGRICULTURAL AND MECHANICAL COLLEGE
**Baton Rouge, Louisiana**

**Contact:** Patrick Carpenter or Carlette Woodard, Recruiters, PO Box 9901, Baton Route, LA 70813. *Phone:* 504-771-2430. *Fax:* 504-771-2500. *Visit location:* Office of Admissions and Recruitment, Room 113, T.H. Harris Hall, PO Box 9901.

## QUICK FACTS

Enrollment: 9,791; UG: 8,340. Entrance: noncompetitive. SAT>500: N/R; ACT>18: 31%. Resident tuition and fees: $2068. Nonresident tuition and fees: $5852. Room and board: $3270. Application deadline: 7/1.

## GENERAL

State-supported, comprehensive, coed. Part of Southern University System. Awards associate, bachelor's, master's, doctoral, and first professional degrees. Founded 1880. Setting: 964-acre suburban campus. Undergraduate faculty: 539 (458 full-time, 81 part-time); student-faculty ratio is 18:1.

## CAMPUS VISITS

**College Calendar 1998–99:** *Regular classes:* Aug. 24–Dec. 2; Jan. 11–Apr. 28; June 9–July 27. *Breaks:* Nov. 26–29; Mar. 28–Apr. 5; July 5; Dec. 11–Jan. 3; May 7–June 4; July 30–Aug. 15. *Final exams:* Dec. 3–9; Apr. 29–May 5; July 28–29. *Special campus days:* Fall Graduation, Dec. 11.

## VISIT OPPORTUNITIES

| | Appointments? | Who? |
|---|---|---|
| **Campus Tour** | required | |
| **Information Session** | not required | open to all |
| **Admission Interview** | not required | open to all |
| **Classroom Visit** | required | |

**Information Sessions:** M–F; 20 minutes.

**Interviews:** M–F; 20 minutes.

**Campus Tours:** Conducted by students and admission reps. M–F; 60 minutes.

**Class Visits:** Arrangement must be made in advance.

## CAMPUS FACILITIES

**Of Special Interest:** John B. Cade Library.

## LOCAL ATTRACTIONS

Red Stick (commemorative spot for the highest point of the Mississippi River).

# TULANE UNIVERSITY
### New Orleans, Louisiana

**Contact:** Office of Undergraduate Admission, 6823 St Charles Avenue, New Orleans, LA 70118-5669. *Phone:* toll-free 800-873-9283. *Web site:* http://www.tulane.edu/ *Visit location:* Undergraduate Admission, Gibson Hall, Room 210, 6823 St. Charles Avenue.

### QUICK FACTS

Enrollment: 10,910; UG: 6,609. Entrance: very difficult. SAT>500: 95% V, 95% M; ACT>18: N/R. Tuition and fees: $22,720. Room and board: $6600. Application deadline: 1/15.

### GENERAL

Independent, university, coed. Awards associate, bachelor's, master's, doctoral, and first professional degrees. Founded 1834. Setting: 110-acre urban campus. Undergraduate faculty: 758 (434 full-time, 324 part-time); student-faculty ratio is 10:1. Most popular recent majors: biology, English, psychology.

### CAMPUS VISITS

**College Calendar 1998–99:** *Regular classes:* Sept. 2–Dec. 10; Jan. 13–Apr. 28. *Breaks:* Nov. 25–29; Feb. 15–16; Mar. 28–Apr. 4. *Final exams:* Dec. 14–22; May 3–11. *Admission office closed:* Good Friday, Apr. 2; Mardi Gras, Feb. 15–16; Yom Kippur, Sept. 30. *Special campus days:* Homecoming, Oct. 17; Parent's Weekend, Oct. 3.

### VISIT OPPORTUNITIES

|  | Appointments? | Who? |
|---|---|---|
| **Campus Tour** | required | open to all |
| **Information Session** | required | open to all |
| **Classroom Visit** | not required | open to all |
| **Faculty Meeting** | required | open to all |
| **Overnight Visit** | required | open to all |

**Information Sessions:** M–F at 9:00 am, 2:00 pm; Sat. during academic year at 9:00 am; 30 minutes.
**Campus Tours:** Conducted by students. M–F at 9:30 am, 2:30 pm; Sat. during academic year at 9:30 am; 75 minutes.

**Class Visits:** Certain predetermined classrooms are open to visitors.
**Overnight Visits:** During the regular academic year, prospective applicants may spend an evening in a residence hall with a student host.
**Video:** Free on request.

### CAMPUS FACILITIES

**Science:** Appointment Required: Boggs Center for Engineering and Biotechnology, Merry I. and Sam Israel, Jr. Environmental Sciences Building.
**Arts:** Appointment Required: Woldenberg Art Center, Elleonora P. McWilliams Hall (Theatre and Dance), Dixon Hall and Dixon Performing Arts Center (Music).
**Athletic:** Reily Recreation Center; Appointment Required: James W. Wilson Center for Intercollegiate Athletics, Turchin Stadium, Goldring Tennis Center and Track Stadium.
**Of Special Interest:** University Center, Howard-Tilton Memorial Library.

### LOCAL ATTRACTIONS

Amistad Research Center for the Study of Ethnic Minorities; Middle American Research Institute; Audubon Parkland Zoological Gardens; Aquarium of the Americas; French Market Garden District; Antique District; Riverboat Cruise.

# MAINE

# BATES COLLEGE
### Lewiston, Maine

**Contact:** Mr. Wylie L. Mitchell, Dean of Admissions, 23 Campus Avenue, Lewiston, ME 04240. *Phone:* 207-786-6000. *Fax:* 207-786-6025. *E-mail:* admissions@bates.edu *Web site:* http://www.bates.edu/ *Visit location:* Admissions Office, Lindholm House, 23 Campus Avenue.

### QUICK FACTS

Enrollment: 1,611; UG: 1,611. Entrance: most difficult. SAT>500: 97% V, 100% M; ACT>18: N/R. Comprehensive fee: $28,650. Room and board: N/App. Application deadline: 1/15.

### GENERAL

Independent, 4-year, coed. Awards bachelor's degrees. Founded 1855. Setting: 109-acre suburban campus. Faculty: 176 (152 full-time, 24 part-time);

*Bates College (continued)*

student-faculty ratio is 11:1. Most popular recent majors: biology, psychology, English.

### CAMPUS VISITS

**College Calendar 1998–99:** *Regular classes:* Sept. 9–Dec. 11; Jan. 11–Apr. 9; Apr. 26–May 28. *Breaks:* Oct. 20–25; Apr. 17–25; Nov. 21–29. *Final exams:* Dec. 15–19; Apr. 13. *Special campus days:* Alumni Weekend, June 11–13; Commencement, May 31.

### VISIT OPPORTUNITIES

|  | Appointments? | Who? |
|---|---|---|
| **Campus Tour** | not required | open to all |
| **Admission Interview** | required | open to all |
| **Classroom Visit** | not required | open to all |
| **Faculty Meeting** | required | open to all |
| **Overnight Visit** | required | open to all |

**Interviews:** M–F; 50 minutes.

**Campus Tours:** Conducted by students. M–F at 10:00 am, 11:00 am, 12:00 pm, 2:00 pm, 3:00 pm, 4:00 pm; M–F (Dec.–Mar.) at 10:00 am, 12:00 pm, 2:00 pm, 4:00 pm; 60 minutes.

**Class Visits:** Prospective students may attend a class in their area of interest.

**Overnight Visits:** During the regular academic year, prospective applicants may spend an evening in a residence hall with a student host.

**Video:** Available, fee charged.

### CAMPUS FACILITIES

**Of Special Interest:** Ladd Library.

# BOWDOIN COLLEGE
**Brunswick, Maine**

**Contact:** Kristin Steinman, 5000 College Station, Admissions Office, Brunswick, ME 04011-8441. *Phone:* 207-725-3100. *Fax:* 207-725-3101. *E-mail:* ksteinma@henry.bowdoin.edu *Web site:* http://www.bowdoin.edu/ *Visit location:* Admissions Office, Chamberlain Hall, College Street.

### QUICK FACTS

Enrollment: 1,597; UG: 1,597. Entrance: most difficult. SAT>500: 96% V, 99% M; ACT>18: N/App. Tuition and fees: $22,905. Room and board: $6115. Application deadline: 1/1.

### GENERAL

Independent, 4-year, coed. Awards bachelor's degrees. Founded 1794. Setting: 110-acre small-town campus with easy access to Portland. Faculty: 163 (137 full-time, 26 part-time); student-faculty ratio is 11:1. Most popular recent majors: political science, biology, history.

### CAMPUS VISITS

**College Calendar 1998–99:** *Regular classes:* Sept. 3–Dec. 9; Jan. 25–May 11. *Breaks:* Oct. 16–21; Mar. 19–Apr. 5; Nov. 25–30. *Final exams:* Dec. 14–21; May 16–22. *Special campus days:* Commencement, May 29; Homecoming, Oct. 24.

### VISIT OPPORTUNITIES

|  | Appointments? | Who? |
|---|---|---|
| **Campus Tour** | not required | open to all |
| **Information Session** | not required | open to all |
| **Admission Interview** | required | open to all |
| **Classroom Visit** | not required | open to all |
| **Overnight Visit** | required | open to all |

**Information Sessions:** M–F and select Sat. during academic year; M–F and Sat. during summer; 60 minutes.

**Interviews:** M–F, select Sat.; available Sat. mornings Sept.–Dec.; 45 minutes.

**Campus Tours:** Conducted by students. M–F, select Sat. at 9:00 am, 11:00 am, 2:00 pm, 4:00 pm; Sat. at 11:00 am; call for vacation period schedule.

**Class Visits:** Prospective students may attend a class in their area of interest.

**Overnight Visits:** During the regular academic year, prospective applicants may spend an evening in a residence hall with a student host.

### CAMPUS FACILITIES

**Science:** Druckenmiller Hall, Coastal Studies Center.

**Arts:** Bowdoin College Museum of Art, Visual Arts Center.

**Athletic:** Farley Field House, Watson Fitness Center.

**Of Special Interest:** Arctic Museum, Smith Union.

### LOCAL ATTRACTIONS

Joshua Chamberlain Museum.

# COLBY COLLEGE
### Waterville, Maine

**Contact:** Admissions and Financial Aid Office, 4800 Mayflower Hill, Waterville, ME 04901-8848. *Phone:* 207-872-3168 or toll-free 800-723-3032. *Fax:* 207-872-3474. *E-mail:* admissions@colby.edu *Web site:* http://www.colby.edu/ *Visit location:* Office of Admissions and Financial Aid, Lunder House, 4800 Mayflower Hill.

## QUICK FACTS
Enrollment: 1,753; UG: 1,753. Entrance: most difficult. SAT>500: 99% V, 99% M; ACT>18: 100%. Comprehensive fee: $29,190. Room and board: N/App. Application deadline: 1/15.

## GENERAL
Independent, 4-year, coed. Awards bachelor's degrees. Founded 1813. Setting: 714-acre small-town campus. Faculty: 157 (145 full-time, 12 part-time); student-faculty ratio is 11:1. Most popular recent majors: biology, English, political science.

## CAMPUS VISITS
**College Calendar 1998–99:** *Regular classes:* Sept. 9–Dec. 11; Jan. 4–28; Feb. 3–May 7. *Breaks:* Oct. 19–20; Jan. 29–Feb. 1; Mar. 20–28; Nov. 25–29. *Final exams:* Dec. 16–21; May 12–17.

## VISIT OPPORTUNITIES

|                     | Appointments? | Who?        |
|---------------------|---------------|-------------|
| **Campus Tour**     | not required  | open to all |
| **Information Session** | not required | open to all |
| **Admission Interview** | required  | open to all |
| **Classroom Visit** | recommended   | open to all |
| **Overnight Visit** | required      | open to all |

**Information Sessions:** M–F at 10:45 am, 2:45 pm; group sessions only Jan. through May 1; 45 minutes.

**Interviews:** M–F 8:45 am–3:45 pm; Sat. at 8:45 am, 9:45 am, 10:45 am; no individual interviews Jan. 15–May 1; 45 minutes.

**Campus Tours:** Conducted by students. M–F at 9:30 am, 10:30 am, 11:30 am, 1:30 pm, 2:30 pm, 3:30 pm; Sat. at 9:30 am, 10:30 am, 11:30 am; M–F (Jun. 1 to mid-Dec.) at 9:30 am, 10:30 am, 11:30 am, 12:30 pm, 1:30 pm, 2:30 pm, 3:30 pm; M–F (mid Jan. to May 31) at 9:30 am, 11:30 am, 1:30 pm, 3:30 pm; Sat. (Labor Day to Jan. 15) at 9:30 am, 10:30 am, 11:30 am; Sat. (Jan. 15 to May 1) at 9:30 am, 11:30 am, 1:30 pm, 3:30 pm; Sat. during Apr. at 11:00 am; 60 minutes.

**Class Visits:** Prospective students may attend a class in their area of interest.

**Overnight Visits:** During the regular academic year, prospective applicants may spend an evening in a residence hall with a student host.

## CAMPUS FACILITIES
**Science:** Olin Science Center.

**Arts:** Colby Art Museum.

**Athletic:** Harold Alfond Athletic Center.

**Of Special Interest:** Cotter Union (Student Center), Miller Library.

# SAINT JOSEPH'S COLLEGE
### Standish, Maine

**Contact:** Kathy Armstrong, St. Joseph's College, 278 Whites Bridge Road, Standish, ME 04084. *Phone:* toll-free 800-338-7057. *Fax:* 207-893-7862. *E-mail:* admissions@sjcme.edu *Web site:* http://www.sjcme. edu/ *Visit location:* Office of Admissions, St. George Hall, St. Joseph's College.

## QUICK FACTS
Enrollment: 4,630; UG: 3,600. Entrance: moderately difficult. SAT>500: 53% V, 48% M; ACT>18: N/R. Tuition and fees: $11,710. Room and board: $5530. Application deadline: rolling.

## GENERAL
Independent, comprehensive, coed, Roman Catholic Church. Awards associate, bachelor's, and master's degrees. Founded 1912. Setting: 330-acre small-town campus. Undergraduate faculty: 96 (53 full-time, 43 part-time). Most popular recent majors: nursing, business administration, elementary education.

## CAMPUS VISITS
**College Calendar 1998–99:** *Regular classes:* Sept. 8–Dec. 15; Jan. 11–Apr. 28. *Breaks:* Oct. 10–13; Mar. 6–14; Nov. 25–29; Apr. 1–5. *Final exams:* Dec. 16–19; Apr. 29–May 4. *Special campus days:* Commencement Exercises, May 8; Fall Open House, Oct. 23.

*Saint Joseph's College (continued)*

## VISIT OPPORTUNITIES

| | Appointments? | Who? |
|---|---|---|
| **Campus Tour** | recommended | applicants and parents |
| **Admission Interview** | recommended | applicants and parents |
| **Classroom Visit** | required | applicants and parents |
| **Faculty Meeting** | required | applicants and parents |
| **Overnight Visit** | required | |

**Interviews:** M–F, select Sat.; unavailable during breaks in academic year.

**Campus Tours:** Conducted by students. M–F, select Sat.; unavailable during breaks in academic year; available in summer; 60 minutes.

**Class Visits:** Classroom visits are determined by the visit schedule.

**Overnight Visits:** During the regular academic year, prospective applicants may spend an evening in a residence hall with a student host.

## CAMPUS FACILITIES
**Of Special Interest:** Wellehan Library.

## LOCAL ATTRACTIONS
Old Port—Portland; L.L. Bean, Maine Mall; Point Sebago; Portland Museum of Art; Sunday River Ski Resort; Sebago Lake State Park.

# UNITY COLLEGE
**Unity, Maine**

**Contact:** Lucie Poirier, Assistant to the Dean for Admissions, PO Box 532, Unity, ME 04988-0532. *Phone:* 207-948-3131. *Fax:* 207-948-6277. *E-mail:* admissions@unity.unity.edu *Web site:* http://www.unity.edu/ *Visit location:* Admissions Office, Allison Hall Welcome Center, Unity College, Quaker Hill Road.

## QUICK FACTS
Enrollment: 505; UG: 505. Entrance: moderately difficult. SAT>500: 18% V, 13% M; ACT>18: N/R. Tuition and fees: $11,200. Room and board: $5200. Application deadline: rolling.

## GENERAL
Independent, 4-year, coed. Awards bachelor's degrees. Founded 1965. Setting: 205-acre rural campus. Faculty: 55 (36 full-time, 19 part-time); student-faculty ratio is 14:1.

## CAMPUS VISITS
**College Calendar 1998–99:** *Regular classes:* Sept. 2–Dec. 11; Jan. 27–May 7. *Breaks:* Nov. 23–27; Mar. 15–19; Dec. 17–Jan. 27. *Final exams:* Dec. 15–17; May 11–13.

## VISIT OPPORTUNITIES

| | Appointments? | Who? |
|---|---|---|
| **Campus Tour** | required | open to all |
| **Admission Interview** | required | open to all |
| **Classroom Visit** | required | open to all |
| **Faculty Meeting** | required | open to all |
| **Overnight Visit** | required | open to all |

**Interviews:** M–F, select Sat.; 60 minutes.

**Campus Tours:** Conducted by students and admission reps. M–F 9:00 am–3:00 pm; select Sat. 8:30 am–12:00 pm; 60 minutes.

**Class Visits:** Prospective students may attend a class in their area of interest.

**Overnight Visits:** During the regular academic year, prospective applicants may spend an evening in a residence hall with a student host.

**Video:** Free on request.

## CAMPUS FACILITIES
**Of Special Interest:** Dorothy Webb Quimby Library.

# UNIVERSITY OF MAINE
**Orono, Maine**

**Contact:** Admissions Office, 5713 Chadbourne Hall, Orono, ME 04469-5713. *Phone:* 207-581-1561. *Fax:* 207-581-1213. *E-mail:* um-admit@maine.edu *Web site:* http://www.ume.maine.edu/ *Visit location:* Visitors Center, Chadbourne Hall.

## QUICK FACTS
Enrollment: 8,406; UG: 6,451. Entrance: moderately difficult. SAT>500: 73% V, 74% M; ACT>18: N/R.

Resident tuition and fees: $4344. Nonresident tuition and fees: $11,214. Room and board: $4906. Application deadline: rolling.

## GENERAL

State-supported, university, coed. Part of University of Maine System. Awards bachelor's, master's, and doctoral degrees. Founded 1865. Setting: 3,298-acre small-town campus. Undergraduate faculty: 634 (486 full-time, 148 part-time); student-faculty ratio is 14:1. Most popular recent majors: business administration, elementary education, nursing.

## CAMPUS VISITS

**College Calendar 1998–99:** *Regular classes:* Aug. 31–Dec. 11; Dec. 28–Jan. 8; Jan. 11–Apr. 30. *Breaks:* Oct. 9–13; Feb. 26–Mar. 15; Nov. 25–30. *Final exams:* Dec. 14–18; May 3–7. *Special campus days:* Commencement, May 8; Family and Friends, Sept. 25–27; Homecoming, Oct. 16–18; Maine Day, Apr. 21.

## VISIT OPPORTUNITIES

| | Appointments? | Who? |
|---|---|---|
| **Campus Tour** | recommended, not required | applicants and parents |
| **Information Session** | recommended, not required | |
| **Admission Interview** | recommended | applicants and parents |
| **Classroom Visit** | recommended, not required | |
| **Faculty Meeting** | required | applicants and parents |
| **Overnight Visit** | required | |

**Information Sessions:** M–F, Sat. at 9:00 am, 11:00 am, 1:00 pm; 15 minutes.
**Interviews:** M–F; 30 minutes.
**Campus Tours:** Conducted by students. M–F, Sat.; 60 minutes.
**Class Visits:** Certain predetermined classrooms are open to visitors.
**Overnight Visits:** During the regular academic year.
**Video:** Free on request.

## CAMPUS FACILITIES

**Science:** Global Sciences Center, Sawyer Environmental Research Center, Advanced Wood Composites Engineering Center, Ornamental Gardens.
**Arts:** Carnegie Art Museum, Hudson Museum, Class of 1944 Hall, Pavilion Theatre.

**Athletic:** Alfond Sports Arena, Latti Fitness Center, Alfond Stadium.
**Of Special Interest:** Planetarium, Mahaney Diamond Clubhouse, D.P. Corbett Business Building.

# UNIVERSITY OF NEW ENGLAND
### Biddeford, Maine

**Contact:** Mary Sinkewjz, Office of Admissions, Hills Beach Road, Biddeford, ME 04005. *Phone:* 207-283-0171 Ext. 2287 or toll-free 800-477-4UNE. *Fax:* 207-286-3678. *E-mail:* msinkewjz@mailbox.une.edu *Web site:* http://www.une.edu/ *Visit location:* Admissions Office, Admissions House, 592 Pool Road.

## QUICK FACTS

Enrollment: 2,416; UG: 1,324. Entrance: moderately difficult. SAT>500: 54% V, 59% M; ACT>18: N/R. Tuition and fees: $14,830. Room and board: $5820. Application deadline: rolling.

## GENERAL

Independent, comprehensive, coed. Awards associate, bachelor's, master's, and first professional degrees. Founded 1953. Setting: 410-acre small-town campus. Undergraduate faculty: 179 (110 full-time, 69 part-time); student-faculty ratio is 19:1. Most popular recent majors: occupational therapy, physical therapy, nursing.

## CAMPUS VISITS

**College Calendar 1998–99:** *Regular classes:* Sept. 8–Dec. 17; Jan. 12–May 13. *Final exams:* Dec. 17–21; May 3–7. *Special campus days:* Commencement, May 8.

## VISIT OPPORTUNITIES

| | Appointments? | Who? |
|---|---|---|
| **Campus Tour** | required | open to all |
| **Information Session** | required | open to all |
| **Admission Interview** | required | open to all |
| **Classroom Visit** | required | |
| **Faculty Meeting** | required | applicants and parents |
| **Overnight Visit** | required | admitted applicants only |

**Information Sessions:** M–F at 10:00 am, 1:00 pm; 60 minutes.

*University of New England (continued)*

**Interviews:** M–F; 60 minutes.

**Campus Tours:** Conducted by students and admission reps. M–F at 10:00 am, 1:00 pm; Sat. at 1:00 pm; 60 minutes.

**Class Visits:** Prospective students may attend a class in their area of interest.

**Overnight Visits:** During the regular academic year, prospective applicants may spend an evening in a residence hall with a student host.

### CAMPUS FACILITIES

**Science:** Alfond Center for Health Science—University Campus.

**Arts:** Appointment Required: Payson Gallery—West Brook College Campus.

**Athletic:** Campus Center—University Campus.

**Of Special Interest:** Children Center—Westbrook College Campus.

### LOCAL ATTRACTIONS

Resort areas of Kennebunkport, Old Orchard Beach; Old Port Section of Portland.

# MARYLAND

## HOOD COLLEGE
### Frederick, Maryland

**Contact:** Gina Gruden, Assistant to the Director of Admission, 401 Rosemont Avenue, Frederick, MD 21701. *Phone:* toll-free 800-922-1599. *Fax:* 301-696-3819. *E-mail:* ggruden@nimue.hood.edu *Web site:* http://www.hood.edu *Visit location:* Admissions Office, Strawn Cottage, 401 Rosemont Avenue.

### QUICK FACTS

Enrollment: 1,856; UG: 1,022. Entrance: moderately difficult. SAT>500: 80% V, 77% M; ACT>18: N/R. Tuition and fees: $16,418. Room and board: $6592. Application deadline: 3/1.

### GENERAL

Independent, comprehensive, primarily women, United Church of Christ. Awards bachelor's and master's degrees (also offers adult program with significant enrollment not reflected in profile). Founded 1893. Setting: 50-acre suburban campus with easy access to Baltimore and Washington, DC. Undergraduate faculty: 86 (72 full-time, 14 part-

time); student-faculty ratio is 10:1. Most popular recent majors: business administration, education, biology.

### CAMPUS VISITS

**College Calendar 1998–99:** *Regular classes:* Aug. 24–Dec. 9. *Breaks:* Oct. 8–12; Nov. 25–30. *Final exams:* Dec. 11–15. *Special campus days:* Blazer Days, Sept. 24–25, Oct. 15–16, Nov. 14, Jan. 28–29; Scholars' Weekend, Nov. 22–23, Feb. 21–22; Spring Reception, Apr. 10.

### VISIT OPPORTUNITIES

|  | Appointments? | Who? |
|---|---|---|
| **Campus Tour** | recommended, not required | open to all |
| **Information Session** | recommended, not required | open to all |
| **Admission Interview** | required | open to all |
| **Classroom Visit** | required | open to all |
| **Faculty Meeting** | required | open to all |
| **Overnight Visit** | required | open to all |

**Information Sessions:** Vary with related campus programs; inquire for schedule.

**Interviews:** M–F, select Sat.; inquire for schedule during campus programs; 30 minutes.

**Campus Tours:** Conducted by students. M–F, Sat. 9:00 am–4:30 pm; 50 minutes.

**Class Visits:** Prospective students may attend a class in their area of interest.

**Overnight Visits:** During the regular academic year, prospective applicants may spend an evening in a residence hall with a student host.

**Video:** Free on request.

### CAMPUS FACILITIES

**Of Special Interest:** Campus Center, Language Lab, Child Development Lab.

### LOCAL ATTRACTIONS

Downtown historic Frederick, original Hood College site.

## JOHNS HOPKINS UNIVERSITY
### Baltimore, Maryland

**Contact:** Office of Undergraduate Admissions, 3400 North Charles Street/140 Garland Hall, Baltimore,

MD 21218-2699. *Phone:* 410-516-8171. *Fax:* 410-516-6025. *Web site:* http://www.jhu.edu/ *Visit location:* Office of Undergraduate Admissions, 140 Garland Hall, 3400 North Charles Street.

## QUICK FACTS

Enrollment: 5,022; UG: 3,656. Entrance: most difficult. SAT>500: 99% V, 100% M; ACT>18: 100%. Tuition and fees: $21,700. Room and board: $7355. Application deadline: 1/1.

## GENERAL

Independent, university, coed. Awards bachelor's, master's, and doctoral degrees. Founded 1876. Setting: 140-acre urban campus with easy access to Washington, DC. Undergraduate faculty: 413 (361 full-time, 52 part-time); student-faculty ratio is 10:1. Most popular recent majors: biology, bioengineering, international relations.

## CAMPUS VISITS

**College Calendar 1998–99:** *Regular classes:* Sept. 3–Dec. 8; Jan. 25–May 3. *Breaks:* Nov. 26–29; Mar. 15–21; Dec. 19–Jan. 3. *Final exams:* Dec. 11–18; May 7–14. *Admission office closed:* Martin Luther King, Jr. Day, Jan. 18; Presidents Day, Feb. 15; mid-year vacation, Dec. 19–Jan. 3. *Special campus days:* Commencement, May 27; Moving-in Day, Aug. 29; Open House Program; Registration, Sept. 1–2.

## VISIT OPPORTUNITIES

|  | Appointments? | Who? |
| --- | --- | --- |
| **Campus Tour** | not required | open to all |
| **Information Session** | not required | open to all |
| **Admission Interview** | required | open to all |
| **Classroom Visit** | not required | open to all |
| **Faculty Meeting** | recommended | open to all |
| **Overnight Visit** | required | open to all |

**Information Sessions:** M–F at 11:00 am, 2:00 pm; select Sat. at 11:00 am; check school's campus visit planner Web page; 60 minutes.

**Interviews:** M–F; two weeks notice recommended; local alumni interviews available around the country; 55 minutes.

**Campus Tours:** Conducted by students. M–F at 10:00 am, 12:00 pm, 3:00 pm; select Sat. at 12:00 pm; check school's campus visit planner Web page; 60 minutes.

**Class Visits:** Prospective students may attend a class in their area of interest, certain predetermined classrooms are open to visitors.

**Overnight Visits:** During the regular academic year, prospective applicants may spend an evening in a residence hall with a student host.

## CAMPUS FACILITIES

**Science:** Center for Alternatives to Animal Testing, Center for Language and Speech Processing, Chemical Propulsion Agency, Genome Database (Human Genome Project), Krieger Mind/Brain Institute, Applied Physics Laboratory (APL); Appointment Required: The John Hopkins School of Medicine, School of Nursing, School of Hygiene and Public Health and Hospital, Hopkins-Ultraviolet Telescope, which has flown twice in the Space Shuttle with a Hopkins physicist as accompany scientist (1990s), The Space Telescope Science Institute (STScI).

**Arts:** The Peabody Institute, The Baltimore Museum of Art And Bufano Sculpture Gardens.

**Athletic:** Indoor rock climbing wall, competition-size pool, separate diving pool, 2 gymnasia, squash, handball, paddleball and basketball courts, fencing, wrestling, dance, aerobics, conditioning, weight rooms, sauna, outdoor track, outdoor tennis courts,, lacrosse/football/soccer/field hockey stadium, baseball field, boat house, The National Lacrosse Hall of Fame.

**Of Special Interest:** Levering Union, Language Teaching Center, Center for Digital Media Research and Development, Archaeology Museum, Milton S. Eisenhower Library.

## LOCAL ATTRACTIONS

National Aquarium; Maryland Science Center and Davis Planetarium at the Inner Harbor; Orioles Park and Ravens Stadium at Camden Yards; shopping, dining and live music in Little Italy and Fell's Point; The Walter's Art Gallery; Edgar Allen Poe House and Museum; the Baltimore Zoo; Great Blacks in Wax Museum; Star-spangled Banner Flag House and 1812 Museum.

# LOYOLA COLLEGE
**Baltimore, Maryland**

**Contact:** Undergraduate Admissions Office, 4501 North Charles Street, Baltimore, MD 21210. *Phone:* toll-free 800-221-9107 Ext. 2252 (in-state). *Web site:*

*Loyola College (continued)*

http://www.loyola.edu/ *Visit location:* Undergraduate Admissions Office, Humanities Building, 4501 North Charles Street.

## QUICK FACTS
Enrollment: 6,191; UG: 3,234. Entrance: moderately difficult. SAT>500: 93% V, 93% M; ACT>18: N/App. Tuition and fees: $16,560. Room and board: $7240. Application deadline: 1/15.

## GENERAL
Independent Roman Catholic (Jesuit), comprehensive, coed. Awards bachelor's, master's, and doctoral degrees and post-master's certificates. Founded 1852. Setting: 89-acre urban campus with easy access to Washington, DC. Undergraduate faculty: 452 (225 full-time, 227 part-time); student-faculty ratio is 14:1. Most popular recent majors: business administration, psychology, communications.

## CAMPUS VISITS
**College Calendar 1998–99:** *Regular classes:* Aug. 31–Dec. 9; Jan. 11–Apr. 28. *Breaks:* Nov. 25–29; Mar. 1–7. *Final exams:* Dec. 11–19; Apr. 30–May 8. *Admission office closed:* Christmas, Dec. 24–Jan. 1; Thanksgiving, Nov. 26–27. *Special campus days:* College Days, Oct. 24; Open House, Nov. 21, Feb. 6; Parents' Weekend, Sept. 25–27; Undergraduate Commencement, May 15.

### VISIT OPPORTUNITIES

|                      | Appointments?              | Who?        |
| -------------------- | -------------------------- | ----------- |
| **Campus Tour**      | recommended, not required  | open to all |
| **Information Session** | recommended, not required | open to all |
| **Admission Interview** | required                | open to all |
| **Classroom Visit**  | required                   | open to all |
| **Faculty Meeting**  | required                   | open to all |

**Information Sessions:** M–F at 10:00 am, 1:30 pm; available Sept. 12, Sept. 19, Oct. 3, Oct. 10, Oct. 31, Nov. 7, Nov. 14, Dec. 5, Jan. 16, Jan. 23, Jan. 30, Feb. 13, Mar. 13, and Mar. 20 at 11:00 am; 45 minutes.

**Interviews:** M–F; 20 minutes.

**Campus Tours:** Conducted by students. M–F; follows information session; may not be available during final exams; 45 minutes.

**Class Visits:** Prospective students may attend a class in their area of interest.

**Video:** Free on request.

## CAMPUS FACILITIES
**Science:** The Donnelly Science Complex.

**Arts:** Art Gallery/Julio Fine Arts wing.

**Athletic:** Three court gymnasium, Olympic-sized indoor pool, fitness centers, world's fifth largest artificial turf athletic field.

**Of Special Interest:** Loyola/Notre Dame Library, Alumni Memorial Chapel; Appointment Required: Nine multimedia classrooms, Speech and hearing clinic.

## LOCAL ATTRACTIONS
Baltimore's Inner Harbor; Oriole Park at Camden Yards.

# MARYLAND INSTITUTE, COLLEGE OF ART
**Baltimore, Maryland**

**Contact:** Debra Lally, Administrative Assistant, 1300 Mount Royal Avenue, Baltimore, MD 21217. *Phone:* 410-225-2222. *Fax:* 410-225-2337. *E-mail:* admissions@mica.edu *Web site:* http://www.mica.edu/ *Visit location:* Office of Undergraduate Admission, Main Building, 1300 Mount Royal Avenue.

## QUICK FACTS
Enrollment: 1,143; UG: 991. Entrance: very difficult. SAT>500: 88% V, 75% M; ACT>18: N/R. Tuition and fees: $16,760. Room and board: $5200. Application deadline: 2/1.

## GENERAL
Independent, comprehensive, coed. Awards bachelor's and master's degrees. Founded 1826. Setting: 12-acre urban campus. Undergraduate faculty: 178 (82 full-time, 96 part-time); student-faculty ratio is 6:1. Most popular recent majors: art, graphic design/commercial art/illustration, painting.

## CAMPUS VISITS
**College Calendar 1998–99:** *Regular classes:* Aug. 31–Dec. 18; Jan. 19–May 7. *Breaks:* Oct. 17–20; Mar. 21–28; Nov. 25–29. *Final exams:* Dec. 14–22; May 3–11. *Admission office closed:* Dec. 22–Jan. 3. *Special campus days:* Commencement, May 19; Parents Weekend, Feb. 26–28; Portfolio Day/Open House, Dec. 6; Spring Open House, Apr. 11.

## VISIT OPPORTUNITIES

|                      | Appointments? | Who?                        |
| -------------------- | ------------- | --------------------------- |
| Campus Tour          | required      | open to all                 |
| Information Session  | required      | admitted applicants only    |
| Admission Interview  | required      | open to all                 |
| Classroom Visit      | required      | open to all                 |
| Faculty Meeting      | required      | applicants only             |
| Overnight Visit      | required      | admitted applicants only    |

**Information Sessions:** Selected Apr. weekdays; limited to accepted scholarship finalist applicants.

**Interviews:** M–F; summer available in Jul. only; 60 minutes.

**Campus Tours:** Conducted by students. M–F at 10:30 am, 1:30 pm; available when classes in session; 75 minutes.

**Class Visits:** Prospective students may attend a class in their area of interest.

**Overnight Visits:** During the regular academic year, prospective applicants may spend an evening in a residence hall with a student host.

## CAMPUS FACILITIES

**Arts:** Major Art Galleries on campus exhibiting works of students, faculty, alumni and other renowned artists.

**Of Special Interest:** Computer Facilities, Residential Housing; Appointment Required: Independent Studios.

## LOCAL ATTRACTIONS

Baltimore's Seaport—the Inner Harbor; Major Art Museums.

# MOUNT SAINT MARY'S COLLEGE AND SEMINARY
### Emmitsburg, Maryland

**Contact:** Mount Saint Mary's College, Admissions Office, 16300 Old Emmitsburg Road, Emmitsburg, MD 21727. *Phone:* toll-free 800-448-4347. *Fax:* 301-447-5755. *Web site:* http://www.msmary.edu/ *Visit location:* Admissions Office, Bradley Building, 16300 Old Emmitsburg Road.

## QUICK FACTS

Enrollment: 1,758; UG: 1,358. Entrance: moderately difficult. SAT>500: 75% V, 71% M; ACT>18: N/R. Tuition and fees: $15,650. Room and board: $6450. Application deadline: 3/1.

## GENERAL

Independent Roman Catholic, comprehensive, coed. Awards bachelor's, master's, and first professional degrees. Founded 1808. Setting: 1,400-acre rural campus with easy access to Baltimore and Washington, DC. Undergraduate faculty: 149 (106 full-time, 43 part-time); student-faculty ratio is 15:1. Most popular recent majors: business administration, accounting, elementary education.

## CAMPUS VISITS

**College Calendar 1998–99:** *Regular classes:* Aug. 24–Dec. 11; Jan. 11–Apr. 30. *Breaks:* Oct. 10–18; Feb. 27–Mar. 7. *Final exams:* Dec. 14–18; May 3–7. *Admission office closed:* Christmas Break, Dec. 25–Jan. 1; Easter Break, Apr. 1–5; Thanksgiving Break, Nov. 26–27; Winter Holiday, Mar. 8. *Special campus days:* Baccalaureate, May 15; Commencement, May 16; Easter Break, Apr. 1–6; Family Weekend, Sept. 25–27; Honors Convocation, Apr. 25; New Student Orientation, Aug. 21–23; Thanksgiving Break, Nov. 25–29.

## VISIT OPPORTUNITIES

|                      | Appointments?             | Who?        |
| -------------------- | ------------------------- | ----------- |
| Campus Tour          | recommended, not required | open to all |
| Information Session  | recommended               | open to all |
| Admission Interview  | recommended, not required | open to all |
| Classroom Visit      | recommended               | open to all |
| Faculty Meeting      | required                  | open to all |
| Overnight Visit      | required                  | open to all |

**Information Sessions:** Available during Open Houses, call for schedule.

**Interviews:** M–F, select Sat.; arrangements for time and dates may be made through Admissions.

**Campus Tours:** Conducted by students. M–F, select Sat.; 60 minutes.

**Class Visits:** Prospective students may attend a class in their area of interest.

**Overnight Visits:** During the regular academic year, prospective applicants may spend an evening in a residence hall with a student host.

*Mount Saint Mary's College and Seminary (continued)*

**Video:** Free on request.

### CAMPUS FACILITIES
**Science:** COAD Science Building.

**Arts:** Flynn Hall (Visual and Performing Arts Building); Appointment Required: Barrett Hall (Art Building).

**Athletic:** ARCC (Athletic Recreation Convocation Complex).

### LOCAL ATTRACTIONS
The Grotto of Lourdes Shrine; Saint Elizabeth Ann Seton Shrine; Gettysburg Battlefield.


## ST. JOHN'S COLLEGE
### Annapolis, Maryland

**Contact:** Mr. John Christensen, Director of Admission, PO Box 2800, Annapolis, MD 21404. *Phone:* toll-free 800-727-9238. *Fax:* 410-269-7916. *E-mail:* admissions@sjca.edu *Web site:* http://www.sjca.edu/ *Visit location:* Admissions Office, Carroll-Barrister House, St. John's College.

### QUICK FACTS
Enrollment: 534; UG: 455. Entrance: moderately difficult. SAT>500: 99% V, 90% M; ACT>18: N/App. Tuition and fees: $21,180. Room and board: $6010. Application deadline: rolling.

### GENERAL
Independent, comprehensive, coed. Awards bachelor's and master's degrees. Founded 1784. Setting: 36-acre small-town campus with easy access to Baltimore and Washington, DC. Undergraduate faculty: 78 (65 full-time, 13 part-time); student-faculty ratio is 8:1.

### CAMPUS VISITS
**College Calendar 1998–99:** *Regular classes:* Aug. 27–Dec. 10; Jan. 4–May 14. *Breaks:* Dec. 11–Jan. 3; Feb. 26–Mar. 14. *Admission office closed:* Dec. 24–Jan. 1.

### VISIT OPPORTUNITIES

|  | Appointments? | Who? |
| --- | --- | --- |
| **Campus Tour** | required | open to all |
| **Information Session** | required | open to all |

|  | Appointments? | Who? |
| --- | --- | --- |
| **Admission Interview** | required | open to all |
| **Classroom Visit** | required | open to all |
| **Overnight Visit** | required | open to all |

**Information Sessions:** M–F at 10:00 am, 2:00 pm; 60 minutes.

**Interviews:** Tue. and Fri. for students participating in overnight visit program; 30 minutes.

**Campus Tours:** Conducted by students and admission reps. M–F at 10:00 am, 2:00 pm; campus tour and interactive talk with student guide and/or admissions counselor; 60 minutes.

**Class Visits:** Certain predetermined classrooms are open to visitors, classroom visits are determined by the visit schedule, classroom visit includes a full sample freshman schedule.

**Overnight Visits:** During the regular academic year and over the summer, prospective applicants may spend an evening in a residence hall.

### CAMPUS FACILITIES
**Arts:** Art Gallery.

**Athletic:** Gymnasium.

**Of Special Interest:** McDowall Hall (historic building—1742)).

### LOCAL ATTRACTIONS
Historic Annapolis; U.S. Naval Academy.


## ST. MARY'S COLLEGE OF MARYLAND
### St. Mary's City, Maryland

**Contact:** Office of Admissions, Somerset 102, St. Mary's City, MD 20686. *Phone:* toll-free 800-492-7181. *Fax:* 301-862-0906. *E-mail:* admissions@honors.smcm.edu *Web site:* http://www.smcm.edu/ *Visit location:* Office of Admissions.

### QUICK FACTS
Enrollment: 1,523; UG: 1,523. Entrance: very difficult. SAT>500: 97% V, 95% M; ACT>18: N/R. Resident tuition and fees: $6875. Nonresident tuition and fees: $11,125. Room and board: $5645. Application deadline: 1/15.

## GENERAL

State-supported, 4-year, coed. Part of Maryland State Colleges and Universities System. Awards bachelor's degrees. Founded 1840. Setting: 275-acre rural campus. Faculty: 162 (110 full-time, 52 part-time); student-faculty ratio is 14:1. Most popular recent majors: biology, psychology, economics.

## CAMPUS VISITS

**College Calendar 1998–99:** *Regular classes:* Aug. 31–Dec. 11; Jan. 18–May 4. *Breaks:* Nov. 24–30; Mar. 15–20. *Final exams:* Dec. 14–18; May 6–11. *Admission office closed:* Christmas break, Dec. 21–Jan. 4; Thanksgiving break, Nov. 25–29. *Special campus days:* Commencement, May 15.

## VISIT OPPORTUNITIES

|  | Appointments? | Who? |
|---|---|---|
| **Campus Tour** | required | open to all |
| **Admission Interview** | required | applicants and parents |
| **Classroom Visit** | required | applicants only |
| **Faculty Meeting** | required | applicants and parents |

**Interviews:** M–F; 60 minutes.

**Campus Tours:** Conducted by students. M–F; 90 minutes.

**Class Visits:** Prospective students may attend a class in their area of interest.

**Video:** Free on request.

## CAMPUS FACILITIES

**Of Special Interest:** Baltimore Hall.

## LOCAL ATTRACTIONS

Historic St. Mary's City.

# UNIVERSITY OF MARYLAND, COLLEGE PARK

## College Park, Maryland

**Contact:** Undergraduate Admissions, College Park, MD 20742-5045. *Phone:* toll-free 800-422-5867. *E-mail:* um-admit@uga.umd.edu *Web site:* http://www.umcp.umd.edu/ *Visit location:* Office of Undergraduate Admissions, Mitchell Building.

QUICK FACTS

## QUICK FACTS

Enrollment: 32,041; UG: 23,784. Entrance: moderately difficult. SAT>500: 89% V, 89% M; ACT>18: N/R. Resident tuition and fees: $4460. Nonresident tuition and fees: $10,589. Room and board: $5667. Application deadline: 2/15.

## GENERAL

State-supported, university, coed. Part of University System of Maryland. Awards bachelor's, master's, and doctoral degrees and post-master's certificates. Founded 1856. Setting: 3,773-acre suburban campus with easy access to Baltimore and Washington, DC. Undergraduate faculty: 1,955 (1,519 full-time, 436 part-time); student-faculty ratio is 13:1. Most popular recent majors: criminology, psychology, accounting.

## CAMPUS VISITS

**College Calendar 1998–99:** *Regular classes:* Aug. 31–Dec. 11; Jan. 28–May 14. *Breaks:* Nov. 26–29; Mar. 22–28; Dec. 20–Jan. 27. *Final exams:* Dec. 14–19; May 17–22. *Admission office closed:* Dec. 25–Jan. 1, Mar. 22–23. *Special campus days:* All-Niter, Sept. 25; Commencement, May 24; Family Weekend, Oct. 2–4; First Look Fair, Sept. 23–24; Homecoming, Oct. 12–18.

## VISIT OPPORTUNITIES

|  | Appointments? | Who? |
|---|---|---|
| **Campus Tour** | not required | open to all |
| **Information Session** | required | open to all |
| **Admission Interview** | recommended, not required | open to all |
| **Classroom Visit** | required | open to all |
| **Faculty Meeting** | required | open to all |
| **Overnight Visit** | required | open to all |

**Information Sessions:** M–F at 11:00 am; Sat. at 10:00 am; 60 minutes.

**Interviews:** M–F; Dec. 1 to Feb. 1; 30 minutes.

**Campus Tours:** Conducted by students. M–F at 10:00 am, 11:00 am, 1:00 pm, 3:00 pm; Sat. at 10:00 am; call for times during Dec., Jan., Jun., Jul., and Aug.; 60 minutes.

**Class Visits:** Classroom visits are determined by the visit schedule.

**Overnight Visits:** During the regular academic year, prospective applicants may spend an evening in a residence hall with a student host.

*University of Maryland, College Park (continued)*

## CAMPUS FACILITIES
**Science:** Appointment Required: Engineering Wind Tunnel, Space Systems Laboratory.
**Arts:** Art Gallery; Appointment Required: Maryland Center for the Performing Arts.
**Athletic:** Campus Recreation Center, Cole Field House, Byrd Stadium.

## LOCAL ATTRACTIONS
Washington, D.C., National Mall, Monuments, Museums; Baltimore Inner Harbor.

# UNIVERSITY OF MARYLAND EASTERN SHORE
**Princess Anne, Maryland**

**Contact:** Recruitment Office, Bird Hall, Princess Anne, MD 21853. *Phone:* toll-free 800-232-UMES. *Fax:* 410-651-7922. *Web site:* http://www.umes.umd. edu/ *Visit location:* Recruitment, Bird Hall, University of Maryland Eastern Shore.

## QUICK FACTS
Enrollment: 3,204; UG: 2,908. Entrance: moderately difficult. SAT>500: 23% V, 18% M; ACT>18: N/R. Resident tuition and fees: $3240. Nonresident tuition and fees: $7777. Room and board: $4330. Application deadline: rolling.

## GENERAL
State-supported, university, coed. Part of University System of Maryland. Awards bachelor's, master's, and doctoral degrees. Founded 1886. Setting: 700-acre rural campus. Undergraduate faculty: 280 (215 full-time, 65 part-time).

## CAMPUS VISITS
**College Calendar 1998–99:** *Regular classes:* Aug. 31–Dec. 11. *Final exams:* Dec. 14–18.

## VISIT OPPORTUNITIES

|  | Appointments? | Who? |
|---|---|---|
| **Campus Tour** | recommended, not required | open to all |
| **Information Session** | recommended | open to all |
| **Admission Interview** | recommended | open to all |
| **Classroom Visit** | required | |

|  | Appointments? | Who? |
|---|---|---|
| **Faculty Meeting** | required | open to all |

**Information Sessions:** M–F 9:00 am–2:00 pm; 60 minutes.
**Interviews:** M–F, select Sat.; 60 minutes.
**Campus Tours:** Conducted by students and admission reps. M–F 9:00 am–2:00 pm; Sat. 10:00 am–12:00 pm; 45 minutes.
**Class Visits:** Certain predetermined classrooms are open to visitors.
**Video:** Free on request.

## CAMPUS FACILITIES
**Science:** Appointment Required: George Washington Carver Hall, Henry O. Tanner Hall.
**Arts:** Appointment Required: Mosely Art Gallery, Ella Fitzgerald Center for the Performing Arts.
**Athletic:** Physical and Health Education Center.
**Of Special Interest:** Appointment Required: Richard A. Henson Center.

# WASHINGTON COLLEGE
**Chestertown, Maryland**

**Contact:** Kevin L. Coveney, Vice President for Admissions, 300 Washington Avenue, Chestertown, MD 21620. *Phone:* toll-free 800-422-1782 Ext. 7700. *Fax:* 410-778-7287. *E-mail:* kevin.coveney@washcoll. edu *Web site:* http://www.washcoll.edu/ *Visit location:* Admission Office, Casey Academic Center, Washington College 300 Washington Avenue.

## QUICK FACTS
Enrollment: 1,083; UG: 1,003. Entrance: moderately difficult. SAT>500: 78% V, 74% M; ACT>18: N/R. Tuition and fees: $18,250. Room and board: $5740. Application deadline: 2/15.

## GENERAL
Independent, comprehensive, coed. Awards bachelor's and master's degrees. Founded 1782. Setting: 120-acre small-town campus with easy access to Baltimore and Washington, DC. Undergraduate faculty: 103 (74 full-time, 29 part-time); student-faculty ratio is 12:1. Most popular recent majors: English, psychology, business administration.

## CAMPUS VISITS
**College Calendar 1998–99:** *Regular classes:* Aug. 31–Dec. 11; Jan. 20–May 6. *Breaks:* Dec. 20–Jan. 20. *Final exams:* Dec. 14–19; May 10–14.

## VISIT OPPORTUNITIES

| | Appointments? | Who? |
|---|---|---|
| **Campus Tour** | required | open to all |
| **Information Session** | required | open to all |
| **Admission Interview** | required | open to all |
| **Classroom Visit** | required | open to all |
| **Faculty Meeting** | required | open to all |
| **Overnight Visit** | required | open to all |

**Information Sessions:** Select Sat.; 90 minutes.
**Interviews:** M–F, select Sat.; 45 minutes.
**Campus Tours:** Conducted by students. M–F, select Sat.; 45 minutes.
**Class Visits:** Prospective students may attend a class in their area of interest.
**Overnight Visits:** During the regular academic year, prospective applicants may spend an evening in a residence hall with a student host.
**Video:** Available.

## CAMPUS FACILITIES
**Of Special Interest:** Clifton M. Miller Library.

# WESTERN MARYLAND COLLEGE
## Westminster, Maryland

**Contact:** Donna Phipps, Admissions Coordinator for Campus Visitations, 2 College Hill, Westminster, MD 21157. *Phone:* toll-free 800-638-5005. *Fax:* 410-857-2757. *E-mail:* admissio@wmdc.edu *Web site:* http://www.wmdc.edu/ *Visit location:* Admissions Office, Carroll Hall, 2 College Hill.

## QUICK FACTS
Enrollment: 2,739; UG: 1,464. Entrance: moderately difficult. SAT>500: 73% V, 71% M; ACT>18: N/App. Tuition and fees: $17,730. Room and board: $5350. Application deadline: 3/15.

## GENERAL
Independent, comprehensive, coed. Awards bachelor's and master's degrees. Founded 1867. Setting: 160-acre small-town campus with easy access to Baltimore and Washington, DC. Undergraduate

faculty: 213 (89 full-time, 124 part-time); student-faculty ratio is 13:1. Most popular recent majors: sociology, communications, biology.

## CAMPUS VISITS
**College Calendar 1998–99:** *Regular classes:* Aug. 31–Dec. 11; Jan. 4–22; Jan. 25–May 7. *Breaks:* Oct. 9–14; Mar. 12–22; Nov. 24–29. *Final exams:* Dec. 14–18; May 10–14. *Admission office closed:* Dec. 24–Jan. 3. *Special campus days:* Commencement, May 22; Fall Open House, Nov. 1, Nov. 15; Homecoming, Oct. 17; New Students Orientation, Aug. 27–30; Senior Week, May 15–21; Winter Visit Day, Feb. 7.

## VISIT OPPORTUNITIES

| | Appointments? | Who? |
|---|---|---|
| **Campus Tour** | recommended | open to all |
| **Admission Interview** | required | open to all |
| **Classroom Visit** | required | open to all |
| **Faculty Meeting** | required | open to all |

**Interviews:** M–F; select Sat. 9:00 am–12:00 pm; 30 minutes.
**Campus Tours:** Conducted by students. M–F at 10:30 am, 2:00 pm; Sat. 9:00 am–12:00 pm; 60 minutes.
**Class Visits:** Prospective students may attend a class in their area of interest.

## CAMPUS FACILITIES
**Science:** Appointment Required: Lewis Hall of Science.
**Arts:** Alumni Hall; Appointment Required: Art Studio, Peterson Hall and Rice Art Gallery.
**Athletic:** Appointment Required: Gill Gym, Gill Physical Education Learning Center.
**Of Special Interest:** Appointment Required: Hoover Library, Hill Hall.

## LOCAL ATTRACTIONS
Carroll County Farm Museum; college hosts NFL Baltimore Ravens Summer Training Camp; Union Mills Homestead; Antietam; Cascade Lake; Catoctin State Park; Gettysburg; Ski Liberty.

# MASSACHUSETTS

# AMHERST COLLEGE
## Amherst, Massachusetts

**Contact:** Admission Officer, PO Box 5000, South Pleasant Street, Amherst, MA 01002. *Phone:* 413-542-

*Amherst College (continued)*

2328. *Fax:* 413-542-2040. *E-mail:* admissions@ amhurst.edu *Web site:* http://www.amherst.edu/ *Visit location:* Office of Admissions, Wilson Admission, South Pleasant Street.

## QUICK FACTS

Enrollment: 1,642; UG: 1,642. Entrance: most difficult. SAT>500: 100% V, 100% M; ACT>18: 100%. Tuition and fees: $23,027. Room and board: $6080. Application deadline: 12/31.

## GENERAL

Independent, 4-year, coed. Awards bachelor's degrees. Founded 1821. Setting: 964-acre small-town campus. Faculty: 204 (179 full-time, 25 part-time); student-faculty ratio is 9:1. Most popular recent majors: English, economics, biology.

## CAMPUS VISITS

**College Calendar 1998–99:** *Regular classes:* Sept. 8–Dec. 15; Jan. 4–22; Jan. 25–May 7. *Breaks:* Oct. 12–13; Mar. 13–21; Nov. 21–29. *Final exams:* Dec. 18–22; May 10–14. *Admission office closed:* Nov. 25–27, Dec. 24, July 3. *Special campus days:* Commencement, May 23; Family Weekend, Oct. 30–Nov. 1; Homecoming, Nov. 13–15; Reunion, May 26–30.

## VISIT OPPORTUNITIES

|  | Appointments? | Who? |
| --- | --- | --- |
| **Campus Tour** | not required | open to all |
| **Information Session** | not required | open to all |
| **Classroom Visit** | not required | open to all |
| **Faculty Meeting** | required | open to all |
| **Overnight Visit** | required | open to all |

**Information Sessions:** For groups M–F (Aug. 1 to Sept. 4) at 9:00 am, 11:00 am, 1:00 pm, 3:00 pm, M-F (Sept. 8 to Nov. 20) at 10:00 am, 12:00 pm, 2:00 pm; M–F (Dec. 7-23, Dec. 28-30) at 10:00 am; M–F (Jan. 4, 1999 to Jan. 22, 1999) at 10:00 am; M–F (Feb. 15-19 and Mar. 22 to May 28) at 10:00 am, 2:00 pm; Sat. (Aug. 15, 22, 29 and Sep. 19 to Nov. 14) at 11:00 am; 60 minutes.

**Campus Tours:** Conducted by students. M–F (Aug. to Sept. 4) at 10: am, 12:00 pm, 2:00 pm, 4:00 pm; M–F (Sept. 8 to Dec. 11 and Feb. 8 to May 7 and May 31 to Aug. 27) at 9:00 am, 11:00 am, 1:00 pm, 3:00 pm except Thanksgiving week; Sat. (Sept. 19 to Nov. 12, Dec. 5 and 12 ) at 10:00 am, 12:00 pm, 2:00

pm; Sun. (Sept. 20 to Nov. 14, Dec. 6 and 13) at 10:00 am, 12:00 pm, 2:00 pm; please call to confirm schedule; 60 minutes.

**Class Visits:** Prospective students may attend a class in their area of interest.

**Overnight Visits:** During the regular academic year, prospective applicants may spend an evening in a residence hall with a student host.

## CAMPUS FACILITIES

**Science:** Pratt Museum of Natural History, Merrill Science Center, Life Sciences Building.

**Arts:** Mead Art Museum, Fayerweather Hall.

**Athletic:** Athletic Complex.

**Of Special Interest:** Robert Frost Library, The Campus Center; Appointment Required: Emily Dickinson Homestead.

# ASSUMPTION COLLEGE
## Worcester, Massachusetts

**Contact:** Mary Bresnahan, Kathleen Murphy, Directors of Admission, 500 Salisbury Street, Worcester, MA 01615. *Phone:* toll-free 888-882-7786. *Fax:* 508-799-4412. *E-mail:* ugrad__admiss@assumption. edu *Web site:* http://www.assumption.edu/ *Visit location:* Office of Admissions, La Maison Francais, 500 Salisbury Street.

## QUICK FACTS

Enrollment: 2,574; UG: 2,203. Entrance: moderately difficult. SAT>500: 64% V, 57% M; ACT>18: N/R. Tuition and fees: $15,595. Room and board: $6400. Application deadline: 3/1.

## GENERAL

Independent Roman Catholic, comprehensive, coed. Awards associate, bachelor's, and master's degrees and post-master's certificates. Founded 1904. Setting: 145-acre urban campus with easy access to Boston. Undergraduate faculty: 221 (122 full-time, 99 part-time); student-faculty ratio is 14:1. Most popular recent majors: rehabilitation therapy, psychology, English.

## CAMPUS VISITS

**College Calendar 1998–99:** *Regular classes:* Aug. 31–Dec. 9; Jan. 20–May 5. *Breaks:* Mar. 6–14. *Final exams:* Dec. 10–18; May 6–15. *Special campus days:* Commencement, May 22; Parent/Alumni Weekend, Oct. 2–4.

## VISIT OPPORTUNITIES

| | Appointments? | Who? |
|---|---|---|
| **Campus Tour** | required | open to all |
| **Information Session** | required | open to all |
| **Admission Interview** | required | open to all |
| **Classroom Visit** | required | open to all |
| **Faculty Meeting** | required | open to all |

**Information Sessions:** Select Sat. during fall.

**Interviews:** M–F; 30 minutes.

**Campus Tours:** Conducted by students. M–F, select Sat.; 45 minutes.

**Class Visits:** Classroom visits are determined by the visit schedule.

**Video:** Free on request.

## CAMPUS FACILITIES

**Science:** Kennedy Science Building.

**Athletic:** Plourde Athletic Complex.

**Of Special Interest:** Living Learning Residence Hall, Library.

# BABSON COLLEGE

**Wellesley, Massachusetts**

**Contact:** Martha Heaney, Admission Service Team Member, Undergraduate Admission Office, Mustard Hall, Babson College, Babson Park, MA 02157. *Phone:* toll-free 800-488-3696. *Fax:* 781-239-4006. *E-mail:* ugradadmission@babson.edu *Web site:* http://www.babson.edu/ *Visit location:* Undergraduate Admission, Mustard Hall.

## QUICK FACTS

Enrollment: 3,336; UG: 1,692. Entrance: very difficult. SAT>500: 90% V, 96% M; ACT>18: N/R. Tuition and fees: $20,365. Room and board: $8100. Application deadline: 2/1.

## GENERAL

Independent, comprehensive, coed. Awards bachelor's and master's degrees. Founded 1919. Setting: 450-acre suburban campus with easy access to Boston. Undergraduate faculty: 204 (151 full-time, 53 part-time); student-faculty ratio is 11:1. Most popular recent majors: finance, business administration, business marketing and marketing management.

## CAMPUS VISITS

**College Calendar 1998–99:** *Regular classes:* Sept. 2–Dec. 11; Jan. 22–Apr. 30. *Breaks:* Nov. 21–29; Mar. 15–19; Dec. 20–Jan. 21. *Final exams:* Dec. 15–19; May 5–11. *Admission office closed:* Nov. 27, Dec. 24–25, Dec. 28–31, Jan. 1. *Special campus days:* Family Weekend, Oct. 30–Nov. 1; Founder's Day, Apr. 16; Graduation, May 15; Homecoming, Oct. 16; Orientation, Aug. 30–Sept. 1; Reunion, June 4–7; Student Organization Carnival, Sept. 4.

## VISIT OPPORTUNITIES

| | Appointments? | Who? |
|---|---|---|
| **Campus Tour** | not required | open to all |
| **Information Session** | not required | open to all |
| **Admission Interview** | required | open to all |
| **Classroom Visit** | required | open to all |
| **Overnight Visit** | required | open to all |

**Information Sessions:** Fri. at 2:00 pm; Sat. in the fall; 20 minutes.

**Interviews:** M–F, select Sat.; alumni interviews in local areas may be arranged by appointment; 45 minutes.

**Campus Tours:** Conducted by students. M–F at 9:45 am, 11:00 am, 1:15 pm, 3:00 pm; Sat. at 10:00 am, 2:00 pm; summer tours at 10:00 am, 2:00 pm; 60 minutes.

**Class Visits:** Prospective students may attend a class in their area of interest.

**Overnight Visits:** During the regular academic year, prospective applicants may spend an evening in a residence hall with a student host.

**Video:** Free on request.

## CAMPUS FACILITIES

**Arts:** The Richard Sorenson Center for the Arts, The Gallery (Horn Library).

**Athletic:** Webster Center.

**Of Special Interest:** The Donald W. Reynolds Campus Center, The Glaish Family Chapel.

## LOCAL ATTRACTIONS

Historic Boston, quaint center of Wellesley, and the Natick Mall.

# BERKLEE COLLEGE OF MUSIC

**Boston, Massachusetts**

**Contact:** Jackie Landry, Assistant Director of Admissions, 1140 Boylston Street, Boston, MA 02215.

*Berklee College of Music (continued)*

*Phone:* toll-free 800-421-0084 Ext. 2365. *Fax:* 617-747-2047. *E-mail:* admissions@berklee.edu *Web site:* http://www.berklee.edu/ *Visit location:* Office of Admissions, Uchida Building, 921 Boylston Street.

### QUICK FACTS
Enrollment: 2,933; UG: 2,933. Entrance: moderately difficult. SAT>500: N/App; ACT>18: N/App. Tuition and fees: $15,100. Room and board: $7890. Application deadline: rolling.

### GENERAL
Independent, 4-year, coed. Awards bachelor's degrees. Founded 1945. Faculty: 359 (142 full-time, 217 part-time); student-faculty ratio is 9:1.

### CAMPUS VISITS
**College Calendar 1998–99:** *Regular classes:* Sept. 8–Dec. 10; Jan. 19–Apr. 30. *Breaks:* Nov. 26–29; Mar. 13–21; Dec. 18–Jan. 12. *Final exams:* Dec. 11–17; May 3–7. *Special campus days:* Convocation; Freshman Orientation; Graduation, May 8; Welcome Barbecue.

### VISIT OPPORTUNITIES

|  | Appointments? | Who? |
|---|---|---|
| **Campus Tour** | recommended, not required | open to all |
| **Information Session** | recommended, not required | open to all |
| **Admission Interview** | recommended, not required | open to all |
| **Faculty Meeting** | required | |

**Information Sessions:** M–F at 10:00 am, 2:00 pm; select Sat. at 12:30 pm; reduced schedule during midterms, finals, and school breaks; 90 minutes.

**Interviews:** M–F, select Sat.; reduced schedule during midterms, finals, and school breaks; 45 minutes.

**Campus Tours:** Conducted by students. M–F, select Sat.; reduced schedule during midterms, finals, and school breaks; 90 minutes.

**Video:** Free on request.

### CAMPUS FACILITIES
**Of Special Interest:** Appointment Required: recording studios, midi-synthesizer labs, Berklee Performance Center.

### LOCAL ATTRACTIONS
City of Boston cultural and entertainment attractions.

# BOSTON COLLEGE
## Chestnut Hill, Massachusetts

**Contact:** Office of Undergraduate Admissions, Devlin Hall 208, Boston College, Chestnut Hill, MA 02167. *Phone:* toll-free 800-360-2522. *Fax:* 617-552-3290. *Web site:* http://www.bc.edu/ *Visit location:* Office of Undergraduate Admission, Devlin Hall 208, Boston College, 140 Commonwealth Avenue.

### QUICK FACTS
Enrollment: 13,640; UG: 8,921. Entrance: very difficult. SAT>500: 97% V, 99% M; ACT>18: N/R. Tuition and fees: $20,292. Room and board: $7770. Application deadline: 1/15.

### GENERAL
Independent Roman Catholic (Jesuit), university, coed. Awards bachelor's, master's, doctoral, and first professional degrees and post-master's certificates (also offers continuing education program with significant enrollment not reflected in profile). Founded 1863. Setting: 240-acre suburban campus with easy access to Boston. Undergraduate faculty: 1,117 (615 full-time, 502 part-time); student-faculty ratio is 15:1. Most popular recent majors: English, finance, psychology.

### CAMPUS VISITS
**College Calendar 1998–99:** *Regular classes:* Sept. 2–Dec. 8; Jan. 19–May 4. *Breaks:* Dec. 19–Jan. 18; Mar. 1–5; Apr. 1–5. *Final exams:* Dec. 11–18; May 7–14. *Admission office closed:* Sept. 7, Nov. 26–27, Dec. 21–25, Jan. 18, Apr. 2, Apr. 18, May 31. *Special campus days:* Commencement, May 24; Evening Football game, Oct. 8; Parents' Weekend, Sept. 18–20.

### VISIT OPPORTUNITIES

|  | Appointments? | Who? |
|---|---|---|
| **Campus Tour** | not required | open to all |
| **Information Session** | not required | open to all |
| **Classroom Visit** | required | open to all |
| **Faculty Meeting** | required | |

**Information Sessions:** M–F at 10:00 am, 2:00 pm; Columbus Day Oct. 12 at 9:00 am, 11:00 am;

available Sat. Sept. 26, Oct. 10, Oct. 31, Nov. 14, Nov. 21, Dec. 5; summer Jun. 2 to Aug. 21 at 10:30 am, 11:30 pm, 12:30 pm, 2:00 pm, 3:00 pm; not available Aug. 22 to Sept. 20, Nov. 23 to Nov. 29, Dec. 6 to Feb.14, Mar. 1 to Mar. 7, Apr. 1 to Apr. 5, May 1 to Jun. 2; 60 minutes.

**Campus Tours:** Conducted by students. M–F at 11:00 am, 12:00 pm, 1:00 pm, 3:00 pm; Sat. at 9:00 am, 11:00 am; Columbus Day Oct. 12 at 10:00 am, 12:00 pm; available Sat. Sept. 26, Oct. 10, Oct. 31, Nov. 14, Nov. 21, Dec. 5; summer Jun. 2 to Aug. 22 at 10:30 am, 11:30 am, 12:30 pm, 2:00 pm, 3:00 pm; not available Aug 22 to Sept. 20, Nov. 23 to Nov. 29, Dec. 6 to Feb. 14, Mar. 1 to Mar. 7, Apr.1 to Apr. 5, May, 1 to Jun. 2; 75 minutes.

**Class Visits:** Prospective students may attend a class in their area of interest.

## CAMPUS FACILITIES
**Science:** Merker Chemistry Center.
**Arts:** McMullen Art Museum.
**Athletic:** Conte Forum.
**Of Special Interest:** O'Neill Library, Bapst Library.

## LOCAL ATTRACTIONS
City of Boston; Freedom Trail; Paul Revere's Home; Museum of Fine Arts; Museum of Science; Quincy Market; The North End; Lexington and Concord; Harvard Square; Copley Square.

# BRADFORD COLLEGE
**Haverhill, Massachusetts**

**Contact:** Maryann Swochak, Admission Receptionist, 320 South Main Street, Haverhill, MA 01845. *Phone:* 978-372-7161 Ext. 5271 or toll-free 800-336-6448. *Fax:* 978-372-5240. *E-mail:* maswochak@bnet. bradford.edu *Web site:* http://www.Bradford.edu/ *Visit location:* Office of Admissions and Financial Advising, Greenleaf House, 11 Kingsbury Avenue.

## QUICK FACTS
Enrollment: 575; UG: 575. Entrance: moderately difficult. SAT>500: N/R; ACT>18: N/R. Tuition and fees: $16,315. Room and board: $6720. Application deadline: rolling.

## GENERAL
Independent, 4-year, coed. Awards bachelor's degrees. Founded 1803. Setting: 80-acre suburban campus with easy access to Boston. Faculty: 75 (33 full-time, 42 part-time); student-faculty ratio is 12:1.

Most popular recent majors: psychology, art, business marketing and marketing management.

## CAMPUS VISITS
**College Calendar 1998–99:** *Regular classes:* Sept. 9–Dec. 15; Jan. 13–Apr. 27. *Breaks:* Dec. 20–Jan. 12; Mar. 6–14. *Final exams:* Dec. 17–20; Apr. 29–May 3. *Special campus days:* Commencement, May 8.

## VISIT OPPORTUNITIES

|  | **Appointments?** | **Who?** |
|---|---|---|
| **Campus Tour** | required | applicants and parents |
| **Information Session** | required | |
| **Admission Interview** | required | applicants and parents |
| **Classroom Visit** | required | applicants and parents |
| **Faculty Meeting** | required | applicants and parents |
| **Overnight Visit** | required | |

**Information Sessions:** M–F at 10:00 am, 2:00 pm; call for special arrangements; 45 minutes.

**Interviews:** M–F; inquire for special events schedule; 45 minutes.

**Campus Tours:** Conducted by students. M–F at 9:00 am, 11:00 am, 1:00 pm, 3:00 pm; call for special arrangements; 45 minutes.

**Class Visits:** Prospective students may attend a class in their area of interest, classroom visits are determined by the visit schedule.

**Overnight Visits:** During the regular academic year, prospective applicants may spend an evening in a residence hall with a student host.

## CAMPUS FACILITIES
**Science:** Labs; Appointment Required: environmental/ecology site.
**Arts:** Visual arts studios, dance studio, theaters, art gallery.
**Athletic:** Appointment Required: Cederdale.
**Of Special Interest:** Dormitories, library; Appointment Required: support facilities.

## LOCAL ATTRACTIONS
Historical and seaside attractions.

# BRANDEIS UNIVERSITY
## Waltham, Massachusetts

**Contact:** Marilyn Walsh, Administrative, Brandeis University, Office of Admissions (MS003), Waltham, MA 02254. *Phone:* 781-736-3500 or toll-free 800-622-0622 (out-of-state). *Fax:* 781-736-3536. *E-mail:* sendinfo@brandeis.edu *Web site:* http://www.brandeis.edu/ *Visit location:* Admissions Office, Shapiro Admissions Center, 415 South Street.

## QUICK FACTS
Enrollment: 4,216; UG: 2,976. Entrance: very difficult. SAT>500: 99% V, 98% M; ACT>18: N/R. Tuition and fees: $22,851. Room and board: $6970. Application deadline: 2/1.

## GENERAL
Independent, university, coed. Awards bachelor's, master's, doctoral, and first professional degrees. Founded 1948. Setting: 235-acre suburban campus with easy access to Boston. Undergraduate faculty: 498 (342 full-time, 156 part-time); student-faculty ratio is 10:1. Most popular recent majors: psychology, economics, biology.

## CAMPUS VISITS
**College Calendar 1998–99:** *Regular classes:* Sept. 13–Dec. 14; Jan. 19–May 4. *Breaks:* Dec. 24–Jan. 18; Feb. 22–26. *Final exams:* Dec. 16–23; May 6–13.

## VISIT OPPORTUNITIES

|  | Appointments? | Who? |
| --- | --- | --- |
| **Campus Tour** | not required | open to all |
| **Information Session** | not required | open to all |
| **Admission Interview** | required | open to all |
| **Classroom Visit** | not required | open to all |
| **Faculty Meeting** | recommended | |
| **Overnight Visit** | required | open to all |

**Information Sessions:** M–F; available summer months only; call for other times and schedule; 45 minutes.

**Interviews:** M–F; 30 minutes.

**Campus Tours:** Conducted by students. M–F; weekends during Oct., Apr.; call for details; 60 minutes.

**Class Visits:** Prospective students may attend a class in their area of interest.

**Overnight Visits:** During the regular academic year, prospective applicants may spend an evening in a residence hall with a student host.

## CAMPUS FACILITIES
**Science:** Volen/National Center for Complex Systems, Gerstenzang Science Library, Science Labs/Classroom Complex, Rosenstiel Basic Medical Sciences Research Center.

**Arts:** Slosberg Music Center, Spingold Theatre, Goldman Schwartz-Pollack Art Building; Appointment Required: Rose Art Museum.

**Athletic:** Gosman Sports and Convocation Center.

**Of Special Interest:** Usdan Student Center, Goldfarb/Farber Library; Appointment Required: Residence Halls.

## LOCAL ATTRACTIONS
Historic Boston.

# CLARK UNIVERSITY
## Worcester, Massachusetts

**Contact:** Marisa Dionis, Campus Visit Coordinator, 950 Main Street, ATTN: Admissions House, Worcester, MA 01610. *Phone:* 508-793-7431 or toll-free 800-GO-CLARK (out-of-state). *Fax:* 508-793-8821. *E-mail:* mdionis@admissions.clarku.edu *Web site:* http://www.clarku.edu/ *Visit location:* Admissions House, 950 Main Street.

## QUICK FACTS
Enrollment: 2,861; UG: 2,047. Entrance: moderately difficult. SAT>500: 81% V, 82% M; ACT>18: 92%. Tuition and fees: $20,940. Room and board: $4250. Application deadline: 2/1.

## GENERAL
Independent, university, coed. Awards bachelor's, master's, and doctoral degrees and post-master's certificates. Founded 1887. Setting: 50-acre urban campus with easy access to Boston. Undergraduate faculty: 260 (172 full-time, 88 part-time); student-faculty ratio is 11:1. Most popular recent majors: psychology, political science, business administration.

## CAMPUS VISITS
**College Calendar 1998–99:** *Regular classes:* Aug. 29–Dec. 10; Jan. 19–May 3. *Breaks:* Oct. 16–21; Mar. 5–15. *Final exams:* Dec. 14–18; May 6–12. *Special campus days:* Academic Spree Day, Apr. 23; Commencement, May 23; Family Weekend, Oct. 2–4.

## VISIT OPPORTUNITIES

|  | Appointments? | Who? |
| --- | --- | --- |
| **Campus Tour** | recommended, not required | open to all |
| **Information Session** | recommended, not required | open to all |
| **Admission Interview** | required | open to all |
| **Classroom Visit** | required | open to all |
| **Faculty Meeting** | required | open to all |
| **Overnight Visit** | required | open to all |

**Information Sessions:** Sat. at 12:00 pm; M–F Jul. through Sept. 10:00 am–2:00 pm; call for available schedule; 45 minutes.

**Interviews:** M–F, Sat.; unavailable Sat. in Mar., Jun., Jul.; 30 minutes.

**Campus Tours:** Conducted by students. M–F at 10:30 am, 11:30 am, 2:30 pm, 3:30 pm; Sat. at 12:00 pm; Sat. tours unavailable during Jun. and Jul.; 45 minutes.

**Class Visits:** Prospective students may attend a class in their area of interest, certain predetermined classrooms are open to visitors.

**Overnight Visits:** During the regular academic year, prospective applicants may spend an evening in a residence hall with a student host.

### CAMPUS FACILITIES
**Of Special Interest:** Robert Hutchings Goddard Library.

# COLLEGE OF THE HOLY CROSS
**Worcester, Massachusetts**

**Contact:** Ann Bowe McDermott, Director of Admissions, 1 College Street, Worcester, MA 01610. *Phone:* 508-793-2443 or toll-free 800-442-2421. *Fax:* 508-793-3888. *E-mail:* admissions@holycross.edu *Web site:* http://www.holycross.edu/ *Visit location:* Admissions Office, Fenwick Hall, 1 College Street.

### QUICK FACTS
Enrollment: 2,710; UG: 2,710. Entrance: very difficult. SAT>500: 98% V, 97% M; ACT>18: N/App. Tuition and fees: $22,005. Room and board: $7100. Application deadline: 1/15.

### GENERAL
Independent Roman Catholic (Jesuit), 4-year, coed. Awards bachelor's degrees. Founded 1843. Setting: 174-acre suburban campus with easy access to Boston. Faculty: 261 (215 full-time, 46 part-time); student-faculty ratio is 13:1. Most popular recent majors: English, psychology, economics.

### CAMPUS VISITS
**College Calendar 1998–99:** *Regular classes:* Sept. 1–Dec. 7; Jan. 19–May 3. *Breaks:* Nov. 24–30; Mar. 5–15; Mar. 31–Apr. 6. *Final exams:* Dec. 11–18; May 7–14. *Admission office closed:* Good Friday, Apr. 2; day after Thanksgiving, Nov. 27. *Special campus days:* Commencement, May 28; Homecoming, Sept. 26; Open House for Prospective Students, Oct. 18, Nov. 15.

## VISIT OPPORTUNITIES

|  | Appointments? | Who? |
| --- | --- | --- |
| **Campus Tour** | not required | open to all |
| **Information Session** | not required | open to all |
| **Admission Interview** | required | open to all |
| **Classroom Visit** | required | open to all |
| **Faculty Meeting** | required | open to all |
| **Overnight Visit** | required | open to all |

**Information Sessions:** Available during summer and select Sat. in the fall; 30 minutes.

**Interviews:** M–F, select Sat.; Jun. 1 to Jan. 15 for seniors only.

**Campus Tours:** Conducted by students. M–F 9:00 am–4:00 pm; select Sat. at 10:00 am, 12:00 pm; fall semester 9:00 am–4:00 pm daily, when in session; remainder of year 9:00 am, 12:00 pm, 3:00 pm; 45 minutes.

**Class Visits:** Prospective students may attend a class in their area of interest.

**Overnight Visits:** During the regular academic year, prospective applicants may spend an evening in a residence hall with a student host.

**Video:** Free on request.

### CAMPUS FACILITIES
**Of Special Interest:** Dinand Library.

# EMERSON COLLEGE
**Boston, Massachusetts**

**Contact:** Office of Undergraduate Admission, 100 Beacon Street, Boston, MA 02116. *Phone:* 617-824-

*Emerson College (continued)*

8600. *Fax:* 617-824-8609. *E-mail:* admiss@emerson. edu *Web site:* http://www.emerson.edu/admiss/ *Visit location:* Office of Admission, The Berkeley Building, 420 Boylston Street, 3rd Floor.

## QUICK FACTS
Enrollment: 3,885; UG: 2,983. Entrance: moderately difficult. SAT>500: 94% V, 79% M; ACT>18: 94%. Tuition and fees: $17,826. Room and board: $8250. Application deadline: 2/1.

## GENERAL
Independent, comprehensive, coed. Awards bachelor's, master's, and doctoral degrees and first professional certificates. Founded 1880. Undergraduate faculty: 285 (101 full-time, 184 part-time); student-faculty ratio is 17:1. Most popular recent majors: mass communications, theater arts/drama, public relations.

## CAMPUS VISITS
**College Calendar 1998–99:** *Regular classes:* Sept. 14–Dec. 17; Jan. 19–Apr. 28. *Breaks:* Nov. 24–30; Mar. 6–14; Dec. 23–Jan. 18. *Final exams:* Dec. 19–22; Apr. 30–May 4. *Special campus days:* Athletic Open House, Feb. 13; Commencement, May 17; Family Weekend, Oct. 30–Nov. 1; Open House, Oct. 3, Nov. 14.

### VISIT OPPORTUNITIES

|  | Appointments? | Who? |
|---|---|---|
| **Campus Tour** | required | applicants and parents |
| **Information Session** | recommended | |
| **Admission Interview** | recommended | applicants and parents |
| **Classroom Visit** | | open to all |
| **Faculty Meeting** | required | |
| **Overnight Visit** | | applicants only |

**Information Sessions:** Mon., Tue., Thu., Fri.; select Sat. during academic year only; Mon., Wed., and Fri. during summer; held in conjunction with tour.

**Interviews:** M–F; select Sat.; 45 minutes.

**Campus Tours:** Conducted by students. Mon., Tue., Thu., Fri. at 10:00 am, 12:00 pm, 2:00 pm; select Sat. during academic year only; Mon., Wed., and Fri. during summer; 90 minutes.

**Class Visits:** Certain predetermined classrooms are open to visitors.

**Overnight Visits:** During the regular academic year, prospective applicants may spend an evening in a residence hall with a student host.

## CAMPUS FACILITIES
**Science:** The Robbins Speech, Language and Hearing Center, Thayer Lindsley Patient-Centered Nursery for hearing impaired children and their families.

**Arts:** Emerson Majestic Theatre, The Ansin Building.

**Athletic:** The Fitness Center.

**Of Special Interest:** The Library.

## LOCAL ATTRACTIONS
The Freedom Trail; Fanueil Hall; The Museum of Fine Arts; Fenway Park; Gardener Museum.

# ENDICOTT COLLEGE
**Beverly, Massachusetts**

**Contact:** Mr. Thomas J. Redman, Vice President of Admissions and Financial Aid, 376 Hale Street, Beverly, MA 01915. *Phone:* 978-921-1000 or toll-free 800-325-1114 (out-of-state). *Fax:* 978-232-2520. *Web site:* http://www.endicott.edu/ *Visit location:* Admissions, College Hall, 376 Hale Street.

## QUICK FACTS
Enrollment: 1,270; UG: 1,230. Entrance: moderately difficult. SAT>500: 43% V, 36% M; ACT>18: N/App. Tuition and fees: $14,040. Room and board: $7160. Application deadline: rolling.

## GENERAL
Independent, comprehensive, coed. Awards associate, bachelor's, and master's degrees. Founded 1939. Setting: 150-acre suburban campus with easy access to Boston. Undergraduate faculty: 161 (58 full-time, 103 part-time); student-faculty ratio is 12:1. Most popular recent majors: nursing, psychology, physical therapy assistant.

## CAMPUS VISITS
**College Calendar 1998–99:** *Regular classes:* Sept. 1–Dec. 11; Feb. 1–May 10. *Breaks:* Mar. 20–29. *Final exams:* Dec. 14–18; May 12–18.

## VISIT OPPORTUNITIES

| | Appointments? | Who? |
|---|---|---|
| **Campus Tour** | required | open to all |
| **Information Session** | required | open to all |
| **Admission Interview** | required | open to all |
| **Classroom Visit** | required | open to all |
| **Faculty Meeting** | required | open to all |
| **Overnight Visit** | required | open to all |

**Information Sessions:** Select Sat.; 240 minutes.

**Interviews:** M–F, select Sat.; 120 minutes.

**Campus Tours:** Conducted by students. M–F, select Sat.; 120 minutes.

**Class Visits:** Prospective students may attend a class in their area of interest.

**Overnight Visits:** During the regular academic year, prospective applicants may spend an evening in a residence hall with a student host.

**Video:** Free on request.

### CAMPUS FACILITIES

**Of Special Interest:** Appointment Required: Student Center, Residence Halls, Library.

# FRAMINGHAM STATE COLLEGE

**Framingham, Massachusetts**

**Contact:** Office of Admissions Services, 100 State Street, PO Box 9101, Framingham, MA 01701-9101. *Phone:* 508-626-4500. *Fax:* 508-626-4017. *Web site:* http://www.framingham.edu/ *Visit location:* Office of Admissions Services, Dwight Hall, Room 229, 100 State Street.

### QUICK FACTS

Enrollment: 4,584; UG: 3,530. Entrance: moderately difficult. SAT>500: 57% V, 46% M; ACT>18: N/R. Resident tuition and fees: $3150. Nonresident tuition and fees: $7830. Room and board: $3944. Application deadline: 3/15.

### GENERAL

State-supported, comprehensive, coed. Part of Massachusetts Public Higher Education System. Awards bachelor's and master's degrees. Founded 1839. Setting: 73-acre suburban campus with easy access to Boston. Undergraduate faculty: 288 (168 full-time, 120 part-time). Most popular recent majors: business administration, psychology, elementary education.

### CAMPUS VISITS

**College Calendar 1998–99:** *Regular classes:* Sept. 2–Dec. 14; Jan. 21–May 7. *Breaks:* Dec. 22–Jan. 17. *Final exams:* Dec. 16–22; May 10–14. *Special campus days:* Commencement, May 23.

## VISIT OPPORTUNITIES

| | Appointments? | Who? |
|---|---|---|
| **Campus Tour** | required | open to all |
| **Information Session** | required | open to all |
| **Admission Interview** | required | |
| **Classroom Visit** | required | open to all |

**Information Sessions:** Select Sat. at 10:00 am; Fri. at 10:00 am; offered fall and spring terms; 30 minutes.

**Interviews:** M–F; 30 minutes.

**Campus Tours:** Conducted by students. M–F 11:00 am–4:00 pm; select Sat. at 10:00 am; 45 minutes.

**Class Visits:** Prospective students may attend a class in their area of interest.

### CAMPUS FACILITIES

**Science:** Appointment Required: Planetarium, Food Pilot Plant Laboratory.

**Arts:** Mazmanian Gallery.

**Of Special Interest:** Curriculum Library; Appointment Required: Television Studio, Christa Corrigan McAuliffe Center.

# GORDON COLLEGE

**Wenham, Massachusetts**

**Contact:** Heidi Forget, Visitation Associate, 255 Grapevine Road, Wenham, MA 01984. *Phone:* toll-free 800-343-1379. *Fax:* 978-524-3722. *E-mail:* hforget@hope.gordonc.edu *Web site:* http://www.gordonc.edu/ *Visit location:* Admissions Office, Frost Hall, 255 Grapevine Road.

### QUICK FACTS

Enrollment: 1,375; UG: 1,348. Entrance: moderately difficult. SAT>500: 87% V, 79% M; ACT>18: N/R. Tuition and fees: $15,760. Room and board: $4950. Application deadline: rolling.

### GENERAL

Independent Christian, comprehensive, coed. Awards bachelor's and master's degrees. Founded 1889.

*Gordon College (continued)*

Setting: 500-acre small-town campus with easy access to Boston. Undergraduate faculty: 110 (75 full-time, 35 part-time); student-faculty ratio is 18:1. Most popular recent majors: English, psychology, biblical studies.

## CAMPUS VISITS

**College Calendar 1998–99:** *Regular classes:* Aug. 26–Dec. 10; Jan. 13–May 5. *Breaks:* Oct. 16–19; Mar. 6–15. *Final exams:* Dec. 14–17; May 7–12. *Special campus days:* Commencement, May 15; Homecoming, Oct. 9–11.

### VISIT OPPORTUNITIES

|  | Appointments? | Who? |
|---|---|---|
| Campus Tour | required | applicants and parents |
| Admission Interview | required |  |
| Classroom Visit | required | applicants and parents |
| Faculty Meeting | required | applicants and parents |
| Overnight Visit | required |  |

**Interviews:** M–F, Sat.; 45 minutes.

**Campus Tours:** Conducted by students. M–F, Sat.; 60 minutes.

**Class Visits:** Prospective students may attend a class in their area of interest.

**Overnight Visits:** During the regular academic year, prospective applicants may spend an evening in a residence hall with a student host.

**Video:** Free on request.

## CAMPUS FACILITIES

**Athletic:** Bennett Recreation and Athletic Center.

**Of Special Interest:** A.J. Gordon Memorial Chapel, Lane Student Center.

## LOCAL ATTRACTIONS

Local beaches; Salem, Cape Ann; Boston.

# HAMPSHIRE COLLEGE

**Amherst, Massachusetts**

**Contact:** Admissions Office, 893 West Street, Amherst, MA 01002. *Phone:* 413-582-5471. *Fax:*

413-582-5631. *E-mail:* haad@hampshire.edu *Web site:* http://www.hampshire.edu/ *Visit location:* Admissions Office, Stiles House, 893 West Street.

## QUICK FACTS

Enrollment: 1,141; UG: 1,141. Entrance: moderately difficult. SAT>500: 98% V, 86% M; ACT>18: 100%. Tuition and fees: $23,780. Room and board: $6225. Application deadline: 2/1.

## GENERAL

Independent, 4-year, coed. Awards bachelor's degrees. Founded 1965. Setting: 800-acre rural campus. Faculty: 92 (84 full-time, 8 part-time); student-faculty ratio is 12:1. Most popular recent majors: art, theater arts/drama, creative writing.

## CAMPUS VISITS

**College Calendar 1998–99:** *Regular classes:* Sept. 3–Dec. 10; Jan. 28–May 1. *Breaks:* Oct. 11–14; Mar. 14–22. *Final exams:* Dec. 11–16; May 4–8. *Special campus days:* Commencement, May 16; Family and Friends Weekend, Oct. 24–26; Student Orientation, Aug. 27–Sept. 2.

**Class Visits:** Faculty chooses appropriate class.

**Overnight Visits:** During the regular academic year, prospective applicants may spend an evening in a residence hall with a student host.

## CAMPUS FACILITIES

**Science:** Cole Science Lab, Farm Center.

**Arts:** Main gallery—library, film and photo gallery—Longsworth Arts Village.

**Athletic:** Robert Crown Center, Multi-sports Facility.

**Of Special Interest:** Canopy walk.

## LOCAL ATTRACTIONS

National Yiddish Book Center (Hampshire Campus); Emily Dickinson Homestead (Amherst Center).

# HARVARD UNIVERSITY

**Cambridge, Massachusetts**

**Contact:** Office of Admissions, Byerly Hall, 8 Garden Street, Cambridge, MA 02138. *Phone:* 617-495-1551. *Web site:* http://www.fas.harvard.edu/ *Visit location:* Office of Admissions, Byerly Hall, 8 Garden Street.

## QUICK FACTS

Enrollment: 17,425; UG: 6,630. Entrance: most difficult. SAT>500: N/R; ACT>18: N/R. Tuition and fees: $22,802. Room and board: $7278. Application deadline: 1/1.

## GENERAL

Independent, university, coed. Awards bachelor's, master's, doctoral, and first professional degrees. Founded 1636. Setting: 380-acre urban campus with easy access to Boston. Undergraduate faculty: 1,746; student-faculty ratio is 8:1. Most popular recent majors: economics, biology, political science.

## CAMPUS VISITS

**College Calendar 1998–99:** *Regular classes:* Sept. 16–Dec. 17; Feb. 3–May 7. *Breaks:* Dec. 18–Jan. 13; Mar. 27–Apr. 4; Jan. 28–Feb. 2. *Final exams:* Jan. 16–27; May 20–29.

## VISIT OPPORTUNITIES

|  | Appointments? | Who? |
|---|---|---|
| **Campus Tour** | not required | applicants and parents |
| **Information Session** | not required | |
| **Admission Interview** | required | |
| **Classroom Visit** | not required | |
| **Faculty Meeting** | required | |
| **Overnight Visit** | required | |

**Information Sessions:** M–F at 2:00 pm; M–F Apr. 1 to Nov. 26 at 10:00 am; Sat. Sept. 20 to Nov. 22 at 10:00 am; 60 minutes.

**Interviews:** M–F; available on campus Jun. through Aug. and Sept. through Nov.; applicants receive alumni/ae interviews in their local areas; 30 minutes.

**Campus Tours:** Conducted by students. M–F at 11:00 am, 3:00 pm; Sat. at 11:00 am; 75 minutes.

**Class Visits:** Certain predetermined classrooms are open to visitors.

**Overnight Visits:** During the regular academic year, prospective applicants may spend an evening in a residence hall with a student host.

**Video:** Available, fee charged.

## CAMPUS FACILITIES

**Of Special Interest:** Widener Library.

## LOCAL ATTRACTIONS

Cambridge and Boston attractions.

# MASSACHUSETTS COLLEGE OF LIBERAL ARTS

**North Adams, Massachusetts**

**Contact:** Admissions Office, 375 Church Street, North Adams, MA 01247-7100. *Phone:* toll-free 800-292-6632 (in-state). *Fax:* 413-662-5179. *E-mail:* admissions@mcla.mass.edu *Web site:* http://www.mcla.mass.edu/ *Visit location:* Admissions Office, Church Street.

## QUICK FACTS

Enrollment: 1,539; UG: 1,412. Entrance: moderately difficult. SAT>500: 50% V, 38% M; ACT>18: N/App. Resident tuition and fees: $3437. Nonresident tuition and fees: $8017. Room and board: $4840. Application deadline: rolling.

## GENERAL

State-supported, comprehensive, coed. Part of Massachusetts Public Higher Education System. Awards bachelor's and master's degrees. Founded 1894. Setting: 80-acre small-town campus. Undergraduate faculty: 136 (98 full-time, 38 part-time); student-faculty ratio is 14:1. Most popular recent majors: business administration, English, sociology.

## CAMPUS VISITS

**College Calendar 1998–99:** *Regular classes:* Sept. 1–Dec. 11; Jan. 20–May 19. *Breaks:* Dec. 19–Jan. 19; Mar. 15–28. *Final exams:* Dec. 12–18; May 20–26. *Admission office closed:* Nov. 27, Dec. 24–Jan. 4.

## VISIT OPPORTUNITIES

|  | Appointments? | Who? |
|---|---|---|
| **Campus Tour** | required | open to all |
| **Information Session** | required | open to all |
| **Admission Interview** | required | applicants only |
| **Classroom Visit** | required | open to all |
| **Faculty Meeting** | required | open to all |
| **Overnight Visit** | required | admitted applicants only |

**Information Sessions:** M–F at 12:00 pm; 30 minutes.

**Interviews:** M–F; 30 minutes.

**Campus Tours:** Conducted by students. M–F at 12:00 pm; 60 minutes.

*Massachusetts College of Liberal Arts (continued)*

**Class Visits:** Classroom visits are determined by the visit schedule.

**Overnight Visits:** During the regular academic year, prospective applicants may spend an evening in a residence hall with a student host.

## CAMPUS FACILITIES
**Of Special Interest:** Freel Library.

# MASSACHUSETTS INSTITUTE OF TECHNOLOGY
**Cambridge, Massachusetts**

**Contact:** Admissions Office, Room 3-108, 77 Massachusetts Avenue, Cambridge, MA 02139. *Phone:* 617-258-5515. *Fax:* 617-258-8304. *E-mail:* mitfrosh@ mit.edu *Web site:* http://web.mit.edu/ *Visit location:* Admissions Office or Information Center, Rogers Building, 77 Massachusetts Avenue.

## QUICK FACTS
Enrollment: 9,862; UG: 4,363. Entrance: most difficult. SAT>500: 99% V, 100% M; ACT>18: 100%. Tuition and fees: $23,100. Room and board: $5610. Application deadline: 1/1.

## GENERAL
Independent, university, coed. Awards bachelor's, master's, and doctoral degrees. Founded 1861. Setting: 154-acre urban campus with easy access to Boston. Undergraduate faculty: 925 (903 full-time, 22 part-time); student-faculty ratio is 5:1. Most popular recent majors: electrical/electronics engineering, computer science, mechanical engineering.

## CAMPUS VISITS
**College Calendar 1998–99:** *Regular classes:* Sept. 9–Dec. 10; Jan. 4–29; Feb. 2–May 13. *Breaks:* Dec. 19–Jan. 3; Mar. 22–26. *Final exams:* Dec. 14–18; May 17–21. *Admission office closed:* Nov. 27. *Special campus days:* Commencement, June 4; Family Weekend, Oct. 16–17; Freshman Orientation (start date), Aug. 26.

## VISIT OPPORTUNITIES

| | Appointments? | Who? |
|---|---|---|
| **Campus Tour** | not required | open to all |
| **Information Session** | not required | open to all |

## VISIT OPPORTUNITIES—continued

| | Appointments? | Who? |
|---|---|---|
| **Admission Interview** | | applicants only |
| **Classroom Visit** | not required | open to all |
| **Faculty Meeting** | required | open to all |
| **Overnight Visit** | required | open to all |

**Information Sessions:** M–F, select Sat.; immediately follow campus tours; 45 minutes.

**Interviews:** Admissions interview are conducted in the applicant's home area by MIT alumni; waived if no alumni available; 60 minutes.

**Campus Tours:** Conducted by students. M–F at 10:00 am, 2:00 pm; Sat. in Apr. at 10:00 am; unavailable on national or legal holidays; 90 minutes.

**Class Visits:** Prospective students may attend a class in their area of interest.

**Overnight Visits:** During the regular academic year, prospective applicants may spend an evening in a residence hall with a student host.

## CAMPUS FACILITIES
**Science:** Academic Departments within the School of Science, Whitaker College of Health Sciences and Technology, Interdisciplinary Labs.

**Arts:** MIT Museum, List Visual Arts Center, Wolk Gallery and Compton Gallery, Wiesner Gallery.

**Athletic:** DuPont Athletic Center, Johnson Athletics Center.

**Of Special Interest:** Edgerton Center, Student Center, MIT Libraries.

## LOCAL ATTRACTIONS
Freedom Trail; Museum of Science and Fine Arts; Quincy Market.

# MOUNT HOLYOKE COLLEGE
**South Hadley, Massachusetts**

**Contact:** Anita Smith, Director of Admission, Office of Admission, South Hadley, MA 01075. *Phone:* 413-538-2023. *Fax:* 413-538-2409. *Web site:* http:// www.mtholyoke.edu/ *Visit location:* Admission, Newhall, 50 College Street.

## QUICK FACTS
Enrollment: 1,860; UG: 1,849. Entrance: very difficult. SAT>500: 99% V, 96% M; ACT>18:

100%. Tuition and fees: $22,340. Room and board: $6525. Application deadline: 1/15.

## GENERAL
Independent, 4-year, women only. Awards bachelor's degrees. Founded 1837. Setting: 800-acre small-town campus. Most popular recent majors: English, psychology, biology.

## CAMPUS VISITS
**College Calendar 1998–99:** *Regular classes:* Sept. 10–Dec. 22; Jan. 27–May 13. *Breaks:* Dec. 22–Jan. 26. *Final exams:* Dec. 18–22; May 7–13. *Special campus days:* Commencement, May 29; Preview for accepted students, Apr. 18–20; Spotlight program for juniors and seniors, Oct. 25–26.

### VISIT OPPORTUNITIES

| | Appointments? |
|---|---|
| **Campus Tour** | not required |
| **Information Session** | not required |
| **Admission Interview** | required |
| **Classroom Visit** | not required |
| **Faculty Meeting** | required |
| **Overnight Visit** | required |

**Information Sessions:** M–F at 11:00 am, 2:00 pm; available during Jun., Jul., and Aug.; 60 minutes.
**Interviews:** M–F, Sat.; 60 minutes.
**Campus Tours:** Conducted by students. M–F at 9:00 am, 10:00 am, 11:00 am, 1:00 pm, 2:00 pm, 3:00 pm; Sat. at 10:00 am, 11:00 am.
**Class Visits:** Certain predetermined classrooms are open to visitors.
**Overnight Visits:** During the regular academic year, prospective applicants may spend an evening in a residence hall with a student host.
**Video:** Free on request.

## CAMPUS FACILITIES
**Arts:** Appointment Required: Museum, Bronzing Studio.
**Athletic:** Appointment Required: Equestrian Center.

# NICHOLS COLLEGE
## Dudley, Massachusetts

**Contact:** Susan Montville, Admissions Assistant, PO Box 5000, Dudley, MA 01571. *Phone:* toll-free 800-470-3379. *Fax:* 508-943-9885. *E-mail:* admissions@nichols.edu *Web site:* http://www.nichols.edu/ *Visit location:* Office of Admission, Admissions and Financial Aid, PO Box 5000 (Center Road).

## QUICK FACTS
Enrollment: 1,542; UG: 1,266. Entrance: moderately difficult. SAT>500: 38% V, 38% M; ACT>18: N/R. Tuition and fees: $11,325. Room and board: $6400. Application deadline: rolling.

## GENERAL
Independent, comprehensive, coed. Awards associate, bachelor's, and master's degrees. Founded 1815. Setting: 210-acre rural campus with easy access to Boston. Undergraduate faculty: 76 (39 full-time, 37 part-time); student-faculty ratio is 22:1. Most popular recent majors: business administration, accounting, business marketing and marketing management.

## CAMPUS VISITS
**College Calendar 1998–99:** *Regular classes:* Aug. 31–Dec. 11; Jan. 11–Apr. 27. *Breaks:* Dec. 18–Nov. 11; Mar. 12–22. *Final exams:* Dec. 14–18; Apr. 29–May 4. *Special campus days:* Admissions Open House and Parents Day, Oct. 3; Alumni Career Day, Oct. 20; Athletic Open House, Nov. 21; Commencement, May 8; Homecoming, Oct. 24; Honors Banquet, Apr. 10; Spring Weekend, Apr. 17–18.
**Class Visits:** Classroom visits are determined by the visit schedule.
**Overnight Visits:** During the regular academic year, prospective applicants may spend an evening in a residence hall with a student host.

## CAMPUS FACILITIES
**Athletic:** Appointment Required: Chalmers Field House, Nichols College Golf Course.
**Of Special Interest:** Davis Hall, the Currier Center Institute for American Values, Shamic Hall—largest residence hall.

## LOCAL ATTRACTIONS
Old Sturbridge Village, Worcester Common Outlets, Worcester Art Museum, New England Science Center.

# NORTHEASTERN UNIVERSITY
## Boston, Massachusetts

**Contact:** Admissions Visitor Center, 139 Richards Hall, Boston, MA 02115. *Phone:* 617-373-2211. *Fax:*

*Northeastern University (continued)*

617-373-8780. *Web site:* http://www.neu.edu/ *Visit location:* Undergraduate Admissions Visitor Center, Richards Hall 139, 360 Huntington Avenue.

## QUICK FACTS
Enrollment: 24,325; UG: 19,691. Entrance: moderately difficult. SAT>500: 71% V, 75% M; ACT>18: 89%. Tuition and fees: $16,511. Room and board: $8265. Application deadline: rolling.

## GENERAL
Independent, university, coed. Awards associate, bachelor's, master's, doctoral, and first professional degrees and post-master's certificates. Founded 1898. Setting: 57-acre urban campus. Undergraduate faculty: 2,172 (733 full-time, 1,439 part-time); student-faculty ratio is 11:1. Most popular recent majors: criminal justice/law enforcement administration, nursing, physical therapy.

## CAMPUS VISITS
**College Calendar 1998–99:** *Regular classes:* Sept. 23–Dec. 8; Jan. 6–Mar. 12; Mar. 31–June 4. *Breaks:* Nov. 25–29; Mar. 22–26; May 31. *Final exams:* Dec. 11–17; Mar. 15–19; June 7–11. *Special campus days:* Commencement, June 19.

## VISIT OPPORTUNITIES

| | Appointments? | Who? |
|---|---|---|
| **Campus Tour** | not required | open to all |
| **Information Session** | not required | open to all |
| **Admission Interview** | required | open to all |

**Information Sessions:** M–F at 10:00 am, 2:00 pm; Sat. at 10:00 am, 11:00 am; Sat. unavailable during summer; 60 minutes.

**Interviews:** M–F 9:00 am–3:30 pm; 30 minutes.

**Campus Tours:** Conducted by students. M–F 9:00 am–3:00 pm; Sat. at 9:00 am, 10:00 am, 11:00 am; Sat. unavailable during summer; 60 minutes.

## CAMPUS FACILITIES
**Athletic:** Marino Recreation Center.

## LOCAL ATTRACTIONS
Boston Museum of Fine Arts; Boston Aquarium; Fanueil Hall, Quincy Market; Newbury Street.

# SMITH COLLEGE
## Northampton, Massachusetts

**Contact:** Office of Admission, Smith College, Office of Admission, 7 College Lane, Northampton, MA 01063. *Phone:* 413-585-2523. *Fax:* 413-585-2527. *E-mail:* admission@smith.edu *Web site:* http://www.smith.edu/ *Visit location:* Office of Admission, 7 College Lane.

## QUICK FACTS
Enrollment: 3,199; UG: 2,630. Entrance: very difficult. SAT>500: 99% V, 97% M; ACT>18: 100%. Tuition and fees: $21,512. Room and board: $7250. Application deadline: 1/15.

## GENERAL
Independent, comprehensive, women only. Awards bachelor's, master's, and doctoral degrees. Founded 1871. Setting: 125-acre urban campus with easy access to Hartford. Undergraduate faculty: 276 (254 full-time, 22 part-time); student-faculty ratio is 10:1. Most popular recent majors: political science, psychology, English.

## CAMPUS VISITS
**College Calendar 1998–99:** *Regular classes:* Sept. 8–Dec. 15; Jan. 25–Apr. 30. *Breaks:* Dec. 23–Jan. 24; Mar. 13–21; Oct. 10–13. *Final exams:* Dec. 19–22; May 4–7. *Special campus days:* Commencement, May 16; Family Weekend, Oct. 23–25; Opening Convocation, Sept. 7; Otelia Cromwell Day, Nov. 3; Rally Day, Feb. 17.

## VISIT OPPORTUNITIES

| | Appointments? | Who? |
|---|---|---|
| **Campus Tour** | not required | open to all |
| **Information Session** | not required | open to all |
| **Admission Interview** | required | open to all |
| **Classroom Visit** | not required | open to all |
| **Faculty Meeting** | recommended | open to all |
| **Overnight Visit** | required | open to all |

**Information Sessions:** M–F (Mar. 15–Jan. 31), Sat. (Jul. 19–Aug. 23) at 10:30 am and 12:00 pm; Sat. (Sept. 6–Jan. 24) at 10:30 am and 12:00 pm; 60 minutes.

**Interviews:** M–F (Mar. 15–Jan. 31) 9:00 am–3:00 pm, Sat. (Sept. 6–Jan.24) 9:00 am–12:00 pm; 45 minutes.

**Campus Tours:** Conducted by students. Sat. (Jul. 19–Aug. 23) at 9:30 am and 11:00 am; Sat. (Sept. 6–Jan. 24) at 10:00 am and 11:00 am; 60 minutes.

**Class Visits:** Prospective students may attend a class in their area of interest.

**Overnight Visits:** During the regular academic year, prospective applicants may spend an evening in a residence hall with a student host.

**Video:** Free on request.

### CAMPUS FACILITIES

**Science:** Clark Science Center, McConnell Hall, Bass Science Center.

**Arts:** Sage Hall (music), Mendenhall Center for Performing Arts, Berensen Dance Studio, Theater 14.

**Athletic:** Ainsworth Gym, Indoor Track and Tennis Facilities, Riding Stables and Rings.

**Of Special Interest:** Lyman Plant House and Botanical Garden, The Smith College Museum of Art, Unity House.

### LOCAL ATTRACTIONS

Five College Consortium; City of Northampton.

# SPRINGFIELD COLLEGE
## Springfield, Massachusetts

**Contact:** Mary DeAngelo, Interim Director of Undergraduate Admissions, 263 Alden Street, Springfield, MA 01109. *Phone:* toll-free 800-343-1257 (out-of-state). *Fax:* 413-748-3694. *Web site:* http:// www.spfldcol.edu/ *Visit location:* Admissions Office, Doggett Memorial, 263 Alden Street.

### QUICK FACTS

Enrollment: 2,490; UG: 1,890. Entrance: moderately difficult. SAT>500: N/R; ACT>18: N/R. Tuition and fees: $14,825. Room and board: $5018. Application deadline: 4/1.

### GENERAL

Independent, comprehensive, coed. Awards bachelor's, master's, and doctoral degrees. Founded 1885. Setting: 167-acre suburban campus. Undergraduate faculty: 232 (174 full-time, 58 part-time); student-faculty ratio is 15:1.

### CAMPUS VISITS

**College Calendar 1998–99:** *Regular classes:* Aug. 31–Dec. 11; Jan. 19–May 4. *Breaks:* Dec. 18–Jan. 18.

*Final exams:* Dec. 14–17; May 6–11. *Special campus days:* Commencement, May 16; Homecoming, Oct. 17.

### VISIT OPPORTUNITIES

| | Appointments? | Who? |
|---|---|---|
| **Campus Tour** | recommended | open to all |
| **Information Session** | not required | |
| **Admission Interview** | required | applicants and parents |
| **Classroom Visit** | required | |
| **Faculty Meeting** | | applicants and parents |
| **Overnight Visit** | required | |

**Information Sessions:** Call for available schedule.

**Interviews:** M–F; Sat. Oct.–Mar.; 60 minutes.

**Campus Tours:** Conducted by students. M–F at 10:00 am, 11:00 am, 12:00 pm, 1:00 pm, 2:00 pm, 3:00 pm; Sat. at 11:00 am, 12:30 pm; call for availability during break periods; 60 minutes.

**Class Visits:** Classroom visits are determined by the visit schedule.

**Overnight Visits:** During the regular academic year, prospective applicants may spend an evening in a residence hall with a student host.

### CAMPUS FACILITIES

**Science:** Benis Hall, Allied Health Science Center.

**Arts:** Visual Arts Center.

**Athletic:** Blake Arena, Linkletter Natatorium, Judd Gymnasium.

# SUFFOLK UNIVERSITY
## Boston, Massachusetts

**Contact:** Carolyn Long, Appointment Coordinator, 8 Ashburton Place, Boston, MA 02108-2770. *Phone:* 617-573-8460 or toll-free 800-6-SUFFOLK. *Fax:* 617-742-4291. *E-mail:* admissions@admin.suffolk. edu *Web site:* http://www.suffolk.edu/ *Visit location:* Undergraduate Admission Office, The Claflin Building, Twenty Beacon Street.

### QUICK FACTS

Enrollment: 6,139; UG: 2,909. Entrance: moderately difficult. SAT>500: 54% V, 42% M; ACT>18: N/App. Tuition and fees: $12,920. Room and board: $8350. Application deadline: rolling.

*Suffolk University (continued)*

## GENERAL

Independent, comprehensive, coed. Awards associate, bachelor's, master's, doctoral, and first professional degrees and post-master's and first professional certificates (doctoral degree in law). Founded 1906. Setting: 2-acre urban campus. Undergraduate faculty: 619 (269 full-time, 350 part-time); student-faculty ratio is 12:1. Most popular recent majors: sociology, finance, accounting.

## CAMPUS VISITS

**College Calendar 1998–99:** *Regular classes:* Sept. 9–Dec. 10; Jan. 19–Apr. 28. *Breaks:* Nov. 25–29; Mar. 8–14; Dec. 20–Jan. 17. *Final exams:* Dec. 14–19; May 3–8. *Special campus days:* Open House for prospective students, Nov. 7.

## VISIT OPPORTUNITIES

| | Appointments? | Who? |
|---|---|---|
| **Campus Tour** | required | applicants and parents |
| **Information Session** | required | |
| **Admission Interview** | required | applicants and parents |
| **Classroom Visit** | required | |
| **Faculty Meeting** | required | applicants and parents |

**Information Sessions:** Sat. 10:00 am–1:00 pm.

**Interviews:** M–F, select Sat.; 35 minutes.

**Campus Tours:** Conducted by students. M–F 9:30 am–3:30 pm; during Jun.–Aug. please call well in advance; 60 minutes.

**Class Visits:** Classroom visits are determined by the visit schedule.

## CAMPUS FACILITIES

**Science:** Appointment Required: Archer Building.

**Arts:** Appointment Required: New England School of Art and Design at Suffolk University, C. Walsh Theatre.

**Athletic:** Appointment Required: Ridgeway Athletic Center.

**Of Special Interest:** Appointment Required: Residence Hall, Geno A. Ballotti Learning Center.

## LOCAL ATTRACTIONS

State House, Faneuil Hall/Quincy Market/Boston's Public Gardens.

# TUFTS UNIVERSITY
## Medford, Massachusetts

**Contact:** Undergraduate Admissions, Bendetson Hall, Medford, MA 02155. *Phone:* 617-627-3170. *Fax:* 617-627-3860. *E-mail:* uadmiss_inquiry@infonet.tufts. edu *Web site:* http://www.tufts.edu/ *Visit location:* Office of Undergraduate Admission, Bendetson Hall.

## QUICK FACTS

Enrollment: 8,727; UG: 4,738. Entrance: most difficult. SAT>500: 97% V, 99% M; ACT>18: 100%. Tuition and fees: $22,811. Room and board: $6804. Application deadline: 1/1.

## GENERAL

Independent, university, coed. Awards bachelor's, master's, doctoral, and first professional degrees. Founded 1852. Setting: 150-acre suburban campus with easy access to Boston. Undergraduate faculty: 1,018 (575 full-time, 443 part-time); student-faculty ratio is 13:1. Most popular recent majors: biology, international relations, English.

## CAMPUS VISITS

**College Calendar 1998–99:** *Regular classes:* Sept. 8–Dec. 10; Jan. 21–May 3. *Breaks:* Dec. 23–Jan. 20; Mar. 20–28. *Final exams:* Dec. 15–22; May 7–14. *Special campus days:* Commencement, May 23; Homecoming, Oct. 24; Parent's Weekend, Oct. 16–18.

## VISIT OPPORTUNITIES

| | Appointments? | Who? |
|---|---|---|
| **Campus Tour** | recommended, not required | open to all |
| **Information Session** | recommended, not required | open to all |
| **Classroom Visit** | | open to all |
| **Faculty Meeting** | recommended | open to all |
| **Overnight Visit** | required | open to all |

**Information Sessions:** M–F at 10:30 am, 1:30 pm; M–F (mid Jan.–Mar. 12:30 pm); Sat. (Sept. to Nov. and Apr.); unavailable mid-Dec. to mid-Jan.; during Jul. and Aug. 9:00 am session available; 60 minutes.

**Campus Tours:** Conducted by students. M–F 11:30 am–2:30 pm; during Jul. and Aug. 10:00 am tour available; Feb.–May 9:30 am tour also available; Sat. (Sept. to Nov., Apr.) at 10:30 am.

**Class Visits:** Certain predetermined classrooms are open to visitors.

**Overnight Visits:** During the regular academic year, prospective applicants may spend an evening in a residence hall with a student host.

## CAMPUS FACILITIES
**Science:** Sci/Tech Center, Anderson Hall (Engineering), Pearson (Chemistry), Barnum Hall (Biology).

**Arts:** Balch Arena Theater, Art Gallery.

**Athletic:** Fitness Center.

**Of Special Interest:** Tisch Library, Mayer Campus Center.

## LOCAL ATTRACTIONS
City of Boston; Davis Square.

# WENTWORTH INSTITUTE OF TECHNOLOGY
**Boston, Massachusetts**

**Contact:** Admissions Office, 550 Huntington Avenue, Boston, MA 02115. *Phone:* toll-free 800-556-0610. *Fax:* 617-989-4010. *E-mail:* admissions@wit.edu *Web site:* http://www.wit.edu/ *Visit location:* Admissions Office, Main Building, 550 Huntington Avenue.

## QUICK FACTS
Enrollment: 3,013; UG: 3,013. Entrance: moderately difficult. SAT>500: N/R; ACT>18: N/R. Tuition and fees: $11,500. Room and board: $6200. Application deadline: rolling.

## GENERAL
Independent, 4-year, coed. Awards associate and bachelor's degrees. Founded 1904. Setting: 35-acre urban campus. Faculty: 164 (95 full-time, 69 part-time); student-faculty ratio is 18:1. Most popular recent majors: electrical/electronic engineering technology, architectural engineering technology, mechanical engineering technology.

## CAMPUS VISITS
**College Calendar 1998–99:** *Regular classes:* Aug. 13–Dec. 8; Jan. 11–Apr. 20. *Breaks:* Dec. 17–Jan. 10. *Final exams:* Dec. 10–16; Apr. 24–29. *Special campus days:* Commencement; Fall Open House, Oct. 18, Nov. 1, Nov. 22.

## VISIT OPPORTUNITIES

| | Appointments? | Who? |
|---|---|---|
| **Campus Tour** | required | open to all |
| **Information Session** | required | open to all |
| **Admission Interview** | required | open to all |
| **Classroom Visit** | required | open to all |
| **Faculty Meeting** | required | open to all |
| **Overnight Visit** | required | open to all |

**Information Sessions:** Select Sat. during Feb. and Apr. vacation week at 11:00 am and 1:00 pm.

**Interviews:** M–F 9:00 am–4:00 pm; 30 minutes.

**Campus Tours:** Conducted by students and admission reps. M–F at 10:00 am, 11:00 am, 1:00 pm, 2:00 pm; select Sat. at 10:00 am, 12:00 pm; summer schedule: M–F at 10:00 am and 2:00 pm.

**Class Visits:** Classroom visits are determined by the visit schedule.

**Overnight Visits:** During the regular academic year, prospective applicants may spend an evening in a residence hall with a student host.

## CAMPUS FACILITIES
**Arts:** Architecture Studios.

**Athletic:** Sweeney Field.

## LOCAL ATTRACTIONS
Museum of Fine Arts; Isabella Stewart Gardner Museum; Fanueil Hall and Quincy Market; Fenway Park.

# WESTERN NEW ENGLAND COLLEGE
**Springfield, Massachusetts**

**Contact:** Admissions Office, 1215 Wilbraham Road, Springfield, MA 01119. *Phone:* toll-free 800-325-1122 Ext. 1321. *Fax:* 413-782-1777. *E-mail:* ugradmis@wnec.edu *Web site:* http://www.wnec.edu/ *Visit location:* Admissions Office, Admissions, 1268 Wilbraham Road.

## QUICK FACTS
Enrollment: 4,632; UG: 2,997. Entrance: moderately difficult. SAT>500: 44% V, 49% M; ACT>18: N/R. Tuition and fees: $11,448. Room and board: $6120. Application deadline: rolling.

*Western New England College (continued)*

## GENERAL

Independent, comprehensive, coed. Awards associate, bachelor's, master's, and first professional degrees. Founded 1919. Setting: 185-acre suburban campus. Undergraduate faculty: 314 (134 full-time, 180 part-time); student-faculty ratio is 17:1. Most popular recent majors: business administration, accounting, criminal justice/law enforcement administration.

## CAMPUS VISITS

**College Calendar 1998–99:** *Regular classes:* Aug. 31–Dec. 11; Jan. 19–May 7. *Breaks:* Oct. 10–13; Mar. 15–21; Nov. 25–29. *Final exams:* Dec. 14–19; May 10–15. *Admission office closed:* December (Winter Recess), Dec. 25–Jan. 1. *Special campus days:* Commencement, May 16; Homecoming, Sept. 25–27; Open House programs October through April.

## VISIT OPPORTUNITIES

| | Appointments? | Who? |
|---|---|---|
| **Campus Tour** | required | open to all |
| **Admission Interview** | required | open to all |
| **Classroom Visit** | required | open to all |
| **Faculty Meeting** | required | open to all |
| **Overnight Visit** | required | admitted applicants only |

**Interviews:** M–F, select Sat.; 30 minutes.

**Campus Tours:** Conducted by students. M–F, select Sat. 9:00 am–3:00 pm; 75 minutes.

**Class Visits:** Prospective students may attend a class in their area of interest.

**Overnight Visits:** During the regular academic year and over the summer, prospective applicants may spend an evening in a residence hall with a student host.

**Video:** Free on request.

## CAMPUS FACILITIES

**Athletic:** Alumni Healthful Living Center.

**Of Special Interest:** Engineering Labs.

## LOCAL ATTRACTIONS

Basketball Hall of Fame, Springfield Symphony, Springfield Falcons hockey team, Eastern States Expo; the Berkshires.

# WHEATON COLLEGE
## Norton, Massachusetts

**Contact:** Claudia Inglese, Office of Admission, East Main Street, Norton, MA 02766. *Phone:* 508-285-8251 or toll-free 800-394-6003. *Fax:* 508-285-8271. *E-mail:* admission@wheatonma.edu *Web site:* http://www.wheatonma.edu/ *Visit location:* Admission Office, Admission.

## QUICK FACTS

Enrollment: 1,432; UG: 1,432. Entrance: moderately difficult. SAT>500: N/R; ACT>18: N/R. Tuition and fees: $20,820. Room and board: $6470. Application deadline: 2/1.

## GENERAL

Independent, 4-year, coed. Awards bachelor's degrees. Founded 1834. Setting: 385-acre small-town campus with easy access to Boston. Faculty: 135 (93 full-time, 42 part-time); student-faculty ratio is 13:1. Most popular recent majors: psychology, English, sociology.

## CAMPUS VISITS

**College Calendar 1998–99:** *Regular classes:* Sept. 2–Dec. 11; Feb. 1–May 11. *Breaks:* Oct. 12–13; Mar. 15–19. *Final exams:* Dec. 14–18; May 14–17. *Admission office closed:* Dec. 24–Jan. 2, Nov. 27. *Special campus days:* Academic Festival, Apr. 17; Commencement/Reunion Weekend, May 15–17; Distinguished Fellows Program, Mar. 4; Family Weekend, Apr. 17–19; Otis Social Justice Award, Apr. 6; Spring Weekend, Apr. 24–26.

## VISIT OPPORTUNITIES

| | Appointments? | Who? |
|---|---|---|
| **Campus Tour** | recommended | open to all |
| **Information Session** | recommended | |
| **Admission Interview** | required | open to all |
| **Classroom Visit** | not required | open to all |
| **Overnight Visit** | required | open to all |

**Information Sessions:** Select Sat. during the fall; 60 minutes.

**Interviews:** M–F; available Sat. mid-Sept.–Jan. 31; 60 minutes.

**Campus Tours:** Conducted by students. M–F at 9:30 am, 10:30 am, 11:30 am, 1:30 pm, 2:30 pm, 3:30 pm; available Sat. mid-Sept.–Jan. 31 at 9:30 am, 10:30 am, 11:30 am, 1:30 pm, 2:30 pm, 3:30 pm; 60 minutes.

**Class Visits:** Prospective students may attend a class in their area of interest.

**Overnight Visits:** During the regular academic year, prospective applicants may spend an evening in a residence hall with a student host.

**Video:** Free on request.

## CAMPUS FACILITIES
**Of Special Interest:** Madeleine Clark Wallace Library.

## LOCAL ATTRACTIONS
Historic Boston; Providence, RI; Cape Cod; Premium Outlet Mall in Wrentham.

# WILLIAMS COLLEGE
**Williamstown, Massachusetts**

**Contact:** Office of Admission, 988 Main Street, Williamstown, MA 01267. *Phone:* 413-597-2211. *Fax:* 413-597-4052. *Web site:* http://www.williams.edu/ *Visit location:* Office of Admission, Mather House, 988 Main Street.

## QUICK FACTS
Enrollment: 2,011; UG: 1,970. Entrance: most difficult. SAT>500: 99% V, 99% M; ACT>18: 100%. Tuition and fees: $22,990. Room and board: $6300. Application deadline: 1/1.

## GENERAL
Independent, comprehensive, coed. Awards bachelor's and master's degrees. Founded 1793. Setting: 450-acre small-town campus with easy access to Albany. Undergraduate faculty: 262 (236 full-time, 26 part-time); student-faculty ratio is 11:1. Most popular recent majors: English, economics, history.

## CAMPUS VISITS
**College Calendar 1998–99:** *Regular classes:* Sept. 10–Dec. 10; Jan. 4–28; Feb. 4–May 14. *Breaks:* Dec. 20–Jan. 4; Mar. 19–Apr. 5. *Final exams:* Dec. 15–20; May 19–24. *Special campus days:* Commencement, June 6; Homecoming, Nov. 7; Winter Carnival, Feb. 19–20.

## VISIT OPPORTUNITIES

|  | Appointments? | Who? |
|---|---|---|
| **Campus Tour** | not required | open to all |
| **Information Session** | not required | open to all |

## VISIT OPPORTUNITIES—*continued*

|  | Appointments? | Who? |
|---|---|---|
| **Admission Interview** | required | open to all |
| **Classroom Visit** | not required | open to all |
| **Faculty Meeting** | recommended | open to all |
| **Overnight Visit** | required | open to all |

**Information Sessions:** M–F, select Sat.; call for schedule; 60 minutes.

**Interviews:** M–F; 30 minutes.

**Campus Tours:** Conducted by students. M–F, select Sat.; call for schedule; 60 minutes.

**Class Visits:** Prospective students may attend a class in their area of interest.

**Overnight Visits:** During the regular academic year, prospective applicants may spend an evening in a residence hall with a student host.

**Video:** Available, fee charged.

## CAMPUS FACILITIES
**Science:** Bronfman Science Center, Old Hopkins Observatory.

**Arts:** Spencer Studio Art Building, Williams College Museum of Art.

**Athletic:** Chandler Athletic Center.

# WORCESTER POLYTECHNIC INSTITUTE
**Worcester, Massachusetts**

**Contact:** Office of Admissions, 100 Institute Road, Worcester, MA 01609. *Phone:* 508-831-5286. *Fax:* 508-831-5875. *E-mail:* admissions@wpi.edu *Web site:* http://www.wpi.edu/ *Visit location:* Office of Admissions, Boynton Hall, 100 Institute Road.

## QUICK FACTS
Enrollment: 3,725; UG: 2,693. Entrance: very difficult. SAT>500: 96% V, 99% M; ACT>18: N/R. Tuition and fees: $18,910. Room and board: $6240. Application deadline: 2/15.

## GENERAL
Independent, university, coed. Awards bachelor's, master's, and doctoral degrees. Founded 1865. Setting: 80-acre suburban campus with easy access to Boston. Undergraduate faculty: 294; student-faculty

*Worcester Polytechnic Institute (continued)*

ratio is 12:1. Most popular recent majors: mechanical engineering, electrical/electronics engineering, computer science.

## CAMPUS VISITS
**College Calendar 1998–99:** *Regular classes:* Aug. 27–Oct. 15; Oct. 28–Dec. 18; Jan. 14–Mar. 4; Mar. 18–May 6. *Special campus days:* Commencement, May 22; Homecoming, Oct. 3; New Student Orientation, Aug. 22–26.

## VISIT OPPORTUNITIES

|  | Appointments? | Who? |
|---|---|---|
| **Campus Tour** | not required | applicants and parents |
| **Information Session** | not required |  |
| **Classroom Visit** | required |  |
| **Faculty Meeting** | required | applicants and parents |
| **Overnight Visit** | required | open to all |

**Information Sessions:** M–F at 10:00 am, 11:00 am, 3:00 pm; select Sat. at 9:30 am, 11:00 am; 60 minutes.

**Campus Tours:** Conducted by students. M–F 9:00 am–4:00 pm; select Sat. at 10:30 am, 12:00 pm; 60 minutes.

**Class Visits:** Classroom visits are determined by the visit schedule.

**Overnight Visits:** During the regular academic year, prospective applicants may spend an evening in a residence hall with a student host.

**Video:** Free on request.

## CAMPUS FACILITIES
**Science:** Nuclear reactor, Robotics lab, Laser labs.

# MICHIGAN

## ANDREWS UNIVERSITY
### Berrien Springs, Michigan

**Contact:** Admissions Office, Berrien Springs, MI 49104. *Phone:* 616-471-6324 or toll-free 800-253-2874. *Fax:* 616-471-3228. *Web site:* http://www.cs.andrews.edu/ *Visit location:* Enrollment Services, Administration Building, 1st Floor.

## QUICK FACTS
Enrollment: 3,051; UG: 1,746. Entrance: moderately difficult. SAT>500: N/R; ACT>18: N/R. Tuition and fees: $11,577. Room and board: $3510. Application deadline: rolling.

## GENERAL
Independent Seventh-day Adventist, university, coed. Awards associate, bachelor's, master's, doctoral, and first professional degrees. Founded 1874. Setting: 1,650-acre small-town campus. Undergraduate faculty: 318 (259 full-time, 59 part-time); student-faculty ratio is 14:1. Most popular recent majors: anatomy, nursing, medical technology.

## CAMPUS VISITS
**College Calendar 1998–99:** *Regular classes:* Sept. 29–Dec. 10; Jan. 5–Mar. 11; Mar. 30–May 27. *Breaks:* Dec. 17–Jan. 3; Mar. 18–28. *Final exams:* Dec. 13–16; Mar. 14–17; May 30–June 2. *Special campus days:* Alumni Weekend, Apr. 22–25; College Days for Academy and High School Seniors, Oct. 18–19; Commencement Weekend, June 4–6; International Student Week, Apr. 25–May 1.

## VISIT OPPORTUNITIES

|  | Who? |
|---|---|
| **Campus Tour** | open to all |
| **Admission Interview** | open to all |
| **Classroom Visit** | open to all |
| **Faculty Meeting** | open to all |
| **Overnight Visit** | open to all |

**Interviews:** M–F at 8:00 am, 12:00 pm; Mon., Tue., Wed., Thu. at 1:00 pm, 5:00 pm; unavailable during holidays.

**Campus Tours:** Conducted by students. M–F at 8:00 am, 12:00 pm; Mon., Tue., Wed., Thu. at 1:00 pm, 5:00 pm; 45 minutes.

**Class Visits:** Prospective students may attend a class in their area of interest.

**Overnight Visits:** During the regular academic year, prospective applicants may spend an evening in a residence hall.

**Video:** Free on request.

## CAMPUS FACILITIES
**Science:** Greenhouse, Natural History Museum.
**Arts:** Gallery Shows, University Choir, University Orchestra, Wind Symphony.

**Athletic:** Gymnics, Health Clubs.

**Of Special Interest:** Andrews Airpark, Archeology and Horn Museum, Computer Labs, Religious Heritage Museum.

# BAKER COLLEGE OF MOUNT CLEMENS
## Clinton Township, Michigan

**Contact:** Ms. Annette M. Looser, Director of Admissions, 34950 Little Mack Avenue, Clinton Township, MI 48035. *Phone:* 810-791-6610. *Fax:* 810-791-6611. *E-mail:* looser_a@mtclemens.baker. edu *Web site:* http://www.baker.edu *Visit location:* Admissions Office, Baker College of Mount Clemens, 34950 Little Mack Avenue.

## QUICK FACTS
Enrollment: 1,261; UG: 1,261. Entrance: noncompetitive. SAT>500: N/App; ACT>18: N/App. Tuition and fees: $6300. Room and board: N/Avail. Application deadline: rolling.

## GENERAL
Independent, 4-year, coed. Part of Baker College System. Awards associate and bachelor's degrees. Founded 1990. Faculty: 64 (5 full-time, 59 part-time); student-faculty ratio is 16:1. Most popular recent major: business administration.

## CAMPUS VISITS
**College Calendar 1998–99:** *Regular classes:* Sept. 21–Dec. 5; Jan. 12–Mar. 21; Apr. 6–June 13; June 22–Aug. 21. *Breaks:* Dec. 6–Jan. 10. *Final exams:* Nov. 30–Dec. 5; Mar. 18–21; June 10–12; Aug. 17–20. *Special campus days:* Commencement, June 7.

## VISIT OPPORTUNITIES

|  | Appointments? | Who? |
| --- | --- | --- |
| **Campus Tour** | recommended, not required | open to all |
| **Information Session** | recommended, not required | open to all |
| **Admission Interview** | recommended, not required | open to all |
| **Classroom Visit** | required | |
| **Faculty Meeting** | required | |

**Information Sessions:** M–F 9:00 am–6:00 pm; 60 minutes.

**Interviews:** M–F; some evenings by appointment; 60 minutes.

**Campus Tours:** Conducted by admission reps. M–F 9:00 am–6:00 pm; tours available with information sessions and/or presentations on specific career fields; 30 minutes.

**Class Visits:** Prospective students may attend a class in their area of interest, specific tours available to meet students needs.

**Video:** Free on request.

## CAMPUS FACILITIES
**Science:** Medical labs.

**Of Special Interest:** Surgical Technology Operating Room.

# CALVIN COLLEGE
## Grand Rapids, Michigan

**Contact:** Natasha Meyer Turner, Special Visit Coordinator, Calvin College, 3201 Burton Street, SE, Grand Rapids, MI 49546. *Phone:* 616-957-6106 or toll-free 800-668-0122. *Fax:* 616-957-8513. *E-mail:* karrca@calvin.edu *Web site:* http://www.calvin.edu/ *Visit location:* Admissions Reception Center, Spoelhof College Center, Calvin College 3201 Burton Street, SE.

## QUICK FACTS
Enrollment: 3,977; UG: 3,935. Entrance: moderately difficult. SAT>500: 86% V, 86% M; ACT>18: 99%. Tuition and fees: $12,250. Room and board: $4340. Application deadline: rolling.

## GENERAL
Independent, comprehensive, coed, Christian Reformed Church. Awards bachelor's and master's degrees. Founded 1876. Setting: 370-acre suburban campus. Undergraduate faculty: 317 (262 full-time, 55 part-time); student-faculty ratio is 17:1. Most popular recent majors: education, business administration, English.

## CAMPUS VISITS
**College Calendar 1998–99:** *Regular classes:* Sept. 8–Dec. 11; Jan. 7–27; Feb. 1–May 12. *Breaks:* Dec. 18–Jan. 7; Mar. 19–30. *Final exams:* Dec. 14–18; May 14–19. *Special campus days:* Commencement, June 22; Fridays at Calvin (campus visit days); Homecoming, Feb. 20; Opening Convocation, Sept. 8.

*Calvin College (continued)*

## VISIT OPPORTUNITIES

|  | Appointments? | Who? |
|---|---|---|
| **Campus Tour** | recommended | open to all |
| **Information Session** | recommended, not required | open to all |
| **Classroom Visit** | required | open to all |
| **Faculty Meeting** | required | open to all |
| **Overnight Visit** | required | open to all |

**Information Sessions:** M–F 8:00 am–5:00 pm; Sat. 9:00 am–12:00 pm; 45 minutes.

**Campus Tours:** Conducted by students. M–F 8:00 am–5:00 pm; Sat. 9:00 am–12:00 pm; 60 minutes.

**Class Visits:** Prospective students may attend a class in their area of interest, certain predetermined classrooms are open to visitors.

**Overnight Visits:** During the regular academic year, prospective applicants may spend an evening in a residence hall with a student host.

**Video:** Free on request.

## CAMPUS FACILITIES
**Science:** Laboratories, Computer Facilities, Observatory, Ecosystem Preserve.

**Arts:** Art Gallery, Music Computer Lab, Auditoriums.

**Athletic:** Natatorium, Gymnasium.

**Of Special Interest:** Library, Computer Laboratories.

## LOCAL ATTRACTIONS
Downtown Grand Rapids.

# EASTERN MICHIGAN UNIVERSITY
## Ypsilanti, Michigan

**Contact:** Kathryn B. Orscheln, Assistant Director of Admissions, 202 Pierce Hall, Ypsilanti, MI 48197. *Phone:* 734-487-2222 or toll-free 800-GO TO EMU. *Fax:* 734-487-8946. *E-mail:* kathy-orscheln@emich. edu *Web site:* http://www.emich.edu/ *Visit location:* Admissions, Pierce Hall, 400 Pierce Hall.

## QUICK FACTS
Enrollment: 22,557; UG: 17,528. Entrance: moderately difficult. SAT>500: N/R; ACT>18: 93%. Resident tuition and fees: $3529. Nonresident tuition and fees: $8419. Room and board: $4528. Application deadline: 7/31.

## GENERAL
State-supported, comprehensive, coed. Awards bachelor's, master's, and doctoral degrees and post-master's certificates. Founded 1849. Setting: 460-acre suburban campus with easy access to Detroit and Toledo. Undergraduate faculty: 1,202 (702 full-time, 500 part-time); student-faculty ratio is 18:1. Most popular recent majors: elementary education, psychology, social work.

## CAMPUS VISITS
**College Calendar 1998–99:** *Regular classes:* Sept. 12–Dec. 12; Jan. 6–Apr. 19. *Breaks:* Dec. 19–Jan. 6. *Final exams:* Dec. 14–19; Apr. 20–26. *Special campus days:* Explore Eastern, Oct. 17, Nov. 14, Feb. 13, Mar. 13; Family Day, Oct. 10; Summer Open House, Aug. 1.

## VISIT OPPORTUNITIES

|  | Appointments? | Who? |
|---|---|---|
| **Campus Tour** | recommended, not required | open to all |
| **Information Session** |  | open to all |
| **Admission Interview** | required | open to all |
| **Classroom Visit** | required | open to all |
| **Faculty Meeting** | required | open to all |
| **Overnight Visit** | required | admitted applicants only |

**Information Sessions:** M–F, Sat. at 10:00 am, 2:00 pm; unavailable during special visit programs and when university is closed; 10 minutes.

**Interviews:** M–F, Sat.; Sat. unavailable during special visit programs or when university closed; 30 minutes.

**Campus Tours:** Conducted by students. M–F, Sat.; unavailable when university is closed; 90 minutes.

**Class Visits:** Prospective students may attend a class in their area of interest.

**Overnight Visits:** During the regular academic year, prospective applicants may spend an evening in a residence hall with a student host.

## CAMPUS FACILITIES

**Science:** Appointment Required: Sherzer Observatory.

**Arts:** Appointment Required: WEMU-public radio station on campus.

**Athletic:** Appointment Required: New convocation center.

**Of Special Interest:** New Library.

# HILLSDALE COLLEGE
### Hillsdale, Michigan

**Contact:** Mr. Jeff Lantis, Director of Admissions, 33 East College Street, Hillsdale, MI 49242. *Phone:* 517-437-7341. *Fax:* 517-437-0190. *E-mail:* admissions@ac.hillside.edu *Web site:* http://www.hillsdale.edu/ *Visit location:* Admissions Office, Central Hall, 33 East College Street.

## QUICK FACTS
Enrollment: 1,197; UG: 1,197. Entrance: very difficult. SAT>500: 91% V, 90% M; ACT>18: 100%. Tuition and fees: $12,680. Room and board: $5430. Application deadline: rolling.

## GENERAL
Independent, 4-year, coed. Awards bachelor's degrees. Founded 1844. Setting: 200-acre small-town campus. Faculty: 117 (83 full-time, 34 part-time); student-faculty ratio is 11:1. Most popular recent majors: business administration, biology, education.

## CAMPUS VISITS
**College Calendar 1998–99:** *Regular classes:* Aug. 26–Dec. 11; Jan. 20–May 7. *Breaks:* Dec. 18–Jan. 18. *Final exams:* Dec. 14–18; May 10–14. *Special campus days:* CCA Lecture series, Sept. 13–17, Nov. 8–12, Feb. 7–11, Mar. 7–11; Commencement, May 15; Homecoming, Oct. 10; Junior visitation day, Oct. 15; Spring Convocation, Apr. 8; Summer school, May 17–June 25.

## VISIT OPPORTUNITIES

|  | Appointments? |
| --- | --- |
| **Campus Tour** | required |
| **Admission Interview** | required |
| **Classroom Visit** | required |
| **Faculty Meeting** | required |
| **Overnight Visit** | required |

**Interviews:** M–F; select Sat. 9:00 am–12:00 pm; 30 minutes.

**Campus Tours:** Conducted by students. M–F 8:30 am–5:00 pm; select Sat. 9:00 am–12:00 pm; during summer M–F 8:30 am–4:00 pm; 60 minutes.

**Class Visits:** Prospective students may attend a class in their area of interest, classroom visits are determined by the visit schedule.

**Overnight Visits:** During the regular academic year, prospective applicants may spend an evening in a residence hall.

**Video:** Free on request.

## CAMPUS FACILITIES
**Science:** Herbert Henry Dow Science Building, Strosacker Science Center.

**Arts:** Sage Center of the Arts.

**Athletic:** George Roche Health Education and Sports Complex.

**Of Special Interest:** Hillside Academy (K-12 Private School), Mossey Learning Resource Center, Heritage Room Special Collections Library.

# HOPE COLLEGE
### Holland, Michigan

**Contact:** Barbara Muller, Visit Coordinator, PO Box 9000, Holland, MI 49422-9000. *Phone:* toll-free 800-968-7850. *Fax:* 616-395-7130. *E-mail:* muller@hope.edu *Web site:* http://www.hope.edu/ *Visit location:* Admissions Office, Admissions, 69 East 10th Street.

## QUICK FACTS
Enrollment: 2,795; UG: 2,795. Entrance: moderately difficult. SAT>500: 86% V, 92% M; ACT>18: 99%. Tuition and fees: $14,878. Room and board: $4534. Application deadline: rolling.

## GENERAL
Independent, 4-year, coed, Reformed Church in America. Awards bachelor's degrees. Founded 1866. Setting: 45-acre small-town campus with easy access to Grand Rapids. Faculty: 275 (204 full-time, 71 part-time); student-faculty ratio is 13:1. Most popular recent majors: business administration, psychology, biology.

## CAMPUS VISITS
**College Calendar 1998–99:** *Regular classes:* Sept. 1–Dec. 11; Jan. 12–Apr. 30. *Breaks:* Oct. 16–21; Feb. 12–17; Nov. 26–30; Mar. 19–29. *Final exams:* Dec. 14–18; May 3–7. *Special campus days:* Baccalaureate

*Hope College (continued)*

and Commencement, May 9; Critical Issues Symposium, Oct. 6–7; Homecoming, Oct. 10; Junior Day, Apr. 9, Apr. 23; Visitation Day, Oct. 9, Oct. 23, Nov. 6, Nov. 20, Jan. 18, Feb. 5, Feb. 26, Mar. 12.

## VISIT OPPORTUNITIES

|                     | Appointments? | Who?        |
|---------------------|---------------|-------------|
| **Campus Tour**     | required      | open to all |
| **Admission Interview** | required  | open to all |
| **Classroom Visit** | required      | open to all |
| **Faculty Meeting** | required      | open to all |
| **Overnight Visit** | required      | open to all |

**Interviews:** M–F; Sat. mornings; 45 minutes.

**Campus Tours:** Conducted by students and admission reps. M–F 8:00 am–5:00 pm; Sat. 9:00 am–12:00 pm; 60 minutes.

**Class Visits:** Prospective students may attend a class in their area of interest, visits are limited to two classes.

**Overnight Visits:** During the regular academic year, prospective applicants may spend an evening in a residence hall with a student host.

## CAMPUS FACILITIES

**Science:** Peale Science Center, Vander Werf Hall.

**Arts:** Nykerk Hall of Music, De Pree Art Center and Gallery.

**Athletic:** Dow Health and Physical Education Center, Ekdal J. Buys Athletic Complex, De Witt Tennis Center.

**Of Special Interest:** Dimnent Memorial Chapel, Van Wylan Library; Appointment Required: Hayworth Conference and Learning Center.

## LOCAL ATTRACTIONS

Holland State Park and Lake Michigan; Downtown Holland.

# KETTERING UNIVERSITY
**Flint, Michigan**

**Contact:** Office of Admissions, 1700 West Third Avenue, Flint, MI 40504-4898. *Phone:* toll-free 800-955-4464 Ext. TOUR. *Fax:* 810-762-9837. *E-mail:* admissions@kettering.edu *Web site:* http://www.

kettering.edu/ *Visit location:* Office of Admissions, Campus Center, 1700 West Third Avenue.

## QUICK FACTS

Enrollment: 3,225; UG: 2,468. Entrance: very difficult. SAT>500: 90% V, 100% M; ACT>18: 99%. Tuition and fees: $14,232. Room and board: $3863. Application deadline: rolling.

## GENERAL

Independent, comprehensive, coed. Awards bachelor's and master's degrees. Founded 1919. Setting: 45-acre suburban campus with easy access to Detroit. Undergraduate faculty: 156 (138 full-time, 18 part-time); student-faculty ratio is 12:1. Most popular recent majors: mechanical engineering, electrical/electronics engineering, industrial engineering.

## CAMPUS VISITS

**College Calendar 1998–99:** *Regular classes:* July 6–Sept. 18; Sept. 28–Dec. 11; Jan. 4–Mar. 19; Mar. 29–June 11. *Final exams:* Sept. 21–24; Dec. 14–17; Mar. 22–25; June 14–17. *Special campus days:* Commencement, Dec. 4, June 18; Holiday, Dec. 21–Jan. 3; Martin Luther King, Jr. Holiday, Jan. 18.

## VISIT OPPORTUNITIES

|                         | Appointments? | Who?        |
|-------------------------|---------------|-------------|
| **Campus Tour**         | required      | open to all |
| **Information Session** | required      | open to all |
| **Admission Interview** | required      | open to all |
| **Classroom Visit**     | required      | open to all |
| **Faculty Meeting**     | required      | open to all |
| **Overnight Visit**     | required      | open to all |

**Information Sessions:** Held as part of tour; 30 minutes.

**Interviews:** M–F; please call for availability during weekend programs and at off campus programs; 30 minutes.

**Campus Tours:** Conducted by admission reps. M–F at 9:30 am, 1:30 pm; call for availability during weekend programs; 120 minutes.

**Class Visits:** Classroom visits are determined by the visit schedule.

**Overnight Visits:** During the regular academic year and over the summer, prospective applicants may spend an evening in a residence hall with a student host.

**Video:** Free on request.

## CAMPUS FACILITIES
**Science:** Laboratories.

**Arts:** Art Gallery.

**Athletic:** Recreation Center.

**Of Special Interest:** Food Service, Wellness Center, Residence Hall.

## LOCAL ATTRACTIONS
Sloan Museum, Flint Institute of Arts, Crossroads Village, Robert T. Longway Planetarium.

# LAKE SUPERIOR STATE UNIVERSITY
**Sault Sainte Marie, Michigan**

**Contact:** Admissions Office, 650 West Easterday Avenue, Sault Sainte Marie, MI 49783. *Phone:* toll-free 888-800-LSSU Ext. 2231. *Fax:* 906-635-6669. *E-mail:* admissions@lakers.lssu.edu *Web site:* http://www.lssu.edu/ *Visit location:* Admissions Office, Fletcher Center, 650 West Easterday Avenue.

## QUICK FACTS
Enrollment: 3,369; UG: 3,224. Entrance: moderately difficult. SAT>500: N/App; ACT>18: N/R. Resident tuition and fees: $3642. Nonresident tuition and fees: $7158. Room and board: $4646. Application deadline: 8/15.

## GENERAL
State-supported, comprehensive, coed. Awards associate, bachelor's, and master's degrees. Founded 1946. Setting: 121-acre small-town campus. Undergraduate faculty: 191 (114 full-time, 77 part-time); student-faculty ratio is 22:1. Most popular recent majors: criminal justice/law enforcement administration, business administration, education.

## CAMPUS VISITS
**College Calendar 1998–99:** *Regular classes:* Aug. 31–Dec. 11; Jan. 11–Apr. 23. *Breaks:* Dec. 19–Jan. 11; Feb. 26–Mar. 8. *Final exams:* Dec. 14–18; Apr. 26–30. *Admission office closed:* Dec. 21–Jan. 4.

## VISIT OPPORTUNITIES

|  | Appointments? | Who? |
| --- | --- | --- |
| **Campus Tour** | not required | open to all |
| **Information Session** | recommended | open to all |
| **Admission Interview** | recommended | open to all |

## VISIT OPPORTUNITIES—*continued*

|  | Appointments? | Who? |
| --- | --- | --- |
| **Classroom Visit** | required | open to all |
| **Faculty Meeting** | required | open to all |
| **Overnight Visit** | required | |

**Information Sessions:** M–F; select Sat. by appointment; 50 minutes.

**Interviews:** M–F, select Sat.; Sat. during academic year by appointment only; 50 minutes.

**Campus Tours:** Conducted by students. M–F at 10:15 am, 1:30 pm; Sat. during academic year at 10:00 am, 1:00 pm; 90 minutes.

**Class Visits:** Prospective students may attend a class in their area of interest, classroom visits are arranged with permission of instructor.

**Overnight Visits:** During the regular academic year, prospective applicants may spend an evening in a residence hall.

## CAMPUS FACILITIES
**Science:** Crawford Hall of Science, Center for Applied Science and Engineering.

**Athletic:** Norris Center Recreation Facility, Taffy Abel Ice Cream Arena.

**Of Special Interest:** Kenneth Shouldice Library; Appointment Required: LSSU Aquatic Lab.

## LOCAL ATTRACTIONS
The Soo Locks, Tahquamenon Falls, Agawa Canyon train tour, five local golf courses, Sault area, downhill skiing, cross country skiing, and snowmobile trails.

# LAWRENCE TECHNOLOGICAL UNIVERSITY
**Southfield, Michigan**

**Contact:** Jan Richards, Admission Counselor—Coordinator of Special Events, 21000 West Ten Mile Road, Southfield, MI 48075. *Phone:* 248-204-3174 or toll-free 800-225-5588. *Fax:* 248-204-3188. *E-mail:* richards@ltu.edu *Web site:* http://www.ltu.edu/ *Visit location:* Admissions Office, Buell Management Building, 21000 West Ten Mile Road.

*Lawrence Technological University (continued)*

## QUICK FACTS

Enrollment: 3,645; UG: 3,063. Entrance: moderately difficult. SAT>500: N/R; ACT>18: 98%. Tuition and fees: $9340. Room only: $2800. Application deadline: 8/11.

## GENERAL

Independent, comprehensive, coed. Awards associate, bachelor's, and master's degrees. Founded 1932. Setting: 110-acre suburban campus with easy access to Detroit. Undergraduate faculty: 328 (109 full-time, 219 part-time); student-faculty ratio is 14:1. Most popular recent majors: mechanical engineering, architecture, electrical/electronics engineering.

## CAMPUS VISITS

**College Calendar 1998–99:** *Regular classes:* Aug. 26–Dec. 18; Jan. 11–May 8; May 12–June 23; May 12–July 22. *Breaks:* Mar. 8–13. *Final exams:* Dec. 14–18; May 3–8; June 22–23; July 20–22. *Special campus days:* Annual College Night, Oct. 8; Annual Open House Weekend, Apr. 24–25.

## VISIT OPPORTUNITIES

| | Appointments? | Who? |
|---|---|---|
| **Campus Tour** | required | applicants and parents |
| **Information Session** | recommended | |
| **Admission Interview** | not required | applicants and parents |
| **Classroom Visit** | required | applicants and parents |

**Information Sessions:** M–F; 60 minutes.

**Interviews:** M–F; 60 minutes.

**Campus Tours:** Conducted by students and admission reps. M–F; 60 minutes.

**Class Visits:** Prospective students may attend a class in their area of interest.

**Video:** Free on request.

## CAMPUS FACILITIES

**Science:** Computer Labs, Chemistry Labs, Physics Labs, Biology Labs.

**Arts:** School of Architecture Studios, School of Architecture Gallery.

**Athletic:** Intramural Field House.

**Of Special Interest:** Engineering Projects, Engineering Labs.

# MICHIGAN STATE UNIVERSITY
**East Lansing, Michigan**

**Contact:** Office of Admissions and Scholarship, 250 Hannah Adminstration Building, East Lansing, MI 48824. *Phone:* 517-355-8332. *Fax:* 517-353-1647. *E-mail:* admis@pilot.msu.edu *Web site:* http://www.msu.edu/ *Visit location:* Office of Admissions and Scholarship, 250 Hannah Administration Building.

## QUICK FACTS

Enrollment: 42,327; UG: 33,032. Entrance: moderately difficult. SAT>500: 70% V, 75% M; ACT>18: 89%. Resident tuition and fees: $4789. Nonresident tuition and fees: $11,854. Room and board: $4052. Application deadline: 7/30.

## GENERAL

State-supported, university, coed. Awards bachelor's, master's, doctoral, and first professional degrees. Founded 1855. Setting: 5,000-acre suburban campus with easy access to Detroit. Undergraduate faculty: 3,426 (3,006 full-time, 420 part-time); student-faculty ratio is 12:1. Most popular recent majors: psychology, accounting, finance.

## CAMPUS VISITS

**College Calendar 1998–99:** *Regular classes:* Aug. 31–Dec. 11; Jan. 11–Apr. 30. *Breaks:* Mar. 8–12. *Final exams:* Dec. 14–18; May 3–7. *Special campus days:* Fall Commencement, Dec. 11–12; Spring Commencement, May 7–8.

## VISIT OPPORTUNITIES

| | Appointments? | Who? |
|---|---|---|
| **Campus Tour** | not required | open to all |
| **Information Session** | not required | open to all |
| **Admission Interview** | required | open to all |
| **Classroom Visit** | required | open to all |
| **Faculty Meeting** | required | open to all |
| **Overnight Visit** | required | open to all |

**Information Sessions:** Mon.; Fri.; select Sat.

**Interviews:** M–F; 30 minutes.

**Campus Tours:** Conducted by students. Mon.; Fri.; select Sat.

**Class Visits:** Classroom visits are determined by the visit schedule.

**Overnight Visits:** During the regular academic year, prospective applicants may spend an evening in a residence hall with a student host.

## CAMPUS FACILITIES

**Arts:** Kresge Art Museum; Appointment Required: Wharton Center for Performing Arts.

**Athletic:** Breslin Student Events Center.

**Of Special Interest:** Library.

# MICHIGAN TECHNOLOGICAL UNIVERSITY
**Houghton, Michigan**

**Contact:** Admissions Office, 1400 Townsend Drive, Houghton, MI 49931. *Phone:* 906-487-2335. *Fax:* 906-487-2125. *E-mail:* mtu4u@mtu.edu *Web site:* http://www.mtu.edu/ *Visit location:* Admissions Office, Administration and Student Services Building, 1400 Townsend Drive.

## QUICK FACTS

Enrollment: 6,170; UG: 5,542. Entrance: moderately difficult. SAT>500: 83% V, 93% M; ACT>18: 98%. Resident tuition and fees: $4062. Nonresident tuition and fees: $9702. Room and board: $4420. Application deadline: rolling.

## GENERAL

State-supported, university, coed. Awards associate, bachelor's, master's, and doctoral degrees. Founded 1885. Setting: 240-acre small-town campus. Undergraduate faculty: 406 (374 full-time, 32 part-time); student-faculty ratio is 12:1. Most popular recent majors: mechanical engineering, electrical/electronics engineering, civil engineering.

## CAMPUS VISITS

**College Calendar 1998–99:** *Regular classes:* Sept. 8–Nov. 13; Nov. 30–Feb. 19; Mar. 8–May 14. *Breaks:* Nov. 23–27; Dec. 18–Jan. 4; Mar. 1–5. *Final exams:* Nov. 16–20; Feb. 22–26; May 17–21. *Admission office closed:* Dec. 21–Jan. 1. *Special campus days:* Homecoming, Sept. 25–26; Mid Year Commencement, Nov. 21; Spring Commencement, May 22; Winter Carnival, Feb. 3–6.

## VISIT OPPORTUNITIES

| | Appointments? | Who? |
| --- | --- | --- |
| **Campus Tour** | recommended, not required | open to all |
| **Admission Interview** | recommended, not required | open to all |
| **Classroom Visit** | recommended | open to all |
| **Faculty Meeting** | recommended | open to all |
| **Overnight Visit** | required | open to all |

**Interviews:** M–F; 30 minutes.

**Campus Tours:** Conducted by students. M–F at 10:00 am, 2:00 pm; 120 minutes.

**Class Visits:** Classroom visits are determined by the visit schedule.

**Overnight Visits:** During the regular academic year and over the summer, prospective applicants may spend an evening in a residence hall with a student host.

**Video:** Free on request.

## CAMPUS FACILITIES

**Science:** Seaman Mineral Museum.

**Athletic:** Mount Ripley Ski area, Portage Lake Golf Course, Student Development Center.

## LOCAL ATTRACTIONS

Quincy Mine; scenic areas.

# MINNESOTA

# BETHEL COLLEGE
**St. Paul, Minnesota**

**Contact:** Grace Okongo-Gwoke, Campus Visit Coordinator, Admissions Department, Bethel College, 3900 Bethel Drive, St. Paul, MN 55112. *Phone:* 612-638-6242 or toll-free 800-255-8706. *Fax:* 612-635-1490. *E-mail:* j-okongo-gwoke@bethel.edu *Web site:* http://www.bethel.edu/ *Visit location:* Office of Admissions, "RC" Building, 3900 Bethel Drive.

## QUICK FACTS

Enrollment: 2,540; UG: 2,319. Entrance: moderately difficult. SAT>500: 80% V, 81% M; ACT>18: N/R. Tuition and fees: $13,840. Room and board: $4950. Application deadline: rolling.

*Bethel College (continued)*

## GENERAL

Independent, comprehensive, coed, Baptist General Conference. Awards associate, bachelor's, and master's degrees. Founded 1871. Setting: 231-acre suburban campus. Undergraduate faculty: 228 (121 full-time, 107 part-time); student-faculty ratio is 16:1. Most popular recent majors: education, nursing, business administration.

## CAMPUS VISITS

**College Calendar 1998–99:** *Regular classes:* Sept. 1–Dec. 11; Feb. 1–May 14. *Breaks:* Nov. 25–30; Mar. 26–Apr. 6; Oct. 30–Nov. 2. *Final exams:* Dec. 14–18; May 17–21. *Admission office closed:* Christmas, Dec. 24–28; Martin Luther King Day, Jan. 18; Thanksgiving, Nov. 26–27. *Special campus days:* CV Weekend, Feb. 4–6, Nov. 5–7; Homecoming, Oct. 2–3; Parent's Weekend, Oct. 16–17; Spring Preview, May 1; Spring Reception, Apr. 10, Apr. 24, Apr. 26, Apr. 10.

## VISIT OPPORTUNITIES

|  | Appointments? | Who? |
|---|---|---|
| **Campus Tour** | recommended, not required | open to all |
| **Information Session** | required | open to all |
| **Admission Interview** | recommended, not required | open to all |
| **Classroom Visit** | required | open to all |
| **Faculty Meeting** | required | open to all |
| **Overnight Visit** | required | open to all |

**Information Sessions:** Sessions scheduled for specific events, not on a regular basis.

**Interviews:** M–F, Sat.; 60 minutes.

**Campus Tours:** Conducted by students. Call for available schedule; 60 minutes.

**Class Visits:** Prospective students may attend a class in their area of interest.

**Overnight Visits:** During the regular academic year, prospective applicants may spend an evening in a residence hall with a student host.

**Video:** Free on request.

## CAMPUS FACILITIES

**Of Special Interest:** The Great Hall Chapel.

# CONCORDIA COLLEGE
## Moorhead, Minnesota

**Contact:** Fern Elofson, Campus Visit Coordinator, 901 South 8th Street, Moorhead, MN 56562. *Phone:* toll-free 800-699-9897. *Fax:* 218-299-3947. *E-mail:* elofson@cord.edu *Web site:* http://www.cord.edu/ *Visit location:* Admissions Office, Lorentzsen Hall, 901 South 8th Street.

## QUICK FACTS

Enrollment: 2,858; UG: 2,858. Entrance: moderately difficult. SAT>500: 80% V, 83% M; ACT>18: 96%. Tuition and fees: $12,655. Room and board: $3645. Application deadline: rolling.

## GENERAL

Independent, 4-year, coed, Evangelical Lutheran Church in America. Awards bachelor's degrees. Founded 1891. Setting: 120-acre suburban campus. Faculty: 270 (180 full-time, 90 part-time); student-faculty ratio is 15:1. Most popular recent majors: business administration, biology, communications.

## CAMPUS VISITS

**College Calendar 1998–99:** *Regular classes:* Sept. 3–Dec. 15; Jan. 5–Apr. 26. *Breaks:* Oct. 26–27; Mar. 1–5. *Final exams:* Dec. 16–18; Apr. 28–30. *Admission office closed:* Nov. 27; Good Friday, Apr. 2. *Special campus days:* Graduation, May 2; Homecoming, Oct. 2–4.

## VISIT OPPORTUNITIES

|  | Appointments? | Who? |
|---|---|---|
| **Campus Tour** | recommended | open to all |
| **Information Session** | recommended | open to all |
| **Admission Interview** | recommended, not required | open to all |
| **Classroom Visit** | recommended | open to all |
| **Faculty Meeting** | recommended | open to all |
| **Overnight Visit** | recommended | open to all |

**Information Sessions:** M–F, Sat.

**Interviews:** M–F; Sat. during academic year; 30 minutes.

**Campus Tours:** Conducted by students. M–F 8:00 am–5:00 pm; Sat. 9:00 am–1:00 pm; 60 minutes.

**Class Visits:** Prospective students may attend a class in their area of interest.

**Overnight Visits:** During the regular academic year, prospective applicants may spend an evening in a residence hall with a student host.

## CAMPUS FACILITIES
**Of Special Interest:** Carl B. Ylvisaker Library.

# MACALESTER COLLEGE
St. Paul, Minnesota

**Contact:** Admissions Office, 1600 Grand Avenue, St. Paul, MN 55105-1899. *Phone:* toll-free 800-231-7974. *Fax:* 651-696-6724. *E-mail:* admissions@ macalester.edu *Web site:* http://www.macalester.edu/ *Visit location:* Admissions Office, Weyerhaeuser Hall, 62 Macalester Street.

## QUICK FACTS
Enrollment: 1,729; UG: 1,729. Entrance: very difficult. SAT>500: 99% V, 99% M; ACT>18: 100%. Tuition and fees: $18,758. Room and board: $5430. Application deadline: 1/15.

## GENERAL
Independent Presbyterian, 4-year, coed. Awards bachelor's degrees. Founded 1874. Setting: 53-acre urban campus. Faculty: 205 (144 full-time, 61 part-time); student-faculty ratio is 11:1. Most popular recent majors: psychology, English, economics.

## CAMPUS VISITS
**College Calendar 1998–99:** *Regular classes:* Sept. 9–Dec. 15; Feb. 1–May 11. *Breaks:* Oct. 29–Nov. 1; Mar. 27–Apr. 4; Dec. 21–Jan. 31. *Final exams:* Dec. 17–21; May 13–18. *Admission office closed:* Dec. 24. *Special campus days:* Commencement, May 23; Parents' Weekend/Fall Festival, Oct. 16; Scottish Country Fair, May 1.

## VISIT OPPORTUNITIES

| | Appointments? | Who? |
|---|---|---|
| **Campus Tour** | required | open to all |
| **Information Session** | recommended | open to all |
| **Admission Interview** | required | open to all |
| **Classroom Visit** | required | open to all |
| **Faculty Meeting** | required | open to all |
| **Overnight Visit** | required | open to all |

**Information Sessions:** M–F, select Sat.; M–F May–Jan. and Sat. during fall semester; 45 minutes.

**Interviews:** M–F, select Sat.; M–F May–Jan. and Sat. during fall semester; 45 minutes.

**Campus Tours:** Conducted by students. M–F, select Sat.; M–F May–Apr. and Sat. during fall semester; 45 minutes.

**Class Visits:** Prospective students may attend a class in their area of interest, classroom visits are determined by the visit schedule.

**Overnight Visits:** During the regular academic year, prospective applicants may spend an evening in a residence hall with a student host.

## CAMPUS FACILITIES
**Of Special Interest:** DeWitt Wallace Library.

## LOCAL ATTRACTIONS
The Hungry Mind Bookstore; Summit Avenue; Grand Avenue; retail and restaurant area.

# MANKATO STATE UNIVERSITY
Mankato, Minnesota

**Contact:** Admissions Office, MSU 55 PO Box 8400, Mankato, MN 56002-8400. *Phone:* 507-389-1822 or toll-free 800-722-0544. *Fax:* 507-389-5114. *E-mail:* admissions@mankato.msus.edu *Web site:* http://www. mankato.msus.edu/ *Visit location:* Admissions Office, Wigley Administration Building, Second Floor, MSU Box 55—PO Box 8400.

## QUICK FACTS
Enrollment: 12,166; UG: 10,009. Entrance: moderately difficult. SAT>500: N/App; ACT>18: 89%. Resident tuition and fees: $2983. Nonresident tuition and fees: $6170. Room and board: $2965. Application deadline: rolling.

## GENERAL
State-supported, comprehensive, coed. Part of Minnesota State Colleges and Universities System. Awards associate, bachelor's, and master's degrees. Founded 1868. Setting: 303-acre small-town campus with easy access to Minneapolis–St. Paul. Undergraduate faculty: 574 (521 full-time, 53 part-time); student-faculty ratio is 19:1. Most popular recent majors: business administration, education, accounting.

## CAMPUS VISITS
**College Calendar 1998–99:** *Regular classes:* Aug. 24–Dec. 18; Jan. 11–May 7. *Breaks:* Dec. 24–Jan. 10. *Final exams:* Dec. 14–18; May 3–7.

*Mankato State University (continued)*

## VISIT OPPORTUNITIES

|  | Appointments? | Who? |
|---|---|---|
| **Campus Tour** | recommended | open to all |
| **Information Session** | recommended | open to all |
| **Admission Interview** | recommended | open to all |
| **Faculty Meeting** | recommended | open to all |

**Information Sessions:** Call for schedule.

**Interviews:** M–F; 20 minutes.

**Campus Tours:** Conducted by students. M–F at 10:00 am, 2:00 pm; call for schedule during summer and finals weeks; 60 minutes.

## CAMPUS FACILITIES

**Science:** Lecture Hall, Science Labs, Microcomputer Clean Rooms.

**Arts:** Conkling Gallery; Appointment Required: Theater.

**Athletic:** Fieldhouse, Fitness Center.

**Of Special Interest:** Appointment Required: Residence Hall Rooms.

# MOORHEAD STATE UNIVERSITY
## Moorhead, Minnesota

**Contact:** Brenda Soule, Admissions Tour Coordinator, Moorhead State University, Owens Hall, Moorhead, MN 56563. *Phone:* toll-free 800-593-7246 Ext. 1. *Fax:* 218-236-2168. *Web site:* http://www.moorhead.msus.edu/ *Visit location:* Admissions Office, Owens Hall, 1104 Seventh Avenue South.

### QUICK FACTS

Enrollment: 5,986; UG: 5,668. Entrance: moderately difficult. SAT>500: N/App; ACT>18: N/App. Resident tuition and fees: $2908. Nonresident tuition and fees: $6020. Room and board: $3256. Application deadline: 8/7.

### GENERAL

State-supported, comprehensive, coed. Part of Minnesota State Colleges and Universities System. Awards associate, bachelor's, and master's degrees and post-master's certificates. Founded 1885. Setting: 118-acre urban campus. Undergraduate faculty: 340 (255 full-time, 85 part-time); student-faculty ratio is 18:1. Most popular recent majors: business administration, accounting.

### CAMPUS VISITS

**College Calendar 1998–99:** *Regular classes:* Aug. 24–Dec. 10; Jan. 6–Apr. 29. *Breaks:* Nov. 26–29; Mar. 8–12; Dec. 18–Jan. 6. *Final exams:* Dec. 11–17; Apr. 30–May 6. *Special campus days:* Fall Breather, Oct. 9–12; Spring Commencement, May 7; Winter Commencement, Dec. 18.

### VISIT OPPORTUNITIES

|  | Appointments? | Who? |
|---|---|---|
| **Campus Tour** | recommended, not required | open to all |
| **Information Session** | recommended | open to all |
| **Admission Interview** | required | open to all |
| **Classroom Visit** | required | open to all |
| **Faculty Meeting** | required | open to all |
| **Overnight Visit** | required | open to all |

**Information Sessions:** M–F at 10:00 am, 2:00 pm; Sat. at 10:30 am; 15 minutes.

**Interviews:** M–F, select Sat.; 20 minutes.

**Campus Tours:** Conducted by students. M–F at 10:00 am, 2:00 pm; Sat. at 11:00 am; unavailable during term breaks; 60 minutes.

**Class Visits:** Prospective students may attend a class in their area of interest.

**Overnight Visits:** During the regular academic year and over the summer, prospective applicants may spend an evening in a residence hall.

**Video:** Free on request.

### CAMPUS FACILITIES

**Science:** Appointment Required: Planetarium, Chemistry/Physics/Biology Departments.

**Arts:** Appointment Required: Main Stage, Thrust Stage, Art Gallery, Graphic Design Studio.

**Athletic:** Main Fieldhouse; Appointment Required: Pool.

**Of Special Interest:** Library; Appointment Required: Regional Science Center, Residence Halls.

### LOCAL ATTRACTIONS

Fargo Dome; Hefitage Hjemkomst Center; West Acres Mall.

# ST. CLOUD STATE UNIVERSITY
St. Cloud, Minnesota

**Contact:** Shana Moses, Visit Center Coordinator, AS 115 St.Cloud State University 4th Avenue South, St. Cloud, MN 56301-4498. *Phone:* 320-255-2244 or toll-free 800-369-4260. *Fax:* 320-255-2243. *E-mail:* scsu4u@stcloudstate.edu *Web site:* http://www.stcloud.state.edu/ *Visit location:* Admissions Visitor Center, Administrative Services Building, 720 4th Avenue South.

## QUICK FACTS
Enrollment: 13,946; UG: 12,570. Entrance: moderately difficult. SAT>500: N/App; ACT>18: N/App. Resident tuition and fees: $3082. Nonresident tuition and fees: $6106. Room and board: $3066. Application deadline: 5/1.

## GENERAL
State-supported, comprehensive, coed. Part of Minnesota State Colleges and Universities System. Awards associate, bachelor's, master's, and doctoral degrees. Founded 1869. Setting: 82-acre suburban campus with easy access to Minneapolis–St. Paul. Undergraduate faculty: 627 (573 full-time, 54 part-time); student-faculty ratio is 21:1. Most popular recent majors: elementary education, psychology, mass communications.

## CAMPUS VISITS
**College Calendar 1998–99:** *Regular classes:* Aug. 24–Dec. 11; Jan. 11–Apr. 30. *Breaks:* Nov. 25–29; Mar. 8–12. *Final exams:* Dec. 14–18; May 3–7. *Special campus days:* Fall Commencement, Dec. 18; Homecoming; Spring Commencement, May 7.

## VISIT OPPORTUNITIES

|  | Appointments? | Who? |
|---|---|---|
| **Campus Tour** | recommended | open to all |
| **Information Session** | recommended | open to all |
| **Admission Interview** | required | open to all |
| **Classroom Visit** | required | open to all |
| **Faculty Meeting** | required | open to all |
| **Overnight Visit** | required | open to all |

**Information Sessions:** M–F, select Sat., except during school breaks; 20 minutes.
**Interviews:** M–F, select Sat.; 20 minutes.
**Campus Tours:** Conducted by students. M–F, select Sat., except during school breaks; 90 minutes.

**Class Visits:** Classroom visits are determined by the visit schedule.
**Overnight Visits:** During the regular academic year, prospective applicants may spend an evening in a residence hall with a student host.

## CAMPUS FACILITIES
**Science:** Planetarium, Observatory, Weather Labs.
**Arts:** Kiehle Visual Center, SCSU Performing Arts Center, Mass Communication Studios, Atwood Center gallery.
**Athletic:** National Hockey Center, Halenbeck Recreational Facilities, Human Performance Lab.
**Of Special Interest:** Beaver Island trails and Talahi woods, American Indian Center, Minority Culture Center.

## LOCAL ATTRACTIONS
Mississippi River, Barden Park, Clemets gardens.

# SAINT MARY'S UNIVERSITY OF MINNESOTA
Winona, Minnesota

**Contact:** Mr. Anthony M. Piscitiello, Vice President for Admissions, 700 Terrace Heights #2, Winona, MN 55987. *Phone:* 507-457-1700 or toll-free 800-635-5987. *Fax:* 507-457-1722. *E-mail:* admissions@smumn.edu *Web site:* http://www.smumn.edu/ *Visit location:* Admissions, The Hendrickson Center, 700 Terrace Heights.

## QUICK FACTS
Enrollment: 5,083; UG: 1,667. Entrance: moderately difficult. SAT>500: N/R; ACT>18: 86%. Tuition and fees: $12,495. Room and board: $4120. Application deadline: rolling.

## GENERAL
Independent Roman Catholic, comprehensive, coed. Awards bachelor's, master's, and doctoral degrees and post-master's certificates. Founded 1912. Setting: 350-acre small-town campus. Undergraduate faculty: 303 (96 full-time, 207 part-time); student-faculty ratio is 14:1. Most popular recent majors: biology, psychology, elementary education.

## CAMPUS VISITS
**College Calendar 1998–99:** *Regular classes:* Sept. 1–Dec. 22; Jan. 11–May 11. *Breaks:* Oct. 17–20; Feb. 13–21; Nov. 25–30; Mar. 27–Apr. 5. *Final exams:* Dec. 18–22; May 7–11. *Admission office closed:* Nov. 26–27,

*Saint Mary's University of Minnesota (continued)*

Dec. 24–25. *Special campus days:* Commencement, May 15; Homecoming, June 18–20; Parents' Weekend, Oct. 2–4.

## VISIT OPPORTUNITIES

| | Appointments? | Who? |
|---|---|---|
| **Campus Tour** | recommended | open to all |
| **Information Session** | recommended | open to all |
| **Admission Interview** | recommended | open to all |
| **Classroom Visit** | recommended | open to all |
| **Faculty Meeting** | required | open to all |
| **Overnight Visit** | required | open to all |

**Information Sessions:** Included with admission interview.

**Interviews:** M–F 8:30 am–4:30 pm; Sat. 10:00 am–2:00 pm; 30 minutes.

**Campus Tours:** Conducted by students and admission reps. M–F 8:30 am–4:30 pm; Sat. 10:00 am–2:00 pm; 60 minutes.

**Class Visits:** Prospective students may attend a class in their area of interest.

**Overnight Visits:** During the regular academic year, prospective applicants may spend an evening in a residence hall with a student host.

**Video:** Free on request.

### CAMPUS FACILITIES
**Science:** Adducci Science Center.

**Arts:** Performance Center.

**Athletic:** The Recreation and Athletic Center (RAC).

**Of Special Interest:** Residence Halls, Michael H. Toner Student Center, Fitzgerald Library and McEnery Center.

# ST. OLAF COLLEGE
### Northfield, Minnesota

**Contact:** Janice Manning, Visit Coordinator, 1520 St. Olaf Avenue, Northfield, MN 55057. *Phone:* toll-free 800-275-6523 or toll-free 800-800-3025 (in-state). *Fax:* 507-646-3832. *Web site:* http://www.stolaf.edu/ *Visit location:* Admissions Office, Administration Building, 1520 St. Olaf Avenue.

### QUICK FACTS
Enrollment: 2,845; UG: 2,845. Entrance: very difficult. SAT>500: 90% V, 93% M; ACT>18: 99%. Tuition and fees: $16,500. Room and board: $4020. Application deadline: rolling.

### GENERAL
Independent Lutheran, 4-year, coed. Awards bachelor's degrees. Founded 1874. Setting: 350-acre small-town campus with easy access to Minneapolis–St. Paul. Faculty: 366 (222 full-time, 144 part-time); student-faculty ratio is 11:1. Most popular recent majors: biology, English, psychology.

### CAMPUS VISITS
**College Calendar 1998–99:** *Regular classes:* Sept. 10–Dec. 11; Jan. 4–28; Feb. 8–May 12. *Breaks:* Oct. 24–27; Mar. 27–Apr. 5; Nov. 25–29. *Final exams:* Dec. 14–18; Jan. 29; May 14–19.

## VISIT OPPORTUNITIES

| | Appointments? | Who? |
|---|---|---|
| **Campus Tour** | recommended | open to all |
| **Information Session** | required | open to all |
| **Admission Interview** | required | open to all |
| **Classroom Visit** | required | open to all |
| **Faculty Meeting** | required | open to all |
| **Overnight Visit** | required | open to all |

**Information Sessions:** M–F, select Sat.; 60 minutes.

**Interviews:** M–F; select Sat. until 12:00 pm except in the summer; 60 minutes.

**Campus Tours:** Conducted by students. M–F, select Sat.; 60 minutes.

**Class Visits:** Prospective students may attend a class in their area of interest.

**Overnight Visits:** During the regular academic year, prospective applicants may spend an evening in a residence hall with a student host.

### CAMPUS FACILITIES
**Athletic:** Skoglund Athletic Center, Manitou Field House.

**Of Special Interest:** New Student Commons.

# UNIVERSITY OF MINNESOTA, DULUTH
### Duluth, Minnesota

**Contact:** Office of Admissions, 23 Campus Center - 10 University Drive, Duluth, MN 55812. *Phone:*

toll-free 800-232-1339. *Fax:* 218-726-6394. *E-mail:* umdadmis@d.umn.edu *Web site:* http://www.d.umn. edu/ *Visit location:* Office of Admissions, Campus Center—Room 23, 10 University Drive.

## QUICK FACTS

Enrollment: 9,568; UG: 8,941. Entrance: moderately difficult. SAT>500: N/R; ACT>18: 96%. Resident tuition and fees: $4316. Nonresident tuition and fees: $11,196. Room and board: $3912. Application deadline: 2/1.

## GENERAL

State-supported, comprehensive, coed. Part of University of Minnesota System. Awards bachelor's and master's degrees. Founded 1947. Setting: 250-acre suburban campus. Undergraduate faculty: 510 (345 full-time, 165 part-time); student-faculty ratio is 18:1. Most popular recent majors: business administration, criminology.

## CAMPUS VISITS

**College Calendar 1998–99:** *Regular classes:* Sept. 8–Nov. 13; Nov. 30–Feb. 22; Mar. 8–May 14. *Breaks:* Nov. 21–29; Feb. 28–Mar. 7. *Final exams:* Nov. 16–20; Feb. 23–27; May 17–21. *Special campus days:* Commencement, May 22.

## VISIT OPPORTUNITIES

|  | Appointments? | Who? |
| --- | --- | --- |
| **Campus Tour** | recommended | open to all |
| **Information Session** | recommended | open to all |
| **Admission Interview** | recommended | open to all |
| **Classroom Visit** | recommended | open to all |
| **Faculty Meeting** | required | open to all |
| **Overnight Visit** | required | open to all |

**Information Sessions:** Fri. and Sat. during school year; call for available schedule; 120 minutes.

**Interviews:** M–F; 45 minutes.

**Campus Tours:** Conducted by students. M–F, select Sat. at 10:00 am, 2:00 pm; during summer M–F and select Sat. at 12:00 pm; 75 minutes.

**Class Visits:** Classroom visits are determined by the visit schedule.

**Overnight Visits:** During the regular academic year, prospective applicants may spend an evening in a residence hall.

## CAMPUS FACILITIES

**Science:** Appointment Required: Marshall W. Alworth Planetarium, Olga Lakela Herbarium.

**Arts:** Tweed Museum of Art, Marshall Performing Arts Center.

**Athletic:** Sports and Health Center.

## LOCAL ATTRACTIONS

Canal Park; Park Point Recreation Area; Glensheen Mansion; William A Irwin Ore Ship; Duluth area attractions.

# UNIVERSITY OF MINNESOTA, TWIN CITIES CAMPUS
**Minneapolis, Minnesota**

**Contact:** VISITLINE, 240 Williamson Hall, 231 Pillsbury Avenue SE, Minneapolis, MN 55455. *Phone:* toll-free 800-752-1000. *Fax:* 612-626-1693. *E-mail:* admissions@tc.umn.edu *Web site:* http://www1. umn.edu/tc/ *Visit location:* Office of Admissions, 240 Williamson Hall, 231 Pillsbury Drive SE.

## QUICK FACTS

Enrollment: 39,140; UG: 26,072. Entrance: moderately difficult. SAT>500: 81% V, 85% M; ACT>18: 95%. Resident tuition and fees: $4450. Nonresident tuition and fees: $11,852. Room and board: $4311. Application deadline: rolling.

## GENERAL

State-supported, university, coed. Part of University of Minnesota System. Awards bachelor's, master's, doctoral, and first professional degrees. Founded 1851. Setting: 2,000-acre urban campus. Undergraduate faculty: 2,722 (2,345 full-time, 377 part-time); student-faculty ratio is 15:1. Most popular recent majors: psychology, mechanical engineering, chemical engineering.

## CAMPUS VISITS

**College Calendar 1998–99:** *Regular classes:* Sept. 24–Dec. 4; Jan. 4–Mar. 12; Mar. 29–June 4. *Breaks:* Dec. 13–Jan. 3; Mar. 21–28. *Final exams:* Dec. 7–12; Mar. 15–20; June 7–12. *Admission office closed:* Nov. 27, Dec. 24, Mar. 26, July 5. *Special campus days:* Commencement, Dec. 12, Mar. 20, June 12; Homecoming, Oct. 24; Open House Events—available Saturdays in Fall.

*University of Minnesota, Twin Cities Campus (continued)*

## VISIT OPPORTUNITIES

| | Appointments? | Who? |
|---|---|---|
| **Campus Tour** | recommended, not required | open to all |
| **Information Session** | recommended, not required | open to all |
| **Classroom Visit** | | open to all |
| **Faculty Meeting** | | open to all |
| **Overnight Visit** | | open to all |

**Information Sessions:** M–F at 10:00 am, 1:00 pm; Sat. during academic year at 10:00 am; 60 minutes.

**Campus Tours:** Conducted by students and admission reps. M–F at 11:15 am, 2:15 pm; Sat. during academic year at 11:15 am; 60 minutes.

**Class Visits:** Prospective students may attend a class in their area of interest.

**Overnight Visits:** During the summer, prospective applicants may spend an evening in a residence hall.

**Video:** Free on request.

## CAMPUS FACILITIES
**Science:** Electrical Engineering and Computer Science Building, Basic Biology and Biochemistry Building, Civil Engineering Building.

**Arts:** Weisman Art Museum, Goldstein Gallery.

**Athletic:** Mariucci Hockey Arena, Williams Arena, University Recreation Center, Sports Pavilion.

## LOCAL ATTRACTIONS
Mall of America; Walker Art Center; Ordway Theater; Valleyfair Amusement Park; Major league sporting events.

# UNIVERSITY OF ST. THOMAS
## St. Paul, Minnesota

**Contact:** Visit Coordinator, 2115 Summit Avenue #32F-1, St. Paul, MN 55105-1096. *Phone:* toll-free 800-328-6819 Ext. 26154. *Fax:* 612-962-6160. *E-mail:* admissions@stthomas.edu *Web site:* http://www. stthomas.edu/ *Visit location:* Office of Admissions, 32 Finn.

## QUICK FACTS
Enrollment: 10,197; UG: 4,888. Entrance: moderately difficult. SAT>500: 81% V, 81% M; ACT>18: 98%. Tuition and fees: $14,660. Room and board: $4769. Application deadline: rolling.

## GENERAL
Independent Roman Catholic, university, coed. Awards bachelor's, master's, doctoral, and first professional degrees. Founded 1885. Setting: 78-acre urban campus with easy access to Minneapolis. Undergraduate faculty: 723 (341 full-time, 382 part-time); student-faculty ratio is 17:1. Most popular recent majors: business administration, sociology, journalism.

## CAMPUS VISITS
**College Calendar 1998–99:** *Regular classes:* Sept. 9–Dec. 11; Feb. 1–May 14. *Breaks:* Oct. 30–Nov. 1; Mar. 29–Apr. 5; Dec. 19–Jan. 31. *Final exams:* Dec. 15–18; May 18–21. *Special campus days:* Fall Commencement, Dec. 18; Spring Commencement, May 22.

## VISIT OPPORTUNITIES

| | Appointments? | Who? |
|---|---|---|
| **Campus Tour** | recommended | open to all |
| **Information Session** | not required | open to all |
| **Admission Interview** | recommended | open to all |
| **Classroom Visit** | required | open to all |
| **Faculty Meeting** | required | open to all |
| **Overnight Visit** | required | open to all |

**Information Sessions:** Scheduled events by invitation to prospective students; 180 minutes.

**Interviews:** M–F, select Sat.; 45 minutes.

**Campus Tours:** Conducted by students. M–F, select Sat.; 75 minutes.

**Class Visits:** Classroom visits are determined by the visit schedule.

**Overnight Visits:** During the regular academic year, prospective applicants may spend an evening in a residence hall with a student host.

## CAMPUS FACILITIES
**Science:** Frey Science and Engineering Center, Owens Science Hall.

**Of Special Interest:** Television Studio.

## LOCAL ATTRACTIONS
The Twin Cities, Mississippi River.

# WINONA STATE UNIVERSITY
Winona, Minnesota

**Contact:** Dr. Jim Mootz, Director of Admission, Somsen Hall - 106, Winona, MN 55987. *Phone:* toll-free 800-DIAL-WSU. *Fax:* 507-457-5620. *E-mail:* admissions@vaxz.winona.msus.edu *Web site:* http://www.winona.msus.edu/ *Visit location:* Office of Admission, Somsen Hall—106.

## QUICK FACTS
Enrollment: 6,531; UG: 5,860. Entrance: moderately difficult. SAT>500: N/R; ACT>18: 100%. Resident tuition and fees: $3019. Nonresident tuition and fees: $6147. Room and board: $3150. Application deadline: rolling.

## GENERAL
State-supported, comprehensive, coed. Part of Minnesota State Colleges and Universities System. Awards associate, bachelor's, and master's degrees and post-master's certificates. Founded 1858. Setting: 40-acre small-town campus. Undergraduate faculty: 350 (325 full-time, 25 part-time); student-faculty ratio is 21:1. Most popular recent majors: business administration, liberal arts and studies, nursing.

## CAMPUS VISITS
**College Calendar 1998–99:** *Regular classes:* Aug. 24–Dec. 10; Jan. 12–May 14. *Breaks:* Nov. 26–29; Mar. 6–21. *Final exams:* Dec. 11–17; May 17–20.

## VISIT OPPORTUNITIES

|  | Appointments? | Who? |
|---|---|---|
| **Campus Tour** | recommended, not required | open to all |
| **Information Session** | recommended, not required | open to all |
| **Admission Interview** | recommended, not required | open to all |
| **Classroom Visit** | recommended, not required | open to all |
| **Faculty Meeting** | recommended, not required | open to all |
| **Overnight Visit** | required | |

**Information Sessions:** M–F, select Sat.; 60 minutes.
**Interviews:** M–F, select Sat.; 60 minutes.
**Campus Tours:** Conducted by students. M–F at 9:00 am, 1:00 pm; Sat. at 10:00 am; 60 minutes.

**Class Visits:** Prospective students may attend a class in their area of interest, classroom visits are determined by the visit schedule.
**Overnight Visits:** During the regular academic year and over the summer.
**Video:** Available, fee charged.

## CAMPUS FACILITIES
**Science:** Engineering Labs, Nursing Skills Lab, Biology Area, Computer Facilities.
**Arts:** Theatres, Music Rooms, Art Studios.
**Athletic:** Field House, Training Facilities, Handball/Racquetball Courts.
**Of Special Interest:** Residential College, Library/Media Center, Technology Center.

## LOCAL ATTRACTIONS
Garvin Heights; Mississippi River Front.

# MISSISSIPPI

## MISSISSIPPI STATE UNIVERSITY
Mississippi State, Mississippi

**Contact:** Barbara Carver, Staff Assistant, Office of Enrollment Services, Box 6334, Mississippi, MS 39762. *Phone:* 601-325-3076. *Fax:* 601-325-1678. *E-mail:* barbara@saffairs.msstate.edu *Web site:* http://www.msstate.edu/ *Visit location:* Enrollment Services, Lee Hall, Lee Boulevard.

## QUICK FACTS
Enrollment: 15,533; UG: 12,527. Entrance: moderately difficult. SAT>500: N/R; ACT>18: 91%. Resident tuition and fees: $2731. Nonresident tuition and fees: $5551. Room and board: $4100. Application deadline: 7/26.

## GENERAL
State-supported, university, coed. Awards bachelor's, master's, doctoral, and first professional degrees and post-master's certificates. Founded 1878. Setting: 4,200-acre small-town campus. Undergraduate faculty: 823 (822 full-time, 1 part-time); student-faculty ratio is 17:1. Most popular recent majors: elementary education, business administration, business marketing and marketing management.

## CAMPUS VISITS
**College Calendar 1998–99:** *Regular classes:* Aug. 24–Dec. 11; Jan. 11–May 5. *Breaks:* Dec. 18–Jan. 10.

*Mississippi State University (continued)*

*Final exams:* Dec. 12–17; May 7–12. *Admission office closed:* Sept. 7, Nov. 26–27, Dec. 23–Jan. 1, Jan. 18. *Special campus days:* Commencement, Dec. 18, May 13; Homecoming, Oct. 17; Orientation, June 13–14, June 27–28, June 18–19; Super Bulldog Weekend, Apr. 24–26.

## VISIT OPPORTUNITIES

|                     | Appointments? | Who?                  |
|---------------------|---------------|-----------------------|
| **Campus Tour**     | recommended   | applicants and parents|
| **Information Session** | recommended |                    |
| **Classroom Visit** | recommended   | applicants and parents|
| **Faculty Meeting** | recommended   | applicants and parents|

**Information Sessions:** M–F 8:00 am–5:00 pm; 45 minutes.

**Campus Tours:** Conducted by students. M–F 8:00 am–5:00 pm; call to schedule Sat. visit; 60 minutes.

**Class Visits:** Prospective students may attend a class in their area of interest.

**Video:** Free on request.

## CAMPUS FACILITIES

**Science:** Appointment Required: High Voltage Laboratory, Raspet Flight Laboratory, Engineering Research Center, College of Veterinary Medicine.

**Arts:** Appointment Required: McComas Hall Theatre, Stafford and Freeman Hall, Giles Architecture Building.

**Athletic:** Appointment Required: Sanderson Student Center, Dudy-Noble Baseball Stadium, Humphrey Coliseum.

**Of Special Interest:** Appointment Required: Dairy Science—Ice Cream and Cheese making.

## LOCAL ATTRACTIONS

Golf Course, Old Waverly Golf Course, Equine Center.

# MISSOURI

## COLLEGE OF THE OZARKS
**Point Lookout, Missouri**

**Contact:** Dr. M. Glen Cameron, Dean of Admissions, Point Lookout, MO 65726. *Phone:* 417-334-

6411 Ext. 4217 or toll-free 800-222-0525. *Fax:* 417-335-2618. *E-mail:* admiss4@cofo.edu *Web site:* http://www.cofo.edu/ *Visit location:* Admissions, Administration Building.

## QUICK FACTS

Enrollment: 1,563; UG: 1,563. Entrance: moderately difficult. SAT>500: N/R; ACT>18: 98%. Tuition and fees: $150. Room and board: $2200. Application deadline: rolling.

## GENERAL

Independent Presbyterian, 4-year, coed. Awards bachelor's degrees. Founded 1906. Setting: 1,000-acre small-town campus. Faculty: 110 (83 full-time, 27 part-time); student-faculty ratio is 14:1. Most popular recent majors: education, business administration, psychology.

## CAMPUS VISITS

**College Calendar 1998–99:** *Regular classes:* Aug. 24–Dec. 10; Jan. 11–May 1. *Breaks:* Nov. 23–27; Mar. 15–19; Dec. 21–Jan. 6. *Final exams:* Dec. 12–17; May 3–7. *Admission office closed:* Nov. 23–27, Dec. 21–27, Jan. 1. *Special campus days:* Commencement, May 9; Homecoming, Oct. 17.

## VISIT OPPORTUNITIES

|                     | Appointments?            | Who?                  |
|---------------------|--------------------------|-----------------------|
| **Campus Tour**     | recommended, not required| open to all           |
| **Information Session** | recommended, not required | open to all       |
| **Admission Interview** | recommended          | applicants and parents|
| **Classroom Visit** | required                 |                       |
| **Faculty Meeting** | recommended              | applicants and parents|

**Information Sessions:** M–F 8:00 am–5:00 pm; summer hours 7:30 am–4:00 pm; 30 minutes.

**Interviews:** M–F; 30 minutes.

**Campus Tours:** Conducted by students. M–F 9:00 am–4:00 pm; summer hours 9:00 am–3:00 pm; 45 minutes.

**Class Visits:** Prospective students may attend a class in their area of interest.

## CAMPUS FACILITIES

**Of Special Interest:** Chapel.

## LOCAL ATTRACTIONS

Ralph Foster Museum; Grist Mill; Fruitcake and Jelly Kitchen; Branson area attractions.

# CULVER-STOCKTON COLLEGE

Canton, Missouri

**Contact:** Admissions Office, #1 College Hill, Canton, MO 63435. *Phone:* toll-free 800-537-1883 (out-of-state). *Fax:* 217-231-6611. *E-mail:* admissions@culver.edu *Web site:* http://www.culver.edu/ *Visit location:* Admissions Office, Henderson Hall, #1 College Hill.

## QUICK FACTS

Enrollment: 994; UG: 994. Entrance: moderately difficult. SAT>500: 36% V, 50% M; ACT>18: 94%. Tuition and fees: $9200. Room and board: $4230. Application deadline: rolling.

## GENERAL

Independent, 4-year, coed, Christian Church (Disciples of Christ). Awards bachelor's degrees. Founded 1853. Setting: 143-acre rural campus. Faculty: 76 (53 full-time, 23 part-time); student-faculty ratio is 17:1. Most popular recent majors: nursing, business administration, elementary education.

## CAMPUS VISITS

**College Calendar 1998–99:** *Regular classes:* Aug. 25–Dec. 7; Jan. 18–May 5. *Breaks:* Nov. 25–29; Mar. 8–12; Apr. 2–5. *Final exams:* Dec. 9–15; May 7–12.

## VISIT OPPORTUNITIES

|  | Appointments? | Who? |
|---|---|---|
| **Campus Tour** | recommended, not required | open to all |
| **Information Session** | recommended, not required | open to all |
| **Admission Interview** | recommended | |
| **Classroom Visit** | required | |
| **Faculty Meeting** | recommended | |
| **Overnight Visit** | required | |

**Information Sessions:** M–F, select Sat.; 30 minutes.
**Interviews:** M–F, Sat.; select Sun.; 30 minutes.
**Campus Tours:** Conducted by students and admission reps. M–F, Sat.; select Sun.; 60 minutes.

**Class Visits:** Prospective students may attend a class in their area of interest.
**Overnight Visits:** During the regular academic year and over the summer, prospective applicants may spend an evening in a residence hall with a student host.
**Video:** Free on request.

## CAMPUS FACILITIES

**Of Special Interest:** Johann Memorial Library.

# EVANGEL COLLEGE

Springfield, Missouri

**Contact:** Sherry Clopine, Campus Visit Coordinator, 1111 North Glenstone, Springfield, MO 65802. *Phone:* 417-865-2811 or toll-free 800-382-6435 (in-state). *Fax:* 417-865-9599. *E-mail:* clopines@mail.evangel.edu *Web site:* http://www.evangel.edu/ *Visit location:* Enrollment, Administration, 111 North Glenstone.

## QUICK FACTS

Enrollment: 1,595; UG: 1,595. Entrance: moderately difficult. SAT>500: N/R; ACT>18: 94%. Tuition and fees: $8850. Room and board: $3550. Application deadline: 8/15.

## GENERAL

Independent, 4-year, coed, Assemblies of God. Awards associate and bachelor's degrees. Founded 1955. Setting: 80-acre urban campus. Faculty: 122 (84 full-time, 38 part-time); student-faculty ratio is 18:1. Most popular recent majors: business administration, education, mass communications.

## CAMPUS VISITS

**College Calendar 1998–99:** *Regular classes:* Aug. 27–Dec. 15; Jan. 14–May 7. *Breaks:* Oct. 19–22; Mar. 5–14. *Final exams:* Dec. 11–15; May 3–6.

## VISIT OPPORTUNITIES

|  | Appointments? |
|---|---|
| **Campus Tour** | recommended |
| **Information Session** | recommended |
| **Admission Interview** | recommended |
| **Classroom Visit** | recommended |
| **Faculty Meeting** | recommended |
| **Overnight Visit** | required |

*Evangel College (continued)*

**Information Sessions:** M–F; 30 minutes.

**Interviews:** M–F; 20 minutes.

**Campus Tours:** Conducted by students and admission reps. M–F; 30 minutes.

**Class Visits:** Classroom visits are determined by the visit schedule.

**Overnight Visits:** During the regular academic year, prospective applicants may spend an evening in a residence hall with a student host.

**Video:** Free on request.

### CAMPUS FACILITIES
**Of Special Interest:** Claude Kendrick Library.


# KANSAS CITY ART INSTITUTE
## Kansas City, Missouri

**Contact:** Larry Stone, Vice President, Enrollment Management, 4415 Warwick Boulevard, Kansas City, MO 64111. *Phone:* 816-931-5224 or toll-free 800-522-5224. *Fax:* 816-531-6296. *E-mail:* admiss@kcai.edu *Web site:* http://www.kcai.edu/ *Visit location:* Admissions Office, Mineral Hall, 4340 Oak.

### QUICK FACTS
Enrollment: 607; UG: 607. Entrance: moderately difficult. SAT>500: 64% V, 57% M; ACT>18: 83%. Tuition and fees: $16,930. Room and board: $4964. Application deadline: rolling.

### GENERAL
Independent, 4-year, coed. Awards bachelor's degrees. Founded 1885. Setting: 12-acre urban campus. Faculty: 81 (48 full-time, 33 part-time); student-faculty ratio is 12:1.

### CAMPUS VISITS
**College Calendar 1998–99:** *Regular classes:* Aug. 31–Dec. 16; Jan. 20–May 11. *Breaks:* Mar. 12–21. *Final exams:* Dec. 10–16; May 5–11. *Special campus days:* Commencement, May 15.

### VISIT OPPORTUNITIES

|  | Appointments? | Who? |
| --- | --- | --- |
| **Campus Tour** | required | open to all |
| **Information Session** | required | open to all |
| **Admission Interview** | required | open to all |

|  | Appointments? | Who? |
| --- | --- | --- |
| **Classroom Visit** | required | open to all |
| **Faculty Meeting** | required | open to all |
| **Overnight Visit** | required | open to all |

**Information Sessions:** Available Fri. 9:30 am–12:00 pm twice a month.

**Interviews:** M–F, select Sat.; 60 minutes.

**Campus Tours:** Conducted by students. M–F, select Sat.; 60 minutes.

**Class Visits:** Prospective students may attend a class in their area of interest.

**Overnight Visits:** During the regular academic year, prospective applicants may spend an evening in a residence hall with a student host.

### CAMPUS FACILITIES
**Arts:** Student gallery, Department Studios.

### LOCAL ATTRACTIONS
Nelson-Atkins Museum of Art; Kemper Museum of Contemporary Art.


# LINDENWOOD UNIVERSITY
## St. Charles, Missouri

**Contact:** Tonie Isenhour, Director of Undergraduate Admissions, 209 South Kings Highway, St. Charles, MO 63301. *Phone:* 314-949-4949. *Fax:* 314-949-4910. *E-mail:* isenhour@lindenwood.edu *Web site:* http://www.lindenwood.edu/ *Visit location:* Undergraduate Admissions, Gables, Lindenwood University.

### QUICK FACTS
Enrollment: 4,732; UG: 3,147. Entrance: moderately difficult. SAT>500: N/R; ACT>18: 80%. Tuition and fees: $10,150. Room and board: $5000. Application deadline: rolling.

### GENERAL
Independent Presbyterian, comprehensive, coed. Awards bachelor's and master's degrees. Founded 1827. Setting: 268-acre suburban campus with easy access to St. Louis. Undergraduate faculty: 278 (124 full-time, 154 part-time); student-faculty ratio is 17:1. Most popular recent majors: business administration, mass communications, education.

## CAMPUS VISITS

**College Calendar 1998–99:** *Regular classes:* Aug. 24–Dec. 11; Jan. 11–May 7. *Breaks:* Nov. 26–27; Mar. 8–12. *Final exams:* Dec. 12–17; May 8–13. *Special campus days:* Commencement, May 15; Homecoming.

## VISIT OPPORTUNITIES

|  | Appointments? | Who? |
|---|---|---|
| **Campus Tour** | recommended, not required | open to all |
| **Information Session** | recommended | open to all |
| **Admission Interview** | recommended, not required | open to all |
| **Classroom Visit** | recommended | open to all |
| **Faculty Meeting** | recommended | open to all |

**Information Sessions:** M–F, Sat.; 30 minutes.

**Interviews:** M–F, Sat.; 30 minutes.

**Campus Tours:** Conducted by students and admission reps. M–F, Sat.; 45 minutes.

**Class Visits:** Classroom visits are determined by the visit schedule.

**Video:** Free on request.

## CAMPUS FACILITIES

**Arts:** Hendren Art Gallery, Lindenwood University Cultural Arts Center, Jekyl Theatre.

**Athletic:** Hyland Performance Arena, Fitness Center.

**Of Special Interest:** KCLC Radio Station, Dance Studio.

# MISSOURI VALLEY COLLEGE

Marshall, Missouri

**Contact:** Ms. Debbie Bultman, Office Coordinator, 500 East College, Marshall, MO 65340. *Phone:* 660-831-4114. *Fax:* 660-831-4039. *E-mail:* mo-valley@juno.com *Web site:* http://www.murlin.com/~webfx/mvc/ *Visit location:* Admission Office, Baity Hall #209, 500 East College.

## QUICK FACTS

Enrollment: 1,250; UG: 1,250. Entrance: moderately difficult. SAT>500: 10% V, 10% M; ACT>18: 77%. Tuition and fees: $10,500. Room and board: $5000. Application deadline: rolling.

## GENERAL

Independent, 4-year, coed, Presbyterian Church. Awards associate and bachelor's degrees. Founded 1889. Setting: 140-acre small-town campus with easy access to Kansas City. Faculty: 68 (59 full-time, 9 part-time); student-faculty ratio is 20:1. Most popular recent majors: business administration, education, psychology.

## CAMPUS VISITS

**College Calendar 1998–99:** *Regular classes:* Aug. 24–Dec. 11; Jan. 26–May 14. *Breaks:* Dec. 18–Jan. 3; Mar. 19–28. *Final exams:* Dec. 14–17; May 17–20. *Special campus days:* Homecoming/Alumni Weekend, Oct. 3.

## VISIT OPPORTUNITIES

|  | Appointments? | Who? |
|---|---|---|
| **Campus Tour** | recommended | applicants and parents |
| **Information Session** | recommended | |
| **Admission Interview** | recommended | applicants and parents |
| **Classroom Visit** | recommended | |
| **Faculty Meeting** | recommended | applicants and parents |
| **Overnight Visit** | | applicants only |

**Information Sessions:** Inquire for available schedule; 30 minutes.

**Interviews:** M–F, Sat.; 60 minutes.

**Campus Tours:** Conducted by students and admission reps. M–Sat., select Sun.

**Class Visits:** Classroom visits are determined by the visit schedule.

**Overnight Visits:** During the regular academic year, prospective applicants may spend an evening in a residence hall with a student host.

## CAMPUS FACILITIES

**Of Special Interest:** Murrell Memorial Library.

# NORTHWEST MISSOURI STATE UNIVERSITY

Maryville, Missouri

**Contact:** Visitor's Center, 800 University Drive, Maryville, MO 64468. *Phone:* toll-free 800-633-1175.

*Northwest Missouri State University (continued)*

*Fax:* 660-562-1121. *E-mail:* admissions@acad. nwmissouri.edu *Visit location:* Mabel Cook Admissions Office, Mabel Cook House, 800 University Drive.

### QUICK FACTS
Enrollment: 6,035; UG: 5,059. Entrance: moderately difficult. SAT>500: N/R; ACT>18: N/R. Resident tuition and fees: $2813. Nonresident tuition and fees: $4823. Room and board: $3890. Application deadline: rolling.

### GENERAL
State-supported, comprehensive, coed. Part of Missouri Coordinating Board for Higher Education. Awards bachelor's and master's degrees. Founded 1905. Setting: 240-acre small-town campus with easy access to Kansas City. Undergraduate faculty: 259 (228 full-time, 31 part-time); student-faculty ratio is 27:1. Most popular recent majors: business economics, education.

### CAMPUS VISITS
**College Calendar 1998–99:** *Regular classes:* Aug. 24–Dec. 4; Jan. 11–Apr. 23. *Breaks:* Dec. 11–Jan. 11. *Final exams:* Dec. 7–11; Apr. 26–30. *Special campus days:* Commencement, May 1, July 29; Family Day, Sept. 26; Homecoming, Oct. 10; Sneak Preview, Oct. 24.

### VISIT OPPORTUNITIES

|  | Appointments? | Who? |
|---|---|---|
| **Campus Tour** | recommended | open to all |
| **Information Session** | recommended, not required | open to all |
| **Admission Interview** | required | open to all |
| **Classroom Visit** |  | open to all |
| **Faculty Meeting** | required | open to all |

**Information Sessions:** M–F 9:00 am–3:00 pm; Sat. at 10:30 am; 30 minutes.
**Interviews:** M–F, Sat.; 30 minutes.
**Campus Tours:** Conducted by students and admission reps. M–F 9:00 am–3:00 pm; Sat. at 10:30 am; 75 minutes.
**Video:** Free on request.

### CAMPUS FACILITIES
**Science:** Garrett-Strong Science Building.

**Arts:** Fine Arts Building, Mary Lynn Performing Arts Center.
**Athletic:** Bearcat Arena, Student Recreation Center, Aquatic Center.
**Of Special Interest:** Colden Hall, Wells Hall (television and radio stations), Student Union, B.D. Owens library; resident halls; Appointment Required: agriculture facilities.

# ROCKHURST COLLEGE
**Kansas City, Missouri**

**Contact:** Ms. Kimberly Six, 1100 Rockhurst Road, Kansas City, MO 64110. *Phone:* toll-free 800-842-6776. *Fax:* 816-501-4241. *Web site:* http://www. rockhurst.edu/ *Visit location:* Admission Office, Massman Hall, second floor, 1100 Rockhurst Road.

### QUICK FACTS
Enrollment: 2,772; UG: 2,029. Entrance: moderately difficult. SAT>500: 76% V, 74% M; ACT>18: 95%. Tuition and fees: $11,850. Room and board: $4760. Application deadline: rolling.

### GENERAL
Independent Roman Catholic (Jesuit), comprehensive, coed. Awards bachelor's and master's degrees. Founded 1910. Setting: 35-acre urban campus. Undergraduate faculty: 192 (108 full-time, 84 part-time); student-faculty ratio is 11:1. Most popular recent majors: nursing, biology, psychology.

### CAMPUS VISITS
**College Calendar 1998–99:** *Regular classes:* Aug. 26–Dec. 12; Jan. 13–May 5. *Breaks:* Oct. 16–19; Mar. 8–13; Apr. 2–5. *Final exams:* Dec. 14–19; May 6–12. *Admission office closed:* Good Friday, Apr. 2. *Special campus days:* Commencement, May 16.

### VISIT OPPORTUNITIES

|  | Appointments? | Who? |
|---|---|---|
| **Campus Tour** | required | open to all |
| **Information Session** | required | open to all |
| **Admission Interview** | required | open to all |
| **Classroom Visit** | required | open to all |
| **Faculty Meeting** | required | open to all |
| **Overnight Visit** | required | open to all |

**Information Sessions:** Select programs in certain cities for general information sessions; 45 minutes.

**Interviews:** M–F; first Sat. of month from Sept.–May; 60 minutes.

**Campus Tours:** Conducted by students and admission reps. M–F, select Sat.; 60 minutes.

**Class Visits:** Prospective students may attend a class in their area of interest, classroom visits are determined by the visit schedule.

**Overnight Visits:** During the regular academic year, prospective applicants may spend an evening in a residence hall with a student host.

**Video:** Free on request.

## CAMPUS FACILITIES

**Science:** Richardson Science Center.

**Arts:** Appointment Required: Van Ackeren Gallery of Religious Art.

**Athletic:** Mason-Halpin Fieldhouse, Physical Education and Convocation Center.

**Of Special Interest:** St. Francis Xavier Catholic Center.

## LOCAL ATTRACTIONS

The Country Club Plaza; Nelson-Atkins Museum of Art; NCAA headquarters; Arthur Bryant bar-b-que.

# SOUTHEAST MISSOURI STATE UNIVERSITY

Cape Girardeau, Missouri

**Contact:** Wenke Buttl, Campus Visit Coordinator, One University Plaza, Cape Girardeau, MO 63701. *Phone:* 573-651-5945. *Fax:* 573-651-5936. *E-mail:* wbuttl@semovm.semo.edu *Web site:* http://www.semo.edu/ *Visit location:* Admissions Office, Academic Hall, One University Plaza.

## QUICK FACTS

Enrollment: 7,896; UG: 7,011. Entrance: moderately difficult. SAT>500: N/R; ACT>18: N/R. Resident tuition and fees: $3000. Nonresident tuition and fees: $5400. Room and board: $6920. Application deadline: 7/15.

## GENERAL

State-supported, comprehensive, coed. Part of Missouri Coordinating Board for Higher Education. Awards associate, bachelor's, and master's degrees. Founded 1873. Setting: 693-acre small-town campus with easy access to St. Louis. Undergraduate faculty:

378 (377 full-time, 1 part-time); student-faculty ratio is 19:1. Most popular recent majors: business administration, education, mass communications.

## CAMPUS VISITS

**College Calendar 1998–99:** *Regular classes:* Aug. 24–Dec. 11; Jan. 19–May 18. *Breaks:* Nov. 25–27; Mar. 15–19. *Final exams:* Dec. 14–18; May 17–21.

## VISIT OPPORTUNITIES

|  | Appointments? | Who? |
|---|---|---|
| **Campus Tour** | required | open to all |
| **Information Session** | required | open to all |
| **Admission Interview** | required | open to all |
| **Classroom Visit** | required | open to all |
| **Faculty Meeting** | required | open to all |

**Information Sessions:** M–F, Sat.; 30 minutes.

**Interviews:** M–F, Sat.; 30 minutes.

**Campus Tours:** Conducted by students. M–F, Sat. 9:00 am–1:00 pm; 90 minutes.

**Class Visits:** Classroom visits are assigned to available classes.

**Video:** Available, fee charged.

## CAMPUS FACILITIES

**Science:** Appointment Required: Horticulture Green House, Crime Lab, Children's Educational Lab.

**Arts:** Theater, University Museum.

**Athletic:** Football Building.

# STEPHENS COLLEGE

Columbia, Missouri

**Contact:** Office of Admission, 1200 East Broadway Box 2121, Columbia, MO 65215. *Phone:* toll-free 800-876-7207. *Fax:* 573-876-7237. *E-mail:* apply@sc.stephens.edu *Web site:* http://www.stephens.edu/ *Visit location:* Admission Office, Visitor's Center, 1215 East Broadway.

## QUICK FACTS

Enrollment: 819; UG: 808. Entrance: moderately difficult. SAT>500: N/R; ACT>18: N/R. Tuition and fees: $14,830. Room and board: $5700. Application deadline: 7/31.

*Stephens College (continued)*

## GENERAL
Independent, comprehensive, women only. Awards associate, bachelor's, and master's degrees. Founded 1833. Setting: 244-acre urban campus. Undergraduate faculty: 59 (51 full-time, 8 part-time); student-faculty ratio is 10:1. Most popular recent majors: fashion merchandising, theater arts/drama, business administration.

## CAMPUS VISITS
**College Calendar 1998–99:** *Regular classes:* Aug. 24–Dec. 11; Jan. 11–Apr. 30. *Breaks:* Dec. 18–Jan. 10. *Final exams:* Dec. 14–17; May 3–6. *Admission office closed:* Dec. 23–Jan. 4. *Special campus days:* Campus Visit Day, Sept. 25, Feb. 8, Apr. 12; Commencement, May 8; Preview Day Weekend, Oct. 11–12, Mar. 14–15; Stephens College Academic Scholarship Program, Nov. 6–7.

## VISIT OPPORTUNITIES

|  | Appointments? | Who? |
|---|---|---|
| **Campus Tour** | not required | open to all |
| **Information Session** | not required | open to all |
| **Admission Interview** | not required | open to all |
| **Classroom Visit** | recommended | open to all |
| **Faculty Meeting** |  | open to all |
| **Overnight Visit** | recommended | open to all |

**Information Sessions:** M–F 8:00 am–5:00 pm; call for Preview Day Events schedule; 60 minutes.

**Interviews:** M–F; call for Preview Day Event schedule; 30 minutes.

**Campus Tours:** Conducted by students and admission reps. M–F 8:00 am–5:00 pm; call for Preview Day Events schedule.

**Class Visits:** Prospective students may attend a class in their area of interest, classroom visits are determined by the visit schedule.

**Overnight Visits:** During the regular academic year, prospective applicants may spend an evening in a residence hall with a student host.

**Video:** Free on request.

## CAMPUS FACILITIES
**Science:** Prunty House Plan, Pillsbury Science Center.

**Arts:** MacKlanburg Gallery and Playhouse, Davis Art Gallery, Historic Costume Collection, Harriet Ann Gray Dance Studio.

**Athletic:** Basketball Arena, Olympic size Swimming Pool, Golf Course and Lake.

**Of Special Interest:** Firestone Baars Chapel, Stephens Stables.

## LOCAL ATTRACTIONS
Downtown Columbia; historic University of Missouri—Columbia.

# TRUMAN STATE UNIVERSITY
### Kirksville, Missouri

**Contact:** Campus Visit Coordinator, 205 McClain Hall, Kirksville, MO 63501. *Phone:* 660-785-4135 or toll-free 800-892-7792 (in-state). *Fax:* 660-785-7456. *E-mail:* admission@truman.edu *Web site:* http://www. truman.edu/ *Visit location:* Office of Admission, 205 McClain Hall, 100 East Normal Street.

## QUICK FACTS
Enrollment: 6,328; UG: 5,957. Entrance: moderately difficult. SAT>500: 94% V, 93% M; ACT>18: 100%. Resident tuition and fees: $3274. Nonresident tuition and fees: $5754. Room and board: $3992. Application deadline: 3/1.

## GENERAL
State-supported, comprehensive, coed. Awards bachelor's and master's degrees. Founded 1867. Setting: 140-acre small-town campus. Undergraduate faculty: 399 (356 full-time, 43 part-time); student-faculty ratio is 16:1. Most popular recent majors: business administration, biology, English.

## CAMPUS VISITS
**College Calendar 1998–99:** *Regular classes:* Aug. 24–Dec. 15; Jan. 6–May 4. *Breaks:* Oct. 16–19; Mar. 8–15; Apr. 2–5. *Final exams:* Dec. 10–15; Apr. 29–May 4. *Special campus days:* Homecoming, Oct. 24; Spring Commencement, May 8; Winter Commencement, Dec. 19.

## VISIT OPPORTUNITIES

|  | Appointments? | Who? |
|---|---|---|
| **Campus Tour** | recommended | open to all |
| **Admission Interview** | recommended | open to all |
| **Classroom Visit** | required | open to all |

## VISIT OPPORTUNITIES—*continued*

| | Appointments? | Who? |
|---|---|---|
| **Faculty Meeting** | required | open to all |
| **Overnight Visit** | required | open to all |

**Interviews:** M–F, select Sat.

**Campus Tours:** Conducted by students. M–F 9:30 am–3:30 pm; select Sat.; 90 minutes.

**Overnight Visits:** During the regular academic year, prospective applicants may spend an evening in a residence hall with a student host.

### CAMPUS FACILITIES

**Athletic:** Student Recreation Center.

**Of Special Interest:** Pickler Memorial Library, Vollette Hall.

# UNIVERSITY OF MISSOURI–ROLLA

**Rolla, Missouri**

**Contact:** Carolyn Cassidy, 106 Parker Hall, 1870 Miner Circle, Rolla, MO 65409-1060. *Phone:* toll-free 800-522-0938. *Fax:* 573-341-4082. *E-mail:* umrolla@umr.edu *Web site:* http://www.umr.edu/ *Visit location:* Admissions-Room 106, Parker Hall, 1870 Miner Circle.

### QUICK FACTS

Enrollment: 4,898; UG: 4,034. Entrance: very difficult. SAT>500: 94% V, 97% M; ACT>18: 100%. Resident tuition and fees: $4194. Nonresident tuition and fees: $11,637. Room and board: $4220. Application deadline: 7/1.

### GENERAL

State-supported, university, coed. Part of University of Missouri System. Awards bachelor's, master's, and doctoral degrees. Founded 1870. Setting: 284-acre small-town campus. Undergraduate faculty: 383 (320 full-time, 63 part-time); student-faculty ratio is 14:1. Most popular recent majors: mechanical engineering, electrical/electronics engineering, civil engineering.

### CAMPUS VISITS

**College Calendar 1998–99:** *Regular classes:* Aug. 24–Dec. 11; Jan. 11–May 7. *Breaks:* Dec. 19–Jan. 10. *Final exams:* Dec. 14–18; May 10–14. *Special campus days:* Commencement, May 14–15; Fall Open House, Oct. 17; Homecoming, Oct. 2–3; Rolla Review, Oct.

15–16; Science and Engineering Fair, Apr. 2–3; Spring Open House, Apr. 3.

### VISIT OPPORTUNITIES

| | Appointments? | Who? |
|---|---|---|
| **Campus Tour** | recommended, not required | open to all |
| **Information Session** | recommended, not required | open to all |
| **Classroom Visit** | recommended, not required | open to all |
| **Faculty Meeting** | recommended, not required | open to all |
| **Overnight Visit** | recommended, not required | open to all |

**Information Sessions:** M–F, select Sat.; 60 minutes.

**Campus Tours:** Conducted by students. M–F, select Sat.; 60 minutes.

**Class Visits:** Prospective students may attend a class in their area of interest.

**Overnight Visits:** During the regular academic year and over the summer, prospective applicants may spend an evening in a residence hall.

**Video:** Free on request.

### CAMPUS FACILITIES

**Science:** Appointment Required: Laboratories.

**Arts:** Appointment Required: Theater, Music Rehearsal Halls.

**Athletic:** Appointment Required: Practice Field/facilities.

**Of Special Interest:** Stonehenge.

### LOCAL ATTRACTIONS

Missouri Wine Country, Ozark National Scenic Riverways, Lake of the Ozarks, Branson, St. Louis Arch; Kansas City Plaza Area, Meramec and Onondaga Caverns, Professional Sports Teams.

# WASHINGTON UNIVERSITY IN ST. LOUIS

**St. Louis, Missouri**

**Contact:** Office of Undergraduate Admissions, Campus Box 1089, One Brookings Drive, St. Louis, MO 63130-4899. *Phone:* toll-free 800-638-0700. *Fax:* 314-935-4290. *E-mail:* admission@wustl.edu *Web site:* http://www.wustl.edu/ *Visit location:* Office of Under-

*Washington University in St. Louis (continued)*

graduate Admissions, South Brookings Hall, One Brookings Drive (Campus Box 1089).

## QUICK FACTS

Enrollment: 11,017; UG: 5,493. Entrance: very difficult. SAT>500: 93% V, 100% M; ACT>18: 100%. Tuition and fees: $22,422. Room and board: $6922. Application deadline: 1/15.

## GENERAL

Independent, university, coed. Awards bachelor's, master's, doctoral, and first professional degrees. Founded 1853. Setting: 169-acre suburban campus. Undergraduate faculty: 2,452 (1,948 full-time, 504 part-time); student-faculty ratio is 7:1. Most popular recent majors: engineering, business administration, biology.

## CAMPUS VISITS

**College Calendar 1998–99:** *Regular classes:* Aug. 26–Dec. 21; Jan. 11–May 6. *Breaks:* Oct. 16–18; Mar. 1–7. *Final exams:* Dec. 14–21; Apr. 29–May 6. *Admission office closed:* Nov. 27, Dec. 24. *Special campus days:* Commencement, May 14.

## VISIT OPPORTUNITIES

|  | Appointments? | Who? |
|---|---|---|
| **Campus Tour** | recommended, not required | open to all |
| **Information Session** | recommended, not required | open to all |
| **Admission Interview** | recommended | open to all |
| **Classroom Visit** | recommended | open to all |
| **Faculty Meeting** | recommended | open to all |
| **Overnight Visit** | required | open to all |

**Information Sessions:** M–F, select Sat.; 60 minutes.

**Interviews:** M–F, select Sat.; alumni interviews available; call for schedule.

**Campus Tours:** Conducted by students. M–F, select Sat.; contact Undergraduate Admissions to arrange individualized tours; 90 minutes.

**Class Visits:** Prospective students may attend a class in their area of interest.

**Overnight Visits:** During the regular academic year, prospective applicants may spend an evening in a residence hall with a student host.

**Video:** Free on request.

## CAMPUS FACILITIES

**Science:** Appointment Required: Laboratory Tours, Observatory.

**Arts:** Steinberg Gallery of Art, Edison Theatre, International Writers Center, Performing Arts Department, Music and Dance Facilities; Appointment Required: School of Art and School of Architecture.

**Athletic:** Athletic Complex.

**Of Special Interest:** Libraries; Appointment Required: Freshmen Residence Halls, Business School, Engineering School.

## LOCAL ATTRACTIONS

Gateway Arch; Forest Park; Missouri Botanical Gardens; Fox Theatre; symphony; sporting events; concerts; The Loop; Central West End; Crayton.

# MONTANA

## MONTANA STATE UNIVERSITY–BOZEMAN

**Bozeman, Montana**

**Contact:** Visit Coordinator, 120 Hamilton Hall, Bozeman, MT 59717. *Phone:* toll-free 888-MSU-CATS. *Fax:* 406-994-1923. *E-mail:* zami202@montana. edu *Web site:* http://www.montana.edu/ *Visit location:* New Student Services, 120 Hamilton Hall, Montana State University.

## QUICK FACTS

Enrollment: 11,489; UG: 10,287. Entrance: moderately difficult. SAT>500: 68% V, 74% M; ACT>18: 92%. Resident tuition and fees: $2677. Nonresident tuition and fees: $7692. Room and board: $4025. Application deadline: 7/1.

## GENERAL

State-supported, university, coed. Part of Montana University System. Awards bachelor's, master's, and doctoral degrees. Founded 1893. Setting: 1,170-acre small-town campus. Undergraduate faculty: 641 (507 full-time, 134 part-time); student-faculty ratio is 18:1.

## CAMPUS VISITS

**College Calendar 1998–99:** *Regular classes:* Aug. 31–Dec. 18; Jan. 13–May 7. *Breaks:* Mar. 15–19. *Final exams:* Dec. 14–18; May 3–7. *Special campus days:* Commencement, May 8.

## VISIT OPPORTUNITIES

|                     | Appointments? | Who?        |
|---------------------|---------------|-------------|
| **Campus Tour**        | not required  | open to all |
| **Information Session** |               | open to all |
| **Admission Interview** | recommended   | open to all |
| **Faculty Meeting**     | recommended   | open to all |
| **Overnight Visit**     | required      | open to all |

**Interviews:** M–F; weekends by appointment; 30 minutes.

**Campus Tours:** Conducted by students and admission reps. M–F at 9:00 am, 2:00 pm; weekends by appointment; 60 minutes.

**Overnight Visits:** During the regular academic year, prospective applicants may spend an evening in a residence hall with a student host.

## CAMPUS FACILITIES
**Of Special Interest:** Renne Library.

## LOCAL ATTRACTIONS
Museum of the Rockies.

# THE UNIVERSITY OF MONTANA–MISSOULA
**Missoula, Montana**

**Contact:** Admissions and New Student Services, The University of Montana, Lodge 101, Missoula, MT 59812. *Phone:* 406-243-6266 or toll-free 800-462-8636. *Fax:* 406-243-5711. *E-mail:* admiss@selway.umt.edu *Web site:* http://www.umt.edu/ *Visit location:* Admissions and New Student Services, Lodge, Room 101.

## QUICK FACTS
Enrollment: 12,124; UG: 10,433. Entrance: moderately difficult. SAT>500: 72% V, 69% M; ACT>18: 91%. Resident tuition and fees: $2630. Nonresident tuition and fees: $7192. Room and board: $3917. Application deadline: 7/1.

## GENERAL
State-supported, university, coed. Part of Montana University System. Awards associate, bachelor's, master's, doctoral, and first professional degrees. Founded 1893. Setting: 220-acre urban campus. Undergraduate faculty: 590 (421 full-time, 169

part-time); student-faculty ratio is 19:1. Most popular recent majors: business administration, education, forestry.

## CAMPUS VISITS
**College Calendar 1998–99:** *Regular classes:* Aug. 31–Dec. 11; Jan. 25–May 7. *Breaks:* Dec. 18–Jan. 24; Mar. 15–19; Nov. 25–27. *Final exams:* Dec. 14–18; May 10–14.

## VISIT OPPORTUNITIES

|                     | Appointments?                | Who?        |
|---------------------|------------------------------|-------------|
| **Campus Tour**        | recommended, not required   | open to all |
| **Information Session** | recommended, not required   | open to all |
| **Classroom Visit**    | required                     | open to all |
| **Faculty Meeting**    | required                     | open to all |
| **Overnight Visit**    | required                     | open to all |

**Campus Tours:** Conducted by students. M–F at 10:00 am, 1:00 pm, 3:00 pm; 60 minutes.

**Class Visits:** Prospective students may attend a class in their area of interest.

**Overnight Visits:** During the regular academic year, prospective applicants may spend an evening in a residence hall.

**Video:** Free on request.

## CAMPUS FACILITIES
**Science:** Biological Station at Flathead Lake, Lubrecht Forest, Stella Duncan Memorial Research Institute.

**Arts:** Gallery of Visual Arts, Paxon Art Gallery, University Center Art Gallery.

**Athletic:** Harry Adams Fieldhouse, Washington-Grizzly Stadium.

**Of Special Interest:** Broadcast Media Center, Center at Salmon Lake, Center for Rocky Mountain West.

## LOCAL ATTRACTIONS
Missoula Carousel, Missoula Smoke Jumpers Center, Mount Sentinel, Rocky Mountain Elk Foundation, Mission Bison Range, Flathead Lake.

# NEBRASKA

# CREIGHTON UNIVERSITY
**Omaha, Nebraska**

**Contact:** Office of Admissions, 2500 California Plaza, Omaha, NE 68178-0001. *Phone:* toll-free

*Creighton University (continued)*

800-282-5835 (in-state). *Fax:* 402-280-2685. *E-mail:* admissions@creighton.edu *Web site:* http://www.creighton.edu/ *Visit location:* Undergraduate Office of Admissions, Swanson Hall, 2500 California Plaza.

## QUICK FACTS
Enrollment: 5,898; UG: 3,585. Entrance: moderately difficult. SAT>500: N/R; ACT>18: 99%. Tuition and fees: $12,756. Room and board: $4940. Application deadline: rolling.

## GENERAL
Independent Roman Catholic (Jesuit), university, coed. Awards associate, bachelor's, master's, doctoral, and first professional degrees. Founded 1878. Setting: 85-acre urban campus. Undergraduate faculty: 835 (625 full-time, 210 part-time); student-faculty ratio is 14:1. Most popular recent majors: nursing, biology, psychology.

## CAMPUS VISITS
**College Calendar 1998–99:** *Regular classes:* Aug. 26–Dec. 19; Jan. 13–May 8. *Breaks:* Oct. 17–25; Mar. 6–14. *Final exams:* Dec. 14–19; May 3–8. *Special campus days:* University Commencement, May 15.

## VISIT OPPORTUNITIES

|  | Appointments? | Who? |
|---|---|---|
| **Campus Tour** | required | open to all |
| **Information Session** | required | open to all |
| **Admission Interview** | required | open to all |
| **Classroom Visit** | required | open to all |
| **Faculty Meeting** | required | open to all |
| **Overnight Visit** | required | open to all |

**Information Sessions:** M–F.

**Interviews:** M–F; Sat. appointments during academic year; 45 minutes.

**Campus Tours:** Conducted by students. M–F, select Sat.; 60 minutes.

**Class Visits:** Prospective students may attend a class in their area of interest, classroom visits are determined by the visit schedule.

**Overnight Visits:** During the regular academic year, prospective applicants may spend an evening in a residence hall with a student host.

**Video:** Free on request.

## CAMPUS FACILITIES
**Science:** Biomedical Information Center.

**Arts:** Lied Center for the Fine and Performing Arts.

**Athletic:** Kiewit Physical Fitness Center.

**Of Special Interest:** V.J. and Angela Skutt Student Center.

## LOCAL ATTRACTIONS
Henry Doorly Zoo, Riverfront "Old Market" district featuring Victorian storefronts, horse-drawn carriage rides, specialty boutiques and sidewalk cafes.

# GRACE UNIVERSITY
**Omaha, Nebraska**

**Contact:** Emily Hulling, Admissions Assistant, 1311 South Ninth Street, Omaha, NE 68108. *Phone:* toll-free 800-383-1422. *Fax:* 402-341-9587. *E-mail:* admissions@graceu.edu *Web site:* http://www.graceu.edu/ *Visit location:* Admissions, Administrative, 1311 South Ninth Street.

## QUICK FACTS
Enrollment: 519; UG: 439. Entrance: moderately difficult. SAT>500: N/App; ACT>18: N/App. Tuition and fees: $7484. Room and board: $3230. Application deadline: rolling.

## GENERAL
Independent nondenominational, comprehensive, coed. Awards associate, bachelor's, and master's degrees. Founded 1943. Undergraduate faculty: 40 (26 full-time, 14 part-time); student-faculty ratio is 14:1.

## CAMPUS VISITS
**College Calendar 1998–99:** *Regular classes:* Aug. 18–Dec. 13; Jan. 4–8; Jan. 12–May 7. *Breaks:* Oct. 12–13; Mar. 22–26; Nov. 26–30. *Final exams:* Dec. 14–17; May 10–13.

## VISIT OPPORTUNITIES

|  | Appointments? |
|---|---|
| **Campus Tour** | recommended |
| **Information Session** | recommended |
| **Admission Interview** | recommended |
| **Classroom Visit** | recommended |
| **Faculty Meeting** | recommended |
| **Overnight Visit** | recommended |

**Information Sessions:** M–F 7:00 am–9:00 pm; Sat. 9:00 am–2:00 pm.

**Interviews:** M–F 7:00 am–9:00 pm; Sat. 9:00 am–2:00 pm; 45 minutes.

**Campus Tours:** Conducted by admission reps. M–F 7:00 am–9:00 pm; Sat. 9:00 am–2:00 pm.

**Class Visits:** Prospective students may attend a class in their area of interest, classroom visits are determined by the visit schedule.

**Overnight Visits:** During the regular academic year, prospective applicants may spend an evening in a residence hall with a student host.

**Video:** Free on request.

### LOCAL ATTRACTIONS
Henry Doorley Zoo; Omaha Royals baseball team.

## HASTINGS COLLEGE
Hastings, Nebraska

**Contact:** Mr. Michael Karloff, Director of Admissions, 800 North Turner, Hastings, NE 68901. *Phone:* toll-free 800-532-7642 (in-state), 800-461-7480 (out-of-state). *Fax:* 402-461-7490. *E-mail:* mkarloff@ hastings.edu *Web site:* http://www.hastings.edu/ *Visit location:* Admissions Office, Hurley-McDonald Hall, 800 North Turner.

### QUICK FACTS
Enrollment: 1,036; UG: 1,007. Entrance: moderately difficult. SAT>500: 70% V, 71% M; ACT>18: 90%. Tuition and fees: $11,368. Room and board: $3758. Application deadline: 7/15.

### GENERAL
Independent Presbyterian, comprehensive, coed. Awards bachelor's and master's degrees. Founded 1882. Setting: 88-acre small-town campus. Undergraduate faculty: 101 (72 full-time, 29 part-time); student-faculty ratio is 13:1. Most popular recent majors: business administration, education, psychology.

### CAMPUS VISITS
**College Calendar 1998–99:** *Regular classes:* Aug. 31–Dec. 11; Jan. 5–26; Feb. 1–May 14. *Breaks:* Dec. 17–Jan. 5; Jan. 26–Feb. 1. *Final exams:* Dec. 14–17; May 17–20.

### VISIT OPPORTUNITIES

| | Appointments? | Who? |
|---|---|---|
| **Campus Tour** | required | open to all |
| **Information Session** | required | open to all |
| **Admission Interview** | required | open to all |
| **Classroom Visit** | required | open to all |
| **Faculty Meeting** | required | open to all |
| **Overnight Visit** | required | open to all |

**Information Sessions:** M–F, select Sat.; inquire for schedule during holidays; 30 minutes.

**Interviews:** M–F, select Sat.; inquire for schedule during holidays; 30 minutes.

**Campus Tours:** Conducted by students and admission reps. M–F, select Sat.; inquire for schedule during holidays.

**Class Visits:** Prospective students may attend a class in their area of interest.

**Overnight Visits:** During the regular academic year, prospective applicants may spend an evening in a residence hall with a student host.

**Video:** Free on request.

### CAMPUS FACILITIES
**Science:** Steinhart Hall of Science, Observatory.

**Arts:** Art Gallery, Scott Studio Theater, Fuhr Music Hall.

**Athletic:** Kiewit Athletic Department, Indoor Pool.

**Of Special Interest:** Gray Center for Communication Arts—Radio/TV Broadcasting, Campus Golf Course.

### LOCAL ATTRACTIONS
Hastings Museum/IMAX Theater; Lochland Golf Course; Southern Hills Golf Course; Lake Hastings Recreational Area; Imperial Mall.

## UNIVERSITY OF NEBRASKA– LINCOLN
Lincoln, Nebraska

**Contact:** Duane M. Willes, Campus Visits Coordinator, Alexander Building East-1410 Q Street PO Box 880417, Lincoln, NE 68588-0417. *Phone:* toll-free 800-742-8800 Ext. 8545. *Fax:* 402-272-0670. *E-mail:* dwilesl@unl.edu *Web site:* http://www. unl.edu/ *Visit location:* Office of Admissions, Alexander Building East 1410 Q Street, PO Box 880417.

*University of Nebraska–Lincoln (continued)*

## QUICK FACTS

Enrollment: 22,760; UG: 18,179. Entrance: moderately difficult. SAT>500: 78% V, 80% M; ACT>18: 98%. Resident tuition and fees: $2829. Nonresident tuition and fees: $6872. Room and board: $3700. Application deadline: 6/30.

## GENERAL

State-supported, university, coed. Part of University of Nebraska System. Awards associate, bachelor's, master's, doctoral, and first professional degrees. Founded 1869. Setting: 616-acre urban campus with easy access to Omaha. Undergraduate faculty: 1,519 (1,239 full-time, 280 part-time); student-faculty ratio is 13:1. Most popular recent majors: political science, biology, finance.

## CAMPUS VISITS

**College Calendar 1998–99:** *Regular classes:* Aug. 24–Dec. 12; Jan. 11–May 1. *Breaks:* Dec. 18–Jan. 11. *Final exams:* Dec. 14–18; May 3–7. *Admission office closed:* Dec. 24–Jan. 2, Nov. 27. *Special campus days:* Commencement Fall, Dec. 19; Commencement Spring, May 8; Distinguished Scholar Day and World Herald Dinner, Oct. 27; Homecoming; People of Color in Predominately White Institutions Conference; Principal Counselor Conference; Red Letter Day, Oct. 16, Oct. 23, Oct. 30, Nov. 6, Nov. 18, Nov. 20, Dec. 4, Dec. 11, Feb. 15.

## VISIT OPPORTUNITIES

|                     | Appointments? | Who?        |
| ------------------- | ------------- | ----------- |
| **Campus Tour**     | recommended   | open to all |
| **Information Session** | recommended | open to all |
| **Classroom Visit** | recommended   | open to all |
| **Faculty Meeting** | required      | open to all |

**Information Sessions:** M–F at 9:00 am, 1:00 pm; Sat. at 10:00 am; 45 minutes.

**Campus Tours:** Conducted by students. M–F at 9:45 am, 1:45 pm; Sat. at 10:45 am; 60 minutes.

**Class Visits:** Prospective students may attend a class in their area of interest.

## CAMPUS FACILITIES

**Science:** Animal Science Facility, Plant Industry (EC), Hamilton Hall; Appointment Required: Beadle Center.

**Arts:** Quilt Display—Morrill Hall, Kimball Recital Hall; Appointment Required: Lied Center for Performing Arts, Sheldon Art Gallery.

**Athletic:** Memorial Stadium, Bob Devaney Center; Appointment Required: Hewitt Center.

**Of Special Interest:** Recreation Center, Cook Pavilion, Morrill Hall.

## LOCAL ATTRACTIONS

Historical Haymarket.

# WAYNE STATE COLLEGE
**Wayne, Nebraska**

**Contact:** Jane Rademacher, 1111 Main Street, Wayne, NE 68787. *Phone:* toll-free 800-228-9972. *Fax:* 402-375-7204. *E-mail:* wscadmit@wscgate.wsc. edu *Web site:* http://www.wsc.edu/ *Visit location:* 1111 Main Street.

## QUICK FACTS

Enrollment: 3,670; UG: 3,032. Entrance: noncompetitive. SAT>500: N/R; ACT>18: N/R. Resident tuition and fees: $2140. Nonresident tuition and fees: $3931. Room and board: $2860. Application deadline: rolling.

## GENERAL

State-supported, comprehensive, coed. Part of Nebraska State College System. Awards bachelor's and master's degrees and post-master's certificates. Founded 1910. Setting: 128-acre small-town campus. Undergraduate faculty: 228 (123 full-time, 105 part-time); student-faculty ratio is 23:1. Most popular recent majors: business administration, education, criminal justice/law enforcement administration.

## CAMPUS VISITS

**College Calendar 1998–99:** *Regular classes:* Aug. 24–Dec. 17; Jan. 11–May 6. *Final exams:* Dec. 14–17; May 3–6. *Special campus days:* Homecoming, Sept. 26; commencement, Dec. 18, May 8.

## VISIT OPPORTUNITIES

|                     | Appointments?              | Who?           |
| ------------------- | -------------------------- | -------------- |
| **Campus Tour**     | required                   | open to all    |
| **Information Session** | recommended, not required | open to all |
| **Admission Interview** |                        | applicants only |

## VISIT OPPORTUNITIES—*continued*

| | Appointments? | Who? |
|---|---|---|
| **Faculty Meeting** | required | open to all |

**Information Sessions:** Available select Fri. during fall semester at 9:00 am; please call one week in advance to request specific department session.

**Interviews:** M–F.

**Campus Tours:** Conducted by students. M–F at 11:00 am, 2:00 pm.

## CAMPUS FACILITIES

**Of Special Interest:** U. S. Conn Library.

# NEVADA

## UNIVERSITY OF NEVADA, RENO

Reno, Nevada

**Contact:** Steve Maples, Admissions and Recruitment Coordinator, 9th and Center University of Nevada, Reno, Reno, NV 89557. *Phone:* 702-784-4865 or toll-free 800-622-4867 (in-state). *Fax:* 702-784-1852. *E-mail:* smaples@scs.unr.edu *Web site:* http://www.unr. edu/ *Visit location:* Office for Prospective Students, Jone Visitor Center, 9th and Center.

## QUICK FACTS

Enrollment: 11,803; UG: 8,428. Entrance: moderately difficult. SAT>500: 61% V, 62% M; ACT>18: 89%. Resident tuition and fees: $2109. Nonresident tuition and fees: $7544. Room and board: $5095. Application deadline: 3/1.

## GENERAL

State-supported, university, coed. Part of University and Community College System of Nevada. Awards bachelor's, master's, doctoral, and first professional degrees. Founded 1874. Setting: 200-acre urban campus. Undergraduate faculty: 668 (597 full-time, 71 part-time); student-faculty ratio is 20:1. Most popular recent majors: elementary education, general studies, special education.

## CAMPUS VISITS

**College Calendar 1998–99:** *Regular classes:* Aug. 24–Dec. 8; Jan. 19–May 4. *Breaks:* Dec. 21–Jan. 8; Mar. 13–21. *Final exams:* Dec. 10–16; May 6–12.

*Special campus days:* Fall Commencement, Dec. 5; Homecoming, Oct. 16; Spring Commencement, May 16.

## VISIT OPPORTUNITIES

| | Appointments? | Who? |
|---|---|---|
| **Campus Tour** | recommended | open to all |
| **Information Session** | required | open to all |
| **Admission Interview** | required | open to all |
| **Classroom Visit** | required | open to all |
| **Faculty Meeting** | required | |
| **Overnight Visit** | | open to all |

**Interviews:** M–F; 30 minutes.

**Campus Tours:** Conducted by students. M–F, select Sat.; 60 minutes.

**Class Visits:** Prospective students may attend a class in their area of interest.

**Overnight Visits:** During the summer.

## CAMPUS FACILITIES

**Science:** Mackay Science Mining Museum, Laxalt Mineral Engineering—Seismology Lab.

**Arts:** Church Fine Arts.

**Athletic:** Lombardi Recreation Facility.

**Of Special Interest:** Thompson Student Services Building.

# NEW HAMPSHIRE

## COLBY-SAWYER COLLEGE

New London, New Hampshire

**Contact:** Admissions Office, 100 Main Street, New London, NH 03257. *Phone:* toll-free 800-272-1015 (out-of-state). *Fax:* 603-526-3452. *E-mail:* csadmiss@ colby-sawyer.edu *Web site:* http://www.colby-sawyer. edu/ *Visit location:* Admissions, Colgate Hall, 100 Main Street.

## QUICK FACTS

Enrollment: 775; UG: 775. Entrance: moderately difficult. SAT>500: N/R; ACT>18: N/R. Tuition and fees: $16,310. Room and board: $6240. Application deadline: rolling.

*Colby-Sawyer College (continued)*

### GENERAL

Independent, 4-year, coed. Awards associate and bachelor's degrees. Founded 1837. Setting: 196-acre small-town campus. Faculty: 90 (40 full-time, 50 part-time); student-faculty ratio is 12:1. Most popular recent majors: athletic training/sports medicine, developmental/child psychology, business administration.

### CAMPUS VISITS

**College Calendar 1998–99:** *Regular classes:* Sept. 8–Dec. 11; Jan. 19–May 6. *Breaks:* Nov. 25–30; Feb. 15–17; Mar. 20–29. *Final exams:* Dec. 14–17; May 7–12. *Special campus days:* Commencement, May 15; Family Weekend, Oct. 9–11.

### VISIT OPPORTUNITIES

|  | Appointments? | Who? |
|---|---|---|
| **Campus Tour** | recommended, not required | open to all |
| **Information Session** | recommended | open to all |
| **Admission Interview** | recommended | open to all |
| **Classroom Visit** | required | open to all |
| **Faculty Meeting** | required | open to all |
| **Overnight Visit** | required | admitted applicants only |

**Information Sessions:** Select Sat.; 30 minutes.

**Interviews:** M–F, select Sat.; during summer no Sat. interviews and on select Fri. the college closes at noon; 30 minutes.

**Campus Tours:** Conducted by students. M–F at 10:00 am, 11:00 am, 2:00 pm, 3:00 pm; Sat. at 9:00 am, 10:00 am, 11:00 am, 11:30 am; during summer no Sat. tours; 60 minutes.

**Class Visits:** Classroom visits are determined by the visit schedule.

**Overnight Visits:** During the regular academic year, prospective applicants may spend an evening in a residence hall with a student host.

### CAMPUS FACILITIES

**Of Special Interest:** Appointment Required: equestrian facilities.

## DANIEL WEBSTER COLLEGE
### Nashua, New Hampshire

**Contact:** Mr. Paul D. La Barre, Director of Admissions, 20 University Drive, Nashua, NH 03063. *Phone:* toll-free 800-325-6876 (in-state). *Fax:* 603-577-6001. *E-mail:* admissions@dwc.edu *Web site:* http://www.dwc.edu/ *Visit location:* Office of Admissions, Daniel Webster Hall, 20 University Drive.

### QUICK FACTS

Enrollment: 877; UG: 877. Entrance: moderately difficult. SAT>500: 51% V, 55% M; ACT>18: N/R. Tuition and fees: $14,310. Room and board: $5662. Application deadline: rolling.

### GENERAL

Independent, 4-year, coed. Awards associate and bachelor's degrees. Founded 1965. Setting: 50-acre suburban campus with easy access to Boston. Faculty: 77 (26 full-time, 51 part-time); student-faculty ratio is 14:1. Most popular recent majors: aviation management, aircraft pilot (professional), business administration.

### CAMPUS VISITS

**College Calendar 1998–99:** *Regular classes:* Sept. 2–Dec. 14; Jan. 21–May 7. *Breaks:* Dec. 19–Jan. 19. *Final exams:* Dec. 16–19; May 10–14. *Admission office closed:* Fri. at 3:00 pm during the summer. *Special campus days:* Fall Open House, Oct. 11, Oct. 25; Spring Open House, Mar. 28.

### VISIT OPPORTUNITIES

|  | Appointments? | Who? |
|---|---|---|
| **Campus Tour** | required | open to all |
| **Admission Interview** | required | open to all |
| **Classroom Visit** | required | open to all |
| **Faculty Meeting** | required | open to all |
| **Overnight Visit** | required | applicants only |

**Interviews:** M–F, select Sat.

**Campus Tours:** Conducted by students. M–F, select Sat. at 9:00 am, 10:00 am, 11:00 am, 12:00 pm, 1:00 pm, 2:00 pm; 60 minutes.

**Class Visits:** Certain predetermined classrooms are open to visitors.

**Overnight Visits:** During the regular academic year, prospective applicants may spend an evening in a residence hall with a student host.

## CAMPUS FACILITIES
**Of Special Interest:** Ann Bridge Baddour Library and Learning Center.

## LOCAL ATTRACTIONS
American Stage Festival (Milford, NH); Currier Gallery of Art (Manchester); Lakes Region Outlet Mall (Tilton); Boston.

# DARTMOUTH COLLEGE
**Hanover, New Hampshire**

**Contact:** Office of Admissions, 6016 McNutt Hall, Hanover, NH 03755. *Phone:* 603-646-2875. *E-mail:* admissions.office@dartmouth.edu *Web site:* http://www. dartmouth.edu/ *Visit location:* Office of Admissions, McNutt Hall, 6016 McNutt Hall.

## QUICK FACTS
Enrollment: 4,307; UG: 4,307. Entrance: most difficult. SAT>500: 100% V, 100% M; ACT>18: N/R. Tuition and fees: $23,012. Room and board: $6495. Application deadline: 1/1.

## GENERAL
Independent, university, coed. Awards bachelor's, master's, and doctoral degrees. Founded 1769. Setting: 265-acre rural campus. Undergraduate faculty: 487 (339 full-time, 148 part-time); student-faculty ratio is 12:1. Most popular recent majors: political science, history, engineering.

## CAMPUS VISITS
**College Calendar 1998–99:** *Regular classes:* Sept. 24–Dec. 2; Jan. 4–Mar. 9; Mar. 29–June 1; June 24–Aug. 25. *Final exams:* Dec. 5–9; Mar. 12–16; June 4–8; Aug. 28–31. *Special campus days:* Commencement, June 13; Green Key, May 14; Homecoming, Oct. 16; Winter Carnival, Feb. 11.

## VISIT OPPORTUNITIES

|  | Appointments? | Who? |
|---|---|---|
| **Campus Tour** | not required | open to all |
| **Information Session** | not required | open to all |
| **Admission Interview** | required | open to all |
| **Classroom Visit** | not required |  |
| **Overnight Visit** | required | open to all |

**Information Sessions:** M–F, select Sat.; group sessions vary during academic year; call for schedule; 60 minutes.

**Interviews:** M–F, select Sat.; 30 minutes.

**Campus Tours:** Conducted by students. M–F, Sat.; vary during academic year; call for schedule; 60 minutes.

**Class Visits:** Prospective students may attend a class in their area of interest.

**Overnight Visits:** During the regular academic year, prospective applicants may spend an evening in a residence hall with a student host.

**Video:** Available.

## CAMPUS FACILITIES
**Science:** Burke Laboratory, Fairchild Physical Sciences Center, Shattuck Observatory, Sndikoff Laboratory.

**Arts:** Hopkins Center, Hood Museum of Art.

**Athletic:** Alumni Gymnasium, Berry Sports Center.

**Of Special Interest:** The Rockefeller Center for the Social Sciences, Collis Center.

# FRANKLIN PIERCE COLLEGE
**Rindge, New Hampshire**

**Contact:** Admissions Office, College Road PO Box 60, Rindge, NH 03461. *Phone:* toll-free 800-437-0048. *Fax:* 603-899-4372. *E-mail:* admission@rindge.fpc.edu *Web site:* http://www.fpc.edu/ *Visit location:* Admissions, Rindge Hall, College Road PO Box 60.

## QUICK FACTS
Enrollment: 3,114; UG: 2,936. Entrance: moderately difficult. SAT>500: 46% V, 35% M; ACT>18: 64%. Tuition and fees: $16,170. Room and board: $5050. Application deadline: rolling.

## GENERAL
Independent, comprehensive, coed. Awards bachelor's and master's degrees (continuing education sites: Keene, Concord, Salem, Nashua, Portsmouth, Lebanon). Founded 1962. Setting: 1,000-acre rural campus. Undergraduate faculty: 130 (65 full-time, 65 part-time). Most popular recent majors: elementary education, history, mass communications.

## CAMPUS VISITS
**College Calendar 1998–99:** *Regular classes:* Sept. 7–Dec. 15; Jan. 21–May 5. *Breaks:* Dec. 20–Jan. 19. *Final exams:* Dec. 16–19; May 6–10. *Admission office*

*Franklin Pierce College (continued)*

*closed:* Dec. 24–Jan. 3. *Special campus days:* Commencement, May 16; Fall Open House, Nov. 14; Homecoming, Oct. 2–4; Spring Open House, Apr. 17.

## VISIT OPPORTUNITIES

|  | Appointments? | Who? |
|---|---|---|
| **Campus Tour** | recommended, not required | open to all |
| **Admission Interview** | recommended | open to all |
| **Classroom Visit** |  | open to all |
| **Faculty Meeting** |  | open to all |
| **Overnight Visit** | required | applicants only |

**Interviews:** M–F; Sat.; closed on some holidays and Sat. during summer; call to confirm schedule; 30 minutes.

**Campus Tours:** Conducted by students. M–F, Sat. 9:00 am–3:00 pm; 45 minutes.

**Class Visits:** Prospective students may attend a class in their area of interest.

**Overnight Visits:** During the regular academic year, prospective applicants may spend an evening in a residence hall with a student host.

**Video:** Free on request.

## CAMPUS FACILITIES

**Science:** Marcucella Hall.

**Arts:** Ravencroft Theatre, Warehouse Theatre, Dance Studio, Glassblowing Studio.

**Athletic:** Fieldhouse, Airframe Recreation Center.

## LOCAL ATTRACTIONS

Cathedral of the Pines; Mount Monadnock.

# KEENE STATE COLLEGE

**Keene, New Hampshire**

**Contact:** Mrs. Kathryn Dodge, Director of Admissions, 229 Main Street, Keene State College, Keene, NH 03435-2604. *Phone:* 603-358-2276 or toll-free 800-572-1909. *Fax:* 603-358-2767. *E-mail:* admissions@keene.edu *Web site:* http://www.keene.edu/ *Visit location:* Admissions, Elliott Hall, 229 Main Street.

## QUICK FACTS

Enrollment: 4,016; UG: 3,794. Entrance: moderately difficult. SAT>500: 50% V, 43% M; ACT>18: N/App. Resident tuition and fees: $4340. Nonresident tuition and fees: $9840. Room and board: $4660. Application deadline: 3/1.

## GENERAL

State-supported, comprehensive, coed. Part of University System of New Hampshire. Awards associate, bachelor's, and master's degrees and post-master's certificates. Founded 1909. Setting: 160-acre small-town campus. Most popular recent majors: elementary education, psychology, business administration.

## CAMPUS VISITS

**College Calendar 1998–99:** *Regular classes:* Aug. 31–Dec. 11; Jan. 25–May 6. *Final exams:* Dec. 14–19; May 10–13. *Special campus days:* Commencement, May 16; Fall Honors Convocation, Oct. 25.

## VISIT OPPORTUNITIES

|  | Appointments? | Who? |
|---|---|---|
| **Campus Tour** | required | open to all |
| **Information Session** | required | open to all |
| **Admission Interview** | required | open to all |
| **Classroom Visit** | required | open to all |
| **Faculty Meeting** | required | open to all |

**Information Sessions:** Sat. when classes are in session; 120 minutes.

**Interviews:** M–F, except holidays; 30 minutes.

**Campus Tours:** Conducted by students. M–F, Sat., except holidays; 60 minutes.

**Class Visits:** Prospective students may attend a class in their area of interest.

**Video:** Free on request.

## CAMPUS FACILITIES

**Science:** Science Center.

**Arts:** Arts Center on Brickyard Pond, Thorne Sagendorf Art Gallery.

**Athletic:** Spaulding Gymnasium, Athletic Fields.

**Of Special Interest:** Child Development Center.

# NEW ENGLAND COLLEGE

**Henniker, New Hampshire**

**Contact:** Lois Richards, Coordinator of Campus Visits, 26 Bridge Street, Henniker, NH 03242. *Phone:*

toll-free 800-521-7642 (out-of-state). *Fax:* 603-428-7230. *E-mail:* admis@necl.nec.edu *Web site:* http://www.nec.edu/ *Visit location:* Admission Office, Davis House, Bridge Street.

## QUICK FACTS
Enrollment: 842; UG: 784. Entrance: moderately difficult. SAT>500: N/R; ACT>18: N/R. Tuition and fees: $15,784. Room and board: $5920. Application deadline: rolling.

## GENERAL
Independent, comprehensive, coed. Awards bachelor's and master's degrees. Founded 1946. Setting: 225-acre small-town campus with easy access to Boston. Undergraduate faculty: 92 (49 full-time, 43 part-time); student-faculty ratio is 12:1. Most popular recent majors: business administration, education, mass communications.

## CAMPUS VISITS
**College Calendar 1998–99:** *Regular classes:* Sept. 2–Dec. 14; Jan. 18–Apr. 30. *Breaks:* Oct. 16–20; Mar. 6–14; Dec. 19–Jan. 17. *Final exams:* Dec. 16–19; May 3–6. *Special campus days:* Homecoming, Oct. 9–11; Parent's Weekend, Oct. 30–Nov. 1.

## VISIT OPPORTUNITIES

|  | Appointments? | Who? |
|---|---|---|
| **Campus Tour** | recommended, not required | open to all |
| **Admission Interview** | recommended, not required | open to all |
| **Classroom Visit** |  | open to all |
| **Faculty Meeting** | recommended, not required | open to all |
| **Overnight Visit** | required | admitted applicants only |

**Interviews:** M–F, select Sat.; 45 minutes.

**Campus Tours:** Conducted by students. M–F, Sat. at 10:00 am, 12:00 pm; 60 minutes.

**Class Visits:** Prospective students may attend a class in their area of interest, classroom visits are determined by the visit schedule.

**Overnight Visits:** During the regular academic year, prospective applicants may spend an evening in a residence hall with a student host.

## CAMPUS FACILITIES
**Science:** Science building, computer center.
**Arts:** Art gallery.
**Athletic:** Gymnasium, hockey arena, physical fitness center.
**Of Special Interest:** Library, residence halls.

# PLYMOUTH STATE COLLEGE OF THE UNIVERSITY SYSTEM OF NEW HAMPSHIRE
**Plymouth, New Hampshire**

**Contact:** Admission Office, 17 High Street, Plymouth, NH 03264-1595. *Phone:* toll-free 800-842-6900. *Fax:* 603-535-2714. *E-mail:* pscadmit@psc.plymouth.edu *Web site:* http://www.plymouth.edu/ *Visit location:* Admission Office, Russell House, 17 High Street.

## QUICK FACTS
Enrollment: 4,062; UG: 3,489. Entrance: moderately difficult. SAT>500: N/R; ACT>18: N/App. Resident tuition and fees: $4342. Nonresident tuition and fees: $9842. Room and board: $4564. Application deadline: 4/1.

## GENERAL
State-supported, comprehensive, coed. Part of University System of New Hampshire. Awards associate, bachelor's, and master's degrees and post-master's certificates. Founded 1871. Setting: 170-acre small-town campus. Undergraduate faculty: 295 (168 full-time, 127 part-time); student-faculty ratio is 18:1. Most popular recent majors: physical education, child care/development, business administration.

## CAMPUS VISITS
**College Calendar 1998–99:** *Regular classes:* Sept. 2–Dec. 11; Jan. 25–May 7. *Breaks:* Nov. 25–29; Mar. 19–29. *Final exams:* Dec. 14–18; May 10–14. *Special campus days:* Commencement, May 15; Homecoming, Sept. 25–27.

## VISIT OPPORTUNITIES

|  | Appointments? | Who? |
|---|---|---|
| **Campus Tour** | recommended, not required | open to all |
| **Information Session** | recommended, not required | open to all |
| **Admission Interview** | required | open to all |

*Plymouth State College of the University System of New Hampshire (continued)*

## VISIT OPPORTUNITIES—*continued*

| | Appointments? | Who? |
|---|---|---|
| **Classroom Visit** | required | open to all |
| **Faculty Meeting** | required | open to all |

**Information Sessions:** M–F at 10:00 am, 2:00 pm; Sat., Oct., Nov. 21 and Dec. 5, Sun. Nov. 15 at 10:30 am; 30 minutes.

**Interviews:** M–F; 30 minutes.

**Campus Tours:** Conducted by students. M–F at 10:00 am, 2:30 pm; Sat. Oct., Nov. 21, and Dec. 5; Sun. Nov. 15 at 11:15 am; 60 minutes.

**Class Visits:** Certain predetermined classrooms are open to visitors.

### CAMPUS FACILITIES
**Science:** Planetarium, the weather center, meteorology lab.

**Arts:** Silver Cultural Arts Center, Art Gallery, Graphic Design studio and lab.

**Athletic:** Physical Education Center, 35 acres playing fields.

**Of Special Interest:** Lamson Library, Hartman Student Union Building, Prospect Dining Hall.

### LOCAL ATTRACTIONS
Waterville Valley Resort, Loon Mountain Resort, Franconia State Park, Polar Caves.

# SAINT ANSELM COLLEGE
**Manchester, New Hampshire**

**Contact:** Jane E. Yerrington, Office Manager, 100 Saint Anselm Drive, Manchester, NH 03102. *Phone:* toll-free 888-4ANSELM. *Fax:* 603-641-7550. *E-mail:* admissions@anselm.edu *Web site:* http://www.anselm.edu/ *Visit location:* Office of Admissions, Alumni Hall, 100 Saint Anselm Drive.

### QUICK FACTS
Enrollment: 1,924; UG: 1,924. Entrance: moderately difficult. SAT>500: 78% V, 74% M; ACT>18: N/R. Tuition and fees: $16,670. Room and board: $6160. Application deadline: rolling.

### GENERAL
Independent Roman Catholic, 4-year, coed. Awards bachelor's degrees. Founded 1889. Setting: 450-acre suburban campus with easy access to Boston. Faculty: 163 (114 full-time, 49 part-time); student-faculty ratio is 15:1. Most popular recent majors: biology, business economics, history.

### CAMPUS VISITS
**College Calendar 1998–99:** *Regular classes:* Sept. 1–Dec. 11; Jan. 18–May 4. *Breaks:* Nov. 25–30; Mar. 5–15; Mar. 31–Apr. 6. *Final exams:* Dec. 14–21; May 6–13. *Special campus days:* Alumni Weekend; Commencement, May 22; Family Weekend, Oct. 16–18; Freshman Orientation Weekend, Aug. 13–15.

### VISIT OPPORTUNITIES

| | Appointments? | Who? |
|---|---|---|
| **Campus Tour** | required | open to all |
| **Admission Interview** | required | open to all |
| **Classroom Visit** | required | open to all |
| **Faculty Meeting** | required | open to all |
| **Overnight Visit** | required | open to all |

**Interviews:** M–F; Sat. 9:00 am–12:00 pm during the academic year; 30 minutes.

**Campus Tours:** Conducted by students. M–F; Sat. morning during the academic year; unavailable during examination periods; 60 minutes.

**Class Visits:** Prospective students may attend a class in their area of interest, classroom visits are determined by the visit schedule.

**Overnight Visits:** During the regular academic year, prospective applicants may spend an evening in a residence hall with a student host.

### CAMPUS FACILITIES
**Science:** Goulet Science Center, Gadbois Hall Nursing Center.

**Arts:** Chapel Art Center, Dana Center /Koonz Theatre, College Fine Arts Studio.

**Athletic:** Stoutenurgh Gymnasium, Carr Center, football stadium, soccer fields.

**Of Special Interest:** Davison Hall—dining facility, Bernard Court—town houses.

# UNIVERSITY OF NEW HAMPSHIRE
**Durham, New Hampshire**

**Contact:** University of New Hampshire, Admissions Office, Grant House, 4 Garrison Avenue, Durham,

NH 03824. *Phone:* 603-862-1360. *Fax:* 603-862-0077. *E-mail:* admissions@unhf.unh.edu *Web site:* http://www.unh.edu/ *Visit location:* Admissions Office, Grant House, 4 Garrison Avenue.

## QUICK FACTS

Enrollment: 13,960; UG: 11,155. Entrance: moderately difficult. SAT>500: 77% V, 78% M; ACT>18: N/App. Resident tuition and fees: $5889. Nonresident tuition and fees: $14,749. Room and board: $4524. Application deadline: 2/1.

## GENERAL

State-supported, university, coed. Part of University System of New Hampshire. Awards associate, bachelor's, master's, and doctoral degrees. Founded 1866. Setting: 200-acre small-town campus with easy access to Boston. Undergraduate faculty: 883 (613 full-time, 270 part-time); student-faculty ratio is 17:1. Most popular recent majors: business administration, English, biology.

## CAMPUS VISITS

**College Calendar 1998–99:** *Regular classes:* Sept. 2–Dec. 14; Jan. 19–May 10. *Breaks:* Nov. 26–27; Mar. 15–19. *Final exams:* Dec. 17–22; May 13–20. *Admission office closed:* July 3, Nov. 11, Nov. 27, Dec. 24–Jan. 2. *Special campus days:* Commencement, May 22; Homecoming; Parents' Weekend.

### VISIT OPPORTUNITIES

| | Appointments? | Who? |
|---|---|---|
| **Campus Tour** | not required | open to all |
| **Information Session** | not required | open to all |
| **Admission Interview** | required | open to all |
| **Classroom Visit** | not required | open to all |
| **Overnight Visit** | required | |

**Information Sessions:** Included with tour; 150 minutes.
**Interviews:** M–F; available from late Sept. until early Dec., Feb. until early May, and Jul., Aug.; 40 minutes.
**Campus Tours:** Conducted by students. M–F at 10:00 am, 12:00 pm, 2:00 pm; Sat. in spring at 2:00 pm.; Sun. during fall and spring at 2:00 pm.; M–F offered late Sept. until early Dec., Feb. until early May, and Jul., Aug.; 60 minutes.
**Class Visits:** Prospective students may attend a class in their area of interest, certain predetermined classrooms are open to visitors, classroom visits are determined by the visit schedule.

**Overnight Visits:** Prospective applicants may spend an evening in a residence hall with a student host.

## CAMPUS FACILITIES

**Science:** Rudman Hall and Spaulding Life Science Center, Institute of Earth, Ocean, Space; Appointment Required: Jackson Estaurine Laboratory, Isle of Shoals Marine Laboratory.

**Arts:** Paul Creative Arts Center, The Whiltemore Center, Hamel Center; Appointment Required: The Gallery at Paul Creative Arts Center.

**Athletic:** The Whiltemore Center Ice Hockey Arena, UNH Field House and Cowell Stadium, The Browne Center, The Hamel Center.

**Of Special Interest:** College Woods Nature Recreational Center, Memorial Union Building—Student Activities Center, New England Center.

## LOCAL ATTRACTIONS

Portsmouth, N.H.; New England Coastline; White Mountains; Boston; Portland, ME.

# NEW JERSEY

## DREW UNIVERSITY

**Madison, New Jersey**

**Contact:** Office of College Admission, 36 Madison Avenue, Madison, NJ 07940. *Phone:* 973-408-DREW. *Fax:* 973-408-3068. *E-mail:* cadm@drew.edu *Web site:* http://www.drew.edu/ *Visit location:* Office of College Admission, Wesley House, 36 Madison Avenue.

## QUICK FACTS

Enrollment: 2,254; UG: 1,491. Entrance: very difficult. SAT>500: 95% V, 93% M; ACT>18: N/App. Tuition and fees: $21,396. Room and board: $6114. Application deadline: 2/15.

## GENERAL

Independent, university, coed, United Methodist Church. Awards bachelor's, master's, doctoral, and first professional degrees. Founded 1867. Setting: 186-acre suburban campus with easy access to New York City. Undergraduate faculty: 255 (136 full-time, 119 part-time); student-faculty ratio is 13:1. Most popular recent majors: political science, psychology, English.

*Drew University (continued)*

## CAMPUS VISITS

**College Calendar 1998–99:** *Regular classes:* Aug. 31–Dec. 9; Jan. 28–May 7. *Breaks:* Mar. 12–21. *Final exams:* Dec. 12–18; May 12–18. *Special campus days:* Academic Convocation, Aug. 31; Commencement, May 22; Orientation, Aug. 25–30.

## VISIT OPPORTUNITIES

|  | Appointments? | Who? |
|---|---|---|
| **Campus Tour** | not required | open to all |
| **Information Session** | not required | open to all |
| **Admission Interview** | required | open to all |
| **Classroom Visit** | required | open to all |
| **Faculty Meeting** | required | open to all |
| **Overnight Visit** | required | open to all |

**Information Sessions:** M–F at 11:00 am, 2:00 pm; summer months only; 45 minutes.

**Interviews:** M–F, Sat.; not available between Feb. and mid-Apr.; 45 minutes.

**Campus Tours:** Conducted by students. M–F at 10:00 am, 11:00 am, 2:00 pm, 3:00 pm, 3:45 pm, 12:00 pm; Sat. in fall 10:00 am, 10:30 am, 11:15 am, 12:00 pm; Jan. and summer M–F at 10:00 am, 12:00 pm, 3:00 pm; 60 minutes.

**Class Visits:** Prospective students may attend a class in their area of interest.

**Overnight Visits:** During the regular academic year, prospective applicants may spend an evening in a residence hall with a student host.

## CAMPUS FACILITIES

**Arts:** Renovated Bowne Theatre.

**Athletic:** Simon Forum and Athletic Center.

**Of Special Interest:** Mead Hall.

## LOCAL ATTRACTIONS

Washington's Headquarters; Jockey Hollow; New York City.

# PRINCETON UNIVERSITY
## Princeton, New Jersey

**Contact:** Orange Key Guide Services, Maclean House, Princeton, NJ 08544. *Phone:* 609-258-3603. *Web site:* http://www.princeton.edu/ *Visit location:* Orange Key, Maclean House.

## QUICK FACTS

Enrollment: 6,351; UG: 4,600. Entrance: most difficult. SAT>500: 100% V, 100% M; ACT>18: N/App. Tuition and fees: $23,820. Room and board: $6711. Application deadline: 1/2.

## GENERAL

Independent, university, coed. Awards bachelor's, master's, and doctoral degrees. Founded 1746. Setting: 600-acre suburban campus with easy access to New York City and Philadelphia. Undergraduate faculty: 886 (698 full-time, 188 part-time); student-faculty ratio is 5:1. Most popular recent majors: economics, history, molecular biology.

## CAMPUS VISITS

**College Calendar 1998–99:** *Regular classes:* Sept. 17–Jan. 4; Feb. 1–May 3. *Breaks:* Oct. 31–Nov. 8; Mar. 13–21; Dec. 18–Jan. 3. *Final exams:* Jan. 13–23; May 12–22. *Admission office closed:* Good Friday, Apr. 2; Martin Luther King Day, Jan. 18. *Special campus days:* Baccalaureate, May 30; Class Day, May 31; Commencement Day, June 1; Undergraduate Registration, Sept. 12.

## VISIT OPPORTUNITIES

|  | Appointments? | Who? |
|---|---|---|
| **Campus Tour** | not required | applicants and parents |
| **Information Session** | not required |  |
| **Admission Interview** | required | open to all |
| **Classroom Visit** | required | open to all |
| **Faculty Meeting** | required | open to all |
| **Overnight Visit** | required | open to all |

**Information Sessions:** M–F Apr. through mid-Dec. at 12:30 pm; 60 minutes.

**Interviews:** Available May through mid-Dec.; call 609-258-5397 several weeks in advance to schedule an appointment; 60 minutes.

**Campus Tours:** Conducted by students. M–F, Sat. at 10:00 am, 11:00 am, 1:30 pm, 3:30 pm; Sun. at 1:30 pm, 3:30 pm; Engineering Quadrangle Tours available M–F during the academic year except during semester recesses and examination periods; call (609) 258-4554 to schedule engineering tour or faculty member meeting; 60 minutes.

**Class Visits:** Prospective students may attend a class in their area of interest, classroom visit appointments are made with the department office.

**Overnight Visits:** During the regular academic year, prospective applicants may spend an evening in a residence hall with a student host.

## CAMPUS FACILITIES
**Of Special Interest:** Nassau Hall, University Chapel.

# RAMAPO COLLEGE OF NEW JERSEY
### Mahwah, New Jersey

**Contact:** Peter Goetz, Assistant Director of Admissions, 505 Ramapo Valley Road, Mahwah, NJ 07430. *Phone:* 201-529-6486 or toll-free 800-9RAMAPO (in-state). *Fax:* 201-529-7603. *E-mail:* pgoetz@orion. ramapo.edu *Web site:* http://www.ramapo.edu/ *Visit location:* Admissions, The Mansion, 505 Ramapo Valley Road.

## QUICK FACTS
Enrollment: 4,202; UG: 4,062. Entrance: moderately difficult. SAT>500: 57% V, 57% M; ACT>18: N/R. Resident tuition and fees: $4206. Nonresident tuition and fees: $6576. Room and board: $5734. Application deadline: 3/15.

## GENERAL
State-supported, comprehensive, coed. Part of New Jersey State College System. Awards bachelor's and master's degrees. Founded 1969. Setting: 315-acre suburban campus with easy access to New York City. Undergraduate faculty: 293 (151 full-time, 142 part-time); student-faculty ratio is 17:1. Most popular recent majors: business administration, psychology, mass communications.

## CAMPUS VISITS
**College Calendar 1998–99:** *Regular classes:* Sept. 2–Dec. 21; Feb. 1–May 22. *Final exams:* Dec. 15–21; May 17–22. *Admission office closed:* Fri. in summer. *Special campus days:* Commencement, May 27; Fall Fest, Oct. 10.

## VISIT OPPORTUNITIES

|  | Appointments? | Who? |
|---|---|---|
| **Campus Tour** | not required | open to all |
| **Information Session** | recommended | open to all |
| **Admission Interview** | required | open to all |
| **Classroom Visit** | required | open to all |

VISIT OPPORTUNITIES—*continued*

|  | Appointments? | Who? |
|---|---|---|
| **Faculty Meeting** | required | open to all |
| **Overnight Visit** | required | open to all |

**Information Sessions:** Available at Sun. Open House, call for schedule.

**Interviews:** M–F; 20 minutes.

**Campus Tours:** Conducted by students. M–F, select Sat. at 1:00 pm; unavailable Fri. in summer.

**Class Visits:** Prospective students may attend a class in their area of interest, classroom visits are determined by the visit schedule.

**Overnight Visits:** During the regular academic year, prospective applicants may spend an evening in a residence hall with a student host.

**Video:** Free on request.

## CAMPUS FACILITIES
**Of Special Interest:** Residence Halls.

## LOCAL ATTRACTIONS
New York City; United States Military Academy at West Point.

# RIDER UNIVERSITY
### Lawrenceville, New Jersey

**Contact:** Admissions Office, 2083 Lawrenceville Road, Lawrenceville, NJ 08648. *Phone:* 609-896-5042 or toll-free 800-257-9026. *Fax:* 609-895-6645. *E-mail:* admissions@rider.edu *Web site:* http://www.rider.edu/ *Visit location:* Office of Admissions, Admissions Building, 2083 Lawrenceville Road.

## QUICK FACTS
Enrollment: 5,055; UG: 3,855. Entrance: moderately difficult. SAT>500: 54% V, 57% M; ACT>18: N/R. Tuition and fees: $15,410. Room and board: $6270. Application deadline: rolling.

## GENERAL
Independent, comprehensive, coed. Awards bachelor's and master's degrees. Founded 1865. Setting: 340-acre suburban campus with easy access to Philadelphia and New York City. Undergraduate faculty: 403 (227 full-time, 176 part-time); student-faculty ratio is 13:1. Most popular recent majors: accounting, elementary education, business administration.

*Rider University (continued)*

## CAMPUS VISITS

**College Calendar 1998–99:** *Regular classes:* Sept. 10–Dec. 12; Jan. 25–May 1. *Breaks:* Nov. 25–29; Mar. 13–21. *Final exams:* Dec. 14–22; May 3–11. *Admission office closed:* Mar. 19, Dec. 24–Jan. 2. *Special campus days:* Commencement, May 14; Homecoming.

## VISIT OPPORTUNITIES

|  | Appointments? | Who? |
|---|---|---|
| **Campus Tour** | not required | open to all |
| **Information Session** | recommended | open to all |
| **Admission Interview** | required | open to all |
| **Classroom Visit** | required | open to all |
| **Faculty Meeting** | required | open to all |

**Information Sessions:** Select days during the summer; 120 minutes.

**Interviews:** M–F, select Sat.; 30 minutes.

**Campus Tours:** Conducted by students. M–F, select Sat.; restricted availability during breaks, nonacademic periods, and summer; 60 minutes.

**Class Visits:** Prospective student attends class of a "matched" ambassador.

## CAMPUS FACILITIES

**Of Special Interest:** Franklin F. Moore Library.


# RUTGERS, THE STATE UNIVERSITY OF NEW JERSEY, COLLEGE OF ENGINEERING

**Piscataway, New Jersey**

**Contact:** Campus Information Services, 542 George Street, New Brunswick, NJ 08901. *Phone:* 732-932-INFO. *Fax:* 732-932-9359. *Web site:* http://www.rutgers.edu/ *Visit location:* Welcome Center, Van Nest Hall, College Avenue.

## QUICK FACTS

Enrollment: 2,202; UG: 2,202. Entrance: very difficult. SAT>500: 83% V, 97% M; ACT>18: N/R. Resident tuition and fees: $5836. Nonresident tuition and fees: $10,730. Room and board: $5314. Application deadline: 12/15.

## GENERAL

State-supported, 4-year, coed. Part of Rutgers, The State University of New Jersey. Awards bachelor's degrees (master of science, master of philosophy, and doctor of philosophy degrees are offered through the Graduate School, New Brunswick). Founded 1864. Setting: 2,695-acre small-town campus with easy access to New York City and Philadelphia. Faculty: 136 (all full-time); student-faculty ratio is 10:1. Most popular recent majors: mechanical engineering, electrical/electronics engineering, chemical engineering.

## CAMPUS VISITS

**College Calendar 1998–99:** *Regular classes:* Sept. 1–Dec. 10; Jan. 19–May 3. *Breaks:* Dec. 23–Jan. 18. *Final exams:* Dec. 15–22; May 5–12. *Special campus days:* Commencement, May 20.

## VISIT OPPORTUNITIES

|  | Appointments? | Who? |
|---|---|---|
| **Campus Tour** | required | applicants and parents |
| **Information Session** | required |  |
| **Classroom Visit** | required |  |
| **Faculty Meeting** | required | applicants and parents |

**Information Sessions:** M–F, select Sat. at 9:00 am, 10:30 am; 45 minutes.

**Campus Tours:** Conducted by students. M–F at 9:00 am, 10:30 am; M–F, select Sat. at 9:00 am, 10:30 am, 12:30 pm, 1:00 pm, 1:30 pm, 2:00 pm; walking tours available on Fri. at 1:00 pm; call 732-445-2212 for information; 60 minutes.

## CAMPUS FACILITIES

**Science:** Geology Museum.

**Arts:** Zimmerli Museum.

**Athletic:** Football Stadium, Sonny Werblin Recreation Center, Athletic Center.


# RUTGERS, THE STATE UNIVERSITY OF NEW JERSEY, COOK COLLEGE

**New Brunswick, New Jersey**

**Contact:** Campus Information Services, 542 George Street, New Brunswick, NJ 08901. *Phone:* 732-932-

INFO. *Fax:* 732-932-9359. *Web site:* http://www.
rutgers.edu/ *Visit location:* Welcome Center, Van Nest
Hall, College Avenue.

## QUICK FACTS
Enrollment: 3,194; UG: 3,194. Entrance: very
difficult. SAT>500: 83% V, 87% M; ACT>18: N/R.
Resident tuition and fees: $5817. Nonresident tuition
and fees: $10,711. Room and board: $5314. Application deadline: 12/15.

## GENERAL
State-supported, 4-year, coed. Part of Rutgers, The
State University of New Jersey. Awards bachelor's
degrees. Founded 1921. Setting: 2,695-acre small-
town campus with easy access to New York City and
Philadelphia. Most popular recent majors: environmental science, biology, natural resources management.

## CAMPUS VISITS
**College Calendar 1998–99:** *Regular classes:* Sept.
1–Dec. 10; Jan. 19–May 3. *Breaks:* Dec. 23–Jan. 18.
*Final exams:* Dec. 15–22; May 5–12. *Special campus
days:* Commencement, May 20.

## VISIT OPPORTUNITIES

|  | Appointments? | Who? |
|---|---|---|
| **Campus Tour** | required | applicants and parents |
| **Information Session** | required | |
| **Classroom Visit** | required | |
| **Faculty Meeting** | required | applicants and parents |

**Information Sessions:** M–F, select Sat. at 9:00 am,
10:30 am; 45 minutes.

**Campus Tours:** Conducted by students. M–F, select
Sat. at 9:00 am, 10:30 am, 12:30 pm, 1:00 pm, 1:30
pm, 2:00 pm; walking tours available Wed. and Fri. at
1:15 pm; 60 minutes.

## CAMPUS FACILITIES
**Science:** Institute of Marine and Coastal Science,
Agricultural Museum, Geology Museum.

**Arts:** Zimmerli Museum.

**Athletic:** Football Stadium, Sonny Werblin Recreation Center, Athletic Center.

**Of Special Interest:** Display Gardens.

# RUTGERS, THE STATE UNIVERSITY OF NEW JERSEY, DOUGLASS COLLEGE
**New Brunswick, New Jersey**

**Contact:** Campus Information Services, 542 George
Street, New Brunswick, NJ 08901. *Phone:* 732-932-
INFO. *Fax:* 732-932-9359. *Web site:* http://www.
rutgers.edu/ *Visit location:* Welcome Center, Van Nest
Hall, College Avenue.

## QUICK FACTS
Enrollment: 2,997; UG: 2,997. Entrance: moderately
difficult. SAT>500: 77% V, 74% M; ACT>18: N/R.
Resident tuition and fees: $5349. Nonresident tuition
and fees: $9763. Room and board: $5314. Application
deadline: 12/15.

## GENERAL
State-supported, 4-year, women only. Part of Rutgers,
The State University of New Jersey. Awards bachelor's degrees. Founded 1918. Setting: 2,695-acre
small-town campus with easy access to New York
City and Philadelphia. Most popular recent majors:
psychology, English, political science.

## CAMPUS VISITS
**College Calendar 1998–99:** *Regular classes:* Sept.
1–Dec. 10; Jan. 19–May 3. *Breaks:* Dec. 23–Jan. 18.
*Final exams:* Dec. 15–22; May 5–12. *Special campus
days:* Commencement, May 20.

## VISIT OPPORTUNITIES

|  | Appointments? | Who? |
|---|---|---|
| **Campus Tour** | required | applicants and parents |
| **Information Session** | required | |
| **Classroom Visit** | required | |
| **Faculty Meeting** | required | applicants and parents |

**Information Sessions:** M–F, select Sat. at 9:00 am,
10:30 am; 45 minutes.

**Campus Tours:** Conducted by students. M–F, select
Sat. at 9:00 am, 10:30 am, 12:00 pm, 1:00 pm, 1:30
pm, 2:00 pm; walking tours (including an information
session) available Thu. and Fri. at 11:00 am; no
appointment necessary; 60 minutes.

*Rutgers, The State University of New Jersey, Douglass College (continued)*

## CAMPUS FACILITIES

**Science:** Geology Museum.

**Arts:** Zimmerli Museum.

**Athletic:** Football Stadium, Sonny Werblin Recreation Center, Athletic Center.

# RUTGERS, THE STATE UNIVERSITY OF NEW JERSEY, LIVINGSTON COLLEGE

**Piscataway, New Jersey**

**Contact:** Campus Information Services, 542 George Street, New Brunswick, NJ 08901. *Phone:* 732-932-INFO. *Fax:* 732-932-9359. *Web site:* http://www.rutgers.edu/ *Visit location:* Welcome Center, Van Nest Hall, College Avenue.

## QUICK FACTS

Enrollment: 3,149; UG: 3,149. Entrance: moderately difficult. SAT>500: 78% V, 84% M; ACT>18: N/R. Resident tuition and fees: $5382. Nonresident tuition and fees: $9796. Room and board: $5314. Application deadline: 12/15.

## GENERAL

State-supported, 4-year, coed. Part of Rutgers, The State University of New Jersey. Awards bachelor's degrees. Founded 1969. Setting: 2,695-acre small-town campus with easy access to New York City and Philadelphia. Most popular recent majors: psychology, economics, criminal justice/law enforcement administration.

## CAMPUS VISITS

**College Calendar 1998–99:** *Regular classes:* Sept. 1–Dec. 10; Jan. 19–May 3. *Break:* Dec. 23–Jan. 18. *Final exams:* Dec. 15–22; May 5–12. *Special campus days:* Commencement, May 20.

## VISIT OPPORTUNITIES

|  | Appointments? | Who? |
|---|---|---|
| **Campus Tour** | required | applicants and parents |
| **Information Session** | required | |
| **Classroom Visit** | required | |

## VISIT OPPORTUNITIES—*continued*

|  | Appointments? | Who? |
|---|---|---|
| **Faculty Meeting** | required | applicants and parents |

**Information Sessions:** M–F, select Sat. at 9:00 am, 10:30 am; 45 minutes.

**Campus Tours:** Conducted by students. M–F; M–F, select Sat. at 9:00 am, 10:30 am, 12:30 pm, 1:00 pm, 1:30 pm, 2:00 pm; walking tours available by appointment M–Sat. at 1:10 pm; call 732-445-4124 for arrangements; 60 minutes.

## CAMPUS FACILITIES

**Science:** Geology Museum.

**Arts:** Zimmerli Museum.

**Athletic:** Football Stadium, Sonny Werblin Recreation Center, Athletic Center.

# RUTGERS, THE STATE UNIVERSITY OF NEW JERSEY, NEWARK COLLEGE OF ARTS AND SCIENCES

**Newark, New Jersey**

**Contact:** Admissions Office, 249 University Avenue, Newark, NJ 07102. *Phone:* 973-353-5206. *Fax:* 973-353-1440. *Web site:* http://www.rutgers.edu/ *Visit location:* Admissions Office, Blumenthal Hall, 249 University Avenue.

## QUICK FACTS

Enrollment: 3,600; UG: 3,600. Entrance: moderately difficult. SAT>500: 50% V, 54% M; ACT>18: N/R. Resident tuition and fees: $5151. Nonresident tuition and fees: $9565. Room and board: $5314. Application deadline: 12/15.

## GENERAL

State-supported, 4-year, coed. Part of Rutgers, The State University of New Jersey. Awards bachelor's degrees. Founded 1946. Setting: 34-acre urban campus with easy access to New York City. Most popular recent majors: accounting, biology, psychology.

## CAMPUS VISITS
**College Calendar 1998–99:** *Regular classes:* Sept. 1–Dec. 10; Jan. 19–May 3. *Breaks:* Dec. 23–Jan. 18. *Final exams:* Dec. 15–22; May 5–12.

## VISIT OPPORTUNITIES

|  | Appointments? | Who? |
| --- | --- | --- |
| **Campus Tour** | required | applicants and parents |
| **Information Session** | required |  |
| **Classroom Visit** | required |  |
| **Faculty Meeting** | required | applicants and parents |

**Information Sessions:** Mon. at 11:30 am; Wed. at 2:30 pm; 45 minutes.
**Campus Tours:** Conducted by students. Mon. at 11:30 am; Wed. at 2:30 pm; 60 minutes.

## CAMPUS FACILITIES
**Athletic:** Golden Dome.
**Of Special Interest:** Institute of Jazz Studies.

## LOCAL ATTRACTIONS
Performing Arts Center.


# RUTGERS, THE STATE UNIVERSITY OF NEW JERSEY, RUTGERS COLLEGE
New Brunswick, New Jersey

**Contact:** Campus Information Services, 542 George Street, New Brunswick, NJ 08901. *Phone:* 732-932-INFO. *Fax:* 732-932-9359. *Web site:* http://www.rutgers.edu/ *Visit location:* Welcome Center, Van Nest Hall, College Avenue.

## QUICK FACTS
Enrollment: 10,559; UG: 10,559. Entrance: very difficult. SAT>500: 87% V, 89% M; ACT>18: N/R. Resident tuition and fees: $5386. Nonresident tuition and fees: $9800. Room and board: $5314. Application deadline: 12/15.

## GENERAL
State-supported, comprehensive, coed. Part of Rutgers, The State University of New Jersey. Awards bachelor's degrees. Founded 1766. Setting: 2,695-acre small-town campus with easy access to New York

City and Philadelphia. Most popular recent majors: psychology, biology, English.

## CAMPUS VISITS
**College Calendar 1998–99:** *Regular classes:* Sept. 1–Dec. 10; Jan. 19–May 3. *Breaks:* Dec. 23–Jan. 18. *Final exams:* Dec. 15–22; May 5–12. *Special campus days:* Commencement, May 20.

## VISIT OPPORTUNITIES

|  | Appointments? | Who? |
| --- | --- | --- |
| **Campus Tour** | required | applicants and parents |
| **Information Session** | required |  |
| **Classroom Visit** | required |  |
| **Faculty Meeting** | required | applicants and parents |

**Information Sessions:** M–F, select Sat. at 9:00 am, 10:30 am; 45 minutes.
**Campus Tours:** Conducted by students. M–F, select Sat. at 9:00 am, 10:30 am, 12:30 pm, 1:00 pm, 1:30 pm, 2:00 pm; walking tours are available M–F at 1:15 pm and selected Sat. at 12:30 pm; 60 minutes.

## CAMPUS FACILITIES
**Science:** Geology Museum.
**Arts:** Zimmerli Museum.
**Athletic:** Football Stadium, Sonny Werblin Recreation Center, Athletic Center.


# SETON HALL UNIVERSITY
South Orange, New Jersey

**Contact:** Gregg A. Meyer, Director of Enrollment Services, 400 South Orange Avenue, South Orange, NJ 07079-2680. *Phone:* toll-free 800-THE-HALL. *Fax:* 973-761-9452. *E-mail:* thehall@shu.edu *Web site:* http://www.shu.edu/ *Visit location:* Admissions Lobby, Bayley Hall, 400 South Orange Avenue.

## QUICK FACTS
Enrollment: 9,297; UG: 4,715. Entrance: moderately difficult. SAT>500: 59% V, 62% M; ACT>18: 50%. Tuition and fees: $13,600. Room and board: $7020. Application deadline: 3/1.

## GENERAL
Independent Roman Catholic, university, coed. Awards bachelor's, master's, doctoral, and first professional

*Seton Hall University (continued)*

degrees and post-master's certificates. Founded 1856. Setting: 58-acre suburban campus with easy access to New York City. Undergraduate faculty: 733 (343 full-time, 390 part-time); student-faculty ratio is 16:1. Most popular recent majors: communications, nursing, criminal justice studies.

## CAMPUS VISITS

**College Calendar 1998–99:** *Regular classes:* Aug. 31–Dec. 14; Jan. 21–May 13. *Breaks:* Oct. 9–14; Mar. 8–13; Dec. 22–Jan. 20. *Final exams:* Dec. 15–21; May 14–20. *Admission office closed:* Easter recess, Apr. 1–3; Martin Luther King, Jr. Day, Jan. 18; Thanksgiving recess, Nov. 26–28. *Special campus days:* Charter Day, Mar. 7; Commencement, May 24; Open House, Oct. 25, Nov. 8; University Day, Oct. 7.

## VISIT OPPORTUNITIES

| | Appointments? | Who? |
|---|---|---|
| **Campus Tour** | required | open to all |
| **Information Session** | not required | open to all |
| **Admission Interview** | required | open to all |
| **Classroom Visit** | required | applicants only |
| **Faculty Meeting** | required | applicants only |
| **Overnight Visit** | required | admitted applicants only |

**Information Sessions:** Select Sat. at 11:30 am; unavailable holidays, test dates, university events, and summer months; 10 minutes.

**Interviews:** M–F, select Sat.; unavailable holidays, test dates, university events, and summer months; 30 minutes.

**Campus Tours:** Conducted by students. M–F at 11:00 am, 2:30 pm; select Sat. at 11:30 am; unavailable holidays, test dates, university events, and summer months; 60 minutes.

**Class Visits:** Prospective students may attend a class in their area of interest.

**Overnight Visits:** During the regular academic year, prospective applicants may spend an evening in a residence hall with a student host.

**Video:** Free on request.

## CAMPUS FACILITIES

**Athletic:** Brennan Recreation Center.
**Of Special Interest:** Immaculate Conception Chapel.

## LOCAL ATTRACTIONS

Village of South Orange; South Mountain Arena; Meadowlands Sports Complex; New York City.

# STEVENS INSTITUTE OF TECHNOLOGY
## Hoboken, New Jersey

**Contact:** Daniel Gallagher, Director of Undergraduate Admissions, Castle Point on Hudson, Hoboken, NJ 07030. *Phone:* toll-free 800-458-5323. *Fax:* 201-216-8348. *Web site:* http://www.stevens-tech.edu/ *Visit location:* Undergraduate Admissions, Wesley J. Howe Center, 8th Floor.

## QUICK FACTS

Enrollment: 3,245; UG: 1,448. Entrance: very difficult. SAT>500: 81% V, 97% M; ACT>18: N/R. Tuition and fees: $19,360. Room and board: $6724. Application deadline: 3/1.

## GENERAL

Independent, university, coed. Awards bachelor's, master's, and doctoral degrees. Founded 1870. Setting: 55-acre urban campus with easy access to New York City. Undergraduate faculty: 201 (121 full-time, 80 part-time); student-faculty ratio is 9:1. Most popular recent majors: mechanical engineering, chemical engineering, computer engineering.

## CAMPUS VISITS

**College Calendar 1998–99:** *Regular classes:* Aug. 31–Dec. 11; Jan. 19–May 5. *Breaks:* Nov. 25–29; Mar. 14–21; Dec. 24–Jan. 19. *Final exams:* Dec. 13–23; May 6–17. *Admission office closed:* Dec. 24–Jan. 2. *Special campus days:* Boken—third or last week in April; Graduate Commencement, May 27; Techfest—Halloween weekend; Undergraduate Commencement, May 26.

## VISIT OPPORTUNITIES

| | Appointments? | Who? |
|---|---|---|
| **Campus Tour** | recommended | applicants and parents |
| **Information Session** | recommended | open to all |
| **Admission Interview** | required | open to all |

## VISIT OPPORTUNITIES—*continued*

| | Appointments? | Who? |
|---|---|---|
| **Classroom Visit** | required | open to all |
| **Faculty Meeting** | required | open to all |
| **Overnight Visit** | required | open to all |

**Information Sessions:** Select weekdays throughout the year; high school seniors only during fall semester; high school juniors only during summer.

**Interviews:** M–F, Sat.; unavailable holidays; 30 minutes.

**Campus Tours:** Conducted by students. M–F 10:00 am–3:00 pm; Sat. 10:00 am–12:00 pm; unavailable holidays; 45 minutes.

**Class Visits:** Prospective students may attend a class in their area of interest.

**Overnight Visits:** During the regular academic year, prospective applicants may spend an evening in a residence hall with a student host.

### CAMPUS FACILITIES
**Science:** Materials lab, Advance Software Design lab.
**Athletic:** Charles V. Schaefer, Jr. Athletic and Recreation Center.
**Of Special Interest:** Residence hall.

### LOCAL ATTRACTIONS
Washington Street.

# NEW MEXICO

## EASTERN NEW MEXICO UNIVERSITY
**Portales, New Mexico**

**Contact:** Ms. Pat Dodd, Admissions Specialist, ENMU, #7, Portales, NM 88130. *Phone:* toll-free 800-367-3668. *Fax:* 505-562-2118. *E-mail:* pat.dodd@enmu.edu *Web site:* http://www.enmu.edu/ *Visit location:* Office of Admissions, Student Academic Services Building.

### QUICK FACTS
Enrollment: 3,453; UG: 2,923. Entrance: minimally difficult. SAT>500: 26% V, 51% M; ACT>18: N/R. Resident tuition and fees: $1716. Nonresident tuition and fees: $6378. Room and board: $2942. Application deadline: rolling.

### GENERAL
State-supported, comprehensive, coed. Part of Eastern New Mexico University System. Awards associate, bachelor's, and master's degrees. Founded 1934. Setting: 240-acre rural campus. Undergraduate faculty: 226 (151 full-time, 75 part-time). Most popular recent majors: education, sociology, liberal arts and studies.

### CAMPUS VISITS
**College Calendar 1998–99:** *Regular classes:* Aug. 20–Dec. 4; Jan. 19–May 7. *Breaks:* Dec. 11–Jan. 18; Mar. 22–26. *Final exams:* Dec. 5–10; May 8–13. *Special campus days:* Commencement, Dec. 11, May 15; Homecoming, Sept. 25–26; Peanut Valley Arts and Crafts Festival, Oct. 23–25.

### VISIT OPPORTUNITIES

| | Appointments? | Who? |
|---|---|---|
| **Campus Tour** | recommended, not required | open to all |
| **Information Session** | recommended, not required | open to all |
| **Admission Interview** | recommended, not required | open to all |
| **Classroom Visit** | recommended | open to all |
| **Faculty Meeting** | required | open to all |
| **Overnight Visit** | required | open to all |

**Information Sessions:** M–F; Sat. and Sun. available upon request; 30 minutes.

**Interviews:** M–F; appointments available Sat. and Sun.; 30 minutes.

**Campus Tours:** Conducted by students. M–F; Sat. and Sun. available upon request; 60 minutes.

**Class Visits:** Prospective students may attend a class in their area of interest.

**Overnight Visits:** During the regular academic year, prospective applicants may spend an evening in a residence hall with a student host.

**Video:** Free on request.

### CAMPUS FACILITIES
**Science:** Natural History Museum; Appointment Required: Biology Student Labs, Laser Technology Lab, Fishery Lab.

**Arts:** University Theatre Center, Buchanan Hall—Music Building; Appointment Required: MIDI Lab, Computer Animation Lab—Liberal Arts Building.

**Athletic:** Greyhound Arena.

*Eastern New Mexico University (continued)*

**Of Special Interest:** University Computer Center, Golden Library, Broadcast Center; Appointment Required: Communicative Disorders Clinic, Blackwater Draw Archeological Museum and Site.

## LOCAL ATTRACTIONS
Valencia Peanut Processing Plants; Roosevelt County Museum.

# NEW MEXICO INSTITUTE OF MINING AND TECHNOLOGY
**Socorro, New Mexico**

**Contact:** Admission Office, 801 Leroy Place, Socorro, NM 87801. *Phone:* toll-free 800-428-TECH. *Fax:* 505-835-5989. *E-mail:* admission@admin.nmt.edu *Web site:* http://www.nmt.edu/ *Visit location:* Admission Office, Brown Hall—Room 118, 801 Leroy Place.

## QUICK FACTS
Enrollment: 1,284; UG: 1,026. Entrance: moderately difficult. SAT>500: N/R; ACT>18: 99%. Resident tuition and fees: $2073. Nonresident tuition and fees: $6611. Room and board: $3530. Application deadline: 8/1.

## GENERAL
State-supported, university, coed. Awards associate, bachelor's, master's, and doctoral degrees. Founded 1889. Setting: 320-acre small-town campus with easy access to Albuquerque. Undergraduate faculty: 117 (108 full-time, 9 part-time); student-faculty ratio is 11:1. Most popular recent majors: environmental engineering, biology, mathematics.

## CAMPUS VISITS
**College Calendar 1998–99:** *Regular classes:* Aug. 25–Dec. 11; Jan. 19–May 7. *Breaks:* Mar. 15–19. *Final exams:* Dec. 14–18; May 10–14. *Admission office closed:* Nov. 26–27, Dec. 18–Jan. 2, Mar. 15–19. *Special campus days:* 49ers (homecoming), Oct. 23; Commencement, May 15; Spring Fling, Apr. 2.

## VISIT OPPORTUNITIES

| | Appointments? | Who? |
|---|---|---|
| **Campus Tour** | recommended | open to all |
| **Information Session** | recommended | open to all |
| **Admission Interview** | recommended | open to all |

| | Appointments? | Who? |
|---|---|---|
| **Classroom Visit** | recommended | open to all |
| **Faculty Meeting** | recommended | open to all |
| **Overnight Visit** | recommended | open to all |

**Information Sessions:** M–F 8:00 am–3:00 pm; 30 minutes.

**Interviews:** M–F; 45 minutes.

**Campus Tours:** Conducted by students. M–F 8:00 am–3:00 pm; 45 minutes.

**Class Visits:** Prospective students may attend a class in their area of interest, certain predetermined classrooms are open to visitors.

**Overnight Visits:** During the regular academic year, prospective applicants may spend an evening in a residence hall with a student host.

**Video:** Available.

## CAMPUS FACILITIES
**Of Special Interest:** New Mexico Tech Library.

## LOCAL ATTRACTIONS
VLA Radio Telescope; Bosque Del Apache Wildlife Refuge; San Miguel Mission.

# NEW MEXICO STATE UNIVERSITY
**Las Cruces, New Mexico**

**Contact:** Admissions Office, Box 30001, MSC 3A, Las Cruces, NM 88003-8001. *Phone:* toll-free 800-662-6678. *Fax:* 505-646-6330. *E-mail:* admissions@nmsu.edu *Web site:* http://www.nmsu.edu/ *Visit location:* Office of Admissions, Educational Services Building, Box 30001, MSC 3A.

## QUICK FACTS
Enrollment: 13,959; UG: 11,136. Entrance: moderately difficult. SAT>500: N/R; ACT>18: 80%. Resident tuition and fees: $2196. Nonresident tuition and fees: $7152. Room and board: $3390. Application deadline: 8/14.

## GENERAL
State-supported, university, coed. Part of New Mexico State University System. Awards associate, bachelor's, master's, and doctoral degrees. Founded 1888. Setting: 900-acre suburban campus with easy

access to El Paso. Undergraduate faculty: 670 (644 full-time, 26 part-time); student-faculty ratio is 18:1. Most popular recent majors: education, business marketing and marketing management, criminal justice/law enforcement administration.

## CAMPUS VISITS

**College Calendar 1998–99:** *Regular classes:* Aug. 19–Dec. 11; Jan. 13–May 14. *Final exams:* Dec. 7–11; May 10–14. *Admission office closed:* Nov. 27, Dec. 23–Jan. 1, Jan. 18, Apr. 2. *Special campus days:* Commencement, Dec. 12, May 15; Homecoming, Oct. 30–31.

## VISIT OPPORTUNITIES

| | Appointments? | Who? |
|---|---|---|
| **Campus Tour** | recommended | open to all |
| **Information Session** | recommended | open to all |
| **Admission Interview** | recommended | open to all |
| **Classroom Visit** | required | open to all |
| **Faculty Meeting** | required | open to all |
| **Overnight Visit** | required | open to all |

**Information Sessions:** M–F 8:00 am–5:00 pm; 30 minutes.

**Interviews:** M–F; 30 minutes.

**Campus Tours:** Conducted by students and admission reps. M–F 8:00 am–5:00 pm; 45 minutes.

**Class Visits:** Prospective students may attend a class in their area of interest.

**Overnight Visits:** During the regular academic year and over the summer, prospective applicants may spend an evening in a residence hall.

**Video:** Free on request.

## CAMPUS FACILITIES

**Arts:** University Museum.
**Athletic:** Student Activity Center.
**Of Special Interest:** Libraries.

## LOCAL ATTRACTIONS

White Sands National Park; Elephant Butte Lake; Old Mesilla.

# ST. JOHN'S COLLEGE
## Santa Fe, New Mexico

**Contact:** Heather Giles, Visit Coordinator, 1160 Camino Cruz Blanca, Santa Fe, NM 87501. *Phone:*

toll-free 800-331-5232. *Fax:* 505-984-6003. *E-mail:* admissions@mail.sjcsf.edu *Web site:* http://www.sjcsf.edu/ *Visit location:* Admissions, Weigle Hall, 1160 Camino Cruz Blanca.

## QUICK FACTS

Enrollment: 488; UG: 382. Entrance: moderately difficult. SAT>500: 96% V, 89% M; ACT>18: 98%. Tuition and fees: $19,700. Room and board: $6116. Application deadline: rolling.

## GENERAL

Independent, comprehensive, coed. Administratively affiliated with St. John's College (MD). Awards bachelor's and master's degrees. Founded 1964. Setting: 250-acre small-town campus. Undergraduate faculty: 60 (55 full-time, 5 part-time); student-faculty ratio is 8:1.

## CAMPUS VISITS

**College Calendar 1998–99:** *Regular classes:* Aug. 27–Dec. 17; Jan. 18–May 21. *Breaks:* Nov. 26–29; Mar. 13–28; Dec. 18–Jan. 17. *Admission office closed:* the last Fri. of spring break. *Special campus days:* Commencement; Convocation, Aug. 27.

## VISIT OPPORTUNITIES

| | Appointments? | Who? |
|---|---|---|
| **Campus Tour** | required | open to all |
| **Information Session** | required | open to all |
| **Admission Interview** | required | open to all |
| **Classroom Visit** | required | open to all |
| **Overnight Visit** | required | open to all |

**Interviews:** M–F; 30 minutes.

**Campus Tours:** Conducted by students. M–F, select Sun.; spring tours for accepted students only; 90 minutes.

**Class Visits:** Classroom visits are determined by the visit schedule.

**Overnight Visits:** During the regular academic year and over the summer, prospective applicants may spend an evening in a residence hall.

## CAMPUS FACILITIES

**Arts:** The St. John's gallery.

*St. John's College (continued)*

**LOCAL ATTRACTIONS**
Georgia O'Keefe Museum; The Santa Fe Opera; Museum of Fine Arts; Museum of Indian Arts and Culture; Museum of International Folk Art; The Plaza.

# NEW YORK

## BARD COLLEGE
**Annandale-on-Hudson, New York**

**Contact:** Jane Brien, Admissions Coordinator, Admissions Office, Bard College, Annandale-on-Hudson, NY 12504. *Phone:* 914-758-7472. *Fax:* 914-758-5208. *E-mail:* admissions@bard.edu *Web site:* http://www. bard.edu/ *Visit location:* Admissions Office, Hopson Cottage, Bard College.

**QUICK FACTS**
Enrollment: 1,186; UG: 1,126. Entrance: very difficult. SAT>500: 100% V, 97% M; ACT>18: N/R. Tuition and fees: $22,220. Room and board: $6812. Application deadline: 1/31.

**GENERAL**
Independent, comprehensive, coed. Awards bachelor's, master's, and doctoral degrees. Founded 1860. Setting: 600-acre rural campus. Undergraduate faculty: 160 (99 full-time, 61 part-time); student-faculty ratio is 9:1. Most popular recent majors: social sciences, art, literature.

**CAMPUS VISITS**
College Calendar 1998–99: *Regular classes:* Sept. 2–Dec. 18; Jan. 27–May 19. *Breaks:* Oct. 12–16; Mar. 26–Apr. 4. *Admission office closed:* Dec. 24–Jan. 2.

**VISIT OPPORTUNITIES**

| | Appointments? | Who? |
|---|---|---|
| **Campus Tour** | required | open to all |
| **Admission Interview** | required | open to all |
| **Classroom Visit** | required | open to all |
| **Faculty Meeting** | required | |
| **Overnight Visit** | required | applicants only |

**Interviews:** M–F; interviews unavailable Feb.–Mar.; 60 minutes.
**Campus Tours:** Conducted by students. M–F at 9:00 am, 10:30 am, 11:00 am, 1:00 pm, 2:00 pm, 3:00 pm; 60 minutes.
**Class Visits:** Prospective students may attend a class in their area of interest, classroom visits are determined by the visit schedule.
**Overnight Visits:** During the regular academic year, prospective applicants may spend an evening in a residence hall with a student host.

**CAMPUS FACILITIES**
**Science:** Hegeman-Rose Science Building, Field Station, ecology research facilities.
**Arts:** Fisher Arts Center, Avery Center for the Arts, Edith C. Blum Institute, Preston Film Center, Woods Studio—photographic darkrooms, welding studio.
**Athletic:** Stevenson Gymnasium, Tennis Courts, Soccer/Rugby Field.
**Of Special Interest:** Stevenson Library, Olin Humanities Building, The Jerome Levy Economics Institute Blithewood Mansion of the Hudson River, Bertelsmann Campus Center.

**LOCAL ATTRACTIONS**
Tivoli–neighboring village, thriving artistic community; Historic Hudson Valley homes–including the home of Franklin Delano Roosevelt, Eleanor Roosevelt, and painter Frederick Church; natural beauty of scenic Hudson River and nearby Catskill Mountains.

## BARUCH COLLEGE OF THE CITY UNIVERSITY OF NEW YORK
**New York, New York**

**Contact:** Lynn Salmon, 151 East 25th Street, New York, NY 10010. *Phone:* 212-802-2321. *Fax:* 212-802-2310. *E-mail:* lynn__salmon@newton.baruch.cuny.edu *Web site:* http://www.baruch.cuny.edu/ *Visit location:* Admissions, Newman Library, 151 East 25th Street, 7th Floor.

**QUICK FACTS**
Enrollment: 14,736; UG: 12,313. Entrance: moderately difficult. SAT>500: N/App; ACT>18: N/App.

Resident tuition and fees: $3330. Nonresident tuition and fees: $6930. Room and board: N/Avail. Application deadline: 6/15.

## GENERAL

State and locally supported, comprehensive, coed. Part of City University of New York System. Awards bachelor's, master's, and doctoral degrees and post-master's certificates. Founded 1919. Undergraduate faculty: 770 (420 full-time, 350 part-time); student-faculty ratio is 31:1. Most popular recent majors: accounting, finance, human resources management.

## CAMPUS VISITS

**College Calendar 1998–99:** *Regular classes:* Aug. 30–Dec. 15; Jan. 30–May 10. *Final exams:* Dec. 16–23; May 11–20. *Admission office closed:* Fri. in Jun., Jul., and Aug. *Special campus days:* Commencement, June 6.

## VISIT OPPORTUNITIES

|  | Appointments? | Who? |
|---|---|---|
| **Campus Tour** | required | applicants and parents |
| **Information Session** | not required | |
| **Admission Interview** | recommended | applicants and parents |

**Information Sessions:** M–F 9:15 am–5:30 pm.

**Interviews:** M–F; 30 minutes.

**Campus Tours:** Conducted by students and admission reps. Fri. at 11:00 am, 2:00 pm.

## CAMPUS FACILITIES

**Of Special Interest:** The William and Anita Newman Library.

# CLARKSON UNIVERSITY
## Potsdam, New York

**Contact:** Office of Undergraduate Admission, Holcroft House, Potsdam, NY 13699-5605. *Phone:* toll-free 800-527-6577 (in-state), 800-527-6578 (out-of-state). *Fax:* 315-268-7647. *E-mail:* admission@agent. clarkson.edu *Web site:* http://www.clarkson.edu/ *Visit location:* Undergraduate Admission Office, Holcroft House, Clarkson University.

QUICK FACTS

Enrollment: 2,745; UG: 2,424. Entrance: very difficult. SAT>500: 88% V, 98% M; ACT>18: N/R. Tuition and fees: $18,593. Room and board: $6510. Application deadline: 3/15.

## GENERAL

Independent, university, coed. Awards bachelor's, master's, and doctoral degrees. Founded 1896. Setting: 640-acre small-town campus. Undergraduate faculty: 183 (153 full-time, 30 part-time); student-faculty ratio is 16:1. Most popular recent majors: civil engineering, mechanical engineering, chemical engineering.

## CAMPUS VISITS

**College Calendar 1998–99:** *Regular classes:* Aug. 31–Dec. 12; Jan. 18–Apr. 30. *Breaks:* Oct. 2–7; Mar. 12–22; Nov. 24–30. *Final exams:* Dec. 14–18; May 3–7. *Admission office closed:* Nov. 26–28. *Special campus days:* Commencement, May 16.

## VISIT OPPORTUNITIES

|  | Appointments? | Who? |
|---|---|---|
| **Campus Tour** | recommended | open to all |
| **Admission Interview** | recommended | open to all |
| **Classroom Visit** | recommended | open to all |
| **Faculty Meeting** | required | open to all |
| **Overnight Visit** | required | open to all |

**Interviews:** M–F, Sat.; 60 minutes.

**Campus Tours:** Conducted by students. M–F, Sat.; 60 minutes.

**Class Visits:** Prospective students may attend a class in their area of interest.

**Overnight Visits:** During the regular academic year, prospective applicants may spend an evening in a residence hall with a student host.

**Video:** Free on request.

## CAMPUS FACILITIES

**Science:** CAMP (Center for Advanced Materials Processing), Science Center, Rowley Labs, CAISE (Center for the Advancement of Instruction in Science and Engineering).

**Athletic:** Indoor Recreation Center, Cheel Campus Center–Hockey Arena, Fitness Center.

**Of Special Interest:** CLED (Center for Leadership and Entrepreneurial Development).

# COLGATE UNIVERSITY
**Hamilton, New York**

**Contact:** Office of Admission, 13 Oak Drive, Hamilton, NY 13346. *Phone:* 315-228-7401. *Fax:* 315-228-7544. *E-mail:* admission@mail.colgate.edu *Web site:* http://www.colgate.edu/ *Visit location:* Office of Admission, James B. Colgate Hall, 13 Oak Drive.

## QUICK FACTS
Enrollment: 2,847; UG: 2,842. Entrance: very difficult. SAT>500: 98% V, 98% M; ACT>18: 100%. Tuition and fees: $22,765. Room and board: $6110. Application deadline: 1/15.

## GENERAL
Independent, comprehensive, coed. Awards bachelor's and master's degrees. Founded 1819. Setting: 515-acre rural campus. Undergraduate faculty: 258 (188 full-time, 70 part-time); student-faculty ratio is 11:1. Most popular recent majors: economics, political science, English.

## CAMPUS VISITS
**College Calendar 1998–99:** *Regular classes:* Aug. 31–Dec. 11; Jan. 18–Apr. 30. *Breaks:* Oct. 17–20; Mar. 13–21; Nov. 25–29. *Final exams:* Dec. 14–18; May 3–7. *Special campus days:* Commencement, May 16; Family Weekend, Sept. 25–27; Homecoming, Oct. 10.

## VISIT OPPORTUNITIES

|  | Appointments? | Who? |
| --- | --- | --- |
| **Campus Tour** | not required | open to all |
| **Information Session** | not required | open to all |
| **Admission Interview** | required | applicants only |
| **Classroom Visit** |  | applicants only |
| **Faculty Meeting** | recommended | open to all |
| **Overnight Visit** | required | applicants only |

**Information Sessions:** M–F at 10:30 am, 1:15 pm, 2:30 pm; call for Sat. and holiday schedule; 60 minutes.

**Interviews:** M–F; May through Dec.; 45 minutes.

**Campus Tours:** Conducted by students. M–F at 10:30 am, 12:00 pm, 2:00 pm, 3:30 pm; call for Sat. and holiday schedule; 60 minutes.

**Class Visits:** Prospective students may attend a class in their area of interest.

**Overnight Visits:** During the regular academic year, prospective applicants may spend an evening in a residence hall with a student host.

## CAMPUS FACILITIES
**Science:** Geology Museum, The George R. Cooley Herbarium, The Observatory.

**Arts:** Picker Art Gallery (museum collection), Gallery of Department of Art and Art History, Longyear Museum of Anthropology.

**Athletic:** Brian Little Fitness Center, Lineberry Natatorium/Huntington Gym, Reid Athletic Center /Starr Rink and Cotterell Court.

**Of Special Interest:** ALANA Cultural Center, Center for Women's Studies, Keck Humanities Center, Ho Center for Chinese Studies, Chapel House.

# COLUMBIA COLLEGE
**New York, New York**

**Contact:** Office of Undergraduate Admissions, 1130 Amsterdam Avenue MC 2807, New York, NY 10027. *Phone:* 212-854-2522. *Fax:* 212-854-1209. *E-mail:* ugrad-admiss@columbia.edu *Web site:* http://www. columbia.edu/ *Visit location:* Visitor Center, 213 Low Memorial Library, 116th Street and Broadway.

## QUICK FACTS
Enrollment: 3,763; UG: 3,763. Entrance: most difficult. SAT>500: N/R; ACT>18: N/R. Tuition and fees: $22,650. Room and board: $7344. Application deadline: 1/1.

## GENERAL
Independent, 4-year, coed. Part of Columbia University. Awards bachelor's degrees. Founded 1754. Setting: 35-acre urban campus. Faculty: 527 (all full-time); student-faculty ratio is 7:1. Most popular recent majors: English, history, political science.

## CAMPUS VISITS
**College Calendar 1998–99:** *Regular classes:* Sept. 8–Dec. 14; Jan. 19–May 3. *Breaks:* Mar. 13–21. *Final exams:* Dec. 16–23; May 7–14.

|  | Appointments? | Who? |
|---|---|---|
| **Campus Tour** | not required | open to all |
| **Information Session** | not required | open to all |
| **Classroom Visit** | not required | open to all |
| **Faculty Meeting** |  | applicants only |
| **Overnight Visit** | required | open to all |

**Information Sessions:** M–F at 10:00 am, 2:00 pm; Sat. available mid-Sept. to mid-Dec. at 10:00 am, excluding Thanksgiving weekend; 60 minutes.

**Campus Tours:** Conducted by students. M–F at 11:00 am, 3:00 pm; Sat. available mid-Sept. to mid-Dec. at 11:00 am, excluding Thanksgiving weekend; 60 minutes.

**Class Visits:** Prospective students may attend a class in their area of interest.

**Overnight Visits:** During the regular academic year, prospective applicants may spend an evening in a residence hall with a student host.

### CAMPUS FACILITIES
**Of Special Interest:** Butler Library.

# COLUMBIA UNIVERSITY, SCHOOL OF ENGINEERING AND APPLIED SCIENCE
New York, New York

**Contact:** Office of Undergraduate Admissions, 1130 Amsterdam Avenue MC 2807, New York, NY 10027. *Phone:* 212-854-2522. *Fax:* 212-854-1209. *E-mail:* ugrad-admiss@columbia.edu *Web site:* http://www.columbia.edu/ *Visit location:* Visitor Center, 213 Low Memorial Library, 116th Street and Broadway.

### QUICK FACTS
Enrollment: 1,178; UG: 1,178. Entrance: most difficult. SAT>500: N/R; ACT>18: N/R. Tuition and fees: $22,650. Room and board: $7344. Application deadline: 1/1.

### GENERAL
Independent, university, coed. Part of Columbia University. Awards bachelor's, master's, and doctoral degrees. Founded 1864. Undergraduate faculty: 95

(all full-time). Most popular recent majors: computer science, electrical/electronics engineering, mechanical engineering.

### CAMPUS VISITS
**College Calendar 1998–99:** *Regular classes:* Sept. 8–Dec. 14; Jan. 19–May 3. *Breaks:* Mar. 13–21. *Final exams:* Dec. 16–23; May 7–14.

## VISIT OPPORTUNITIES

|  | Appointments? | Who? |
|---|---|---|
| **Campus Tour** | not required | open to all |
| **Information Session** | not required | open to all |
| **Classroom Visit** | not required | open to all |
| **Faculty Meeting** |  | applicants only |
| **Overnight Visit** | required | open to all |

**Information Sessions:** M–F at 10:00 am, 2:00 pm; Sat. from mid-Sept. to mid-Dec. at 10:00 am; 60 minutes.

**Campus Tours:** Conducted by students. M–F at 11:00 am, 3:00 pm; Sat. from mid-Sept. to mid-Dec. at 11:00 am; 60 minutes.

**Class Visits:** Prospective students may attend a class in their area of interest.

**Overnight Visits:** During the regular academic year, prospective applicants may spend an evening in a residence hall with a student host.

### CAMPUS FACILITIES
**Of Special Interest:** Butler Library.

# CORNELL UNIVERSITY
Ithaca, New York

**Contact:** Information Referral Center, Day Hall Lobby, Ithaca, NY 14853. *Phone:* 607-254-4636. *Fax:* 607-255-5396. *E-mail:* info-mailbox@cornell.edu *Web site:* http://www.cornell.edu/ *Visit location:* Undergraduate Admissions Office, 410 Thurston Avenue.

### QUICK FACTS
Enrollment: 18,397; UG: 13,263. Entrance: most difficult. SAT>500: 97% V, 99% M; ACT>18: N/R. Tuition and fees: $21,914. Room and board: $7110. Application deadline: 1/1.

*Cornell University (continued)*

## GENERAL
Independent, university, coed. Awards bachelor's, master's, doctoral, and first professional degrees. Founded 1865. Setting: 745-acre small-town campus with easy access to Syracuse. Undergraduate faculty: 1,526 (1,467 full-time, 59 part-time); student-faculty ratio is 9:1. Most popular recent majors: biology, economics, mechanical engineering.

## CAMPUS VISITS
**College Calendar 1998–99:** *Regular classes:* Aug. 27–Dec. 5; Jan. 25–May 8. *Breaks:* Oct. 10–13; Mar. 20–28; Nov. 25–29. *Final exams:* Dec. 10–18; May 13–21. *Special campus days:* Commencement, May 30.

## VISIT OPPORTUNITIES

|  | Appointments? | Who? |
| --- | --- | --- |
| **Campus Tour** | not required | open to all |
| **Information Session** | not required | open to all |
| **Classroom Visit** | not required | open to all |
| **Overnight Visit** | required | open to all |

**Information Sessions:** Jun.–Nov. M–F at 9:00 am, 11:00 am, 1:00 pm; Sat. at 9:00 am, 1:00 pm; Dec.–May M-Sat. at 11:00 am; call for schedule of group admissions conferences offered by individual colleges; unavailable Nov. 26–29, Dec. 25–Jan. 1, and during major holidays; 60 minutes.

**Campus Tours:** Conducted by students. Apr. 1 through Nov. 30 M–F at 9:00 am, 11:00 am, 1:00 pm, 3:00 pm; Sat. at 9:00 am, 1:00 pm; Sun. at 1:00 pm; Dec. 1 through Mar. 31 M–Sun. at 1:00 pm; unavailable Nov. 26 to Nov. 29, Dec. 25 to Jan. 1; call for 1999 schedule; 75 minutes.

**Class Visits:** Certain predetermined classrooms are open to visitors.

**Overnight Visits:** During the regular academic year, prospective applicants may spend an evening in a residence hall with a student host.

**Video:** Available, fee charged.

## CAMPUS FACILITIES
**Science:** Center for the Environment, Comstock Hall.

**Arts:** Cornell Center for Theatre Arts, Herbert F. Johnson Museum of Art.

**Athletic:** Fieldhouse, Reis Tennis Center, Oxley Equestrian Center; Appointment Required: Lindseth Climbing Wall.

**Of Special Interest:** Africana Studies and Research Center, Cornell Plantation, Carl A. Kroch Library.

## LOCAL ATTRACTIONS
Ithaca College; Ithaca Performing Arts Center; Kitchen Theatre; Ithaca Falls; Taughennock Falls State Park; Sapsucker Woods and Sanctuary; Sciencenter.

# D'YOUVILLE COLLEGE
**Buffalo, New York**

**Contact:** Admissions Office, 320 Porter Avenue, Buffalo, NY 14201. *Phone:* toll-free 800-777-3921. *Fax:* 716-881-7790. *Web site:* http://www.dyc.edu/ *Visit location:* Admissions Office, Administration Building, 320 Porter Avenue.

## QUICK FACTS
Enrollment: 1,798; UG: 1,149. Entrance: moderately difficult. SAT>500: 58% V, 60% M; ACT>18: 90%. Tuition and fees: $10,040. Room and board: $4760. Application deadline: rolling.

## GENERAL
Independent, comprehensive, coed. Awards bachelor's and master's degrees. Founded 1908. Setting: 7-acre urban campus. Undergraduate faculty: 161 (88 full-time, 73 part-time); student-faculty ratio is 13:1. Most popular recent majors: physical therapy, occupational therapy, nursing.

## CAMPUS VISITS
**College Calendar 1998–99:** *Regular classes:* Aug. 31–Dec. 12; Jan. 20–May 8. *Breaks:* Nov. 25–29; Apr. 2–11. *Final exams:* Dec. 14–19; May 10–15. *Special campus days:* Commencement, May 22; Home Coming, Sept. 24–27; Open House, Nov. 14, Apr. 17.

## VISIT OPPORTUNITIES

|  | Appointments? | Who? |
| --- | --- | --- |
| **Campus Tour** | required | open to all |
| **Information Session** | required | open to all |
| **Admission Interview** | not required | open to all |
| **Classroom Visit** | required | open to all |
| **Faculty Meeting** | required | open to all |
| **Overnight Visit** | required | open to all |

**Information Sessions:** Select Sat.; highlights specific majors; 120 minutes.

**Interviews:** M–F, select Sat.; 45 minutes.

**Campus Tours:** Conducted by students. M–F 8:30 am–4:00 pm; Sat. 9:00 am–2:30 pm; 45 minutes.

**Class Visits:** Certain predetermined classrooms are open to visitors.

**Overnight Visits:** During the regular academic year, prospective applicants may spend an evening in a residence hall with a student host.

**Video:** Free on request.

## CAMPUS FACILITIES
**Of Special Interest:** D'Youville College Library.


# ELMIRA COLLEGE
Elmira, New York

**Contact:** Suzanne Giancoli, Office of Admissions Manager, One Park Place, Elmira, NY 14901. *Phone:* 607-735-1724 or toll-free 800-935-6472. *Fax:* 607-735-1718. *E-mail:* admissions@elmira.edu *Web site:* http://www.elmira.edu/ *Visit location:* Office of Admissions, Hamilton Hall, College Avenue and Washington Avenue.

## QUICK FACTS
Enrollment: 1,958; UG: 1,576. Entrance: moderately difficult. SAT>500: 85% V, 83% M; ACT>18: 96%. Tuition and fees: $20,276. Room and board: $6690. Application deadline: 4/15.

## GENERAL
Independent, comprehensive, coed. Awards bachelor's and master's degrees. Founded 1855. Setting: 42-acre small-town campus. Undergraduate faculty: 74 (all full-time); student-faculty ratio is 15:1. Most popular recent majors: psychology, business administration, elementary education.

## CAMPUS VISITS
**College Calendar 1998–99:** *Regular classes:* Sept. 7–Dec. 11; Jan. 11–Apr. 9; Apr. 26–June 2. *Breaks:* Oct. 17–21; Feb. 19–Mar. 1. *Final exams:* Dec. 14–18; Apr. 12–16. *Special campus days:* Commencement, June 6; Octagon Fair, Sept. 26.

## VISIT OPPORTUNITIES

| | Appointments? | Who? |
|---|---|---|
| **Campus Tour** | recommended | open to all |
| **Admission Interview** | recommended | open to all |

**VISIT OPPORTUNITIES**— *continued*

| | Appointments? | Who? |
|---|---|---|
| **Classroom Visit** | recommended | open to all |
| **Faculty Meeting** | recommended | open to all |
| **Overnight Visit** | recommended | open to all |

**Interviews:** M–F; Sat. morning; 45 minutes.

**Campus Tours:** Conducted by students. M–F at 10:30 am, 1:00 pm, 3:00 pm; Sat. at 9:30 am, 10:30 am, 11:30 am; 75 minutes.

**Class Visits:** Prospective students may attend a class in their area of interest.

**Overnight Visits:** During the regular academic year, prospective applicants may spend an evening in a residence hall with a student host.

**Video:** Free on request.

## CAMPUS FACILITIES
**Of Special Interest:** Gannet-Tripp Library.


# HAMILTON COLLEGE
Clinton, New York

**Contact:** Mary Lou Millar, Admissions Office, 198 College Hill Road, Clinton, NY 13323-1296. *Phone:* 315-859-4421 or toll-free 800-843-2655. *Fax:* 315-859-4457. *E-mail:* mlmillar@hamilton.edu *Web site:* http://www.hamilton.edu/ *Visit location:* Office of Admission, Elihu Root House, 198 College Hill Road.

## QUICK FACTS
Enrollment: 1,694; UG: 1,694. Entrance: very difficult. SAT>500: 96% V, 95% M; ACT>18: N/R. Tuition and fees: $22,700. Room and board: $5650. Application deadline: 1/15.

## GENERAL
Independent, 4-year, coed. Awards bachelor's degrees. Founded 1812. Setting: 1,200-acre rural campus. Faculty: 177 full-time, 28 part-time; student-faculty ratio is 10:1. Most popular recent majors: economics, English, political science.

## CAMPUS VISITS
**College Calendar 1998–99:** *Regular classes:* Aug. 31–Dec. 11; Jan. 18–May 7. *Breaks:* Oct. 2–7; Mar. 12–29; Nov. 24–30. *Final exams:* Dec. 15–20; May 5–11. *Special campus days:* Commencement, May 23.

*Hamilton College (continued)*

## VISIT OPPORTUNITIES

| | Appointments? | Who? |
|---|---|---|
| **Campus Tour** | not required | open to all |
| **Information Session** | not required | open to all |
| **Admission Interview** | required | open to all |
| **Classroom Visit** | recommended, not required | open to all |
| **Faculty Meeting** | required | open to all |
| **Overnight Visit** | required | open to all |

**Information Sessions:** M–F; M–F (Apr.-Nov.) 12:15 pm, Sat. (July 11–Aug. 22) at 10:00 am, Sat. (Sept. 12–Dec. 5) at 12:30 pm; 50 minutes.

**Interviews:** M–F, select Sat.; 45 minutes.

**Campus Tours:** Conducted by students. M–F at 10:00 am, 11:00 am, 1:00 pm, 2:00 pm, 3:00 pm; Sat. available in the fall at 9:30 am, 10:15 am, 11:00 am, 11:45 am, 12:30 pm, 1:15 pm; additional daily times at 12:00 pm and 4:00 pm during Jul. and Aug.; 75 minutes.

**Class Visits:** Prospective students may attend a class in their area of interest.

**Overnight Visits:** During the regular academic year, prospective applicants may spend an evening in a residence hall with a student host.

**Video:** Free on request.

### CAMPUS FACILITIES
**Science:** Saunders Hall of Chemistry, Science Building; Appointment Required: Observatory.
**Arts:** Schambach Center for the Performing Arts, List Studio, Emerson Gallery; Appointment Required: Minor Theater.
**Athletic:** Sage Ring, Ade Fitness Center and Fieldhouse, Bristol Pool.
**Of Special Interest:** Beinecke Student Activities Village, Fillius Events Barn, Root Glen.

### LOCAL ATTRACTIONS
Adirondack State Park; Munson Williams Proctor Institute of Arts; Baseball Hall of Fame, Cooperstown, NY.

# HOBART AND WILLIAM SMITH COLLEGES
**Geneva, New York**

**Contact:** Donna Wolfe or Nancy Caves, 639 South Main Street, Geneva, NY 14456-3397. *Phone:* toll-free 800-245-0100. *Fax:* 315-781-3471. *E-mail:* hoadm@hws.edu or wsadm@hws.edu *Web site:* http://www.hws.edu/ *Visit location:* Admissions, Hobart Admissions or William Smith Admissions, 639 South Main Street.

### QUICK FACTS
Enrollment: 1,829; UG: 1,829. Entrance: very difficult. SAT>500: 88% V, 87% M; ACT>18: N/R. Tuition and fees: $22,380. Room and board: $6564. Application deadline: 2/1.

### GENERAL
Independent, 4-year, coed. Awards bachelor's degrees. Founded 1822. Setting: 200-acre small-town campus with easy access to Rochester and Syracuse. Faculty: 172 (138 full-time, 34 part-time); student-faculty ratio is 13:1. Most popular recent majors: English, economics, interdisciplinary studies.

### CAMPUS VISITS
**College Calendar 1998–99:** *Regular classes:* Sept. 9–Nov. 17; Jan. 4–Mar. 12; Mar. 29–June 4. *Breaks:* Nov. 24–Jan. 3; Mar. 18–28. *Final exams:* Nov. 21–24; Mar. 15–18; June 6–9. *Admission office closed:* Dec. 24–Jan. 3. *Special campus days:* Alumni/ae Weekend, Oct. 2–4; Commencement, June 13; Parents Weekend, Oct. 23–25.

## VISIT OPPORTUNITIES

| | Appointments? | Who? |
|---|---|---|
| **Campus Tour** | recommended | open to all |
| **Information Session** | required | open to all |
| **Admission Interview** | required | open to all |
| **Classroom Visit** | required | open to all |
| **Faculty Meeting** | required | open to all |
| **Overnight Visit** | required | open to all |

**Information Sessions:** Call for available schedule in select cities during fall and spring.

**Interviews:** M–F at 9:00 am, 10:00 am, 11:00 am, 1:00 pm, 2:00 pm, 3:00 pm; Sat. during academic year at 9:00 am, 10:00 am, and 11:00 am; 45 minutes.

**Campus Tours:** Conducted by students. M–F at 9:00 am, 10:00 am, 11:00 am, 1:00 pm, 2:00 pm, 3:00 pm; Sat. morning during academic year; 60 minutes.

**Class Visits:** Prospective students may attend a class in their area of interest.

**Overnight Visits:** During the regular academic year, prospective applicants may spend an evening in a residence hall with a student host.

**Video:** Available, fee charged.

## CAMPUS FACILITIES

**Science:** Rosenberg Science Center, Hanley Nature Preserve.

**Arts:** Houghton House.

**Athletic:** Bristol and Winn-Seeley Gymnasia, Bristol Sport and Recreation Center.

**Of Special Interest:** Mercy Academic Center, Scandling Student Center.

## LOCAL ATTRACTIONS

Finger Lakes Region; Corning Glass; Sonnenberg Gardens; Wineries; Parks; Falls.

# HOFSTRA UNIVERSITY
## Hempstead, New York

**Contact:** Office of Admissions, 100 Hofstra University, Hempstead, NY 11549-1000. *Phone:* toll-free 800-HOFSTRA. *Fax:* 516-463-5100. *E-mail:* hofstra@hofstra.edu *Web site:* http://www.hofstra.edu/ *Visit location:* Bernon Hall—Admissions Center, 100 Hofstra University.

## QUICK FACTS

Enrollment: 12,439; UG: 8,568. Entrance: moderately difficult. SAT>500: 71% V, 73% M; ACT>18: 91%. Tuition and fees: $13,544. Room and board: $6730. Application deadline: rolling.

## GENERAL

Independent, university, coed. Awards associate, bachelor's, master's, doctoral, and first professional degrees. Founded 1935. Setting: 238-acre suburban campus with easy access to New York City. Undergraduate faculty: 1,104 (461 full-time, 643 part-time); student-faculty ratio is 13:1. Most popular recent majors: psychology, accounting, business marketing and marketing management.

## CAMPUS VISITS

**College Calendar 1998–99:** *Regular classes:* Aug. 31–Dec. 13; Jan. 4–25; Jan. 27–May 16. *Breaks:* Nov. 25–29; Mar. 31–Apr. 11; Dec. 20–Jan. 3. *Final exams:* Dec. 14–19; May 17–22. *Special campus days:* Commencement, May 23–24; Homecoming, Oct. 17–18.

## VISIT OPPORTUNITIES

| | Appointments? | Who? |
|---|---|---|
| **Campus Tour** | required | open to all |
| **Information Session** | required | open to all |
| **Admission Interview** | required | open to all |
| **Classroom Visit** | required | open to all |
| **Overnight Visit** | required | open to all |

**Information Sessions:** M–F at 11:15 am, 2:00 pm; Sat. at 9:30 am, 11:00 am; 45 minutes.

**Interviews:** M–F, Sat.; 30 minutes.

**Campus Tours:** Conducted by students. M–F at 12:15 pm, 3:00 pm; Sat. at 10:30 am, 12:00 pm; 60 minutes.

**Class Visits:** Classroom visits are determined by the visit schedule.

**Overnight Visits:** During the regular academic year, prospective applicants may spend an evening in a residence hall with a student host.

## CAMPUS FACILITIES

**Arts:** Hofstra Museum, Hofstra Aboretum; Appointment Required: John Adams Playhouse.

**Athletic:** Appointment Required: Hofstra Stadium, Physical Fitness Center, Recreation Center.

**Of Special Interest:** Appointment Required: School of Communication.

## LOCAL ATTRACTIONS

Nassau Coliseum shows; New York City; Bronx Zoo.

# HOUGHTON COLLEGE
## Houghton, New York

**Contact:** Diane Galloway, Coordinator of Campus Visits, One Willard Avenue, Houghton, NY 14744. *Phone:* toll-free 800-777-2556. *Fax:* 716-567-9522'. *E-mail:* admissions@houghton.edu *Web site:* http://www.houghton.edu/ *Visit location:* Admission Office, Fancher Building, One Willard Avenue.

## QUICK FACTS

Enrollment: 1,411; UG: 1,411. Entrance: moderately difficult. SAT>500: 90% V, 81% M; ACT>18: 100%. Tuition and fees: $12,765. Room and board: $4238. Application deadline: 3/1.

*Houghton College (continued)*

## GENERAL

Independent Wesleyan, 4-year, coed. Awards associate and bachelor's degrees. Founded 1883. Setting: 1,300-acre rural campus with easy access to Buffalo and Rochester. Faculty: 135 (102 full-time, 33 part-time); student-faculty ratio is 15:1. Most popular recent majors: elementary education, biology, psychology.

## CAMPUS VISITS

**College Calendar 1998–99:** *Regular classes:* Sept. 1–Dec. 11; Jan. 12–Apr. 28. *Breaks:* Oct. 15–18; Feb. 20–23; Nov. 25–29; Mar. 27–Apr. 5. *Final exams:* Dec. 14–18; Apr. 30–May 5. *Special campus days:* Baccalaureate, May 9; Commencement, May 10; First Year Parents Weekend, Oct. 23–24; Homecoming, Oct. 2–3; Upperclass Parents Weekend, Oct. 9–10.

## VISIT OPPORTUNITIES

|  | Appointments? |
| --- | --- |
| **Campus Tour** | required |
| **Information Session** | required |
| **Admission Interview** | required |
| **Classroom Visit** | required |
| **Faculty Meeting** | required |
| **Overnight Visit** | required |

**Information Sessions:** M–F; unavailable during summer and college breaks; 30 minutes.

**Interviews:** M–F, Sat.; 30 minutes.

**Campus Tours:** Conducted by students. M–F, Sat.; 90 minutes.

**Class Visits:** Classroom visits are determined by the visit schedule.

**Overnight Visits:** During the regular academic year, prospective applicants may spend an evening in a residence hall.

## CAMPUS FACILITIES

**Science:** Appointment Required: Paine Science and Mathematics Building.

**Arts:** Appointment Required: Stevens Art Building.

**Athletic:** Appointment Required: Nielsen Physical Education Center.

**Of Special Interest:** Appointment Required: Equestrian Center.

# HUNTER COLLEGE OF THE CITY UNIVERSITY OF NEW YORK
**New York, New York**

**Contact:** Barbara Austin-King, Admissions Counselor, 695 Park Avenue, New York, NY 10021. *Phone:* 212-772-4045. *Fax:* 212-650-3336. *Web site:* http://www.hunter.cuny.edu/ *Visit location:* Welcome Center, Room 100, North, 695 Park Avenue.

## QUICK FACTS

Enrollment: 18,548; UG: 14,219. Entrance: moderately difficult. SAT>500: 50% V, 48% M; ACT>18: N/App. Resident tuition and fees: $3329. Nonresident tuition and fees: $6929. Room only: $1700. Application deadline: 1/15.

## GENERAL

State and locally supported, comprehensive, coed. Part of City University of New York System. Awards bachelor's and master's degrees. Founded 1870. Undergraduate faculty: 1,299 (620 full-time, 679 part-time); student-faculty ratio is 18:1. Most popular recent majors: psychology, English, sociology.

## CAMPUS VISITS

**College Calendar 1998–99:** *Regular classes:* Aug. 31–Dec. 16; Jan. 28–May 19. *Breaks:* Nov. 26–29; Mar. 31–Apr. 11. *Final exams:* Dec. 17–Jan. 4; May 21–28. *Admission office closed:* Nov. 27, Dec. 24, Dec. 31; Fri. during summer. *Special campus days:* spring commencement, June 2–3; winter commencement, Jan. 26.

## VISIT OPPORTUNITIES

|  | Appointments? | Who? |
| --- | --- | --- |
| **Campus Tour** | required | applicants and parents |
| **Information Session** | required | |
| **Admission Interview** | not required | |
| **Classroom Visit** | required | |
| **Faculty Meeting** | required | |

**Information Sessions:** Mon., Tue., Wed., Thu. at 10:00 am, 6:00 pm; Fri. at 10:00 am, 4:00 pm.

**Interviews:** Mon., Tue., Wed., Thu. at 10:00 am, 6:00 pm; Fri. at 10:00 am, 4:00 pm; 20 minutes.

**Campus Tours:** Conducted by students. Fri. at 3:00 pm; unavailable during the summer and holidays; 120 minutes.

**Class Visits:** Prospective students may attend a class in their area of interest.

## CAMPUS FACILITIES

**Science:** Academic Computing Facility, Schools of Nursing and Health Science; Appointment Required: Geography Remote Sensing Lab.

**Arts:** Dance Studios, Leubsdorf Art Gallery; Appointment Required: Voorhees Campus, Kaye Playhouse, Lang Recital Hall.

**Athletic:** Main Competition Gymnasium; Appointment Required: Fitness Gym, Pool, Handball/Raquetball Courts.

**Of Special Interest:** School of Social Work; Appointment Required: Residence Hall, Library.

## LOCAL ATTRACTIONS

Central Park; Metropolitan Museum of Art; Times Square; Ellis Island; Greenwich Village; Lincoln Center.

# ITHACA COLLEGE
### Ithaca, New York

**Contact:** Office of Admission, 100 Job Hall, Ithaca, NY 14850-7020. *Phone:* toll-free 800-429-4274. *Fax:* 607-274-1900. *E-mail:* admission@ithaca.edu *Web site:* http://www.ithaca.edu/ *Visit location:* Admission Office, 100 Job Hall.

## QUICK FACTS

Enrollment: 5,824; UG: 5,556. Entrance: moderately difficult. SAT>500: 86% V, 87% M; ACT>18: N/R. Tuition and fees: $16,900. Room and board: $7340. Application deadline: 3/1.

## GENERAL

Independent, comprehensive, coed. Awards bachelor's and master's degrees. Founded 1892. Setting: 757-acre small-town campus with easy access to Syracuse. Undergraduate faculty: 513 (409 full-time, 104 part-time); student-faculty ratio is 11:1. Most popular recent majors: physical therapy, radio/television broadcasting, music.

## CAMPUS VISITS

**College Calendar 1998–99:** *Regular classes:* Aug. 26–Dec. 11; Jan. 18–Apr. 30. *Breaks:* Oct. 14–18; Mar. 5–14. *Final exams:* Dec. 14–18; May 3–7. *Special*

*campus days:* Commencement, May 15; Homecoming, Sept. 25–27; Parent's Weekend, Oct. 23–25.

## VISIT OPPORTUNITIES

|  | Appointments? | Who? |
|---|---|---|
| **Campus Tour** | not required | open to all |
| **Admission Interview** | required | open to all |
| **Classroom Visit** | required | open to all |
| **Faculty Meeting** | required | open to all |
| **Overnight Visit** | required | open to all |

**Interviews:** M–F, select Sat.; 30 minutes.

**Campus Tours:** Conducted by students. M–F 9:00 am–3:00 pm; select Sat. 9:00–11:00 am; call for available schedule; 60 minutes.

**Class Visits:** Classroom visits are determined by the visit schedule.

**Overnight Visits:** During the regular academic year, prospective applicants may spend an evening in a residence hall with a student host.

**Video:** Available, fee charged.

## CAMPUS FACILITIES

**Science:** New Science Building, Williams Hall, New health sciences facility.

**Arts:** Dillingham Center—Theater Arts, Ford Hall—Music; Appointment Required: Ceracche Center—Art.

**Athletic:** Hill Center, New recreation facility.

**Of Special Interest:** Center for Trading and Analysis of Financial Investments; Appointment Required: Roy H. Park School of Communications.

## LOCAL ATTRACTIONS

The Commons in downtown Ithaca, Finger Lakes area wineries, scenic vistas.

# THE JUILLIARD SCHOOL
### New York, New York

**Contact:** Ms. Mary K. Gray, Director of Admissions, 60 Lincoln Center Plaza, New York, NY 10023-6588. *Phone:* 212-799-5000. *Web site:* http://www.juilliard.edu/ *Visit location:* Admissions Office, The Juilliard School, 60 Lincoln Center Plaza.

*The Juilliard School (continued)*

## QUICK FACTS
Enrollment: 781; UG: 464. Entrance: most difficult. SAT>500: N/App; ACT>18: N/App. Tuition and fees: $15,000. Room and board: $6500. Application deadline: 12/1.

## GENERAL
Independent, comprehensive, coed. Awards bachelor's, master's, and doctoral degrees. Founded 1905. Undergraduate faculty: 241 (104 full-time, 137 part-time); student-faculty ratio is 4:1. Most popular recent majors: music (piano and organ performance), stringed instruments, dance.

## CAMPUS VISITS
**College Calendar 1998–99:** *Regular classes:* Sept. 3–Dec. 13; Jan. 11–May 7. *Breaks:* Nov. 26–29; Feb. 27–Mar. 14; Dec. 19–Jan. 10. *Final exams:* Dec. 14–18; May 10–14. *Admission office closed:* Dec. 19–Jan. 10, Feb. 27–Mar. 14.

## VISIT OPPORTUNITIES

|  | Appointments? | Who? |
|---|---|---|
| **Campus Tour** | recommended | applicants and parents |
| **Information Session** | required |  |
| **Admission Interview** |  | applicants only |
| **Classroom Visit** |  | open to all |
| **Overnight Visit** | required |  |

**Information Sessions:** M–F at 3:00 pm.

**Interviews:** M–F.

**Campus Tours:** Conducted by students. M–F at 3:00 pm.

**Class Visits:** Prospective students may attend a class in their area of interest, classroom visits are determined by the visit schedule.

**Overnight Visits:** During the regular academic year, prospective applicants may spend an evening in a residence hall with a student host.

## CAMPUS FACILITIES
**Of Special Interest:** Lila Acheson Wallace Library.

# LONG ISLAND UNIVERSITY, C.W. POST CAMPUS
**Brookville, New York**

**Contact:** Barbara Gottlieb, Admissions Secretary, C.W. Post Admissions, 720 Northern Boulevard, Brookville, NY 11548. *Phone:* 516-299-2070 or toll-free 800-LIU-PLAN. *Fax:* 516-299-2137. *E-mail:* bgottlieb@john.liunet.edu *Web site:* http://www.liu. edu/ *Visit location:* Admissions, College Hall, 720 Northern Boulevard.

## QUICK FACTS
Enrollment: 8,171; UG: 4,613. Entrance: moderately difficult. SAT>500: 62% V, 68% M; ACT>18: N/R. Tuition and fees: $14,530. Room and board: $6025. Application deadline: rolling.

## GENERAL
Independent, comprehensive, coed. Part of Long Island University. Awards associate, bachelor's, master's, and doctoral degrees. Founded 1954. Setting: 308-acre suburban campus with easy access to New York City. Undergraduate faculty: 1,076 (309 full-time, 767 part-time); student-faculty ratio is 9:1. Most popular recent majors: liberal arts and studies, business administration, education.

## CAMPUS VISITS
**College Calendar 1998–99:** *Regular classes:* Sept. 9–Dec. 16; Jan. 19–Apr. 28. *Breaks:* Dec. 24–Jan. 19. *Final exams:* Dec. 17–23; Apr. 29–May 7. *Admission office closed:* Nov. 27, Dec. 26. *Special campus days:* Commencement, May 9; Homecoming, Family Day and Alumni Weekend, Oct. 17–18.

## VISIT OPPORTUNITIES

|  | Appointments? | Who? |
|---|---|---|
| **Campus Tour** | recommended, not required | open to all |
| **Information Session** | recommended | open to all |
| **Admission Interview** | required | open to all |
| **Classroom Visit** | required | open to all |
| **Faculty Meeting** | required | open to all |
| **Overnight Visit** | required | open to all |

**Information Sessions:** Fri. on Post Preview Day at 9:00 am, 1:00 pm.

**Interviews:** M–F, Sat.; 30 minutes.

**Campus Tours:** Conducted by students. M–F, Sat.; call for schedule; 60 minutes.

**Class Visits:** Prospective students may attend a class in their area of interest.

**Overnight Visits:** During the regular academic year, prospective applicants may spend an evening in a residence hall with a student host.

## CAMPUS FACILITIES

**Science:** Special Laboratories for Molecular Biology, Chemistry Laboratory, Earth and Environmental Studies Laboratories, Physics Laboratories.

**Arts:** Tilles Center for the Performing Arts, Hutchins Gallery, Hillwood Art Museum; Appointment Required: C.W. Post Little Theater.

**Athletic:** Hickox Field, Equestrian Center; Appointment Required: Pioneer Field House.

**Of Special Interest:** Appointment Required: Television Studio, Computer Graphics Laboratory, Radio Station.

## LOCAL ATTRACTIONS

Sagamore Hill—Theodore Roosevelt's Home; Jones Beach; Vanderbilt Museum and Planetarium.

# MANHATTAN SCHOOL OF MUSIC

New York, New York

**Contact:** Lee Ciappa, Director of Admissions, 120 Claremont Avenue, New York, NY 10027. *Phone:* 212-749-2802 Ext. 445. *Fax:* 212-749-5471. *E-mail:* admission@msmnyc.edu *Web site:* http://www.msmnyc.edu/ *Visit location:* Office of Admission and Financial Aid, Broadway and 122nd Street.

## QUICK FACTS

Enrollment: 834; UG: 408. Entrance: very difficult. SAT>500: N/R; ACT>18: N/R. Tuition and fees: $17,900. Room and board: $9000. Application deadline: 3/15.

## GENERAL

Independent, comprehensive, coed. Awards bachelor's, master's, and doctoral degrees. Founded 1917. Setting: 1-acre urban campus. Undergraduate faculty: 277 (36 full-time, 241 part-time); student-faculty ratio is 10:1. Most popular recent majors: music (voice and choral/opera performance), music (piano and organ performance), jazz.

## CAMPUS VISITS

**College Calendar 1998–99:** *Regular classes:* Sept. 3–Dec. 11; Jan. 11–Apr. 30. *Breaks:* Nov. 26–29; Feb. 28–Mar. 14. *Final exams:* Dec. 14–18; May 3–10. *Admission office closed:* Nov. 26–27, Dec. 21–Jan. 1, Jan. 18. *Special campus days:* Commencement, May 16; Family Weekend, Oct. 2–4.

### VISIT OPPORTUNITIES

| | Appointments? | Who? |
|---|---|---|
| **Campus Tour** | required | open to all |
| **Admission Interview** | required | open to all |
| **Classroom Visit** | required | open to all |
| **Faculty Meeting** | required | open to all |

**Interviews:** M–F; unavailable during Mar. and May audition weeks; 30 minutes.

**Campus Tours:** Conducted by students. M–F; unavailable holidays Dec. 31–Jan. 1.

**Class Visits:** Classroom visits are determined by the visit schedule.

## CAMPUS FACILITIES

**Of Special Interest:** Francis Hall Ballard Library.

# MARIST COLLEGE

Poughkeepsie, New York

**Contact:** Director of Admissions, 290 North Road, Poughkeepsie, NY 12601. *Phone:* toll-free 800-436-5483. *Fax:* 914-575-3215. *E-mail:* admissions@marist.edu *Web site:* http://www.marist.edu/ *Visit location:* Admissions Office Marist College, Greystone Hall, 290 North Road.

## QUICK FACTS

Enrollment: 4,505; UG: 3,949. Entrance: moderately difficult. SAT>500: 76% V, 74% M; ACT>18: N/R. Tuition and fees: $13,098. Room and board: $6772. Application deadline: 3/1.

## GENERAL

Independent, comprehensive, coed. Awards bachelor's and master's degrees. Founded 1929. Setting: 135-acre small-town campus with easy access to Albany and New York City. Undergraduate faculty: 388 (162 full-time, 226 part-time); student-faculty ratio is 15:1. Most popular recent majors: mass communications, business administration, psychology.

*Marist College (continued)*

## CAMPUS VISITS

**College Calendar 1998–99:** *Regular classes:* Sept. 1–Dec. 12; Jan. 20–May 6. *Breaks:* Oct. 16–18; Mar. 13–21. *Final exams:* Dec. 14–19; May 8–14. *Special campus days:* Commencement, May 22.

## VISIT OPPORTUNITIES

| | Appointments? | Who? |
|---|---|---|
| **Campus Tour** | required | applicants and parents |
| **Information Session** | required | |
| **Admission Interview** | required | |
| **Classroom Visit** | required | |
| **Faculty Meeting** | required | applicants and parents |
| **Overnight Visit** | required | admitted applicants only |

**Information Sessions:** Available fall (Sept. to Dec.) M–Sun.; call for spring schedule; 60 minutes.

**Interviews:** M–F; available fall (Sept. to Dec.) M–Sun.; spring M–Sat. 9:00 am to 12:00 pm; 40 minutes.

**Campus Tours:** Conducted by students. Fall (Sept. to Dec.) M–Sun.; call for spring and summer schedule; 45 minutes.

**Class Visits:** Prospective students may attend a class in their area of interest, classroom visits are scheduled by Visit Coordinator.

**Overnight Visits:** During the regular academic year, prospective applicants may spend an evening in a residence hall with a student host.

## CAMPUS FACILITIES

**Arts:** Gallery; Appointment Required: Studios.

**Athletic:** Recreation Center, Athletic Center, Athletic Fields.

**Of Special Interest:** Dyson Center, Student Center, Book Store, Theater.

## LOCAL ATTRACTIONS

Franklin D. Roosevelt Library and Home; Mohawk Mountain House; Vanderbilt Mansion; other historic facilities.

# MARYMOUNT MANHATTAN COLLEGE
### New York, New York

**Contact:** Admissions Office, 221 East 71st Street, New York, NY 10021. *Phone:* toll-free 800-MARYMOUNT (out-of-state). *Fax:* 212-517-0413. *E-mail:* admissions@marymount.mmm.edu *Web site:* http://www.marymount.mmm.edu/ *Visit location:* Admissions, Main Building, 221 East 71st Street.

## QUICK FACTS

Enrollment: 1,962; UG: 1,962. Entrance: moderately difficult. SAT>500: 60% V, 42% M; ACT>18: N/R. Tuition and fees: $12,290. Room only: $3182. Application deadline: rolling.

## GENERAL

Independent, 4-year, coed. Awards bachelor's degrees. Founded 1936. Setting: 1-acre urban campus. Faculty: 156 (62 full-time, 94 part-time); student-faculty ratio is 17:1. Most popular recent majors: theater arts/drama, business administration, mass communications.

## CAMPUS VISITS

**College Calendar 1998–99:** *Regular classes:* Sept. 10–Dec. 19; Feb. 6–May 22. *Breaks:* Nov. 26–29; Mar. 29–Apr. 4. *Final exams:* Dec. 14–19; May 17–22. *Admission office closed:* Fri. during summer; Good Friday, Apr. 2; Holy Thursday, Apr. 1; holiday break, Dec. 24–Jan. 2. *Special campus days:* Homecoming, Oct. 24–25; Open House for High School Juniors/Seniors, Nov. 15.

## VISIT OPPORTUNITIES

| | Appointments? | Who? |
|---|---|---|
| **Campus Tour** | recommended | open to all |
| **Information Session** | recommended | open to all |
| **Admission Interview** | required | open to all |
| **Classroom Visit** | required | open to all |
| **Faculty Meeting** | required | open to all |

**Information Sessions:** Inquire for time schedule; 90 minutes.

**Interviews:** M–F, select Sat.; college is closed Fri. and Sat. during summer; 30 minutes.

**Campus Tours:** Conducted by students. M–F, select Sat. at 12:00 pm, 3:00 pm; closed Fri. and Sat. during summer; call to confirm times of tour; 90 minutes.

**Class Visits:** Prospective students may attend a class in their area of interest.

### CAMPUS FACILITIES

**Science:** Freeman Science Center.

**Arts:** Marymount Manhattan College Gallery.

**Of Special Interest:** Appointment Required: Multimedia Suites for Communication Arts, Marymount Manhattan College Theatre, Residence Halls.

# NEW YORK UNIVERSITY
**New York, New York**

**Contact:** New York University, Undergraduate Admissions Office, 22 Washington Square North, New York, NY 10011. *Phone:* 212-998-4500. *Fax:* 212-995-4902. *E-mail:* nyuadmit@uccvm.nyu.edu *Web site:* http://www.nyu.edu/ *Visit location:* Undergraduate Admissions, 22 Washington Square North.

### QUICK FACTS

Enrollment: 36,284; UG: 17,153. Entrance: most difficult. SAT>500: 99% V, 97% M; ACT>18: 100%. Tuition and fees: $21,730. Room and board: $8170. Application deadline: 1/15.

### GENERAL

Independent, university, coed. Awards associate, bachelor's, master's, doctoral, and first professional degrees. Founded 1831. Setting: 28-acre urban campus. Undergraduate faculty: 4,722 (2,274 full-time, 2,448 part-time); student-faculty ratio is 12:1. Most popular recent majors: business administration, theater arts/drama, social sciences.

### CAMPUS VISITS

**College Calendar 1998–99:** *Regular classes:* Sept. 8–Dec. 14; Jan. 19–May 3. *Breaks:* Dec. 24–Jan. 16; Mar. 15–20. *Final exams:* Dec. 16–23; May 5–12. *Special campus days:* Commencement, May 13.

### VISIT OPPORTUNITIES

| | Appointments? | Who? |
|---|---|---|
| **Campus Tour** | not required | applicants and parents |
| **Information Session** | required | |
| **Classroom Visit** | not required | |
| **Overnight Visit** | required | admitted applicants only |

**Information Sessions:** M–F; call for Sat. schedule; 60 minutes.

**Campus Tours:** Conducted by students. M–F, select Sat.; 60 minutes.

**Class Visits:** Certain predetermined classrooms are open to visitors.

**Overnight Visits:** During the regular academic year, prospective applicants may spend an evening in a residence hall with a student host.

### CAMPUS FACILITIES

**Arts:** Grey Art Gallery.

**Athletic:** Coles Sports and Recreation Center.

**Of Special Interest:** Bobst Library.

### LOCAL ATTRACTIONS

Greenwich Village; Chinatown; Soho; Little Italy.

# NIAGARA UNIVERSITY
**Niagara Falls, New York**

**Contact:** Office of Admissions, Bailo Hall, PO Box 2011, Niagara University, NY 14109-2011. *Phone:* toll-free 800-462-2111. *Fax:* 716-286-8710. *E-mail:* admission@niagara.edu *Web site:* http://www.niagara.edu/ *Visit location:* Office of Admissions, Bailo Hall, PO Box 2011, Niagara University.

### QUICK FACTS

Enrollment: 3,033; UG: 2,406. Entrance: moderately difficult. SAT>500: 61% V, 60% M; ACT>18: N/R. Tuition and fees: $12,890. Room and board: $5658. Application deadline: 8/1.

### GENERAL

Independent, comprehensive, coed. Awards associate, bachelor's, and master's degrees. Founded 1856. Setting: 160-acre suburban campus with easy access to Buffalo and Toronto. Undergraduate faculty: 265 (118 full-time, 147 part-time); student-faculty ratio is 16:1. Most popular recent majors: business administration, travel-tourism management, social sciences.

### CAMPUS VISITS

**College Calendar 1998–99:** *Regular classes:* Sept. 1–Dec. 22; Jan. 12–May 8. *Breaks:* Nov. 24–30; Feb. 17–22; Oct. 12–13; Mar. 27–Apr. 7. *Final exams:* Dec. 17–22; May 4–8.

*Niagara University (continued)*

## VISIT OPPORTUNITIES

| | Appointments? | Who? |
|---|---|---|
| **Campus Tour** | required | applicants and parents |
| **Information Session** | required | open to all |
| **Admission Interview** | required | applicants and parents |
| **Classroom Visit** | required | open to all |
| **Faculty Meeting** | required | open to all |
| **Overnight Visit** | required | open to all |

**Information Sessions:** Call for details; 180 minutes.

**Interviews:** M–F, select Sat.; during summer open to 12:00 pm Fri.; available selected Sat. during fall and spring; 40 minutes.

**Campus Tours:** Conducted by students. M–F 9:30 am–3:30 pm; Sat. 10:00 am–12:00 pm; call to verify times; 60 minutes.

**Class Visits:** Prospective students may attend a class in their area of interest, classroom visits are determined by the visit schedule.

**Overnight Visits:** During the regular academic year, prospective applicants may spend an evening in a residence hall with a student host.

## CAMPUS FACILITIES
**Science:** De Paul Hall, Dunleavy Hall.

**Arts:** Castellani Art Museum; Appointment Required: Theatre.

**Athletic:** Keirnan Athletic and Recreation Center; Appointment Required: Ice Hockey Arena.

**Of Special Interest:** Alumni Chapel, Library.

## LOCAL ATTRACTIONS
Niagara Falls; Fort Niagara; Maid of the Mist; Aquarium; Wintergarden; Outlet Malls; Artpark; Fantasy Island Amusement Park; Casino Niagara.

# PACE UNIVERSITY
**New York, New York**

**Contact:** Richard Alvarez, Director of Admissions NYC, One Pace Plaza, New York, NY 10038. *Phone:* 212-346-1225 or toll-free 800-874-7223. *Fax:* 212-346-1040. *E-mail:* ugnyc@fsmail.pace.edu *Web site:* http://www.pace.edu/ *Visit location:* Office of Undergraduate Admission, Civic Center Building, One Pace Plaza.

## QUICK FACTS
Enrollment: 12,054; UG: 7,779. Entrance: moderately difficult. SAT>500: 49% V, 57% M; ACT>18: N/R. Tuition and fees: $13,820. Room and board: $6100. Application deadline: 8/15.

## GENERAL
Independent, university, coed. Part of Pace University. Awards associate, bachelor's, master's, doctoral, and first professional degrees and post-master's and first professional certificates (setting: 3-acre urban New York City campus, 200-acre small-town Pleasantville campus). Founded 1906. Undergraduate faculty: 1,266 (429 full-time, 837 part-time); student-faculty ratio is 11:1. Most popular recent majors: accounting, finance, computer science.

## CAMPUS VISITS
**College Calendar 1998–99:** *Regular classes:* Sept. 8–Dec. 14; Jan. 25–May 3. *Breaks:* Dec. 24–Jan. 24; Mar. 15–21. *Final exams:* Dec. 16–23; May 6–15. *Admission office closed:* Christmas–New Year's Day break.

## VISIT OPPORTUNITIES

| | Appointments? | Who? |
|---|---|---|
| **Campus Tour** | recommended | open to all |
| **Information Session** | recommended | open to all |
| **Admission Interview** | recommended | open to all |
| **Classroom Visit** | required | open to all |
| **Faculty Meeting** | required | open to all |
| **Overnight Visit** | required | open to all |

**Information Sessions:** M–F, select Sat.; call for available dates and times; 30 minutes.

**Interviews:** M–F, select Sat.; 30 minutes.

**Campus Tours:** Conducted by students. M–F; call for available times.

**Class Visits:** Classroom visits are determined by the visit schedule.

**Overnight Visits:** During the regular academic year, prospective applicants may spend an evening in a residence hall with a student host.

## CAMPUS FACILITIES
**Science:** Appointment Required: science labs.

**Arts:** Art building in Pleasantville, Schimmel Theatre art gallery in New York City.

**Of Special Interest:** Residence halls.


# PARSONS SCHOOL OF DESIGN, NEW SCHOOL FOR SOCIAL RESEARCH

**New York, New York**

**Contact:** Ms. Nadine M. Bourgeois, Director of Admissions, 66 Fifth Avenue, New York, NY 10011-8878. *Phone:* 212-229-8910 or toll-free 800-252-0852. *Fax:* 212-229-8975. *E-mail:* parsadm@ newschool.edu *Web site:* http://www.parsons.edu/ *Visit location:* Office of Admissions, 2 West 13th Avenue, Ground Floor.

## QUICK FACTS

Enrollment: 2,011; UG: 1,788. Entrance: very difficult. SAT>500: 69% V, 60% M; ACT>18: N/R. Tuition and fees: $18,540. Room and board: $8555. Application deadline: rolling.

## GENERAL

Independent, comprehensive, coed. Part of New School for Social Research. Awards associate, bachelor's, and master's degrees. Founded 1896. Setting: 2-acre urban campus. Undergraduate faculty: 403 (38 full-time, 365 part-time); student-faculty ratio is 14:1. Most popular recent majors: fashion design/ illustration, graphic design/commercial art/illustration.

## CAMPUS VISITS

**College Calendar 1998–99:** *Regular classes:* Sept. 8–Dec. 23; Jan. 25–May 15. *Breaks:* Dec. 24–Jan. 19; Mar. 22–28.

## CAMPUS FACILITIES

**Arts:** Appointment Required: galleries, computer facilities, library.

## LOCAL ATTRACTIONS

Greenwich Village and New York City.


# PRATT INSTITUTE

**Brooklyn, New York**

**Contact:** Ms. Judith Aaron, Vice President, Enrollment, 200 Willoughby Avenue, Brooklyn, NY 11205.

*Phone:* toll-free 800-331-0834. *Fax:* 718-636-3670. *E-mail:* info@pratt.edu *Web site:* http://www.pratt. edu/ *Visit location:* Admissions, DeKalb, 2nd Floor, 200 Willoughby Avenue.

## QUICK FACTS

Enrollment: 3,640; UG: 2,272. Entrance: moderately difficult. SAT>500: 65% V, 56% M; ACT>18: N/R. Tuition and fees: $17,151. Room and board: $7153. Application deadline: rolling.

## GENERAL

Independent, comprehensive, coed. Awards associate, bachelor's, and master's degrees. Founded 1887. Setting: 25-acre urban campus. Undergraduate faculty: 502 (141 full-time, 361 part-time); student-faculty ratio is 12:1. Most popular recent majors: architecture, art.

## CAMPUS VISITS

**College Calendar 1998–99:** *Regular classes:* Sept. 3–Dec. 20; Jan. 29–May 23. *Breaks:* Dec. 20–Jan. 29. *Final exams:* Dec. 16–20; May 17–23. *Special campus days:* Commencement, May 28; Exhibition Days, May 25–26.

## VISIT OPPORTUNITIES

|  | Appointments? | Who? |
| --- | --- | --- |
| **Campus Tour** | required | open to all |
| **Information Session** | recommended | open to all |
| **Admission Interview** | required | open to all |
| **Classroom Visit** | required | open to all |
| **Faculty Meeting** | required | open to all |
| **Overnight Visit** | required | open to all |

**Information Sessions:** National Portfolio Day Nov. 21; open houses held three times a year on selected Sat.; call for scheduled dates.

**Interviews:** M–F; 30 minutes.

**Campus Tours:** Conducted by students. M–F at 11:00 am, 2:30 pm; 60 minutes.

**Overnight Visits:** During the regular academic year.

## CAMPUS FACILITIES

**Arts:** Various Galleries on Campus.

**Of Special Interest:** Appointment Required: Pratt Library.

## LOCAL ATTRACTIONS

Manhattan Museums and Galleries.

# PURCHASE COLLEGE, STATE UNIVERSITY OF NEW YORK

**Purchase, New York**

**Contact:** Hilary Blackman, Michelle Cost or Lisa Labeille, Anderson Hill Road, Purchase, NY 10577. *Phone:* 914-251-6300. *Fax:* 914-251-6314. *E-mail:* admissions@purchase.edu *Web site:* http://www.purchase.edu/ *Visit location:* Office of Admissions, Administration Building—Purchase College, Anderson Hill Road.

## QUICK FACTS

Enrollment: 2,548; UG: 2,468. Entrance: moderately difficult. SAT>500: 69% V, 59% M; ACT>18: 91%. Resident tuition and fees: $3879. Nonresident tuition and fees: $8779. Room and board: $5264. Application deadline: rolling.

## GENERAL

State-supported, comprehensive, coed. Part of State University of New York System. Awards bachelor's and master's degrees. Founded 1967. Setting: 500-acre small-town campus with easy access to New York City. Undergraduate faculty: 252 (114 full-time, 138 part-time); student-faculty ratio is 20:1. Most popular recent majors: art, literature, liberal arts and studies.

## CAMPUS VISITS

**College Calendar 1998–99:** *Regular classes:* Aug. 31–Dec. 22; Jan. 20–May 12. *Breaks:* Nov. 26–29; Mar. 13–21. *Final exams:* Dec. 16–22; May 6–12. *Special campus days:* Commencement, May 16; Spring Weekend "Culture Shock", Apr. 16–18.

### VISIT OPPORTUNITIES

| | Appointments? | Who? |
|---|---|---|
| **Campus Tour** | recommended, not required | open to all |
| **Information Session** | recommended, not required | open to all |
| **Classroom Visit** | recommended | open to all |
| **Overnight Visit** | | admitted applicants only |

**Information Sessions:** M–F at 10:00 am, 12:00 pm; information sessions are available by appointment during regular hours Mon. through Fri.; 30 minutes.
**Campus Tours:** Conducted by students, admission reps, and administrators/staff. Fri. at 10:00 am, 12:00 pm; Mon. at 10:00 am, 12:00 pm; tours are available by appointment during regular hours Mon. through Fri.; 60 minutes.
**Class Visits:** Certain predetermined classrooms are open to visitors.

## CAMPUS FACILITIES

**Science:** Natural Sciences Building.
**Arts:** Performing Arts Center, Art and Design/Visual Arts Building, Neuberger Museum, Dance Building, Music Building.
**Athletic:** Gym.
**Of Special Interest:** Campus centers, residence halls.

## LOCAL ATTRACTIONS

Pepsico Sculpture Gardens; Westchester Mall.

# RENSSELAER POLYTECHNIC INSTITUTE

**Troy, New York**

**Contact:** Campus Visit Coordinator, 110 8th Street, Troy, NY 12180. *Phone:* 518-276-6216 or toll-free 800-448-6562. *Fax:* 518-276-4072. *E-mail:* admissions@rpi.edu *Web site:* http://www.rpi.edu/ *Visit location:* Office of Undergraduate Admissions, Admissions/Financial Aid Building, Sage Avenue and Eaton Road.

## QUICK FACTS

Enrollment: 6,315; UG: 4,307. Entrance: very difficult. SAT>500: 91% V, 97% M; ACT>18: N/R. Tuition and fees: $20,604. Room and board: $6786. Application deadline: 1/1.

## GENERAL

Independent, university, coed. Awards bachelor's, master's, and doctoral degrees. Founded 1824. Setting: 260-acre suburban campus with easy access to Albany. Undergraduate faculty: 342 (341 full-time, 1 part-time); student-faculty ratio is 12:1. Most popular recent majors: mechanical engineering, electrical/electronics engineering, computer science.

## CAMPUS VISITS

**College Calendar 1998–99:** *Regular classes:* Aug. 24–Dec. 7; Jan. 11–Apr. 28. *Breaks:* Oct. 9–14; Feb. 15–16; Dec. 17–Jan. 11; Mar. 5–15. *Final exams:* Dec. 10–16; May 3–7. *Special campus days:* Commencement, May 14; Honors Convocation and Family

Weekend, Nov. 6–8; Rensselaer 175th Anniversary Celebration begins, Sept. 12.

## VISIT OPPORTUNITIES

| | Appointments? | Who? |
|---|---|---|
| **Campus Tour** | not required | open to all |
| **Information Session** | not required | open to all |
| **Admission Interview** | required | open to all |
| **Classroom Visit** | recommended | open to all |
| **Faculty Meeting** | required | open to all |

**Information Sessions:** M–F, Sat. at 1:00 pm; 60 minutes.

**Interviews:** M–F; 45 minutes.

**Campus Tours:** Conducted by students. M–F, Sat. at 11:00 am, 2:00 pm; 60 minutes.

**Class Visits:** Prospective students may attend a class in their area of interest.

**Video:** Free on request.

## CAMPUS FACILITIES

**Of Special Interest:** Folsom Library.

# ST. BONAVENTURE UNIVERSITY
## St. Bonaventure, New York

**Contact:** Mr. Alexander P. Nazemetz, Director of Admissions, Office of Admissions, PO Box D, St. Bonaventure, NY 14778. *Phone:* toll-free 800-462-5050. *Fax:* 716-375-2005. *E-mail:* admissions@sbu.edu *Web site:* http://www.sbu.edu/ *Visit location:* Office of Admissions, Hopkins Hall, St. Bonaventure University.

## QUICK FACTS

Enrollment: 2,711; UG: 2,027. Entrance: moderately difficult. SAT>500: 68% V, 67% M; ACT>18: N/R. Tuition and fees: $13,100. Room and board: $5378. Application deadline: 3/1.

## GENERAL

Independent, comprehensive, coed, Roman Catholic Church. Awards bachelor's and master's degrees. Founded 1858. Setting: 600-acre small-town campus. Undergraduate faculty: 173 (127 full-time, 46 part-time); student-faculty ratio is 17:1. Most popular recent majors: accounting, elementary education, mass communications.

## CAMPUS VISITS

**College Calendar 1998–99:** *Regular classes:* Aug. 24–Dec. 8; Jan. 16–May 5. *Breaks:* Oct. 10–13; Feb. 27–Mar. 7; Nov. 21–29; Apr. 1–5. *Final exams:* Dec. 10–15; May 7–12. *Special campus days:* Baccalaureate Mass, May 15; Commencement, May 16; December Recognition (Graduation), Dec. 16.

## VISIT OPPORTUNITIES

| | Appointments? | Who? |
|---|---|---|
| **Campus Tour** | recommended, not required | open to all |
| **Information Session** | recommended, not required | open to all |
| **Admission Interview** | recommended, not required | open to all |
| **Classroom Visit** | required | open to all |
| **Faculty Meeting** | required | open to all |
| **Overnight Visit** | required | applicants only |

**Information Sessions:** Select Sat.; includes brunch and student led tour.

**Interviews:** M–F, select Sat.; 45 minutes.

**Campus Tours:** Conducted by students and admission reps. M–F 9:00 am–3:30 pm; select Sat. at 10:00 am; includes information session and brunch; 60 minutes.

**Class Visits:** Prospective students may attend a class in their area of interest, classroom visits are determined by the visit schedule.

**Overnight Visits:** During the regular academic year, prospective applicants may spend an evening in a residence hall with a student host.

## CAMPUS FACILITIES

**Science:** De la Roche Hall; Appointment Required: Observatory.

**Arts:** Regina A. Quick Center for the Arts.

**Athletic:** Rielly Center, Tripodi Fitness Center, St. Bonaventure Golf Course, McGraw-Jennings Athletics Fields.

**Of Special Interest:** Friedsam Memorial Library.

# ST. FRANCIS COLLEGE
## Brooklyn Heights, New York

**Contact:** Br. George Larkin, OSF, Dean of Admissions, 180 Remsen Street, Brooklyn, NY 11201.

*St. Francis College (continued)*

*Phone:* 718-489-5200. *Fax:* 718-802-0453. *E-mail:* glarkin@stfranciscollege.edu *Web site:* http://www. stfranciscollege.edu/ *Visit location:* Admissions, 180 Remsen Street.

## QUICK FACTS

Enrollment: 2,136; UG: 2,136. Entrance: moderately difficult. SAT>500: N/App; ACT>18: N/App. Tuition and fees: $7680. Room and board: $3150. Application deadline: rolling.

## GENERAL

Independent Roman Catholic, 4-year, coed. Awards associate and bachelor's degrees. Founded 1884. Setting: 1-acre urban campus with easy access to New York City. Faculty: 157 (62 full-time, 95 part-time); student-faculty ratio is 27:1. Most popular recent majors: business administration, liberal arts and studies, psychology.

## CAMPUS VISITS

**College Calendar 1998–99:** *Regular classes:* Sept. 9–Dec. 15; Jan. 25–May 14. *Breaks:* Dec. 23–Jan. 25. *Final exams:* Dec. 12–23; May 17–21. *Admission office closed:* June 25, July 2, July 9, July 16, July 23, July 30, Aug. 6. *Special campus days:* Charter Day; Commencement; Event celebrating the life and talent of Hispanics.

## VISIT OPPORTUNITIES

|                      | Appointments?              | Who?        |
| -------------------- | -------------------------- | ----------- |
| **Campus Tour**      | recommended, not required  | open to all |
| **Information Session** | recommended, not required | open to all |
| **Admission Interview** | recommended, not required | open to all |
| **Classroom Visit**  | recommended, not required  | open to all |
| **Faculty Meeting**  | required                   |             |

**Information Sessions:** M–F 9:00 am–5:00 pm; 30 minutes.

**Interviews:** M–F 9:00 am–5:00 pm; 30 minutes.

**Campus Tours:** Conducted by students. M–F 9:00 am–5:00 pm; 30 minutes.

**Class Visits:** Prospective students may attend a class in their area of interest, classroom visits are determined by the visit schedule.

**Video:** Free on request.

## CAMPUS FACILITIES
**Of Special Interest:** McGarry Library.

## LOCAL ATTRACTIONS
New York Harbor Promenade.

# ST. LAWRENCE UNIVERSITY
**Canton, New York**

**Contact:** Office of Admissions, St. Lawrence University, Canton, NY 13617. *Phone:* toll-free 800-285-1856. *Fax:* 315-229-5818. *E-mail:* admiss@music. stlawu.edu *Web site:* http://www.stlawu.edu/ *Visit location:* Office of Admissions, Payson Hall.

## QUICK FACTS

Enrollment: 1,992; UG: 1,892. Entrance: very difficult. SAT>500: 83% V, 84% M; ACT>18: N/R. Tuition and fees: $21,435. Room and board: $6340. Application deadline: 2/15.

## GENERAL

Independent, comprehensive, coed. Awards bachelor's and master's degrees. Founded 1856. Setting: 1,000-acre small-town campus with easy access to Ottawa. Undergraduate faculty: 181 (151 full-time, 30 part-time); student-faculty ratio is 12:1. Most popular recent majors: English, psychology, biology.

## CAMPUS VISITS

**College Calendar 1998–99:** *Regular classes:* Aug. 27–Dec. 11; Jan. 25–May 7. *Breaks:* Oct. 15–17; Mar. 12–19. *Final exams:* Dec. 14–19; May 10–17.

## VISIT OPPORTUNITIES

|                        | Appointments? | Who?        |
| ---------------------- | ------------- | ----------- |
| **Campus Tour**        | required      | open to all |
| **Admission Interview** | required     | open to all |
| **Classroom Visit**    | required      | open to all |
| **Faculty Meeting**    | required      | open to all |

**Interviews:** M–F, select Sat.; 60 minutes.

**Campus Tours:** Conducted by students. M–F, select Sat.; 60 minutes.

**Class Visits:** Prospective students may attend a class in their area of interest.

## CAMPUS FACILITIES
**Of Special Interest:** Owen D. Young Library.

# ST. THOMAS AQUINAS COLLEGE
**Sparkill, New York**

**Contact:** Mr. Joseph L. Chillo, Executive Director of Enrollment Services, 125 Route 340, Sparkill, NY 10976. *Phone:* 914-398-4100 or toll-free 800-999-STAC. *Fax:* 914-398-4224. *E-mail:* jchillo@stacmail. stac.edu *Web site:* http://www.stac.edu/ *Visit location:* Office of Admissions and Financial Aid, Spellman Hall, 125 Route 340.

## QUICK FACTS
Enrollment: 1,685; UG: 1,508. Entrance: moderately difficult. SAT>500: 32% V, 31% M; ACT>18: N/R. Tuition and fees: $10,700. Room and board: $6700. Application deadline: rolling.

## GENERAL
Independent, comprehensive, coed. Awards bachelor's and master's degrees and post-master's certificates. Founded 1952. Setting: 46-acre suburban campus with easy access to New York City. Undergraduate faculty: 150 (76 full-time, 74 part-time); student-faculty ratio is 17:1. Most popular recent majors: education, business administration, psychology.

## CAMPUS VISITS
**College Calendar 1998–99:** *Regular classes:* Sept. 8–Dec. 18; Jan. 25–May 7. *Final exams:* Dec. 14–18; May 3–7. *Admission office closed:* Dec. 24–Jan. 3.

## VISIT OPPORTUNITIES

|  | Appointments? | Who? |
|---|---|---|
| **Campus Tour** | recommended | open to all |
| **Information Session** | required | open to all |
| **Admission Interview** | required | open to all |
| **Classroom Visit** | required | open to all |
| **Faculty Meeting** | required | open to all |
| **Overnight Visit** | required | applicants only |

**Information Sessions:** M–F, Sat.; 60 minutes.
**Interviews:** M–F, Sat.; 60 minutes.

**Campus Tours:** Conducted by students. M–F at 10:00 am, 1:00 pm, 4:00 pm; Sat. at 10:00 am; 45 minutes.

**Class Visits:** Prospective students may attend a class in their area of interest.

**Overnight Visits:** During the regular academic year, prospective applicants may spend an evening in a residence hall with a student host.

**Video:** Free on request.

## CAMPUS FACILITIES
**Arts:** Mac Lab, Graphic Studio.
**Athletic:** Gymnasium.
**Of Special Interest:** Computer Lab, Technology Classrooms, Theatre.

## LOCAL ATTRACTIONS
Piermont, New York; historic Dewitt House.

# SARAH LAWRENCE COLLEGE
**Bronxville, New York**

**Contact:** Admissions Office, 1 Mead Way, Bronxville, NY 10708-5999. *Phone:* toll-free 800-888-2858. *Fax:* 914-395-2510. *E-mail:* slcadmit@mail.slc.edu *Web site:* http://www.slc.edu/ *Visit location:* Office of Admissions, Westlands, 1 Mead Way.

## QUICK FACTS
Enrollment: 1,388; UG: 1,111. Entrance: very difficult. SAT>500: 98% V, 89% M; ACT>18: 100%. Tuition and fees: $23,076. Room and board: $7219. Application deadline: 2/1.

## GENERAL
Independent, comprehensive, coed. Awards bachelor's and master's degrees. Founded 1926. Setting: 40-acre suburban campus with easy access to New York City. Undergraduate faculty: 238 (173 full-time, 65 part-time); student-faculty ratio is 6:1. Most popular recent majors: literature, creative writing, theater arts/drama.

## CAMPUS VISITS
**College Calendar 1998–99:** *Regular classes:* Sept. 7–Dec. 18; Jan. 19–May 14. *Breaks:* Nov. 25–29; Mar. 13–28; Dec. 20–Jan. 18. *Admission office closed:* winter break, Dec. 21–Jan. 1. *Special campus days:* Commencement, May 21.

*Sarah Lawrence College (continued)*

## VISIT OPPORTUNITIES

| | Appointments? | Who? |
|---|---|---|
| **Campus Tour** | recommended | open to all |
| **Information Session** | recommended | open to all |
| **Admission Interview** | required | open to all |
| **Classroom Visit** | required | open to all |
| **Faculty Meeting** | required | open to all |
| **Overnight Visit** | required | open to all |

**Information Sessions:** M–F; Sat. during fall semester; 30 minutes.

**Interviews:** M–F; Sat. during fall semester; 45 minutes.

**Campus Tours:** Conducted by students. M–F; Sat. during fall semester; 45 minutes.

**Class Visits:** Prospective students may attend a class in their area of interest.

**Overnight Visits:** During the regular academic year, prospective applicants may spend an evening in a residence hall with a student host.

## CAMPUS FACILITIES
**Science:** Science Center.

**Arts:** Performing Arts Center, Visual Arts Studios, Music building.

**Athletic:** Campbell Sport's Center.

**Of Special Interest:** Library, Ruth Leff Siegel Student Center, Residence Halls.

## LOCAL ATTRACTIONS
New York City.

# SKIDMORE COLLEGE
## Saratoga Springs, New York

**Contact:** Ms. Mary Lou W. Bates, Director of Admissions, 815 North Broadway, Saratoga Springs, NY 12866. *Phone:* 518-580-5570 or toll-free 800-867-6007. *Fax:* 518-581-7462. *E-mail:* admissions@scott.skiomore.edu *Web site:* http://www.skidmore.edu/ *Visit location:* Admissions, Eissner Admissions Center, 815 North Broadway.

## QUICK FACTS
Enrollment: 2,559; UG: 2,499. Entrance: very difficult. SAT>500: 92% V, 91% M; ACT>18: N/R. Tuition and fees: $21,988. Room and board: $6354. Application deadline: 2/1.

## GENERAL
Independent, comprehensive, coed. Awards bachelor's and master's degrees. Founded 1903. Setting: 800-acre small-town campus with easy access to Albany. Undergraduate faculty: 185 (173 full-time, 12 part-time); student-faculty ratio is 11:1. Most popular recent majors: business administration, English, psychology.

## CAMPUS VISITS
**College Calendar 1998–99:** *Regular classes:* Sept. 9–Dec. 11; Jan. 25–May 4. *Breaks:* Dec. 23–Jan. 23; Mar. 13–21. *Final exams:* Dec. 16–22; May 10–14. *Special campus days:* Commencement, May 23; Family Weekend, Oct. 16–18; Thanksgiving, Nov. 25–29.

## VISIT OPPORTUNITIES

| | Appointments? | Who? |
|---|---|---|
| **Campus Tour** | recommended, not required | open to all |
| **Information Session** | required | open to all |
| **Admission Interview** | required | open to all |
| **Classroom Visit** | required | open to all |
| **Overnight Visit** | required | open to all |

**Information Sessions:** M–F at 10:30 am, 2:30 pm; available Apr. 1 through Sept. 1; 45 minutes.

**Interviews:** M–F; Sat. mornings except in Feb., Mar., Jun., Jul., and Aug.; 45 minutes.

**Campus Tours:** Conducted by students. M–F 9:30–11:30 am, 1:30–4:00 pm; Sat. 9:30 am–11:30 am except in Feb., Mar., Jun., Jul., and Aug.

**Class Visits:** Prospective students may attend a class in their area of interest, certain predetermined classrooms are open to visitors.

**Overnight Visits:** During the regular academic year, prospective applicants may spend an evening in a residence hall with a student host.

**Video:** Available, fee charged.

## CAMPUS FACILITIES
**Science:** Dana Science Center.

**Arts:** Saisselin Art Building, Bernhard Theater, Filene Music Building, Dance Theater and Studios.

**Athletic:** Sports and Recreation Center, Artificial Turf Field/Stadium/Track, Van Lennup Riding Center.

**Of Special Interest:** Scribner Library.

## LOCAL ATTRACTIONS
Saratoga Performing Arts Center, historic Saratoga Race Course, National Museum of Dance, National Museum of Racing, Main street Saratoga Springs.

# STATE UNIVERSITY OF NEW YORK AT ALBANY
Albany, New York

**Contact:** Ms. Sheila Mahan, Assistant Vice President for Academic Affairs, 1400 Washington Avenue, Office of Admissions, Albany, NY 12222. *Phone:* 518-442-5435. *Web site:* http://www.albany.edu/ *Visit location:* Administration, Admissions–AD101, 1400 Washington Avenue.

## QUICK FACTS
Enrollment: 15,213; UG: 10,209. Entrance: moderately difficult. SAT>500: 83% V, 86% M; ACT>18: N/R. Resident tuition and fees: $4173. Nonresident tuition and fees: $9073. Room and board: $5241. Application deadline: rolling.

## GENERAL
State-supported, university, coed. Part of State University of New York System. Awards bachelor's, master's, and doctoral degrees and post-master's certificates. Founded 1844. Setting: 560-acre suburban campus. Undergraduate faculty: 835 (591 full-time, 244 part-time); student-faculty ratio is 16:1. Most popular recent majors: English, psychology, business administration.

## CAMPUS VISITS
**College Calendar 1998–99:** *Regular classes:* Aug. 31–Dec. 9; Jan. 27–May 12. *Final exams:* Dec. 11–18.

## VISIT OPPORTUNITIES

| | Appointments? |
|---|---|
| **Campus Tour** | recommended, not required |
| **Information Session** | recommended, not required |
| **Admission Interview** | recommended, not required |

| | Appointments? |
|---|---|
| **Classroom Visit** | not required |
| **Faculty Meeting** | required |
| **Overnight Visit** | required |

**Information Sessions:** M–F, Sat. at 12:30 pm; unavailable during school breaks; call for summer schedule; 60 minutes.

**Interviews:** M–F; 30 minutes.

**Campus Tours:** Conducted by students. M–F at 11:00 am, 1:30 pm; Sat. at 2:00 pm; Sun. at 2:00 pm; unavailable during school breaks; call for summer schedule and group tours; 75 minutes.

**Class Visits:** Certain predetermined classrooms are open to visitors.

**Overnight Visits:** During the regular academic year.

## CAMPUS FACILITIES
**Science:** Center for Environmental Science and Technology Management, Atmospheric Science Department.

**Arts:** Art Museum.

**Athletic:** Recreation and Convocation Center, Physical Education Building, Fitness Centers.

## LOCAL ATTRACTIONS
The Capitol; Empire Plaza; New York State Museum.

# STATE UNIVERSITY OF NEW YORK AT BINGHAMTON
Binghamton, New York

**Contact:** Office of Admissions, Box 6001, Binghamton, NY 13902-6001. *Phone:* 607-777-2171. *Fax:* 607-777-4445. *E-mail:* admit@binghamton.edu *Web site:* http://www.binghamton.edu/ *Visit location:* PO Box 6000.

## QUICK FACTS
Enrollment: 11,981; UG: 9,285. Entrance: very difficult. SAT>500: 90% V, 96% M; ACT>18: 100%. Resident tuition and fees: $4110. Nonresident tuition and fees: $9010. Room and board: $5114. Application deadline: 2/15.

*State University of New York at Binghamton (continued)*

## GENERAL

State-supported, university, coed. Part of State University of New York System. Awards bachelor's, master's, and doctoral degrees and post-master's certificates. Founded 1946. Setting: 606-acre suburban campus. Undergraduate faculty: 838 (466 full-time, 372 part-time); student-faculty ratio is 17:1. Most popular recent majors: psychology, biology, English.

## CAMPUS VISITS

**College Calendar 1998–99:** *Regular classes:* Aug. 31–Dec. 11; Jan. 25–May 7. *Breaks:* Sept. 21–23; Mar. 13–22; Nov. 25–30; Mar. 31–Apr. 6. *Final exams:* Dec. 14–18; May 10–13. *Special campus days:* Commencement, May 16.

## VISIT OPPORTUNITIES

|  | Appointments? | Who? |
|---|---|---|
| **Campus Tour** | required | open to all |
| **Information Session** | required | open to all |
| **Classroom Visit** | recommended | open to all |
| **Overnight Visit** | required | open to all |

**Information Sessions:** M–F, select Sat. at 12:15 pm; visits to campus should be scheduled 1–2 weeks in advance; schools and community agencies may request special arrangements; students/parents without reservation are welcome but are seated as space is available; 60 minutes.

**Campus Tours:** Conducted by students. M–F, select Sat.; following information sessions; 90 minutes.

**Class Visits:** Admission staff or student hosts recommend classes or take students visitors to class.

**Overnight Visits:** During the regular academic year, prospective applicants may spend an evening in a residence hall with a student host.

**Video:** Available, fee charged.

## CAMPUS FACILITIES

**Arts:** Anderson Center for Fine and Performing Arts.

**Of Special Interest:** Couper Building, Residential Communities, Dickinson, Hinman, Newing and College in the woods.

## LOCAL ATTRACTIONS

Roberson Center (art galleries, planetarium); several historic carousels (operational April through October); Ross Park Zoo and Carousel.

# STATE UNIVERSITY OF NEW YORK AT BUFFALO

**Buffalo, New York**

**Contact:** Visit UB Program - Office of Admissions, Caper Hall Room 17, Buffalo, NY 14260-1660. *Phone:* toll-free 888-UB-ADMIT. *Fax:* 716-645-6411. *E-mail:* ub-admissions@admissions.buffalo.edu *Web site:* http://www.buffalo.edu/ *Visit location:* Visit UB Program, Talbert Hall, Room 107, North Campus.

## QUICK FACTS

Enrollment: 23,429; UG: 15,552. Entrance: very difficult. SAT>500: 80% V, 89% M; ACT>18: N/R. Resident tuition and fees: $4340. Nonresident tuition and fees: $9240. Room and board: $5604. Application deadline: rolling.

## GENERAL

State-supported, university, coed. Part of State University of New York System. Awards bachelor's, master's, doctoral, and first professional degrees. Founded 1846. Setting: 1,350-acre suburban campus. Undergraduate faculty: 1,484 (1,099 full-time, 385 part-time); student-faculty ratio is 13:1. Most popular recent majors: business administration, social sciences, psychology.

## CAMPUS VISITS

**College Calendar 1998–99:** *Regular classes:* Aug. 31–Dec. 14; Jan. 19–May 3. *Breaks:* Nov. 25–27; Mar. 8–12. *Final exams:* Dec. 15–22; May 6–13. *Admission office closed:* Commencement Weekend, May 14–16; Holiday Curtailment, Dec. 23–Jan. 4; Rosh Hashanah; Yom Kippur; call for summer schedule (May–Aug.). *Special campus days:* Commencement Weekend, May 14–16; Discover UB (Undergraduate Open House), Oct. 17; Homecoming, Oct. 10; Preview Day (Open House for Accepted Undergraduates), Apr. 17.

## VISIT OPPORTUNITIES

|  | Appointments? | Who? |
|---|---|---|
| **Campus Tour** | required | open to all |
| **Information Session** | required | open to all |
| **Admission Interview** | recommended | |
| **Classroom Visit** | required | |
| **Faculty Meeting** | required | |

**Information Sessions:** M–F at 1:00 pm; select Sat. at 1:00 pm; two-week advance appointment recommended; 60 minutes.

**Interviews:** M–F; 30 minutes.

**Campus Tours:** Conducted by students. M–F, select Sat.; follow Information Sessions; occasional morning tours available; call for schedule; 120 minutes.

**Class Visits:** Prospective students may attend a class in their area of interest, certain predetermined classrooms are open to visitors.

**Video:** Free on request.

## CAMPUS FACILITIES

**Science:** Departments of Social Sciences; Appointment Required: School of Engineering, Departments of Biological Science, Chemistry, Computer Science, Biology, Mathematics, Physics.

**Arts:** Appointment Required: Center for the Arts, Department of Art, Media Studies, Theatre and Dance, and Music.

**Athletic:** Appointment Required: Alumni Arena, recreation and sports facilities.

**Of Special Interest:** School of Pharmacy; Appointment Required: School of Management, School of Architecture and Planning, School of Health Related Professions, Residence Halls on South Campus, School of Nursing.

## LOCAL ATTRACTIONS

Buffalo theater, sports and arts events; Niagara Falls.

# STATE UNIVERSITY OF NEW YORK AT NEW PALTZ
New Paltz, New York

**Contact:** Office of Admissions, 75 South Manheim Boulevard, Suite 1, New Paltz, NY 12561-2499. *Phone:* 914-257-3200 or toll-free 888-NEWPLTZ (in-state). *Fax:* 914-257-3209. *E-mail:* admiss@npvm. newpaltz.edu *Web site:* http://www.newpaltz.edu/ *Visit location:* Office of Admissions, Hopfer Alumni and Admissions Center, 75 South Manheim Boulevard, Suite 1.

## QUICK FACTS

Enrollment: 7,186; UG: 5,618. Entrance: moderately difficult. SAT>500: N/R; ACT>18: N/R. Resident tuition and fees: $3885. Nonresident tuition and fees: $8785. Room and board: $5020. Application deadline: 5/1.

## GENERAL

State-supported, comprehensive, coed. Part of State University of New York System. Awards bachelor's and master's degrees. Founded 1828. Setting: 216-acre small-town campus. Undergraduate faculty: 534 (270 full-time, 264 part-time); student-faculty ratio is 19:1. Most popular recent majors: elementary education, psychology, business administration.

## CAMPUS VISITS

**College Calendar 1998–99:** *Regular classes:* Aug. 24–Dec. 9; Jan. 25–May 12. *Breaks:* Dec. 18–Jan. 25. *Final exams:* Dec. 14–18; May 17–21.

## VISIT OPPORTUNITIES

|  | Appointments? | Who? |
|---|---|---|
| **Campus Tour** | required | open to all |
| **Information Session** | required | open to all |
| **Admission Interview** | required | applicants only |
| **Classroom Visit** | required | open to all |
| **Faculty Meeting** | required | open to all |

**Information Sessions:** M–F, select Sat.; unavailable Dec. 9 to Feb. 1; 30 minutes.

**Interviews:** M–F; 30 minutes.

**Campus Tours:** Conducted by students. M–F, select Sat.; unavailable Dec. 9 to Feb. 1; 90 minutes.

**Class Visits:** Prospective students may attend a class in their area of interest.

## CAMPUS FACILITIES

**Science:** Appointment Required: lab facilities, research facilities.

**Of Special Interest:** Appointment Required: Media Center (Radio/TV/Journalism), Communication Disorders Center/Clinic, Engineering Labs/Research Facilities.

## LOCAL ATTRACTIONS

Huguenot Street National Historic Site; Mononk Mountain House and Preserve; regional wineries.

# STATE UNIVERSITY OF NEW YORK AT STONY BROOK
Stony Brook, New York

**Contact:** Ms. Gigi Lamens, Dean of Admissions, State University of New York at Stony Brook, Stony Brook, NY 11794-1901. *Phone:* 516-632-6868. *Fax:* 516-632-9898. *Web site:* http://www.sunysb.edu/www/

*State University of New York at Stony Brook (continued)*

studinfo.html *Visit location:* Office of Admissions, Administration Building, State University of New York at Stony Brook.

## QUICK FACTS

Enrollment: 17,831; UG: 11,769. Entrance: very difficult. SAT>500: 62% V, 76% M; ACT>18: N/App. Resident tuition and fees: $3932. Nonresident tuition and fees: $8832. Room and board: $5758. Application deadline: rolling.

## GENERAL

State-supported, university, coed. Part of State University of New York System. Awards bachelor's, master's, doctoral, and first professional degrees and post-master's certificates. Founded 1957. Setting: 1,100-acre small-town campus with easy access to New York City. Undergraduate faculty: 1,682 (1,226 full-time, 456 part-time); student-faculty ratio is 17:1. Most popular recent majors: psychology, biology, business administration.

## CAMPUS VISITS

**College Calendar 1998–99:** *Regular classes:* Aug. 31–Dec. 15; Jan. 20–May 4. *Breaks:* Sept. 21–22; Mar. 29–Apr. 2; Nov. 26–29. *Final exams:* Dec. 16–22; May 6–12.

---

### VISIT OPPORTUNITIES

| | Appointments? | Who? |
|---|---|---|
| **Campus Tour** | recommended | open to all |
| **Information Session** | recommended | open to all |
| **Admission Interview** | recommended | open to all |
| **Classroom Visit** | | admitted applicants only |
| **Faculty Meeting** | | open to all |
| **Overnight Visit** | | open to all |

---

**Information Sessions:** Sat.; unavailable during school holidays; 45 minutes.

**Interviews:** M–F, select Sat.; unavailable during school holidays; 30 minutes.

**Campus Tours:** Conducted by students. M–F at 12:45 pm, 3:45 pm; Sat. at 10:00 am, 11:00 am, 12:00 pm; 60 minutes.

**Class Visits:** Classroom visits are determined by the visit schedule.

**Overnight Visits:** During the regular academic year, prospective applicants may spend an evening in a residence hall with a student host.

**Video:** Free on request.

## CAMPUS FACILITIES

**Science:** Health Sciences Center; Appointment Required: Brookhaven National Laboratory, Marine Sciences Research Center, Center for Biotechnology.

**Arts:** Staller Center for the Arts.

**Athletic:** Indoor Sports Complex, Pritchard Gymnasium, Eugene Weidman Wellness Center.

**Of Special Interest:** Frank Melville Jr. Memorial Library, University Hospital, Student Activities Center.

## LOCAL ATTRACTIONS

Historic Stony Brook Village, Museums at Stony Brook, Stony Brook Grist Mill, Three Village Inn, Long Island Sound, Pollack–Krasner House and Study Center.

# SYRACUSE UNIVERSITY
### Syracuse, New York

---

**Contact:** Office of Admissions, 201 Tolley Administrative Building, Syracuse, NY 13244-1100. *Phone:* 315-443-3611. *Fax:* 315-443-4226. *E-mail:* orange@syr.edu *Web site:* http://www.syr.edu/ *Visit location:* The Office of Admissions, Tolley Administration Building, 201 Tolley.

## QUICK FACTS

Enrollment: 10,394; UG: 10,394. Entrance: very difficult. SAT>500: 88% V, 90% M; ACT>18: N/R. Tuition and fees: $18,056. Room and board: $7760. Application deadline: 1/15.

## GENERAL

Independent, university, coed. Awards bachelor's, master's, doctoral, and first professional degrees and post-master's certificates. Founded 1870. Setting: 200-acre urban campus. Undergraduate faculty: 1,377 (807 full-time, 570 part-time); student-faculty ratio is 12:1. Most popular recent majors: information sciences/systems, psychology, architecture.

## CAMPUS VISITS

**College Calendar 1998–99:** *Regular classes:* Aug. 31–Dec. 11; Jan. 19–May 4. *Breaks:* Oct. 16–18; Mar. 14–21; Nov. 25–29. *Final exams:* Dec. 16–22; May

7–13. *Special campus days:* Commencement, May 16; Homecoming, Nov. 13–15; Parents Weekend, Oct. 30–Nov. 1.

## VISIT OPPORTUNITIES

|  | Appointments? | Who? |
| --- | --- | --- |
| **Campus Tour** | required | open to all |
| **Information Session** | required | open to all |
| **Admission Interview** | required | open to all |
| **Classroom Visit** | required | open to all |
| **Faculty Meeting** | required | open to all |
| **Overnight Visit** | required | admitted applicants only |

**Information Sessions:** M–F, select Sat.; 90 minutes.

**Interviews:** M–F; during the fall term; 30 minutes.

**Campus Tours:** Conducted by students. M–F, select Sat.; 60 minutes.

**Class Visits:** Certain predetermined classrooms are open to visitors.

**Overnight Visits:** During the regular academic year.

**Video:** Available, fee charged.

## CAMPUS FACILITIES

**Science:** The Center for Advanced Technology in Computer Applications and Software Engineering, The Center of Science and Technology, The Institute for Sensory Research.

**Arts:** Lowe Art Gallery, Mensche I Gallery, Crouse College, Comstock Art Facility.

**Athletic:** Carrier Dome, Flanagan Gymnasium, Goldstein Fitness Center.

**Of Special Interest:** Schine Student Center, Goldstein Student Center, Maxwell School of Citizenship and Public Affairs.

## LOCAL ATTRACTIONS

Everson Museum of Art, Burnett Park Zoo, Carousel Shopping Center, Armory Square, numerous recreational facilities.

# VASSAR COLLEGE
## Poughkeepsie, New York

**Contact:** Office of Admission, 124 Raymond Avenue, Poughkeepsie, NY 12604. *Phone:* toll-free 800-827-7270. *Fax:* 914-437-7063. *E-mail:* admissions@vassar.

edu *Web site:* http://www.vassar.edu/ *Visit location:* Admissions, Kautz House, Vassar College, 124 Raymond Avenue.

## QUICK FACTS
Enrollment: 2,361; UG: 2,361. Entrance: very difficult. SAT>500: 99% V, 98% M; ACT>18: N/R. Tuition and fees: $22,090. Room and board: $6470. Application deadline: 1/1.

## GENERAL
Independent, comprehensive, coed. Awards bachelor's and master's degrees. Founded 1861. Setting: 1,000-acre suburban campus with easy access to New York City. Undergraduate faculty: 258 (215 full-time, 43 part-time); student-faculty ratio is 9:1. Most popular recent majors: English, political science, psychology.

## CAMPUS VISITS
**College Calendar 1998–99:** *Regular classes:* Aug. 31–Dec. 8; Jan. 18–May 4. *Breaks:* Oct. 17–25; Mar. 6–21; Nov. 25–29. *Final exams:* Dec. 14–18; May 12–18. *Admission office closed:* July 3, Nov. 27, Dec. 24, Dec. 28–31, Apr. 2. *Special campus days:* Commencement, May 23.

## VISIT OPPORTUNITIES

|  | Appointments? | Who? |
| --- | --- | --- |
| **Campus Tour** | not required | open to all |
| **Information Session** | not required | open to all |
| **Classroom Visit** | required | open to all |
| **Faculty Meeting** | required | open to all |
| **Overnight Visit** | required | open to all |

**Information Sessions:** M–F at 1:00 pm; select Sat. at 11:00 am; additional 10:00 am session Jun. 29–Nov. 13; 45 minutes.

**Campus Tours:** Conducted by students. M–F at 11:30 am, 2:00 pm; select Sat. at 9:30 am, 12:00 pm; additional 9:00 am tour Jun. 29–Nov. 13; 60 minutes.

**Class Visits:** Prospective students may attend a class in their area of interest.

**Overnight Visits:** During the regular academic year, prospective applicants may spend an evening in a residence hall with a student host.

## CAMPUS FACILITIES
**Science:** Biology or Chemistry Labs; Appointment Required: Observatory.

**Arts:** Skinner Hall of Music.

*Vassar College (continued)*

**Athletic:** Walker Field House.
**Of Special Interest:** Library.

# NORTH CAROLINA

## APPALACHIAN STATE UNIVERSITY
### Boone, North Carolina

**Contact:** Patrick Setzer, Assistant Director, Office of Admission, Boone, NC 28608. *Phone:* 704-262-2179. *Fax:* 704-262-3296. *E-mail:* setzerp@appstate.edu *Visit location:* Office of Admission, John E. Thomas Building.

### QUICK FACTS
Enrollment: 12,108; UG: 11,163. Entrance: moderately difficult. SAT>500: 74% V, 84% M; ACT>18: N/R. Resident tuition and fees: $1840. Nonresident tuition and fees: $8968. Room and board: $3008. Application deadline: 4/15.

### GENERAL
State-supported, comprehensive, coed. Part of University of North Carolina System. Awards bachelor's, master's, and doctoral degrees. Founded 1899. Setting: 255-acre small-town campus. Undergraduate faculty: 828 (583 full-time, 245 part-time); student-faculty ratio is 15:1. Most popular recent majors: business administration, mass communications, elementary education.

### CAMPUS VISITS
**College Calendar 1998–99:** *Regular classes:* Aug. 19–Dec. 9; Jan. 11–May 5. *Final exams:* Dec. 11–16; May 7–12.

### VISIT OPPORTUNITIES

|  | Appointments? | Who? |
| --- | --- | --- |
| **Campus Tour** | required | |
| **Information Session** | recommended | |
| **Admission Interview** | not required | |
| **Classroom Visit** | | open to all |
| **Faculty Meeting** | | open to all |

**Information Sessions:** M–F at 9:00 am, 10:30 am, 12:00 pm, 1:30 pm; Sat. at 10:00 am; 30 minutes.
**Interviews:** M–F, Sat.; 15 minutes.
**Campus Tours:** Conducted by students. M–F at 9:30 am, 11:00 am, 12:30 pm, 2:00 pm; Sat. at 10:30 am; 60 minutes.
**Class Visits:** Prospective students may attend a class in their area of interest.

### CAMPUS FACILITIES
**Of Special Interest:** Carol Grotnes Belk Library.

### LOCAL ATTRACTIONS
Blue Ridge Parkway.

## BELMONT ABBEY COLLEGE
### Belmont, North Carolina

**Contact:** Admissions Office, 100 Belmont-Mt. Holly Road, Belmont, NC 28012. *Phone:* 704-825-6665 or toll-free 888-BAC-0110. *Fax:* 704-825-6220. *Web site:* http://www.bac.edu/ *Visit location:* Admission, Robert L. Stowe Hall, 100 Belmont-Mt. Holy Road.

### QUICK FACTS
Enrollment: 890; UG: 822. Entrance: moderately difficult. SAT>500: 53% V, 44% M; ACT>18: N/R. Tuition and fees: $11,034. Room and board: $5666. Application deadline: 8/15.

### GENERAL
Independent Roman Catholic, comprehensive, coed. Awards bachelor's and master's degrees. Founded 1876. Setting: 650-acre small-town campus with easy access to Charlotte. Undergraduate faculty: 69 (37 full-time, 32 part-time); student-faculty ratio is 16:1. Most popular recent majors: business administration, education, accounting.

### CAMPUS VISITS
**College Calendar 1998–99:** *Regular classes:* Aug. 25–Dec. 7; Jan. 12–May 3. *Breaks:* Dec. 17–Jan. 10; Mar. 6–14; Nov. 25–29; Apr. 1–5. *Final exams:* Dec. 9–16; May 5–12. *Special campus days:* Fall Break, Oct. 15–18; Feast of Immaculate Conception, Dec. 8; Martin Luther King, Jr. Day, Jan. 18; Reading Day, May 4.

## VISIT OPPORTUNITIES

| | Appointments? | Who? |
|---|---|---|
| **Campus Tour** | recommended | open to all |
| **Information Session** | recommended | open to all |
| **Admission Interview** | required | open to all |
| **Classroom Visit** | required | open to all |
| **Faculty Meeting** | required | open to all |
| **Overnight Visit** | required | open to all |

**Information Sessions:** M–F, Sat.; 30 minutes.

**Interviews:** M–F, select Sat.; 30 minutes.

**Campus Tours:** Conducted by students and admission reps. M–F; Sat. at 10:00 am, 12:00 pm; 90 minutes.

**Class Visits:** Classroom visits are determined by the visit schedule.

**Overnight Visits:** During the regular academic year.

## CAMPUS FACILITIES

**Science:** Gaston Science building.

**Arts:** Music Building.

**Athletic:** Wheeler Center.

**Of Special Interest:** Writing center, career service center, curriculum resource center, Windows 95 computer lab.

## LOCAL ATTRACTIONS

Downtown Charlotte, downtown Belmont.

# CAMPBELL UNIVERSITY

**Buies Creek, North Carolina**

**Contact:** Admissions Office, PO Box 546, Buies Creek, NC 27506. *Phone:* 910-893-1290 or toll-free 800-334-4111 (out-of-state). *Fax:* 910-893-1288. *Web site:* http://www.campbell.edu/ *Visit location:* Admissions Office, Mc Leod House, 110 Main Street.

## QUICK FACTS

Enrollment: 3,359; UG: 2,231. Entrance: moderately difficult. SAT>500: 61% V, 58% M; ACT>18: N/R. Tuition and fees: $10,003. Room and board: $3610. Application deadline: rolling.

## GENERAL

Independent Baptist, university, coed. Awards associate, bachelor's, master's, doctoral, and first professional degrees. Founded 1887. Setting: 850-acre rural

campus with easy access to Raleigh. Undergraduate faculty: 349 (159 full-time, 190 part-time); student-faculty ratio is 18:1. Most popular recent majors: business administration, (pre)law, mass communications.

## CAMPUS VISITS

**College Calendar 1998–99:** *Regular classes:* Aug. 26–Dec. 14; Jan. 6–Apr. 29. *Final exams:* Dec. 7–14; Apr. 23–29. *Special campus days:* Graduation, May 10; Homecoming, Oct. 3.

## VISIT OPPORTUNITIES

| | Appointments? | Who? |
|---|---|---|
| **Campus Tour** | recommended | open to all |
| **Information Session** | not required | open to all |
| **Admission Interview** | required | applicants only |
| **Classroom Visit** | required | open to all |
| **Faculty Meeting** | required | open to all |

**Information Sessions:** M–F; 60 minutes.

**Interviews:** M–F; scholarship interviews scheduled during Nov. and Feb.; 45 minutes.

**Campus Tours:** Conducted by students and admission reps. M–F; 30 minutes.

**Class Visits:** Classroom visits are determined by the visit schedule.

**Video:** Free on request.

## CAMPUS FACILITIES

**Arts:** Fine Arts Building.

**Athletic:** Training Facilities, Swimming Pool.

**Of Special Interest:** Student Center, Library.

## LOCAL ATTRACTIONS

Raleigh—state capital.

# CATAWBA COLLEGE

**Salisbury, North Carolina**

**Contact:** Melanie Mock, Administrative Assistant, 2300 West Innes Street, Salisbury, NC 28144. *Phone:* 704-637-4402 or toll-free 800-CATAWBA (out-of-state). *Fax:* 704-637-4222. *Web site:* http://www.catawba.edu/ *Visit location:* Admissions Office, Hedrick Hall/Administration, 2300 Innes Street.

*Catawba College (continued)*

## QUICK FACTS
Enrollment: 1,307; UG: 1,283. Entrance: moderately difficult. SAT>500: 51% V, 49% M; ACT>18: N/R. Tuition and fees: $11,352. Room and board: $4500. Application deadline: rolling.

## GENERAL
Independent, comprehensive, coed, United Church of Christ. Awards bachelor's and master's degrees. Founded 1851. Setting: 210-acre small-town campus with easy access to Charlotte. Undergraduate faculty: 96 (64 full-time, 32 part-time); student-faculty ratio is 17:1. Most popular recent majors: business administration, education, mass communications.

## CAMPUS VISITS
**College Calendar 1998–99:** *Regular classes:* Aug. 27–Dec. 9; Jan. 12–Apr. 29. *Breaks:* Oct. 10–13; Feb. 27–Mar. 7; Nov. 25–29; Apr. 2–4. *Final exams:* Dec. 11–16; May 1–5. *Special campus days:* Family Weekend, Sept. 11–13; Homecoming, Nov. 13–15.

## VISIT OPPORTUNITIES

|  | Appointments? | Who? |
|---|---|---|
| **Campus Tour** | required | applicants and parents |
| **Admission Interview** | required | applicants and parents |
| **Classroom Visit** | required | applicants and parents |
| **Faculty Meeting** | required | applicants and parents |
| **Overnight Visit** | required | |

**Interviews:** M–F; Sat. 9:00 am–12:00 pm.
**Campus Tours:** Conducted by students. M–F, Sat.; 55 minutes.
**Class Visits:** Prospective students may attend a class in their area of interest.
**Video:** Free on request.

## CAMPUS FACILITIES
**Science:** Ecological Preserve.
**Arts:** Appointment Required: Catawba Experimental Theatre, Dance Studio.
**Athletic:** Appointment Required: Athletic Training Facility.
**Of Special Interest:** Omwake-Dearborn Chapel; Appointment Required: Child Development Center.

## LOCAL ATTRACTIONS
Historic Salisbury; North Carolina Transportation Museum.

# CHOWAN COLLEGE
### Murfreesboro, North Carolina

**Contact:** Stephanie Harrell, Director of Admissions, PO Box 1848, Murfreesboro, NC 27855. *Phone:* 919-398-6314 or toll-free 800-488-4101. *Fax:* 919-398-1190. *E-mail:* admissions@micah.chowan.edu *Web site:* http://www.chowan.edu/ *Visit location:* Admissions Office, McDowell Columns Building, PO Box 1848.

## QUICK FACTS
Enrollment: 755; UG: 755. Entrance: minimally difficult. SAT>500: 30% V, 24% M; ACT>18: 65%. Tuition and fees: $10,760. Room and board: $4170. Application deadline: rolling.

## GENERAL
Independent Baptist, 4-year, coed. Awards associate and bachelor's degrees. Founded 1848. Setting: 300-acre rural campus with easy access to Norfolk. Faculty: 70 (58 full-time, 12 part-time); student-faculty ratio is 11:1. Most popular recent majors: business administration, physical education, graphic/printing equipment.

## CAMPUS VISITS
**College Calendar 1998–99:** *Regular classes:* Aug. 25–Dec. 11; Jan. 13–May 6. *Breaks:* Oct. 16–21; Mar. 5–15; Nov. 24–30. *Final exams:* Dec. 14–18; May 7–13. *Admission office closed:* Dec. 19–Jan. 4, Mar. 8–9. *Special campus days:* Commencement, May 15; Family Day, Sept. 19; Homecoming, Oct. 31.

## VISIT OPPORTUNITIES

|  | Appointments? | Who? |
|---|---|---|
| **Campus Tour** | recommended, not required | open to all |
| **Information Session** | recommended, not required | open to all |
| **Admission Interview** | recommended, not required | open to all |
| **Classroom Visit** | required | open to all |
| **Faculty Meeting** | required | open to all |
| **Overnight Visit** | required | open to all |

**Information Sessions:** M–F at 9:30 am, 1:30 pm; Sat. at 9:30 am; 40 minutes.

**Interviews:** M–F, Sat.; 30 minutes.

**Campus Tours:** Conducted by students and admission reps. M–F at 10:00 am, 2:00 pm; Sat. at 10:00 am; 60 minutes.

**Class Visits:** Classroom visits are determined by the visit schedule.

**Overnight Visits:** During the regular academic year, prospective applicants may spend an evening in a residence hall with a student host.

## CAMPUS FACILITIES
**Science:** Labs, Classroom.

**Arts:** Graphic Communications, Graphic Design.

**Athletic:** Gymnasium, Pool, Weight Room.

**Of Special Interest:** Chapel, Library, Cafeteria.

## LOCAL ATTRACTIONS
Historic Murfreesboro Tour, Outer Banks, Colonial Williamsburg.

# DAVIDSON COLLEGE
**Davidson, North Carolina**

**Contact:** Bonnie Kemmler, Campus Visit Coordinator, PO Box 573, Davidson, NC 28036. *Phone:* toll-free 800-768-0380. *Fax:* 704-892-2016. *E-mail:* bokemmle@davidson.edu *Web site:* http://www.davidson.edu *Visit location:* Office of Admission, Grey House, 405 North Main Street.

## QUICK FACTS
Enrollment: 1,623; UG: 1,623. Entrance: very difficult. SAT>500: 99% V, 99% M; ACT>18: 100%. Tuition and fees: $20,595. Room and board: $5918. Application deadline: 1/15.

## GENERAL
Independent Presbyterian, 4-year, coed. Awards bachelor's degrees. Founded 1837. Setting: 464-acre small-town campus with easy access to Charlotte. Faculty: 155 (139 full-time, 16 part-time); student-faculty ratio is 11:1. Most popular recent majors: biology, English, history.

## CAMPUS VISITS
**College Calendar 1998–99:** *Regular classes:* Aug. 24–Dec. 4; Jan. 11–Apr. 27. *Breaks:* Dec. 18–Jan. 11; Feb. 27–Mar. 7; Nov. 25–29. *Final exams:* Dec. 10–17; May 5–12. *Admission office closed:* May 13–14. *Special campus days:* Alumni Weekend, Apr. 23–25; Com-

mencement, May 16; Fall Break, Oct. 12–13; Homecoming, Oct. 23–24; Martin Luther King, Jr. Celebration, Jan. 18.

## VISIT OPPORTUNITIES

|  | Appointments? | Who? |
|---|---|---|
| **Campus Tour** | recommended | open to all |
| **Information Session** | recommended | open to all |
| **Admission Interview** | required | open to all |
| **Classroom Visit** | not required | open to all |
| **Overnight Visit** | required | applicants only |

**Information Sessions:** Mon., Tue., Thu., Fri. at 10:30 am, 11:30 am, 2:30 pm, 3:30 pm; Wed. at 2:30 pm, 3:30 pm; Sat. at 1:00 pm; schedule modified during school holidays; 45 minutes.

**Interviews:** M–F; not available Wed. mornings; 45 minutes.

**Campus Tours:** Conducted by students. Mon., Tue., Thu., Fri. at 9:00 am, 10:00 am, 1:00 pm, 2:00 pm; Wed. at 1:00 pm, 2:00 pm; Sat. at 11:30 am, 2:00 pm; schedule modified during school holidays; 90 minutes.

**Class Visits:** Faculty volunteer and visitors select from office schedule.

**Overnight Visits:** During the regular academic year, prospective applicants may spend an evening in a residence hall with a student host.

**Video:** Available, fee charged.

## CAMPUS FACILITIES
**Science:** Baker-Watt Life Science Complex.

**Arts:** Visual Arts Center.

**Athletic:** Baker Sports Complex.

**Of Special Interest:** Lake Campus.

## LOCAL ATTRACTIONS
City of Charlotte.

# DUKE UNIVERSITY
**Durham, North Carolina**

**Contact:** Admissions Office, 2138 Campus Drive, Box 90586, Durham, NC 27708-0586. *Phone:* 919-684-3214. *Fax:* 919-681-8941. *E-mail:* askduke@

*Duke University (continued)*

admiss.duke.edu *Web site:* http://www.duke.edu/ *Visit location:* Undergraduate Admissions, 2138 Campus Drive.

## QUICK FACTS
Enrollment: 11,459; UG: 6,245. Entrance: most difficult. SAT>500: 98% V, 99% M; ACT>18: N/R. Tuition and fees: $22,173. Room and board: $6853. Application deadline: 1/2.

## GENERAL
Independent, university, coed, United Methodist Church. Awards bachelor's, master's, doctoral, and first professional degrees. Founded 1838. Setting: 8,500-acre suburban campus. Undergraduate faculty: 2,100 (all full-time); student-faculty ratio is 11:1. Most popular recent majors: biology, psychology, history.

## CAMPUS VISITS
**College Calendar 1998–99:** *Regular classes:* Aug. 31–Dec. 10; Jan. 14–Apr. 28. *Breaks:* Oct. 9–14; Mar. 12–22; Nov. 25–30. *Final exams:* Dec. 14–19; May 3–8. *Special campus days:* Founder's Day, Oct. 4; Homecoming, Sept. 25–27; New Student Orientation, Aug. 26; Parent's Weekend, Oct. 23–25.

---

### VISIT OPPORTUNITIES

|  | **Appointments?** | **Who?** |
|---|---|---|
| **Campus Tour** | not required | open to all |
| **Information Session** | not required | open to all |
| **Admission Interview** | required | open to all |
| **Classroom Visit** | not required | open to all |
| **Faculty Meeting** | required | open to all |
| **Overnight Visit** | required | open to all |

---

**Information Sessions:** M–F, Sat. at 10:00 am; 2:00 pm information session available M–F during Jun., Jul., and Aug. and on Mon. and Fri. in Sept., Oct., Apr., and May; 60 minutes.

**Interviews:** M–F; Jun. 1 to Dec.15 for seniors only; 30 minutes.

**Campus Tours:** Conducted by students. M–F at 9:00 am, 11:30 am, 3:00 pm; Sat. at 11:30 am; 9:00 am tour M–F during Jun., Jul., and Aug.; 60 minutes.

**Class Visits:** Certain predetermined classrooms are open to visitors.

**Overnight Visits:** During the regular academic year, prospective applicants may spend an evening in a residence hall with a student host.

**Video:** Available, fee charged.

## CAMPUS FACILITIES
**Science:** Appointment Required: Primate Center, School of Engineering.

**Arts:** Duke Museum of Art, Mary Duke Biddle Music Building.

**Athletic:** Cameron Indoor Stadium, Wallace Wade Stadium.

**Of Special Interest:** Duke Gardens, Duke Chapel, Perkins Library.

# EAST CAROLINA UNIVERSITY
**Greenville, North Carolina**

**Contact:** Admissions Office, 106 Whichard Building, Greenville, NC 27858-4353. *Phone:* 252-328-6640. *Fax:* 252-328-6945. *Web site:* http://www.ecu.edu/ *Visit location:* Office of Undergraduate Admissions, 106 Whichard Building.

## QUICK FACTS
Enrollment: 18,205; UG: 14,714. Entrance: moderately difficult. SAT>500: 54% V, 53% M; ACT>18: 75%. Resident tuition and fees: $1848. Nonresident tuition and fees: $8960. Room and board: $3680. Application deadline: 3/15.

## GENERAL
State-supported, university, coed. Part of University of North Carolina System. Awards bachelor's, master's, doctoral, and first professional degrees and post-master's certificates. Founded 1907. Setting: 465-acre urban campus. Undergraduate faculty: 1,351 (1,184 full-time, 167 part-time); student-faculty ratio is 19:1. Most popular recent majors: nursing, elementary education, biology.

## CAMPUS VISITS
**College Calendar 1998–99:** *Regular classes:* Aug. 19–Dec. 5; Jan. 11–Apr. 27. *Breaks:* Oct. 14–18; Mar. 7–14; Nov. 25–29. *Final exams:* Dec. 7–12; Apr. 29–May 6. *Admission office closed:* Nov. 27, Dec. 22–25. *Special campus days:* Fall Open House, Nov. 21; Spring Open House, Apr. 17.

## VISIT OPPORTUNITIES

|  | Appointments? | Who? |
| --- | --- | --- |
| **Campus Tour** | recommended | open to all |
| **Information Session** | recommended | open to all |
| **Admission Interview** | recommended | open to all |

**Information Sessions:** M–F at 10:30 am, 2:15 pm; call for summer times; 30 minutes.

**Interviews:** Call for available schedule.

**Campus Tours:** Conducted by students. M–F at 10:30 am, 2:15 pm; call for summer times; 60 minutes.

### CAMPUS FACILITIES
**Arts:** Art School Building.

**Athletic:** Student Recreation Center.

**Of Special Interest:** The Student Center, general classroom building, residence hall, dining facilities.

# ELON COLLEGE
### Elon College, North Carolina

**Contact:** Julia Hughes Tabor, Coordinator of Campus Visits, Admissions Campus Box 2700, Elon College, Elon College, NC 27244. *Phone:* toll-free 800-334-8448. *Fax:* 336-398-3986. *E-mail:* taborj@numen.elon.edu *Web site:* http://www.elon.edu/ *Visit location:* Admissions Office, Powell Building, Haggard Avenue.

### QUICK FACTS
Enrollment: 3,633; UG: 3,481. Entrance: moderately difficult. SAT>500: 73% V, 74% M; ACT>18: N/R. Tuition and fees: $11,542. Room and board: $4170. Application deadline: rolling.

### GENERAL
Independent, comprehensive, coed, United Church of Christ. Awards bachelor's and master's degrees. Founded 1889. Setting: 500-acre suburban campus with easy access to Raleigh. Undergraduate faculty: 260 (158 full-time, 102 part-time); student-faculty ratio is 17:1. Most popular recent majors: business administration, communications, education.

### CAMPUS VISITS
**College Calendar 1998–99:** *Regular classes:* Aug. 26–Dec. 4; Jan. 5–25; Feb. 3–May 11. *Breaks:* Oct. 9–14; Mar. 19–29; Nov. 24–30. *Final exams:* Dec. 7–11; May 13–18. *Special campus days:* Fall Open House, Oct. 24, Nov. 21; Homecoming, Nov. 14; Spring Open House, Apr. 10.

## VISIT OPPORTUNITIES

|  | Appointments? |
| --- | --- |
| **Campus Tour** | recommended |
| **Information Session** | recommended |
| **Admission Interview** | recommended |
| **Classroom Visit** | required |
| **Faculty Meeting** | required |

**Information Sessions:** M–F at 9:00 am, 11:00 am, 1:30 pm, 3:00 pm; Sat. at 9:00 am, 10:00 am, 11:00 am; inquire for holiday closure dates; 30 minutes.

**Interviews:** M–F; 30 minutes.

**Campus Tours:** Conducted by students. Immediately following Information Session; 60 minutes.

**Class Visits:** Prospective students may attend a class in their area of interest, classroom visits are determined by the visit schedule.

**Video:** Free on request.

### CAMPUS FACILITIES
**Science:** New Science Facilities.

**Arts:** Faith Rockefeller Model Center for the Arts, communication and dance facilities, McCrary Theater /Yeager Recital Hall, Television Studio, art, music, drama facilities.

**Athletic:** Alumni Memorial Gymnasium, Stewart Fitness Center, Koury Center.

**Of Special Interest:** Moseley Center, McKinnon Hall, Octogon Cafe.

# GARDNER-WEBB UNIVERSITY
### Boiling Springs, North Carolina

**Contact:** Admissions Office, PO Box 997, Boiling Springs, NC 28017. *Phone:* toll-free 800-253-6472, 800-222-2311 (in-state). *Fax:* 704-434-4488. *E-mail:* admissions@gardner-webb.edu *Web site:* http://www.gardner-webb.edu/ *Visit location:* Admissions Office, Washburn Hall.

### QUICK FACTS
Enrollment: 2,913; UG: 2,383. Entrance: moderately difficult. SAT>500: 53% V, 53% M; ACT>18: N/R. Tuition and fees: $9620. Room and board: $4630. Application deadline: rolling.

*Gardner-Webb University (continued)*

## GENERAL

Independent Baptist, comprehensive, coed. Awards associate, bachelor's, and master's degrees. Founded 1905. Setting: 200-acre small-town campus with easy access to Charlotte. Undergraduate faculty: 174 (90 full-time, 84 part-time); student-faculty ratio is 17:1. Most popular recent majors: business administration, education, biology.

## CAMPUS VISITS

**College Calendar 1998–99:** *Regular classes:* Aug. 26–Dec. 11; Jan. 13–May 5. *Breaks:* Oct. 24–28; Mar. 6–15; Dec. 20–Jan. 11. *Final exams:* Dec. 14–19; May 7–13. *Admission office closed:* Oct. 26, Mar. 8. *Special campus days:* Commencement, May 15; Family Weekend, Sept. 11–12; Homecoming, Oct. 2–3.

## VISIT OPPORTUNITIES

|  | Appointments? | Who? |
|---|---|---|
| **Campus Tour** | recommended | applicants and parents |
| **Information Session** | recommended | |
| **Admission Interview** | required | |
| **Classroom Visit** | required | applicants and parents |
| **Faculty Meeting** | required | applicants and parents |
| **Overnight Visit** | required | |

**Information Sessions:** M–F 8:00 am–5:00 pm; Sat., call for available day and time; 60 minutes.

**Interviews:** M–F; 45 minutes.

**Campus Tours:** Conducted by students and admission reps. M–F 8:00 am–5:00 pm; Sat., call for availability days and times; 60 minutes.

**Class Visits:** Classroom visits are determined by the visit schedule.

**Overnight Visits:** During the regular academic year, prospective applicants may spend an evening in a residence hall with a student host.

**Video:** Free on request.

## CAMPUS FACILITIES

**Arts:** O. Max Gardner Memorial Hall, Kathleen Nolan Dover Theater.

**Athletic:** Lutz-Yelton Convocation Center, Paul Porter Arena, Ernest W. Spangler Memorial Stadium.

**Of Special Interest:** Lake Hollifield Complex.

# GUILFORD COLLEGE
**Greensboro, North Carolina**

**Contact:** Ms. Nancy Houston, Coordinator of Visitor Services, 5800 West Friendly Avenue, Greensboro, NC 27910. *Phone:* toll-free 800-992-7759. *Fax:* 336-316-2954. *E-mail:* houstonn1@rascal.guilford. edu *Web site:* http://www.guilford.edu/ *Visit location:* Admission, New Garden Hall, 5800 West Friendly Avenue.

## QUICK FACTS

Enrollment: 1,362; UG: 1,362. Entrance: moderately difficult. SAT>500: 83% V, 73% M; ACT>18: 100%. Tuition and fees: $14,750. Room and board: $5270. Application deadline: 2/1.

## GENERAL

Independent, 4-year, coed, Society of Friends. Awards bachelor's degrees. Founded 1837. Setting: 340-acre suburban campus. Faculty: 123 (88 full-time, 35 part-time); student-faculty ratio is 15:1. Most popular recent majors: psychology, English, business administration.

## CAMPUS VISITS

**College Calendar 1998–99:** *Regular classes:* Aug. 25–Dec. 10; Jan. 12–Apr. 27. *Breaks:* Oct. 16–26; Mar. 5–15; Nov. 25–30. *Final exams:* Dec. 14–18; Apr. 30–May 4. *Special campus days:* Family Weekend, Sept. 18–20; Homecoming, Oct. 9–11; Open House for admitted students, Apr. 10; Preferred Candidates' Preview Day.

## VISIT OPPORTUNITIES

|  | Appointments? | Who? |
|---|---|---|
| **Campus Tour** | recommended | open to all |
| **Information Session** | required | open to all |
| **Admission Interview** | required | open to all |
| **Classroom Visit** | required | open to all |
| **Overnight Visit** | required | open to all |

**Information Sessions:** M–F, select Sat.; 45 minutes.

**Interviews:** M–F, select Sat.; 45 minutes.

**Campus Tours:** Conducted by students. M–F at 9:00 am, 10:00 am, 1:00 pm, 2:00 pm; Sat. at 10:00 am, 11:30 am; during summer M–F at 10:00 am, and 2:00 pm; 60 minutes.

**Class Visits:** Prospective students may attend a class in their area of interest, classroom visits are determined by the visit schedule.

**Overnight Visits:** During the regular academic year, prospective applicants may spend an evening in a residence hall with a student host.

## CAMPUS FACILITIES

**Arts:** Hege Library Art Gallery.

**Of Special Interest:** Bauman Telecommunications and Computing Center.

# HIGH POINT UNIVERSITY
## High Point, North Carolina

**Contact:** Mr. James L. Schlimmer, Dean of Enrollment Management, University Station, Montlieu Avenue, High Point, NC 27262. *Phone:* toll-free 800-345-6993. *Fax:* 336-841-4599. *E-mail:* admiss@ acme.highpoint.edu *Web site:* http://www.highpoint. edu/ *Visit location:* Office of Admissions, Wrenn, 833 Montlieu Avenue.

## QUICK FACTS

Enrollment: 2,676; UG: 2,530. Entrance: moderately difficult. SAT>500: 52% V, 49% M; ACT>18: N/R. Tuition and fees: $11,120. Room and board: $5300. Application deadline: rolling.

## GENERAL

Independent United Methodist, comprehensive, coed. Awards bachelor's and master's degrees. Founded 1924. Setting: 77-acre suburban campus with easy access to Charlotte. Undergraduate faculty: 196 (109 full-time, 87 part-time); student-faculty ratio is 17:1. Most popular recent majors: business administration, accounting, elementary education.

## CAMPUS VISITS

**College Calendar 1998–99:** *Regular classes:* Aug. 26–Dec. 10; Jan. 12–Apr. 29. *Breaks:* Oct. 16–26; Mar. 5–15. *Final exams:* Dec. 11–17; Apr. 30–May 6. *Special campus days:* Commencement; Family Weekend, Nov. 6–7; Homecoming, Oct. 3; New Student Pre-Registration; Open Houses in March and November; Presidential Scholarship Weekend.

## VISIT OPPORTUNITIES

| | Appointments? | Who? |
|---|---|---|
| **Campus Tour** | recommended, not required | open to all |
| **Information Session** | recommended, not required | open to all |
| **Admission Interview** | recommended, not required | open to all |
| **Classroom Visit** | recommended, not required | open to all |
| **Faculty Meeting** | recommended, not required | open to all |

**Information Sessions:** M–F, select Sat.; 30 minutes.

**Interviews:** M–F; select Sat. 9:00 am–12:00 pm; 30 minutes.

**Campus Tours:** Conducted by students. M–F 9:00 am–3:00 pm; select Sat. 9:00–11:00 am; 60 minutes.

**Class Visits:** Prospective students may attend a class in their area of interest.

## CAMPUS FACILITIES

**Of Special Interest:** Herman and Louise Smith Library.

# JOHNSON C. SMITH UNIVERSITY
## Charlotte, North Carolina

**Contact:** Ms. Sonji Young, Administrative Assistant, 100 Beatties Ford Road, Charlotte, NC 28216. *Phone:* toll-free 800-782-7303. *Fax:* 704-378-1242. *Visit location:* Admissions Office Room #3, Biddle Hall, 100 Beatties Ford Road.

## QUICK FACTS

Enrollment: 1,357; UG: 1,357. Entrance: minimally difficult. SAT>500: 3% V, 10% M; ACT>18: N/R. Tuition and fees: $8469. Room and board: $3328. Application deadline: 8/1.

## GENERAL

Independent, 4-year, coed. Awards bachelor's degrees. Founded 1867. Setting: 105-acre urban campus. Faculty: 88 (81 full-time, 7 part-time); student-faculty ratio is 17:1. Most popular recent majors: business administration, mass communications, computer science.

*Johnson C. Smith University (continued)*

## CAMPUS VISITS

**College Calendar 1998–99:** *Regular classes:* Aug. 21–Dec. 7; Jan. 5–Apr. 22. *Breaks:* Oct. 15–19; Apr. 2–5; Dec. 18–Jan. 3. *Final exams:* Dec. 9–12; Apr. 23–28. *Special campus days:* Commencement, May 2; Graduating Senior Activities, Apr. 30–May 2; Homecoming, Oct. 24.

## VISIT OPPORTUNITIES

|  | Appointments? | Who? |
| --- | --- | --- |
| **Campus Tour** | recommended | open to all |
| **Information Session** | recommended | open to all |
| **Admission Interview** | required | open to all |
| **Classroom Visit** | required | open to all |
| **Faculty Meeting** | required | open to all |
| **Overnight Visit** | required | admitted applicants only |

**Information Sessions:** M–F 8:30 am–4:00 pm; 20 minutes.

**Interviews:** M–F.

**Campus Tours:** Conducted by students and admission reps. M–F 8:30 am–4:00 pm; 40 minutes.

**Class Visits:** Certain predetermined classrooms are open to visitors.

**Overnight Visits:** During the regular academic year, prospective applicants may spend an evening in a residence hall with a student host.

**Video:** Free on request.

## CAMPUS FACILITIES

**Science:** Appointment Required: Technology Center.

**Of Special Interest:** Biddle Hall Auditorium, Honors College Residents Hall, new Residents Hall.

## LOCAL ATTRACTIONS

Ericcson Stadium, Charlotte Coliseum, downtown Charlotte, and South Park Mall.

# LENOIR-RHYNE COLLEGE

**Hickory, North Carolina**

**Contact:** Carrie Whitlock, Admissions Receptionist, 7th Avenue and 8th Street, NE, Hickory, NC 28601. *Phone:* toll-free 800-277-5721. *Fax:* 704-328-7378.

*E-mail:* admissions@arc.edu *Web site:* http://www.lrc.edu/ *Visit location:* Admissions, Admissions House, 510 7th Avenue, NE.

## QUICK FACTS

Enrollment: 1,533; UG: 1,391. Entrance: moderately difficult. SAT>500: 49% V, 51% M; ACT>18: 93%. Tuition and fees: $12,386. Room and board: $4500. Application deadline: rolling.

## GENERAL

Independent Lutheran, comprehensive, coed. Awards bachelor's and master's degrees. Founded 1891. Setting: 100-acre small-town campus with easy access to Charlotte. Undergraduate faculty: 137 (102 full-time, 35 part-time); student-faculty ratio is 13:1. Most popular recent majors: nursing, education, business administration.

## CAMPUS VISITS

**College Calendar 1998–99:** *Regular classes:* Aug. 25–Dec. 9; Jan. 12–May 5. *Breaks:* Dec. 16–Jan. 12. *Final exams:* Dec. 11–15; May 7–11. *Admission office closed:* Nov. 25–27.

## VISIT OPPORTUNITIES

|  | Appointments? | Who? |
| --- | --- | --- |
| **Campus Tour** | recommended | open to all |
| **Information Session** | recommended | open to all |
| **Admission Interview** | recommended | open to all |
| **Classroom Visit** | recommended | open to all |
| **Faculty Meeting** | required | open to all |
| **Overnight Visit** | required | open to all |

**Information Sessions:** Sat. at 9:30 am.

**Interviews:** M–F; Sat. mornings; 30 minutes.

**Campus Tours:** Conducted by students. M–F; Sat. at 10:30 am; 45 minutes.

**Class Visits:** Prospective students may attend a class in their area of interest.

**Overnight Visits:** During the regular academic year, prospective applicants may spend an evening in a residence hall with a student host.

## CAMPUS FACILITIES

**Of Special Interest:** Carl Rudisill Library.

# LIVINGSTONE COLLEGE
**Salisbury, North Carolina**

**Contact:** Ms. Diedre Stewart, Recruitment Coordinator, 701 West Monroe Street, Salisbury, NC 28144. *Phone:* 704-638-5502 or toll-free 800-835-3435. *Fax:* 704-638-5426. *Visit location:* Enrollment Management-Admissions, Price Administration, 701 West Monroe Street.

## QUICK FACTS

Entrance: minimally difficult. SAT>500: N/R; ACT>18: N/App. Tuition and fees: $6900. Room and board: $3600. Application deadline: rolling.

## GENERAL

Independent, 4-year, coed, African Methodist Episcopal Zion Church. Awards bachelor's degrees. Founded 1879. Setting: 272-acre small-town campus. Faculty: 68 (51 full-time, 17 part-time); student-faculty ratio is 15:1. Most popular recent majors: business administration, education, computer science.

## CAMPUS VISITS

**College Calendar 1998–99:** *Regular classes:* Aug. 25–Dec. 13; Jan. 12–May 2. *Breaks:* Oct. 17–20; Mar. 16–23; Dec. 13–Jan. 12. *Final exams:* Dec. 9–13; May 4–7. *Admission office closed:* Christmas Holidays; Easter Break; Thanksgiving Holidays. *Special campus days:* Bear Fest, Apr. 1–4; Commencement, May 8; Homecoming, Nov. 8.

## VISIT OPPORTUNITIES

|  | Appointments? | Who? |
|---|---|---|
| **Campus Tour** | required | open to all |
| **Information Session** | recommended | open to all |
| **Classroom Visit** | required | applicants and parents |
| **Overnight Visit** | required | |

**Information Sessions:** M–F 8:00 am–5:00 pm; 30 minutes.

**Campus Tours:** Conducted by students and admission reps. M–F 10:00 am–2:00 pm; 30 minutes.

**Class Visits:** Prospective students may attend a class in their area of interest.

**Overnight Visits:** During the summer, prospective applicants may spend an evening in a residence hall with a student host.

**Video:** Free on request.

## CAMPUS FACILITIES

**Science:** Duncan Science.

**Arts:** Heritage Hall, Tubman Theatre.

**Athletic:** Appointment Required: Gymnasium, Football Stadium.

**Of Special Interest:** Varick Auditorium, Library.

# MARS HILL COLLEGE
**Mars Hill, North Carolina**

**Contact:** Susan Bryson, Admissions Office, Mars Hill College Admissions Office, Mars Hill, NC 28754. *Phone:* toll-free 800-543-1514. *Fax:* 704-689-1473. *Web site:* http://www.mhc.edu/ *Visit location:* Admissions Office, Blackwell Hall.

## QUICK FACTS

Enrollment: 1,244; UG: 1,244. Entrance: moderately difficult. SAT>500: 57% V, 56% M; ACT>18: 100%. Tuition and fees: $8900. Room and board: $3800. Application deadline: rolling.

## GENERAL

Independent Baptist, 4-year, coed. Awards bachelor's degrees. Founded 1856. Setting: 194-acre small-town campus. Faculty: 123 (80 full-time, 43 part-time); student-faculty ratio is 13:1. Most popular recent majors: recreation and leisure studies, education, business administration.

## CAMPUS VISITS

**College Calendar 1998–99:** *Regular classes:* Aug. 26–Dec. 9; Jan. 13–Apr. 28. *Breaks:* Oct. 16–21; Mar. 12–22; Nov. 24–30. *Final exams:* Dec. 10–16; Apr. 29–May 5.

## VISIT OPPORTUNITIES

|  | Appointments? | Who? |
|---|---|---|
| **Campus Tour** | recommended, not required | open to all |
| **Information Session** | recommended, not required | open to all |
| **Admission Interview** | recommended, not required | open to all |
| **Classroom Visit** | recommended, not required | open to all |
| **Faculty Meeting** | recommended, not required | open to all |

*Mars Hill College (continued)*

## VISIT OPPORTUNITIES—*continued*

| | Appointments? | Who? |
|---|---|---|
| **Overnight Visit** | recommended, not required | open to all |

**Information Sessions:** M–F 8:00 am–5:00 pm; select Sat.; we will accommodate the students needs; 30 minutes.

**Interviews:** M–F, select Sat.

**Campus Tours:** Conducted by students. M–F 8:00 am–5:00 pm; select Sat. 9:00 am–1:00 pm; we will accommodate students' needs; 60 minutes.

**Class Visits:** Prospective students may attend a class in their area of interest.

**Overnight Visits:** During the regular academic year, prospective applicants may spend an evening in a residence hall with a student host.

## CAMPUS FACILITIES
**Science:** Wall Science Building.

**Arts:** Moore Auditorium, Owen Theater, Harris Media Center.

**Athletic:** Chambers Gym.

**Of Special Interest:** Rural Life Museum, Broyhill Chapel, Renfro Library.

## LOCAL ATTRACTIONS
Biltmore Estates, Grove Park Inn, Asheville, NC.


# METHODIST COLLEGE
## Fayetteville, North Carolina

**Contact:** Eric Brandon, Director of Admissions, 5400 Ramsey Street, Fayetteville, NC 28311-1420. *Phone:* 910-630-7027 or toll-free 800-488-7110. *Fax:* 910-630-7285. *Visit location:* Admissions Office, Stout Hall, 5400 Ramsey Street.

## QUICK FACTS
Enrollment: 1,720; UG: 1,720. Entrance: moderately difficult. SAT>500: 33% V, 36% M; ACT>18: N/R. Tuition and fees: $11,900. Room and board: $4580. Application deadline: rolling.

## GENERAL
Independent United Methodist, 4-year, coed. Awards associate and bachelor's degrees. Founded 1956. Setting: 600-acre suburban campus. Faculty: 134 (84 full-time, 50 part-time); student-faculty ratio is 17:1. Most popular recent majors: business administration, education, sociology.

## CAMPUS VISITS
**College Calendar 1998–99:** *Regular classes:* Aug. 25–Dec. 8; Jan. 12–Apr. 27. *Breaks:* Dec. 17–Jan. 11. *Final exams:* Dec. 10–17; Apr. 29–May 6.

## VISIT OPPORTUNITIES

| | Appointments? | Who? |
|---|---|---|
| **Campus Tour** | recommended | applicants and parents |
| **Information Session** | recommended | |
| **Admission Interview** | recommended | applicants and parents |
| **Classroom Visit** | required | applicants and parents |
| **Faculty Meeting** | required | applicants and parents |
| **Overnight Visit** | required | |

**Information Sessions:** Call for schedule; 45 minutes.

**Interviews:** M–F, Sat.; 30 minutes.

**Campus Tours:** Conducted by students and admission reps. Sat. 9:00 am–12:00 pm; M–F 8:00 am–5:00 pm; 45 minutes.

**Class Visits:** Prospective students may attend a class in their area of interest.

**Overnight Visits:** During the regular academic year, prospective applicants may spend an evening in a residence hall with a student host.

**Video:** Free on request.

## CAMPUS FACILITIES
**Science:** Science Laboratories, Computer Science Lab.

**Arts:** Art Department, Auditorium, Music Department, Theatre Department.

**Athletic:** Golf Course and Pro Shop, Gymnasium and Weight Room, Tennis Courts, Football, Baseball, and Soccer Fields.

**Of Special Interest:** Student Union, Dormitories, Chapel and Library.

# NORTH CAROLINA STATE UNIVERSITY
## Raleigh, North Carolina

**Contact:** Office of Undergraduate Admissions, 112 Peele Hall, Box 7103, Raleigh, NC 27695-7103. *Phone:* 919-515-2434. *Fax:* 919-515-5039. *E-mail:* undergrad_admissions@ncsu.edu *Web site:* http://www.ncsu.edu/ *Visit location:* Undergraduate Admissions, 112 Peele Hall.

## QUICK FACTS
Enrollment: 19,533; UG: 19,235. Entrance: very difficult. SAT>500: 84% V, 89% M; ACT>18: 91%. Resident tuition and fees: $2270. Nonresident tuition and fees: $11,256. Room and board: $3910. Application deadline: 2/1.

## GENERAL
State-supported, university, coed. Part of University of North Carolina System. Awards associate, bachelor's, master's, doctoral, and first professional degrees and first professional certificates. Founded 1887. Setting: 1,623-acre suburban campus. Undergraduate faculty: 1,593 (1,531 full-time, 62 part-time); student-faculty ratio is 14:1. Most popular recent majors: business administration, electrical/electronics engineering, mechanical engineering.

## CAMPUS VISITS
**College Calendar 1998–99:** *Regular classes:* Aug. 17–Dec. 4; Jan. 4–Apr. 30. *Breaks:* Oct. 9–13; Mar. 8–12. *Final exams:* Dec. 7–15; May 3–11.

## VISIT OPPORTUNITIES

| | Appointments? | Who? |
|---|---|---|
| **Campus Tour** | not required | applicants and parents |
| **Information Session** | not required | |
| **Admission Interview** | required | applicants and parents |
| **Classroom Visit** | not required | applicants and parents |
| **Faculty Meeting** | required | applicants and parents |

**Information Sessions:** Mon., Wed., Fri. at 10:30 am; Tue., Thu. at 1:30 pm; selected Sat., call for schedule; 60 minutes.

**Interviews:** M–F; 30 minutes.

**Campus Tours:** Conducted by students. M–F at 12:20 pm.

**Class Visits:** Certain predetermined classrooms are open to visitors.

**Video:** Available, fee charged.

## CAMPUS FACILITIES
**Science:** Nuclear Reactor.

**Arts:** University Student Center Art Gallery.

**Athletic:** Reynolds Coliseum.

## LOCAL ATTRACTIONS
North Carolina Museum of Art; Museum of Natural History; State Capitol Building.

# NORTH CAROLINA WESLEYAN COLLEGE
## Rocky Mount, North Carolina

**Contact:** Katie Campbell, Campus Visit Coordinator, 3400 North Wesleyan Boulevard, Rocky Mount, NC 27804. *Phone:* toll-free 800-488-6292. *Fax:* 919-985-5295. *E-mail:* kcampbell@ncwc.edu *Web site:* http://www.ncwc.edu/ *Visit location:* Admissions Office, Bellemonte House, 3400 North Wesleyan Boulevard.

## QUICK FACTS
Enrollment: 1,582; UG: 1,582. Entrance: moderately difficult. SAT>500: 29% V, 31% M; ACT>18: N/R. Tuition and fees: $8144. Room and board: $4952. Application deadline: rolling.

## GENERAL
Independent, 4-year, coed, United Methodist Church. Awards bachelor's degrees (also offers adult part-time degree program with significant enrollment not reflected in profile). Founded 1956. Setting: 200-acre suburban campus. Faculty: 65 (33 full-time, 32 part-time). Most popular recent majors: business administration, information sciences/systems.

## CAMPUS VISITS
**College Calendar 1998–99:** *Regular classes:* Oct. 1–Dec. 4; Feb. 1–May 7. *Breaks:* Oct. 19–20; Mar. 29–Apr. 6; Nov. 25–27. *Final exams:* Dec. 7–10; May 10–13. *Special campus days:* Commencement, Dec. 12, May 15; Honors Convocation, Apr. 25; Parent's Weekend, Nov. 6–8.

*North Carolina Wesleyan College (continued)*

## VISIT OPPORTUNITIES

|  | Appointments? | Who? |
| --- | --- | --- |
| **Campus Tour** | recommended, not required | open to all |
| **Information Session** | recommended, not required | open to all |
| **Admission Interview** | recommended, not required | open to all |
| **Classroom Visit** | recommended, not required | open to all |
| **Faculty Meeting** | recommended | open to all |
| **Overnight Visit** | required | open to all |

**Information Sessions:** M–F; 15 minutes.

**Interviews:** M–F, Sat.; 20 minutes.

**Campus Tours:** Conducted by students. M–F, Sat.; 60 minutes.

**Class Visits:** Classroom visits are determined by the visit schedule.

**Overnight Visits:** During the regular academic year, prospective applicants may spend an evening in a residence hall with a student host.

## CAMPUS FACILITIES

**Science:** Biology Labs, Chemistry Labs.

**Arts:** Dunn Center for Performing Arts.

**Athletic:** Fitness and weight room, softball, baseball, and soccer fields.

# SHAW UNIVERSITY
## Raleigh, North Carolina

**Contact:** Mr. Keith Smith, Director of Admissions and Recruitment, 118 East South Street, Raleigh, NC 27601. *Phone:* toll-free 800-214-6683. *Fax:* 919-546-8271. *E-mail:* ksmith@shawu.edu *Visit location:* Admissions and Recruitment, Tyler Hall, 118 East South Street.

## QUICK FACTS

Enrollment: 2,327; UG: 2,327. Entrance: minimally difficult. SAT>500: N/App; ACT>18: N/App. Tuition and fees: $6304. Room and board: $4052. Application deadline: 7/30.

## GENERAL

Independent Baptist, 4-year, coed. Awards associate and bachelor's degrees. Founded 1865. Setting: 18-acre urban campus. Faculty: 276 (84 full-time, 192 part-time); student-faculty ratio is 14:1. Most popular recent majors: business administration, social sciences, criminal justice studies.

## CAMPUS VISITS

**College Calendar 1998–99:** *Regular classes:* Aug. 17–Dec. 4; Jan. 13–Apr. 30. *Breaks:* Sept. 7; Mar. 6–14; Nov. 26–29; Apr. 9–12. *Final exams:* Dec. 5–11; Apr. 26–May 7. *Admission office closed:* Apr. 2–5; Christmas break (usually 2–3 days before Christmas Eve through New Year's). *Special campus days:* Baccalaureate and Commencement; Bessie Boyd-Holman Lecture Series on Ethics and Values; Coronation of Miss Shaw University; Founders Day/Homecoming; Martin Luther King, Jr. Commemorative Service; New Students/Parents Orientation; Religious Emphasis Week; University Awards Day.

## VISIT OPPORTUNITIES

|  | Appointments? | Who? |
| --- | --- | --- |
| **Campus Tour** | recommended | |
| **Information Session** | | open to all |
| **Admission Interview** | required | |
| **Classroom Visit** | recommended | |
| **Faculty Meeting** | required | |

**Information Sessions:** M–F; 30 minutes.

**Interviews:** M–F; 35 minutes.

**Campus Tours:** Conducted by students, admission reps, and alumni. M–F; 60 minutes.

**Class Visits:** Prospective students may attend a class in their area of interest.

## CAMPUS FACILITIES

**Science:** Robert Science Hall.

**Of Special Interest:** James E. Cheek Learning Resources Center, Talbert O. Shaw Living/Learning Center, Estey Hall.

# THE UNIVERSITY OF NORTH CAROLINA AT CHAPEL HILL
## Chapel Hill, North Carolina

**Contact:** Undergraduate Admissions, CB #2200 Jackson Hall, UNC-CH, Chapel Hill, NC 27599-

2200. *Phone:* 919-966-3621. *Fax:* 919-962-3045. *E-mail:* uadmtour@unc.edu *Web site:* http://www.unc. edu/ *Visit location:* Undergraduate Admissions, Jackson Hall, Campus Box 2200, Jackson Hall.

## QUICK FACTS
Enrollment: 23,936; UG: 15,068. Entrance: very difficult. SAT>500: 93% V, 93% M; ACT>18: N/R. Resident tuition and fees: $2224. Nonresident tuition and fees: $11,210. Room and board: $4760. Application deadline: 1/15.

## GENERAL
State-supported, university, coed. Part of University of North Carolina System. Awards bachelor's, master's, doctoral, and first professional degrees. Founded 1789. Setting: 789-acre suburban campus with easy access to Raleigh-Durham. Undergraduate faculty: 2,640 (2,417 full-time, 223 part-time); student-faculty ratio is 14:1. Most popular recent majors: biology, business administration, psychology.

## CAMPUS VISITS
**College Calendar 1998–99:** *Regular classes:* Aug. 18–Dec. 7; Jan. 6–Apr. 29. *Breaks:* Oct. 15–18; Mar. 6–14; Nov. 25–29. *Final exams:* Dec. 9–16; May 1–8. *Admission office closed:* Christmas break, Dec. 23–25; Good Friday, Apr. 2; Martin Luther King, Jr. Day, Jan. 18; Thanksgiving, Nov. 26–27. *Special campus days:* Fall Commencement, Dec. 20; Homecoming, Oct. 10; Spring Commencement, May 16; University Day, Oct. 12.

## VISIT OPPORTUNITIES

|  | Appointments? | Who? |
| --- | --- | --- |
| **Campus Tour** | recommended, not required | open to all |
| **Information Session** | recommended, not required | open to all |
| **Admission Interview** | recommended, not required | open to all |
| **Classroom Visit** | required | open to all |
| **Faculty Meeting** | required | open to all |

**Information Sessions:** M–F at 11:00 am, 3:00 pm; unavailable during university holidays; 60 minutes.

**Interviews:** M–F; unavailable during university holidays.

**Campus Tours:** Conducted by students. M–F at 10:00 am, 2:00 pm; unavailable during student breaks Dec. 15–Jan. 7, Jan. 18, Apr. 2, and university holidays; 60 minutes.

**Class Visits:** Students call department of interest for appointment to visit class.

## CAMPUS FACILITIES
**Science:** Botanical Gardens; Appointment Required: Sitterson Virtual Reality Computer Lab, Kenan Chemistry Labs, Morehead Planetarium Telescope.

**Arts:** Ackland Art Museum, Hanes Art Center, Paul Greene Theatre, Play Makers Theatre.

**Athletic:** Student Recreation Center; Appointment Required: Dean Smith Center, Kenan Stadium.

**Of Special Interest:** Student Union, Lenoir Cafeteria, Wilson and Davis Libraries.

## LOCAL ATTRACTIONS
Franklin Street, Ackland Art Museum; Visitors Center; McCall Building.

# UNIVERSITY OF NORTH CAROLINA AT CHARLOTTE
**Charlotte, North Carolina**

**Contact:** Undergraduate Admissions Office, 9201 University City Boulevard, Charlotte, NC 28223. *Phone:* 704-547-2213. *Fax:* 704-510-6483. *E-mail:* unccadm@email.uncc.edu *Web site:* http://www.uncc. edu/ *Visit location:* Undergraduate Admissions, Reese Building-1st Floor, 9201 University City Boulevard.

## QUICK FACTS
Enrollment: 15,436; UG: 12,747. Entrance: moderately difficult. SAT>500: 54% V, 54% M; ACT>18: 74%. Resident tuition and fees: $1777. Nonresident tuition and fees: $8905. Room and board: $3446. Application deadline: 7/1.

## GENERAL
State-supported, university, coed. Part of University of North Carolina System. Awards bachelor's, master's, and doctoral degrees and post-master's certificates. Founded 1946. Setting: 1,000-acre urban campus. Undergraduate faculty: 931 (643 full-time, 288 part-time); student-faculty ratio is 16:1. Most popular recent majors: psychology, English, criminal justice/law enforcement administration.

*University of North Carolina at Charlotte (continued)*

## CAMPUS VISITS

**College Calendar 1998–99:** *Regular classes:* Aug. 24–Dec. 11; Jan. 13–May 5. *Breaks:* Oct. 12; Jan. 18; Nov. 25–27; Mar. 8–12. *Final exams:* Dec. 12–18; May 6–12. *Special campus days:* Commencement, May 15.

## VISIT OPPORTUNITIES

|  | Appointments? | Who? |
|---|---|---|
| **Campus Tour** | recommended, not required | open to all |
| **Information Session** | recommended, not required | open to all |
| **Admission Interview** | not required | open to all |
| **Faculty Meeting** | recommended, not required | open to all |

**Information Sessions:** M–F at 3:00 pm; Sat. at 11:00 am; department presentations: Engineering – Mon. at 1:00 pm; Computer Science – Mon. at 1:00 pm; Nursing and Health Fitness – Tue. at 4:00 pm; Architecture – Thu. at 4:00 pm; Arts and Sciences – Thu. at 4:00 pm; Education – Fri. at 4:00 pm; 45 minutes.

**Interviews:** M–F, Sat.; 30 minutes.

**Campus Tours:** Conducted by students. M–F at 2:00 pm; Sat. at 10:00 am; 60 minutes.

## CAMPUS FACILITIES
**Of Special Interest:** Student Activity Center.

# WAKE FOREST UNIVERSITY
**Winston-Salem, North Carolina**

**Contact:** Office of Admissions, PO Box 7305, Winston-Salem, NC 27109. *Phone:* 336-758-5201. *E-mail:* admissions@wfu.edu *Web site:* http://www.wfu. edu/ *Visit location:* Welcome Center/Admissions House, 2601 Wake Forest Road.

## QUICK FACTS
Enrollment: 5,931; UG: 3,800. Entrance: very difficult. SAT>500: 98% V, 97% M; ACT>18: N/App. Tuition and fees: $19,450. Room and board: $5450. Application deadline: 1/15.

## GENERAL
Independent, university, coed. Awards bachelor's, master's, doctoral, and first professional degrees.

Founded 1834. Setting: 350-acre suburban campus. Undergraduate faculty: 1,708 (1,066 full-time, 642 part-time); student-faculty ratio is 12:1. Most popular recent majors: business administration, biology, psychology.

## CAMPUS VISITS

**College Calendar 1998–99:** *Regular classes:* Aug. 26–Dec. 4; Jan. 3–Apr. 30. *Breaks:* Nov. 25–29; Mar. 6–14; Oct. 9; Apr. 2. *Final exams:* Dec. 7–12; May 3–8. *Special campus days:* Commencement, May 17; Family Weekend, Oct. 31; Homecoming, Oct. 3.

## VISIT OPPORTUNITIES

|  | Appointments? | Who? |
|---|---|---|
| **Campus Tour** | required | open to all |
| **Information Session** | required | open to all |
| **Admission Interview** | required | open to all |
| **Classroom Visit** | required | open to all |
| **Faculty Meeting** | required | open to all |
| **Overnight Visit** | required | open to all |

**Information Sessions:** M–F, select Sat.; 45 minutes.

**Interviews:** M–F during summer for high school seniors; 20 minutes.

**Campus Tours:** Conducted by students. M–F, select Sat.; call for appointment during breaks in school; 50 minutes.

**Class Visits:** Prospective students may attend a class in their area of interest.

**Overnight Visits:** During the regular academic year, prospective applicants may spend an evening in a residence hall with a student host.

**Video:** Free on request.

## CAMPUS FACILITIES
**Science:** Appointment Required: Olin Physical Lab.

**Arts:** Scales Fine Arts Center, Wake Forest University Fine Arts Gallery.

**Athletic:** Appointment Required: Lawrence Joel Veterans Memorial Coliseum.

**Of Special Interest:** Museum of Anthropology.

## LOCAL ATTRACTIONS
Old Salem; Reynolda House Museum of American Art; Reynolda Gardens/Reynolda Village.

## WARREN WILSON COLLEGE
### Asheville, North Carolina

**Contact:** Monique A. Cote, Campus Visit Coordinator, PO Box 9000, Asheville, NC 28815-9000. *Phone:* toll-free 800-934-3536. *Fax:* 704-298-1440. *Web site:* http://www.warren-wilson.edu/ *Visit location:* Admission Office, Dodge House.

### QUICK FACTS
Enrollment: 723; UG: 645. Entrance: moderately difficult. SAT>500: 88% V, 70% M; ACT>18: N/R. Tuition and fees: $12,250. Room and board: $4000. Application deadline: 3/15.

### GENERAL
Independent, comprehensive, coed, Presbyterian Church (U.S.A.). Awards bachelor's and master's degrees. Founded 1894. Setting: 1,100-acre small-town campus. Undergraduate faculty: 132 (92 full-time, 40 part-time); student-faculty ratio is 11:1. Most popular recent majors: environmental science, recreation and leisure studies, art.

### CAMPUS VISITS
**College Calendar 1998–99:** *Regular classes:* Aug. 26–Dec. 19; Jan. 19–May 15. *Special campus days:* Open House, Oct. 31.

### VISIT OPPORTUNITIES

|  | Appointments? | Who? |
|---|---|---|
| **Campus Tour** | required | open to all |
| **Information Session** | required | open to all |
| **Admission Interview** | required | open to all |
| **Classroom Visit** | required | open to all |
| **Faculty Meeting** | required | open to all |
| **Overnight Visit** | required | open to all |

**Information Sessions:** M–F, select Sat.

**Interviews:** M–F, select Sat.; 30 minutes.

**Campus Tours:** Conducted by students. M–F, select Sat.

**Class Visits:** Prospective students may attend a class in their area of interest.

**Overnight Visits:** During the regular academic year, prospective applicants may spend an evening in a residence hall with a student host.

**Video:** Free on request.

### CAMPUS FACILITIES
**Of Special Interest:** Martha Ellison Library.

# NORTH DAKOTA

## NORTH DAKOTA STATE UNIVERSITY
### Fargo, North Dakota

**Contact:** Cindy Larson, Campus Visit Coordinator, University Station, Fargo, ND 58105. *Phone:* toll-free 800-488-NDSU. *Fax:* 701-231-8802. *E-mail:* nuadmiss@plains.nodak.edu *Web site:* http://www.ndsu.nodak.edu/ *Visit location:* Office of Admission, Ceres Hall, Room 124, Administration Avenue/NDSU.

### QUICK FACTS
Enrollment: 8,500; UG: 8,500. Entrance: moderately difficult. SAT>500: N/R; ACT>18: N/R. Resident tuition and fees: $2566. Nonresident tuition and fees: $6300. Room and board: $3135. Application deadline: rolling.

### GENERAL
State-supported, university, coed. Part of North Dakota University System. Awards bachelor's, master's, doctoral, and first professional degrees. Founded 1890. Setting: 2,100-acre urban campus. Undergraduate faculty: 530 (478 full-time, 52 part-time); student-faculty ratio is 19:1. Most popular recent majors: civil engineering, business administration, mechanical engineering.

### CAMPUS VISITS
**College Calendar 1998–99:** *Regular classes:* Aug. 25–Dec. 10; Jan. 5–Apr. 29. *Breaks:* Dec. 21–Jan. 4; Mar. 8–12; Apr. 2–5. *Final exams:* Dec. 14–18; May 3–7. *Special campus days:* Family Weekend, Oct. 23–24; Homecoming Week, Sept. 28–Oct. 3; Spring Commencement, May 8; Winter Commencement, Dec. 18.

### VISIT OPPORTUNITIES

|  | Appointments? | Who? |
|---|---|---|
| **Campus Tour** | recommended | open to all |
| **Information Session** | recommended | open to all |
| **Admission Interview** | recommended | open to all |
| **Classroom Visit** | recommended | open to all |

*North Dakota State University (continued)*

## VISIT OPPORTUNITIES—*continued*

| | Appointments? | Who? |
|---|---|---|
| **Faculty Meeting** | recommended | open to all |

**Information Sessions:** "Discover NDSU" Open House dates: Oct. 8–9, 15–16, 1998, Nov. 6–7 1998, April 16–17, 1999. These sessions are large-group information gatherings, including a campus tour, student panel, parent session, and academic interest session; 180 minutes.

**Interviews:** M–F, select Sat.; 30 minutes.

**Campus Tours:** Conducted by students. M–F 8:00 am–5:00 pm; Sat. at 11:30 am, 1:00 pm; summer (mid-May through Aug.) office hours 7:30 am to 4:00 pm with tours scheduled at 10:00 am, 12:00 pm, 2:00 pm; 60 minutes.

**Class Visits:** Certain predetermined classrooms are open to visitors.

**Video:** Free on request.

## CAMPUS FACILITIES
**Science:** Industrial Agriculture and Communications Center (Computer Center).

**Arts:** Reineke Fine Arts Center.

**Athletic:** Bison Sports Arena, Newman Baseball Complex, Ellig Track and Soccer Complex.

**Of Special Interest:** Memorial Union, Varsity Mart Bookstore and Food Court, residence halls.

## LOCAL ATTRACTIONS
Fargo Dome.

# OHIO

## CASE WESTERN RESERVE UNIVERSITY
Cleveland, Ohio

**Contact:** Scheduling Coordinator, Office of Undergraduate Admission, Office of Undergraduate Admission, Tomlinson Hall, Cleveland, OH 44122. *Phone:* 216-368-4450. *Fax:* 216-368-5111. *E-mail:* xx329@po. cwru.edu *Web site:* http://www.cwru.edu/ *Visit location:* Office of Undergraduate Admission, Tomlinson Hall, 10900 Euclid Avenue.

## QUICK FACTS
Enrollment: 9,605; UG: 3,306. Entrance: very difficult. SAT>500: 94% V, 97% M; ACT>18: 99%. Tuition and fees: $17,940. Room and board: $5050. Application deadline: 2/1.

## GENERAL
Independent, university, coed. Awards bachelor's, master's, doctoral, and first professional degrees. Founded 1826. Setting: 128-acre urban campus. Undergraduate faculty: 1,949 (all full-time); student-faculty ratio is 8:1. Most popular recent majors: biology, psychology, chemical engineering.

## CAMPUS VISITS
**College Calendar 1998–99:** *Regular classes:* Aug. 24–Dec. 4; Jan. 11–Apr. 26. *Breaks:* Nov. 26–29; Mar. 8–12; Oct. 19–20. *Final exams:* Dec. 9–16; Apr. 29–May 6. *Admission office closed:* Nov. 27, Dec. 24–25. *Special campus days:* Commencement, May 16.

## VISIT OPPORTUNITIES

| | Appointments? | Who? |
|---|---|---|
| **Campus Tour** | recommended | open to all |
| **Information Session** | recommended | open to all |
| **Admission Interview** | required | open to all |
| **Classroom Visit** | recommended | open to all |
| **Faculty Meeting** | required | open to all |
| **Overnight Visit** | required | open to all |

**Information Sessions:** Select Sat. 12:00–3:00 pm; call for available schedule; 60 minutes.

**Interviews:** M–F; 30 minutes.

**Campus Tours:** Conducted by students. M–F, select Sat. at 9:00 am, 11:30 am, 12:00 pm, 1:30 pm, 2:30 pm; select Sat.; 90 minutes.

**Class Visits:** Certain predetermined classrooms are open to visitors.

**Overnight Visits:** During the regular academic year, prospective applicants may spend an evening in a residence hall with a student host.

**Video:** Available, fee charged.

## CAMPUS FACILITIES
**Science:** Case School of Engineering, Kent Smith Building.

**Arts:** Eldred Theater, Mather House.

**Athletic:** Veale Convocation, Recreation and Athletic Center.

**Of Special Interest:** Thwing Student Center, Kelvin H. Smith Library.

## LOCAL ATTRACTIONS
The Cleveland Museum of Art, Severance Hall, home of the Cleveland Orchestra, the Rock and Roll Hall of Fame, Great Lakes Science Center.

# CEDARVILLE COLLEGE
Cedarville, Ohio

**Contact:** Guest Coordinator, PO Box 601, Cedarville, OH 45314. *Phone:* toll-free 800-CEDARVILLE. *Fax:* 937-766-7575. *E-mail:* admissions@cedarville.edu *Web site:* http://www.cedarville.edu/ *Visit location:* Admissions Office, College Center, Cedarville College.

## QUICK FACTS
Enrollment: 2,550; UG: 2,550. Entrance: moderately difficult. SAT>500: 87% V, 83% M; ACT>18: 100%. Tuition and fees: $9312. Room and board: $4716. Application deadline: rolling.

## GENERAL
Independent Baptist, 4-year, coed. Awards associate and bachelor's degrees. Founded 1887. Setting: 300-acre rural campus with easy access to Columbus and Dayton. Faculty: 173 (133 full-time, 40 part-time); student-faculty ratio is 16:1. Most popular recent majors: elementary education, nursing, biology.

## CAMPUS VISITS
**College Calendar 1998–99:** *Regular classes:* Sept. 24–Dec. 8; Jan. 4–Mar. 9; Mar. 22–June 1. *Breaks:* Nov. 25–Dec. 1; Mar. 13–21; Apr. 2–5; Dec. 12–Jan. 3. *Final exams:* Dec. 9–11; Mar. 10–12; June 2–4. *Admission office closed:* Nov. 26–27, Dec. 21–25, Apr. 5. *Special campus days:* Commencement, June 5; Engineering Day; Homecoming, Oct. 16–18; Leadership Conference, Jan. 8–9; Lil Sibs Weekend; Music Showcase; Science and Math Day, Nov. 7; Summer Previews.

## VISIT OPPORTUNITIES

| | Appointments? | Who? |
|---|---|---|
| **Campus Tour** | recommended, not required | applicants and parents |
| **Information Session** | recommended, not required | |

| | Appointments? | Who? |
|---|---|---|
| **Admission Interview** | required | |
| **Classroom Visit** | recommended, not required | applicants and parents |
| **Faculty Meeting** | required | applicants and parents |
| **Overnight Visit** | required | |

**Information Sessions:** M–F at 2:00 pm; Sat. by appointment only; 60 minutes.

**Interviews:** M–F, select Sat.; 60 minutes.

**Campus Tours:** Conducted by students. M–F at 9:00 am, 11:00 am, 12:00 pm, 1:00 pm; Sat. by appointment only; 90 minutes.

**Class Visits:** Prospective students may attend a class in their area of interest.

**Overnight Visits:** During the regular academic year and over the summer, prospective applicants may spend an evening in a residence hall with a student host.

**Video:** Available, fee charged.

## CAMPUS FACILITIES
**Of Special Interest:** Chapel.

# THE COLLEGE OF WOOSTER
Wooster, Ohio

**Contact:** Ms. Carol D. Wheatley, Director of Admissions, Galpin Hall, Wooster, OH 44691. *Phone:* toll-free 800-877-9905. *Fax:* 330-263-2621. *E-mail:* admissions@acs.wooster.edu *Web site:* http://www. wooster.edu/ *Visit location:* Office of Admissions, Galpin Hall.

## QUICK FACTS
Enrollment: 1,700; UG: 1,700. Entrance: moderately difficult. SAT>500: 88% V, 85% M; ACT>18: 89%. Tuition and fees: $19,230. Room and board: $5070. Application deadline: 2/15.

## GENERAL
Independent, 4-year, coed, Presbyterian Church (U.S.A.). Awards bachelor's degrees. Founded 1866. Setting: 320-acre small-town campus with easy access to Cleveland. Faculty: 144 (128 full-time, 16 part-time); student-faculty ratio is 11:1. Most popular recent majors: English, biology, economics.

*The College of Wooster (continued)*

## CAMPUS VISITS

**College Calendar 1998–99:** *Regular classes:* Aug. 31–Dec. 11; Jan. 12–Apr. 30. *Breaks:* Dec. 17–Jan. 12. *Final exams:* Dec. 14–17; May 3–6.

## VISIT OPPORTUNITIES

|  | Appointments? | Who? |
| --- | --- | --- |
| **Campus Tour** | recommended | applicants and parents |
| **Admission Interview** | required | |
| **Classroom Visit** | required | |
| **Faculty Meeting** | required | |
| **Overnight Visit** | required | |

**Interviews:** M–F; Sat. during academic year; 45 minutes.

**Campus Tours:** Conducted by students. M–F 9:00 am–4:00 pm; Sat. 9:00 am–12:00 pm; 60 minutes.

**Class Visits:** Prospective students may attend a class in their area of interest.

**Overnight Visits:** During the regular academic year, prospective applicants may spend an evening in a residence hall with a student host.

**Video:** Free on request.

## CAMPUS FACILITIES

**Science:** Timlar Science Library, Mattar Hall (Biology), Servance Hall (Chemistry), Taylor Hall (Physics, math, computer science), Scorel Hall (Geology).

**Arts:** Ebest Art Center, Sussel Gallery, Freedlander Theatre, Scheide Music Center.

**Athletic:** Armington Physical Education Center.

**Of Special Interest:** Flo K. Gault Library for Independent Study.

# FRANCISCAN UNIVERSITY OF STEUBENVILLE

**Steubenville, Ohio**

**Contact:** Mrs. Margaret Weber, Director of Admissions, 1235 University Boulevard, Steubenville, OH 43952. *Phone:* toll-free 800-783-6220. *Fax:* 740-284-5456. *E-mail:* admissions@franuniv.edu *Web site:* http://esoptron.umd.edu/FUSFOLDER/francisc. html *Visit location:* Admissions Office, Starvaggi Hall, 1235 University Boulevard.

## QUICK FACTS

Enrollment: 1,971; UG: 1,579. Entrance: moderately difficult. SAT>500: 87% V, 68% M; ACT>18: 95%. Tuition and fees: $11,370. Room and board: $4730. Application deadline: 6/30.

## GENERAL

Independent Roman Catholic, comprehensive, coed. Awards associate, bachelor's, and master's degrees. Founded 1946. Setting: 100-acre suburban campus with easy access to Pittsburgh. Undergraduate faculty: 137 (91 full-time, 46 part-time); student-faculty ratio is 16:1. Most popular recent majors: theology, elementary education, business administration.

## CAMPUS VISITS

**College Calendar 1998–99:** *Regular classes:* Aug. 25–Dec. 3; Jan. 12–Apr. 28. *Breaks:* Dec. 10–Jan. 8. *Final exams:* Dec. 5–10; Apr. 30–May 5. *Admission office closed:* holy days of the Catholic church. *Special campus days:* Commencement, May 8; Parents Weekend, Oct. 2–3.

## VISIT OPPORTUNITIES

|  | Appointments? | Who? |
| --- | --- | --- |
| **Campus Tour** | required | open to all |
| **Information Session** | required | open to all |
| **Admission Interview** | required | open to all |
| **Classroom Visit** | required | open to all |
| **Faculty Meeting** | required | open to all |
| **Overnight Visit** | required | open to all |

**Information Sessions:** M–F; Sat. for spring and fall open house or for special visiting persons and groups; 60 minutes.

**Interviews:** M–F at 2:00 pm; select Sat.; Sat. for spring and fall open house or for special visiting persons and groups; 60 minutes.

**Campus Tours:** Conducted by students, admission reps, and faculty/administrators. M–F; Sat. for spring and fall open house or for special visiting persons and groups; 60 minutes.

**Class Visits:** Prospective students may attend a class in their area of interest, certain predetermined classrooms are open to visitors, classroom visits are determined by the visit schedule.

**Overnight Visits:** During the regular academic year, prospective applicants may spend an evening in a residence hall with a student host.

**Video:** Free on request.

## CAMPUS FACILITIES

**Science:** Nursing Labs, Biology and Chemistry Labs.

**Arts:** Anathan Theater (Drama).

**Athletic:** Finnegan Fieldhouse, Various outdoor fields and courts.

**Of Special Interest:** Radio/TV Labs, Portiuncula Chapel/Outdoor "Stations of the Cross"/Tomb of the Unborn Child, Education Clinical Labs and Psychology Labs.

## LOCAL ATTRACTIONS

Steubenville, "The City of Murals"—large artistic paintings on many downtown buildings; mural tours available.

# JOHN CARROLL UNIVERSITY
## University Heights, Ohio

**Contact:** Mr. Thomas P. Fanning, Director of Admission, 20700 North Park Boulevard, University Heights, OH 44118. *Phone:* 216-397-4294. *Fax:* 216-397-3098. *E-mail:* admission@jcvaxa.jcu.edu *Web site:* http://www.jcu.edu/ *Visit location:* Admission Office, Administration Building, 20700 North Park Boulevard.

## QUICK FACTS

Enrollment: 4,280; UG: 3,401. Entrance: moderately difficult. SAT>500: 86% V, 82% M; ACT>18: 95%. Tuition and fees: $14,620. Room and board: $5804. Application deadline: rolling.

## GENERAL

Independent Roman Catholic (Jesuit), comprehensive, coed. Awards bachelor's and master's degrees. Founded 1886. Setting: 60-acre suburban campus with easy access to Cleveland. Undergraduate faculty: 392 (226 full-time, 166 part-time); student-faculty ratio is 10:1. Most popular recent majors: mass communications, psychology, biology.

## CAMPUS VISITS

**College Calendar 1998–99:** *Regular classes:* Aug. 31–Dec. 12; Jan. 11–Apr. 29. *Breaks:* Oct. 15–19; Feb. 27–Mar. 8; Nov. 24–30; Mar. 31–Apr. 6. *Final exams:* Dec. 14–18; May 3–7. *Admission office closed:* Mar. 30–31.

## VISIT OPPORTUNITIES

| | Appointments? | Who? |
|---|---|---|
| **Campus Tour** | required | open to all |
| **Information Session** | required | open to all |
| **Admission Interview** | required | open to all |
| **Classroom Visit** | required | open to all |
| **Faculty Meeting** | required | open to all |
| **Overnight Visit** | required | admitted applicants only |

**Information Sessions:** Sat.; 45 minutes.

**Interviews:** M–F; 60 minutes.

**Campus Tours:** Conducted by students. M–F, Sat.; 60 minutes.

**Class Visits:** Prospective students may attend a class in their area of interest.

**Overnight Visits:** During the regular academic year, prospective applicants may spend an evening in a residence hall with a student host.

**Video:** Free on request.

## CAMPUS FACILITIES

**Science:** Bohanen Science Center.

**Arts:** O'Malley Center for Communication and Language Arts.

**Athletic:** D. J. Lombardo Student Center, Don Shula Sports Center.

## LOCAL ATTRACTIONS

Rock and Roll Hall of Fame; Great Lakes Science Center; Gateway Complex—Gund Arena and Jacobs Field.

# KENYON COLLEGE
## Gambier, Ohio

**Contact:** Mr. John W. Anderson, Dean of Admissions and Financial Aid, Admissions and Financial Aid Office, Ransom Hall, Gambier, OH 43022-9623. *Phone:* 740-427-5776 or toll-free 800-848-2468. *Fax:* 740-427-2634. *E-mail:* admissions@kenyon.edu *Web site:* http://www.kenyon.edu/ *Visit location:* Admissions and Financial Aid Office, Ransom Hall.

## QUICK FACTS

Enrollment: 1,536; UG: 1,536. Entrance: very difficult. SAT>500: 100% V, 99% M; ACT>18:

*Kenyon College (continued)*

100%. Tuition and fees: $22,850. Room and board: $3990. Application deadline: 2/1.

## GENERAL

Independent, 4-year, coed. Awards bachelor's degrees. Founded 1824. Setting: 800-acre rural campus with easy access to Columbus. Faculty: 145 (128 full-time, 17 part-time); student-faculty ratio is 10:1. Most popular recent majors: English, history, psychology.

## CAMPUS VISITS

**College Calendar 1998–99:** *Regular classes:* Aug. 27–Dec. 11; Jan. 18–May 7. *Breaks:* Oct. 6–10; Mar. 6–22; Nov. 21–30. *Final exams:* Dec. 12–19; May 8–17. *Special campus days:* Commencement, May 23; Family Weekend, Oct. 16–18; Homecoming, Sept. 25–27; Orientation for First Year and Transfer Students, Aug. 23–26.

## VISIT OPPORTUNITIES

| | Appointments? | Who? |
|---|---|---|
| **Campus Tour** | recommended | open to all |
| **Admission Interview** | required | open to all |
| **Classroom Visit** | recommended | open to all |
| **Faculty Meeting** | required | open to all |
| **Overnight Visit** | required | open to all |

**Interviews:** M–F; Sat. during academic year; alumni representatives available for local interview, call for details; 60 minutes.

**Campus Tours:** Conducted by students. M–F, select Sat.; call for available times; 60 minutes.

**Class Visits:** Prospective students may attend a class in their area of interest.

**Overnight Visits:** During the regular academic year, prospective applicants may spend an evening in a residence hall with a student host.

**Video:** Free on request.

## CAMPUS FACILITIES

**Science:** Samuel Mather Hall, Philip Mather Hall.

**Arts:** Bexley Hall, Bolton Dance Studio, Bolton Theater, Mayer Art Center.

**Athletic:** Wertheimer Fieldhouse, McBride Field, Ernst Athletic Recreation Convocation Center.

**Of Special Interest:** Chalmers Library, Olin Library, Church of the Holy Spirit.

## LOCAL ATTRACTIONS

The College Bookstore.

# MARIETTA COLLEGE
## Marietta, Ohio

**Contact:** Ms. Sharon Warden, Visit Coordinator, 215 Fifth Street, Marietta, OH 45750. *Phone:* toll-free 800-331-7896. *Fax:* 740-346-8888. *E-mail:* admit@marietta.edu *Web site:* http://www.marietta. edu/ *Visit location:* Admission Office, Admission House, 215 Fifth Street.

## QUICK FACTS

Enrollment: 1,280; UG: 1,209. Entrance: moderately difficult. SAT>500: 71% V, 66% M; ACT>18: 100%. Tuition and fees: $16,150. Room and board: $4586. Application deadline: 4/15.

## GENERAL

Independent, comprehensive, coed. Awards associate, bachelor's, and master's degrees. Founded 1835. Setting: 120-acre small-town campus. Undergraduate faculty: 109 (75 full-time, 34 part-time); student-faculty ratio is 12:1. Most popular recent majors: business administration, mass communications, education.

## CAMPUS VISITS

**College Calendar 1998–99:** *Regular classes:* Aug. 24–Dec. 11; Jan. 12–Apr. 26. *Breaks:* Nov. 21–29; Mar. 6–14. *Final exams:* Oct. 12–19; Apr. 27–30. *Special campus days:* Commencement, May 9; Homecoming, Oct. 17.

## VISIT OPPORTUNITIES

| | Appointments? | Who? |
|---|---|---|
| **Campus Tour** | recommended, not required | open to all |
| **Information Session** | recommended, not required | open to all |
| **Admission Interview** | recommended, not required | open to all |
| **Classroom Visit** | required | open to all |
| **Faculty Meeting** | required | open to all |
| **Overnight Visit** | required | applicants only |

**Information Sessions:** Call for schedule of Apr. information sessions for juniors.

**Interviews:** M–F, select Sat.; 60 minutes.

**Campus Tours:** Conducted by students. M–F 9:00 am–5:00 pm; select Sat. 9:00 am–12:00 pm; not available during breaks or late Dec.; 60 minutes.

**Class Visits:** Prospective students may attend a class in their area of interest.

**Overnight Visits:** During the regular academic year, prospective applicants may spend an evening in a residence hall with a student host.

**Video:** Free on request.

## CAMPUS FACILITIES

**Science:** Selby Science—Greenhouse.

**Arts:** Graphic Arts Computer Lab, Hermann Fine Arts Center, Hermann Gallery.

**Athletic:** McCoy Athletic Center, Baw Johnson Field House.

**Of Special Interest:** McDonough Center for Leadership and Business.

## LOCAL ATTRACTIONS

Valley Gem Sternwheel Boat Ride, historic Marietta, River Museum, Campus Martins History Museum.

# MIAMI UNIVERSITY
## Oxford, Ohio

**Contact:** Visit Coordinator, Admission Office, Oxford, OH 45056. *Phone:* 513-529-4632. *Fax:* 513-529-1550. *E-mail:* admission@muohio.edu *Web site:* http://www.muohio.edu/ *Visit location:* Office of Admission, Campus Avenue Building, 301 South Campus Avenue.

## QUICK FACTS

Enrollment: 16,190; UG: 14,594. Entrance: moderately difficult. SAT>500: 91% V, 94% M; ACT>18: 99%. Resident tuition and fees: $5512. Nonresident tuition and fees: $11,612. Room and board: $4810. Application deadline: 1/31.

## GENERAL

State-related, university, coed. Part of Miami University System. Awards bachelor's, master's, and doctoral degrees. Founded 1809. Setting: 2,000-acre small-town campus with easy access to Cincinnati. Undergraduate faculty: 1,290 (750 full-time, 540 part-time); student-faculty ratio is 18:1. Most popular recent majors: business marketing and marketing management, elementary education, zoology.

## CAMPUS VISITS

**College Calendar 1998–99:** *Regular classes:* Aug. 25–Dec. 11; Jan. 11–Apr. 30. *Breaks:* Oct. 16–18; Mar. 7–14; Nov. 25–29. *Final exams:* Dec. 14–18; May 3–7. *Special campus days:* Commencement, Dec. 18, May 9; Homecoming, Oct. 10; Parents Weekend, Oct. 30–31.

## VISIT OPPORTUNITIES

|  | Appointments? |
| --- | --- |
| **Campus Tour** | required |
| **Information Session** | required |
| **Admission Interview** | required |
| **Classroom Visit** | required |
| **Faculty Meeting** | required |
| **Overnight Visit** | required |

**Information Sessions:** M–F at 10:00 am, 2:00 pm; Sat. at 10:00 am; Sat. unavailable May through late Aug.; 60 minutes.

**Interviews:** M–F; 30 minutes.

**Campus Tours:** Conducted by students. M–F at 11:00 am, 3:00 pm; Sat. at 11:00 pm; Sat. unavailable May through late Aug.; 75 minutes.

**Class Visits:** Classroom visits are determined by the visit schedule.

**Overnight Visits:** During the regular academic year, prospective applicants may spend an evening in a residence hall with a student host.

**Video:** Available, fee charged.

## CAMPUS FACILITIES

**Science:** Pearson Hall (biological sciences); Appointment Required: Shideler Hall (geology), Upham Hall (zoology, herbarium).

**Arts:** Art Museum, Hiestand Hall, Art Building.

**Athletic:** Recreational Sports Center, Goggin Ice Arena, Millett Hall.

**Of Special Interest:** King Library, Conrad Formal Gardens/Dogwood Grove; Appointment Required: McGuffey Museum.

## LOCAL ATTRACTIONS
Hueston Woods State Park.

# OBERLIN COLLEGE
## Oberlin, Ohio

**Contact:** Leslie Curtis, Campus Visit Office, Oberlin, OH 44074-1090. *Phone:* toll-free 800-622-OBIE.

*Oberlin College (continued)*

*Web site:* http://www.oberlin.edu/ *Visit location:* Admissions Office, Carnegie Building, 101 North Professor Street.

## QUICK FACTS

Enrollment: 2,904; UG: 2,904. Entrance: very difficult. SAT>500: 98% V, 95% M; ACT>18: 99%. Tuition and fees: $22,438. Room and board: $6358. Application deadline: 1/15.

## GENERAL

Independent, 4-year, coed. Awards bachelor's degrees. Founded 1833. Setting: 440-acre small-town campus with easy access to Cleveland. Faculty: 339 (245 full-time, 94 part-time); student-faculty ratio is 12:1. Most popular recent majors: English, history, biology.

## CAMPUS VISITS

**College Calendar 1998–99:** *Regular classes:* Sept. 2–Dec. 14; Jan. 5–Feb. 1; Feb. 8–May 15. *Breaks:* Oct. 17–26; Mar. 20–29. *Final exams:* Dec. 18–22; May 19–23. *Admission office closed:* Dec. 20–Jan. 4. *Special campus days:* Commencement, May 31.

## VISIT OPPORTUNITIES

|  | Appointments? | Who? |
|---|---|---|
| **Campus Tour** | not required | open to all |
| **Information Session** | not required | open to all |
| **Admission Interview** | required | open to all |
| **Classroom Visit** | not required | open to all |
| **Overnight Visit** | required | open to all |

**Information Sessions:** M–F at 1:30 pm; Sat. at 11:00 am; 60 minutes.

**Interviews:** M–F, select Sat.; unavailable Sat. during summer; 30 minutes.

**Campus Tours:** Conducted by students. M–F at 10:00 am, 12:00 pm, 2:30 pm, 4:30 pm; select Sat. at 10:00 am, 12:00 pm; unavailable Sat. during summer; abbreviated schedule during breaks; 60 minutes.

**Class Visits:** Prospective students may attend a class in their area of interest.

**Overnight Visits:** During the regular academic year, prospective applicants may spend an evening in a residence hall with a student host.

## CAMPUS FACILITIES

**Arts:** Alla Art Museum.
**Athletic:** Philips Athletic Center.
**Of Special Interest:** Library, Conservatory of Music, Student Union, Student Residences.

# OHIO NORTHERN UNIVERSITY
## Ada, Ohio

**Contact:** Jane Crace, Executive Secretary, 525 South Main Street, Ada, OH 45810. *Phone:* 419-772-2260. *Fax:* 419-772-2313. *E-mail:* admissions-ug@onu.edu *Web site:* http://www.onu.edu/ *Visit location:* Office of Admissions, Student Personnel Center, 525 South Main Street.

## QUICK FACTS

Enrollment: 2,902; UG: 2,465. Entrance: moderately difficult. SAT>500: N/R; ACT>18: 99%. Tuition and fees: $19,815. Room and board: $4875. Application deadline: 8/15.

## GENERAL

Independent United Methodist, comprehensive, coed. Awards bachelor's and first professional degrees. Founded 1871. Setting: 260-acre small-town campus. Undergraduate faculty: 240 (179 full-time, 61 part-time); student-faculty ratio is 13:1. Most popular recent majors: pharmacy, mechanical engineering, elementary education.

## CAMPUS VISITS

**College Calendar 1998–99:** *Regular classes:* Sept. 8–Nov. 20; Nov. 30–Feb. 22; Mar. 8–May 21. *Breaks:* Nov. 21–29; Dec. 19–Jan. 4; Feb. 27–Mar. 7. *Final exams:* Nov. 16–20; Feb. 22–26; May 17–21. *Special campus days:* Commencement, May 23; Founders Day, Apr. 7; Homecoming, Oct. 17; Honors Day, May 5.

## VISIT OPPORTUNITIES

|  | Appointments? | Who? |
|---|---|---|
| **Campus Tour** | recommended, not required | open to all |
| **Information Session** | recommended | open to all |
| **Admission Interview** | recommended | open to all |
| **Classroom Visit** | recommended | open to all |
| **Faculty Meeting** | recommended | open to all |
| **Overnight Visit** | required | applicants only |

**Information Sessions:** M–F 8:00 am–4:30 pm; Sat. 8:00 am–12:00 pm; 45 minutes.

**Interviews:** M–F 8:00 am–4:30 pm; Sat. 8:00 am–12:00 pm; 45 minutes.

**Campus Tours:** Conducted by students. M–F 8:00 am–4:30 pm; Sat. 8:00 am–12:00 pm; 45 minutes.

**Class Visits:** Classroom visits are determined by the visit schedule.

**Overnight Visits:** During the regular academic year, prospective applicants may spend an evening in a residence hall with a student host.

**Video:** Free on request.

## CAMPUS FACILITIES

**Science:** Meyer Hall of Science, Biggs Engineering Building, Robertson-Evans Pharmacy Building, Nature Center (located in Tuscarawus County, Ohio).

**Arts:** Freed Center for the Performing Arts, Presser Hall of Music, Wilson Art Center and Elzay Gallery.

**Athletic:** ONU Sports Center.

**Of Special Interest:** McIntosh Student Center, Wesley Center Complex and English Chapel, Heterick Memorial Library, Pharmacy Museum located in Robertson-Evans Pharmacy Building.

## LOCAL ATTRACTIONS

Wilson Football Factory.

# THE OHIO STATE UNIVERSITY
## Columbus, Ohio

**Contact:** Admissions, Lincoln Tower, 3rd Floor, 1800 Cannon Drive, Columbus, OH 43210. *Phone:* 614-292-3980. *Fax:* 614-292-3240. *Web site:* http://www.ohio-state.edu/ *Visit location:* Student Visitor Center, 131 Enarson Hall, 154 West 12th Avenue.

## QUICK FACTS

Enrollment: 48,049; UG: 35,418. Entrance: moderately difficult. SAT>500: 76% V, 79% M; ACT>18: 94%. Resident tuition and fees: $3660. Nonresident tuition and fees: $10,869. Room and board: $5094. Application deadline: 2/15.

## GENERAL

State-supported, university, coed. Awards bachelor's, master's, doctoral, and first professional degrees and post-master's certificates. Founded 1870. Setting: 2,905-acre urban campus. Undergraduate faculty: 4,151 (2,930 full-time, 1,221 part-time); student-

faculty ratio is 12:1. Most popular recent majors: psychology, English, communications.

## CAMPUS VISITS

**College Calendar 1998–99:** *Regular classes:* Sept. 23–Dec. 4; Jan. 4–Mar. 12; Mar. 29–June 4. *Breaks:* Dec. 11–Jan. 3; Mar. 19–29. *Final exams:* Dec. 7–10; Mar. 15–18; June 7–10. *Admission office closed:* Nov. 27, Dec. 24, Jan. 18; Veteran's Day. *Special campus days:* Commencement, Dec. 11, Mar. 19, June 11.

## VISIT OPPORTUNITIES

| | Appointments? | Who? |
|---|---|---|
| **Campus Tour** | required | open to all |
| **Information Session** | required | open to all |
| **Admission Interview** | not required | open to all |
| **Faculty Meeting** | required | open to all |

**Information Sessions:** M–F at 9:00 am, 1:00 pm; select Sat. at 9:30 am; 60 minutes.

**Interviews:** M–F, select Sat.

**Campus Tours:** Conducted by students. M–F at 10:00 am, 2:00 pm; select Sat. at 10:30 am; 105 minutes.

**Video:** Free on request.

## CAMPUS FACILITIES

**Science:** Chadwick Arboretum; Appointment Required: Orton Geological Museum.

**Arts:** Ohio Union Galleries; Appointment Required: Wexner Center for the Arts, The Historic Costume and Textiles Collection.

**Athletic:** Ohio Stadium, Larkins Hall; Appointment Required: Woody Hayes Athletic Facility.

**Of Special Interest:** Ohio Union and Drake Union.

## LOCAL ATTRACTIONS

Downtown Columbus; Short North Area; German Village; Center for Science and Industry.

# OHIO UNIVERSITY
## Athens, Ohio

**Contact:** Office of Admissions, 120 Chubb Hall, Athens, OH 45701-2979. *Phone:* 740-593-4100. *Fax:* 740-593-0560. *Web site:* http://www.ohiou.edu/ *Visit location:* Office of Undergraduate Admissions, Chubb Hall, 120 Chubb Hall.

*Ohio University (continued)*

## QUICK FACTS

Enrollment: 19,564; UG: 16,481. Entrance: moderately difficult. SAT>500: 80% V, 78% M; ACT>18: 97%. Resident tuition and fees: $4275. Nonresident tuition and fees: $8994. Room and board: $4698. Application deadline: 2/1.

## GENERAL

State-supported, university, coed. Part of Ohio Board of Regents. Awards associate, bachelor's, master's, doctoral, and first professional degrees. Founded 1804. Setting: 1,700-acre small-town campus. Undergraduate faculty: 1,186 (852 full-time, 334 part-time); student-faculty ratio is 19:1. Most popular recent majors: biology, journalism, elementary education.

## CAMPUS VISITS

**College Calendar 1998–99:** *Regular classes:* Sept. 12–Nov. 17; Jan. 5–Mar. 12; Mar. 30–June 5. *Breaks:* Nov. 26–Jan. 2; Mar. 22–26. *Final exams:* Mar. 15–19; June 7–11. *Special campus days:* Commencement, June 12; Homecoming, Oct. 16–18; Parents Weekend, Nov. 6–8.

### VISIT OPPORTUNITIES

| | Appointments? | Who? |
|---|---|---|
| **Campus Tour** | recommended | applicants and parents |
| **Information Session** | recommended | |
| **Classroom Visit** | recommended | |
| **Faculty Meeting** | recommended | applicants and parents |

**Information Sessions:** M–F at 11:00 am, 1:00 pm; Sat. at 11:00 am; 60 minutes.

**Campus Tours:** Conducted by students. M–F at 10:00 am, 12:00 pm, 2:00 pm; Sat. at 12:00 pm; 60 minutes.

**Class Visits:** Prospective students may attend a class in their area of interest.

**Video:** Free on request.

## CAMPUS FACILITIES

**Science:** Appointment Required: Biological Sciences, Chemistry /Physics, Computer Science, College of Engineering.

**Arts:** School of Music, School of Theatre; Appointment Required: School of Art, School of Dance.

**Athletic:** Ping Recreation Center, Aquatic Center, Bird Ice Arena.

**Of Special Interest:** Appointment Required: School of Radio/TV, School of Journalism, College of Business.

## LOCAL ATTRACTIONS

Wayne National Forest, Caves, Waterfalls, Lakes.

# OHIO WESLEYAN UNIVERSITY
### Delaware, Ohio

**Contact:** Admissions Office, 61 South Sandusky Street, Delaware, OH 43015. *Phone:* 740-368-3020 or toll-free 800-922-8953. *Fax:* 740-368-3314. *E-mail:* owuadmit@cc.owu.edu *Web site:* http://www.owu.edu/ *Visit location:* Admission, Slocum Hall, 75 South Sandusky Street.

## QUICK FACTS

Enrollment: 1,870; UG: 1,870. Entrance: very difficult. SAT>500: 82% V, 85% M; ACT>18: 95%. Tuition and fees: $20,040. Room and board: $6370. Application deadline: 3/1.

## GENERAL

Independent United Methodist, 4-year, coed. Awards bachelor's degrees. Founded 1842. Setting: 200-acre small-town campus with easy access to Columbus. Faculty: 172 (122 full-time, 50 part-time); student-faculty ratio is 14:1. Most popular recent majors: zoology, psychology, business administration.

## CAMPUS VISITS

**College Calendar 1998–99:** *Regular classes:* Aug. 24–Dec. 10; Jan. 11–Apr. 29. *Breaks:* Oct. 10–12; Mar. 6–14; Nov. 21–29. *Final exams:* Dec. 12–17; May 1–6. *Admission office closed:* Dec. 24. *Special campus days:* Commencement, May 9; Fallfest (Homecoming), Oct. 30–Nov. 1; Monnett Weekend/Parents Weekend, Apr. 9–11.

### VISIT OPPORTUNITIES

| | Appointments? | Who? |
|---|---|---|
| **Campus Tour** | recommended | open to all |
| **Information Session** | recommended, not required | open to all |
| **Admission Interview** | recommended | open to all |
| **Classroom Visit** | required | open to all |
| **Faculty Meeting** | required | open to all |

## VISIT OPPORTUNITIES—*continued*

| | Appointments? | Who? |
|---|---|---|
| **Overnight Visit** | required | open to all |

**Information Sessions:** Select Sat. at 10:00 am, 11:00 am, 9:00 am; 50 minutes.

**Interviews:** M–F at 9:00 am, 11:00 am, 1:15 pm, 3:15 pm; Sat. available during fall and spring semester at 9:00 am, 10:00 am, 11:00 am; 50 minutes.

**Campus Tours:** Conducted by students. M–F at 9:45 am, 12:00 pm, 2:00 pm, 4:00 pm; Sat. available during fall and spring semester at 10:00 am, 11:00 am; 60 minutes.

**Class Visits:** Prospective students may attend a class in their area of interest.

**Overnight Visits:** During the regular academic year, prospective applicants may spend an evening in a residence hall with a student host.

**Video:** Free on request.

### CAMPUS FACILITIES

**Science:** Bigelow-Rice Hall, Stewart Hall; Appointment Required: Perkins Observatory.

**Arts:** Humphreys Art Hall.

**Athletic:** Branch Rickey Physical Education Center, Edwards Gymnasium and Pfeiffer Natatorium, Selby Stadium.

**Of Special Interest:** University Hall and Gray Chapel, Sanborn Hall (music), Hamilton-Williams Student Center.

### LOCAL ATTRACTIONS

Delaware County Arts Castle; Columbus Zoo.

# UNIVERSITY OF DAYTON
## Dayton, Ohio

**Contact:** Campus Visit Coordinator, 300 College Park, Dayton, OH 45469-1611. *Phone:* toll-free 800-837-7433. *Fax:* 937-229-4545. *E-mail:* admission@ udayton.edu *Web site:* http://www.udayton.edu/ *Visit location:* Office of Admission, St. Mary's Hall, 300 College Park.

### QUICK FACTS

Enrollment: 10,038; UG: 6,492. Entrance: moderately difficult. SAT>500: 79% V, 80% M; ACT>18: 98%. Tuition and fees: $14,670. Room and board: $4670. Application deadline: rolling.

### GENERAL

Independent Roman Catholic, university, coed. Awards bachelor's, master's, doctoral, and first professional degrees. Founded 1850. Setting: 110-acre suburban campus with easy access to Cincinnati. Undergraduate faculty: 772 (400 full-time, 372 part-time); student-faculty ratio is 14:1. Most popular recent majors: mass communications, elementary education, business marketing and marketing management.

### CAMPUS VISITS

**College Calendar 1998–99:** *Regular classes:* Aug. 26–Dec. 11; Jan. 4–Apr. 29. *Breaks:* Dec. 18–Jan. 3; Feb. 27–Mar. 7. *Final exams:* Dec. 12–18; May 1–7. *Special campus days:* Christmas on Campus, Dec. 8; Commencement (First Term), Dec. 19; Commencement (Second Term), May 9; Homecoming, Oct. 16–18; Parents Weekend, Nov. 6–8.

### VISIT OPPORTUNITIES

| | Appointments? | Who? |
|---|---|---|
| **Campus Tour** | recommended | open to all |
| **Admission Interview** | recommended | open to all |
| **Classroom Visit** | required | open to all |
| **Faculty Meeting** | required | open to all |
| **Overnight Visit** | required | open to all |

**Interviews:** M–F, Sat.; Sat. not available Jun., Jul., and Aug.; 45 minutes.

**Campus Tours:** Conducted by students. M–F 9:00 am–4:00 pm; Sat. at 10:00 am, 12:15 pm; Sat. not available Jun., Jul., and Aug.; 60 minutes.

**Class Visits:** Classroom visits are determined by the visit schedule.

**Overnight Visits:** During the regular academic year, prospective applicants may spend an evening in a residence hall with a student host.

**Video:** Free on request.

### CAMPUS FACILITIES

**Science:** Sherman Hall, Wohlleben Hall, William S. Anderson Information Sciences Center; Appointment Required: Kettering Labs.

**Arts:** Rike Center for Fine Arts, Music/Theatre Building; Appointment Required: Sears Recital Hall, Boll Theatre.

**Athletic:** Physical Activities Center, Frericks Center.

**Of Special Interest:** Appointment Required: Residence Halls.

*University of Dayton (continued)*

## LOCAL ATTRACTIONS

Dayton Art Institute; Air Force Museum; Sun Watch Prehistoric Indian Village; Dayton Museum of Discovery.

# UNIVERSITY OF TOLEDO
## Toledo, Ohio

**Contact:** Mary Schneider, Campus Visit Coordinator, University of Toledo, Stranahan Hall 2030, Toledo, OH 43606. *Phone:* toll-free 800-5TOLEDO (in-state). *Fax:* 419-530-4504. *E-mail:* enroll@utnet. utoledo.edu *Web site:* http://www.utoledo.edu/ *Visit location:* Office of Undergraduate Admission, Stranahan Hall 2030, 2801 West Bancroft Street.

## QUICK FACTS

Enrollment: 19,546; UG: 16,150. Entrance: noncompetitive. SAT>500: 66% V, 65% M; ACT>18: 87%. Resident tuition and fees: $3952. Nonresident tuition and fees: $9544. Room and board: $4194. Application deadline: rolling.

## GENERAL

State-supported, university, coed. Awards associate, bachelor's, master's, doctoral, and first professional degrees. Founded 1872. Setting: 407-acre suburban campus with easy access to Detroit. Undergraduate faculty: 1,346 (843 full-time, 503 part-time); student-faculty ratio is 20:1. Most popular recent majors: mass communications, business marketing and marketing management.

## CAMPUS VISITS

**College Calendar 1998–99:** *Regular classes:* Aug. 26–Dec. 10; Jan. 10–Apr. 28. *Breaks:* Nov. 24–28; Mar. 6–10. *Final exams:* Dec. 13–17; May 1–5. *Admission office closed:* Nov. 27, Dec. 24. *Special campus days:* Commencement, Dec. 12, May 6; Fall Campus Open House, Oct. 30–31; Homecoming, Oct. 3.

## VISIT OPPORTUNITIES

| | Appointments? | Who? |
|---|---|---|
| **Campus Tour** | recommended, not required | open to all |
| **Information Session** | recommended, not required | open to all |
| **Admission Interview** | recommended, not required | open to all |

| | Appointments? | Who? |
|---|---|---|
| **Classroom Visit** | required | open to all |
| **Faculty Meeting** | required | open to all |
| **Overnight Visit** | required | open to all |

**Information Sessions:** Fri.; select Sat.; call for dates and times; 45 minutes.

**Interviews:** Mon., Tue., Wed., Thu.; 45 minutes.

**Campus Tours:** Conducted by students. M–F, select Sat.; call for times; 75 minutes.

**Class Visits:** Classroom visits are determined by the visit schedule.

**Overnight Visits:** During the regular academic year, prospective applicants may spend an evening in a residence hall with a student host.

## CAMPUS FACILITIES

**Science:** Appointment Required: College of Engineering, College of Pharmacy.

**Arts:** Appointment Required: Center for Visual Arts.

**Of Special Interest:** Student Recreation Center.

# XAVIER UNIVERSITY
## Cincinnati, Ohio

**Contact:** Nancy Broxterman, Campus Visit Coordinator, 3800 Victory Parkway, Cincinnati, OH 45207-5311. *Phone:* toll-free 800-344-4698 Ext. 2940. *Fax:* 513-745-4319. *E-mail:* broxtcr@admin.xu.edu *Web site:* http://www.xu.edu/ *Visit location:* Office of Admission, Buschmann Hall, 3800 Victory Parkway.

## QUICK FACTS

Enrollment: 6,180; UG: 3,591. Entrance: moderately difficult. SAT>500: 79% V, 77% M; ACT>18: 98%. Tuition and fees: $14,520. Room and board: $5900. Application deadline: rolling.

## GENERAL

Independent Roman Catholic, comprehensive, coed. Awards associate, bachelor's, master's, and doctoral degrees. Founded 1831. Setting: 100-acre suburban campus. Undergraduate faculty: 530 (252 full-time, 278 part-time); student-faculty ratio is 7:1. Most popular recent majors: business administration, education, liberal arts and studies.

## CAMPUS VISITS

**College Calendar 1998–99:** *Regular classes:* Aug. 26–Dec. 11; Jan. 11–Apr. 30. *Breaks:* Oct. 8–9; Mar. 1–7; Apr. 1–5. *Final exams:* Dec. 12–17; May 1–6. *Special campus days:* Commencement, Dec. 17, May 15; Homecoming, Nov. 21–22; Midnight Madness, Oct. 16.

## VISIT OPPORTUNITIES

|  | Appointments? | Who? |
| --- | --- | --- |
| **Campus Tour** | recommended | open to all |
| **Information Session** | recommended | open to all |
| **Admission Interview** | required | open to all |
| **Classroom Visit** | required | applicants only |
| **Faculty Meeting** | required | open to all |
| **Overnight Visit** | required | admitted applicants only |

**Information Sessions:** Select Sat.; call for available schedule; 45 minutes.

**Interviews:** M–F, select Sat.; 45 minutes.

**Campus Tours:** Conducted by students. M–F, select Sat.; 60 minutes.

**Class Visits:** Prospective students may attend a class in their area of interest.

**Overnight Visits:** During the regular academic year, prospective applicants may spend an evening in a residence hall with a student host.

**Video:** Free on request.

## CAMPUS FACILITIES

**Of Special Interest:** McDonald Library.

# OKLAHOMA

## OKLAHOMA CITY UNIVERSITY
### Oklahoma City, Oklahoma

**Contact:** Undergraduate Admissions Office, 2501 North Blackwelder, Oklahoma City, OK 73106. *Phone:* toll-free 800-633-7242 Ext. 1. *Fax:* 405-521-5916. *E-mail:* uadmissions@frodo.okcu.edu *Web site:* http://www.okcu.edu/ *Visit location:* Undergraduate Admissions, Clara E. Jones Administration Building, Room 320, 2501 North Blackwelder.

## QUICK FACTS

Enrollment: 4,323; UG: 2,174. Entrance: moderately difficult. SAT>500: 72% V, 79% M; ACT>18: 96%. Tuition and fees: $8512. Room and board: $3990. Application deadline: rolling.

## GENERAL

Independent United Methodist, comprehensive, coed. Awards bachelor's, master's, and first professional degrees. Founded 1904. Setting: 68-acre urban campus. Undergraduate faculty: 355 (177 full-time, 178 part-time); student-faculty ratio is 14:1. Most popular recent majors: business administration, dance, mass communications.

## CAMPUS VISITS

**College Calendar 1998–99:** *Regular classes:* Aug. 19–Dec. 3; Jan. 12–Apr. 29. *Breaks:* Oct. 12–13; Mar. 15–19; Nov. 25–29; Apr. 2. *Final exams:* Dec. 7–11; May 3–7. *Admission office closed:* Apr. 2. *Special campus days:* Commencement, May 8.

## VISIT OPPORTUNITIES

|  | Appointments? | Who? |
| --- | --- | --- |
| **Campus Tour** | required | open to all |
| **Information Session** | required | open to all |
| **Admission Interview** | required | open to all |
| **Classroom Visit** | required | open to all |
| **Faculty Meeting** | required | open to all |
| **Overnight Visit** |  | open to all |

**Information Sessions:** M–F 8:00 am–5:00 pm.

**Interviews:** M–F; 90 minutes.

**Campus Tours:** Conducted by admission reps. M–F.

**Class Visits:** Prospective students may attend a class in their area of interest.

**Overnight Visits:** During the regular academic year, prospective applicants may spend an evening in a residence hall.

**Video:** Free on request.

## CAMPUS FACILITIES

**Of Special Interest:** Dulaney Brown Library.

## LOCAL ATTRACTIONS

National Cowboy Hall of Fame.; Omniplex Museum.

# OKLAHOMA STATE UNIVERSITY
## Stillwater, Oklahoma

**Contact:** Dr. Larry Kruse, Director, High School and College Relations, 210 Student Union, Stillwater, OK 74078. *Phone:* 405-744-5358 or toll-free 800-233-5019 (in-state), 800-852-1255 (out-of-state). *Fax:* 405-744-7092. *Web site:* http://www.okstate.edu/ *Visit location:* High School and College Relations, Student Union, 210 Student Union.

### QUICK FACTS

Enrollment: 19,282; UG: 14,664. Entrance: moderately difficult. SAT>500: 78% V, 77% M; ACT>18: 95%. Resident tuition and fees: $2357. Nonresident tuition and fees: $6377. Room and board: $4344. Application deadline: rolling.

### GENERAL

State-supported, university, coed. Part of Oklahoma State University. Awards bachelor's, master's, doctoral, and first professional degrees. Founded 1890. Setting: 840-acre small-town campus with easy access to Oklahoma City and Tulsa. Undergraduate faculty: 1,173 (1,066 full-time, 107 part-time); student-faculty ratio is 18:1. Most popular recent majors: education, management information systems/business data processing, business marketing and marketing management.

### CAMPUS VISITS

**College Calendar 1998–99:** *Regular classes:* Aug. 17–Dec. 11; Jan. 11–May 7. *Breaks:* Oct. 10–13; Mar. 15–19. *Final exams:* Dec. 7–11; May 3–7. *Admission office closed:* Dec. 23–Jan. 2.

#### VISIT OPPORTUNITIES

|  | Appointments? | Who? |
| --- | --- | --- |
| **Campus Tour** | recommended | open to all |
| **Information Session** | recommended | open to all |
| **Admission Interview** | recommended | open to all |
| **Classroom Visit** | required | |
| **Overnight Visit** | required | |

**Information Sessions:** M–F 8:00 am–5:00 pm; Sat. 9:00 am–12:00 pm; 45 minutes.

**Interviews:** M–F, Sat.; unavailable during holidays; 90 minutes.

**Campus Tours:** Conducted by students and admission reps. M–F at 11:00 am, 1:30 pm; Sat. at 11:00 am; 60 minutes.

**Class Visits:** Prospective students may attend a class in their area of interest.

**Overnight Visits:** During the regular academic year and over the summer, prospective applicants may spend an evening in a residence hall.

### CAMPUS FACILITIES

**Science:** Appointment Required: Noble Research Center, Laser Lab.

**Arts:** Seretean Center; Appointment Required: Bartlett Center.

**Athletic:** Appointment Required: Gallagher-Iba Arena.

**Of Special Interest:** Appointment Required: Veterinary Medicine Teaching Hospital, College of Osteopathic Medicine.

# ORAL ROBERTS UNIVERSITY
## Tulsa, Oklahoma

**Contact:** Reuben Maher, Visitation Coordinator, 7777 South Lewis Avenue, Tulsa, OK 74171-0001. *Phone:* 918-495-7429 or toll-free 800-678-8876 (out-of-state). *Fax:* 918-495-6222. *E-mail:* rmaher@oru.edu *Web site:* http://www.oru.edu/ *Visit location:* Admissions Office, Graduate Center Building, 7777 South Lewis Avenue.

### QUICK FACTS

Enrollment: 3,966; UG: 3,229. Entrance: moderately difficult. SAT>500: 61% V, 42% M; ACT>18: N/R. Tuition and fees: $10,460. Room and board: $4728. Application deadline: rolling.

### GENERAL

Independent interdenominational, university, coed. Awards bachelor's, master's, and doctoral degrees. Founded 1963. Setting: 500-acre urban campus. Undergraduate faculty: 223 (187 full-time, 36 part-time); student-faculty ratio is 16:1. Most popular recent majors: business administration, telecommunications, elementary education.

### CAMPUS VISITS

**College Calendar 1998–99:** *Regular classes:* Aug. 20–Dec. 11; Jan. 6–Apr. 23. *Breaks:* Oct. 16–26; Feb. 27–Mar. 8. *Final exams:* Dec. 14–19; Mar. 24–Apr. 1. *Special campus days:* Fall College Weekend, Nov. 6–8; Spring College Weekend, Mar. 26–28.

## VISIT OPPORTUNITIES

| | Appointments? |
|---|---|
| **Campus Tour** | recommended |
| **Admission Interview** | not required |
| **Classroom Visit** | required |
| **Faculty Meeting** | required |
| **Overnight Visit** | required |

**Interviews:** M–F; 30 minutes.

**Campus Tours:** Conducted by students and admission reps. M–F 8:00 am–4:30 pm; 40 minutes.

**Class Visits:** Prospective students may attend a class in their area of interest, classroom visits are determined by the visit schedule.

**Overnight Visits:** During the regular academic year, prospective applicants may spend an evening in a residence hall with a student host.

**Video:** Available, fee charged.

## CAMPUS FACILITIES

**Science:** Graduate Center Building.

**Arts:** Timke Barton Musical Building.

**Athletic:** Mabee Center, Kenneth Cooper Aerobic Facility.

**Of Special Interest:** Prayer Tower, Baby Mabee Center, Christ's Chapel.

# UNIVERSITY OF CENTRAL OKLAHOMA
## Edmond, Oklahoma

**Contact:** Stacy McNeiland, Director Prospective Student Services, 100 North University Drive, Edmond, OK 73034. *Phone:* 405-341-2980. *Fax:* 405-341-4964. *E-mail:* mcneilan@aixl.ucok.edu *Web site:* http://www.ucok.edu/ *Visit location:* Prospective Student Services/Scholarships, University Center, 100 North University Drive.

## QUICK FACTS

Enrollment: 13,928; UG: 11,288. Entrance: minimally difficult. SAT>500: N/R; ACT>18: 88%. Resident tuition and fees: $1806. Nonresident tuition and fees: $4161. Room and board: $2481. Application deadline: rolling.

## GENERAL

State-supported, comprehensive, coed. Part of Oklahoma State Regents for Higher Education. Awards bachelor's and master's degrees. Founded 1890. Setting: 200-acre suburban campus with easy access to Oklahoma City. Undergraduate faculty: 701 (386 full-time, 315 part-time); student-faculty ratio is 21:1. Most popular recent majors: liberal arts and studies, elementary education, nursing.

## CAMPUS VISITS

**College Calendar 1998–99:** *Regular classes:* Aug. 24–Dec. 11; Jan. 18–May 7. *Breaks:* Oct. 15–18; Mar. 15–21; Nov. 25–29. *Final exams:* Dec. 14–18; May 10–14. *Admission office closed:* spring break and fall break. *Special campus days:* Stampede week — first week of fall semester.

## VISIT OPPORTUNITIES

| | Appointments? | Who? |
|---|---|---|
| **Campus Tour** | recommended, not required | applicants and parents |
| **Information Session** | not required | open to all |
| **Admission Interview** | not required | open to all |
| **Classroom Visit** | recommended | open to all |
| **Faculty Meeting** | recommended, not required | open to all |

**Information Sessions:** M–F 8:00 am–5:00 pm; 60 minutes.

**Interviews:** M–F; 15 minutes.

**Campus Tours:** Conducted by students. M–F at 11:00 am, 1:00 pm, 3:00 pm; specific appointments available; 60 minutes.

**Class Visits:** Prospective students may attend a class in their area of interest, certain predetermined classrooms are open to visitors.

## CAMPUS FACILITIES

**Of Special Interest:** Max Chambers Library.

# UNIVERSITY OF OKLAHOMA
## Norman, Oklahoma

**Contact:** J.P Audas, Director of Prospective Student Services, 550 Parrington Oval, Norman, OK 73019. *Phone:* toll-free 800-234-6868. *Fax:* 405-325-7478.

*University of Oklahoma (continued)*

*E-mail:* ou-pss@ou.edu *Web site:* http://www.ou.edu/ *Visit location:* Visitor's Center, Jacobson Hall, 550 Parrington Oval.

## QUICK FACTS

Enrollment: 25,975; UG: 17,378. Entrance: moderately difficult. SAT>500: N/R; ACT>18: 96%. Resident tuition and fees: $2311. Nonresident tuition and fees: $6351. Room and board: $3800. Application deadline: 7/15.

## GENERAL

State-supported, university, coed. Awards bachelor's, master's, doctoral, and first professional degrees. Founded 1890. Setting: 3,200-acre suburban campus with easy access to Oklahoma City. Undergraduate faculty: 2,021 (1,672 full-time, 349 part-time); student-faculty ratio is 15:1. Most popular recent majors: management information systems/business data processing, accounting, psychology.

## CAMPUS VISITS

**College Calendar 1998–99:** *Regular classes:* Aug. 17–Dec. 4; Jan. 11–Apr. 30. *Breaks:* Nov. 25–29; Mar. 13–21. *Final exams:* Dec. 7–11; May 3–7. *Special campus days:* Commencement, May 8; Dad's Day, Oct. 31; Homecoming, Oct. 3; Mom's Day, Apr. 10.

## VISIT OPPORTUNITIES

|                     | Appointments?              | Who?        |
|---------------------|----------------------------|-------------|
| **Campus Tour**     | recommended, not required  | open to all |
| **Information Session** | required               | open to all |
| **Classroom Visit** | required                   | open to all |
| **Faculty Meeting** | required                   | open to all |
| **Overnight Visit** | required                   | open to all |

**Information Sessions:** M–F at 2:00 pm; Sat. at 9:30 am; 30 minutes.

**Campus Tours:** Conducted by students. M–F at 2:00 pm; Sat. at 9:30 am; 120 minutes.

**Class Visits:** Prospective students may attend a class in their area of interest, classroom visits are determined by the visit schedule.

**Overnight Visits:** During the regular academic year and over the summer, prospective applicants may spend an evening in a residence hall with a student host.

**Video:** Free on request.

## CAMPUS FACILITIES

**Science:** Sam Noble Oklahoma Museum of Natural History, Sarkeys Energy Center; Appointment Required: Human Genome Sequencing Research Center, Weather Research Center.

**Arts:** Fred Jones Jr. Museum of Art, Holmberg Hall, Rupel Jones Fine Arts Center, Catlett Music Hall.

**Athletic:** Oklahoma Memorial Stadium, Lloyd Noble Stadium, Mitchell Ball Park and Softball Facility.

**Of Special Interest:** Great Reading Room, Huston Huffman Physical Fitness Center; Appointment Required: History of Science Collection (Bizzell Library).

## LOCAL ATTRACTIONS

Brandt Park (Duck Pond); David A. Burr Park; Ada Lois Sipuel Fisher Garden; Gimeno Fountain; OU Golf Course; Campus Corner; Firehouse Art Center; The Jacobson House Art Center.

# OREGON

## LEWIS & CLARK COLLEGE
### Portland, Oregon

**Contact:** Visit Coordinator, 0615 SW Palatine Hill Road, Portland, OR 97219. *Phone:* toll-free 800-444-4111. *Fax:* 503-768-7055. *E-mail:* admissions@lclark.edu *Web site:* http://www.lclark.edu/ *Visit location:* Admissions, Manor House, 0615 SW Palatine Hill Road.

## QUICK FACTS

Enrollment: 3,023; UG: 1,858. Entrance: very difficult. SAT>500: 97% V, 96% M; ACT>18: 100%. Tuition and fees: $18,530. Room and board: $5770. Application deadline: 2/1.

## GENERAL

Independent, comprehensive, coed. Awards bachelor's, master's, and first professional degrees. Founded 1867. Setting: 115-acre suburban campus. Undergraduate faculty: 283 (151 full-time, 132 part-time); student-faculty ratio is 14:1. Most popular recent majors: international relations, psychology, biology.

## CAMPUS VISITS

**College Calendar 1998–99:** *Regular classes:* Sept. 1–Dec. 9; Jan. 11–Apr. 21. *Breaks:* Dec. 19–Jan. 11;

Mar. 20–28. *Final exams:* Dec. 14–18; Apr. 29–30. *Special campus days:* Commencement, May 2; Fall Open House.

## VISIT OPPORTUNITIES

|  | Appointments? | Who? |
|---|---|---|
| **Campus Tour** | recommended, not required | open to all |
| **Information Session** | recommended, not required | open to all |
| **Admission Interview** | required | open to all |
| **Classroom Visit** | required | open to all |
| **Overnight Visit** | required | applicants only |

**Information Sessions:** M–F; follows campus tour; Sat. by appointment; 30 minutes.

**Interviews:** M–F, Sat.; during Feb. and Mar. available to merit scholarship nominees and Early Action deferred applicants; 30 minutes.

**Campus Tours:** Conducted by students. M–F at 9:00 am, 3:00 pm; Sat. at 10:15 am by appointment only.

**Class Visits:** Prospective students may attend a class in their area of interest, classroom visits are determined by the visit schedule.

**Overnight Visits:** During the regular academic year, prospective applicants may spend an evening in a residence hall with a student host.

## CAMPUS FACILITIES

**Science:** Olin Physics/Chemistry Building, Biology, Psychology Building.

**Arts:** Fields Fine Arts Center, Gallery of Contemporary Art in Watzek Library, Agnes Flanagan Chapel, Evans Music Building, Fir Acres Theater.

**Athletic:** Pamplin Sports Center, Griswold Stadium, Zehntbauer Swimming Pavilion.

**Of Special Interest:** Templeton Student Center, Aubrey Watzek Library, Miller Humanities Building.

## LOCAL ATTRACTIONS

Downtown Portland, Tryon Creek State Park, Lower Campus and formal rose gardens.

# LINFIELD COLLEGE
## McMinnville, Oregon

**Contact:** Tami Harrell, Campus Visit Coordinator, 900 SE Baker Street, McMinnville, OR 97128. *Phone:*

toll-free 800-640-2287. *Fax:* 503-434-2472. *E-mail:* admissions@linfield.edu *Web site:* http://www.linfield.edu/ *Visit location:* Office of Admissions, Michelbook House, 450 Linfield Avenue.

## QUICK FACTS
Enrollment: 2,692; UG: 2,692. Entrance: moderately difficult. SAT>500: 73% V, 78% M; ACT>18: 100%. Tuition and fees: $16,960. Room and board: $5180. Application deadline: 2/15.

## GENERAL
Independent American Baptist, 4-year, coed. Awards bachelor's degrees. Founded 1849. Setting: 74-acre small-town campus with easy access to Portland. Most popular recent majors: business administration, elementary education, biology.

## CAMPUS VISITS
**College Calendar 1998–99:** *Regular classes:* Sept. 2–Dec. 14; Jan. 4–29; Feb. 8–May 21. *Breaks:* Oct. 26–27; Mar. 22–26; Nov. 26–27. *Final exams:* Dec. 16–19; May 25–28. *Special campus days:* Fall Commencement, Dec. 20; Homecoming, Oct. 10–11; Parent's Weekend, Oct. 3–4; Spring Commencement Weekend, May 29–30.

## VISIT OPPORTUNITIES

|  | Appointments? | Who? |
|---|---|---|
| **Campus Tour** | not required | open to all |
| **Information Session** | recommended | open to all |
| **Admission Interview** | recommended | open to all |
| **Classroom Visit** | required | open to all |
| **Faculty Meeting** | required | open to all |
| **Overnight Visit** | required | open to all |

**Information Sessions:** M–F; during academic year; 60 minutes.

**Interviews:** M–F; Sat. by appointment; 45 minutes.

**Campus Tours:** Conducted by students and admission reps. M–F, Sat.; M–F during summer and school holidays and vacations; 60 minutes.

**Class Visits:** Prospective students may attend a class in their area of interest.

**Overnight Visits:** During the regular academic year, prospective applicants may spend an evening in a residence hall with a student host.

## CAMPUS FACILITIES
**Of Special Interest:** Emanuel Northup Library.

*Linfield College (continued)*

## LOCAL ATTRACTIONS
Portland, Oregon and the beautiful Oregon coast; the Willamette Valley featuring many vineyards and wineries.

# OREGON STATE UNIVERSITY
## Corvallis, Oregon

**Contact:** Student Visitor Center, Tour (Team of Undergraduate Recruiters) Coordinator, 150 Kerr Administration Building, Corvallis, OR 97331. *Phone:* toll-free 800-291-4192 (in-state). *Fax:* 541-737-6157. *E-mail:* visit.osu@orst.edu *Web site:* http://www.orst. edu/ *Visit location:* Visitor Center, Admission and Orientation, Kerr Administration Building, 150 Kerr Administration Building.

## QUICK FACTS
Enrollment: 14,145; UG: 11,354. Entrance: moderately difficult. SAT>500: 59% V, 69% M; ACT>18: N/R. Resident tuition and fees: $3540. Nonresident tuition and fees: $11,808. Room and board: $5064. Application deadline: 3/1.

## GENERAL
State-supported, university, coed. Part of Oregon State System of Higher Education. Awards bachelor's, master's, doctoral, and first professional degrees. Founded 1868. Setting: 530-acre small-town campus with easy access to Portland. Undergraduate faculty: 2,204 (1,597 full-time, 607 part-time); student-faculty ratio is 8:1. Most popular recent majors: business administration, mechanical engineering, mass communications.

## CAMPUS VISITS
**College Calendar 1998–99:** *Regular classes:* Sept. 28–Dec. 4; Jan. 4–Mar. 12; Mar. 29–June 4. *Breaks:* Dec. 12–Jan. 3; Mar. 20–28. *Final exams:* Dec. 7–11; Mar. 15–19; June 7–11. *Special campus days:* Commencement, June 3; Homecoming, Oct. 17.

## VISIT OPPORTUNITIES

|  | Appointments? | Who? |
|---|---|---|
| **Campus Tour** | not required | open to all |
| **Information Session** | not required | open to all |
| **Admission Interview** | recommended, not required | open to all |

**VISIT OPPORTUNITIES**—*continued*

|  | Appointments? | Who? |
|---|---|---|
| **Classroom Visit** | recommended | open to all |
| **Faculty Meeting** | recommended | open to all |

**Information Sessions:** M–F, select Sat.; 30 minutes.

**Interviews:** M–F, select Sat.; 30 minutes.

**Campus Tours:** Conducted by students. M–F 8:00 am–4:00 pm; select Sat. 10:00 am–12:00 pm; 60 minutes.

**Class Visits:** Prospective students may attend a class in their area of interest.

**Video:** Free on request.

## CAMPUS FACILITIES
**Science:** Hatfield Marine Science Center in Newport; Appointment Required: McDonald Forest and Peary Arboretum, 3-D Biochemistry Classes.

**Arts:** Fairbanks Hall, Benton Hall, OSU Craft Center; Appointment Required: University Theatre.

**Athletic:** Dixon Recreation Center, Rock Climbing Center; Appointment Required: Valley Football Center.

**Of Special Interest:** Memorial Union, Valley Library.

# PACIFIC UNIVERSITY
## Forest Grove, Oregon

**Contact:** Christopher Sweet, Admissions Counselor and Campus Visit Coordinator, 2043 College Way, Forest Grove, OR 97116. *Phone:* toll-free 800-677-6712. *Fax:* 503-359-2975. *E-mail:* sweetcg@pacificu. edu *Web site:* http://www.pacificu.edu/ *Visit location:* Offices of Admissions, Knight Hall, College Way.

## QUICK FACTS
Enrollment: 1,821; UG: 1,053. Entrance: moderately difficult. SAT>500: 79% V, 79% M; ACT>18: 100%. Tuition and fees: $16,695. Room and board: $4564. Application deadline: 2/15.

## GENERAL
Independent, comprehensive, coed. Awards bachelor's, master's, doctoral, and first professional degrees. Founded 1849. Setting: 55-acre small-town campus with easy access to Portland. Undergraduate faculty: 204 (145 full-time, 59 part-time); student-

faculty ratio is 11:1. Most popular recent majors: biology, business administration, psychology.

## CAMPUS VISITS
**College Calendar 1998–99:** *Regular classes:* Aug. 31–Dec. 8; Jan. 4–25; Feb. 1–May 11. *Breaks:* Mar. 22–26. *Final exams:* Dec. 10–16; Jan. 25; May 13–19. *Admission office closed:* Holiday Break, Dec. 24–Jan. 1; Thanksgiving Holiday, Nov. 25–27. *Special campus days:* Commencement; Founders Week; Hawaiian Luau; Homecoming; Parents Weekend; Tom McCall Forum.

## VISIT OPPORTUNITIES

| | Appointments? | Who? |
| --- | --- | --- |
| **Campus Tour** | recommended | open to all |
| **Information Session** | required | open to all |
| **Admission Interview** | required | open to all |
| **Classroom Visit** | required | open to all |
| **Faculty Meeting** | required | open to all |
| **Overnight Visit** | required | open to all |

**Information Sessions:** M–F 9:00 am–4:00 pm; 60 minutes.

**Interviews:** M–F; 60 minutes.

**Campus Tours:** Conducted by students. Mon., Wed., Fri. at 11:00 am, 2:00 pm; Tue., Thu. at 11:00 am, 2:30 pm; 60 minutes.

**Class Visits:** Prospective students may attend a class in their area of interest.

**Overnight Visits:** During the regular academic year, prospective applicants may spend an evening in a residence hall with a student host.

## CAMPUS FACILITIES
**Science:** Appointment Required: Strain Science Center.

**Arts:** Kathrin Cawein Art Gallery, McCready Auditorium, Tom Miles Theatre.

**Athletic:** Swim Center, Pacific Athletic Center, Tom Reynolds Soccer Field.

**Of Special Interest:** Oregon Holocaust Resource Center, Old College Hall Museum.

## LOCAL ATTRACTIONS
Saturday Market, Powell's Bookstore, Pioneer Square—Portland, Mt. Hood, Columbia River Gorge, the Oregon coast.

# REED COLLEGE
### Portland, Oregon

**Contact:** Jessica Selig, Visit Coordinator, 3203 Southeast Woodstock Boulevard, Portland, OR 97202. *Phone:* toll-free 800-547-4750 (out-of-state). *Fax:* 503-777-7553. *E-mail:* admission@reed.edu *Web site:* http://www.reed.edu/ *Visit location:* Office of Admission, Eliot Hall, 3203 Southeast Woodstock Boulevard.

## QUICK FACTS
Enrollment: 1,298; UG: 1,276. Entrance: very difficult. SAT>500: 100% V, 98% M; ACT>18: N/R. Tuition and fees: $22,340. Room and board: $6200. Application deadline: 2/1.

## GENERAL
Independent, comprehensive, coed. Awards bachelor's and master's degrees. Founded 1909. Setting: 98-acre suburban campus. Undergraduate faculty: 121 (106 full-time, 15 part-time); student-faculty ratio is 10:1. Most popular recent majors: biology, English, psychology.

## CAMPUS VISITS
**College Calendar 1998–99:** *Regular classes:* Aug. 31–Dec. 9; Jan. 25–Apr. 30. *Breaks:* Oct. 17–25; Mar. 20–28; Dec. 18–Jan. 24. *Final exams:* Dec. 14–17; May 10–13. *Admission office closed:* Dec. 24–Jan. 4. *Special campus days:* Commencement, May 17; Fall Thesis Parade, Dec. 4; Spring Thesis Parade, Apr. 30; Thanksgiving, Nov. 26–29.

## VISIT OPPORTUNITIES

| | Appointments? | Who? |
| --- | --- | --- |
| **Campus Tour** | recommended | open to all |
| **Information Session** | recommended | open to all |
| **Admission Interview** | | open to all |
| **Classroom Visit** | | open to all |
| **Faculty Meeting** | | open to all |
| **Overnight Visit** | | open to all |

**Information Sessions:** M–F; 60 minutes.

**Interviews:** M–F; 30 minutes.

**Campus Tours:** Conducted by students. M–F; 60 minutes.

**Class Visits:** Classroom visits are determined by the visit schedule.

*Reed College (continued)*

**Overnight Visits:** During the regular academic year, prospective applicants may spend an evening in a residence hall with a student host.

## CAMPUS FACILITIES
**Science:** Appointment Required: Nuclear Reactor.
**Arts:** Appointment Required: Art Gallery.

## LOCAL ATTRACTIONS
Powells Books.

# SOUTHERN OREGON UNIVERSITY
## Ashland, Oregon

**Contact:** Office of Admissions, Southern Oregon University, Ashland, OR 97520. *Phone:* 541-552-6411 or toll-free 800-482-SOSC Ext. 6411 (in-state). *E-mail:* admissions@sou.edu *Visit location:* Office of Admissions, Britt Hall, Room 242.

## QUICK FACTS
Enrollment: 5,035; UG: 4,501. Entrance: moderately difficult. SAT>500: 65% V, 60% M; ACT>18: N/R. Resident tuition and fees: $3204. Nonresident tuition and fees: $9153. Room and board: $4380. Application deadline: rolling.

## GENERAL
State-supported, comprehensive, coed. Part of Oregon State System of Higher Education. Awards associate, bachelor's, and master's degrees. Founded 1926. Setting: 175-acre small-town campus. Undergraduate faculty: 219 (148 full-time, 71 part-time); student-faculty ratio is 18:1.

## CAMPUS VISITS
**College Calendar 1998–99:** *Regular classes:* Sept. 28–Dec. 4; Jan. 4–Mar. 12; Mar. 29–June 4; June 21–Aug. 13. *Breaks:* Dec. 14–Jan. 3; Mar. 22–28; June 14–18; Aug. 16–Sept. 24. *Final exams:* Dec. 7–11; Mar. 15–19; June 7–11; Aug. 9–13.

## VISIT OPPORTUNITIES

|  | Appointments? | Who? |
| --- | --- | --- |
| **Campus Tour** | recommended, not required | open to all |
| **Information Session** | recommended | |

## VISIT OPPORTUNITIES—*continued*

|  | Appointments? | Who? |
| --- | --- | --- |
| **Admission Interview** | recommended | open to all |
| **Classroom Visit** | required | open to all |
| **Faculty Meeting** | required | open to all |
| **Overnight Visit** | required | open to all |

**Information Sessions:** M–F 9:00 am–4:00 pm; 15 minutes.

**Interviews:** M–F; 15 minutes.

**Campus Tours:** Conducted by students. M–F 9:00 am–4:00 pm; separate housing tours available: 30 minute tours of residence hall complexes; offered at hour and half-hour on weekdays; all tours available when classes are in session; 30 minutes.

**Class Visits:** Prospective students may attend a class in their area of interest.

**Overnight Visits:** During the regular academic year, prospective applicants may spend an evening in a residence hall.

## CAMPUS FACILITIES
**Science:** Appointment Required: Science Building.
**Arts:** Appointment Required: Theater Arts, Music, Art.
**Athletic:** Appointment Required: gymnasium and related facilities.
**Of Special Interest:** Appointment Required: radio station studios.

## LOCAL ATTRACTIONS
Shakespeare Festival, Lithia Park, Mt. Ashland, downtown Ashland.

# UNIVERSITY OF OREGON
## Eugene, Oregon

**Contact:** Donna Logan, Visit Coordinator Office of Admissions, 1217 University of Oregon, Eugene, OR 97403. *Phone:* toll-free 800-BEA-DUCK. *Fax:* 541-346-5815. *E-mail:* dlogan@oregon.uoregon.edu *Web site:* http://www.uoregon.edu/ *Visit location:* Office of Admission, 240 Oregon Hall.

## QUICK FACTS
Enrollment: 17,096; UG: 13,481. Entrance: moderately difficult. SAT>500: 74% V, 74% M; ACT>18:

N/R. Resident tuition and fees: $3408. Nonresident tuition and fees: $11,859. Room and board: $4646. Application deadline: 3/2.

## GENERAL
State-supported, university, coed. Part of Oregon State System of Higher Education. Awards bachelor's, master's, doctoral, and first professional degrees. Founded 1872. Setting: 250-acre urban campus. Undergraduate faculty: 1,168 (777 full-time, 391 part-time); student-faculty ratio is 16:1. Most popular recent majors: business administration, psychology, journalism.

## CAMPUS VISITS
**College Calendar 1998–99:** *Regular classes:* Sept. 28–Dec. 4; Jan. 4–Mar. 12; Mar. 29–June 4. *Breaks:* Dec. 12–Jan. 3; Mar. 20–28; June 12–20. *Final exams:* Dec. 7–11; Mar. 15–19; June 7–11. *Admission office closed:* Martin Luther King, Jr. Day, Jan. 18. *Special campus days:* Commencement, June 12; Homecoming and Fall Parent's weekend, Oct. 23–25; Spring Family Weekend, May 15–17.

## VISIT OPPORTUNITIES

| | Appointments? | Who? |
|---|---|---|
| **Campus Tour** | recommended, not required | open to all |
| **Information Session** | recommended | open to all |
| **Admission Interview** | recommended, not required | open to all |
| **Classroom Visit** | recommended | open to all |
| **Faculty Meeting** | recommended | open to all |

**Information Sessions:** Call for available times.
**Interviews:** M–F, Sat.; 45 minutes.
**Campus Tours:** Conducted by students. M–F at 10:00 am, 2:00 pm; Sat. at 10:00 am; 60 minutes.
**Class Visits:** Prospective students may attend a class in their area of interest, classroom visits are determined by the visit schedule.
**Video:** Free on request.

## CAMPUS FACILITIES
**Science:** Willamette Hall, Science Library, Museum of Natural History.
**Arts:** Museum of Art, Laverne Krause Gallery—Lawrence Hall, Adell McMillan Gallery—Student Union.
**Athletic:** Esslinger Hall; Appointment Required: Casanova Athletic Center at Autzen Stadium.

**Of Special Interest:** Knight Library, Erb Memorial Union.

## LOCAL ATTRACTIONS
Fifth Street Public Market in Eugene The Oregon Coastline.

# UNIVERSITY OF PORTLAND
**Portland, Oregon**

**Contact:** Alisha Howe, Admissions Office, 5000 North Willamette Boulevard, Portland, OR 97203. *Phone:* 503-283-7147 or toll-free 800-227-4568 (out-of-state). *Fax:* 503-289-7399. *E-mail:* admissio@up.edu *Web site:* http://www.uofport.edu/ *Visit location:* Admissions, Waldschmidt Hall, 5000 North Willamette Boulevard.

## QUICK FACTS
Enrollment: 2,606; UG: 2,039. Entrance: moderately difficult. SAT>500: 81% V, 77% M; ACT>18: N/R. Tuition and fees: $15,520. Room and board: $4710. Application deadline: rolling.

## GENERAL
Independent Roman Catholic, comprehensive, coed. Awards bachelor's and master's degrees. Founded 1901. Setting: 125-acre suburban campus. Undergraduate faculty: 251 (138 full-time, 113 part-time); student-faculty ratio is 14:1. Most popular recent majors: business administration, education, nursing.

## CAMPUS VISITS
**College Calendar 1998–99:** *Regular classes:* Sept. 1–Dec. 11; Jan. 11–Apr. 2. *Breaks:* Oct. 12–13; Mar. 8–12. *Final exams:* Dec. 14–17; Apr. 26–29. *Admission office closed:* Good Friday, Apr. 2.

## VISIT OPPORTUNITIES

| | Appointments? | Who? |
|---|---|---|
| **Campus Tour** | recommended, not required | open to all |
| **Information Session** | required | open to all |
| **Classroom Visit** | required | open to all |
| **Faculty Meeting** | required | open to all |
| **Overnight Visit** | required | open to all |

**Information Sessions:** M–F, Sat. 9:00 am–4:00 pm; Sat. appointment available during academic year with exception of Christmas break; 60 minutes.

*University of Portland (continued)*

**Campus Tours:** Conducted by students. M–F at 10:30 am, 2:30 pm; Sat. at 10:30 am; 60 minutes.

**Class Visits:** Classroom visits are determined by the visit schedule.

**Overnight Visits:** During the regular academic year, prospective applicants may spend an evening in a residence hall with a student host.

**Video:** Free on request.

## CAMPUS FACILITIES

**Science:** Appointment Required: Engineering Building, Chemistry Annex, Science Building, Starr Observatory.

**Arts:** University Museum/Archives, Mago Hunt Center.

**Athletic:** Chiles Center, Pilot Stadium, Merlo Field.

**Of Special Interest:** Howard Hall, Pilot House.

## LOCAL ATTRACTIONS

International Rose Test Garden; Pioneer Place; Northwest District; Powell's Bookstore; Hawthorne District.

# WILLAMETTE UNIVERSITY
**Salem, Oregon**

**Contact:** Brenda Robinson, Admission Office, 900 State Street, Salem, OR 97301. *Phone:* 503-370-6303. *Fax:* 503-375-5363. *E-mail:* bjrobins@willamette.edu *Web site:* http://www.willamette.edu/ *Visit location:* Office of Admission, Willamette International Student House, 900 State Street.

## QUICK FACTS

Enrollment: 2,389; UG: 1,749. Entrance: very difficult. SAT>500: 95% V, 97% M; ACT>18: 100%. Tuition and fees: $20,290. Room and board: $5280. Application deadline: 2/1.

## GENERAL

Independent United Methodist, comprehensive, coed. Awards bachelor's, master's, and first professional degrees. Founded 1842. Setting: 72-acre urban campus with easy access to Portland. Undergraduate faculty: 237 (168 full-time, 69 part-time); student-faculty ratio is 12:1. Most popular recent majors: economics, political science, psychology.

## CAMPUS VISITS

**College Calendar 1998–99:** *Regular classes:* Sept. 1–Dec. 11; Jan. 19–May 4. *Breaks:* Nov. 25–30; Mar. 19–29; Dec. 19–Jan. 18. *Final exams:* Dec. 14–19; May 7–12. *Special campus days:* Baccalaureate and Commencement, May 16; Mid-Semester Day, Oct. 23.

## VISIT OPPORTUNITIES

|  | Appointments? |
|---|---|
| **Campus Tour** | recommended |
| **Information Session** | recommended |
| **Admission Interview** | recommended |
| **Classroom Visit** | recommended |
| **Faculty Meeting** | recommended |
| **Overnight Visit** | recommended |

**Information Sessions:** M–F; select Sat. in Oct., Nov., Mar., Apr. at 10:00 am; 50 minutes.

**Interviews:** M–F 8:00 am–5:00 pm; M–F in summer at 8:30 am–12:00 pm, 1:00 pm–4:30 pm; available in select cities Sept.–Jan.; 60 minutes.

**Campus Tours:** Conducted by students. M–F at 10:00 am, 11:30 am, 2:00 pm, 3:00 pm; M–F during summer at 10:00 am, 2:00 pm; 60 minutes.

**Class Visits:** Prospective students may attend a class in their area of interest.

**Overnight Visits:** During the regular academic year, prospective applicants may spend an evening in a residence hall with a student host.

## CAMPUS FACILITIES

**Science:** Olin Science Center.

**Arts:** Museum, Fine Arts Center.

**Athletic:** Sparks Athletic Complex.

**Of Special Interest:** Mark O. Hatfield Library, Tokyo International University of America.

## LOCAL ATTRACTIONS

State Capitol; Willamette River; historic downtown Salem.

# PENNSYLVANIA

# ALLEGHENY COLLEGE
**Meadville, Pennsylvania**

**Contact:** Megan K. Murphy, Director of Admissions, 520 North Main Street, Meadville, PA 16335. *Phone:*

toll-free 800-521-5293. *Fax:* 814-337-0431. *E-mail:* admiss@admin.alleg.edu *Web site:* http://www.alleg. edu/ *Visit location:* Admissions Office, Allegheny College, Schultz Hall.

## QUICK FACTS

Enrollment: 1,855; UG: 1,855. Entrance: very difficult. SAT>500: 94% V, 94% M; ACT>18: 97%. Tuition and fees: $19,360. Room and board: $4720. Application deadline: 2/15.

## GENERAL

Independent, 4-year, coed, United Methodist Church. Awards bachelor's degrees. Founded 1815. Setting: 254-acre small-town campus. Faculty: 199 (153 full-time, 46 part-time); student-faculty ratio is 12:1. Most popular recent majors: psychology, biology, environmental science.

## CAMPUS VISITS

**College Calendar 1998–99:** *Regular classes:* Sept. 3–Dec. 16; Jan. 20–May 4. *Breaks:* Oct. 17–20; Mar. 20–28; Nov. 25–29. *Final exams:* Dec. 18–22; May 7–11. *Special campus days:* Commencement, May 16; Fall Campus Visit Day, Oct. 31; Spring Campus Visit Day, Apr. 24.

## VISIT OPPORTUNITIES

|  | Appointments? | Who? |
|---|---|---|
| **Campus Tour** | recommended, not required | open to all |
| **Information Session** | recommended | |
| **Admission Interview** | recommended | open to all |
| **Classroom Visit** | recommended | open to all |
| **Faculty Meeting** | required | open to all |
| **Overnight Visit** | required | open to all |

**Information Sessions:** Select Sat. during fall semester; call for holiday schedule.

**Interviews:** M–F; Sat. 8:30 am–12:00 pm; 45 minutes.

**Campus Tours:** Conducted by students. M–F; Sat. until 12:00 pm; 60 minutes.

**Class Visits:** Prospective students may attend a class in their area of interest, certain predetermined classrooms are open to visitors, classroom visits are determined by the visit schedule.

**Overnight Visits:** During the regular academic year, prospective applicants may spend an evening in a residence hall with a student host.

## CAMPUS FACILITIES

**Science:** Doane Hall of Chemistry, Hall of Advanced Biology, Carr Hall of Mathematics and Physics.

**Arts:** Bowman, Penelec and Megahan Galleries, Doane Hall of Art, Governor Raymond P. Shafer Auditorium.

**Athletic:** Robertson Athletic Field Complex, Wise Sport and Fitness Center, Mellon Pool and Recreation Building.

**Of Special Interest:** Newton Observatory, Ford Memorial Chapel, Pelletier Library.

# ALLEGHENY UNIVERSITY OF THE HEALTH SCIENCES
### Philadelphia, Pennsylvania

**Contact:** Ms. Paula Greenberg, Director Admissions and Recruitment, MS 472, Broad and Vine Streets, Philadelphia, PA 19102. *Phone:* 215-762-4293. *Fax:* 215-762-6194. *E-mail:* greenbergp@auhs.edu *Web site:* http://www.auhs.edu/ *Visit location:* Admissions and Recruitment, SHP Building, 201 North 15th Street.

## QUICK FACTS

Enrollment: 3,106; UG: 968. Entrance: moderately difficult. SAT>500: N/R; ACT>18: N/R. Tuition and fees: $9660. Room only: $4800. Application deadline: rolling.

## GENERAL

Independent, university, coed. Awards associate, bachelor's, master's, doctoral, and first professional degrees and post-master's certificates. Founded 1848. Undergraduate faculty: 1,446 (1,319 full-time, 127 part-time); student-faculty ratio is 12:1. Most popular recent majors: physician assistant, nursing.

## CAMPUS VISITS

**College Calendar 1998–99:** *Regular classes:* Aug. 31–Dec. 11; Jan. 25–May 7. *Breaks:* Dec. 18–Jan. 25; Mar. 29–31. *Final exams:* Dec. 14–18; May 10–14. *Special campus days:* Graduation, May 21.

## VISIT OPPORTUNITIES

|  | Appointments? | Who? |
|---|---|---|
| **Campus Tour** | recommended | |
| **Information Session** | recommended | |

*Allegheny University of the Health Sciences (continued)*

## VISIT OPPORTUNITIES—*continued*

|  | Appointments? | Who? |
|---|---|---|
| **Admission Interview** |  | applicants only |

**Information Sessions:** Open house twice a month; individual appointments available; 60 minutes.

**Campus Tours:** Conducted by admission reps. Open tours twice a month; individual appointments available; 60 minutes.

### CAMPUS FACILITIES

**Science:** Appointment Required: Hospital, Labs, Anatomy Lab.

**Athletic:** Exercise Room.

**Of Special Interest:** Library, Service Offices; Appointment Required: Residence Hall.

### LOCAL ATTRACTIONS

Historic Philadelphia.

## BRYN MAWR COLLEGE

### Bryn Mawr, Pennsylvania

**Contact:** Admissions Assistant, 101 North Merion Avenue, Bryn Mawr, PA 19010-2899. *Phone:* 610-526-5152 or toll-free 800-BMC-1885 (out-of-state). *Fax:* 610-526-7471. *E-mail:* admissions@brynmawr.edu *Web site:* http://www.brynmawr.edu/ *Visit location:* Office of Admissions, Ely House, 101 North Merion Avenue.

### QUICK FACTS

Enrollment: 1,811; UG: 1,238. Entrance: most difficult. SAT>500: 100% V, 97% M; ACT>18: N/R. Tuition and fees: $21,430. Room and board: $7500. Application deadline: 1/15.

### GENERAL

Independent, university, women only. Awards bachelor's, master's, and doctoral degrees. Founded 1885. Setting: 135-acre suburban campus with easy access to Philadelphia. Undergraduate faculty: 221 (152 full-time, 69 part-time); student-faculty ratio is 10:1. Most popular recent majors: biology, English, psychology.

### CAMPUS VISITS

**College Calendar 1998–99:** *Regular classes:* Aug. 31–Dec. 8; Jan. 18–Apr. 30. *Breaks:* Dec. 18–Jan. 18. *Final exams:* Dec. 11–18; May 5–14.

### VISIT OPPORTUNITIES

|  | Appointments? | Who? |
|---|---|---|
| **Campus Tour** | required | open to all |
| **Information Session** | required | open to all |
| **Admission Interview** | required | open to all |
| **Classroom Visit** | recommended | open to all |
| **Faculty Meeting** | required | open to all |
| **Overnight Visit** |  | open to all |

**Information Sessions:** Mon. at 10:00 am, 2:00 pm; Fri. at 10:00 am, 2:00 pm; 45 minutes.

**Interviews:** Mon., Wed., Fri.; Thu.; Sat. interviews available Sept. through Jan.; 45 minutes.

**Campus Tours:** Conducted by students. M–F 9:00 am–4:00 pm; select Sat.; select Sat. Sept. through Jan. at 10:00 am, 11:00 am, 12:00 pm, 1:00 pm; 60 minutes.

**Class Visits:** Prospective students may attend a class in their area of interest, certain predetermined classrooms are open to visitors.

**Overnight Visits:** During the regular academic year, prospective applicants may spend an evening in a residence hall with a student host.

### CAMPUS FACILITIES

**Science:** New Chemistry Wing.

**Of Special Interest:** Erdman Residence Hall—designed by Louis Kahn, Rhys Carpenter Library, Thomas Library—on the National Historic Register.

### LOCAL ATTRACTIONS

Philadelphia—Art Museum, Independence Hall/Historic area; Valley Forge.

## BUCKNELL UNIVERSITY

### Lewisburg, Pennsylvania

**Contact:** Office of Admissions, Freas Hall, Lewisburg, PA 17837. *Phone:* 717-524-1101. *Fax:* 717-524-3538. *E-mail:* admissions@bucknell.edu *Web site:* http://www.bucknell.edu/ *Visit location:* Admissions, Freas Hall.

## QUICK FACTS

Enrollment: 3,496; UG: 3,329. Entrance: very difficult. SAT>500: 96% V, 97% M; ACT>18: N/R. Tuition and fees: $21,210. Room and board: $5200. Application deadline: 1/1.

## GENERAL

Independent, comprehensive, coed. Awards bachelor's and master's degrees. Founded 1846. Setting: 393-acre small-town campus. Undergraduate faculty: 280 (261 full-time, 19 part-time); student-faculty ratio is 13:1. Most popular recent majors: biology, economics, business administration.

## CAMPUS VISITS

**College Calendar 1998–99:** *Regular classes:* Aug. 26–Dec. 8; Jan. 13–Apr. 27. *Breaks:* Oct. 9–14; Mar. 5–15; Nov. 24–30. *Final exams:* Dec. 10–17; Apr. 29–May 6. *Special campus days:* Commencement, May 16; Homecoming, Oct. 24; Parent's Weekend, Sept. 25–26; Reunion, June 3; Spring Weekend, Apr. 9–10.

## VISIT OPPORTUNITIES

|  | Appointments? | Who? |
|---|---|---|
| **Campus Tour** | not required | open to all |
| **Information Session** | recommended | open to all |
| **Admission Interview** | required | open to all |
| **Classroom Visit** | recommended | open to all |
| **Faculty Meeting** | recommended | open to all |
| **Overnight Visit** | required | open to all |

**Information Sessions:** Available when personal interview schedule is full; group sessions Sept. through Jan.; most Mon., Fri. during Jul., Aug., and high school holidays; 45 minutes.

**Interviews:** M–F, select Sat.; offered from mid-Apr. of student's junior year through Jan. of senior year; Sat. available Sept. through Jan.; 45 minutes.

**Campus Tours:** Conducted by students. M–F at 10:30 am, 11:15 am, 12:15 pm, 1:15 pm, 2:15 pm, 3:30 pm; select Sat.; select Sat. Sept. through May at 10:30 am, 11:15 am, 12:00 pm; M–F Jun.–Aug. the 4:15 pm tour is unavailable; 75 minutes.

**Class Visits:** Classroom visits are determined by the visit schedule.

**Overnight Visits:** During the regular academic year, prospective applicants may spend an evening in a residence hall with a student host.

## CAMPUS FACILITIES

**Science:** Dana Engineering, Rooke Chemistry/Biology Buildings; Appointment Required: Animal Behavior Lab.

**Arts:** Weis Center for the Performing Arts, Harvey Powers Theatre, Stadler Poetry Center, Center Gallery.

**Athletic:** Fieldhouse, Davis Gym, Freas-Rooke Pool, Christy Matthewson Memorial Stadium.

**Of Special Interest:** Langone Center, Rooke Chapel, Bertrand Library.

# CARNEGIE MELLON UNIVERSITY

**Pittsburgh, Pennsylvania**

**Contact:** Admission Office, 5000 Forbes Avenue, Pittsburgh, PA 15213. *Phone:* 412-268-2082. *Fax:* 412-268-7838. *E-mail:* undergraduate-admissions@andrew.cmu.edu *Web site:* http://www.cmu.edu/ *Visit location:* Admission Office, Warner Hall, 5000 Forbes Avenue.

## QUICK FACTS

Enrollment: 7,770; UG: 4,875. Entrance: very difficult. SAT>500: 94% V, 100% M; ACT>18: N/R. Tuition and fees: $20,375. Room and board: $6225. Application deadline: 1/15.

## GENERAL

Independent, university, coed. Awards bachelor's, master's, and doctoral degrees. Founded 1900. Setting: 103-acre urban campus. Undergraduate faculty: 810 (703 full-time, 107 part-time); student-faculty ratio is 9:1. Most popular recent majors: electrical/electronics engineering, computer science, business administration.

## CAMPUS VISITS

**College Calendar 1998–99:** *Regular classes:* Aug. 24–Dec. 5; Jan. 11–Apr. 30. *Breaks:* Dec. 16–Jan. 10; Mar. 29–Apr. 2. *Final exams:* Dec. 7–15; May 6–11.

## VISIT OPPORTUNITIES

|  | Appointments? | Who? |
|---|---|---|
| **Campus Tour** | recommended, not required | open to all |
| **Information Session** | required | open to all |
| **Admission Interview** | required | open to all |

*Carnegie Mellon University (continued)*

## VISIT OPPORTUNITIES—*continued*

|  | Appointments? | Who? |
|---|---|---|
| **Classroom Visit** | required | open to all |
| **Faculty Meeting** | required | admitted applicants only |
| **Overnight Visit** | required | open to all |

**Information Sessions:** Available in Apr., Jul., Aug.; 45 minutes.

**Interviews:** M–F, select Sat.; no interviews from mid-Jan. to Apr. 1; 45 minutes.

**Campus Tours:** Conducted by students. M–F, select Sat. at 9:30 am, 11:30 am, 1:30 pm, 3:30 pm; call for available schedule and cancellations; 60 minutes.

**Class Visits:** Prospective students may attend a class in their area of interest.

**Overnight Visits:** During the regular academic year, prospective applicants may spend an evening in a residence hall with a student host.

**Video:** Available, fee charged.

## CAMPUS FACILITIES

**Science:** Appointment Required: Science Labs.

**Arts:** Appointment Required: Concert Hall, Theatre, Studios.

**Athletic:** Gymnasium, Student Center.

## LOCAL ATTRACTIONS

Pittsburgh museums, shops, theaters, sporting events and concerts.

# DELAWARE VALLEY COLLEGE

**Doylestown, Pennsylvania**

**Contact:** Stephen Zenko, Director of Admissions, 200 East Butler Avenue, Doylestown, PA 18901. *Phone:* 215-489-2211 or toll-free 800-2DELVAL (in-state). *Fax:* 215-230-2968. *E-mail:* admitme@divalcol.edu *Visit location:* Admissions, Admissions Building, 700 East Butler Avenue.

## QUICK FACTS

Enrollment: 1,506; UG: 1,506. Entrance: moderately difficult. SAT>500: 51% V, 53% M; ACT>18: N/R. Tuition and fees: $14,929. Room and board: $5655. Application deadline: rolling.

## GENERAL

Independent, 4-year, coed. Awards associate and bachelor's degrees. Founded 1896. Setting: 600-acre suburban campus with easy access to Philadelphia. Faculty: 129 (81 full-time, 48 part-time); student-faculty ratio is 16:1. Most popular recent majors: business administration, ornamental horticulture, animal sciences.

## CAMPUS VISITS

**College Calendar 1998–99:** *Regular classes:* Aug. 31–Dec. 15; Jan. 21–May 7. *Breaks:* Dec. 22–Jan. 21. *Final exams:* Dec. 16–22; May 10–15. *Special campus days:* Commencement, May 22; Family Day, Oct. 16; Founders Day, Apr. 7; Homecoming, Oct. 2; Open House for High School Seniors, Nov. 8.

## VISIT OPPORTUNITIES

|  | Appointments? | Who? |
|---|---|---|
| **Campus Tour** | required | open to all |
| **Information Session** | required | open to all |
| **Admission Interview** | required | open to all |
| **Classroom Visit** | required | open to all |
| **Faculty Meeting** | required | open to all |
| **Overnight Visit** | required | open to all |

**Information Sessions:** Inquire for fall and spring schedules.

**Interviews:** M–F; 30 minutes.

**Campus Tours:** Conducted by students. M–F; 45 minutes.

**Class Visits:** Prospective students may attend a class in their area of interest.

**Overnight Visits:** During the regular academic year, prospective applicants may spend an evening in a residence hall with a student host.

## CAMPUS FACILITIES

**Science:** Mandell Science Building.

**Athletic:** Gymnasuim, Athletic Stadium.

**Of Special Interest:** Greenhouse Complex, Equine Center, Animal Facilities.

## LOCAL ATTRACTIONS

Historic Bucks County.

# DICKINSON COLLEGE
Carlisle, Pennsylvania

**Contact:** Admissions Office, PO Box 1773, Carlisle, PA 17013. *Phone:* toll-free 800-644-1773. *Fax:* 717-245-1442. *E-mail:* admit@dickinson.edu *Web site:* http://www.dickinson.edu/ *Visit location:* Admissions, Robert A. Waidner Admissions House, College and High Street.

## QUICK FACTS
Enrollment: 1,792; UG: 1,792. Entrance: very difficult. SAT>500: 91% V, 89% M; ACT>18: N/R. Tuition and fees: $21,600. Room and board: $5840. Application deadline: 2/15.

## GENERAL
Independent, 4-year, coed. Awards bachelor's degrees. Founded 1773. Setting: 103-acre suburban campus with easy access to Harrisburg. Faculty: 186 (149 full-time, 37 part-time); student-faculty ratio is 10:1. Most popular recent majors: political science, English, psychology.

## CAMPUS VISITS
**College Calendar 1998–99:** *Regular classes:* Sept. 2–Dec. 11; Jan. 20–Apr. 30. *Breaks:* Oct. 14–19; Mar. 12–22; Nov. 24–30. *Final exams:* Dec. 14–20; May 3–11. *Special campus days:* Alumni Weekend; Commencement, May 16; Homecoming, Oct. 23–25; Parents Weekend, Sept. 25–27.

## VISIT OPPORTUNITIES

|  | Appointments? | Who? |
|---|---|---|
| **Campus Tour** | not required | open to all |
| **Information Session** | recommended | open to all |
| **Admission Interview** | required | open to all |
| **Classroom Visit** | not required | open to all |
| **Overnight Visit** | required | open to all |

**Information Sessions:** Mon., Wed., Fri. during Dec. and Jan. at 1:30 pm; Sat. Sept. to Apr. at 9:00 am, 10:30 am except during campus holidays; 60 minutes.
**Interviews:** M–F; not available Mon., Wed., Fri. in Jan. and Mon. in Feb. or Mar. 1 to Mar. 15; 45 minutes.
**Campus Tours:** Conducted by students. M–F 9:00 am–4:00 pm; 60 minutes.
**Class Visits:** Prospective students may attend a class in their area of interest.

**Overnight Visits:** During the regular academic year, prospective applicants may spend an evening in a residence hall with a student host.

## CAMPUS FACILITIES
**Science:** Dana Hall of Biology, Jacob Tomb Scientific Building.
**Arts:** Emil R. Weiss Center for the Arts.
**Athletic:** Kline Life/Sports Learning Center.
**Of Special Interest:** Boyd Lee Spahr Library, Holland Union Building.

## LOCAL ATTRACTIONS
Carlisle Army War College.

# DREXEL UNIVERSITY
Philadelphia, Pennsylvania

**Contact:** Visitation Center, 3141 Chestnut Street, Philadelphia, PA 19104. *Phone:* 215-895-6727 or toll-free 800-2-DREXEL (in-state). *Fax:* 215-895-5939. *Web site:* http://www.drexel.edu/ *Visit location:* Office of Undergraduate Admissions, Main Building–Room #212, Corner of 32nd and Chestnut Streets.

## QUICK FACTS
Enrollment: 9,838; UG: 7,085. Entrance: moderately difficult. SAT>500: 77% V, 86% M; ACT>18: N/App. Tuition and fees: $15,048. Room and board: $7266. Application deadline: 3/1.

## GENERAL
Independent, university, coed. Awards bachelor's, master's, and doctoral degrees. Founded 1891. Setting: 38-acre urban campus. Undergraduate faculty: 832 (402 full-time, 430 part-time); student-faculty ratio is 15:1. Most popular recent majors: electrical/electronics engineering, accounting, finance.

## CAMPUS VISITS
**College Calendar 1998–99:** *Regular classes:* Sept. 21–Dec. 5; Jan. 4–Mar. 14; Mar. 29–June 5; June 21–Aug. 28. *Final exams:* Dec. 7–12; Mar. 15–20; June 7–12; Aug. 30–Sept. 4. *Special campus days:* Accepted Students Day, Apr. 18; Alumni Reunion Weekend, Apr. 30–May 1; Commencement, June 13; Convocation, Sept. 29; Fall Open House I, Oct. 18; Fall Open House II, Nov. 15; Scholars' Day I, Feb. 21; Scholars' Day II, Feb. 27; Scholars' Day III, Feb. 28; Spring Jam Weekend, June 4–6; Welcome Back Days, Sept. 17–20.

*Drexel University (continued)*

## VISIT OPPORTUNITIES

| | Appointments? | Who? |
|---|---|---|
| **Campus Tour** | recommended, not required | open to all |
| **Information Session** | recommended, not required | open to all |
| **Admission Interview** | recommended, not required | open to all |
| **Classroom Visit** | required | open to all |
| **Faculty Meeting** | recommended | open to all |
| **Overnight Visit** | required | applicants only |

**Information Sessions:** M–F at 10:00 am, 1:00 pm; Sat. at 10:00 am; 90 minutes.

**Interviews:** M–F; 30 minutes.

**Campus Tours:** Conducted by students. M–F at 12:30 pm, 1:30 pm; Sat. at 11:00 am; 60 minutes.

**Class Visits:** Prospective students may attend a class in their area of interest.

**Overnight Visits:** During the regular academic year and over the summer, prospective applicants may spend an evening in a residence hall with a student host.

**Video:** Free on request.

## CAMPUS FACILITIES

**Science:** Appointment Required: Disque Labs, Stratton Hall Labs.

**Arts:** Appointment Required: Nesbitt College of Design Arts Studios, Music Studio.

**Of Special Interest:** Residence halls.

# DUQUESNE UNIVERSITY
## Pittsburgh, Pennsylvania

**Contact:** Admissions Office, 600 Forbes Avenue, Pittsburgh, PA 15282. *Phone:* toll-free 800-456-0590. *Fax:* 412-396-5644. *E-mail:* admissions@duq2.cc.duq.edu *Web site:* http://www.duq.edu/ *Visit location:* Admissions Office, Administration Building, McAnulty Drive.

## QUICK FACTS

Enrollment: 9,498; UG: 5,570. Entrance: moderately difficult. SAT>500: 76% V, 74% M; ACT>18: 95%. Tuition and fees: $14,066. Room and board: $5978. Application deadline: 7/1.

## GENERAL

Independent Roman Catholic, university, coed. Awards bachelor's, master's, doctoral, and first professional degrees. Founded 1878. Setting: 43-acre urban campus. Undergraduate faculty: 672 (397 full-time, 275 part-time); student-faculty ratio is 16:1. Most popular recent majors: health science, business administration, pharmacy.

## CAMPUS VISITS

**College Calendar 1998–99:** *Regular classes:* Aug. 31–Dec. 21; Jan. 11–May 6. *Breaks:* Nov. 23–28; Mar. 8–13; Apr. 1–5. *Final exams:* Dec. 16–21; Apr. 30–May 6. *Admission office closed:* Christmas break, Dec. 24–Jan. 2; Easter Break, Apr. 1–2; Thanksgiving, Nov. 26–27; holy day, Aug. 15, Dec. 8, Nov. 1. *Special campus days:* Commencement, May 8, Dec. 22; Freshman Orientation, Aug. 25–30; Greek Carnival, Oct. 8–10; Homecoming, Oct. 9–11; Open Campus ("Duquesne Fest"), Aug. 2.

## VISIT OPPORTUNITIES

| | Appointments? | Who? |
|---|---|---|
| **Campus Tour** | required | open to all |
| **Information Session** | required | open to all |
| **Admission Interview** | required | open to all |
| **Classroom Visit** | required | open to all |
| **Faculty Meeting** | required | open to all |
| **Overnight Visit** | required | open to all |

**Information Sessions:** Unavailable holidays and holy days; held with information session.

**Interviews:** M–F, select Sat.; unavailable holidays and holy days; held with Information Session; 35 minutes.

**Campus Tours:** Conducted by students. M–F at 10:00 am, 12:00 pm, 2:00 pm; select Sat. at 10:00 am, 12:00 pm; no tours on holidays, holy days, final exam days or "study" days; 60 minutes.

**Class Visits:** Classroom visits are determined by the visit schedule.

**Overnight Visits:** During the regular academic year, prospective applicants may spend an evening in a residence hall with a student host.

**Video:** Available, fee charged.

## CAMPUS FACILITIES

**Arts:** Appointment Required: Duquesne Art Gallery.
**Athletic:** Appointment Required: Arthur J. Rooney Field.
**Of Special Interest:** A.J. Palumbo Center.

## LOCAL ATTRACTIONS

Pittsburgh area; Heinz Hall; Benedum Center; The Carnegie Museum; Three Rivers Stadium.

# EAST STROUDSBURG UNIVERSITY OF PENNSYLVANIA
## East Stroudsburg, Pennsylvania

**Contact:** Mr. Alan T. Chesterton, Director of Admission, 200 Prospect Street, East Stroudsburg, PA 18301. *Phone:* 717-422-3542. *Fax:* 717-422-3933. *E-mail:* undergrads@esu.edu *Web site:* http://www.esu.edu/ *Visit location:* Office of Admission, 216 Normal Street, 200 Prospect Street.

## QUICK FACTS

Enrollment: 5,544; UG: 4,678. Entrance: moderately difficult. SAT>500: 43% V, 39% M; ACT>18: N/R. Resident tuition and fees: $4322. Nonresident tuition and fees: $9678. Room and board: $3720. Application deadline: 3/1.

## GENERAL

State-supported, comprehensive, coed. Part of Pennsylvania State System of Higher Education. Awards associate, bachelor's, and master's degrees. Founded 1893. Setting: 183-acre small-town campus. Undergraduate faculty: 271 (254 full-time, 17 part-time); student-faculty ratio is 19:1. Most popular recent majors: elementary education, physical education, biology.

## CAMPUS VISITS

**College Calendar 1998–99:** *Regular classes:* Sept. 8–Dec. 22; Jan. 25–May 21. *Breaks:* Nov. 24–30; Mar. 19–Apr. 5. *Final exams:* Dec. 16–22; May 17–21. *Admission office closed:* Nov. 26–27, Dec. 25–Jan. 1, July 5. *Special campus days:* Celebration of ESU (one week), Oct. 25; Fall Commencement, Dec. 19; Family Day, Sept. 26; Hall of Fame Day, Oct. 24; Homecoming, Oct. 3; Open House, Nov. 7; Spring Commencement, May 22; Super Soccer Saturday, Oct. 10.

## VISIT OPPORTUNITIES

| | Appointments? | Who? |
|---|---|---|
| **Campus Tour** | required | open to all |
| **Information Session** | required | open to all |
| **Admission Interview** | required | open to all |
| **Classroom Visit** | required | open to all |
| **Faculty Meeting** | required | applicants and parents |

**Information Sessions:** Tue., Thu., select Sat. during fall semester; Tue. during spring semester; 60 minutes.
**Interviews:** M–F; 30 minutes.
**Campus Tours:** Conducted by students. Call for tour schedule; 90 minutes.
**Class Visits:** Prospective students should contact specific departments.

## CAMPUS FACILITIES

**Science:** Moore Biology Hall, Gessner Science Hall, DeNike Center for Human Services; Appointment Required: Observatory.
**Arts:** Fine and Performing Arts Center, Stroud Hall.
**Athletic:** Koehler Fieldhouse.
**Of Special Interest:** Kemp Library, University Center, Center for Hospitality Management, McGarry Communications Center Rosenkrans Hall; Appointment Required: Stony Acres.

## LOCAL ATTRACTIONS

Poconos vacation area.

# ELIZABETHTOWN COLLEGE
## Elizabethtown, Pennsylvania

**Contact:** W. Kent Barnds, Director of Admissions, 1 Alpha Drive, Elizabethtown, PA 17022. *Phone:* 717-361-1400. *Fax:* 717-361-1365. *E-mail:* admissions@acad.etown.edu *Web site:* http://www.etown.edu/ *Visit location:* Admissions, Leffler House, College Avenue and Mt. Joy Street.

## QUICK FACTS

Enrollment: 1,703; UG: 1,703. Entrance: moderately difficult. SAT>500: 78% V, 81% M; ACT>18: 81%. Tuition and fees: $16,930. Room and board: $4900. Application deadline: rolling.

*Elizabethtown College (continued)*

## GENERAL

Independent, 4-year, coed, Church of the Brethren. Awards bachelor's degrees. Founded 1899. Setting: 185-acre small-town campus with easy access to Baltimore and Philadelphia. Faculty: 164 (103 full-time, 61 part-time); student-faculty ratio is 13:1. Most popular recent majors: business administration, education, communications.

## CAMPUS VISITS

**College Calendar 1998–99:** *Regular classes:* Aug. 31–Dec. 11; Jan. 4–Apr. 30. *Breaks:* Oct. 3–6; Mar. 6–14; Nov. 26–29; Apr. 2–5. *Final exams:* Dec. 14–19; May 3–8.

## VISIT OPPORTUNITIES

| | Appointments? | Who? |
|---|---|---|
| **Campus Tour** | recommended | applicants and parents |
| **Admission Interview** | recommended | applicants and parents |
| **Classroom Visit** | required | applicants and parents |
| **Faculty Meeting** | required | applicants and parents |
| **Overnight Visit** | required | |

**Interviews:** M–F, select Sat.; individual interviews not available during Open Houses; Sat. appointments unavailable when school not in session; 45 minutes.

**Campus Tours:** Conducted by students. M–F, select Sat.; call for specific times; 60 minutes.

**Overnight Visits:** During the regular academic year, prospective applicants may spend an evening in a residence hall with a student host.

## CAMPUS FACILITIES

**Science:** Musser Hall-Chemistry-MolecVue.

**Arts:** Leffler Chapel and Performance Center-McCormick and Lyet Galleries, Zug Memorial Hall-Hess Gallery.

**Athletic:** Blue Jay Body Shop, Ira Herr Field.

**Of Special Interest:** Bucher Meetinghouse, Young Center for the study of Anabaptist and Pietist Groups.

## LOCAL ATTRACTIONS

Hershey Park; Masonic Homes, Elizabethtown; Amish Country; Ephrata Cloister; historic Harrisburg.

# FRANKLIN AND MARSHALL COLLEGE
**Lancaster, Pennsylvania**

**Contact:** Vicki L. Mumma, Campus Visit Coordinator, PO Box 3003, Lancaster, PA 17604-3003. *Phone:* 717-291-3951. *Fax:* 717-291-4389. *E-mail:* v_mumma@admin.fandm.edu *Web site:* http://www.fandm.edu/ *Visit location:* Admission Office, Wohlsen House, 637 College Avenue.

## QUICK FACTS

Enrollment: 1,807; UG: 1,807. Entrance: very difficult. SAT>500: 98% V, 99% M; ACT>18: 100%. Tuition and fees: $22,664. Room and board: $4906. Application deadline: 2/1.

## GENERAL

Independent, 4-year, coed. Awards bachelor's degrees. Founded 1787. Setting: 125-acre suburban campus with easy access to Philadelphia. Faculty: 172 (154 full-time, 18 part-time); student-faculty ratio is 11:1. Most popular recent majors: political science, English, biology.

## CAMPUS VISITS

**College Calendar 1998–99:** *Regular classes:* Sept. 2–Dec. 11; Jan. 12–Apr. 22. *Breaks:* Oct. 9–14; Feb. 26–Mar. 8. *Final exams:* Dec. 15–20; Apr. 26–May 1. *Special campus days:* Alumni Weekend, Oct. 24–25; Closer Look, Apr. 17; Commencement, May 9; Family Weekend, Oct. 31–Nov. 1; Junior Open House, Apr. 10; Science Building Dedication, Oct. 24–25.

## VISIT OPPORTUNITIES

| | Appointments? | Who? |
|---|---|---|
| **Campus Tour** | not required | open to all |
| **Information Session** | required | open to all |
| **Admission Interview** | required | open to all |
| **Classroom Visit** | required | open to all |
| **Faculty Meeting** | required | open to all |
| **Overnight Visit** | required | open to all |

**Information Sessions:** Select Sat. at 10:00 am; 60 minutes.

**Interviews:** M–F; limited interviews in Mar.; 40 minutes.

**Campus Tours:** Conducted by students. M–F at 10:00 am, 11:00 am, 2:00 pm, 3:00 pm; select Sat. at 11:00 am; individual and large group tours available by special arrangement; 60 minutes.

**Class Visits:** Prospective students may attend a class in their area of interest.

**Overnight Visits:** During the regular academic year, prospective applicants may spend an evening in a residence hall with a student host.

**Video:** Free on request.

**CAMPUS FACILITIES**
**Athletic:** Alumni Sports and Fitness Center.

**LOCAL ATTRACTIONS**
Lancaster's Central Market; Wheatland—Home of President Buchanan; Amish Country; Strasburg Railroad.

# GANNON UNIVERSITY
**Erie, Pennsylvania**

**Contact:** Linda Kish, Campus Visit Coordinator, 109 University Square, Erie, PA 16541-0001. *Phone:* toll-free 800-GANNON-U Ext. 7407. *Fax:* 814-871-5803. *E-mail:* admissions@mail1.gannon.edu *Web site:* http://www.gannon.edu/ *Visit location:* Office of Admissions, AJ Palumbo Academic Center, 824 Peach Street.

**QUICK FACTS**
Enrollment: 3,207; UG: 2,664. Entrance: moderately difficult. SAT>500: 62% V, 63% M; ACT>18: 74%. Tuition and fees: $12,994. Room and board: $4860. Application deadline: rolling.

**GENERAL**
Independent Roman Catholic, comprehensive, coed. Awards associate, bachelor's, and master's degrees. Founded 1925. Setting: 13-acre urban campus with easy access to Cleveland. Undergraduate faculty: 261 (165 full-time, 96 part-time); student-faculty ratio is 13:1. Most popular recent majors: nursing, biology, criminal justice studies.

**CAMPUS VISITS**
**College Calendar 1998–99:** *Regular classes:* Aug. 26–Dec. 18; Jan. 13–May 7. *Breaks:* Nov. 25–29; Feb.

27–Mar. 8; Apr. 1–5. *Final exams:* Dec. 14–18; May 3–7. *Special campus days:* Commencement (spring), May 9; Commencement (winter), Dec. 13; Freshman Convocation, Aug. 23; Homecoming, Oct. 10.

**VISIT OPPORTUNITIES**

|  | Appointments? | Who? |
|---|---|---|
| **Campus Tour** | recommended, not required | open to all |
| **Information Session** | required | open to all |
| **Classroom Visit** | required | applicants only |
| **Faculty Meeting** | required | open to all |
| **Overnight Visit** | required | admitted applicants only |

**Information Sessions:** M–F, select Sat.; 60 minutes.

**Campus Tours:** Conducted by students. Follows information session; 75 minutes.

**Class Visits:** Prospective students may attend a class in their area of interest, classroom visits are determined by the visit schedule.

**Overnight Visits:** During the regular academic year, prospective applicants may spend an evening in a residence hall with a student host.

**CAMPUS FACILITIES**
**Science:** Zurn Science Center; Appointment Required: Cadaver Lab, Materials and Engineering Lab, Computer Integrated Enterprise and Manufacturing Center.

**Arts:** Appointment Required: Schuster Theatre in Scottino Hall.

**Athletic:** Hammermill Center, Student Recreation Center.

**Of Special Interest:** A.J. Palumbo Academic Center, John E. Waldron Campus Center; Appointment Required: WERG FM Radio Station.

**LOCAL ATTRACTIONS**
Presque Isle State Park; Erie Civic Center.

# GROVE CITY COLLEGE
**Grove City, Pennsylvania**

**Contact:** Jeffrey C. Mincey, Director of Admissions, 100 Campus Drive, Grove City, PA 16127-2104. *Phone:* 724-458-2100. *Fax:* 724-458-3395. *E-mail:*

*Grove City College (continued)*

admissions@gcc.edu *Web site:* http://www.gcc.edu/ *Visit location:* Office of Admissions, Crawford Hall, 100 Campus Drive.

## QUICK FACTS

Enrollment: 2,292; UG: 2,267. Entrance: very difficult. SAT>500: 97% V, 97% M; ACT>18: 100%. Tuition and fees: $6576. Room and board: $3816. Application deadline: 2/15.

## GENERAL

Independent Presbyterian, comprehensive, coed. Awards bachelor's and master's degrees. Founded 1876. Setting: 150-acre small-town campus with easy access to Pittsburgh. Undergraduate faculty: 145 (111 full-time, 34 part-time); student-faculty ratio is 21:1. Most popular recent majors: business administration, mechanical engineering, elementary education.

## CAMPUS VISITS

**College Calendar 1998–99:** *Regular classes:* Sept. 2–Dec. 22; Jan. 19–May 12. *Breaks:* Oct. 14–19; Feb. 24–Mar. 1; Nov. 21–30; Mar. 27–Apr. 6. *Final exams:* Dec. 17–22; May 7–12. *Admission office closed:* Sat., May 15–Aug. 24. *Special campus days:* Commencement, May 15; Homecoming, Oct. 3; Parents Weekend, May 1.

## VISIT OPPORTUNITIES

|                      | Appointments? | Who?        |
| -------------------- | ------------- | ----------- |
| **Campus Tour**          | required      | open to all |
| **Information Session**  | required      | open to all |
| **Admission Interview**  | required      | open to all |
| **Classroom Visit**      | required      | open to all |
| **Faculty Meeting**      | required      | open to all |
| **Overnight Visit**      | required      | open to all |

**Information Sessions:** M–F 8:30 am–4:30 pm; Sat. 8:30 am–12:00 pm; 30 minutes.

**Interviews:** M–F; Sat. 8:30 am–12:00 pm; 30 minutes.

**Campus Tours:** Conducted by students and admission reps. M–F 8:30 am–4:30 pm; Sat. 8:30 am–12:00 pm; 60 minutes.

**Class Visits:** Classroom visits are determined by the visit schedule.

**Overnight Visits:** During the regular academic year, prospective applicants may spend an evening in a residence hall with a student host.

## CAMPUS FACILITIES

**Science:** Appointment Required: Rockwell Hall of Science.

**Arts:** Appointment Required: Pew Fine Arts Center.

**Athletic:** Appointment Required: Physical Learning Center.

**Of Special Interest:** Appointment Required: Harbison Chapel, Technological Learning Center, Henry Buhl Library.

## LOCAL ATTRACTIONS

Grove City Outlet Mall; Wendel August Forge.

# KING'S COLLEGE
## Wilkes-Barre, Pennsylvania

**Contact:** Mr. Charles O. Bachman, Dean of Enrollment Management, 133 North River Street, Wilkes-Barre, PA 18911. *Phone:* 717-208-5858 or toll-free 888-KINGSPA. *Fax:* 717-208-5971. *E-mail:* admssns@ leo.kings.edu *Web site:* http://www.kings.edu/ *Visit location:* Office of Admission, Hessel Hall, 134 North Franklin Street.

## QUICK FACTS

Enrollment: 2,222; UG: 2,077. Entrance: moderately difficult. SAT>500: 62% V, 58% M; ACT>18: N/App. Tuition and fees: $14,000. Room and board: $6120. Application deadline: rolling.

## GENERAL

Independent Roman Catholic, comprehensive, coed. Awards associate, bachelor's, and master's degrees. Founded 1946. Setting: 48-acre suburban campus. Undergraduate faculty: 168 (94 full-time, 74 part-time); student-faculty ratio is 17:1. Most popular recent majors: accounting, communications, business administration.

## CAMPUS VISITS

**College Calendar 1998–99:** *Regular classes:* Aug. 31–Dec. 11; Jan. 11–Apr. 28. *Breaks:* Oct. 12; Mar. 1–5; Nov. 25–27; Apr. 1–5. *Final exams:* Dec. 14–19; Apr. 30–May 7. *Special campus days:* Commencement, May 15–16; Convocation Mass of Holy Spirit, Sept. 3; Freshman Orientation, Aug. 27–29; Homecoming, Oct. 31; Honors Convocation, Apr. 18; New Student Orientation, Jan. 10; Parents Weekend, Sept. 18–20; Patron's Day, Nov. 22.

## VISIT OPPORTUNITIES

| | Appointments? | Who? |
|---|---|---|
| **Campus Tour** | recommended | applicants and parents |
| **Admission Interview** | recommended | applicants and parents |
| **Classroom Visit** | required | open to all |
| **Faculty Meeting** | required | open to all |
| **Overnight Visit** | required | open to all |

**Interviews:** M–F; Sat. during school year; 45 minutes.

**Campus Tours:** Conducted by students. M–F; Sat. mornings during school year; 60 minutes.

**Class Visits:** Prospective students may attend a class in their area of interest.

**Overnight Visits:** During the regular academic year, prospective applicants may spend an evening in a residence hall with a student host.

**Video:** Free on request.

### CAMPUS FACILITIES
**Science:** Parente Life Sciences Center.
**Athletic:** Monarch Fields.

### LOCAL ATTRACTIONS
Pocono Mountains.

# LAFAYETTE COLLEGE
Easton, Pennsylvania

**Contact:** Patricia Lorenz, Visitation Coordinator, Lafayette College, Markle Hall, Easton, PA 18042. *Phone:* 610-250-5100. *Fax:* 610-250-5355. *E-mail:* lorenzp@lafayette.edu *Web site:* http://www.lafayette. edu/ *Visit location:* Admissions, Markle Hall, High Street.

### QUICK FACTS
Enrollment: 2,129; UG: 2,129. Entrance: very difficult. SAT>500: 94% V, 97% M; ACT>18: N/App. Tuition and fees: $21,202. Room and board: $6560. Application deadline: 1/1.

### GENERAL
Independent, 4-year, coed, Presbyterian Church (U.S.A.). Awards bachelor's degrees. Founded 1826. Setting: 110-acre suburban campus with easy access to Philadelphia and New York City. Faculty: 232 (183 full-time, 49 part-time); student-faculty ratio is 11:1. Most popular recent majors: biology, business economics, psychology.

### CAMPUS VISITS
**College Calendar 1998–99:** *Regular classes:* Aug. 31–Dec. 11; Jan. 25–May 7. *Breaks:* Oct. 12–13; Mar. 15–19. *Final exams:* Dec. 15–22; May 10–17. *Special campus days:* Fall Open Houses, October and November; Homecoming, Oct. 17; Junior Visiting Day—April; Parents Weekend, Sept. 26–27.

### VISIT OPPORTUNITIES

| | Appointments? | Who? |
|---|---|---|
| **Campus Tour** | not required | open to all |
| **Information Session** | recommended | open to all |
| **Admission Interview** | required | open to all |
| **Classroom Visit** | not required | open to all |
| **Faculty Meeting** | recommended | open to all |
| **Overnight Visit** | required | open to all |

**Information Sessions:** M–F (Apr. and Aug.) at 10:00 am, 2:00 pm; Sat. morning during academic year; 60 minutes.

**Interviews:** Select Sat. in morning for groups; M–F May 1 to Jan. 31 for individual interviews; 40 minutes.

**Campus Tours:** Conducted by students. M–F at 10:00 am, 11:00 am, 1:00 pm, 2:00 pm, 3:15 pm; select Sat.; available during fall and spring breaks at 10:00 am, 2:00 pm; 60 minutes.

**Class Visits:** Prospective students may attend a class in their area of interest, certain predetermined classrooms are open to visitors.

**Overnight Visits:** During the regular academic year, prospective applicants may spend an evening in a residence hall with a student host.

**Video:** Free on request.

### CAMPUS FACILITIES
**Science:** Olin Hall, Kunkel Hall.
**Arts:** Williams Art Center.
**Athletic:** Alumni Gym, Kirby Field House.
**Of Special Interest:** Farinon Student Center, Skillman Library, Markel Hall Theatre.

### LOCAL ATTRACTIONS
Crayola Factory; Twin Rivers.

# LEHIGH UNIVERSITY
## Bethlehem, Pennsylvania

**Contact:** Mr. Jason Honsel, Assistant Director of Admission, 27 Memorial Drive West, Bethlehem, PA 18015. *Phone:* 610-758-3100. *Fax:* 610-758-4361. *E-mail:* inado@lehigh.edu *Web site:* http://www.lehigh.edu/ *Visit location:* Admissions Office, Alumni Memorial Building, 27 Memorial Drive West.

## QUICK FACTS
Enrollment: 6,231; UG: 4,398. Entrance: very difficult. SAT>500: 90% V, 96% M; ACT>18: N/App. Tuition and fees: $21,350. Room and board: $6220. Application deadline: 1/15.

## GENERAL
Independent, university, coed. Awards bachelor's, master's, and doctoral degrees and post-master's certificates. Founded 1865. Setting: 1,600-acre suburban campus with easy access to Philadelphia. Undergraduate faculty: 470 (397 full-time, 73 part-time); student-faculty ratio is 11:1. Most popular recent majors: finance, civil engineering, mechanical engineering.

## CAMPUS VISITS
**College Calendar 1998–99:** *Regular classes:* Aug. 25–Dec. 4; Jan. 12–May 3. *Breaks:* Oct. 10–13; Mar. 6–14; Nov. 26–29; Apr. 1–5. *Final exams:* Dec. 8–16; May 6–14. *Admission office closed:* Christmas–New Years week, Dec. 24–Jan. 1; freshman check-in day.

## VISIT OPPORTUNITIES

|  | Appointments? | Who? |
|---|---|---|
| **Campus Tour** | not required | open to all |
| **Information Session** | not required | open to all |
| **Admission Interview** | required | open to all |
| **Classroom Visit** | not required | open to all |
| **Faculty Meeting** | required | open to all |
| **Overnight Visit** | required | open to all |

**Information Sessions:** M–F at 9:30 am, 10:30 am, 2:30 pm; select Sat. at 9:00 am, 10:00 am, 11:00 am; unavailable Feb. and Mar.; 45 minutes.

**Interviews:** M–F, select Sat.; unavailable Feb. and Mar.; 45 minutes.

**Campus Tours:** Conducted by students. M–F at 10:15 am, 11:15 am, 1:00 pm, 3:00 pm; select Sat. at 10:00 am, 11:00 am, 12:00 pm; call for summer and holiday schedule; 60 minutes.

**Class Visits:** Prospective students may attend a class in their area of interest.

**Overnight Visits:** During the regular academic year, prospective applicants may spend an evening in a residence hall with a student host.

## CAMPUS FACILITIES
**Science:** Engineering Labs, Atlass Lab.
**Arts:** Performing Arts Center.
**Athletic:** Taylor Gym, Goodman Athletic Campus.

## LOCAL ATTRACTIONS
MusikFest (August); Christmas decorations; Philadelphia Eagles training camp.

# LINCOLN UNIVERSITY
## Lincoln University, Pennsylvania

**Contact:** David E. Thomas, Admissions Counselor /Campus Tour Coordinator, Lincoln University, 200 Lincoln Hall, Lincoln University, PA 19352. *Phone:* toll-free 800-790-0191 Ext. 3275. *Fax:* 610-932-1209. *E-mail:* dthomas@lu.lincoln.edu *Web site:* http://www.lincoln.edu/ *Visit location:* Security Office, Azikiwe-Nkrumah Hall.

## QUICK FACTS
Enrollment: 1,974; UG: 1,498. Entrance: moderately difficult. SAT>500: 18% V, 15% M; ACT>18: 56%. Resident tuition and fees: $4762. Nonresident tuition and fees: $6930. Room and board: $4440. Application deadline: rolling.

## GENERAL
State-related, comprehensive, coed. Awards bachelor's and master's degrees. Founded 1854. Setting: 442-acre rural campus with easy access to Philadelphia. Undergraduate faculty: 178 (100 full-time, 78 part-time); student-faculty ratio is 16:1. Most popular recent majors: education, business administration, biology.

## CAMPUS VISITS
**College Calendar 1998–99:** *Regular classes:* Aug. 26–Dec. 4; Jan. 6–Apr. 16. *Final exams:* Dec. 7–11; Apr. 19–23. *Special campus days:* All University Convocation, Sept. 9, Oct. 7, Nov. 4; Black History Convocation, Feb. 10; Homecoming, Oct. 24; Martin Luther King, Jr. Convocation, Jan. 20.

## VISIT OPPORTUNITIES

|  | Appointments? | Who? |
|---|---|---|
| **Campus Tour** | required | applicants and parents |
| **Information Session** | required | |
| **Admission Interview** | required | |
| **Classroom Visit** | required | |
| **Overnight Visit** | required | |

**Information Sessions:** M–F at 10:00 am, 2:00 pm; 30 minutes.

**Interviews:** M–F; 30 minutes.

**Campus Tours:** Conducted by students. M–F at 10:00 am, 2:00 pm; 60 minutes.

**Class Visits:** Classroom visits are assigned to accommodate time of class and require professor's permission.

**Overnight Visits:** During the regular academic year, prospective applicants may spend an evening in a residence hall with a student host.

## CAMPUS FACILITIES

**Of Special Interest:** Langston Hughes Memorial Library.

# LOCK HAVEN UNIVERSITY OF PENNSYLVANIA
## Lock Haven, Pennsylvania

**Contact:** Office of Admissions, Akeley Hall, Lock Haven University, Lock Haven, PA 17745. *Phone:* 717-893-2027 or toll-free 800-332-8900 (in-state), 800-233-8978 (out-of-state). *Fax:* 717-893-2201. *E-mail:* admissions@eagle.lhup.edu *Web site:* http://www.lhup.edu/ *Visit location:* Office of Admissions, Akeley Hall, Lock Haven University.

## QUICK FACTS

Enrollment: 3,430; UG: 3,357. Entrance: moderately difficult. SAT>500: N/App; ACT>18: N/App. Resident tuition and fees: $4062. Nonresident tuition and fees: $9418. Room and board: $3880. Application deadline: rolling.

## GENERAL

State-supported, comprehensive, coed. Part of Pennsylvania State System of Higher Education. Awards associate, bachelor's, and master's degrees. Founded 1870. Setting: 135-acre small-town campus. Under-

graduate faculty: 211 (204 full-time, 7 part-time); student-faculty ratio is 19:1. Most popular recent majors: education, health science, biology.

## CAMPUS VISITS

**College Calendar 1998–99:** *Regular classes:* Aug. 31–Dec. 18; Jan. 18–May 10. *Breaks:* Nov. 24–30; Mar. 5–15. *Final exams:* Dec. 14–18; May 5–10. *Special campus days:* Spring Commencement, May 15; Winter Commencement, Dec. 13.

## VISIT OPPORTUNITIES

|  | Appointments? | Who? |
|---|---|---|
| **Campus Tour** | recommended, not required | open to all |
| **Information Session** | recommended, not required | open to all |
| **Admission Interview** | recommended | open to all |
| **Classroom Visit** | required | open to all |
| **Faculty Meeting** | required | open to all |

**Information Sessions:** Mon., Wed., Fri. at 10:00 am; Sat. at 10:00 am; 40 minutes.

**Interviews:** M–F, select Sat.; 30 minutes.

**Campus Tours:** Conducted by students. M–F at 1:00 pm, 2:00 pm.

## CAMPUS FACILITIES

**Of Special Interest:** Stevenson Library.

# LYCOMING COLLEGE
## Williamsport, Pennsylvania

**Contact:** Admissions Office, 700 College Place, Williamsport, PA 17701. *Phone:* toll-free 800-345-3920. *Fax:* 717-321-4317. *Web site:* http://www.lycoming.edu/ *Visit location:* Admissions Office, Admissions House, 700 College Place.

## QUICK FACTS

Enrollment: 1,409; UG: 1,409. Entrance: moderately difficult. SAT>500: 69% V, 66% M; ACT>18: N/R. Tuition and fees: $16,930. Room and board: $4770. Application deadline: 4/1.

## GENERAL

Independent United Methodist, 4-year, coed. Awards bachelor's degrees. Founded 1812. Setting: 35-acre small-town campus. Faculty: 107 (94 full-time, 13

*Lycoming College (continued)*

part-time); student-faculty ratio is 13:1. Most popular recent majors: psychology, biology, business administration.

## CAMPUS VISITS

**College Calendar 1998–99:** *Regular classes:* Aug. 31–Dec. 11; Jan. 11–Apr. 23. *Breaks:* Nov. 24–29; Feb. 26–Mar. 7. *Final exams:* Dec. 14–18; Apr. 26–30. *Special campus days:* Baccalaureate, May 8; Commencement, May 9; Family Weekend, Oct. 2–4; Home Coming, Oct. 9–11.

## VISIT OPPORTUNITIES

|  | Appointments? | Who? |
| --- | --- | --- |
| **Campus Tour** | recommended, not required | open to all |
| **Admission Interview** | recommended, not required | open to all |
| **Classroom Visit** | required | open to all |
| **Faculty Meeting** | required | open to all |
| **Overnight Visit** | required | applicants only |

**Interviews:** M–F; Sat. by appointment; 45 minutes.

**Campus Tours:** Conducted by students. M–F; Sat. by appointment; 60 minutes.

**Class Visits:** Prospective students may attend a class in their area of interest.

**Overnight Visits:** During the regular academic year, prospective applicants may spend an evening in a residence hall with a student host.

## CAMPUS FACILITIES

**Science:** Heim Biology and Chemistry Building, Planetarium.

**Arts:** Fine Arts Center, Arena Theatre.

**Athletic:** Lamade Gymnasium, Fitness Center.

**Of Special Interest:** Communication Center, Video Conference Facility.

# MANSFIELD UNIVERSITY OF PENNSYLVANIA
**Mansfield, Pennsylvania**

**Contact:** Mr. Brian D. Barden, Director of Admissions, Office of Admissions, Mansfield, PA 16933. *Phone:* 717-662-4243 or toll-free 800-577-6826. *Fax:* 717-662-4121. *E-mail:* admissns@mnsfld.edu *Web site:* http://www.mnsfld.edu/ *Visit location:* Office of Admissions, Alumni Hall, Academy Street.

## QUICK FACTS

Enrollment: 2,715; UG: 2,506. Entrance: moderately difficult. SAT>500: 65% V, 54% M; ACT>18: 100%. Resident tuition and fees: $4404. Nonresident tuition and fees: $9760. Room and board: $3704. Application deadline: N/R.

## GENERAL

State-supported, comprehensive, coed. Part of Pennsylvania State System of Higher Education. Awards associate, bachelor's, and master's degrees. Founded 1857. Setting: 205-acre small-town campus. Undergraduate faculty: 202 (169 full-time, 33 part-time); student-faculty ratio is 16:1. Most popular recent majors: criminal justice/law enforcement administration, elementary education, business administration.

## CAMPUS VISITS

**College Calendar 1998–99:** *Regular classes:* Aug. 24–Dec. 4; Jan. 11–Apr. 30. *Breaks:* Oct. 12; Mar. 8–12; Nov. 25–27. *Final exams:* Dec. 7–10; May 3–6. *Special campus days:* Commencement—Fall, Dec. 12; Commencement—Spring, May 8; Homecoming, Oct. 17; Parents Weekend, Sept. 26.

## VISIT OPPORTUNITIES

|  | Appointments? | Who? |
| --- | --- | --- |
| **Campus Tour** | recommended | open to all |
| **Information Session** | required | open to all |
| **Admission Interview** | required | open to all |
| **Classroom Visit** | required | open to all |
| **Faculty Meeting** | required | open to all |

**Information Sessions:** M–F at 10:00 am, 1:00 pm; select Sat. at 9:30 am; 45 minutes.

**Interviews:** M–F, select Sat.

**Campus Tours:** Conducted by students. M–F at 11:00 am, 2:00 pm; select Sat. at 10:30 am; 45 minutes.

**Class Visits:** Classroom visits are determined by the visit schedule.

## CAMPUS FACILITIES

**Athletic:** Student Fitness Center.

**Of Special Interest:** Library.

# MERCYHURST COLLEGE
Erie, Pennsylvania

**Contact:** Nancy Gullifer, Admissions Office, Mercyhurst College, Erie, PA 16546. *Phone:* 814-824-2202 or toll-free 800-825-1926. *Fax:* 814-824-2871. *E-mail:* admug@mercyhurst.edu *Web site:* http://www.mercyhurst.edu/ *Visit location:* Admissions, Old Main, Mercyhurst College.

## QUICK FACTS
Enrollment: 2,556; UG: 2,439. Entrance: moderately difficult. SAT>500: 75% V, 72% M; ACT>18: 93%. Tuition and fees: $12,750. Room and board: $4884. Application deadline: rolling.

## GENERAL
Independent Roman Catholic, comprehensive, coed. Awards associate, bachelor's, and master's degrees. Founded 1926. Setting: 88-acre suburban campus with easy access to Buffalo. Undergraduate faculty: 190 (109 full-time, 81 part-time); student-faculty ratio is 20:1. Most popular recent majors: business administration, archaeology, music.

## CAMPUS VISITS
**College Calendar 1998–99:** *Regular classes:* Sept. 9–Nov. 17; Dec. 1–Feb. 22; Mar. 9–May 18. *Breaks:* Nov. 20–30; Feb. 25–Mar. 8. *Final exams:* Nov. 18–19; Feb. 23–24; May 19–20.

## VISIT OPPORTUNITIES

|  | Appointments? | Who? |
|---|---|---|
| **Campus Tour** | recommended, not required | open to all |
| **Information Session** | not required | open to all |
| **Admission Interview** | recommended, not required | open to all |
| **Classroom Visit** | required | open to all |
| **Faculty Meeting** | required | open to all |
| **Overnight Visit** | required | open to all |

**Information Sessions:** M–F, Sat.; unavailable Sat. during the summer; 30 minutes.

**Interviews:** M–F, Sat.; 30 minutes.

**Campus Tours:** Conducted by students. M–F, Sat. at 9:00 am, 10:00 am, 11:00 am, 1:00 pm, 2:00 pm; unavailable Sat. during the summer; 30 minutes.

**Class Visits:** Prospective students may attend a class in their area of interest.

**Overnight Visits:** During the regular academic year, prospective applicants may spend an evening in a residence hall with a student host.

**Video:** Free on request.

## CAMPUS FACILITIES
**Science:** Archeology labs; Appointment Required: Planetarium/Observatory.

**Arts:** Cummings Art Gallery, D'Angelo Performing Arts Center.

**Athletic:** Ice Rink, Fitness Center, Athletic Center.

**Of Special Interest:** Hammermill Library.

# MESSIAH COLLEGE
Grantham, Pennsylvania

**Contact:** Connie Marks, Office Coordinator, 1 College Avenue, Grantham, PA 17027. *Phone:* 717-691-6000 or toll-free 800-382-1349 (in-state), 800-233-4220 (out-of-state). *Fax:* 717-796-5374. *E-mail:* admiss@messiah.edu *Web site:* http://www.messiah.edu/ *Visit location:* Admissions Office, Old Main, 1 College Avenue.

## QUICK FACTS
Enrollment: 2,595; UG: 2,595. Entrance: moderately difficult. SAT>500: 85% V, 81% M; ACT>18: 98%. Tuition and fees: $12,990. Room and board: $5500. Application deadline: rolling.

## GENERAL
Independent interdenominational, 4-year, coed. Awards bachelor's degrees. Founded 1909. Setting: 360-acre small-town campus. Faculty: 224 (139 full-time, 85 part-time); student-faculty ratio is 15:1. Most popular recent majors: elementary education, biology, nursing.

## CAMPUS VISITS
**College Calendar 1998–99:** *Regular classes:* Sept. 1–Dec. 11; Jan. 11–29; Feb. 2–May 3. *Breaks:* Oct. 3–6; Jan. 30–Feb. 1; Mar. 13–21; Dec. 19–Jan. 10; Apr. 2–5. *Final exams:* Dec. 14–18; May 4–7.

## VISIT OPPORTUNITIES

|  | Appointments? | Who? |
|---|---|---|
| **Campus Tour** | recommended, not required | applicants and parents |
| **Information Session** | recommended, not required |  |

*Messiah College (continued)*

## VISIT OPPORTUNITIES—*continued*

| | Appointments? | Who? |
|---|---|---|
| **Admission Interview** | required | |
| **Classroom Visit** | recommended, not required | |
| **Faculty Meeting** | required | |
| **Overnight Visit** | required | |

**Information Sessions:** M–F 8:30 am–4:00 pm; 30 minutes.

**Interviews:** M–F; 30 minutes.

**Campus Tours:** Conducted by admission reps. M–F 8:30 am–3:00 pm; 60 minutes.

**Class Visits:** Prospective students may attend a class in their area of interest.

**Overnight Visits:** During the regular academic year, prospective applicants may spend an evening in a residence hall with a student host.

### CAMPUS FACILITIES

**Science:** Kline Hall of Science, Frey Hall.

**Arts:** Climenhaga Fine Arts Center.

**Athletic:** Starry Athletic Complex (outdoor), Sollenberger Sports Center (indoor).

**Of Special Interest:** Library, dormitories/apartments.

### LOCAL ATTRACTIONS

Gettysburg Battlefield, Hershey Park.

# MORAVIAN COLLEGE

**Bethlehem, Pennsylvania**

**Contact:** Admission Office, 1200 Main Street, Bethlehem, PA 18018. *Phone:* 610-861-1320. *Fax:* 610-861-3956. *E-mail:* admissions@moravian.edu *Web site:* http://www.moravian.edu/ *Visit location:* Admission Office, Admission, 1200 Main Street.

### QUICK FACTS

Enrollment: 1,566; UG: 1,448. Entrance: moderately difficult. SAT>500: 78% V, 77% M; ACT>18: N/R. Tuition and fees: $17,276. Room and board: $5580. Application deadline: 3/1.

### GENERAL

Independent, comprehensive, coed, Moravian Church. Awards bachelor's and master's degrees. Founded 1742. Setting: 70-acre suburban campus with easy access to Philadelphia. Undergraduate faculty: 144 (88 full-time, 56 part-time); student-faculty ratio is 14:1. Most popular recent majors: business administration, psychology, biology.

### CAMPUS VISITS

**College Calendar 1998–99:** *Regular classes:* Sept. 1–Dec. 14; Jan. 11–May 1. *Breaks:* Oct. 10–14; Mar. 6–15. *Final exams:* Dec. 16–22; May 3–8. *Special campus days:* Commencement, May 15; Homecoming, Oct. 31.

### VISIT OPPORTUNITIES

| | Appointments? | Who? |
|---|---|---|
| **Campus Tour** | recommended, not required | applicants and parents |
| **Information Session** | recommended, not required | |
| **Admission Interview** | recommended | applicants and parents |
| **Classroom Visit** | required | applicants and parents |
| **Faculty Meeting** | required | applicants and parents |
| **Overnight Visit** | required | |

**Interviews:** M–F; Sat. 9:00–11:30 am; 30 minutes.

**Campus Tours:** Conducted by students. M–F, Sat.; 60 minutes.

**Class Visits:** Prospective students may attend a class in their area of interest.

**Overnight Visits:** During the regular academic year, prospective applicants may spend an evening in a residence hall with a student host.

**Video:** Free on request.

### CAMPUS FACILITIES

**Of Special Interest:** Reeves Library.

# PENNSYLVANIA STATE UNIVERSITY ALTOONA COLLEGE

**Altoona, Pennsylvania**

**Contact:** Office of Student Marketing and Admissions, 3000 Ivyside Park, Altoona, PA 16601. *Phone:*

toll-free 800-848-9843. *Fax:* 814-949-5564. *E-mail:* aaadmit@psu.edu *Web site:* http://www.psu.edu/ *Visit location:* Office of Student Marketing and Admissions, Raymond E. Smith Building, 3000 Ivyside Park.

## QUICK FACTS

Enrollment: 3,414; UG: 3,408. Entrance: moderately difficult. SAT>500: 50% V, 52% M; ACT>18: N/R. Resident tuition and fees: $5682. Nonresident tuition and fees: $8734. Room and board: $4640. Application deadline: rolling.

## GENERAL

State-related, 4-year, coed. Part of Pennsylvania State University. Awards associate and bachelor's degrees. Founded 1929. Setting: 81-acre suburban campus. Faculty: 208 (102 full-time, 106 part-time); student-faculty ratio is 28:1.

## CAMPUS VISITS

**College Calendar 1998–99:** *Regular classes:* Aug. 26–Dec. 11; Jan. 11–Apr. 30. *Breaks:* Dec. 20–Jan. 10. *Final exams:* Dec. 14–19; May 3–8. *Special campus days:* Fall Commencement, Dec. 20; Spring Commencement, May 15.

### VISIT OPPORTUNITIES

|  | Appointments? | Who? |
| --- | --- | --- |
| **Campus Tour** | required | open to all |
| **Information Session** | required | open to all |
| **Admission Interview** | required | open to all |
| **Classroom Visit** | required | open to all |
| **Faculty Meeting** | required | open to all |
| **Overnight Visit** | required | |

**Information Sessions:** Available for groups with tour; 60 minutes.
**Interviews:** M–F, select Sat.; 30 minutes.
**Campus Tours:** Conducted by students. M–F, select Sat.; 60 minutes.
**Class Visits:** Prospective students may attend a class in their area of interest.
**Overnight Visits:** During the regular academic year, prospective applicants may spend an evening in a residence hall with a student host.
**Video:** Free on request.

## CAMPUS FACILITIES

**Science:** Ralph and Helen Force Technology Building, Greenhouse.

**Arts:** Theatre, McLanahan and Sheetz Art Galleries, Ceramic Studio.
**Athletic:** Adler Athletic Complex—Olympic size swimming pool, Racquetball and Tennis Courts, Athletic field.
**Of Special Interest:** Edith Davis Eve Chapel, Reflecting Pond.

## LOCAL ATTRACTIONS

Horseshoe Curve; Lakemont Park, Bland's Park; Blue Knob Ski Resort.

# PHILADELPHIA COLLEGE OF TEXTILES AND SCIENCE
## Philadelphia, Pennsylvania

**Contact:** Susan L. Perrone, Visit Coordinator, School House Lane and Henry Avenue, Philadelphia, PA 19144. *Phone:* 215-951-2921. *Fax:* 215-951-2907. *E-mail:* admissions@philacol.edu *Web site:* http://www.philacol.edu/ *Visit location:* Admissions, White Corners, School House Lane and Henry Avenue.

## QUICK FACTS

Enrollment: 3,232; UG: 2,662. Entrance: moderately difficult. SAT>500: 66% V, 66% M; ACT>18: N/R. Tuition and fees: $13,466. Room and board: $6080. Application deadline: rolling.

## GENERAL

Independent, comprehensive, coed. Awards bachelor's and master's degrees. Founded 1884. Setting: 100-acre suburban campus. Undergraduate faculty: 366 (94 full-time, 272 part-time); student-faculty ratio is 21:1. Most popular recent majors: architecture, fashion design/illustration, fashion merchandising.

## CAMPUS VISITS

**College Calendar 1998–99:** *Regular classes:* Aug. 31–Dec. 8; Jan. 13–Apr. 1. *Breaks:* Dec. 18–Jan. 12; Feb. 27–Mar. 8. *Final exams:* Dec. 11–17; Apr. 3–7. *Admission office closed:* Nov. 27–28, Dec. 24–25, Dec. 31–Jan. 1, Jan. 18, Apr. 2.

### VISIT OPPORTUNITIES

|  | Appointments? | Who? |
| --- | --- | --- |
| **Campus Tour** | required | open to all |
| **Information Session** | required | open to all |

*Philadelphia College of Textiles and Science (continued)*

### VISIT OPPORTUNITIES—*continued*

|  | Appointments? | Who? |
|---|---|---|
| **Admission Interview** | required | open to all |
| **Classroom Visit** | required | open to all |
| **Faculty Meeting** | required | open to all |

**Information Sessions:** M–F 10:00 am–3:00 pm; 45 minutes.

**Interviews:** M–F; Sat. until 11:30 am; 45 minutes.

**Campus Tours:** Conducted by students. M–F 10:00 am–3:00 pm; select Sat. 8:30–11:30 am; 75 minutes.

**Class Visits:** Prospective students may attend a class in their area of interest, certain predetermined classrooms are open to visitors, classroom visits are determined by the visit schedule.

### CAMPUS FACILITIES

**Science:** Appointment Required: Physician Assistant Labs.

**Arts:** Architecture and Design Building and Studios, Industrial Design Studios, Graphic Design Department, Textile Fashion Design Studios.

**Of Special Interest:** Library, Learning Center, Residence Halls.

### LOCAL ATTRACTIONS

Historic Philadelphia; Philadelphia Art Museum.

## SAINT JOSEPH'S UNIVERSITY
### Philadelphia, Pennsylvania

**Contact:** Grace Amer, Visit Coordinator, Saint Thomas Hall/Saint Joseph's University, 5600 City Avenue, Philadelphia, PA 19131. *Phone:* 610-660-1300 or toll-free 888-BEAHAWK (in-state). *Fax:* 610-660-1314. *E-mail:* amer@sju.edu *Web site:* http://www.sju.edu/ *Visit location:* Admissions Office, St. Thomas Hall, Lapsley Lane.

### QUICK FACTS

Enrollment: 6,832; UG: 4,009. Entrance: moderately difficult. SAT>500: 81% V, 78% M; ACT>18: N/R. Tuition and fees: $16,165. Room and board: $6972. Application deadline: rolling.

### GENERAL

Independent Roman Catholic (Jesuit), comprehensive, coed. Awards associate, bachelor's, and master's degrees and post-master's certificates. Founded 1851. Setting: 60-acre suburban campus. Undergraduate faculty: 430 (189 full-time, 241 part-time); student-faculty ratio is 16:1. Most popular recent majors: food sales operations, psychology, business marketing and marketing management.

### CAMPUS VISITS

**College Calendar 1998–99:** *Regular classes:* Aug. 31–Dec. 11; Jan. 19–Apr. 30. *Breaks:* Oct. 19–20; Mar. 8–14; Dec. 20–Jan. 19; Apr. 2–5. *Final exams:* Dec. 14–19; May 3–8. *Admission office closed:* Easter Monday, Apr. 5; Good Friday, Apr. 2; Martin Luther King, Jr. Day, Jan. 18; Thanksgiving, Nov. 26–27. *Special campus days:* Commencement, May 16.

### VISIT OPPORTUNITIES

|  | Appointments? | Who? |
|---|---|---|
| **Campus Tour** | required | open to all |
| **Admission Interview** | required | open to all |
| **Classroom Visit** | required | open to all |
| **Faculty Meeting** | required | open to all |
| **Overnight Visit** | required | admitted applicants only |

**Interviews:** M–F, select Sat.; 30 minutes.

**Campus Tours:** Conducted by students. M–F at 10:00 am, 1:00 pm, 3:00 pm; select Sat. at 10:00 am, 11:00 am, 12:00 pm; during the summer daily tours at 10:00 am and 2:00 pm; 60 minutes.

**Class Visits:** Prospective students may attend a class in their area of interest.

**Overnight Visits:** During the regular academic year, prospective applicants may spend an evening in a residence hall with a student host.

### CAMPUS FACILITIES

**Science:** The Science Center.

**Arts:** Appointment Required: Boland Hall.

**Athletic:** Alumni Memorial Fieldhouse.

### LOCAL ATTRACTIONS

Historic Philadelphia, Philadelphia Museum of Art.

## SHIPPENSBURG UNIVERSITY OF PENNSYLVANIA
### Shippensburg, Pennsylvania

**Contact:** Office of Admissions, Shippensburg University, 1871 Old Main Drive, Shippensburg, PA

17257. *Phone:* toll-free 800-822-8028 (in-state). *Fax:* 717-530-4016. *E-mail:* admiss@ship.edu *Web site:* http://www.ship.edu/ *Visit location:* Office of Admissions, Old Main, Room 105, 1871 Old Main Drive.

## QUICK FACTS
Enrollment: 6,603; UG: 5,602. Entrance: moderately difficult. SAT>500: 69% V, 69% M; ACT>18: N/R. Resident tuition and fees: $4344. Nonresident tuition and fees: $9700. Room and board: $3722. Application deadline: rolling.

## GENERAL
State-supported, comprehensive, coed. Part of Pennsylvania State System of Higher Education. Awards bachelor's and master's degrees. Founded 1871. Setting: 200-acre rural campus. Undergraduate faculty: 363 (336 full-time, 27 part-time); student-faculty ratio is 16:1. Most popular recent major: elementary education.

## CAMPUS VISITS
**College Calendar 1998–99:** *Regular classes:* Aug. 25–Dec. 10; Jan. 13–Apr. 29. *Breaks:* Oct. 16–21; Mar. 6–15. *Final exams:* Dec. 11–18; Apr. 30–May 7. *Special campus days:* Fall Commencement, Dec. 19; Homecoming; Open House with President, Dean, faculty, and students, Sept. 26, Nov. 14, Apr. 17, Mar. 20, Oct. 24; Spring Commencement, May 8.

## VISIT OPPORTUNITIES

|  | Appointments? | Who? |
|---|---|---|
| **Campus Tour** | recommended, not required | open to all |
| **Information Session** | recommended, not required | open to all |
| **Admission Interview** | required | open to all |
| **Classroom Visit** | required | open to all |
| **Faculty Meeting** | required | open to all |

**Information Sessions:** M–F, Sat. at 10:00 am; Campus Visitation Program includes information session followed by campus tour; Summer Visitation Program from mid-May through mid-Aug. starts at 1:00 pm; 50 minutes.
**Interviews:** Tue., Thu.; inquire for available times; 50 minutes.
**Campus Tours:** Conducted by students. M–F, Sat. at 11:00 am.
**Class Visits:** Prospective students may attend a class in their area of interest.

**Video:** Available, fee charged.

## CAMPUS FACILITIES
**Science:** Science labs, computer labs.
**Of Special Interest:** Resident halls, student union, student affairs facilities, library.

# SWARTHMORE COLLEGE
**Swarthmore, Pennsylvania**

**Contact:** Admission Office, 500 College Avenue, Swarthmore, PA 19078. *Phone:* 610-328-8300. *Fax:* 610-328-8580. *E-mail:* admissions@swarthmore.edu *Web site:* http://www.swarthmore.edu/ *Visit location:* Admissions Office, Parrish Hall, 500 College Avenue.

## QUICK FACTS
Enrollment: 1,362; UG: 1,362. Entrance: most difficult. SAT>500: 100% V, 100% M; ACT>18: N/R. Tuition and fees: $22,000. Room and board: $7500. Application deadline: 1/1.

## GENERAL
Independent, 4-year, coed. Awards bachelor's degrees. Founded 1864. Setting: 330-acre suburban campus with easy access to Philadelphia. Faculty: 179 (158 full-time, 21 part-time); student-faculty ratio is 9:1. Most popular recent majors: economics, biology, political science.

## CAMPUS VISITS
**College Calendar 1998–99:** *Regular classes:* Sept. 3–Dec. 11; Jan. 18–Apr. 30. *Breaks:* Oct. 9–19; Mar. 5–15; Dec. 22–Jan. 18. *Final exams:* Dec. 14–22; May 6–15. *Special campus days:* Commencement, May 31; Open House, Sept. 19.

## VISIT OPPORTUNITIES

|  | Appointments? | Who? |
|---|---|---|
| **Campus Tour** | not required | open to all |
| **Information Session** | not required | open to all |
| **Admission Interview** | required | open to all |
| **Classroom Visit** | not required | open to all |
| **Faculty Meeting** | recommended | open to all |
| **Overnight Visit** | required | open to all |

**Information Sessions:** Group sessions available throughout the year; call for schedule; 60 minutes.
**Interviews:** Summer: M–F; fall: M.–Sat.; 30 minutes.

*Swarthmore College (continued)*

**Campus Tours:** Conducted by students. Available throughout the year; call for schedule; 60 minutes.

**Class Visits:** Prospective students may attend a class in their area of interest.

**Overnight Visits:** During the regular academic year, prospective applicants may spend an evening in a residence hall with a student host.

## CAMPUS FACILITIES
**Of Special Interest:** McCabe Library.

# TEMPLE UNIVERSITY
## Philadelphia, Pennsylvania

**Contact:** Admissions Office, 1801 North Broad Street, 103 Conwell Hall, Philadelphia, PA 19122. *Phone:* 215-204-4617 or toll-free 888-267-5870. *Fax:* 215-204-5694. *E-mail:* harvind@mail.temple.edu *Web site:* http://www.temple.edu/ *Visit location:* Office of Undergraduate Admissions, Conwell Hall, Room 103, 1801 North Broad Street.

## QUICK FACTS
Enrollment: 26,454; UG: 16,834. Entrance: moderately difficult. SAT>500: 57% V, 51% M; ACT>18: 59%. Resident tuition and fees: $6150. Nonresident tuition and fees: $11,032. Room and board: $5772. Application deadline: 5/1.

## GENERAL
State-related, university, coed. Awards associate, bachelor's, master's, doctoral, and first professional degrees and first professional certificates. Founded 1884. Setting: 76-acre urban campus. Undergraduate faculty: 2,480 (1,574 full-time, 906 part-time); student-faculty ratio is 24:1. Most popular recent majors: business administration, education, psychology.

## CAMPUS VISITS
**College Calendar 1998–99:** *Regular classes:* Aug. 31–Dec. 12; Jan. 19–May 3. *Breaks:* Nov. 26–29; Mar. 7–15. *Final exams:* Dec. 14–19; May 5–11. *Special campus days:* Commencement, May 20.

## VISIT OPPORTUNITIES

|  | Appointments? | Who? |
|---|---|---|
| **Campus Tour** | not required | open to all |

**VISIT OPPORTUNITIES**—*continued*

|  | Appointments? | Who? |
|---|---|---|
| **Information Session** | not required | open to all |
| **Admission Interview** | recommended | open to all |
| **Classroom Visit** | required | open to all |
| **Faculty Meeting** | required | open to all |
| **Overnight Visit** | required | admitted applicants only |

**Information Sessions:** M–F at 10:00 am, 2:00 pm; select Sat. at 10:00 am; 45 minutes.

**Interviews:** M–F; telephone interviews available; 30 minutes.

**Campus Tours:** Conducted by students. M–F at 11:00 am, 3:00 pm; select Sat. at 11:00 am; unavailable during spring break; 70 minutes.

**Class Visits:** Classroom visits are determined by the visit schedule.

**Overnight Visits:** During the regular academic year, prospective applicants may spend an evening in a residence hall with a student host.

**Video:** Free on request.

## CAMPUS FACILITIES
**Arts:** Appointment Required: Tyler Gallery (at Tyler campus).

**Athletic:** Appointment Required: Independence Blue Cross Student Recreation Center.

**Of Special Interest:** Student Activities Center; Appointment Required: The Apollo of Temple, Temple University Ambler Campus.

## LOCAL ATTRACTIONS
Historic Philadelphia; Philadelphia Museum of Art.

# UNIVERSITY OF PENNSYLVANIA
## Philadelphia, Pennsylvania

**Contact:** General Admissions, 1 College Hall, Philadelphia, PA 19104. *Phone:* 215-898-7507. *Fax:* 215-898-9670. *E-mail:* info@admissions.ugao.upenn.edu *Web site:* http://www.upenn.edu/ *Visit location:* Office of Undergraduate Admissions, College Hall–Room 1.

## QUICK FACTS
Enrollment: 21,641; UG: 11,404. Entrance: most difficult. SAT>500: 99% V, 100% M; ACT>18:

N/R. Tuition and fees: $22,250. Room and board: $7430. Application deadline: 1/1.

## GENERAL
Independent, university, coed. Awards associate, bachelor's, master's, doctoral, and first professional degrees. Founded 1740. Setting: 260-acre urban campus. Undergraduate faculty: 3,632 (2,258 full-time, 1,374 part-time); student-faculty ratio is 6:1. Most popular recent majors: finance, history, communications.

## CAMPUS VISITS
**College Calendar 1998–99:** *Regular classes:* Sept. 9–Dec. 11; Jan. 11–Apr. 23. *Breaks:* Oct. 17–19; Mar. 6–14; Nov. 26–29. *Final exams:* Dec. 15–22; Apr. 29–May 7. *Admission office closed:* Nov. 26–27; Winter Break, Dec. 25–Jan. 1. *Special campus days:* Family Weekend, Oct. 2–4; Homecoming, Oct. 31.

## VISIT OPPORTUNITIES

|  | Appointments? | Who? |
|---|---|---|
| **Campus Tour** |  | open to all |
| **Information Session** |  | open to all |
| **Classroom Visit** |  | open to all |
| **Faculty Meeting** | recommended |  |
| **Overnight Visit** | required |  |

**Information Sessions:** M–F; select Sat.; select Sun.; call for scheduled times and dates; 60 minutes.

**Campus Tours:** Conducted by students. M–F; select Sat.; select Sun.; call for scheduled dates and times; 90 minutes.

**Class Visits:** Certain predetermined classrooms are open to visitors.

**Overnight Visits:** During the regular academic year, prospective applicants may spend an evening in a residence hall with a student host.

**Video:** Available, fee charged.

## CAMPUS FACILITIES
**Of Special Interest:** Van Pelt-Dietrich Library.

# UNIVERSITY OF PITTSBURGH
**Pittsburgh, Pennsylvania**

**Contact:** Office of Admissions and Financial Aid, Second Floor Bruce Hall, Pittsburgh, PA 15260. *Phone:* 412-624-7488. *Fax:* 412-648-8815. *Web site:* http://www.pitt.edu/ *Visit location:* Office of Admissions and Financial Aid, Bruce Hall, Second Floor.

## QUICK FACTS
Enrollment: 24,837; UG: 15,556. Entrance: moderately difficult. SAT>500: 77% V, 77% M; ACT>18: 93%. Resident tuition and fees: $6164. Nonresident tuition and fees: $12,928. Room and board: $5414. Application deadline: rolling.

## GENERAL
State-related, university, coed. Part of University of Pittsburgh System. Awards bachelor's, master's, doctoral, and first professional degrees and post-master's certificates. Founded 1787. Setting: 132-acre urban campus. Undergraduate faculty: 3,394 (2,848 full-time, 546 part-time); student-faculty ratio is 14:1. Most popular recent majors: psychology, nursing, speech/rhetorical studies.

## CAMPUS VISITS
**College Calendar 1998–99:** *Regular classes:* Aug. 31–Dec. 11; Jan. 6–Apr. 16. *Breaks:* Dec. 20–Jan. 5. *Final exams:* Dec. 14–19; Apr. 19–24.

## VISIT OPPORTUNITIES

|  | Appointments? | Who? |
|---|---|---|
| **Campus Tour** | recommended, not required | open to all |
| **Information Session** | recommended, not required | open to all |
| **Admission Interview** | recommended, not required | open to all |
| **Classroom Visit** | not required | open to all |
| **Faculty Meeting** | recommended | open to all |
| **Overnight Visit** | required | open to all |

**Information Sessions:** M–F at 9:30 am, 1:30 pm; select Sat. at 9:30 am; 90 minutes.

**Interviews:** M–F; 30 minutes.

**Campus Tours:** Conducted by students. M–F at 10:00 am, 11:00 am, 12:00 pm, 2:00 pm, 3:00 pm; select Sat. at 11:00 am; 60 minutes.

**Class Visits:** Certain predetermined classrooms are open to visitors.

**Overnight Visits:** During the regular academic year and over the summer, prospective applicants may spend an evening in a residence hall with a student host.

**Video:** Free on request.

*University of Pittsburgh (continued)*

## CAMPUS FACILITIES

**Arts:** Frick Fine Arts Building and Library; Appointment Required: Carnegie Museum of Art and Natural History.

**Athletic:** Fitzgerald Field House, Pitt Stadium, Tress Hall.

## LOCAL ATTRACTIONS

Carnegie Museum of Art and Natural History; Cathedral of Learning Nationality Rooms; City of Pittsburgh; Carnegie Science Center, Pittsburgh, PA.

# UNIVERSITY OF THE SCIENCES IN PHILADELPHIA
## Philadelphia, Pennsylvania

**Contact:** Admission Office, 600 South 43rd Street, Philadelphia, PA 19104-4495. *Phone:* 215-596-8810. *Fax:* 215-895-1100. *E-mail:* admit@pcps.edu *Web site:* http://www.usip.edu *Visit location:* Admission Office, Griffith Hall, 600 South 43rd Street.

## QUICK FACTS

Enrollment: 2,135; UG: 1,967. Entrance: moderately difficult. SAT>500: 84% V, 95% M; ACT>18: 100%. Tuition and fees: $13,290. Room and board: $5985. Application deadline: rolling.

## GENERAL

Independent, university, coed. Awards bachelor's, master's, doctoral, and first professional degrees. Founded 1821. Setting: 35-acre urban campus. Undergraduate faculty: 205 (160 full-time, 45 part-time); student-faculty ratio is 13:1. Most popular recent majors: pharmacy, physical therapy, biology.

## CAMPUS VISITS

**College Calendar 1998–99:** *Regular classes:* Aug. 25–Dec. 12; Jan. 12–May 1. *Breaks:* Nov. 27–28; Mar. 2–6; Dec. 4–5. *Final exams:* Dec. 5–12; Apr. 27–May 1. *Admission office closed:* Fridays, May 15–Aug. 15.

## VISIT OPPORTUNITIES

| | Appointments? | Who? |
|---|---|---|
| **Campus Tour** | required | open to all |
| **Information Session** | required | open to all |
| **Admission Interview** | required | open to all |

| | Appointments? | Who? |
|---|---|---|
| **Classroom Visit** | required | open to all |
| **Faculty Meeting** | required | open to all |
| **Overnight Visit** | required | open to all |

**Information Sessions:** Please call for available schedule; 240 minutes.

**Interviews:** M–F; 30 minutes.

**Campus Tours:** Conducted by students. M–F at 10:00 am, 11:00 am, 1:00 pm, 2:00 pm; unavailable Fri. May 15 through Aug. 15; 30 minutes.

**Class Visits:** Certain predetermined classrooms are open to visitors, classroom visits are determined by the visit schedule.

**Overnight Visits:** During the regular academic year, prospective applicants may spend an evening in a residence hall with a student host.

## CAMPUS FACILITIES

**Of Special Interest:** Appointment Required: Pharmacy Museum.

## LOCAL ATTRACTIONS

Historic Philadelphia; South Street; University City district.

# VILLANOVA UNIVERSITY
## Villanova, Pennsylvania

**Contact:** Office of University Admission, 800 Lancaster Avenue, Villanova, PA 19085. *Phone:* toll-free 800-338-7927. *Fax:* 610-519-6450. *E-mail:* gotovu@email.vill.edu *Web site:* http://www.vill.edu/ *Visit location:* Office of University Admission, Austin Hall, 800 Lancaster Avenue.

## QUICK FACTS

Enrollment: 9,614; UG: 6,704. Entrance: moderately difficult. SAT>500: 96% V, 97% M; ACT>18: N/R. Tuition and fees: $19,133. Room and board: $7400. Application deadline: 1/15.

## GENERAL

Independent Roman Catholic, comprehensive, coed. Awards associate, bachelor's, master's, doctoral, and first professional degrees. Founded 1842. Setting: 222-acre suburban campus with easy access to Philadelphia. Undergraduate faculty: 750 (465 full-time, 285 part-time); student-faculty ratio is 13:1. Most popular recent majors: finance, accounting, nursing.

## CAMPUS VISITS

**College Calendar 1998–99:** *Regular classes:* Aug. 26–Dec. 14; Jan. 11–Apr. 28. *Breaks:* Oct. 16–26; Feb. 26–Mar. 8; Nov. 24–30; Mar. 31–Apr. 6. *Final exams:* Dec. 16–22; May 1–8. *Admission office closed:* Nov. 27, Dec. 23–24, Dec. 31; Easter Monday, Apr. 5; Good Friday, Apr. 2. *Special campus days:* Homecoming, Sept. 12; St. Thomas of Villanova Day, Sept. 10.

## VISIT OPPORTUNITIES

|  | Appointments? | Who? |
|---|---|---|
| **Campus Tour** | not required | applicants and parents |
| **Information Session** | not required | |
| **Classroom Visit** | recommended | |
| **Faculty Meeting** | recommended | applicants and parents |

**Information Sessions:** Mon. at 1:00 pm; Fri. at 1:00 pm; select Sat. at 11:00 am; 30 minutes.

**Campus Tours:** Conducted by students. Mon., Wed., Fri. at 10:30 am, 11:30 am, 1:30 pm, 2:30 pm; Thu. at 10:00 am, 11:30 am, 1:30 pm, 3:00 pm; call for summer schedule; 60 minutes.

**Class Visits:** Prospective students may attend a class in their area of interest.

**Video:** Available, fee charged.

## CAMPUS FACILITIES

**Of Special Interest:** Falvey Library.

# WASHINGTON AND JEFFERSON COLLEGE

**Washington, Pennsylvania**

**Contact:** Cheryl D. Leydig, Acting Director of Admission, 60 South Lincoln Street, Washington, PA 15301. *Phone:* 724-223-6025 or toll-free 888-WANDJAY. *Fax:* 724-223-5271. *E-mail:* cleydig@washjeff.edu *Visit location:* Office of Admission, McMillan Hall, 60 South Lincoln Street.

## QUICK FACTS

Enrollment: 1,097; UG: 1,097. Entrance: moderately difficult. SAT>500: 79% V, 81% M; ACT>18: N/R. Tuition and fees: $18,000. Room and board: $4350. Application deadline: 2/1.

## GENERAL

Independent, 4-year, coed. Awards associate and bachelor's degrees. Founded 1781. Setting: 40-acre small-town campus with easy access to Pittsburgh. Faculty: 111 (94 full-time, 17 part-time); student-faculty ratio is 11:1. Most popular recent majors: biology, psychology, business administration.

## CAMPUS VISITS

**College Calendar 1998–99:** *Regular classes:* Sept. 2–Dec. 4; Jan. 4–29; Feb. 3–May 11. *Breaks:* Mar. 12–22. *Final exams:* Dec. 8–14; May 13–18. *Special campus days:* Commencement, May 22; Family Weekend, Oct. 23–24; Homecoming, Oct. 9–10.

## VISIT OPPORTUNITIES

|  | Appointments? |
|---|---|
| **Campus Tour** | required |
| **Admission Interview** | required |
| **Classroom Visit** | required |
| **Faculty Meeting** | required |
| **Overnight Visit** | required |

**Interviews:** M–F, select Sat. 9:00 am–12:00 pm, except during special campus events; 45 minutes.

**Campus Tours:** Conducted by students and admission reps. M–F, Sat.; 60 minutes.

**Class Visits:** Prospective students may attend a class in their area of interest.

**Overnight Visits:** During the regular academic year, prospective applicants may spend an evening in a residence hall with a student host.

## CAMPUS FACILITIES

**Science:** Deiter-Porter Hall (Biology-Psychology).

**Arts:** Olin Fine Arts Center.

**Athletic:** Henry Memorial Center.

## LOCAL ATTRACTIONS

LeMoyne Crematory; LeMoyne House; Pennsylvania Trolley Museum; Bradford House; City of Pittsburgh.

# WIDENER UNIVERSITY
Chester, Pennsylvania

**Contact:** Admissions Office, 1 University Place, Chester, PA 19013. *Phone:* 610-499-4126 or toll-free 800-870-6481 (in-state). *Fax:* 610-499-4676. *E-mail:* admissions.office@widener.edu *Web site:* http://www.widener.edu/ *Visit location:* Admissions, 1 University Place.

## QUICK FACTS
Enrollment: 7,219; UG: 3,535. Entrance: moderately difficult. SAT>500: N/R; ACT>18: N/R. Tuition and fees: $14,380. Room and board: $6200. Application deadline: rolling.

## GENERAL
Independent, comprehensive, coed. Awards associate, bachelor's, master's, doctoral, and first professional degrees. Founded 1821. Setting: 110-acre suburban campus with easy access to Philadelphia. Undergraduate faculty: 441 (241 full-time, 200 part-time); student-faculty ratio is 12:1. Most popular recent majors: nursing, business administration, psychology.

## CAMPUS VISITS
**College Calendar 1998–99:** *Regular classes:* Sept. 9–Dec. 16; Jan. 12–May 7. *Breaks:* Oct. 30–Nov. 2; Mar. 1–8; Dec. 22–Jan. 11. *Final exams:* Dec. 18–22; Apr. 30–May 7. *Special campus days:* Commencement, May 16; Homecoming, Oct. 17; Open House Programs, Sept. 19, Oct. 24, Nov. 21.

## VISIT OPPORTUNITIES

|  | Appointments? | Who? |
|---|---|---|
| **Campus Tour** | recommended, not required | open to all |
| **Admission Interview** | required | open to all |
| **Classroom Visit** | required | open to all |
| **Faculty Meeting** | required | open to all |
| **Overnight Visit** | required | open to all |

**Interviews:** M–F, select Sat.; 60 minutes.
**Campus Tours:** Conducted by students. M–F, select Sat.; 45 minutes.
**Class Visits:** Classroom visits are determined by the visit schedule.
**Overnight Visits:** During the regular academic year, prospective applicants may spend an evening in a residence hall with a student host.
**Video:** Free on request.

## CAMPUS FACILITIES
**Of Special Interest:** Wolfgram Memorial Library.

# YORK COLLEGE OF PENNSYLVANIA
York, Pennsylvania

**Contact:** Admissions Office, York College of Pennsylvania, York, PA 17405. *Phone:* toll-free 800-455-8018. *Fax:* 717-849-1607. *E-mail:* admissions@ycp.edu *Web site:* http://www.ycp.edu/ *Visit location:* Admissions Office, Miller Administration Building, Country Club Road.

## QUICK FACTS
Enrollment: 4,622; UG: 4,411. Entrance: moderately difficult. SAT>500: 83% V, 80% M; ACT>18: N/R. Tuition and fees: $6100. Room and board: $4390. Application deadline: rolling.

## GENERAL
Independent, comprehensive, coed. Awards associate, bachelor's, and master's degrees. Founded 1787. Setting: 80-acre suburban campus with easy access to Baltimore. Undergraduate faculty: 419 (143 full-time, 276 part-time); student-faculty ratio is 17:1. Most popular recent majors: nursing, elementary education, law enforcement/police science.

## CAMPUS VISITS
**College Calendar 1998–99:** *Regular classes:* Sept. 1–Dec. 15; Jan. 20–May 7. *Breaks:* Oct. 17–21; Feb. 28–Mar. 8; Nov. 25–30; Apr. 1–6. *Final exams:* Dec. 16–21; May 8–13. *Admission office closed:* Fri. mid-May through mid-Aug. at 11:30 am.

## VISIT OPPORTUNITIES

|  | Appointments? | Who? |
|---|---|---|
| **Campus Tour** | recommended, not required | open to all |
| **Information Session** | recommended | open to all |
| **Admission Interview** | required | open to all |
| **Classroom Visit** | required | open to all |
| **Faculty Meeting** | required | applicants and parents |

**Information Sessions:** Group sessions select Sat. 10:00 am and 12:00 pm and specific Federal holidays; 60 minutes.

**Interviews:** M–F; 30 minutes.

**Campus Tours:** Conducted by students. Mon., Tue., Wed., Thu. at 10:00 am, 11:30 am, 1:30 pm, 3:00 pm; Fri. at 10:00 am, 11:30 am, 1:30 pm; 60 minutes.

**Class Visits:** Prospective students may attend a class in their area of interest.

**Video:** Free on request.

### CAMPUS FACILITIES
**Science:** Life Science Building, McKay Hall—houses Mechanical Engineering Labs.

**Arts:** Cora Miller Art Gallery, Collegiate Gallery.

**Athletic:** Wolf Gymnasium.

**Of Special Interest:** Brougher Chapel, York College Bookstore.

### LOCAL ATTRACTIONS
Harley Davidson Motorcycle Museum; York Historical Society; Galleria and West Manchester Malls; Weightlifing Hall of Fame.

# RHODE ISLAND

## BROWN UNIVERSITY
### Providence, Rhode Island

**Contact:** Admission Office, 45 Prospect Street, Providence, RI 02912. *Phone:* 401-863-2378. *Fax:* 401-863-9300. *E-mail:* admission___undergraduate@ brown.edu *Web site:* http://www.brown.edu/ *Visit location:* The College Admission Office, Corliss-Brackett House, 45 Prospect Street.

### QUICK FACTS
Enrollment: 7,372; UG: 5,751. Entrance: most difficult. SAT>500: 98% V, 99% M; ACT>18: 100%. Tuition and fees: $23,124. Room and board: $6776. Application deadline: 1/1.

### GENERAL
Independent, university, coed. Awards bachelor's, master's, doctoral, and first professional degrees. Founded 1764. Setting: 140-acre urban campus with easy access to Boston. Undergraduate faculty: 721 (554 full-time, 167 part-time); student-faculty ratio is 8:1. Most popular recent majors: biology, English, history.

### CAMPUS VISITS
**College Calendar 1998–99:** *Regular classes:* Sept. 8–Dec. 10; Jan. 27–May 11. *Breaks:* Dec. 20–Jan. 26;

Mar. 27–Apr. 4. *Final exams:* Dec. 11–19; May 12–21. *Admission office closed:* Dec. 24–25, Nov. 25–27, Jan. 1, Jan. 16, May 22. *Special campus days:* Commencement Monday, May 31; Homecoming Weekend, Oct. 23–25; Parents' Weekend, Oct. 16–18.

### VISIT OPPORTUNITIES

|  | Appointments? | Who? |
|---|---|---|
| **Campus Tour** | not required | open to all |
| **Information Session** | not required | open to all |
| **Admission Interview** | required | open to all |
| **Classroom Visit** | not required | open to all |
| **Faculty Meeting** | required | open to all |
| **Overnight Visit** | required | open to all |

**Information Sessions:** M–F at 10:00 am, 2:00 pm; select Sat. at 10:00 am, 11:00 am; M–F (mid-Sept.–mid-Nov.) at 10:00 am, 2:00 pm; M–F (Dec.–mid-Apr.) at 2:00 pm; Sat. (Sept. to Nov.) at 10:00 am, 11:00 am; 60 minutes.

**Interviews:** M–F; unavailable Sept. 7, Oct. 12, Nov. 27, and mid-Dec.–May; 30 minutes.

**Campus Tours:** Conducted by students. M–F at 10:00 am, 11:00 am, 1:00 pm, 3:00 pm, 4:00 pm; select Sat. (mid-Sept. –mid-Nov.) at 10:00 am, 11:00 am, and 12:00 pm; only 3:00 pm during vacations in Dec., Jan., and Mar. and exams in Dec. and May; 60 minutes.

**Class Visits:** Prospective students may attend a class in their area of interest.

**Overnight Visits:** During the regular academic year, prospective applicants may spend an evening in a residence hall with a student host.

### CAMPUS FACILITIES
**Science:** Center for Information Technology; Appointment Required: Science Library, Ladd Observatory, Prince Engineering Lab.

**Arts:** List Art Building, Bell Art Gallery, Dill Theatre Complex, Ashamu Dance Studio.

**Athletic:** Pizzitola Gymnasium, Olney-Margolies Athletic Center, Swim Center (Smith Center).

**Of Special Interest:** Faunce House Student Union; Appointment Required: Haffenreffer Museum of Anthropology, John Carter Brown Library (early Americana).

*Brown University (continued)*

### LOCAL ATTRACTIONS
Rhode Island School of Design, Waterplace Park, John Brown House, Rhode Island State Capitol, Roger Williams Park and Zoo.

# JOHNSON & WALES UNIVERSITY
### Providence, Rhode Island

**Contact:** Mr. Kenneth DiSaia, Dean of Admissions, 8 Abbott Park Place, Providence, RI 02903. *Phone:* toll-free 800-342-5598 (out-of-state). *Fax:* 401-598-1835. *E-mail:* admissions@jwu.edu *Web site:* http://www.jwu.edu/ *Visit location:* Admissions Office, University Hall, 111 Dorrance Street.

### QUICK FACTS
Enrollment: 7,979; UG: 7,467. Entrance: minimally difficult. SAT>500: 31% V, 30% M; ACT>18: N/R. Tuition and fees: $12,807. Room and board: $5550. Application deadline: rolling.

### GENERAL
Independent, comprehensive, coed. Awards associate, bachelor's, master's, and doctoral degrees (branch locations: Charleston, SC; Vail, CO; North Miami, FL; Norfolk, VA; Worcester, MA; Gothenberg, Sweden). Founded 1914. Setting: 47-acre urban campus with easy access to Boston. Undergraduate faculty: 332 (229 full-time, 103 part-time); student-faculty ratio is 30:1. Most popular recent majors: culinary arts, hotel and restaurant management, hospitality management.

### CAMPUS VISITS
**College Calendar 1998–99:** *Regular classes:* Sept. 8–Nov. 17; Dec. 1–Feb. 23; Mar. 8–May 18. *Breaks:* Nov. 23–30; Dec. 18–Jan. 3; Feb. 27–Mar. 7. *Final exams:* Nov. 18–20; Feb. 24–26; May 19–21. *Admission office closed:* week between Christmas and New Year's Day. *Special campus days:* Commencement, May 20; Homecoming, Oct. 2–4.

### VISIT OPPORTUNITIES

|  | Appointments? | Who? |
| --- | --- | --- |
| **Campus Tour** | recommended, not required | open to all |
| **Information Session** | required | open to all |

|  | Appointments? | Who? |
| --- | --- | --- |
| **Admission Interview** | required | open to all |
| **Classroom Visit** | required | open to all |
| **Faculty Meeting** | required | open to all |
| **Overnight Visit** | required | open to all |

**Information Sessions:** M–F, select Sat.; 90 minutes.

**Interviews:** M–F, select Sat.; 30 minutes.

**Campus Tours:** Conducted by students. M–F at 9:00 am, 1:00 pm; select Sat.; 120 minutes.

**Class Visits:** Certain predetermined classrooms are open to visitors.

**Overnight Visits:** During the regular academic year.

**Video:** Free on request.

### CAMPUS FACILITIES
**Athletic:** Recreation Center and Delaney Sports Complex.

**Of Special Interest:** University owned hotels, restaurants, travel agency, University owned Women's Retail Store, The Arcade-Indoor Shopping Center.

# SALVE REGINA UNIVERSITY
### Newport, Rhode Island

**Contact:** Admissions Staff, 100 Ochre Point Avenue, Newport, RI 02840. *Phone:* toll-free 888-GO-SALVE. *Fax:* 401-848-2823. *E-mail:* sruadmis@salve.edu *Web site:* http://www.salve.edu/ *Visit location:* Admissions Office, Ochre Court—First Floor, 100 Ochre Point Avenue.

### QUICK FACTS
Enrollment: 2,113; UG: 1,545. Entrance: moderately difficult. SAT>500: 42% V, 31% M; ACT>18: N/R. Tuition and fees: $16,300. Room and board: $7250. Application deadline: rolling.

### GENERAL
Independent Roman Catholic, comprehensive, coed. Awards associate, bachelor's, master's, and doctoral degrees and post-master's certificates. Founded 1934. Setting: 65-acre suburban campus with easy access to Boston. Undergraduate faculty: 195 (105 full-time, 90 part-time); student-faculty ratio is 14:1. Most popular recent majors: business administration, elementary education, nursing.

## CAMPUS VISITS

**College Calendar 1998–99:** *Regular classes:* Aug. 31–Dec. 10; Jan. 12–May 3. *Breaks:* Nov. 25–29; Mar. 13–21; Dec. 19–Jan. 11. *Final exams:* Dec. 14–18; May 6–11. *Special campus days:* Commencement, May 16; Open House, Oct. 25, Nov. 8.

## VISIT OPPORTUNITIES

|  | Appointments? | Who? |
|---|---|---|
| **Campus Tour** | recommended | open to all |
| **Information Session** | required | open to all |
| **Admission Interview** | required | open to all |
| **Classroom Visit** | required | open to all |
| **Faculty Meeting** | required | open to all |
| **Overnight Visit** | required | applicants only |

**Information Sessions:** Select Sat.; during academic year; 60 minutes.

**Interviews:** M–F; 30 minutes.

**Campus Tours:** Conducted by students. M–F, select Sat.; 40 minutes.

**Class Visits:** Prospective students may attend a class in their area of interest, classroom visits are determined by the visit schedule.

**Overnight Visits:** During the regular academic year, prospective applicants may spend an evening in a residence hall with a student host.

**Video:** Free on request.

## CAMPUS FACILITIES

**Of Special Interest:** Our entire campus is in a nationally recognized historic district on the Atlantic Ocean.

## LOCAL ATTRACTIONS

Newport, Mansions, Cliff walk, Ocean drive.

# UNIVERSITY OF RHODE ISLAND
### Kingston, Rhode Island

**Contact:** Admissions Office, University of Rhode Island, 8 Ranger Road, Suite 1, Kingston, RI 02881. *Phone:* 401-874-7000. *Fax:* 401-874-5523. *E-mail:* uriadmit@uriacc.uri.edu *Web site:* http://www.uri.edu/ *Visit location:* Undergraduate Admissions, Green Hall, 8 Ranger Road.

## QUICK FACTS

Enrollment: 9,828; UG: 9,828. Entrance: moderately difficult. SAT>500: 72% V, 73% M; ACT>18: N/R. Resident tuition and fees: $4592. Nonresident tuition and fees: $12,400. Room and board: $5764. Application deadline: 3/1.

## GENERAL

State-supported, university, coed. Part of Rhode Island State System of Higher Education. Awards bachelor's, master's, doctoral, and first professional degrees. Founded 1892. Setting: 1,200-acre small-town campus. Undergraduate faculty: 626 (610 full-time, 16 part-time); student-faculty ratio is 15:1. Most popular recent majors: psychology, individual/ family development, pharmacy.

## CAMPUS VISITS

**College Calendar 1998–99:** *Regular classes:* Sept. 9–Dec. 14; Jan. 19–May 4. *Breaks:* Dec. 23–Jan. 18. *Final exams:* Dec. 17–23; May 7–14. *Special campus days:* Commencement, May 23; Fall Open House, Oct. 24, Nov. 13, Oct. 17; Homecoming, Oct. 10.

## VISIT OPPORTUNITIES

|  | Appointments? | Who? |
|---|---|---|
| **Campus Tour** | recommended | open to all |
| **Information Session** | recommended | open to all |
| **Admission Interview** | required | |
| **Classroom Visit** | recommended | |
| **Faculty Meeting** | required | open to all |

**Information Sessions:** Mon. at 1:30 pm; Fri. at 1:30 pm; select Sat. at 11:30 am; 45 minutes.

**Interviews:** Mon.–Thu. during summer and fall; 45 minutes.

**Campus Tours:** Conducted by students. M–F at 10:00 am, 12:00 pm, 2:00 pm; Sat. at 10:00 am, 2:00 pm; Sat. during summer; 75 minutes.

**Class Visits:** Classroom visits are determined by the visit schedule.

## CAMPUS FACILITIES

**Science:** Engineering Technology Center; Appointment Required: pharmacy building.

**Arts:** Appointment Required: music labs.

**Athletic:** Mackal Field House.

**Of Special Interest:** Student Union, Library.

*University of Rhode Island (continued)*

VISIT OPPORTUNITIES—*continued*

LOCAL ATTRACTIONS
South County beaches.

|  | Appointments? | Who? |
|---|---|---|
| **Overnight Visit** | required | admitted applicants only |

# SOUTH CAROLINA

## THE CITADEL, THE MILITARY COLLEGE OF SOUTH CAROLINA
**Charleston, South Carolina**

**Contact:** Office of Admissions, 171 Moultrie Street, Charleston, SC 29409. *Phone:* 843-953-5230 or toll-free 800-868-1842. *Fax:* 843-953-7630. *E-mail:* admissions@citadel.edu *Web site:* http://www.citadel. edu/ *Visit location:* Admissions, Bond Hall, The Citadel, 171 Moultrie Street.

### QUICK FACTS
Enrollment: 3,709; UG: 1,879. Entrance: moderately difficult. SAT>500: 68% V, 70% M; ACT>18: 100%. Resident tuition and fees: $3499. Nonresident tuition and fees: $8142. Room and board: $3950. Application deadline: 7/1.

### GENERAL
State-supported, comprehensive, coed. Awards bachelor's and master's degrees. Founded 1842. Setting: 130-acre urban campus. Undergraduate faculty: 199 (150 full-time, 49 part-time); student-faculty ratio is 18:1. Most popular recent majors: business administration, political science, civil engineering.

### CAMPUS VISITS
**College Calendar 1998–99:** *Regular classes:* Aug. 22–Dec. 11; Jan. 11–Apr. 26. *Breaks:* Dec. 19–Jan. 6; Mar. 26–Apr. 6. *Final exams:* Dec. 12–19; Apr. 28–May 4.

### VISIT OPPORTUNITIES

|  | Appointments? | Who? |
|---|---|---|
| **Campus Tour** | required | open to all |
| **Information Session** | required | open to all |
| **Admission Interview** | recommended | open to all |
| **Classroom Visit** | required | open to all |
| **Faculty Meeting** | required | open to all |

**Information Sessions:** At off-campus locales for groups varying from 20-100; call for information; 120 minutes.

**Interviews:** M–F; 45 minutes.

**Campus Tours:** Conducted by students. M–F 9:00 am–3:00 pm; 60 minutes.

**Class Visits:** Prospective students may attend a class in their area of interest.

**Overnight Visits:** During the regular academic year.

**Video:** Free on request.

### CAMPUS FACILITIES
**Of Special Interest:** Daniel Library.

### LOCAL ATTRACTIONS
City of Charleston; USS Yorktown Museum.

## CLEMSON UNIVERSITY
**Clemson, South Carolina**

**Contact:** The Visitors Center, Alumni Circle Drive, Clemson, SC 29634. *Phone:* 864-656-4789. *Fax:* 864-656-7451. *E-mail:* mantony@clemson.edu *Web site:* http://www.clemson.edu/ *Visit location:* Visitors Center, Class of 1944 Visitors Center, Alumni Circle Drive.

### QUICK FACTS
Enrollment: 16,288; UG: 12,602. Entrance: moderately difficult. SAT>500: 82% V, 87% M; ACT>18: 98%. Resident tuition and fees: $3392. Nonresident tuition and fees: $8816. Room and board: $3888. Application deadline: 5/1.

### GENERAL
State-supported, university, coed. Awards bachelor's, master's, and doctoral degrees. Founded 1889. Setting: 1,400-acre small-town campus. Undergraduate faculty: 1,339 (1,156 full-time, 183 part-time); student-faculty ratio is 17:1. Most popular recent majors: mechanical engineering, elementary education, nursing.

## CAMPUS VISITS
**College Calendar 1998–99:** *Regular classes:* Aug. 20–Dec. 4; Jan. 6–Apr. 23. *Breaks:* Oct. 31–Nov. 3; Mar. 13–21; Nov. 26–29. *Final exams:* Dec. 7–12; Apr. 26–May 1. *Admission office closed:* July 5, Dec. 22–24, Dec. 27, Nov. 26–27, Dec. 23–25; fall break, Oct. 18; spring break, Mar. 18–19. *Special campus days:* First Friday Parade, Sept. 4; Homecoming, Oct. 10; Parents Weekend, Oct. 10.

## VISIT OPPORTUNITIES

| | Appointments? | Who? |
|---|---|---|
| **Campus Tour** | recommended, not required | open to all |
| **Information Session** | recommended, not required | open to all |
| **Admission Interview** | not required | open to all |
| **Classroom Visit** | required | open to all |
| **Faculty Meeting** | required | open to all |

**Information Sessions:** M–F, Sat. at 9:45 am, 1:45 pm; Sun. at 1:45 pm; unavailable select university holidays; 15 minutes.

**Interviews:** M–F; 30 minutes.

**Campus Tours:** Conducted by students. M–F, Sat. at 9:45 am, 1:45 pm; Sun. at 1:45 pm; unavailable select university holidays; 75 minutes.

**Class Visits:** Prospective students may attend a class in their area of interest.

**Video:** Free on request.

## CAMPUS FACILITIES
**Science:** Appointment Required: Planetarium, Geology Museum.

**Arts:** Appointment Required: Brooks Center for the Performing Arts.

**Athletic:** Walker Golf Course; Appointment Required: Memorial Stadium, Littlejohn Coliseum.

**Of Special Interest:** John C. Calhoun Mansion, Agricultural Sales Center, S.C. Botanical Gardens.

# COASTAL CAROLINA UNIVERSITY
**Conway, South Carolina**

**Contact:** Admissions Office, PO Box 261954, Conway, SC 29528-6054. *Phone:* 803-349-2026 or toll-free 800-277-7000. *Fax:* 803-349-2127. *E-mail:* admissions@coastal.edu *Web site:* http://www.coastal.edu/ *Visit location:* Office of Admissions, Admissions Building, PO Box 261954.

## QUICK FACTS
Enrollment: 4,061; UG: 3,936. Entrance: moderately difficult. SAT>500: 54% V, 49% M; ACT>18: 80%. Resident tuition and fees: $3100. Nonresident tuition and fees: $8320. Room and board: $4640. Application deadline: 8/15.

## GENERAL
State-supported, comprehensive, coed. Awards bachelor's and master's degrees. Founded 1954. Setting: 244-acre suburban campus. Undergraduate faculty: 268 (182 full-time, 86 part-time); student-faculty ratio is 18:1. Most popular recent majors: marine science, elementary education, business administration.

## CAMPUS VISITS
**College Calendar 1998–99:** *Regular classes:* Aug. 20–Dec. 4; Jan. 14–Apr. 30. *Breaks:* Nov. 23–27; Mar. 15–19. *Final exams:* Dec. 7–11; May 3–7. *Special campus days:* CINO Days; Homecoming.

## VISIT OPPORTUNITIES

| | Appointments? | Who? |
|---|---|---|
| **Campus Tour** | recommended, not required | open to all |
| **Information Session** | recommended, not required | open to all |
| **Admission Interview** | recommended, not required | open to all |
| **Classroom Visit** | required | open to all |
| **Faculty Meeting** | required | open to all |

**Information Sessions:** Usually held off-campus at select high schools or special admission programs; 60 minutes.

**Interviews:** M–F at 9:45 am, 2:45 pm; select Sat.; 30 minutes.

**Campus Tours:** Conducted by students and admission reps. M–F at 9:45 am, 2:45 pm; available during special visitation weekends; 60 minutes.

**Class Visits:** Prospective students may attend a class in their area of interest.

**Video:** Free on request.

*Coastal Carolina University (continued)*

**CAMPUS FACILITIES**
**Arts:** Little Theatre Exhibit Room.
**Of Special Interest:** Wheelwright Auditorium.

**LOCAL ATTRACTIONS**
Myrtle Beach and the Atlantic Ocean; over 100 golf courses in area; Brookgreen Gardens.

# COLLEGE OF CHARLESTON
## Charleston, South Carolina

**Contact:** Office of Admissions and Adult Student Services, 66 George Street, Charleston, SC 29424. *Phone:* 843-953-5670. *Fax:* 843-953-6322. *E-mail:* admissions@cofc.edu *Web site:* http://www.cofc.edu/ *Visit location:* Office of Administration and Adult Student Services, Towell Library, 66 George Street.

**QUICK FACTS**
Enrollment: 8,642; UG: 8,642. Entrance: moderately difficult. SAT>500: 89% V, 85% M; ACT>18: 97%. Resident tuition and fees: $3290. Nonresident tuition and fees: $6580. Room and board: $3850. Application deadline: 7/1.

**GENERAL**
State-supported, 4-year, coed. Awards bachelor's degrees (also offers graduate degree programs through University of Charleston, South Carolina). Founded 1770. Setting: 52-acre urban campus. Most popular recent majors: business administration, communications, elementary education.

**CAMPUS VISITS**
**College Calendar 1998–99:** *Regular classes:* Aug. 25–Dec. 7; Jan. 14–Apr. 28. *Breaks:* Oct. 31–Nov. 3; Mar. 6–14; Nov. 25–29. *Final exams:* Dec. 8–16; Apr. 30–May 8. *Admission office closed:* Dec. 23–Jan. 4. *Special campus days:* Commencement, May 15; Mid-Year Commencement, Dec. 20; Open House, Oct. 10, Nov. 14, Mar. 13.

**VISIT OPPORTUNITIES**

|  | Appointments? | Who? |
|---|---|---|
| **Campus Tour** | recommended, not required | open to all |
| **Information Session** | recommended, not required | open to all |

**VISIT OPPORTUNITIES**—*continued*

|  | Appointments? | Who? |
|---|---|---|
| **Faculty Meeting** | required | |

**Information Sessions:** M–F at 10:00 am, 2:00 pm; during summer 10:00 am only; call for appointment; 30 minutes.
**Campus Tours:** Conducted by students. M–F at 10:00 am, 2:00 pm; during summer 10:00 am only; call for appointment; 60 minutes.
**Video:** Free on request.

**CAMPUS FACILITIES**
**Of Special Interest:** Robert Scott Small Library.

**LOCAL ATTRACTIONS**
Magnolia Plantation, Drayton Hall Plantation, Boone Hall Plantation, Middleton Plantation, Charles Towne Landing, Patriots Point Naval Museum.

# FURMAN UNIVERSITY
## Greenville, South Carolina

**Contact:** Mr. J. Carey Thompson, Director of Admissions, 3300 Poinsett Highway, Greenville, SC 29613. *Phone:* 864-294-2034. *Fax:* 864-294-3127. *E-mail:* admissions@furman.edu *Web site:* http://www.furman.edu/ *Visit location:* Office of Admissions, Earle Infirmary, 3300 Poinsett Highway.

**QUICK FACTS**
Enrollment: 2,840; UG: 2,571. Entrance: very difficult. SAT>500: 96% V, 96% M; ACT>18: 100%. Tuition and fees: $16,419. Room and board: $4449. Application deadline: 2/1.

**GENERAL**
Independent, comprehensive, coed. Awards bachelor's and master's degrees. Founded 1826. Setting: 750-acre suburban campus. Undergraduate faculty: 200 (191 full-time, 9 part-time); student-faculty ratio is 12:1. Most popular recent majors: political science, business administration, biology.

**CAMPUS VISITS**
**College Calendar 1998–99:** *Regular classes:* Sept. 15–Dec. 8; Jan. 5–Feb. 19; Mar. 4–May 20. *Breaks:* Apr. 2–5; Nov. 21–29. *Final exams:* Dec. 10–15; Feb. 22–24; May 21–25. *Admission office closed:* Sept. 7,

Nov. 26–27, Dec. 24–Jan. 1. *Special campus days:* Commencement, May 29; Homecoming Weekend, Oct. 16–18.

## VISIT OPPORTUNITIES

|  | Appointments? | Who? |
|---|---|---|
| **Campus Tour** | recommended, not required | open to all |
| **Information Session** | recommended, not required | open to all |
| **Classroom Visit** | required | open to all |
| **Faculty Meeting** | required | open to all |
| **Overnight Visit** | required | open to all |

**Information Sessions:** M–F, select Sat.; inquire for available schedule; 45 minutes.

**Campus Tours:** Conducted by students and admission reps. M–F, select Sat.; 60 minutes.

**Class Visits:** Prospective students may attend a class in their area of interest, classroom visits are determined by the visit schedule.

**Overnight Visits:** During the regular academic year, prospective applicants may spend an evening in a residence hall with a student host.

**Video:** Free on request.

## CAMPUS FACILITIES

**Of Special Interest:** Appointment Required: Residence Halls.

## LOCAL ATTRACTIONS

Peace Center for the Performing Arts; Downtown Greenville; BMW Plant.

# JOHNSON & WALES UNIVERSITY

**Charleston, South Carolina**

**Contact:** Brian Martin, Admissions Assistant, 701 East Bay Street, PCC 1409, Charleston, SC 29403. *Phone:* 803-763-0200 or toll-free 800-868-1522 (out-of-state). *Fax:* 803-763-0318. *E-mail:* admissions@jwu-sc.ed *Web site:* http://www.jwu.edu/ *Visit location:* Admissions, Building 1680, 1680 North Woodmere Drive, Apartment 13.

## QUICK FACTS

Enrollment: 1,325; UG: 1,325. Entrance: minimally difficult. SAT>500: N/App; ACT>18: N/App. Tuition and fees: $13,689. Room only: $3738. Application deadline: rolling.

## GENERAL

Independent, 4-year, coed. Administratively affiliated with Johnson & Wales University (RI). Awards associate and bachelor's degrees. Founded 1984. Faculty: 49 (35 full-time, 14 part-time); student-faculty ratio is 27:1. Most popular recent major: culinary arts.

## CAMPUS VISITS

**College Calendar 1998–99:** *Regular classes:* Sept. 8–Nov. 17; Dec. 1–Feb. 23; Mar. 8–May 18. *Breaks:* Nov. 21–30; Dec. 18–Jan. 3. *Final exams:* Nov. 18–20; Feb. 24–26; May 19–21. *Admission office closed:* Nov. 26, Dec. 24–Jan. 2. *Special campus days:* Family Weekend, Oct. 16–18; Graduation, May 22; Open House, Oct. 25, Nov. 15, Dec. 12, Feb. 20, Mar. 21, Apr. 17, May 16, June 12, July 17, Aug. 14.

## VISIT OPPORTUNITIES

|  | Appointments? | Who? |
|---|---|---|
| **Campus Tour** | recommended | open to all |
| **Information Session** | recommended, not required | open to all |
| **Admission Interview** | recommended, not required | open to all |
| **Faculty Meeting** | required | |
| **Overnight Visit** | required | |

**Information Sessions:** Mon., Tue., Wed., Thu. at 9:30 am, 1:30 pm; Fri. at 9:30 am; select Sat. at 11:00 am; special Mon. holiday Tour N' More at 11:00 am by appointment only; 60 minutes.

**Interviews:** M–F, select Sat.; available during Open House; 30 minutes.

**Campus Tours:** Conducted by students and admission reps. Mon., Tue., Wed., Thu. at 9:30 am, 1:30 pm; Fri. at 9:30 am; select Sat. at 11:00 am; Open House 11:00 am–2:00 pm; 60 minutes.

**Class Visits:** Classrooms are viewed from outside class.

**Overnight Visits:** During the summer.

**Video:** Free on request.

*Johnson & Wales University (continued)*

### CAMPUS FACILITIES
**Arts:** Culinary Labs, Dining Rooms, Pasty Labs, Resource Center.
**Athletic:** Student Center.
**Of Special Interest:** Appointment Required: Local Externship Properties.

### LOCAL ATTRACTIONS
City of Charleston—historic gardens, homes, plantations, beaches, resorts, waterfront park, visitor center.

## PRESBYTERIAN COLLEGE
### Clinton, South Carolina

**Contact:** Admissions Office, 503 South Broad Street, Clinton, SC 29325. *Phone:* toll-free 800-476-7272 Ext. 8230. *Fax:* 864-833-8481. *E-mail:* admissions@presby.edu *Web site:* http://www.presby.edu/ *Visit location:* Admissions Office, Smith Administration Building, 503 South Broad Street.

### QUICK FACTS
Enrollment: 1,093; UG: 1,093. Entrance: very difficult. SAT>500: 71% V, 80% M; ACT>18: 93%. Tuition and fees: $14,806. Room and board: $4216. Application deadline: 4/1.

### GENERAL
Independent Presbyterian, 4-year, coed. Awards bachelor's degrees. Founded 1880. Setting: 215-acre small-town campus. Faculty: 119 (78 full-time, 41 part-time); student-faculty ratio is 12:1. Most popular recent majors: business administration, education, biology.

### CAMPUS VISITS
**College Calendar 1998–99:** *Regular classes:* Sept. 2–Dec. 11; Jan. 12–Apr. 23. *Breaks:* Oct. 16–20; Mar. 5–14; Nov. 25–29; Apr. 1–5. *Final exams:* Dec. 14–18; Apr. 26–30. *Admission office closed:* Oct. 19, Mar. 8. *Special campus days:* Commencement, May 8; Homecoming and Inauguration, Oct. 10; Parents Weekend, Oct. 31.

### VISIT OPPORTUNITIES

|  | Appointments? | Who? |
|---|---|---|
| **Campus Tour** | required | open to all |
| **Information Session** | required | open to all |

### VISIT OPPORTUNITIES—*continued*

|  | Appointments? | Who? |
|---|---|---|
| **Admission Interview** | required | open to all |
| **Classroom Visit** | required | open to all |
| **Faculty Meeting** | required | open to all |
| **Overnight Visit** | required | open to all |

**Information Sessions:** Mon. at 9:00 am, 10:00 am, 11:00 am, 1:30 pm, 2:30 pm, 3:30 pm; Tue. at 9:00 am, 11:00 am, 1:30 pm, 2:30 pm, 3:30 pm; Wed. at 9:00 am, 10:00 am, 11:00 am, 1:30 pm, 2:30 pm, 3:30 pm; Thu. at 9:00 am, 10:00 am, 11:00 am, 1:30 pm, 2:30 pm, 3:30 pm; Fri. at 9:00 am, 10:00 am, 11:00 am, 1:30 pm, 2:30 pm; Sat. at 9:00 am, 10:00 am, 11:00 am during school year; 60 minutes.

**Interviews:** Mon. at 9:00 am, 10:00 am, 11:00 am, 1:30 pm, 2:30 pm, 3:30 pm; Tue. at 9:00 am, 11:00 am, 1:30 pm, 2:30 pm, 3:30 ; Wed. at 9:00 am, 10:00 am, 11:00 am, 1:30 pm, 2:30 pm, 3:30 pm; Thu. at 9:00 am, 10:00 am, 11:00 am, 1:30 pm, 2:30 pm, 3:30 pm; Fri. at 9:00 am, 10:00 am, 11:00 am, 1:30 pm, 2:30 pm; Sat. at 9:00 am, 10:00 am, 11:00 am during school year; 60 minutes.

**Campus Tours:** Conducted by students. Mon. at 10:00 am, 11:00 am, 12:00 pm, 2:30 pm, 3:30 pm, 4:30 pm; Tue. at 10:00 am, 12:00 pm, 2:30 pm, 3:30 pm, 4:30 pm; Wed. at 10:00 am, 11:00 am, 12:00 pm, 2:30 pm, 3:30 pm, 4:30 pm; Thu. at 10:00 am, 11:00 am, 12:00 pm, 2:30 pm, 3:30 pm, 4:30 pm; Fri. at 10:00 am, 11:00 am, 12:00 pm, 2:30 pm, 3:30 pm; Sat. at 10:00 am, 11:00 am, 12:00 pm during school year; 60 minutes.

**Class Visits:** Prospective students may attend a class in their area of interest, certain predetermined classrooms are open to visitors, classroom visits are determined by the visit schedule.

**Overnight Visits:** During the regular academic year, prospective applicants may spend an evening in a residence hall with a student host.

**Video:** Free on request.

### CAMPUS FACILITIES
**Of Special Interest:** James H. Thomason Library.

## UNIVERSITY OF SOUTH CAROLINA
### Columbia, South Carolina

**Contact:** Visitor Center, Carolina Plaza, Columbia, SC 29208. *Phone:* toll-free 800-922-9755 (in-state).

*Fax:* 803-777-0687. *Web site:* http://www.csd.scarolina. edu/ *Visit location:* Visitor Center, Carolina Plaza, Assembly and Pendleton Streets.

## QUICK FACTS

Enrollment: 24,083; UG: 14,464. Entrance: moderately difficult. SAT>500: 67% V, 66% M; ACT>18: 81%. Resident tuition and fees: $3534. Nonresident tuition and fees: $8940. Room and board: $3830. Application deadline: rolling.

## GENERAL

State-supported, university, coed. Part of University of South Carolina System. Awards bachelor's, master's, doctoral, and first professional degrees. Founded 1801. Setting: 242-acre urban campus. Undergraduate faculty: 1,449 (1,125 full-time, 324 part-time); student-faculty ratio is 17:1.

## CAMPUS VISITS

**College Calendar 1998–99:** *Regular classes:* Aug. 20–Dec. 4; Jan. 11–Apr. 28. *Breaks:* Oct. 12–13; Mar. 4–14; Nov. 25–29. *Final exams:* Dec. 7–14; Apr. 30–May 7. *Admission office closed:* Christmas—New Year Break; Day after Thanksgiving, Nov. 27. *Special campus days:* Fall Commencement, Dec. 14; Homecoming, Oct. 17; Spring Commencement, May 7–8.

## VISIT OPPORTUNITIES

|  | **Appointments?** | **Who?** |
|---|---|---|
| **Campus Tour** | recommended, not required | open to all |
| **Admission Interview** | recommended, not required | open to all |
| **Classroom Visit** | required | open to all |
| **Faculty Meeting** | required | open to all |

**Interviews:** M–F, select Sat.; students are encouraged to schedule an appointment with an admissions counselor.

**Campus Tours:** Conducted by students and admission reps. M–F at 10:00 am, 2:00 pm; Sat. at 10:00 am during fall and spring semesters; during summer M–F tour available only at 10:00 am; Housing Tour available during the fall and spring semesters immediately following the Campus Tour; 60 minutes.

**Class Visits:** Prospective students may attend a class in their area of interest.

**Video:** Free on request.

## CAMPUS FACILITIES

**Science:** Pharmacy Museum.

**Arts:** McKiosick Museum; Appointment Required: Koger Center for the Performing Arts, School of Music.

**Athletic:** Recreational Facility; Appointment Required: Gamecock Athletic Facilities.

**Of Special Interest:** Thomas Cooper Library, Historic Horseshoe.

## LOCAL ATTRACTIONS

South Carolina State Museum; Riverbanks Zoo; Congaree Swamps; Lake Murray; area historic homes and museums; Capital City Bombers.

# WINTHROP UNIVERSITY
## Rock Hill, South Carolina

**Contact:** Nancy Draper, Administrative Specialist, Office of Admissions, Stewart House, Rock Hill, SC 29733. *Phone:* 803-323-2191 or toll-free 800-763-0230. *Fax:* 803-323-2137. *Web site:* http://www. winthrop.edu/ *Visit location:* Office of Admissions, Stewart House, Oakland Avenue and Eden Terrace.

## QUICK FACTS

Enrollment: 5,277; UG: 3,997. Entrance: moderately difficult. SAT>500: 61% V, 55% M; ACT>18: 73%. Resident tuition and fees: $3938. Nonresident tuition and fees: $7066. Room and board: $3764. Application deadline: 5/1.

## GENERAL

State-supported, comprehensive, coed. Part of South Carolina Commission on Higher Education. Awards bachelor's and master's degrees. Founded 1886. Setting: 418-acre suburban campus with easy access to Charlotte. Undergraduate faculty: 428 (294 full-time, 134 part-time); student-faculty ratio is 17:1. Most popular recent majors: business administration, elementary education, biology.

## CAMPUS VISITS

**College Calendar 1998–99:** *Regular classes:* Aug. 26–Dec. 8; Jan. 13–Apr. 27. *Breaks:* Oct. 9–12; Mar. 8–13; Nov. 25–28. *Final exams:* Dec. 9–16; Apr. 28–May 5. *Admission office closed:* Nov. 25–28, Dec. 24–Jan. 1, Mar. 8–13. *Special campus days:* Fall Commencement, Dec. 19; Spring Commencement, May 8.

*Winthrop University (continued)*

## VISIT OPPORTUNITIES

| | Appointments? | Who? |
| --- | --- | --- |
| **Campus Tour** | recommended | open to all |
| **Information Session** | recommended | open to all |
| **Admission Interview** | recommended | open to all |
| **Classroom Visit** | required | open to all |
| **Faculty Meeting** | required | open to all |

**Information Sessions:** M–F; Sat. group information session at 11:00 am followed by campus tour on Jan. 16, Mar. 20, and Apr. 24; 30 minutes.

**Interviews:** M–F; group presentations are scheduled on selected Sat.; 20 minutes.

**Campus Tours:** Conducted by students. M–F, select Sat. at 10:00 am, 2:00 pm; unavailable during exam periods or when the school is officially out of session or observing holidays; during summer 11:00 am daily; 60 minutes.

**Class Visits:** Prospective students may attend a class in their area of interest.

**Video:** Free on request.

## CAMPUS FACILITIES
**Science:** Sims Science Building.

**Arts:** Rutledge and Winthrop Galleries, Johnson Hall (theatre and dance departments), Barnes Recital Hall, McLaurin Student Gallery.

**Athletic:** Winthrop Recreational Complex and Lake; Appointment Required: Winthrop Coliseum.

**Of Special Interest:** Tillman Hall, McBryde Hall.

## LOCAL ATTRACTIONS
Glencairn Gardens, Cherry Park, Museum of York County, Historic Brattonsville.

# WOFFORD COLLEGE
**Spartanburg, South Carolina**

**Contact:** Admissions Office, 429 North Charles Street, Spartanburg, SC 29303-3663. *Phone:* 864-597-4130. *Fax:* 864-597-4149. *E-mail:* admissions@wofford.edu *Web site:* http://www.wofford.edu/ *Visit location:* Admissions, Hugh S. Black, 429 North Church Street.

## QUICK FACTS
Enrollment: 1,072; UG: 1,072. Entrance: very difficult. SAT>500: 88% V, 86% M; ACT>18: N/R. Tuition and fees: $15,390. Room and board: $4410. Application deadline: 2/1.

## GENERAL
Independent, 4-year, coed, United Methodist Church. Awards bachelor's degrees. Founded 1854. Setting: 140-acre urban campus with easy access to Charlotte. Faculty: 85 (72 full-time, 13 part-time). Most popular recent majors: biology, English, business economics.

## CAMPUS VISITS
**College Calendar 1998–99:** *Regular classes:* Sept. 1–Dec. 4; Feb. 2–May 7. *Final exams:* Dec. 7–11; May 10–14.

## VISIT OPPORTUNITIES

| | Appointments? | Who? |
| --- | --- | --- |
| **Campus Tour** | recommended | applicants and parents |
| **Information Session** | recommended | |
| **Admission Interview** | recommended | applicants and parents |
| **Classroom Visit** | required | applicants and parents |
| **Faculty Meeting** | required | applicants and parents |
| **Overnight Visit** | required | |

**Information Sessions:** M–F, select Sat. at 9:30 am, 10:30 am, 11:30 am, 2:00 pm, 3:00 pm; 45 minutes.

**Interviews:** M–F; Sat. 9:00 am–12:00 pm; 45 minutes.

**Campus Tours:** Conducted by students and admission reps. M–F, select Sat. at 10:30 am, 11:30 am, 12:30 pm, 3:00 pm, 4:00 pm.

**Class Visits:** Prospective students may attend a class in their area of interest, classroom visits are determined by the visit schedule.

**Overnight Visits:** During the regular academic year, prospective applicants may spend an evening in a residence hall with a student host.

**Video:** Free on request.

## CAMPUS FACILITIES
**Science:** Milliken Science Hall.

**Athletic:** J.J. Richardson Building.

**Of Special Interest:** F. W. Olin Building.

**LOCAL ATTRACTIONS**
The Beacon Drive In.

# SOUTH DAKOTA

## AUGUSTANA COLLEGE
**Sioux Falls, South Dakota**

**Contact:** Carol LaCroix, Campus Visit Coordinator, 2001 South Summit Avenue, Sioux Falls, SD 57197. *Phone:* toll-free 800-727-2844. *Fax:* 605-336-5518. *E-mail:* info@inst.augie.edu *Web site:* http://www.augie. edu/ *Visit location:* Office of Admission, Administration Building, 2001 South Summit Avenue.

**QUICK FACTS**
Enrollment: 1,630; UG: 1,572. Entrance: moderately difficult. SAT>500: 79% V, 92% M; ACT>18: 97%. Tuition and fees: $13,112. Room and board: $3903. Application deadline: rolling.

**GENERAL**
Independent, comprehensive, coed, Evangelical Lutheran Church in America. Awards bachelor's and master's degrees. Founded 1860. Setting: 100-acre urban campus. Undergraduate faculty: 161 (119 full-time, 42 part-time); student-faculty ratio is 12:1. Most popular recent majors: nursing, education, business administration.

**CAMPUS VISITS**
**College Calendar 1998–99:** *Regular classes:* Sept. 2–Dec. 10; Jan. 4–28; Feb. 8–May 20. *Breaks:* Oct. 25–27; Jan. 29–Feb. 7; Mar. 28–Apr. 1; Dec. 17–Jan. 4. *Final exams:* Dec. 12–16; Jan. 28–29; May 19–21. *Special campus days:* Explore Agustana, Oct. 15–16; Viking Days (homecoming), Oct. 15–16.

**VISIT OPPORTUNITIES**

|  | Appointments? | Who? |
|---|---|---|
| **Campus Tour** | required | open to all |
| **Information Session** | required | open to all |
| **Admission Interview** | required | open to all |
| **Classroom Visit** | required | open to all |
| **Faculty Meeting** | required | open to all |
| **Overnight Visit** | required | open to all |

**Interviews:** M–F, select Sat.; unavailable Sat. during breaks and summer; 30 minutes.
**Campus Tours:** Conducted by students. M–F 9:00 am–3:00 pm; Sat. 9:00 am–12:00 pm; 60 minutes.
**Class Visits:** Prospective students may attend a class in their area of interest.
**Overnight Visits:** During the regular academic year, prospective applicants may spend an evening in a residence hall with a student host.

**CAMPUS FACILITIES**
**Of Special Interest:** Mikkelsen Library.

**LOCAL ATTRACTIONS**
Big Sioux River-Falls Park; Empire Mall.

## SOUTH DAKOTA STATE UNIVERSITY
**Brookings, South Dakota**

**Contact:** Christy Osborne, Assistant Director of Admissions, PO Box 2201, ADM 200, Brookings, SD 57007. *Phone:* toll-free 800-952-3541. *Fax:* 605-688-6384. *E-mail:* osbornec@adm.sdstate.edu *Web site:* http://www.sdstate.edu/ *Visit location:* Office of Admissions, Administration Building-Room 200, Box 2201.

**QUICK FACTS**
Enrollment: 8,460; UG: 7,237. Entrance: moderately difficult. SAT>500: N/App; ACT>18: N/App. Resident tuition and fees: $2912. Nonresident tuition and fees: $6680. Room and board: $2482. Application deadline: rolling.

**GENERAL**
State-supported, university, coed. Awards associate, bachelor's, master's, doctoral, and first professional degrees. Founded 1881. Setting: 260-acre small-town campus. Undergraduate faculty: 539 (all full-time); student-faculty ratio is 16:1. Most popular recent majors: nursing, sociology, economics.

**CAMPUS VISITS**
**College Calendar 1998–99:** *Regular classes:* Sept. 1–Dec. 15; Jan. 7–Apr. 30. *Breaks:* Mar. 8–12. *Final exams:* Dec. 16–22; May 3–7. *Special campus days:* Hobo Day Homecoming, Oct. 17; Junior Day visitor program, Feb. 6; Senior Day visitor program, Oct. 3; Thank Goodness It's Friday, High School Students and Parents, Oct. 15–16, Nov. 13, Nov. 20, Jan. 22, Jan. 29, Feb. 19, Feb. 26, Mar. 19, Mar. 26, Apr. 9, Apr. 23, Dec. 4, Dec. 11.

*South Dakota State University (continued)*

## VISIT OPPORTUNITIES

| | Appointments? | Who? |
|---|---|---|
| **Campus Tour** | recommended, not required | open to all |
| **Information Session** | recommended, not required | open to all |
| **Admission Interview** | recommended, not required | open to all |
| **Classroom Visit** | required | applicants and parents |
| **Faculty Meeting** | required | open to all |
| **Overnight Visit** | recommended | |

**Information Sessions:** M–F; prefer prospective student schedule an appointment; 60 minutes.

**Interviews:** M–F 8:00 am–12:00 pm, 1:00–5:00 pm; 60 minutes.

**Campus Tours:** Conducted by students. M–F at 11:00 am, 11:30 am, 1:00 pm, 2:00 pm, 3:00 pm; typical visit includes 1 hour with Admission counselor, 1 hour faculty appointment, and tour; 60 minutes.

**Class Visits:** Classroom visits are determined by the visit schedule.

**Overnight Visits:** During the regular academic year and over the summer, prospective applicants may spend an evening in a residence hall.

**Video:** Free on request.

## CAMPUS FACILITIES
**Science:** Northern Plains Bio-Stress Lab.

**Arts:** South Dakota Art Museum, South Dakota Agricultural Heritage Museum, Lincoln Music Hall.

**Athletic:** Health, Physical Education and Recreation Center.

**Of Special Interest:** McCrory Gardens, University Student Union; Appointment Required: Dairy Bar—detailed tours.

## LOCAL ATTRACTIONS
July—Summer Arts Festival.

# UNIVERSITY OF SOUTH DAKOTA
**Vermillion, South Dakota**

**Contact:** Ms. Paula Tacke, Director of Admission, 414 East Clark Street, Vermillion, SD 57069. *Phone:* 605-677-5012 or toll-free 800-329-2453. *Fax:* 605-677-6753. *E-mail:* ptacke@sundance.usd.edu *Visit location:* Admission Office, Slagle Hall–Room 12, 414 East Clark Street.

## QUICK FACTS
Enrollment: 7,058; UG: 5,065. Entrance: moderately difficult. SAT>500: N/R; ACT>18: 90%. Resident tuition and fees: $3012. Nonresident tuition and fees: $6780. Room and board: $2912. Application deadline: rolling.

## GENERAL
State-supported, university, coed. Awards associate, bachelor's, master's, doctoral, and first professional degrees. Founded 1862. Setting: 216-acre small-town campus. Undergraduate faculty: 356 (330 full-time, 26 part-time); student-faculty ratio is 15:1. Most popular recent majors: business administration, biology, psychology.

## CAMPUS VISITS
**College Calendar 1998–99:** *Regular classes:* Sept. 1–Dec. 15; Jan. 7–Apr. 30. *Breaks:* Dec. 23–Jan. 6. *Final exams:* Dec. 16–22; May 3–7.

## VISIT OPPORTUNITIES

| | Appointments? | Who? |
|---|---|---|
| **Campus Tour** | required | open to all |
| **Information Session** | not required | open to all |
| **Admission Interview** | required | open to all |
| **Classroom Visit** | required | open to all |
| **Faculty Meeting** | required | open to all |
| **Overnight Visit** | required | open to all |

**Information Sessions:** M–F, select Sat. 9:00 am–4:00 pm; 30 minutes.

**Interviews:** M–F, select Sat.; 30 minutes.

**Campus Tours:** Conducted by students. M–F, select Sat. at 10:00 am, 12:00 pm, 2:00 pm; 60 minutes.

**Class Visits:** Prospective students may attend a class in their area of interest.

**Overnight Visits:** During the regular academic year and over the summer, prospective applicants may spend an evening in a residence hall.

## CAMPUS FACILITIES
**Science:** Science labs and classrooms.

**Arts:** Appointment Required: Warren M. Lee Fine Arts Center, Shrine to Music Museum.

**Athletic:** Appointment Required: Dakota Dome.

**Of Special Interest:** Appointment Required: Old Main—Honors Suite/Classrooms, Center for Instructional Delivery and Design.

# TENNESSEE

## AUSTIN PEAY STATE UNIVERSITY
### Clarksville, Tennessee

**Contact:** Admissions, 601 College Street, PO Box 4548, Clarksville, TN 37044. *Phone:* toll-free 800-844-2778 (out-of-state). *Fax:* 931-648-5994. *E-mail:* admissions@apsu01.apsu.edu *Web site:* http://www.apsu.edu/ *Visit location:* Admissions, Ellington Student Services, 601 College Street, P.O. Box 4548.

### QUICK FACTS
Entrance: moderately difficult. SAT>500: 50% V, 47% M; ACT>18: N/R. Resident tuition and fees: $2280. Nonresident tuition and fees: $6876. Room and board: $3260. Application deadline: 7/27.

### GENERAL
State-supported, comprehensive, coed. Part of Tennessee Board of Regents. Awards associate, bachelor's, and master's degrees. Founded 1927. Setting: 200-acre suburban campus with easy access to Nashville. Undergraduate faculty: 486 (284 full-time, 202 part-time); student-faculty ratio is 18:1. Most popular recent majors: elementary education, business administration, nursing.

### CAMPUS VISITS
**College Calendar 1998–99:** *Regular classes:* Aug. 19–Dec. 4; Jan. 11–May 5. *Breaks:* Oct. 9–12; Mar. 6–14; Dec. 11–Jan. 10; Apr. 1. *Final exams:* Dec. 7–11; May 7–13. *Admission office closed:* Dec. 23–Jan. 3. *Special campus days:* AP Day, Nov. 7; Commencement, Dec. 11, May 14; Homecoming, Oct. 17–18.

### VISIT OPPORTUNITIES

| | Appointments? | Who? |
|---|---|---|
| Campus Tour | recommended, not required | admitted applicants only |
| Information Session | recommended, not required | |

| | Appointments? | Who? |
|---|---|---|
| Admission Interview | recommended | |
| Faculty Meeting | required | admitted applicants only |

**Information Sessions:** M–F at 10:00 am, 2:00 pm; Sat. at 9:30 am, 11:00 am; 15 minutes.

**Interviews:** M–F at 10:00 am, 2:00 pm; select Sat. at 9:30 am, 11:00 am; 15 minutes.

**Campus Tours:** Conducted by students. M–F at 10:00 am, 2:00 pm; Sat. at 9:30 am, 11:00 am; 45 minutes.

**Video:** Free on request.

### CAMPUS FACILITIES
**Science:** Appointment Required: McCord Building.

**Arts:** Harned Hall Galleries; Appointment Required: Margaret Fort Trahern Building.

**Athletic:** Appointment Required: Dunn Center, Memorial Health Building (Red Barn).

**Of Special Interest:** Appointment Required: Music/Mass Communications Building.

### LOCAL ATTRACTIONS
Beachaven Vineyards and Winery, Land Between the Lakes, Dunbar Cave State Park, Smith Trahern Mansion, Clarksville-Montgomery County Museum, and Queen of Clarksville.

## BRYAN COLLEGE
### Dayton, Tennessee

**Contact:** Mr. Mark A. Cruver, Assistant Director of Admissions, 130 Mercer Drive, Dayton, TN 37321. *Phone:* toll-free 800-277-9522. *Fax:* 423-775-7199. *E-mail:* cruverma@bryannet.bryan.edu *Web site:* http://www.bryan.edu/ *Visit location:* Admissions Office, Administration Building, 130 Mercer Drive.

### QUICK FACTS
Enrollment: 457; UG: 457. Entrance: moderately difficult. SAT>500: 77% V, 66% M; ACT>18: 91%. Tuition and fees: $10,400. Room and board: $3950. Application deadline: rolling.

### GENERAL
Independent interdenominational, 4-year, coed. Awards associate and bachelor's degrees. Founded 1930.

*Bryan College (continued)*

Setting: 100-acre small-town campus. Faculty: 58 (30 full-time, 28 part-time); student-faculty ratio is 14:1. Most popular recent majors: education, business administration, biology.

## CAMPUS VISITS

**College Calendar 1998–99:** *Regular classes:* Aug. 27–Dec. 11; Jan. 14–Apr. 30. *Breaks:* Oct. 9–18; Mar. 5–14. *Final exams:* Dec. 14–18; May 3–7. *Admission office closed:* July 3, Nov. 26–27, Dec. 24–Jan. 1; Good Friday, Apr. 2. *Special campus days:* Caravan Visitation Days, Sept. 24–25, Nov. 5–6; Caravan/Early Orientation, Mar. 25–27; Commencement, May 8; Preview Day, Jan. 8.

## VISIT OPPORTUNITIES

| | Appointments? | Who? |
|---|---|---|
| **Campus Tour** | recommended, not required | open to all |
| **Information Session** | recommended, not required | open to all |
| **Admission Interview** | recommended, not required | open to all |
| **Classroom Visit** | recommended, not required | open to all |
| **Faculty Meeting** | recommended | open to all |
| **Overnight Visit** | required | open to all |

**Information Sessions:** M–F 8:00 am–5:00 pm; 30 minutes.

**Interviews:** M–F; 30 minutes.

**Campus Tours:** Conducted by students and admission reps. M–F 8:00 am–5:00 pm; inquire for Sat. schedule; 60 minutes.

**Class Visits:** Prospective students may attend a class in their area of interest.

**Overnight Visits:** During the regular academic year, prospective applicants may spend an evening in a residence hall with a student host.

**Video:** Free on request.

## CAMPUS FACILITIES

**Of Special Interest:** Ironside Memorial Library.

# CARSON-NEWMAN COLLEGE

**Jefferson City, Tennessee**

**Contact:** Admissions Office, 1646 Russell Avenue, Jefferson City, TN 37760. *Phone:* toll-free 800-678-9061. *Fax:* 423-471-3502. *E-mail:* sgray@cncadm.cn.edu *Web site:* http://www.cn.edu/ *Visit location:* Undergraduate Admissions, Fite Administration Building, 1646 Russell Avenue.

## QUICK FACTS

Enrollment: 2,264; UG: 2,019. Entrance: moderately difficult. SAT>500: 67% V, 64% M; ACT>18: 94%. Tuition and fees: $10,610. Room and board: $3830. Application deadline: 8/1.

## GENERAL

Independent Southern Baptist, comprehensive, coed. Awards associate, bachelor's, and master's degrees. Founded 1851. Setting: 100-acre small-town campus with easy access to Knoxville. Undergraduate faculty: 193 (121 full-time, 72 part-time); student-faculty ratio is 13:1. Most popular recent majors: education, biology, business administration.

## CAMPUS VISITS

**College Calendar 1998–99:** *Regular classes:* Aug. 27–Dec. 9; Jan. 6–Apr. 28. *Breaks:* Oct. 19–20; Mar. 4–14; Nov. 25–29; Apr. 2–5. *Final exams:* Dec. 11–16; Apr. 30–May 5. *Special campus days:* Commencement, Dec. 19, May 8; Homecoming, Oct. 10; Prime Time, Sept. 24–25, Nov. 19–20, Feb. 18–19; Showcase Saturday, Nov. 7, Jan. 30, Apr. 17.

## VISIT OPPORTUNITIES

| | Appointments? | Who? |
|---|---|---|
| **Campus Tour** | recommended, not required | open to all |
| **Admission Interview** | recommended, not required | open to all |
| **Classroom Visit** | recommended | open to all |
| **Faculty Meeting** | required | open to all |
| **Overnight Visit** | required | open to all |

**Interviews:** M–F; Sat. 9:00 am–12:00 pm; 30 minutes.

**Campus Tours:** Conducted by students. M–F 9:00 am–4:30 pm; Sat. 9:00–11:30 am; available during Showcase Saturday and Prime Time; 45 minutes.

**Class Visits:** Prospective students may attend a class in their area of interest.

**Overnight Visits:** During the regular academic year, prospective applicants may spend an evening in a residence hall with a student host.

**Video:** Free on request.

## CAMPUS FACILITIES

**Arts:** Music Building.

**Athletic:** Student Activities Center.

**Of Special Interest:** Library.

## LOCAL ATTRACTIONS

Great Smoky Mountains National Park; Cherokee Lake.

# CHRISTIAN BROTHERS UNIVERSITY

**Memphis, Tennessee**

**Contact:** Michael J. Daush, Dean of Admissions, 650 East Parkway South, Memphis, TN 38104. *Phone:* 901-321-3205 or toll-free 800-288-7576. *Fax:* 901-321-3202. *E-mail:* admissions@cbu.edu *Web site:* http://www.cbu.edu/ *Visit location:* Admissions Office, Buckman Hall, Suite 127, 650 East Parkway South.

## QUICK FACTS

Enrollment: 1,869; UG: 1,583. Entrance: moderately difficult. SAT>500: N/R; ACT>18: N/R. Tuition and fees: $11,930. Room and board: $3730. Application deadline: 7/1.

## GENERAL

Independent Roman Catholic, comprehensive, coed. Awards bachelor's and master's degrees. Founded 1871. Setting: 70-acre urban campus. Undergraduate faculty: 162 (95 full-time, 67 part-time); student-faculty ratio is 16:1. Most popular recent majors: accounting, psychology, biology.

## CAMPUS VISITS

**College Calendar 1998–99:** *Regular classes:* Aug. 25–Dec. 11; Jan. 13–May 3. *Breaks:* Oct. 17–25; Mar. 6–14. *Final exams:* Dec. 14–18; May 5–11. *Special campus days:* Commencement, May 15.

### VISIT OPPORTUNITIES

|  | Appointments? | Who? |
|---|---|---|
| **Campus Tour** | recommended | open to all |
| **Information Session** | required | open to all |
| **Admission Interview** | required | open to all |
| **Classroom Visit** | required | open to all |
| **Faculty Meeting** | required | open to all |
| **Overnight Visit** | required | open to all |

**Information Sessions:** M–F; call for available schedule; 300 minutes.

**Interviews:** M–F; Sat. available by request; 30 minutes.

**Campus Tours:** Conducted by students and admission reps. M–F; call for available schedule; 40 minutes.

**Class Visits:** Prospective students may attend a class in their area of interest.

**Overnight Visits:** During the regular academic year, prospective applicants may spend an evening in a residence hall with a student host.

## CAMPUS FACILITIES

**Science:** Appointment Required: Science Center and Labs, Computer Labs.

**Arts:** University Gallery, Plough Library, Buckman Hall; Appointment Required: Brother I. Leo O'Donnell Archives.

**Athletic:** Canale Pool, Signiago Soccer Field; Appointment Required: De La Salle Gym.

**Of Special Interest:** Ghandi Institute for Nonviolence, Center for Global Enterprise.

## LOCAL ATTRACTIONS

National Civil Rights Museum; Memphis Zoo; Beale Street; Graceland; Pyramid Sports Complex; Pink Palace Museum, Mississippi Riverfront.

# DAVID LIPSCOMB UNIVERSITY

**Nashville, Tennessee**

**Contact:** Scott Gilmer, Tour Coordinator, 3901 Granny White Pike, Nashville, TN 37204. *Phone:* toll-free 800-333-4358. *Fax:* 615-269-1804. *E-mail:* gilmersw@dlu.edu *Web site:* http://www.dlu.edu/ *Visit location:* Office of Admissions, Crisman Building, 3901 Granny White Pike.

## QUICK FACTS

Enrollment: 2,532; UG: 2,433. Entrance: moderately difficult. SAT>500: 73% V, 66% M; ACT>18: 93%. Tuition and fees: $8470. Room and board: $3910. Application deadline: rolling.

## GENERAL

Independent, comprehensive, coed, Church of Christ. Awards bachelor's and master's degrees. Founded 1891. Setting: 65-acre urban campus. Undergraduate faculty: 194 (92 full-time, 102 part-time); student-faculty ratio is 18:1. Most popular recent majors: business administration, education, history.

*David Lipscomb University (continued)*

## CAMPUS VISITS

**College Calendar 1998–99:** *Regular classes:* Aug. 25–Dec. 11; Jan. 12–Apr. 30. *Breaks:* Nov. 23–27; Apr. 15–19; Dec. 18–Jan. 12. *Final exams:* Dec. 12–17; May 1–6. *Admission office closed:* Christmas holidays; Thanksgiving holiday.

## VISIT OPPORTUNITIES

|  | Appointments? | Who? |
|---|---|---|
| **Campus Tour** | recommended | open to all |
| **Information Session** | recommended | open to all |
| **Admission Interview** | recommended | open to all |
| **Classroom Visit** | recommended | open to all |
| **Faculty Meeting** | recommended | open to all |
| **Overnight Visit** | recommended | open to all |

**Information Sessions:** M–F; follows tour; call for specific appointment time; 60 minutes.

**Interviews:** M–F; weekend appointment available; 60 minutes.

**Campus Tours:** Conducted by students and admission reps. M–F at 10:00 am, 2:00 pm; 60 minutes.

**Class Visits:** Prospective students may attend a class in their area of interest.

**Overnight Visits:** During the regular academic year, prospective applicants may spend an evening in a residence hall with a student host.

**Video:** Free on request.

## CAMPUS FACILITIES

**Science:** McFarland Science Building.

**Athletic:** Mc Quiddy Gymnasium, Dugan Baseball field, Student Activities Center.

**Of Special Interest:** Beaman Library.

## LOCAL ATTRACTIONS

Nashville, historic state capital, Opryland, Percy Priest Lake, Centennial Sportsplex.

# EAST TENNESSEE STATE UNIVERSITY
## Johnson City, Tennessee

**Contact:** Mr. Mike Pitts, Director of Admissions, PO Box 70731, Johnson City, TN 37614. *Phone:* 423-439-4213 or toll-free 800-462-3878. *Fax:* 423-439-7156. *E-mail:* pittsm@etsu.edu *Web site:* http://www.etsu.edu/ *Visit location:* Office of Admissions, Burgin East Dossett Hall, University Parkway.

## QUICK FACTS

Enrollment: 11,480; UG: 9,160. Entrance: moderately difficult. SAT>500: 51% V, 49% M; ACT>18: 86%. Resident tuition and fees: $2100. Nonresident tuition and fees: $6696. Room and board: $2520. Application deadline: rolling.

## GENERAL

State-supported, university, coed. Part of Tennessee Board of Regents. Awards associate, bachelor's, master's, doctoral, and first professional degrees and post-master's certificates. Founded 1911. Setting: 366-acre small-town campus. Undergraduate faculty: 935 (712 full-time, 223 part-time); student-faculty ratio is 19:1. Most popular recent majors: nursing, criminal justice/law enforcement administration, engineering technology.

## CAMPUS VISITS

**College Calendar 1998–99:** *Regular classes:* Aug. 31–Dec. 11; Jan. 11–Apr. 30. *Breaks:* Oct. 30–Nov. 1; Mar. 15–19. *Final exams:* Dec. 12–17; May 1–6. *Admission office closed:* Dec. 25–Jan. 3. *Special campus days:* Fall Commencement, Dec. 19; Homecoming, Oct. 24; Spring Commencement, May 8.

## VISIT OPPORTUNITIES

|  | Appointments? | Who? |
|---|---|---|
| **Campus Tour** | recommended, not required | open to all |
| **Information Session** | recommended, not required | open to all |
| **Admission Interview** | recommended, not required | open to all |
| **Classroom Visit** | required | open to all |
| **Faculty Meeting** | required | open to all |
| **Overnight Visit** | required | open to all |

**Information Sessions:** M–F 8:00 am–4:30 pm; 20 minutes.

**Interviews:** M–F, select Sat.; 30 minutes.

**Campus Tours:** Conducted by students and admission reps. M–F at 10:30 am, 1:30 pm; Sat. at 9:30 am; 45 minutes.

**Class Visits:** Prospective students may attend a class in their area of interest.

**Overnight Visits:** During the regular academic year and over the summer, prospective applicants may spend an evening in a residence hall.

**Video:** Free on request.

## CAMPUS FACILITIES
**Science:** East Tennessee State University Observatory; Appointment Required: Quillen College of Medicine.

**Arts:** Carroll Reese Museum, Slocumb Gallery, Center for Appalachian Studies, Archives of Appalachia.

**Athletic:** Memorial Center.

**Of Special Interest:** Library.

## LOCAL ATTRACTIONS
Historic Jonesborough—oldest town in Tennessee; National Storytelling Festival.

# FISK UNIVERSITY
### Nashville, Tennessee

**Contact:** Mr. Shimane Smith, Admissions Recruiter/Tour Coordinator, Fisk University, 1000 17th Avenue North, Nashville, TN 37208. *Phone:* toll-free 800-443-FISK. *Fax:* 615-329-8774. *E-mail:* sksmith@dubois.fisk.edu *Web site:* http://www.fisk.edu/ *Visit location:* Enrollment Management, Boyd House, 1601 Meharry Boulevard.

## QUICK FACTS
Enrollment: 765; UG: 700. Entrance: moderately difficult. SAT>500: 32% V, 36% M; ACT>18: N/R. Tuition and fees: $7750. Room and board: $4304. Application deadline: 6/15.

## GENERAL
Independent, comprehensive, coed, United Church of Christ. Awards bachelor's and master's degrees. Founded 1866. Setting: 40-acre urban campus. Undergraduate faculty: 97 (63 full-time, 34 part-time); student-faculty ratio is 14:1. Most popular recent majors: business administration, chemistry, psychology.

## CAMPUS VISITS
**College Calendar 1998–99:** *Regular classes:* Aug. 31–Dec. 19; Jan. 13–Apr. 27. *Breaks:* Nov. 26–30; Mar. 8–15. *Final exams:* Dec. 14–18; Apr. 30–May 5. *Admission office closed:* Christmas Break, Dec. 19–Jan.

2. *Special campus days:* Commencement, May 10; Homecoming, Nov. 16–21; Spring Arts Festival, Apr. 5–11.

## VISIT OPPORTUNITIES

|  | Appointments? | Who? |
|---|---|---|
| **Campus Tour** | required | open to all |
| **Information Session** | required | open to all |
| **Admission Interview** | required | open to all |
| **Classroom Visit** | required | open to all |
| **Faculty Meeting** | required | open to all |
| **Overnight Visit** | required | open to all |

**Information Sessions:** M–F 11:00 am–1:00 pm; 20 minutes.

**Interviews:** M–F; 20 minutes.

**Campus Tours:** Conducted by students and admission reps. M–F 9:00 am–3:30 pm; groups should schedule one week in advance; 75 minutes.

**Class Visits:** Prospective students may attend a class in their area of interest, classroom visits are determined by the visit schedule.

**Overnight Visits:** During the regular academic year, prospective applicants may spend an evening in a residence hall with a student host.

**Video:** Free on request.

## CAMPUS FACILITIES
**Science:** Talley-Bradey Hall; Appointment Required: NASA Research Center.

**Arts:** Carl Van Vechten Gallery of Fine Arts, Aaron Douglass Gallery, Cravath Hall, Special Collections.

**Of Special Interest:** Jubilee Hall, Fisk Memorial Chapel, Harris Music Building.

## LOCAL ATTRACTIONS
James Weldon Johnson Home; Cheekwood; Hermitage Plantation.

# FREED-HARDEMAN UNIVERSITY
### Henderson, Tennessee

**Contact:** Admissions, 158 East Main Street, Henderson, TN 38340. *Phone:* toll-free 800-FHU-FHU1. *Fax:* 901-989-6047. *E-mail:* admissions@fhu.edu *Web site:* http://www.fhu.edu/ *Visit location:* Admissions, Old Main Administration Building, 158 East Main Street.

*Freed-Hardeman University (continued)*

## QUICK FACTS

Enrollment: 1,591; UG: 1,266. Entrance: moderately difficult. SAT>500: 77% V, 65% M; ACT>18: 90%. Tuition and fees: $7524. Room and board: $3760. Application deadline: rolling.

## GENERAL

Independent, comprehensive, coed, Church of Christ. Awards bachelor's and master's degrees. Founded 1869. Setting: 96-acre rural campus. Undergraduate faculty: 105 (84 full-time, 21 part-time); student-faculty ratio is 20:1. Most popular recent majors: business administration, education, biblical studies.

## CAMPUS VISITS

**College Calendar 1998–99:** *Regular classes:* Aug. 27–Dec. 13; Jan. 12–May 2. *Breaks:* Dec. 18–Jan. 10. *Final exams:* Dec. 14–18; May 3–7. *Special campus days:* Benefit Dinner (speaker: Elizabeth Dole), Dec. 4; Bible Bowl, Mar. 5–6; Graduation, May 8; Homecoming/Fall Preview Day, Nov. 14; Horizon's (camp), July 11–17; Just for Juniors, Dec. 5; Makin Music, Apr. 2–3; Rush Weekend, Sept. 25–26.

### VISIT OPPORTUNITIES

|                      | Appointments? | Who?        |
| -------------------- | ------------- | ----------- |
| **Campus Tour**      | recommended   | open to all |
| **Information Session** | recommended | open to all |
| **Classroom Visit**  | recommended   | open to all |
| **Faculty Meeting**  | required      | open to all |
| **Overnight Visit**  | recommended   | open to all |

**Information Sessions:** M–F 8:30 am–5:30 pm; weekends available on request; 30 minutes.

**Campus Tours:** Conducted by students and admission reps. M–F 8:30 am–5:30 pm; weekends available on request; 45 minutes.

**Class Visits:** Prospective students may attend a class in their area of interest.

**Overnight Visits:** During the regular academic year, prospective applicants may spend an evening in a residence hall with a student host.

**Video:** Free on request.

## CAMPUS FACILITIES

**Science:** Associates Science Building; Appointment Required: Cancer Research Institute.

**Arts:** Draughon Education Center.

**Athletic:** Sports Center, Bader Gymnasium, Carnes Field.

**Of Special Interest:** Burks Student Center; Appointment Required: 91.5 WFHC Radio Station, TV 40 Television Station.

## LOCAL ATTRACTIONS

Chickasaw State Park, Casey Jones Village, Jackson, TN.

# KING COLLEGE
## Bristol, Tennessee

**Contact:** Sammie N. Playl, Administrative Assistant–Admissions Department, 1350 King College Road, Bristol, TN 37620. *Phone:* 423-652-4861 or toll-free 800-362-0014. *Fax:* 423-652-4727. *E-mail:* admissions@king2.edu *Web site:* http://www.king.edu/ *Visit location:* Admissions Office, Admissions and Financial Aid Building, 1350 King College Road.

## QUICK FACTS

Enrollment: 516; UG: 516. Entrance: moderately difficult. SAT>500: 76% V, 64% M; ACT>18: 93%. Tuition and fees: $10,550. Room and board: $3444. Application deadline: rolling.

## GENERAL

Independent, 4-year, coed, Presbyterian Church (U.S.A.). Awards bachelor's degrees. Founded 1867. Setting: 135-acre suburban campus. Faculty: 70 (42 full-time, 28 part-time); student-faculty ratio is 15:1. Most popular recent majors: behavioral sciences, economics, psychology.

## CAMPUS VISITS

**College Calendar 1998–99:** *Regular classes:* Aug. 26–Dec. 8; Jan. 5–Apr. 22. *Breaks:* Oct. 16–21; Feb. 26–Mar. 8; Nov. 25–30; Apr. 2–6. *Final exams:* Dec. 10–16; Apr. 24–29. *Admission office closed:* Dec. 23–Jan. 4. *Special campus days:* Dogwood Weekend; Fall Ball; Fall, Winter, Spring Preview Weekends.

### VISIT OPPORTUNITIES

|                        | Appointments? |
| ---------------------- | ------------- |
| **Campus Tour**        | recommended   |
| **Admission Interview** | recommended  |
| **Classroom Visit**    | required      |
| **Faculty Meeting**    | required      |

VISIT OPPORTUNITIES—*continued*

|  | **Appointments?** |
|---|---|
| **Overnight Visit** | required |

**Interviews:** M–F 8:00 am–5:00 pm; Sat. 9:00 am–12:00 pm; 45 minutes.

**Campus Tours:** Conducted by students and admission reps. M–F 8:00 am–5:00 pm; Sat. 9:00 am–12:00 pm; 60 minutes.

**Class Visits:** Classroom visits are determined by the visit schedule.

**Overnight Visits:** During the regular academic year, prospective applicants may spend an evening in a residence hall with a student host.

### CAMPUS FACILITIES
**Of Special Interest:** Chapel; Appointment Required: Dormitory.

# LINCOLN MEMORIAL UNIVERSITY
**Harrogate, Tennessee**

**Contact:** Sherry McCreary, Administrative Assistant, Cumberland Gap Parkway, Harrogate, TN 37752-1901. *Phone:* toll-free 800-325-0900 (in-state), 800-325-2506 (out-of-state). *Fax:* 423-869-6370. *E-mail:* admissions@inetlmu.lmunet.edu *Web site:* http://www.lmunet.edu *Visit location:* Admissions Office, Kresge Hall, Cumberland Gap Parkway.

### QUICK FACTS
Enrollment: 1,583; UG: 1,009. Entrance: moderately difficult. SAT>500: N/R; ACT>18: 99%. Tuition and fees: $8000. Room and board: $3500. Application deadline: rolling.

### GENERAL
Independent, comprehensive, coed. Awards associate, bachelor's, and master's degrees. Founded 1897. Setting: 1,000-acre small-town campus. Undergraduate faculty: 116 (73 full-time, 43 part-time); student-faculty ratio is 13:1. Most popular recent major: elementary education.

### CAMPUS VISITS
**College Calendar 1998–99:** *Regular classes:* Aug. 19–Dec. 4; Jan. 12–Apr. 30. *Breaks:* Nov. 26–29; Mar. 22–26. *Final exams:* Dec. 7–11; May 3–7. *Special*

*campus days:* Fall Commencement, Dec. 12; Homecoming, Oct. 22–25; Spring Commencement.

### VISIT OPPORTUNITIES

|  | **Appointments?** | **Who?** |
|---|---|---|
| **Campus Tour** | recommended | applicants and parents |
| **Information Session** | recommended |  |
| **Classroom Visit** | recommended | applicants and parents |

**Information Sessions:** M–F 8:00 am–4:30 pm; appointments encouraged; 30 minutes.

**Campus Tours:** Conducted by admission reps. M–F, select Sat. 8:00 am–4:30 pm; appointments encouraged; 75 minutes.

**Class Visits:** Classroom visits are determined by the visit schedule.

### CAMPUS FACILITIES
**Science:** Appointment Required: Cumberland Mountain Research Center.

**Athletic:** Tex Turner Arena.

**Of Special Interest:** Lincoln Museum.

### LOCAL ATTRACTIONS
Cumberland Gap National Park.

# MARYVILLE COLLEGE
**Maryville, Tennessee**

**Contact:** Karoline Westerling, Coordinator of Campus Visits, 502 East Lamar Alexander Parkway, Maryville, TN 37804. *Phone:* toll-free 800-597-2687. *Fax:* 423-981-8010. *E-mail:* admissions@maryvillecollege.edu *Web site:* http://www.maryvillecollege.edu/ *Visit location:* Office of Admissions, Anderson Hall, Suite 105, 502 East Lamar Alexander Parkway.

### QUICK FACTS
Enrollment: 953; UG: 953. Entrance: moderately difficult. SAT>500: 72% V, 66% M; ACT>18: 98%. Tuition and fees: $14,425. Room and board: $4720. Application deadline: 3/1.

### GENERAL
Independent Presbyterian, 4-year, coed. Awards bachelor's degrees. Founded 1819. Setting: 350-acre suburban campus with easy access to Knoxville.

*Maryville College (continued)*

Faculty: 92 (62 full-time, 30 part-time); student-faculty ratio is 13:1. Most popular recent majors: business administration, psychology, biology.

## CAMPUS VISITS

**College Calendar 1998–99:** *Regular classes:* Sept. 2–Dec. 11; Jan. 25–May 7; Jan. 4–23. *Breaks:* Oct. 9–11; Mar. 13–21; Nov. 25–29. *Final exams:* Dec. 14–17; May 10–13. *Special campus days:* Commencement, May 16.

## VISIT OPPORTUNITIES

| | Appointments? |
|---|---|
| **Campus Tour** | required |
| **Information Session** | recommended |
| **Admission Interview** | required |
| **Classroom Visit** | required |
| **Faculty Meeting** | required |
| **Overnight Visit** | required |

**Interviews:** M–F; 30 minutes.

**Campus Tours:** Conducted by students. Mon., Wed., Fri. at 10:00 am, 2:00 pm; Tue., Thu. at 11:00 am; inquire for special arrangements; 60 minutes.

**Class Visits:** Classroom visits are determined by the visit schedule.

**Overnight Visits:** During the regular academic year, prospective applicants may spend an evening in a residence hall with a student host.

## CAMPUS FACILITIES

**Of Special Interest:** Alpine Tower—Mountain Challenge Program, Residence Hall Room.

## LOCAL ATTRACTIONS

Great Smoky Mountain National Park.

# MIDDLE TENNESSEE STATE UNIVERSITY

**Murfreesboro, Tennessee**

**Contact:** Betty Pedigo, 208 Cope Administration Building, Murfreesboro, TN 37132. *Phone:* toll-free 800-433-MTSU. *Fax:* 615-898-5478. *E-mail:* admissions@mtsu.edu *Web site:* http://www.mtsu.edu/ *Visit location:* Admissions Office, Cope Administration Building, Room 208 Cope Administration Building.

## QUICK FACTS

Enrollment: 18,266; UG: 16,218. Entrance: moderately difficult. SAT>500: N/R; ACT>18: 83%. Resident tuition and fees: $2196. Nonresident tuition and fees: $6792. Room and board: $3343. Application deadline: rolling.

## GENERAL

State-supported, university, coed. Part of Tennessee Board of Regents. Awards associate, bachelor's, master's, and doctoral degrees and post-master's certificates. Founded 1911. Setting: 500-acre urban campus with easy access to Nashville. Undergraduate faculty: 930 (699 full-time, 231 part-time); student-faculty ratio is 19:1. Most popular recent majors: interdisciplinary studies, mass communications, aviation/airway science.

## CAMPUS VISITS

**College Calendar 1998–99:** *Regular classes:* Aug. 19–Dec. 4; Jan. 6–Apr. 27. *Breaks:* Oct. 15–17; Mar. 15–20; Nov. 26–28. *Final exams:* Dec. 5–11; Apr. 28–May 4. *Special campus days:* Fall Commencement, Dec. 12; Fall Preview Day, Oct. 24; Homecoming, Oct. 10.

## VISIT OPPORTUNITIES

| | Appointments? | Who? |
|---|---|---|
| **Campus Tour** | required | open to all |
| **Information Session** | recommended | open to all |
| **Admission Interview** | recommended, not required | open to all |
| **Classroom Visit** | required | open to all |
| **Faculty Meeting** | required | open to all |

**Information Sessions:** M–F at 2:00 pm; select Sat. at 10:30 am.

**Interviews:** M–F, select Sat.; 30 minutes.

**Campus Tours:** Conducted by students. M–F at 2:00 pm; select Sat. at 10:30 am; 60 minutes.

**Class Visits:** Prospective students may attend a class in their area of interest.

**Video:** Free on request.

## CAMPUS FACILITIES

**Athletic:** Newly expanded 30,000 seat football stadium.

**Of Special Interest:** Business/Aerospace Building, Library; Appointment Required: Bragg Mass Communication Building, Student Recreation Center.

## LOCAL ATTRACTIONS

Historic downtown Murfreesboro; Stones River National Battlefield; Nashville area attractions.

# MILLIGAN COLLEGE
### Milligan College, Tennessee

**Contact:** Admissions Counselor, PO Box 210, Milligan College, TN 37682. *Phone:* 423-461-8730 or toll-free 800-262-8337 (in-state). *Fax:* 423-461-8982. *E-mail:* admissions@milligan.edu *Web site:* http://www.milligan.edu *Visit location:* Office of Admissions, McMahan Student Center, PO Box 210.

## QUICK FACTS

Enrollment: 892; UG: 823. Entrance: moderately difficult. SAT>500: N/App; ACT>18: N/App. Tuition and fees: $10,260. Room and board: $3670. Application deadline: rolling.

## GENERAL

Independent Christian, comprehensive, coed. Awards associate, bachelor's, and master's degrees. Founded 1866. Setting: 145-acre suburban campus. Undergraduate faculty: 110 (62 full-time, 48 part-time); student-faculty ratio is 14:1. Most popular recent majors: education, mass communications, biblical studies.

## CAMPUS VISITS

**College Calendar 1998–99:** *Regular classes:* Sept. 1–Dec. 14; Jan. 12–Apr. 30. *Breaks:* Oct. 8–12; Mar. 8–15; Nov. 25–30; Apr. 2–5. *Final exams:* Dec. 15–18; May 3–6.

### VISIT OPPORTUNITIES

| | Appointments? | Who? |
|---|---|---|
| **Campus Tour** | recommended | applicants and parents |
| **Information Session** | recommended | |
| **Admission Interview** | required | |
| **Classroom Visit** | required | applicants and parents |
| **Faculty Meeting** | required | applicants and parents |
| **Overnight Visit** | required | |

**Information Sessions:** M–F, Sat. 9:00 am–5:00 pm; 20 minutes.
**Interviews:** M–F, Sat.; 20 minutes.

**Campus Tours:** Conducted by students and admission reps. M–F, Sat. 9:00 am–5:00 pm; 60 minutes.
**Class Visits:** Prospective students may attend a class in their area of interest.
**Overnight Visits:** During the regular academic year, prospective applicants may spend an evening in a residence hall with a student host.

## CAMPUS FACILITIES

**Of Special Interest:** P. H. Welshimer Memorial Library.

# RHODES COLLEGE
### Memphis, Tennessee

**Contact:** Pat Fetters, Campus Visit Coordinator, 2000 North Parkway, Memphis, TN 38112-1690. *Phone:* toll-free 800-844-5969 (out-of-state). *Fax:* 901-843-3719. *Web site:* http://www.rhodes.edu/ *Visit location:* Admissions Office—Reception Area, Halliburton Tower, 2000 North Parkway.

## QUICK FACTS

Enrollment: 1,399; UG: 1,385. Entrance: very difficult. SAT>500: 100% V, 100% M; ACT>18: 100%. Tuition and fees: $17,518. Room and board: $5110. Application deadline: 2/1.

## GENERAL

Independent Presbyterian, comprehensive, coed. Awards bachelor's and master's degrees (master's degree in accounting only). Founded 1848. Setting: 100-acre suburban campus. Undergraduate faculty: 150 (116 full-time, 34 part-time); student-faculty ratio is 12:1. Most popular recent majors: biology, English, business administration.

## CAMPUS VISITS

**College Calendar 1998–99:** *Regular classes:* Aug. 26–Dec. 9; Jan. 13–Apr. 30. *Breaks:* Oct. 16–21; Mar. 5–15. *Final exams:* Dec. 11–16; May 3–8. *Admission office closed:* Dec. 23–25, Jan. 1, Apr. 2, Nov. 25; Weekends During Summer.

### VISIT OPPORTUNITIES

| | Appointments? | Who? |
|---|---|---|
| **Campus Tour** | required | open to all |
| **Information Session** | required | open to all |
| **Admission Interview** | required | open to all |
| **Classroom Visit** | required | open to all |

*Rhodes College (continued)*

## VISIT OPPORTUNITIES—*continued*

| | Appointments? | Who? |
|---|---|---|
| **Faculty Meeting** | required | open to all |
| **Overnight Visit** | required | open to all |

**Information Sessions:** M–F, Sat.; unavailable Sat. during summer; 30 minutes.

**Interviews:** M–F, Sat.; unavailable Sat. during summer; 30 minutes.

**Campus Tours:** Conducted by students. M–F, Sat.; unavailable Sat. during summer.

**Class Visits:** Prospective students may attend a class in their area of interest.

**Overnight Visits:** During the regular academic year, prospective applicants may spend an evening in a residence hall with a student host.

**Video:** Free on request.

## CAMPUS FACILITIES
**Of Special Interest:** Burrow Library.

# SOUTHERN ADVENTIST UNIVERSITY
## Collegedale, Tennessee

**Contact:** Victor Czerkasij, Director of Admissions and Recruitment, PO Box 370, Collegedale, TN 37315. *Phone:* 423-238-2843 or toll-free 800-768-8437. *Fax:* 423-238-3005. *E-mail:* victor@southern.edu/ *Web site:* http://www.southern.edu/ *Visit location:* Admission Office, Wright Hall, P.O. Box 370.

## QUICK FACTS
Enrollment: 1,695; UG: 1,667. Entrance: moderately difficult. SAT>500: N/R; ACT>18: 82%. Tuition and fees: $9736. Room and board: $3628. Application deadline: rolling.

## GENERAL
Independent Seventh-day Adventist, comprehensive, coed. Awards associate, bachelor's, and master's degrees. Founded 1892. Setting: 1,000-acre small-town campus with easy access to Chattanooga. Undergraduate faculty: 98 (all full-time); student-faculty ratio is 14:1. Most popular recent majors: nursing, business administration, biology.

## CAMPUS VISITS
**College Calendar 1998–99:** *Regular classes:* Aug. 26–Dec. 17; Jan. 5–Apr. 29. *Breaks:* Nov. 25–29; Feb. 26–Mar. 7; Dec. 18–Jan. 3. *Final exams:* Dec. 14–17; Apr. 26–29. *Special campus days:* College Days, Oct. 5–6; Commencement, May 2; Homecoming, Oct. 23–26.

## VISIT OPPORTUNITIES

| | Appointments? | Who? |
|---|---|---|
| **Campus Tour** | recommended, not required | open to all |
| **Information Session** | recommended, not required | open to all |
| **Admission Interview** | recommended, not required | open to all |
| **Classroom Visit** | recommended | |
| **Faculty Meeting** | required | |
| **Overnight Visit** | recommended | open to all |

**Information Sessions:** M–F 9:00 am–12:00 pm, 1:00–4:00 pm; Sun. mornings by appointment; 45 minutes.

**Interviews:** M–F; Sun. by appointment; 60 minutes.

**Campus Tours:** Conducted by students and admission reps. M–F 9:00 am–12:00 pm, 1:00–4:00 pm; 60 minutes.

**Class Visits:** Prospective students may attend a class in their area of interest.

**Overnight Visits:** During the regular academic year and over the summer, prospective applicants may spend an evening in a residence hall.

**Video:** Free on request.

## CAMPUS FACILITIES
**Science:** Appointment Required: Biology, Physics.

**Arts:** Appointment Required: art exhibits.

**Of Special Interest:** Appointment Required: Lincoln Museum, Computer Labs.

## LOCAL ATTRACTIONS
Chattanooga area; Civil War Battle Grounds, TVA Water Power System and Locks, Tennessee Aquarium, IMAX Theater, Creative Discovery Museum, Hunter Museum of Art, Riverboat Cruise, Chattanooga Choo Choo, Incline Railway, Rock City, Ruby Falls.

# THE UNIVERSITY OF MEMPHIS
## Memphis, Tennessee

**Contact:** Office of Student Relations, 159 Administration Building, Memphis, TN 38152. *Phone:* toll-free 800-669-2678, 800-678-9027 (in-state). *Fax:* 901-678-5318. *Web site:* http://www.memphis.edu/ *Visit location:* Student Relations Tour Center, University Center, Room 218, University Drive.

### QUICK FACTS
Enrollment: 19,066; UG: 13,992. Entrance: moderately difficult. SAT>500: 65% V, 63% M; ACT>18: 92%. Resident tuition and fees: $2412. Nonresident tuition and fees: $7008. Room and board: $3500. Application deadline: 8/1.

### GENERAL
State-supported, university, coed. Part of Tennessee Board of Regents. Awards bachelor's, master's, doctoral, and first professional degrees. Founded 1912. Setting: 1,100-acre urban campus. Undergraduate faculty: 1,205 (702 full-time, 503 part-time); student-faculty ratio is 20:1. Most popular recent majors: education, nursing, accounting.

### CAMPUS VISITS
**College Calendar 1998–99:** *Regular classes:* Aug. 31–Dec. 9; Jan. 19–Apr. 28. *Breaks:* Oct. 10–13; Mar. 15–21. *Final exams:* Dec. 11–17; Apr. 30–May 6. *Admission office closed:* Nov. 26–27, Dec. 21–25. *Special campus days:* Campus Day for Seniors, Oct. 17; Commencement, Dec. 19, May 7.

---

#### VISIT OPPORTUNITIES

|  | **Appointments?** | **Who?** |
|---|---|---|
| **Campus Tour** | required | open to all |
| **Information Session** | required | open to all |
| **Classroom Visit** | required | open to all |
| **Faculty Meeting** | required | open to all |
| **Overnight Visit** | required | open to all |

**Information Sessions:** M–F at 1:00 pm; first Sat. of the month at 9:30 am; held before campus tour; 45 minutes.

**Campus Tours:** Conducted by students. M–F at 1:00 pm; first Sat. of the month; 45 minutes.

**Class Visits:** Prospective students may attend a class in their area of interest.

**Overnight Visits:** During the regular academic year, prospective applicants may spend an evening in a residence hall with a student host.

**Video:** Free on request.

### CAMPUS FACILITIES
**Science:** Natural Science Laboratories, Engineering/Technology Laboratories, Center for Earthquake Research Information.

**Arts:** Performing Arts Studios; Appointment Required: Recording Studio.

**Athletic:** Physical Education Complex.

**Of Special Interest:** Ned R. McWherter Library.

### LOCAL ATTRACTIONS
National Civil Rights Museum; Graceland; Memphis Zoo; Beale Street; area Shopping Malls; Dixon Gallery and Gardens; The Pyramid Arena; Memphis Botanic Gardens; Brooks Museum of Art; The Orpheum Theater.

# UNIVERSITY OF THE SOUTH
## Sewanee, Tennessee

**Contact:** Office of Admission, 735 University Avenue, Sewanee, TN 37383. *Phone:* toll-free 800-522-2234. *Fax:* 931-598-1667. *E-mail:* admiss@sewanee.edu *Web site:* http://www.sewanee.edu/ *Visit location:* Office of Admission, Fulford, University Avenue and South Carolina Avenue.

### QUICK FACTS
Enrollment: 1,318; UG: 1,257. Entrance: very difficult. SAT>500: 98% V, 97% M; ACT>18: 100%. Tuition and fees: $17,730. Room and board: $4660. Application deadline: 2/1.

### GENERAL
Independent Episcopal, comprehensive, coed. Awards bachelor's, master's, doctoral, and first professional degrees. Founded 1857. Setting: 10,000-acre small-town campus. Undergraduate faculty: 158 (125 full-time, 33 part-time); student-faculty ratio is 10:1. Most popular recent majors: English, history, psychology.

### CAMPUS VISITS
**College Calendar 1998–99:** *Regular classes:* Aug. 27–Dec. 8; Jan. 19–May 5. *Breaks:* Dec. 16–Jan. 18; Mar. 17–29; Oct. 23–28. *Final exams:* Dec. 10–16;

*University of the South (continued)*

May 7–12. *Admission office closed:* Mar. 26. *Special campus days:* Commencement, May 16; Homecoming, Oct. 16–17.

## VISIT OPPORTUNITIES

|  | Appointments? | Who? |
|---|---|---|
| **Campus Tour** | recommended, not required | applicants and parents |
| **Information Session** | recommended | |
| **Admission Interview** | required | |
| **Classroom Visit** | required | |
| **Overnight Visit** | required | |

**Information Sessions:** Scheduled during application reading season on select weekdays and Sat. depending upon demand; 60 minutes.

**Interviews:** M–F, select Sat.; group sessions offered during application reading season; 45 minutes.

**Campus Tours:** Conducted by students. M–F, select Sat. at 10:00 am, 2:00 pm; 60 minutes.

**Class Visits:** Classroom visits are determined by the visit schedule.

**Overnight Visits:** During the regular academic year, prospective applicants may spend an evening in a residence hall with a student host.

**Video:** Free on request.

## CAMPUS FACILITIES

**Science:** Woods Laboratories.

**Arts:** Tennessee Williams Center.

**Athletic:** Fowler Sports Center, Equestrian facility.

**Of Special Interest:** All Saints' Chapel, duPont Library.

## LOCAL ATTRACTIONS

Scenic mountain vistas.

# VANDERBILT UNIVERSITY
## Nashville, Tennessee

**Contact:** Office of Undergraduate Admissions, 2305 West End Avenue, Nashville, TN 37203. *Phone:* 615-322-2561. *Fax:* 615-343-7765. *E-mail:* admissions@vanderbilt.edu *Web site:* http://www.vanderbilt.edu/ *Visit location:* Office of Undergraduate Admissions, 2305 West End Avenue.

## QUICK FACTS

Enrollment: 10,187; UG: 5,829. Entrance: very difficult. SAT>500: 98% V, 99% M; ACT>18: 100%. Tuition and fees: $21,478. Room and board: $7430. Application deadline: 1/15.

## GENERAL

Independent, university, coed. Awards bachelor's, master's, doctoral, and first professional degrees. Founded 1873. Setting: 330-acre urban campus. Undergraduate faculty: 2,126 (1,817 full-time, 309 part-time); student-faculty ratio is 8:1. Most popular recent majors: psychology, individual/family development, economics.

## CAMPUS VISITS

**College Calendar 1998–99:** *Regular classes:* Aug. 26–Dec. 8; Jan. 13–Apr. 27. *Breaks:* Nov. 21–29; Mar. 6–14; Dec. 18–Jan. 10. *Final exams:* Dec. 9–17; Apr. 28–May 6. *Special campus days:* Commencement, May 14; Freshman Family Weekend, Oct. 10; Homecoming, Oct. 24; Parents Weekend, Mar. 26–28; Residence Halls Open, Aug. 22.

## VISIT OPPORTUNITIES

|  | Appointments? | Who? |
|---|---|---|
| **Campus Tour** | required | open to all |
| **Information Session** | required | open to all |
| **Classroom Visit** | required | open to all |
| **Faculty Meeting** | required | open to all |
| **Overnight Visit** | required | |

**Information Sessions:** M–F; Sat. morning during academic year; 60 minutes.

**Campus Tours:** Conducted by students. M–F; Sat. during academic year; call for availability; 60 minutes.

**Class Visits:** Certain predetermined classrooms are open to visitors.

**Overnight Visits:** During the regular academic year, prospective applicants may spend an evening in a residence hall with a student host.

**Video:** Free on request.

## CAMPUS FACILITIES

**Arts:** Blair School of Music.

**Athletic:** Student Recreational Center.

**Of Special Interest:** Peabody section of campus.

## LOCAL ATTRACTIONS

2nd Avenue area downtown Nashville, The Hermitage tour and museum, Opryland hotel complex, Ryman Auditorium, Cheekwood Botanical garden, Oilers football games, Predators hockey games, TPAC (the performing art center) events.

# TEXAS

## ABILENE CHRISTIAN UNIVERSITY
### Abilene, Texas

**Contact:** Elaine Roberson, Campus Visits Supervisor, ACU Box 29000, Abilene, TX 79699-9000. *Phone:* 915-674-2664 or toll-free 800-888-6228. *E-mail:* roberson@admissions.acu.edu *Web site:* http://www.acu.edu/ *Visit location:* Admissions Office, Zellner Welcome Center.

### QUICK FACTS

Enrollment: 4,438; UG: 3,840. Entrance: moderately difficult. SAT>500: 71% V, 66% M; ACT>18: 90%. Tuition and fees: $9180. Room and board: $3810. Application deadline: rolling.

### GENERAL

Independent, comprehensive, coed, Church of Christ. Awards associate, bachelor's, master's, doctoral, and first professional degrees. Founded 1906. Setting: 208-acre urban campus. Undergraduate faculty: 286 (189 full-time, 97 part-time); student-faculty ratio is 18:1. Most popular recent majors: biology, elementary education, accounting.

### CAMPUS VISITS

**College Calendar 1998–99:** *Regular classes:* Aug. 24–Dec. 4; Jan. 11–Apr. 30. *Breaks:* Oct. 23; Mar. 15–19. *Final exams:* Dec. 8–11; May 4–7. *Special campus days:* Bible Teachers Workshop, July 25–28; Commencement, Dec. 11, Aug. 6, May 8; Fall High School Weekend, Sept. 25–27; Homecoming, Oct. 17; Lectureship, Feb. 21–24; Maymester, May 11–27; Open House, Oct. 16, Jan. 17–18, Apr. 18–19, Nov. 15–16; Sing Song/Open House, Feb. 19–20; Spring High School Weekend, Mar. 26–28; Welcome Week, Aug. 19–22.

### VISIT OPPORTUNITIES

| | Appointments? | Who? |
|---|---|---|
| **Campus Tour** | recommended, not required | open to all |
| **Information Session** | recommended, not required | open to all |
| **Admission Interview** | | open to all |
| **Classroom Visit** | recommended, not required | open to all |
| **Faculty Meeting** | recommended, not required | |
| **Overnight Visit** | required | open to all |

**Information Sessions:** M–F; 30 minutes.

**Interviews:** M–F; 30 minutes.

**Campus Tours:** Conducted by students. M–F at 10:00 am, 2:00 pm; 60 minutes.

**Class Visits:** Prospective students may attend a class in their area of interest.

**Overnight Visits:** During the regular academic year, prospective applicants may spend an evening in a residence hall with a student host.

**Video:** Free on request.

### CAMPUS FACILITIES

**Arts:** Shore Art Gallery.

**Of Special Interest:** Brown Library.

## SOUTHERN METHODIST UNIVERSITY
### Dallas, Texas

**Contact:** Monique Hernandez, Communications Specialist, SMU Box 750181, Dallas, TX 75275-0181. *Phone:* toll-free 800-323-0672. *Fax:* 214-768-0202. *E-mail:* enrol___serv@smu.edu *Web site:* http://www.smu.edu/ *Visit location:* Division of Enrollment Services/Office of Undergraduate Admission, Perkins Administration Building, 6425 Boaz Street.

### QUICK FACTS

Enrollment: 9,573; UG: 5,314. Entrance: moderately difficult. SAT>500: 82% V, 84% M; ACT>18: 98%. Tuition and fees: $16,790. Room and board: $6454. Application deadline: 4/1.

*Southern Methodist University (continued)*

## GENERAL

Independent, university, coed, United Methodist Church. Awards bachelor's, master's, doctoral, and first professional degrees. Founded 1911. Setting: 163-acre suburban campus. Undergraduate faculty: 678 (502 full-time, 176 part-time); student-faculty ratio is 12:1. Most popular recent majors: finance, psychology, accounting.

## CAMPUS VISITS

**College Calendar 1998–99:** *Regular classes:* Aug. 24–Dec. 4; Jan. 11–Apr. 30. *Breaks:* Dec. 13–Jan. 10. *Final exams:* Dec. 7–12; May 3–8. *Admission office closed:* Dec. 19–27. *Special campus days:* Commencement, May 15; Homecoming, Nov. 14; Parents Weekend, Oct. 24.

## VISIT OPPORTUNITIES

|  | Appointments? | Who? |
| --- | --- | --- |
| **Campus Tour** | recommended | open to all |
| **Information Session** | recommended | open to all |
| **Admission Interview** | required | open to all |
| **Classroom Visit** | not required | open to all |
| **Faculty Meeting** | required | open to all |
| **Overnight Visit** | required | open to all |

**Information Sessions:** M–F at 1:00 pm; select Sat. at 11:00 am; 60 minutes.

**Interviews:** M–F; 60 minutes.

**Campus Tours:** Conducted by students. M–F at 11:00 am; Mon., Wed., Fri. at 11:00 am, 2:00 pm; Tue., Thu. at 4:00 pm; Sat. at 10:00 am; during Jun., Jul., and Aug., and holidays at 11:00 am only; 60 minutes.

**Class Visits:** Certain predetermined classrooms are open to visitors.

**Overnight Visits:** During the regular academic year, prospective applicants may spend an evening in a residence hall.

## CAMPUS FACILITIES

**Science:** Seismology Observatory.

**Arts:** Meadows Art Museum, Greer Garson Theatre, Bob Hope Theatre.

**Athletic:** Dedman Center for Lifetime Sports, Moody Coliseum, Ford Stadium.

**Of Special Interest:** John Tower Center for Political Studies.

## LOCAL ATTRACTIONS

West End District, the Sixth Floor, Dallas Aquarium, Dallas Zoo, Cotton Bowl, Dallas Arboretum and Botanical Garden, Six Flags over Texas, Southfork Ranch, Reunion Tower, Dallas Cowboys, Dallas Mavericks, Dallas Stars and Texas Rangers.

# TEXAS A&M UNIVERSITY
## College Station, Texas

**Contact:** Debbie Perez, Academic Advisor, Appelt Aggieland Visitor Center, College Station, TX 77843-1265. *Phone:* 409-845-5851. *Fax:* 409-847-8737. *E-mail:* admissions@tamu.edu *Web site:* http://www.tamu.edu/ *Visit location:* Aggieland Visitors Center, Rudder Tower, Mail Stop 1265.

## QUICK FACTS

Enrollment: 41,442; UG: 33,926. Entrance: moderately difficult. SAT>500: 85% V, 92% M; ACT>18: 100%. Resident tuition and fees: $2777. Nonresident tuition and fees: $9197. Room and board: $4276. Application deadline: 3/1.

## GENERAL

State-supported, university, coed. Part of Texas A&M University System. Awards bachelor's, master's, doctoral, and first professional degrees. Founded 1876. Setting: 5,200-acre suburban campus with easy access to Houston. Undergraduate faculty: 2,299 (1,928 full-time, 371 part-time); student-faculty ratio is 24:1. Most popular recent majors: interdisciplinary studies, animal sciences, accounting.

## CAMPUS VISITS

**College Calendar 1998–99:** *Regular classes:* Aug. 31–Dec. 8; Jan. 19–May 4. *Breaks:* Dec. 16–Jan. 18. *Final exams:* Dec. 11–16; May 7–12. *Admission office closed:* Nov. 26–27, Dec. 21–Jan. 1, Jan. 18. *Special campus days:* Bonfire, Nov. 24; Fall Commencement, Dec. 18–19; Muster, Apr. 21; Spring Commencement, May 14–15.

## VISIT OPPORTUNITIES

|  | Appointments? | Who? |
| --- | --- | --- |
| **Campus Tour** | required | open to all |
| **Information Session** | required | open to all |
| **Faculty Meeting** | required | open to all |

**Information Sessions:** M–F 9:00 am–5:00 pm; scheduled daily for different departments; times vary with the desired appointments scheduled; 60 minutes.

**Campus Tours:** Conducted by students. M–F 9:00 am–5:00 pm; scheduled daily for different departments; times vary with the desired appointments scheduled; 60 minutes.

## CAMPUS FACILITIES

**Science:** Appointment Required: Nuclear Reactor, Wind Tunnel, Cyclotron, Veterinary School.

**Arts:** MSC Forsyth Center Galleries, J. Wayne Stark Galleries, MSC L. T. Jordan Institute-International Collection.

**Athletic:** Student Recreation Center; Appointment Required: Reed Arena, Kyle Field.

**Of Special Interest:** George Bush Presidential Library and Museum.

# TEXAS A&M UNIVERSITY AT GALVESTON
### Galveston, Texas

**Contact:** Paul I. Hille, Associate Director of Student Services, PO Box 1675, Galveston, TX 77550. *Phone:* toll-free 800-850-6376. *Fax:* 409-740-4731. *E-mail:* hillep@tamug.tamu.edu *Visit location:* Office of Student Relations, Building Number 3025, 200 Seawolf Parkway.

## QUICK FACTS

Enrollment: 1,095; UG: 1,095. Entrance: moderately difficult. SAT>500: 67% V, 76% M; ACT>18: 100%. Resident tuition and fees: $2834. Nonresident tuition and fees: $8999. Room and board: $3653. Application deadline: rolling.

## GENERAL

State-supported, 4-year, coed. Part of Texas A&M University System. Awards bachelor's degrees. Founded 1962. Setting: 100-acre suburban campus with easy access to Houston. Faculty: 89 (62 full-time, 27 part-time); student-faculty ratio is 15:1. Most popular recent majors: marine biology, marine science, naval architecture/marine engineering.

## CAMPUS VISITS

**College Calendar 1998–99:** *Regular classes:* Aug. 31–Dec. 8; Jan. 19–May 4. *Breaks:* Nov. 26–27; Mar. 15–19; Dec. 17–Jan. 18. *Final exams:* Dec. 11–16; May 7–12. *Special campus days:* Aggie Muster, Apr. 21;

Bonfire, Nov. 22; Campus Olympics; Maritime Ball, Apr. 3; Parent's Weekend, Apr. 24; Spring Campus Preview, Apr. 24.

## VISIT OPPORTUNITIES

|  | Appointments? | Who? |
|---|---|---|
| **Campus Tour** | recommended | open to all |
| **Information Session** | recommended | open to all |
| **Admission Interview** | required | applicants and parents |
| **Classroom Visit** | required | applicants only |
| **Faculty Meeting** | required | open to all |
| **Overnight Visit** | required | open to all |

**Information Sessions:** Included in campus tour; 45 minutes.

**Interviews:** M–F; not available during holiday breaks; 30 minutes.

**Campus Tours:** Conducted by students. Mon. at 10:00 am, 2:00 pm; Fri. at 10:00 am, 2:00 pm; not available during holiday breaks; 120 minutes.

**Class Visits:** Classroom visits are determined by the visit schedule.

**Overnight Visits:** During the regular academic year and over the summer, prospective applicants may spend an evening in a residence hall.

**Video:** Free on request.

## CAMPUS FACILITIES

**Science:** Appointment Required: Engineering Laboratory, Science Laboratory.

**Athletic:** Appointment Required: Physical Education Facility.

**Of Special Interest:** Appointment Required: United States Training Ship "Texas Clipper II", Sea Turtle Hatchery, Ship Bridge Simulator.

# TEXAS CHRISTIAN UNIVERSITY
### Fort Worth, Texas

**Contact:** Office of Admissions, TCU Box 297013, Fort Worth, TX 76129. *Phone:* toll-free 800-828-3764. *Fax:* 817-257-7268. *E-mail:* frogmail@tcu.edu *Web site:* http://www.tcu.edu/ *Visit location:* Office of Admissions, Sadler Hall, Room 112, 2800 South University Drive.

*Texas Christian University (continued)*

## QUICK FACTS

Enrollment: 7,273; UG: 6,163. Entrance: moderately difficult. SAT>500: N/R; ACT>18: N/R. Tuition and fees: $11,090. Room and board: $3860. Application deadline: 2/15.

## GENERAL

Independent, university, coed, Christian Church (Disciples of Christ). Awards bachelor's, master's, doctoral, and first professional degrees. Founded 1873. Setting: 237-acre suburban campus. Undergraduate faculty: 505 (336 full-time, 169 part-time); student-faculty ratio is 15:1. Most popular recent majors: nursing, psychology, finance.

## CAMPUS VISITS

**College Calendar 1998–99:** *Regular classes:* Aug. 24–Dec. 9; Jan. 19–May 5. *Breaks:* Oct. 23–25; Mar. 15–21. *Final exams:* Dec. 14–18; May 10–14. *Special campus days:* first semester commencement, Dec. 19; second semester commencement, May 15.

## VISIT OPPORTUNITIES

|  | Appointments? | Who? |
| --- | --- | --- |
| **Campus Tour** | recommended | open to all |
| **Information Session** | recommended | open to all |
| **Admission Interview** | recommended | open to all |
| **Classroom Visit** | required | open to all |
| **Faculty Meeting** | required | open to all |
| **Overnight Visit** | required | open to all |

**Information Sessions:** Sat. during academic year; call for available schedule; 50 minutes.

**Interviews:** M–F; 50 minutes.

**Campus Tours:** Conducted by students. M–F, select Sat.; call for available times; 60 minutes.

**Class Visits:** Prospective students may attend a class in their area of interest.

**Overnight Visits:** During the regular academic year, prospective applicants may spend an evening in a residence hall with a student host.

**Video:** Free on request.

## CAMPUS FACILITIES

**Science:** Sid W. Richardson Building.

**Arts:** Mary D. and F. Howard Walsh Performing Arts Center, Moudy Building.

**Athletic:** Amon Carter Stadium, Daniel Meyer Coliseum.

**Of Special Interest:** Dee J. Kelly Alumni and Visitor Center, KTCU campus radio station.

## LOCAL ATTRACTIONS

Kimbell Art Museum; Sundance Square; Fort Worth Stockyards; Billy Bobs Honkey Tonk; downtown Fort Worth; Bass Performing Arts Hall.

# TRINITY UNIVERSITY
### San Antonio, Texas

**Contact:** Office of Admissions, 715 Stadium Drive, San Antonio, TX 78212-7200. *Phone:* toll-free 800-TRINITY. *Fax:* 210-236-8164. *E-mail:* admissions@trinity.edu *Web site:* http://www.trinity.edu/ *Visit location:* Admissions, 715 Stadium Drive.

## QUICK FACTS

Enrollment: 2,560; UG: 2,298. Entrance: very difficult. SAT>500: 97% V, 96% M; ACT>18: 100%. Tuition and fees: $14,724. Room and board: $5970. Application deadline: 2/1.

## GENERAL

Independent, comprehensive, coed, Presbyterian Church. Awards bachelor's and master's degrees. Founded 1869. Setting: 113-acre urban campus. Undergraduate faculty: 281 (220 full-time, 61 part-time); student-faculty ratio is 11:1. Most popular recent majors: business administration, biology, English.

## CAMPUS VISITS

**College Calendar 1998–99:** *Regular classes:* Aug. 27–Dec. 8; Jan. 12–Apr. 27. *Breaks:* Dec. 19–Jan. 10. *Final exams:* Dec. 10–17; Apr. 29–May 6. *Special campus days:* Trinity in Focus—campus visit programs.

## VISIT OPPORTUNITIES

|  | Appointments? | Who? |
| --- | --- | --- |
| **Campus Tour** | required | open to all |
| **Information Session** | required | open to all |
| **Admission Interview** | required | open to all |
| **Classroom Visit** | required | open to all |
| **Faculty Meeting** | required | open to all |
| **Overnight Visit** | required | open to all |

**Information Sessions:** M–F at 10:30 am, 2:30 pm; Sat. at 10:30 am; 45 minutes.

**Interviews:** M–F.

**Campus Tours:** Conducted by students. M–F at 11:30 am, 3:30 pm; Sat. at 11:30 am; 60 minutes.

**Class Visits:** Prospective students may attend a class in their area of interest, classroom visits are determined by the visit schedule.

**Overnight Visits:** During the regular academic year, prospective applicants may spend an evening in a residence hall with a student host.

### CAMPUS FACILITIES
**Athletic:** Bell Center.

### LOCAL ATTRACTIONS
San Antonio's Riverwalk; the Alamo and other historic missions; the San Antonio Museum of Art; McNay Art Museum; Witte Museum; professional sports teams, Sea World of Texas, and Fiesta Texas.

# UNIVERSITY OF DALLAS
Irving, Texas

**Contact:** Larry Webb, Admissions Counselor, 1845 East Northgate Drive, Irving, TX 75062. *Phone:* 972-721-5266 or toll-free 800-628-6999. *Fax:* 972-721-5017. *E-mail:* undadmis@acad.udallas.edu *Visit location:* Undergraduate Admissions, Carpenter Hall, 1845 East Northgate Drive.

### QUICK FACTS
Enrollment: 2,862; UG: 1,096. Entrance: very difficult. SAT>500: 94% V, 92% M; ACT>18: 99%. Tuition and fees: $12,856. Room and board: $4920. Application deadline: 2/15.

### GENERAL
Independent Roman Catholic, university, coed. Awards bachelor's, master's, and doctoral degrees. Founded 1955. Setting: 750-acre suburban campus with easy access to Dallas–Fort Worth. Undergraduate faculty: 211 (109 full-time, 102 part-time); student-faculty ratio is 11:1. Most popular recent majors: biology, English, political science.

### CAMPUS VISITS
**College Calendar 1998–99:** *Regular classes:* Aug. 31–Dec. 10; Jan. 19–May 6. *Breaks:* Mar. 6–14. *Final exams:* Dec. 11–17; May 7–13.

### VISIT OPPORTUNITIES

|  | Appointments? | Who? |
|---|---|---|
| **Campus Tour** | recommended | open to all |
| **Information Session** | recommended | open to all |
| **Admission Interview** | recommended | open to all |
| **Classroom Visit** | required | open to all |
| **Faculty Meeting** | required | open to all |
| **Overnight Visit** | required | open to all |

**Information Sessions:** M–F; 45 minutes.

**Interviews:** M–F, select Sat.; select Sat. during fall semester; 45 minutes.

**Campus Tours:** Conducted by students. M–F; 30 minutes.

**Class Visits:** Classroom visits are determined by the visit schedule.

**Overnight Visits:** During the regular academic year, prospective applicants may spend an evening in a residence hall with a student host.

### CAMPUS FACILITIES
**Of Special Interest:** William A. Blakley Library.

# UNIVERSITY OF HOUSTON
Houston, Texas

**Contact:** Jeff Fuller, Admissions Counselor, 4800 Calhoun, Houston, TX 77204-2161. *Phone:* 713-743-9621 or toll-free 800-741-4449. *Fax:* 713-743-9633. *E-mail:* jfuller@jerson.uh.edu *Web site:* http://www.uh.edu/ *Visit location:* Office of Student Outreach Services, Ezekiel Cullen Building, Room 128, 4805 Calhoun.

### QUICK FACTS
Enrollment: 30,399; UG: 22,369. Entrance: moderately difficult. SAT>500: 56% V, 65% M; ACT>18: 85%. Resident tuition and fees: $1993. Nonresident tuition and fees: $7081. Room and board: $4405. Application deadline: 7/1.

### GENERAL
State-supported, university, coed. Part of University of Houston System. Awards bachelor's, master's, doctoral, and first professional degrees. Founded 1927. Setting: 550-acre urban campus. Undergraduate faculty: 898 (845 full-time, 53 part-time). Most popular recent majors: business administration, biology, psychology.

*University of Houston (continued)*

## CAMPUS VISITS

**College Calendar 1998–99:** *Regular classes:* Aug. 24–Dec. 5; Jan. 19–May 3. *Final exams:* Dec. 9–17; May 5–13. *Special campus days:* Commencement—Spring; Cougar Preview—Fall and Spring; Homecoming—Fall.

## VISIT OPPORTUNITIES

| | Appointments? | Who? |
|---|---|---|
| **Campus Tour** | recommended, not required | open to all |
| **Information Session** | required | open to all |
| **Admission Interview** | recommended | applicants and parents |
| **Classroom Visit** | required | applicants and parents |
| **Faculty Meeting** | required | applicants and parents |
| **Overnight Visit** | required | applicants only |

**Information Sessions:** M–F, select Sat.; 30 minutes.

**Interviews:** M–F; 10 minutes.

**Campus Tours:** Conducted by students. M–F at 10:00 am, 3:00 pm; 60 minutes.

**Class Visits:** Prospective students may attend a class in their area of interest.

**Overnight Visits:** During the regular academic year and over the summer, prospective applicants may spend an evening in a residence hall with a student host.

**Video:** Free on request.

## CAMPUS FACILITIES

**Science:** Appointment Required: Texas Center for Super Conductivity, College of Pharmacy, College of Optometry.

**Arts:** Appointment Required: Moores School of Music, Blaffer Art Gallery.

**Athletic:** Appointment Required: Athletic/Alumni Facility, Hoffeinz Pavilion.

# UNIVERSITY OF NORTH TEXAS
## Denton, Texas

**Contact:** Angela Goin, Tour and Information Desk Superior, PO Box 311070, Denton, TX 76203. *Phone:* 940-565-4104 or toll-free 800-868-8211 (in-state). *Fax:* 940-565-3878. *E-mail:* agoin@pres. admin.unt. edu *Web site:* http://www.unt.edu/ *Visit location:* Public Affairs Information Desk, Eagle Student Services Center, Highland Street-University of North Texas.

## QUICK FACTS

Enrollment: 25,013; UG: 18,719. Entrance: moderately difficult. SAT>500: 68% V, 63% M; ACT>18: N/R. Resident tuition and fees: $2187. Nonresident tuition and fees: $8821. Room and board: $3842. Application deadline: 6/15.

## GENERAL

State-supported, university, coed. Awards bachelor's, master's, and doctoral degrees. Founded 1890. Setting: 456-acre urban campus with easy access to Dallas–Fort Worth. Undergraduate faculty: 979 (726 full-time, 253 part-time); student-faculty ratio is 20:1. Most popular recent majors: biology, psychology, accounting.

## CAMPUS VISITS

**College Calendar 1998–99:** *Regular classes:* Aug. 31–Dec. 18; Jan. 19–May 14. *Final exams:* Dec. 12–18; May 8–14.

## VISIT OPPORTUNITIES

| | Appointments? | Who? |
|---|---|---|
| **Campus Tour** | recommended | applicants and parents |
| **Information Session** | | open to all |
| **Admission Interview** | | applicants and parents |
| **Classroom Visit** | | applicants and parents |
| **Faculty Meeting** | recommended | applicants and parents |
| **Overnight Visit** | | open to all |

**Information Sessions:** M–F, Sat.; available during tour.

**Interviews:** M–F; 60 minutes.

**Campus Tours:** Conducted by students. M–F at 9:00 am, 10:00 am, 2:00 pm, 3:00 pm; Sat. at 10:00 am, 1:00 pm; 90 minutes.

**Class Visits:** Classroom visit depends on department policy.

**Overnight Visits:** During the regular academic year, prospective applicants may spend an evening in a residence hall.

**Video:** Free on request.

## CAMPUS FACILITIES
**Of Special Interest:** Willis Library.

# UTAH

## BRIGHAM YOUNG UNIVERSITY
**Provo, Utah**

**Contact:** Campus Visits Office, Brigham Young University, A-209 ASB, Provo, UT 84602-1229. *Phone:* 801-378-4431. *Fax:* 801-378-4264. *E-mail:* schhol_relations@byu.edu *Web site:* http://www.byu.edu/ *Visit location:* School Relations, Administration Building, A-209 ASB.

### QUICK FACTS
Enrollment: 31,994; UG: 29,259. Entrance: moderately difficult. SAT>500: N/App; ACT>18: 99%. Tuition and fees: $2630. Room and board: $4130. Application deadline: 2/15.

### GENERAL
Independent, university, coed, Church of Jesus Christ of Latter-day Saints. Awards bachelor's, master's, doctoral, and first professional degrees. Founded 1875. Setting: 638-acre suburban campus with easy access to Salt Lake City. Undergraduate faculty: 1,828 (1,388 full-time, 440 part-time); student-faculty ratio is 29:1. Most popular recent majors: family studies, elementary education, accounting.

### CAMPUS VISITS
**College Calendar 1998–99:** *Regular classes:* Aug. 31–Dec. 9; Jan. 4–Apr. 13. *Final exams:* Dec. 12–17; Apr. 16–21. *Special campus days:* Commencement, Apr. 22–23; Homecoming, Oct. 9–10; Thanksgiving Holiday, Nov. 25–29.

### VISIT OPPORTUNITIES

| | Appointments? |
|---|---|
| **Campus Tour** | required |
| **Information Session** | recommended |
| **Faculty Meeting** | required |

**Information Sessions:** M–F 8:00 am–5:00 pm; 45 minutes.

**Campus Tours:** Conducted by students. M–F 8:00 am–5:00 pm; contact Campus Visits 2 weeks in advance for scheduled time and availability; 60 minutes.

## CAMPUS FACILITIES
**Of Special Interest:** Harold B. Lee Library.

# VERMONT

## BENNINGTON COLLEGE
**Bennington, Vermont**

**Contact:** Office of Admissions, Bennington, VT 05201-9993. *Phone:* toll-free 800-833-6845. *Fax:* 802-440-4320. *E-mail:* admissions@bennington.edu *Web site:* http://www.bennington.edu/ *Visit location:* Office of Admissions and The First Year, Bennington College.

### QUICK FACTS
Enrollment: 451; UG: 347. Entrance: very difficult. SAT>500: 90% V, 85% M; ACT>18: N/R. Comprehensive fee: $26,400. Room and board: N/App. Application deadline: 2/1.

### GENERAL
Independent, comprehensive, coed. Awards bachelor's and master's degrees. Founded 1932. Setting: 550-acre small-town campus with easy access to Albany. Undergraduate faculty: 60 (37 full-time, 23 part-time); student-faculty ratio is 6:1. Most popular recent majors: interdisciplinary studies, literature, visual/performing arts.

### CAMPUS VISITS
**College Calendar 1998–99:** *Regular classes:* Sept. 10–Dec. 17; Feb. 23–June 2. *Special campus days:* Admissions Open House, Oct. 11–12, Nov. 8–9; Admitted Students Weekend, Apr. 18–19; Commencement, June 5; Reunion Weekend and Family Weekend, Oct. 1–4.

### VISIT OPPORTUNITIES

| | Appointments? | Who? |
|---|---|---|
| **Campus Tour** | not required | open to all |
| **Information Session** | not required | open to all |
| **Admission Interview** | not required | open to all |
| **Classroom Visit** | recommended | open to all |

*Bennington College (continued)*

## VISIT OPPORTUNITIES—*continued*

| | Appointments? | Who? |
|---|---|---|
| **Faculty Meeting** | recommended | open to all |
| **Overnight Visit** | required | open to all |

**Information Sessions:** M–F 9:00 am–4:00 pm; Sat. 9:00 am–2:00 pm; 30 minutes.

**Interviews:** M–F 9:00 am–4:00 pm; Sat. 9:00 am–1:00 pm; 30 minutes.

**Campus Tours:** Conducted by students. M–F 9:00 am–3:00 pm; Sat. 9:00 am–12:00 pm; 50 minutes.

**Class Visits:** Prospective students may attend a class in their area of interest.

**Overnight Visits:** During the regular academic year, prospective applicants may spend an evening in a residence hall with a student host.

## CAMPUS FACILITIES
**Of Special Interest:** Crossett Library.

# CASTLETON STATE COLLEGE
**Castleton, Vermont**

**Contact:** Admissions Office, Wright House, Castleton, VT 05735. *Phone:* toll-free 800-639-8521. *Fax:* 802-468-1476. *E-mail:* info@sparrow.csc.vsc.edu *Web site:* http://www.csc.vsc.edu *Visit location:* Admissions Office, Wright House.

## QUICK FACTS
Enrollment: 1,774; UG: 1,659. Entrance: moderately difficult. SAT>500: 40% V, 30% M; ACT>18: N/App. Resident tuition and fees: $4506. Nonresident tuition and fees: $9486. Room and board: $5086. Application deadline: rolling.

## GENERAL
State-supported, comprehensive, coed. Part of Vermont State Colleges System. Awards associate, bachelor's, and master's degrees and post-master's certificates. Founded 1787. Setting: 130-acre rural campus. Undergraduate faculty: 169 (92 full-time, 77 part-time); student-faculty ratio is 16:1. Most popular recent majors: business administration, psychology.

## CAMPUS VISITS
**College Calendar 1998–99:** *Regular classes:* Aug. 26–Dec. 11; Jan. 25–May 14. *Final exams:* Dec. 15–19; May 17–21. *Admission office closed:* Christmas/New Year Week, Dec. 25–Jan. 3.

## VISIT OPPORTUNITIES

| | Appointments? | Who? |
|---|---|---|
| **Campus Tour** | recommended | open to all |
| **Information Session** | required | open to all |
| **Admission Interview** | required | open to all |
| **Classroom Visit** | required | open to all |
| **Faculty Meeting** | required | open to all |
| **Overnight Visit** | required | open to all |

**Information Sessions:** M–F at 10:00 am, 2:00 pm; 50 minutes.

**Interviews:** M–F; select Sat. during academic term; 50 minutes.

**Campus Tours:** Conducted by students. M–F at 9:00 am, 11:00 am, 1:00 pm, 3:00 pm; select Sat. at 10:00 am; 60 minutes.

**Class Visits:** Classroom visits are determined by the visit schedule.

**Overnight Visits:** During the regular academic year, prospective applicants may spend an evening in a residence hall with a student host.

## CAMPUS FACILITIES
**Science:** Black Science Building.

**Arts:** Fine Art Center.

**Athletic:** Glenbrook Gymnasium.

## LOCAL ATTRACTIONS
Killington Mountain; Hubbardton Battlefield; Green Mountain National Forest.

# GREEN MOUNTAIN COLLEGE
**Poultney, Vermont**

**Contact:** Alexis Northcross, Assistant Director of Admissions/Campus Visits Coordinator, One College Circle, Poultney, VT 05764. *Phone:* toll-free 800-776-6675 (out-of-state). *Fax:* 802-287-8099. *Web site:* http://www.greenmtn.edu/ *Visit location:* Admissions, Pollock Building, One College Circle.

## QUICK FACTS
Enrollment: 583; UG: 583. Entrance: moderately difficult. SAT>500: 63% V, 45% M; ACT>18: N/R.

Tuition and fees: $15,140. Room and board: $3320. Application deadline: rolling.

## GENERAL
Independent, 4-year, coed, United Methodist Church. Awards bachelor's degrees. Founded 1834. Setting: 155-acre small-town campus. Faculty: 59 (35 full-time, 24 part-time); student-faculty ratio is 14:1. Most popular recent majors: behavioral sciences, business administration.

## CAMPUS VISITS
**College Calendar 1998–99:** *Regular classes:* Aug. 31–Dec. 10; Jan. 11–May 4. *Breaks:* Oct. 12–14; Feb. 12–22; Nov. 24–27; Mar. 26–Apr. 6. *Final exams:* Dec. 12–17; May 6–11. *Special campus days:* Commencement, May 15; Parent's Weekend and Homecoming, Oct. 2–4.

## VISIT OPPORTUNITIES

| | Appointments? | Who? |
|---|---|---|
| **Campus Tour** | required | applicants and parents |
| **Admission Interview** | required | |
| **Classroom Visit** | required | applicants and parents |
| **Overnight Visit** | required | |

**Interviews:** M–F, select Sat.; 30 minutes.

**Campus Tours:** Conducted by students. M–F at 9:00 am, 3:00 pm; select Sat. at 10:00 am, 11:00 am, 1:00 pm, 2:00 pm; call 800-776-6675 for Sat. schedule; 60 minutes.

**Class Visits:** Prospective students may attend a class in their area of interest, classroom visits are determined by the visit schedule.

**Overnight Visits:** During the regular academic year, prospective applicants may spend an evening in a residence hall with a student host.

**Video:** Free on request.

## CAMPUS FACILITIES
**Science:** Appointment Required: labs.

**Arts:** Appointment Required: outdoor kiln, printing press.

**Athletic:** Appointment Required: indoor pool, dance studio.

**Of Special Interest:** Organic garden, weather station.

# LYNDON STATE COLLEGE
**Lyndonville, Vermont**

**Contact:** Admissions Counselor, Vail Hill Road, Lyndonville, VT 05851. *Phone:* 802-626-6413 or toll-free 800-225-1998 (in-state). *Fax:* 802-626-6335. *Web site:* http://www.lsc.vsc.edu/ *Visit location:* Admissions, Vail, Admissions, Lyndon State College.

## QUICK FACTS
Enrollment: 1,190; UG: 1,163. Entrance: moderately difficult. SAT>500: N/App; ACT>18: N/App. Resident tuition and fees: $4516. Nonresident tuition and fees: $9496. Room and board: $5086. Application deadline: rolling.

## GENERAL
State-supported, comprehensive, coed. Part of Vermont State Colleges System. Awards associate, bachelor's, and master's degrees. Founded 1911. Setting: 175-acre rural campus. Undergraduate faculty: 108 (63 full-time, 45 part-time); student-faculty ratio is 17:1. Most popular recent majors: business administration, mass communications, education.

## CAMPUS VISITS
**College Calendar 1998–99:** *Regular classes:* Aug. 31–Dec. 16; Jan. 11–May 7. *Breaks:* Nov. 23–27; Feb. 22–26; Apr. 5–9. *Final exams:* Dec. 17–19; May 10–12. *Special campus days:* Alumni Weekend, Sept. 12–13; Commencement, May 16; Family Weekend, Oct. 2–4.

## VISIT OPPORTUNITIES

| | Appointments? | Who? |
|---|---|---|
| **Campus Tour** | recommended | applicants and parents |
| **Admission Interview** | recommended | |
| **Classroom Visit** | recommended | |
| **Faculty Meeting** | recommended | |
| **Overnight Visit** | recommended | |

**Interviews:** M–F, select Sat.; 20 minutes.

**Campus Tours:** Conducted by students. M–F, select Sat.; 60 minutes.

**Class Visits:** Classroom visits are determined by the visit schedule.

**Overnight Visits:** During the regular academic year, prospective applicants may spend an evening in a residence hall with a student host.

*Lyndon State College (continued)*

## CAMPUS FACILITIES
**Science:** Labs, Science Wing.

**Arts:** Graphic Design Lab, Quimby Art Gallery.

**Athletic:** Pool, Exercise Room/Training Room/Weight Room/Gyms.

**Of Special Interest:** Health Service Building, Dorms.

## LOCAL ATTRACTIONS
Burke Mountain Ski Resort; Local Restaurants.

# MIDDLEBURY COLLEGE
**Middlebury, Vermont**

**Contact:** Director of Admissions, The Emma Willard House, Middlebury, VT 05753. *Phone:* 802-443-3000. *Fax:* 802-443-2056. *E-mail:* admissions@middlebury.edu *Web site:* http://www.middlebury.edu/ *Visit location:* Admissions Office, The Emma Willard House, 131 South Main Street (Route 30).

## QUICK FACTS
Enrollment: 2,169; UG: 2,169. Entrance: very difficult. SAT>500: 98% V, 99% M; ACT>18: 100%. Comprehensive fee: $29,340. Room and board: N/App. Application deadline: 12/31.

## GENERAL
Independent, comprehensive, coed. Awards bachelor's, master's, and doctoral degrees. Founded 1800. Setting: 350-acre small-town campus. Undergraduate faculty: 227 (186 full-time, 41 part-time); student-faculty ratio is 11:1. Most popular recent majors: English, international relations, history.

## CAMPUS VISITS
**College Calendar 1998–99:** *Regular classes:* Sept. 14–Dec. 12; Jan. 4–29; Feb. 8–May 8. *Breaks:* Oct. 15–19; Feb. 25–Mar. 1; Nov. 24–30; Mar. 20–29. *Final exams:* Dec. 14–22; May 11–18. *Special campus days:* Commencement, May 23; Fall Family Weekends, Oct. 2–4, Oct. 9–11; Homecoming, Oct. 23–25.

## VISIT OPPORTUNITIES

|  | Appointments? | Who? |
|---|---|---|
| **Campus Tour** | recommended, not required | open to all |

|  | Appointments? | Who? |
|---|---|---|
| **Information Session** | recommended, not required | open to all |
| **Admission Interview** | required | open to all |
| **Classroom Visit** | not required | open to all |
| **Faculty Meeting** | required | open to all |

**Information Sessions:** M–F at 9:00 am, 1:00 pm; Sat. in fall at 9:00 am; 60 minutes.

**Interviews:** M–F Jun. through Dec.; Sat. groups sessions available in fall; 30 minutes.

**Campus Tours:** Conducted by students. M–F at 10:00 am, 2:00 pm; Sat. in fall at 10:00 am; 60 minutes.

**Class Visits:** Classroom visits are determined by the visit schedule.

**Video:** Free on request.

## CAMPUS FACILITIES
**Science:** Bi-Centennial Hall.

**Arts:** Center for the Arts, Wright Theatre, Johnson Art Center.

**Athletic:** Memorial Field House, Ralph Myhre Golf Course, Middlebury College Snow Bowl (Ski area).

# NORWICH UNIVERSITY
**Northfield, Vermont**

**Contact:** Stephanie Doherty, 65 South Main Street, Northfield, VT 05663. *Phone:* toll-free 800-468-6679 (in-state). *Fax:* 802-485-2032. *Web site:* http://www.norwich.edu/ *Visit location:* Admissions Office, Roberts Hall, 65 South Main Street.

## QUICK FACTS
Enrollment: 2,735; UG: 2,163. Entrance: moderately difficult. SAT>500: 56% V, 55% M; ACT>18: N/R. Tuition and fees: $14,950. Room and board: $5717. Application deadline: rolling.

## GENERAL
Independent, comprehensive, coed. Awards associate, bachelor's, and master's degrees. Founded 1819. Setting: 1,125-acre small-town campus. Undergraduate faculty: 179 (141 full-time, 38 part-time); student-faculty ratio is 14:1. Most popular recent

majors: criminal justice/law enforcement administration, mechanical engineering, business administration.

## CAMPUS VISITS

**College Calendar 1998–99:** *Regular classes:* Aug. 31–Dec. 13; Jan. 11–May 1. *Final exams:* Dec. 13–20; May 2–7.

## VISIT OPPORTUNITIES

|  | Appointments? | Who? |
|---|---|---|
| **Campus Tour** | recommended, not required | open to all |
| **Admission Interview** | recommended, not required | open to all |
| **Classroom Visit** | required | open to all |
| **Faculty Meeting** | required | open to all |
| **Overnight Visit** | required | open to all |

**Interviews:** M–F, Sat.; other individualized appointments available; 30 minutes.

**Campus Tours:** Conducted by students. M–F, Sat.; 60 minutes.

**Class Visits:** Prospective students may attend a class in their area of interest.

**Overnight Visits:** During the regular academic year, prospective applicants may spend an evening in a residence hall with a student host.

## CAMPUS FACILITIES

**Science:** New Mathematics, Science, Engineering Complex, Computer Centers.

**Athletic:** Hockey Ring, Field House.

**Of Special Interest:** Library.

## LOCAL ATTRACTIONS

Stowe; Montpelier, capital of state; Burlington.

# SAINT MICHAEL'S COLLEGE

## Colchester, Vermont

**Contact:** Admission Office, Winooski Park, Colchester, VT 05439. *Phone:* toll-free 800-762-8000. *Fax:* 802-654-2591. *E-mail:* admission@smcvt.edu *Web site:* http://www.smcvt.edu/ *Visit location:* Admission Office, Klein, Winooski Park.

## QUICK FACTS

Enrollment: 2,622; UG: 1,938. Entrance: moderately difficult. SAT>500: 84% V, 81% M; ACT>18: N/R. Tuition and fees: $15,900. Room and board: $7000. Application deadline: 2/1.

## GENERAL

Independent Roman Catholic, comprehensive, coed. Awards bachelor's and master's degrees. Founded 1904. Setting: 440-acre small-town campus with easy access to Montreal. Undergraduate faculty: 212 (145 full-time, 67 part-time); student-faculty ratio is 14:1. Most popular recent majors: psychology, business administration, English.

## CAMPUS VISITS

**College Calendar 1998–99:** *Regular classes:* Sept. 1–Dec. 11; Jan. 11–Apr. 27. *Breaks:* Nov. 24–29; Feb. 19–Mar. 1; Dec. 20–Jan. 9. *Final exams:* Dec. 14–19; Apr. 29–May 4. *Admission office closed:* Nov. 26–27, Dec. 24–25, Dec. 31–Jan. 1, Apr. 2. *Special campus days:* Homecoming, Sept. 19; Parents Weekend, Mar. 20.

## VISIT OPPORTUNITIES

|  | Appointments? | Who? |
|---|---|---|
| **Campus Tour** | recommended, not required | open to all |
| **Information Session** | recommended, not required | open to all |
| **Admission Interview** | required | open to all |
| **Classroom Visit** | required | open to all |
| **Faculty Meeting** | required | open to all |
| **Overnight Visit** | required | admitted applicants only |

**Information Sessions:** Sat. at 10:30 am and selected M–F dates in spring; prospective student Open Houses in fall and spring; call for schedule; 60 minutes.

**Interviews:** M–F; 40 minutes.

**Campus Tours:** Conducted by students. M–F; Sat. at 10:30 am; 60 minutes.

**Class Visits:** Prospective students may attend a class in their area of interest, classroom visits are determined by the visit schedule.

**Overnight Visits:** During the regular academic year, prospective applicants may spend an evening in a residence hall with a student host.

**Video:** Free on request.

*Saint Michael's College (continued)*

## CAMPUS FACILITIES
**Science:** Cheray Science Hall, Observatory.

**Arts:** McCarthy Arts Center.

**Athletic:** Tarrant Recreation Center, Ross Sports Center.

**Of Special Interest:** Durick Library, Alliot Student Center, St. Michael's Chapel.

## LOCAL ATTRACTIONS
Downtown Burlington Church Street Market Place; Ski Resorts—Stowe, Smuggler's Notch Sugarbush; Lake Champlain Waterfront.

# UNIVERSITY OF VERMONT
## Burlington, Vermont

**Contact:** Admissions Office, 194 South Prospect Street, Burlington, VT 05401-3596. *Phone:* 802-656-3370. *Fax:* 802-656-8611. *E-mail:* admissions@uvm.edu *Web site:* http://www.uvm.edu/ *Visit location:* Admissions Office, Clement House, 194 South Prospect Street.

## QUICK FACTS
Enrollment: 9,105; UG: 7,514. Entrance: moderately difficult. SAT>500: 83% V, 82% M; ACT>18: 98%. Resident tuition and fees: $7550. Nonresident tuition and fees: $18,098. Room and board: $5272. Application deadline: 2/1.

## GENERAL
State-supported, university, coed. Awards associate, bachelor's, master's, doctoral, and first professional degrees and post-master's certificates. Founded 1791. Setting: 425-acre suburban campus. Undergraduate faculty: 1,024 (872 full-time, 152 part-time); student-faculty ratio is 13:1. Most popular recent majors: business administration, English, political science.

## CAMPUS VISITS
**College Calendar 1998–99:** *Regular classes:* Sept. 1–Dec. 9; Jan. 20–May 5. *Breaks:* Dec. 18–Jan. 19. *Final exams:* Dec. 12–18; May 7–14. *Admission office closed:* Fall Recess, Oct. 9; Spring Recess, Mar. 15–19; Thanksgiving, Nov. 25–27; Town Meeting Day, Mar. 2. *Special campus days:* Open Houses for Prospective Students, Aug. 21, Oct. 17, Nov. 8, Oct. 25, Sept. 26; Parents Weekend, Oct. 2–4.

## VISIT OPPORTUNITIES

|  | Appointments? | Who? |
|---|---|---|
| **Campus Tour** | recommended, not required | open to all |
| **Information Session** | recommended, not required | open to all |
| **Admission Interview** | required | open to all |
| **Classroom Visit** | required | open to all |
| **Faculty Meeting** | required | open to all |

**Information Sessions:** M–F at 10:00 am, 12:00 pm; Sat. at 9:30 am; call ahead for specific information; not available during university holidays and breaks; 45 minutes.

**Interviews:** M–F; not available during holidays and breaks; alumni representatives interview throughout country, call for details; 30 minutes.

**Campus Tours:** Conducted by students. M–F at 10:00 am, 2:00 pm; not available during university holidays, academic vacations/breaks; call for select weekend dates; 90 minutes.

**Class Visits:** Prospective students may attend a class in their area of interest.

## CAMPUS FACILITIES
**Science:** Science Labs; Appointment Required: UVM Farm, Molecular Biology/Genetics Department.

**Arts:** Recital Hall, practice facilities; Appointment Required: Music Department.

**Of Special Interest:** General residence hall; Appointment Required: speciality residence halls.

## LOCAL ATTRACTIONS
Lake Champlain region; Stowe area; Shelburne Museum–nationally-known collection of Americana; Shelburne Farms.

# VIRGINIA

# COLLEGE OF WILLIAM AND MARY
## Williamsburg, Virginia

**Contact:** Tim Wolfe, Admission Counselor, PO Box 8795, Williamsburg, VA 23187. *Phone:* 757-221-4223. *Fax:* 757-221-1242. *E-mail:* admiss@facstaff.wm.

edu *Web site:* http://www.wm.edu/ *Visit location:* Office of Admission, Blow Memorial Hall, Room 201, Richmond Road.

## QUICK FACTS
Enrollment: 7,511; UG: 5,503. Entrance: very difficult. SAT>500: 98% V, 97% M; ACT>18: 100%. Resident tuition and fees: $5032. Nonresident tuition and fees: $15,404. Room and board: $4586. Application deadline: 1/15.

## GENERAL
State-supported, university, coed. Awards bachelor's, master's, doctoral, and first professional degrees. Founded 1693. Setting: 1,200-acre small-town campus with easy access to Richmond. Undergraduate faculty: 587 (467 full-time, 120 part-time); student-faculty ratio is 12:1. Most popular recent majors: business administration, biology, English.

## CAMPUS VISITS
**College Calendar 1998–99:** *Regular classes:* Aug. 27–Dec. 5; Jan. 21–May 1. *Breaks:* Oct. 11–14; Mar. 7–15; Nov. 25–30. *Final exams:* Dec. 8–19; May 4–13. *Admission office closed:* Dec. 24–Jan. 1. *Special campus days:* Charter Day, Feb. 6; Commencement, May 16; Homecoming, Oct. 24; Opening Convocation, Aug. 28.

## VISIT OPPORTUNITIES

|  | Appointments? | Who? |
|---|---|---|
| **Campus Tour** | not required | open to all |
| **Information Session** | not required | open to all |
| **Admission Interview** | required | open to all |
| **Classroom Visit** | required | open to all |
| **Faculty Meeting** | required | open to all |
| **Overnight Visit** | required | admitted applicants only |

**Information Sessions:** M–F, select Sat.; 45 minutes.
**Interviews:** M–F; 30 minutes.
**Campus Tours:** Conducted by students. M–F, select Sat.; 90 minutes.
**Class Visits:** Certain predetermined classrooms are open to visitors.
**Overnight Visits:** During the regular academic year, prospective applicants may spend an evening in a residence hall with a student host.
**Video:** Available, fee charged.

## CAMPUS FACILITIES
**Science:** Astronomical Observatory, Greenhouse—Millington Hall.

**Arts:** Muscarelle Museum, Andrews Hall Exhibitions.

**Athletic:** William and Mary Hall, McCormack Nagelson Tennis Center, Busch Fields Soccer Complex.

**Of Special Interest:** Wren Building.

## LOCAL ATTRACTIONS
Colonial Williamsburg.

# EASTERN MENNONITE UNIVERSITY
**Harrisonburg, Virginia**

**Contact:** Martha Snavely, Campus Visit Coordinator, 1200 Park Road, Harrisonburg, VA 22802. *Phone:* 540-432-4118 or toll-free 800-368-2665 (out-of-state). *Fax:* 540-432-4444. *E-mail:* admiss@emu.edu *Web site:* http://www.emu.edu/ *Visit location:* Admissions Office, Campus Center, 1200 Park Road.

## QUICK FACTS
Enrollment: 1,199; UG: 987. Entrance: moderately difficult. SAT>500: 68% V, 64% M; ACT>18: 88%. Tuition and fees: $12,600. Room and board: $4700. Application deadline: 8/1.

## GENERAL
Independent Mennonite, comprehensive, coed. Awards associate, bachelor's, master's, and first professional degrees and first professional certificates. Founded 1917. Setting: 92-acre small-town campus. Undergraduate faculty: 129 (75 full-time, 54 part-time); student-faculty ratio is 13:1. Most popular recent majors: education, biology, nursing.

## CAMPUS VISITS
**College Calendar 1998–99:** *Regular classes:* Aug. 26–Dec. 4; Jan. 5–Apr. 16. *Breaks:* Oct. 16–20; Feb. 26–Mar. 5. *Final exams:* Dec. 7–11; Apr. 19–23. *Admission office closed:* Easter weekend; spring break weekends. *Special campus days:* Commencement, Apr. 25; Homecoming, Oct. 10.

*Eastern Mennonite University (continued)*

## VISIT OPPORTUNITIES

| | Appointments? | Who? |
|---|---|---|
| **Campus Tour** | required | applicants and parents |
| **Information Session** | required | |
| **Admission Interview** | required | applicants and parents |
| **Classroom Visit** | required | applicants and parents |
| **Faculty Meeting** | required | applicants and parents |
| **Overnight Visit** | required | |

**Interviews:** M–F, select Sat.; 30 minutes.

**Campus Tours:** Conducted by students. M–F, select Sat. 9:00 am–2:00 pm; 45 minutes.

**Class Visits:** Classroom visits are determined by the visit schedule.

**Overnight Visits:** During the regular academic year, prospective applicants may spend an evening in a residence hall with a student host.

**Video:** Free on request.

## CAMPUS FACILITIES
**Of Special Interest:** Sadie Hartzler Library.

# HAMPDEN-SYDNEY COLLEGE
## Hampden-Sydney, Virginia

**Contact:** Mary M. Brooks, Administrative Secretary, PO Box 667, Hampden-Sydney, VA 23943. *Phone:* 804-223-6120 or toll-free 800-755-0733. *Fax:* 804-223-6346. *E-mail:* maryb1@tiger.hsc.edu *Web site:* http://www.hsc.edu/ *Visit location:* Admissions, Graham Hall, College Road.

## QUICK FACTS
Enrollment: 945; UG: 945. Entrance: moderately difficult. SAT>500: 84% V, 82% M; ACT>18: 100%. Tuition and fees: $15,074. Room and board: $5557. Application deadline: 3/1.

## GENERAL
Independent Presbyterian, 4-year, men only. Awards bachelor's degrees. Founded 1776. Setting: 850-acre rural campus with easy access to Richmond. Faculty:

99 (62 full-time, 37 part-time); student-faculty ratio is 13:1. Most popular recent majors: economics, history, political science.

## CAMPUS VISITS
**College Calendar 1998–99:** *Regular classes:* Aug. 26–Dec. 8; Jan. 12–Apr. 27. *Breaks:* Oct. 17–20; Mar. 13–21; Dec. 17–Jan. 11. *Final exams:* Dec. 11–16; Apr. 30–May 5. *Admission office closed:* Dec. 24–Jan. 1. *Special campus days:* Commencement, May 9; Homecoming, Oct. 10; Parents Weekend, Sept. 25–26.

## VISIT OPPORTUNITIES

| | Appointments? | Who? |
|---|---|---|
| **Campus Tour** | recommended, not required | open to all |
| **Admission Interview** | recommended | open to all |
| **Classroom Visit** | required | open to all |
| **Faculty Meeting** | required | open to all |
| **Overnight Visit** | required | open to all |

**Interviews:** M–F; Sat. mornings during academic year; 45 minutes.

**Campus Tours:** Conducted by students and admission reps. M–F 9:00 am–4:00 pm; select Sat. 9:00 am–12:00 pm during academic year; 60 minutes.

**Class Visits:** Classroom visits are determined by the visit schedule.

**Overnight Visits:** During the regular academic year, prospective applicants may spend an evening in a residence hall with a student host.

## CAMPUS FACILITIES
**Science:** Gilmer Science Building, Compton Gamma Ray Observatory.

**Athletic:** Kirby Field House, Fleet Gymnasium, Leggett Pool.

**Of Special Interest:** Atkinson Museum.

## LOCAL ATTRACTIONS
Historic Virginia including Appomattox, Richmond, and Charlottesville.

# JAMES MADISON UNIVERSITY
## Harrisonburg, Virginia

**Contact:** Campus Visitation Center, Sonner Hall, MSC 0101, Harrisonburg, VA 22807. *Phone:* 540-568-3620. *E-mail:* visit-jum@jmu.edu *Web site:* http://www.

jmu.edu/ *Visit location:* Undergraduate Admission Office, Sonner Hall, James Madison University, Bluestone Drive.

## QUICK FACTS
Enrollment: 13,723; UG: 12,551. Entrance: very difficult. SAT>500: 89% V, 89% M; ACT>18: N/R. Resident tuition and fees: $4148. Nonresident tuition and fees: $8816. Room and board: $4846. Application deadline: 1/15.

## GENERAL
State-supported, comprehensive, coed. Awards bachelor's, master's, and doctoral degrees. Founded 1908. Setting: 472-acre small-town campus. Undergraduate faculty: 880 (581 full-time, 299 part-time); student-faculty ratio is 18:1. Most popular recent majors: psychology, communications, English.

## CAMPUS VISITS
**College Calendar 1998–99:** *Regular classes:* Sept. 1–Dec. 11; Jan. 12–Apr. 30. *Breaks:* Nov. 25–29; Mar. 8–12; Dec. 18–Jan. 10. *Final exams:* Dec. 14–18; May 3–7. *Special campus days:* Fall/Winter Commencement, Dec. 18; Founder's Day, Mar. 17; Homecoming, Oct. 17; Parents Weekend, Oct. 23–25; Spring Commencement, May 8; Spring Preview Days, Mar. 29, Apr. 17.

### VISIT OPPORTUNITIES

|  | Appointments? | Who? |
| --- | --- | --- |
| **Campus Tour** | recommended, not required | open to all |
| **Information Session** | recommended, not required | open to all |
| **Classroom Visit** | recommended | open to all |
| **Faculty Meeting** | recommended | open to all |

**Information Sessions:** M–F at 9:15 am, 2:15 pm; Sat. at 9:00 am, 11:00 am; call to confirm schedule; Sat. unavailable May–Aug.; 45 minutes.

**Campus Tours:** Conducted by students. M–F at 10:00 am, 3:00 pm; Sat. at 10:00 am; call to confirm schedule; Sat. unavailable May–Aug.; 75 minutes.

**Class Visits:** Prospective students may attend a class in their area of interest, student must call department to arrange visit.

## CAMPUS FACILITIES
**Science:** Integrated Science and Technology Building.

**Arts:** Duke Hall, Music Building.
**Athletic:** University Recreation Center.
**Of Special Interest:** Arboretum, Campus Dining Facilities, Bookstore and Student Center, Carrier Library.

## LOCAL ATTRACTIONS
Skyline Drive, Massanutten Ski/four seasons Resort, New Market Battlefield, Shenandoah National Park.

# LONGWOOD COLLEGE
## Farmville, Virginia

**Contact:** Admissions Office, Longwood College, 201 High Street, Farmville, VA 23909. *Phone:* toll-free 800-281-4677. *Fax:* 804-395-2332. *E-mail:* kadmit@ longwood.lwc.edu *Web site:* http://www.lwc.edu/ *Visit location:* Admissions Office, Crafts House, 201 High Street.

## QUICK FACTS
Enrollment: 3,294; UG: 2,906. Entrance: moderately difficult. SAT>500: 68% V, 56% M; ACT>18: N/R. Resident tuition and fees: $4416. Nonresident tuition and fees: $9888. Room and board: $4280. Application deadline: 3/1.

## GENERAL
State-supported, comprehensive, coed. Part of Commonwealth of Virginia Council of Higher Education. Awards bachelor's and master's degrees. Founded 1839. Setting: 154-acre small-town campus with easy access to Richmond. Undergraduate faculty: 212 (157 full-time, 55 part-time); student-faculty ratio is 14:1. Most popular recent majors: business administration, education, psychology.

## CAMPUS VISITS
**College Calendar 1998–99:** *Regular classes:* Aug. 25–Dec. 7; Jan. 12–Apr. 26. *Breaks:* Oct. 9–14; Mar. 5–15; Nov. 25–30. *Final exams:* Dec. 9–15; Apr. 28–May 4. *Admission office closed:* Dec. 22–Jan. 4. *Special campus days:* Graduation, May 8; Oktoberfest, Oct. 3; Spring Weekend, Apr. 16–17.

### VISIT OPPORTUNITIES

|  | Appointments? | Who? |
| --- | --- | --- |
| **Campus Tour** | recommended | open to all |
| **Information Session** | recommended | open to all |

*Longwood College (continued)*

## VISIT OPPORTUNITIES— *continued*

| | Appointments? | Who? |
|---|---|---|
| **Admission Interview** | required | applicants only |
| **Classroom Visit** | required | open to all |
| **Faculty Meeting** | required | open to all |
| **Overnight Visit** | required | applicants only |

**Information Sessions:** M–F at 11:00 am, 2:00 pm; Sat. at 11:00 am; call for additional available schedule; 30 minutes.

**Interviews:** M–F; 20 minutes.

**Campus Tours:** Conducted by students. M–F, select Sat. at 11:30 am, 2:30 pm; 60 minutes.

**Class Visits:** Prospective students may attend a class in their area of interest.

**Overnight Visits:** During the regular academic year, prospective applicants may spend an evening in a residence hall with a student host.

## CAMPUS FACILITIES

**Science:** Jeffers, Stephens, McCorkle.

**Arts:** Bedford Art Building, Longwood College Visual Arts Center.

**Athletic:** Lancer Gym, Iler.

**Of Special Interest:** The Library, The Rotunda.

## LOCAL ATTRACTIONS

Appomattox Courthouse, State recreational area, Green Front Furniture.

# LYNCHBURG COLLEGE

**Lynchburg, Virginia**

**Contact:** Emma Hensley, Visit Coordinator, 1501 Lakeside Drive, Lynchburg, VA 24501. *Phone:* toll-free 800-426-8101. *Fax:* 804-544-8653. *E-mail:* hensley@admvax lynchburg.edu *Web site:* http://www. lynchburg.edu/ *Visit location:* Office of Enrollment, Alumni House, 1501 Lakeside Drive.

## QUICK FACTS

Enrollment: 1,902; UG: 1,553. Entrance: moderately difficult. SAT>500: 54% V, 48% M; ACT>18: N/R. Tuition and fees: $16,415. Room and board: $4400. Application deadline: rolling.

## GENERAL

Independent, comprehensive, coed, Christian Church (Disciples of Christ). Awards bachelor's and master's degrees. Founded 1903. Setting: 214-acre suburban campus. Undergraduate faculty: 165 (104 full-time, 61 part-time); student-faculty ratio is 13:1. Most popular recent majors: education, business administration, mass communications.

## CAMPUS VISITS

**College Calendar 1998–99:** *Regular classes:* Aug. 31–Dec. 11; Jan. 18–May 5. *Breaks:* Oct. 17–20; Mar. 6–14; Dec. 20–Jan. 16. *Final exams:* Dec. 14–19; May 5–11. *Special campus days:* Commencement, May 15; Liberal Arts in Action–Friday afternoons in July and August; Virginia Private College Week.

## VISIT OPPORTUNITIES

| | Appointments? | Who? |
|---|---|---|
| **Campus Tour** | recommended, not required | open to all |
| **Admission Interview** | recommended, not required | open to all |
| **Classroom Visit** | recommended | open to all |
| **Faculty Meeting** | recommended | open to all |
| **Overnight Visit** | required | open to all |

**Interviews:** M–F; Sat. available Sept.–May; 30 minutes.

**Campus Tours:** Conducted by students. M–F at 9:30 am, 11:00 am, 1:00 pm, 3:00 pm; Sat. at 10:00 am, 11:00 am; 60 minutes.

**Class Visits:** Prospective students may attend a class in their area of interest, classroom visits are determined by the visit schedule.

**Overnight Visits:** During the regular academic year, prospective applicants may spend an evening in a residence hall with a student host.

**Video:** Free on request.

## CAMPUS FACILITIES

**Science:** Hobbs Science Center, Organic and Introductory Chemistry labs, Laser physics lab; numerous computer labs.

**Arts:** Dillard Theatre.

**Athletic:** Outdoor track, Field House, Turner Gymnasium.

**Of Special Interest:** Daura Art Gallery–Pierre Daura.

# MARY BALDWIN COLLEGE
**Staunton, Virginia**

**Contact:** Carolyn Hensley, Campus Visit Coordinator, Mary Baldwin College, Office of Admissions, Staunton, VA 24401. *Phone:* toll-free 800-468-2262. *Fax:* 540-886-6634. *E-mail:* chensley@mbc.edu *Web site:* http://www.mbc.edu/ *Visit location:* Admissions Office, Administration Building, Frederick and New Streets.

## QUICK FACTS
Enrollment: 1,421; UG: 1,341. Entrance: moderately difficult. SAT>500: 63% V, 50% M; ACT>18: N/R. Tuition and fees: $14,415. Room and board: $7000. Application deadline: 4/15.

## GENERAL
Independent, comprehensive, primarily women, Presbyterian Church (U.S.A.). Awards bachelor's and master's degrees. Founded 1842. Setting: 54-acre small-town campus. Undergraduate faculty: 126 (71 full-time, 55 part-time); student-faculty ratio is 12:1. Most popular recent majors: psychology, sociology, art.

## CAMPUS VISITS
**College Calendar 1998–99:** *Regular classes:* Aug. 31–Dec. 4; Jan. 6–Apr. 13; Apr. 26–May 14. *Breaks:* Oct. 16–20; Mar. 5–14; Dec. 12–Jan. 5; Apr. 21–25. *Final exams:* Dec. 7–11; Apr. 14–20; May 15. *Admission office closed:* Thanksgiving holiday, Nov. 26–27. *Special campus days:* Commencement, May 23; Homecoming, May 21.

### VISIT OPPORTUNITIES

| | Appointments? | Who? |
|---|---|---|
| **Campus Tour** | recommended, not required | open to all |
| **Information Session** | recommended, not required | open to all |
| **Admission Interview** | recommended, not required | open to all |
| **Classroom Visit** | recommended, not required | open to all |
| **Overnight Visit** | recommended | open to all |

**Interviews:** M–F; Sat. 9:00 am–12:00 pm; 30 minutes.
**Campus Tours:** Conducted by students. M–F; Sat. at 10:00 am; 60 minutes.

**Class Visits:** Prospective students may attend a class in their area of interest.
**Overnight Visits:** During the regular academic year, prospective applicants may spend an evening in a residence hall with a student host.

## CAMPUS FACILITIES
**Of Special Interest:** Dormitories, Library, Dining Hall.

## LOCAL ATTRACTIONS
Woodrow Wilson Birthplace; Statler Brothers Museum; Staunton Historic Districts; Museum of American Frontier Culture; P. Buckley Moss Museum; Grand Caverns Regional Park, Restored C & O Train Station, Valley Bank Museum, Gypsy Hill Park.

# MARY WASHINGTON COLLEGE
**Fredericksburg, Virginia**

**Contact:** Office of Admissions, 1301 College Avenue, Fredericksburg, VA 22401. *Phone:* 540-654-2000 or toll-free 800-468-5614. *Fax:* 540-654-1857. *Web site:* http://www.mwc.edu/ *Visit location:* Admissions, 201 Lee Hall, 1301 College Avenue.

## QUICK FACTS
Enrollment: 3,641; UG: 3,602. Entrance: very difficult. SAT>500: 95% V, 89% M; ACT>18: N/R. Resident tuition and fees: $3556. Nonresident tuition and fees: $8516. Room and board: $5080. Application deadline: 2/1.

## GENERAL
State-supported, comprehensive, coed. Awards bachelor's and master's degrees. Founded 1908. Setting: 176-acre small-town campus with easy access to Richmond and Washington, DC. Undergraduate faculty: 240 (171 full-time, 69 part-time); student-faculty ratio is 18:1. Most popular recent majors: business administration, psychology, English.

## CAMPUS VISITS
**College Calendar 1998–99:** *Regular classes:* Aug. 24–Dec. 4; Jan. 13–Apr. 27. *Breaks:* Oct. 9–14; Mar. 5–15; Nov. 25–30. *Final exams:* Dec. 7–12; May 3–6. *Admission office closed:* Dec. 25–Jan. 3. *Special campus days:* Alumni Weekend, Oct. 24; Family Weekend, Sept. 25; Graduation, May 15.

*Mary Washington College (continued)*

## VISIT OPPORTUNITIES

| | Appointments? |
|---|---|
| **Campus Tour** | recommended |
| **Information Session** | recommended |
| **Admission Interview** | required |
| **Classroom Visit** | required |
| **Faculty Meeting** | required |
| **Overnight Visit** | required |

**Information Sessions:** M–F at 10:30 am, 2:00 pm; Sat. at 9:30 am, 10:30 am; 30 minutes.

**Interviews:** M–F; 20 minutes.

**Campus Tours:** Conducted by students. M–F at 11:00 am, 2:30 pm; Sat. at 10:00 am, 11:00 am; 60 minutes.

**Class Visits:** Prospective students may attend a class in their area of interest.

**Overnight Visits:** During the regular academic year, prospective applicants may spend an evening in a residence hall with a student host.

## CAMPUS FACILITIES
**Arts:** Mary Washington College Galleries, Belmont, The Gari Melchers Estate.

# NORFOLK STATE UNIVERSITY
## Norfolk, Virginia

**Contact:** Ms. Michelle Marable, Admissions Officer, Admissions Office, Norfolk State University, Norfolk, VA 23504. *Phone:* 757-683-8396. *Fax:* 757-683-2078. *Web site:* http://www.nsu.edu/ *Visit location:* Admissions Office, HBWB Administration Building, 2401 Corprew Avenue.

## QUICK FACTS
Enrollment: 7,291; UG: 6,366. Entrance: moderately difficult. SAT>500: N/R; ACT>18: N/R. Resident tuition and fees: $3000. Nonresident tuition and fees: $6802. Room and board: $4166. Application deadline: rolling.

## GENERAL
State-supported, comprehensive, coed. Part of Commonwealth of Virginia Council of Higher Education. Awards associate, bachelor's, master's, and doctoral degrees. Founded 1935. Setting: 130-acre urban campus. Undergraduate faculty: 545 (359 full-time, 186 part-time); student-faculty ratio is 22:1.

## CAMPUS VISITS
**College Calendar 1998–99:** *Regular classes:* Aug. 31–Dec. 11; Jan. 10–May 1. *Breaks:* Dec. 20–Jan. 10. *Final exams:* Dec. 12–19; May 2–9.

**Class Visits:** Classroom visits are determined by the visit schedule.

## CAMPUS FACILITIES
**Science:** Center for Materials Research Lab, Crystal Growth Lab, National Science Institute Facilities (DNIMAS).

**Arts:** Wise Art Gallery, Fine Arts Building.

**Athletic:** Echols Fieldhouse, Dick Price Football Field, Track and Baseball/Softball Facilities.

**Of Special Interest:** Archives and Library, Army and Navy ROTC Units, L. Douglas Wilder Performing Arts Center.

## LOCAL ATTRACTIONS
Waterside Marketplace on Elizabeth River; Nauticus; Virginia Beach Science Museum; Virginia Beach; MacArthur Memorial (Norfolk) Navy Bases and Naval Air Stations.

# RANDOLPH-MACON COLLEGE
## Ashland, Virginia

**Contact:** Dr. Jeffrey Papa, Director of Admissions, PO Box 5005, Ashland, VA 23005. *Phone:* toll-free 800-888-1762. *Fax:* 804-752-4707. *E-mail:* admissions_office@rmc.edu *Web site:* http://www.rmc.edu/ *Visit location:* Admissions, Neville House, 204 East Patrick Street.

## QUICK FACTS
Enrollment: 1,066; UG: 1,066. Entrance: moderately difficult. SAT>500: 74% V, 70% M; ACT>18: N/R. Tuition and fees: $16,240. Room and board: $4175. Application deadline: 3/1.

## GENERAL
Independent United Methodist, 4-year, coed. Awards bachelor's degrees. Founded 1830. Setting: 110-acre suburban campus with easy access to Richmond. Faculty: 155 (92 full-time, 63 part-time); student-faculty ratio is 11:1. Most popular recent majors: business economics, psychology, English.

## CAMPUS VISITS

**College Calendar 1998–99:** *Regular classes:* Sept. 8–Dec. 11; Feb. 9–May 14. *Final exams:* Dec. 14–18; May 17–21.

## VISIT OPPORTUNITIES

|  | Appointments? | Who? |
| --- | --- | --- |
| **Campus Tour** | recommended | open to all |
| **Information Session** | recommended | open to all |
| **Admission Interview** | recommended | open to all |
| **Classroom Visit** | required | open to all |
| **Faculty Meeting** | required | open to all |
| **Overnight Visit** | required | open to all |

**Information Sessions:** Select Sat.; 60 minutes.

**Interviews:** M–F, select Sat.; 30 minutes.

**Campus Tours:** Conducted by students. M–F at 10:00 am, 12:00 pm, 2:00 pm; select Sat.; inquire for Open House and Weekend Program schedule; 60 minutes.

**Class Visits:** Prospective students may attend a class in their area of interest, certain predetermined classrooms are open to visitors.

**Overnight Visits:** During the regular academic year, prospective applicants may spend an evening in a residence hall with a student host.

**Video:** Available, fee charged.

## CAMPUS FACILITIES

**Science:** Copley Science Center.

**Arts:** Pace Armistead Hall.

**Athletic:** Brock Sports and Recreation Center.

**Of Special Interest:** Washington and Franklin Hall, Butler Language Lab, McGraw Page Library.

# SHENANDOAH UNIVERSITY
## Winchester, Virginia

**Contact:** Mr. Michael Carpenter, Director of Admissions, 1460 University Drive, Winchester, VA 22601. *Phone:* toll-free 800-432-2266. *Fax:* 540-665-4627. *E-mail:* admit@su.edu *Web site:* http://www.su.edu/ *Visit location:* Admissions Department, Wilkins Hall, 1460 University Drive.

## QUICK FACTS

Enrollment: 1,890; UG: 1,193. Entrance: moderately difficult. SAT>500: 60% V, 51% M; ACT>18: 94%.

Tuition and fees: $14,400. Room and board: $5050. Application deadline: rolling.

## GENERAL

Independent United Methodist, comprehensive, coed. Awards associate, bachelor's, master's, doctoral, and first professional degrees. Founded 1875. Setting: 72-acre small-town campus with easy access to Baltimore and Washington, DC. Undergraduate faculty: 249 (131 full-time, 118 part-time); student-faculty ratio is 6:1. Most popular recent majors: nursing, music, psychology.

## CAMPUS VISITS

**College Calendar 1998–99:** *Regular classes:* Aug. 24–Dec. 6; Jan. 5–Apr. 26. *Breaks:* Dec. 13–Jan. 4. *Final exams:* Dec. 7–11; Apr. 27–May 7. *Admission office closed:* Apr. 2, Apr. 30.

## VISIT OPPORTUNITIES

|  | Appointments? | Who? |
| --- | --- | --- |
| **Campus Tour** | recommended | open to all |
| **Information Session** | required |  |
| **Admission Interview** | required | applicants and parents |
| **Classroom Visit** | required | open to all |
| **Faculty Meeting** | required | open to all |

**Information Sessions:** M–F 9:00 am–5:00 pm; mini-open-house on Mon. and Fri. at 1:00 pm consisting of a tour of campus and an information session with an Admissions counselor; 45 minutes.

**Interviews:** M–F; 45 minutes.

**Campus Tours:** Conducted by students. M–F at 1:00 pm; reservations may be made for specific tour times Mon.–Fri.; 60 minutes.

**Class Visits:** Prospective students may attend a class in their area of interest.

## CAMPUS FACILITIES

**Science:** Howe Hall, Gregory Hall, Health Professions Building, Physical Therapy, Occupational Therapy.

**Arts:** Ruebush Hall, Ohrstrom-Bryant Theatre, Glaize Studio Theatre, Dorothy Ewing Studio of Dance.

**Athletic:** Shingleton Hall/Gym, Aikens Field (Lacrosse), Moulden Field (Soccer).

*Shenandoah University (continued)*

## LOCAL ATTRACTIONS
Alson H. Smith Jr. Library; Goodson Chapel; Armstrong Concert Hall.

# UNIVERSITY OF RICHMOND
## Richmond, Virginia

**Contact:** Office of Admissions, 28 Westhampton Way, University of Richmond, VA 23173. *Phone:* toll-free 800-700-1662. *E-mail:* admissions@richmond. edu *Web site:* http://www.richmond.edu/ *Visit location:* Office of Admission, Sarah Brunet Hall, 28 Westhampton Way.

## QUICK FACTS
Enrollment: 4,394; UG: 3,606. Entrance: very difficult. SAT>500: 97% V, 96% M; ACT>18: 100%. Tuition and fees: $18,595. Room and board: $4143. Application deadline: 2/1.

## GENERAL
Independent, comprehensive, coed. Awards associate, bachelor's, master's, and first professional degrees. Founded 1830. Setting: 350-acre suburban campus. Undergraduate faculty: 515 (251 full-time, 264 part-time); student-faculty ratio is 11:1. Most popular recent majors: business administration, biology, political science.

## CAMPUS VISITS
**College Calendar 1998–99:** *Regular classes:* Aug. 28–Dec. 8; Jan. 11–Apr. 23. *Breaks:* Oct. 9–14; Mar. 6–12; Nov. 25–29. *Final exams:* Dec. 10–16; Apr. 26–May 1.

### VISIT OPPORTUNITIES

|  | Appointments? | Who? |
|---|---|---|
| **Campus Tour** | recommended | open to all |
| **Information Session** | recommended | open to all |
| **Classroom Visit** | required | open to all |
| **Overnight Visit** | required |  |

**Information Sessions:** Mon., Wed., Fri. at 9:30 am, 1:15 pm; Tue., Thu. at 10:30 am, 1:45 pm; Mon. and Fri. schedules only Jan. through Mar.; during summer M–F May to Mid-Aug. at 9:30 am and 1:45 pm; 45 minutes.

**Campus Tours:** Conducted by students. Mon., Wed., Fri. at 10:15 am, 2:30 pm; Tue., Thu. at 11:15 am, 2:30 pm; Sat. tours available during fall; tours unavailable during fall, spring, and Christmas breaks.

**Class Visits:** Prospective students may attend a class in their area of interest.

**Overnight Visits:** During the regular academic year, prospective applicants may spend an evening in a residence hall with a student host.

**Video:** Free on request.

## CAMPUS FACILITIES
**Science:** Gottwald Science Center.

**Arts:** Madlin Center for the Arts.

**Athletic:** Robins Center.

**Of Special Interest:** Jepson Hall—Student Computer Labs.

## LOCAL ATTRACTIONS
Monument Avenue—Civil War monuments and estates; Carytown shops, art galleries, sidewalk cafes; Shockoe Slip shops and restaurants.

# UNIVERSITY OF VIRGINIA
## Charlottesville, Virginia

**Contact:** Mr. John A. Blackburn, Dean of Admission, PO Box 9017, Charlottesville, VA 22906. *Phone:* 804-982-3200. *Fax:* 804-924-3587. *E-mail:* undergrad-admission@virginia.edu *Web site:* http://www.virginia.edu/ *Visit location:* Office of Admission, Miller Hall, McCormick Road.

## QUICK FACTS
Enrollment: 20,977; UG: 12,281. Entrance: most difficult. SAT>500: 95% V, 97% M; ACT>18: N/App. Resident tuition and fees: $4786. Nonresident tuition and fees: $15,030. Room and board: $4279. Application deadline: 1/2.

## GENERAL
State-supported, university, coed. Awards bachelor's, master's, doctoral, and first professional degrees and post-master's certificates. Founded 1819. Setting: 1,131-acre suburban campus with easy access to Richmond. Undergraduate faculty: 1,866 (1,635 full-time, 231 part-time); student-faculty ratio is 13:1. Most popular recent majors: business, English, biology.

## CAMPUS VISITS

**College Calendar 1998–99:** *Regular classes:* Sept. 2–Dec. 11; Jan. 20–May 4. *Breaks:* Oct. 10–13; Mar. 13–21; Nov. 25–29. *Final exams:* Dec. 14–21; May 7–14.

## VISIT OPPORTUNITIES

|  | Appointments? | Who? |
|---|---|---|
| **Campus Tour** | not required | open to all |
| **Information Session** | not required | open to all |
| **Classroom Visit** | not required | open to all |
| **Faculty Meeting** | recommended, not required | open to all |
| **Overnight Visit** | required | open to all |

**Information Sessions:** M–F at 10:00 am, 1:00 pm; Sat. at 10:00 am; Mon. through Fri. only at 10:00 am Dec.15–Jun.14; please call two weeks in advance to verify schedule and location; 60 minutes.

**Campus Tours:** Conducted by students. M–F at 11:00 am, 2:00 pm; Sat. at 11:00 am; unavailable during University holidays; call two weeks in advance to verify schedule; 85 minutes.

**Class Visits:** Prospective students may attend a class in their area of interest.

**Overnight Visits:** During the regular academic year, prospective applicants may spend an evening in a residence hall with a student host.

## CAMPUS FACILITIES

**Science:** Chemistry Labs, Gilmer Hall, Thornton Hall—Engineering, Physics Building.

**Arts:** Art Studios, Bayly Art Museum, Culbreth Hall—Drama, Old Cabell Hall—Music.

**Athletic:** Aquatic and Fitness Center, Practice Fields, University Hall.

**Of Special Interest:** Rotunda and Lawn Area, Architecture Studios—Campbell Hall, Newcomb Hall—Student Center.

## LOCAL ATTRACTIONS

Monticello—home of Thomas Jefferson; Ashlawn Highland—home of James Monroe; Montpelier—home of James Madison.

# VIRGINIA MILITARY INSTITUTE

**Lexington, Virginia**

**Contact:** Cmdr. Brian L. Quisenberry, Associate Director of Admissions, Admissions Office, Lexington, VA 24450. *Phone:* toll-free 800-767-4207. *Fax:* 540-464-7746. *E-mail:* blqe@vmi.edu *Web site:* http://www.vmi.edu/ *Visit location:* Admissions Office, Pendleton Coles House, 309 Letcher Avenue.

## QUICK FACTS

Enrollment: 1,282; UG: 1,282. Entrance: moderately difficult. SAT>500: 79% V, 79% M; ACT>18: N/R. Resident tuition and fees: $6380. Nonresident tuition and fees: $13,405. Room and board: $3695. Application deadline: 4/1.

## GENERAL

State-supported, 4-year, coed. Awards bachelor's degrees. Founded 1839. Setting: 140-acre small-town campus. Faculty: 134 (105 full-time, 29 part-time); student-faculty ratio is 12:1. Most popular recent majors: economics, history, mechanical engineering.

## CAMPUS VISITS

**College Calendar 1998–99:** *Regular classes:* Aug. 25–Dec. 9; Jan. 19–Apr. 29. *Breaks:* Dec. 19–Jan. 17. *Final exams:* Dec. 11–19; May 1–10. *Special campus days:* Commencement, May 15; Fall break, Oct. 16–19; Founders Day, Nov. 11; Homecoming, Sept. 26; Spring Break, Mar. 5–12; Thanksgiving Break, Nov. 21–29.

## VISIT OPPORTUNITIES

|  | Appointments? | Who? |
|---|---|---|
| **Campus Tour** | recommended, not required | open to all |
| **Information Session** | required | open to all |
| **Admission Interview** | required | open to all |
| **Classroom Visit** | required | open to all |
| **Faculty Meeting** | required | open to all |
| **Overnight Visit** | required | open to all |

**Information Sessions:** M–F 8:00 am–12:00 pm, 1:00–4:30 pm; Sat. 8:00 am–12:00 pm; 30 minutes.

**Interviews:** M–F; Sat. 8:00 am–12:00 pm; 30 minutes.

**Campus Tours:** Conducted by students. M–F at 11:00 am, 3:00 pm; Sat. at 10:00 am, 11:00 am; by specific appointment through Admissions office; 45 minutes.

**Class Visits:** Prospective students may attend a class in their area of interest.

**Overnight Visits:** During the regular academic year, prospective applicants may spend an evening in a residence hall with a student host.

*Virginia Military Institute (continued)*

**Video:** Free on request.

## CAMPUS FACILITIES

**Science:** Science Building (Chemistry-Biology).

**Athletic:** Carmeron Hall (basketball), Patchin Field complex (baseball, soccer, lacrosse, tennis), Swimming facility.

**Of Special Interest:** Virginia Military Institute Museum, George C. Marshall Museum.

## LOCAL ATTRACTIONS

Stonewall Jackson House; Robert E. Lee Chapel; Lexington Visitor Center.

# VIRGINIA POLYTECHNIC INSTITUTE AND STATE UNIVERSITY

**Blacksburg, Virginia**

**Contact:** Office of Undergraduate Admissions, 201 Burruss Hall, Blacksburg, VA 24061. *Phone:* 540-231-6267. *Fax:* 540-231-3242. *E-mail:* vtadmiss@vt.edu *Web site:* http://www.vt.edu/ *Visit location:* Undergraduate Admissions, Burruss Hall.

## QUICK FACTS

Enrollment: 27,191; UG: 20,996. Entrance: moderately difficult. SAT>500: 87% V, 90% M; ACT>18: N/R. Resident tuition and fees: $4147. Nonresident tuition and fees: $11,111. Room and board: $3420. Application deadline: 2/1.

## GENERAL

State-supported, university, coed. Awards associate, bachelor's, master's, doctoral, and first professional degrees. Founded 1872. Setting: 2,600-acre small-town campus. Undergraduate faculty: 1,574 (1,410 full-time, 164 part-time); student-faculty ratio is 17:1. Most popular recent majors: psychology, mechanical engineering, business marketing and marketing management.

## CAMPUS VISITS

**College Calendar 1998–99:** *Regular classes:* Aug. 24–Dec. 9; Jan. 8–May 5. *Breaks:* Nov. 21–29; Mar. 6–14. *Final exams:* Dec. 11–17; May 7–12. *Admission office closed:* Nov. 26–27, Dec. 24–25, Dec. 31, May 31. *Special campus days:* Admissions Open House, Sept. 19–20, Oct. 24–25, Nov. 14–15; Black History Month; Fall Commencement, Dec. 19; Founder's Day; Homecoming, Oct. 17; Military Ball; Parents Day, Oct. 24; Ring Dance; Spring Commencement, May 15; Women's History Month.

## VISIT OPPORTUNITIES

|  | Appointments? | Who? |
|---|---|---|
| **Campus Tour** | not required | open to all |
| **Information Session** | not required | open to all |
| **Classroom Visit** | recommended | open to all |
| **Faculty Meeting** | required | open to all |

**Information Sessions:** M–F at 9:00 am, 2:15 pm; select Sat. at 10:00 am, 12:00 pm; available when classes are in session; 60 minutes.

**Campus Tours:** Conducted by students. M–F, select Sat. at 10:00 am, 11:00 am, 1:00 pm; available when classes are in session; 60 minutes.

**Class Visits:** Prospective students may attend a class in their area of interest.

**Video:** Available, fee charged.

## CAMPUS FACILITIES

**Science:** Appointment Required: Fralin Biotechnology Center, Engineering Labs, The CAVE (Virtual Reality).

**Arts:** Squires Student Center—Art Galleries, Cultural Centers, Burruss Auditorium; Appointment Required: Multimedia Music Lab.

**Athletic:** Cassell Coliseum, Lane Stadium, Rector Fieldhouse.

**Of Special Interest:** Library, Gymnasium/Health and Fitness Center, Dining Facilities, Squires Student Center, Bookstore.

## LOCAL ATTRACTIONS

Mt. Lake Resort; Campus 18-hole Golf Course; New River; Appalachian Trail.

# WASHINGTON AND LEE UNIVERSITY

**Lexington, Virginia**

**Contact:** Admissions office, Washington and Lee University, Lexington, VA 24450-0303. *Phone:* 540-463-8710. *Fax:* 540-463-8062. *E-mail:* admissions@wlu.edu *Web site:* http://www.wlu.edu/ *Visit location:* Office of Admissions and Financial Aid, Gilliam House, Letcher Avenue.

## QUICK FACTS

Enrollment: 2,048; UG: 1,681. Entrance: most difficult. SAT>500: 99% V, 99% M; ACT>18: 100%. Tuition and fees: $16,195. Room and board: $5620. Application deadline: 1/15.

## GENERAL

Independent, comprehensive, coed. Awards bachelor's and first professional degrees. Founded 1749. Setting: 322-acre small-town campus. Undergraduate faculty: 194 (191 full-time, 3 part-time); student-faculty ratio is 10:1. Most popular recent majors: history, journalism, biology.

## CAMPUS VISITS

**College Calendar 1998–99:** *Regular classes:* Sept. 10–Dec. 11; Jan. 4–Apr. 2; Apr. 19–May 28. *Breaks:* Nov. 23–27; Feb. 15–19; Dec. 19–Jan. 3; Apr. 10–18. *Final exams:* Dec. 12–18; Apr. 3–9; May 29–31. *Special campus days:* Alumni Reunion, Apr. 30–May 2; Baccalaureate, June 2; Commencement, June 3; Founders Day, Jan. 19; Homecoming, Oct. 2–4; Parents Weekend, Oct. 23–25; Reading Days, Oct. 15–16.

## VISIT OPPORTUNITIES

|  | Appointments? | Who? |
|---|---|---|
| **Campus Tour** | required | applicants and parents |
| **Information Session** | required | |
| **Admission Interview** | required | applicants and parents |
| **Classroom Visit** | required | applicants and parents |
| **Faculty Meeting** | required | applicants and parents |

**Information Sessions:** Call for availability; 40 minutes.
**Interviews:** M–F, select Sat.; call for availability; 30 minutes.
**Campus Tours:** Conducted by students. M–F, select Sat.; call for availability; 60 minutes.
**Class Visits:** Classroom visits are determined by the visit schedule.
**Video:** Free on request.

## CAMPUS FACILITIES

**Arts:** Appointment Required: Reeves Center and Watson Pavilion.
**Of Special Interest:** Lee Chapel Museum.

## LOCAL ATTRACTIONS

George C. Marshall Museum; Natural Bridge; Stonewall Jackson House.

# WASHINGTON

## GONZAGA UNIVERSITY

**Spokane, Washington**

**Contact:** Steve W. Denny, Visit Director, 502 East Boone Avenue, Spokane, WA 99258. *Phone:* toll-free 800-322-2584. *Fax:* 509-324-5780. *Web site:* http://www.gonzaga.edu/ *Visit location:* Gonzaga Visit Office, Administration, 502 East Boone Avenue.

## QUICK FACTS

Enrollment: 3,947; UG: 2,561. Entrance: moderately difficult. SAT>500: 85% V, 83% M; ACT>18: 100%. Tuition and fees: $16,097. Room and board: $5170. Application deadline: 4/1.

## GENERAL

Independent Roman Catholic, comprehensive, coed. Awards bachelor's, master's, doctoral, and first professional degrees. Founded 1887. Setting: 94-acre urban campus. Undergraduate faculty: 283 (267 full-time, 16 part-time); student-faculty ratio is 20:1. Most popular recent majors: business administration, engineering, psychology.

## CAMPUS VISITS

**College Calendar 1998–99:** *Regular classes:* Aug. 26–Dec. 11; Jan. 12–Apr. 30. *Breaks:* Dec. 17–Jan. 11. *Final exams:* Dec. 14–17; May 3–7.

## VISIT OPPORTUNITIES

|  | Appointments? |
|---|---|
| **Campus Tour** | not required |
| **Information Session** | required |
| **Admission Interview** | required |
| **Classroom Visit** | required |
| **Faculty Meeting** | required |
| **Overnight Visit** | required |

**Information Sessions:** M–F, select Sat.; 45 minutes.
**Interviews:** M–F, select Sat.
**Campus Tours:** Conducted by students. M–F, Sat.; 75 minutes.

*Gonzaga University (continued)*

**Class Visits:** Prospective students may attend a class in their area of interest.

**Overnight Visits:** During the regular academic year, prospective applicants may spend an evening in a residence hall with a student host.

**Video:** Free on request.

## CAMPUS FACILITIES

**Science:** Hughes Center.

**Arts:** Jundt Art Museum.

**Athletic:** Martin Center.

**Of Special Interest:** Foley Library, Crosby Museum.

## LOCAL ATTRACTIONS

Riverfront Park.

# PACIFIC LUTHERAN UNIVERSITY

**Tacoma, Washington**

**Contact:** Admissions Office, Pacific Lutheran University, Tacoma, WA 98447. *Phone:* toll-free 800-274-6758. *Fax:* 253-536-5136. *E-mail:* admissions@plu.edu *Web site:* http://www.plu.edu/ *Visit location:* Admissions, Hauge Administration, 121st and Yakima.

## QUICK FACTS

Enrollment: 3,555; UG: 3,277. Entrance: moderately difficult. SAT>500: 71% V, 74% M; ACT>18: 94%. Tuition and fees: $15,680. Room and board: $4890. Application deadline: rolling.

## GENERAL

Independent, comprehensive, coed, Evangelical Lutheran Church in America. Awards bachelor's and master's degrees. Founded 1890. Setting: 126-acre suburban campus with easy access to Seattle. Undergraduate faculty: 315 (228 full-time, 87 part-time); student-faculty ratio is 13:1. Most popular recent majors: business administration, education, nursing.

## CAMPUS VISITS

**College Calendar 1998–99:** *Regular classes:* Sept. 8–Dec. 11; Feb. 3–May 14. *Breaks:* Nov. 25–30; Mar. 27–Apr. 5. *Final exams:* Dec. 14–18; May 17–21. *Admission office closed:* Dec. 24–Jan. 4; Good Friday, Apr. 2.

## VISIT OPPORTUNITIES

|  | **Appointments?** | **Who?** |
|---|---|---|
| **Campus Tour** | recommended | open to all |
| **Information Session** | not required | open to all |
| **Admission Interview** | recommended | open to all |
| **Classroom Visit** | required | open to all |
| **Faculty Meeting** | required | open to all |
| **Overnight Visit** | required | open to all |

**Information Sessions:** M–F 8:00 am–5:00 pm; first and third Sat. each month at 10:00 am to 2:00 pm; 30 minutes.

**Interviews:** M–F; first and third Sat. of each month; 60 minutes.

**Campus Tours:** Conducted by students. M–F at 9:30 am, 10:30 am, 12:30 pm, 2:30 pm; Sat. at 10:30 am, 12:30 pm; 60 minutes.

**Class Visits:** Prospective students may attend a class in their area of interest.

**Overnight Visits:** During the regular academic year, prospective applicants may spend an evening in a residence hall with a student host.

**Video:** Free on request.

## CAMPUS FACILITIES

**Science:** Rieke Science Center.

**Arts:** Mary Baker Russell Music Center, Wekell Art Gallery.

**Athletic:** Olson Auditorium, Names Fitness Center.

**Of Special Interest:** Mortvedt Library.

# SEATTLE PACIFIC UNIVERSITY

**Seattle, Washington**

**Contact:** Office of Undergraduate Admissions, 3307 Third Avenue West, Seattle, WA 98119-1997. *Phone:* toll-free 800-366-3344. *Fax:* 206-281-2669. *Web site:* http://www.spu.edu/ *Visit location:* Office of Undergraduate Admissions, Demaray Hall 120, 3307 Third Avenue West.

## QUICK FACTS

Enrollment: 3,321; UG: 2,610. Entrance: moderately difficult. SAT>500: 82% V, 77% M; ACT>18: 97%. Tuition and fees: $14,541. Room and board: $5574. Application deadline: 9/1.

## GENERAL

Independent Free Methodist, comprehensive, coed. Awards bachelor's, master's, and doctoral degrees. Founded 1891. Setting: 35-acre urban campus. Undergraduate faculty: 208 (159 full-time, 49 part-time); student-faculty ratio is 15:1. Most popular recent majors: nursing, business administration, psychology.

## CAMPUS VISITS

**College Calendar 1998–99:** *Regular classes:* Sept. 28–Dec. 8; Jan. 4–Mar. 15; Mar. 29–June 7. *Breaks:* Dec. 12–Jan. 3; Mar. 22–26. *Final exams:* Dec. 9–11; Mar. 17–19; June 8–10. *Special campus days:* Campus Preview, Feb. 18–20; S.P.U. Friday Visitations; Senior Preview, Nov. 5–6.

## VISIT OPPORTUNITIES

|                       | Appointments? | Who?        |
| --------------------- | ------------- | ----------- |
| **Campus Tour**       | required      | open to all |
| **Information Session** | required    | open to all |
| **Admission Interview** | required    | open to all |
| **Classroom Visit**   | required      | open to all |
| **Faculty Meeting**   | required      | open to all |
| **Overnight Visit**   | required      | open to all |

**Information Sessions:** M–F; 60 minutes.

**Interviews:** M–F; 60 minutes.

**Campus Tours:** Conducted by students. M–F; 60 minutes.

**Class Visits:** Prospective students may attend a class in their area of interest.

**Overnight Visits:** During the regular academic year and over the summer, prospective applicants may spend an evening in a residence hall with a student host.

## CAMPUS FACILITIES

**Arts:** Art Center.

**Athletic:** Interbay Soccer Stadium.

## LOCAL ATTRACTIONS

Seattle Center, Pike Place Market, Waterfront, Pioneer Square.

# UNIVERSITY OF PUGET SOUND
Tacoma, Washington

**Contact:** Margaret Gibson, Campus Visit Coordinator, 1500 North Warner Street, Tacoma, WA 98416.

*Phone:* 253-756-3211 or toll-free 800-396-7191. *Fax:* 253-756-3500. *E-mail:* admission@ups.edu *Web site:* http://www.ups.edu/ *Visit location:* Office of Admission, Jones Hall, Room 115, 1500 North Warner Street.

## QUICK FACTS

Enrollment: 3,011; UG: 2,734. Entrance: very difficult. SAT>500: 96% V, 95% M; ACT>18: 100%. Tuition and fees: $18,940. Room and board: $4920. Application deadline: 2/1.

## GENERAL

Independent, comprehensive, coed. Awards bachelor's and master's degrees. Founded 1888. Setting: 97-acre suburban campus with easy access to Seattle. Undergraduate faculty: 293 (216 full-time, 77 part-time); student-faculty ratio is 12:1. Most popular recent majors: biology, English, political science.

## CAMPUS VISITS

**College Calendar 1998–99:** *Regular classes:* Aug. 31–Dec. 9; Jan. 19–May 5. *Breaks:* Oct. 16–20; Mar. 12–21; Dec. 18–Jan. 18. *Final exams:* Dec. 14–18; May 10–14. *Special campus days:* Commencement, May 16; Fall Family Weekend, Oct. 9–11; Homecoming, Oct. 23–25.

## VISIT OPPORTUNITIES

|                       | Appointments? | Who?        |
| --------------------- | ------------- | ----------- |
| **Campus Tour**       | recommended   | open to all |
| **Information Session** | recommended | open to all |
| **Admission Interview** | recommended | open to all |
| **Classroom Visit**   | required      | open to all |
| **Faculty Meeting**   | required      | open to all |
| **Overnight Visit**   | required      | open to all |

**Information Sessions:** Sat. Oct. and Nov. at 10:00 am, 11:00 am; 60 minutes.

**Interviews:** M–F; Sat. sessions Aug.–Apr. 9:00 am to 12:00 pm; group sessions available Sat. during Oct.–Nov.; 60 minutes.

**Campus Tours:** Conducted by students. M–F 9:00 am–4:00 pm; Sat. 9:00 am–12:00 pm; 60 minutes.

**Class Visits:** Prospective students may attend a class in their area of interest.

**Overnight Visits:** During the regular academic year, prospective applicants may spend an evening in a residence hall with a student host.

*University of Puget Sound (continued)*

## CAMPUS FACILITIES

**Science:** Thompson Hall.

**Arts:** Inside Theatre, Music Building—Performance Hall, Kittredge Art Gallery/Hall and Ceramics Building.

**Athletic:** Pamplin Athletic Center, Warner Street Pool.

**Of Special Interest:** Residence Halls, Wheelock Student Center, Collins Memorial Library.

# WESTERN WASHINGTON UNIVERSITY

**Bellingham, Washington**

**Contact:** Joy Mbajah, Admissions Counselor, Office of Admissions, Bellingham, WA 98225-9009. *Phone:* 360-650-3861. *Fax:* 360-650-7369. *E-mail:* admit@cc.wwu.edu *Web site:* http://www.wwu.edu/ *Visit location:* Western Washington University Office of Admissions, Old Main 200, 516 High Street.

## QUICK FACTS

Enrollment: 11,470; UG: 10,687. Entrance: moderately difficult. SAT>500: 76% V, 73% M; ACT>18: 95%. Resident tuition and fees: $2772. Nonresident tuition and fees: $9207. Room and board: $4635. Application deadline: 3/1.

## GENERAL

State-supported, comprehensive, coed. Awards bachelor's and master's degrees. Founded 1893. Setting: 223-acre small-town campus with easy access to Seattle and Vancouver. Undergraduate faculty: 564 (414 full-time, 150 part-time); student-faculty ratio is 21:1. Most popular recent majors: business administration, English.

## CAMPUS VISITS

**College Calendar 1998–99:** *Regular classes:* Sept. 23–Dec. 11; Jan. 5–Mar. 19; Mar. 30–June 11; June 22–Aug. 20. *Breaks:* Dec. 12–Jan. 4; Mar. 20–29; June 12–21; Aug. 21–Sept. 21. *Final exams:* Dec. 7–11; Mar. 15–19; June 7–11; Aug. 16–20. *Admission office closed:* Nov. 26–27, Dec. 24. *Special campus days:* Fall Commencement, Dec. 12; Spring Commencement, June 12; Summer Commencement, Aug. 21; Winter Commencement, Mar. 20.

## VISIT OPPORTUNITIES

|  | Appointments? | Who? |
|---|---|---|
| **Campus Tour** | not required | open to all |
| **Information Session** | recommended | open to all |
| **Admission Interview** |  | open to all |
| **Classroom Visit** | required | open to all |
| **Faculty Meeting** | required | applicants only |
| **Overnight Visit** | required | applicants only |

**Information Sessions:** Selected Fri. – "Discovery Days" at 1:00 pm-3:00 pm, reservations required; 120 minutes.

**Interviews:** M–F 1:00–4:00 pm.

**Campus Tours:** Conducted by students. Sat. at 11:00 am, 2:00 pm; 2 weeks advance registration required; 60 minutes.

**Class Visits:** Prospective students may attend a class in their area of interest, certain predetermined classrooms are open to visitors.

**Overnight Visits:** During the regular academic year and over the summer, prospective applicants may spend an evening in a residence hall.

## CAMPUS FACILITIES

**Science:** Science Lecture halls, Resource Learning Center, Labs (Science and Computers), Automotive Technology (solar car plant).

**Arts:** Performing Arts Center, Fine Arts building, Music Library, dance studio; Appointment Required: Western Gallery.

**Athletic:** Gymnasiums, track and football field; Appointment Required: Lap pool, fitness centers, wrestling mats.

**Of Special Interest:** Fairhaven College, Environmental Studies building, Book Store; Appointment Required: Wilson Library.

## LOCAL ATTRACTIONS

Sehome hill arboretum, Parks, shopping mall, Sehome Village, Civic Field, out door sculpture collection.

# WHITMAN COLLEGE

**Walla Walla, Washington**

**Contact:** Carol Harshman, Visit Coordinator, Whitman Office of Admission, 515 Boyer Avenue,

Walla Walla, WA 99362. *Phone:* 509-522-4423. *Fax:* 509-527-4967. *E-mail:* admission@whitman.edu *Web site:* http://www.whitman.edu/ *Visit location:* Whitman Office of Admission, Penrose House, 515 Boyer Avenue.

### QUICK FACTS
Enrollment: 1,375; UG: 1,375. Entrance: very difficult. SAT>500: 99% V, 97% M; ACT>18: N/R. Tuition and fees: $19,756. Room and board: $5640. Application deadline: 2/1.

### GENERAL
Independent, 4-year, coed. Awards bachelor's degrees. Founded 1859. Setting: 55-acre small-town campus. Faculty: 177 (102 full-time, 75 part-time); student-faculty ratio is 10:1. Most popular recent majors: English, biology, psychology.

### CAMPUS VISITS
**College Calendar 1998–99:** *Regular classes:* Sept. 2–Dec. 11; Jan. 19–May 11. *Breaks:* Dec. 19–Jan. 18; Mar. 13–29. *Final exams:* Dec. 14–18; May 13–19. *Special campus days:* Commencement, May 23; Homecoming Weekend, Sept. 25–27; Parents Weekend, Oct. 23–25.

#### VISIT OPPORTUNITIES

| | Appointments? | Who? |
|---|---|---|
| **Campus Tour** | recommended, not required | open to all |
| **Admission Interview** | required | open to all |
| **Classroom Visit** | required | open to all |
| **Faculty Meeting** | required | open to all |
| **Overnight Visit** | required | open to all |

**Interviews:** M–F 8:30 am–3:30 pm; Sat. 9:00 am–12:00 pm; during summer M–F 8:00 am–3:00 pm only; 45 minutes.

**Campus Tours:** Conducted by students. M–F at 9:00 am, 10:00 am, 2:30 pm; Sat. at 11:00 am; available additionally at 10:00 am, 2:00 pm, during vacations and summer; 50 minutes.

**Class Visits:** Prospective students may attend a class in their area of interest.

**Overnight Visits:** During the regular academic year, prospective applicants may spend an evening in a residence hall with a student host.

**Video:** Free on request.

### CAMPUS FACILITIES
**Science:** Hall of Science; Appointment Required: Laboratories.

**Arts:** Harper Joy Theatre; Appointment Required: Chism Recital Hall in the Hall of Music, Communications Arts and Technology Center, Ceramics Laboratory.

**Athletic:** Appointment Required: Sherwood Center, Brattain Tennis Center.

**Of Special Interest:** Penrose Memorial Library, Lyman Hall, Prentiss Hall.

### LOCAL ATTRACTIONS
Whitman Mission, Fort Walla Walla, Pioneer Park Aviary.

## WHITWORTH COLLEGE
### Spokane, Washington

**Contact:** Kimberly Reynolds, Assistant Director of Admissions, 300 West Hawthorne Road, Spokane, WA 99251. *Phone:* toll-free 800-533-4668 (out-of-state). *Fax:* 509-777-3758. *E-mail:* kreynolds @ whitworth.edu *Web site:* http://www.whitworth.edu/ *Visit location:* Admissions, Mac Kay Hall, 300 West Hawthorne.

### QUICK FACTS
Enrollment: 2,043; UG: 1,798. Entrance: very difficult. SAT>500: 50% V, 69% M; ACT>18: N/R. Tuition and fees: $15,593. Room and board: $5300. Application deadline: 3/1.

### GENERAL
Independent Presbyterian, comprehensive, coed. Awards bachelor's and master's degrees. Founded 1890. Setting: 200-acre suburban campus. Undergraduate faculty: 102 (84 full-time, 18 part-time); student-faculty ratio is 16:1. Most popular recent majors: elementary education, business administration, history.

### CAMPUS VISITS
**College Calendar 1998–99:** *Regular classes:* Sept. 9–Dec. 14; Jan. 4–26; Feb. 2–May 10. *Breaks:* Oct. 23–26; Dec. 19–Jan. 3; Mar. 22–26. *Final exams:* Dec. 15–18; Jan. 27–Feb. 1; May 11–14. *Special campus days:* Campus Close-up (seniors and parents), Feb. 14–15; Commencement, May 16; Fall Preview (seniors), Nov. 8–9; Fall musical Production, Oct. 29–31; Great Escape (visit weekend for seniors), Oct. 17–19; Hawaiian Luau, Apr. 17; Homecoming, Oct.

*Whitworth College (continued)*

3; Sneak Preview (juniors and parents), Apr. 18–19; Spring Formal, Apr. 10; Spring Theatre Production, Apr. 22–24; Theatre Production, Oct. 16–17.

## VISIT OPPORTUNITIES

|  | Appointments? | Who? |
|---|---|---|
| **Campus Tour** | recommended, not required | open to all |
| **Information Session** | required | open to all |
| **Admission Interview** | recommended | open to all |
| **Classroom Visit** | required | open to all |
| **Faculty Meeting** | required | open to all |
| **Overnight Visit** | required | open to all |

**Interviews:** M–F; Sat. in Mar., Apr., and May excluding Easter break; 60 minutes.

**Campus Tours:** Conducted by students. M–F at 11:15 am, 2:30 pm; Sat. at 10:00 am; morning tours available with advance notice; 60 minutes.

**Class Visits:** Prospective students may attend a class in their area of interest.

**Overnight Visits:** During the regular academic year, prospective applicants may spend an evening in a residence hall with a student host.

**Video:** Free on request.

## CAMPUS FACILITIES

**Science:** Appointment Required: Science Auditorium.

**Arts:** Appointment Required: Fine Arts Building.

**Athletic:** Fieldhouse, Aquatic Center.

**Of Special Interest:** Chapel, Campus Center, Stan the Man's Espresso Stand (located in the Campus Center).

## LOCAL ATTRACTIONS

The Garland Dollar Theatre, and Riverfront Park.

# WEST VIRGINIA

# BETHANY COLLEGE
**Bethany, West Virginia**

**Contact:** Jackie Andrews, Admission Office, Bethany, WV 26032. *Phone:* 304-829-7611 or toll-free 800-922-7611 (out-of-state). *Fax:* 304-829-7142. *E-mail:* j.andrews@mail.bethanywv.edu *Web site:* http://www.bethanywv.edu/ *Visit location:* Admission, Bethany House.

## QUICK FACTS

Enrollment: 736; UG: 736. Entrance: moderately difficult. SAT>500: 69% V, 73% M; ACT>18: 98%. Tuition and fees: $17,349. Room and board: $5716. Application deadline: rolling.

## GENERAL

Independent, 4-year, coed, Christian Church (Disciples of Christ). Awards bachelor's degrees. Founded 1840. Setting: 1,600-acre rural campus with easy access to Pittsburgh. Faculty: 62 (58 full-time, 4 part-time); student-faculty ratio is 13:1. Most popular recent majors: psychology, communications, education.

## CAMPUS VISITS

**College Calendar 1998–99:** *Regular classes:* Aug. 30–Dec. 10; Jan. 18–May 7. *Final exams:* Dec. 11–15; May 10–13.

## VISIT OPPORTUNITIES

|  | Appointments? | Who? |
|---|---|---|
| **Campus Tour** | required | open to all |
| **Information Session** | required | open to all |
| **Admission Interview** | required | open to all |
| **Classroom Visit** | required | open to all |
| **Faculty Meeting** | required | open to all |
| **Overnight Visit** | required | admitted applicants only |

**Interviews:** M–F, select Sat.; 20 minutes.

**Campus Tours:** Conducted by students. M–F, select Sat.; 60 minutes.

**Class Visits:** Prospective students may attend a class in their area of interest.

**Overnight Visits:** During the regular academic year, prospective applicants may spend an evening in a residence hall with a student host.

**Video:** Free on request.

## CAMPUS FACILITIES

**Science:** Appointment Required: Richardson Science Center, Oglesbay Hall.

**Arts:** West Virginia Watercolors Collection; Appointment Required: Steinman Fine Arts Center, Grace Phillips Johnson Fine Arts Center.

**Athletic:** Johnson Recreation Center, Ewing Tennis Complex, Hummel Fieldhouse.

**Of Special Interest:** Appointment Required: Old Main and Commencement Hall, WTVX Television Station, WVBC Radio Station.

## LOCAL ATTRACTIONS

Alexander Campbell Mansion; Oglebay Park and Mansion; Delta Tau Delta Founders House; Wheeling Independence Hall.

# MARSHALL UNIVERSITY
### Huntington, West Virginia

**Contact:** Sabrina D. Simpson, Tour Coordinator, 401 Hal Greer Boulevard, Huntington, WV 25755. *Phone:* toll-free 800-642-3499 (in-state). *Fax:* 304-696-6858. *E-mail:* simpson@marshall.edu *Web site:* http://www.marshall.edu/ *Visit location:* Admissions, Welcome Center, 1801 5th Avenue.

## QUICK FACTS

Enrollment: 13,366; UG: 9,019. Entrance: minimally difficult. SAT>500: N/App; ACT>18: N/App. Resident tuition and fees: $2184. Nonresident tuition and fees: $6066. Room and board: $4420. Application deadline: rolling.

## GENERAL

State-supported, comprehensive, coed. Part of University System of West Virginia. Awards associate, bachelor's, master's, doctoral, and first professional degrees. Founded 1837. Setting: 70-acre urban campus. Undergraduate faculty: 881 (553 full-time, 328 part-time); student-faculty ratio is 20:1. Most popular recent majors: elementary education, criminal justice/law enforcement administration, psychology.

## CAMPUS VISITS

**College Calendar 1998–99:** *Regular classes:* Aug. 24–Dec. 8; Jan. 11–Apr. 30. *Breaks:* Nov. 23–28; Apr. 2–9; Dec. 15–Jan. 11. *Final exams:* Dec. 9–15; May 3–7. *Admission office closed:* Dec. 23–Jan. 1; Thanksgiving, Nov. 26–27. *Special campus days:* Commencement, May 8; Homecoming, Nov. 7; Open House, Oct. 3, Oct. 17.

## VISIT OPPORTUNITIES

| | Appointments? | Who? |
|---|---|---|
| **Campus Tour** | required | open to all |
| **Information Session** | recommended, not required | open to all |
| **Classroom Visit** | required | open to all |
| **Faculty Meeting** | required | open to all |
| **Overnight Visit** | required | open to all |

**Information Sessions:** M–F 8:00 am–4:30 pm; 30 minutes.

**Campus Tours:** Conducted by students and admission reps. M–F at 10:00 am, 1:00 pm; select Sat. at 10:00 am; 90 minutes.

**Class Visits:** Prospective students may attend a class in their area of interest.

**Overnight Visits:** During the regular academic year, prospective applicants may spend an evening in a residence hall.

## CAMPUS FACILITIES

**Arts:** Appointment Required: Fine and Performing Arts Center.

**Athletic:** Henderson Center (basketball arena), Fitness Center; Appointment Required: Football Stadium.

**Of Special Interest:** Library/Information Center, Memorial Student Center; Appointment Required: Residence Halls.

## LOCAL ATTRACTIONS

Huntington Museum of Art, Blenko Glass Company, Pilgrim Glass Corporation, Heritage Village, Huntington Mall, Museum of Radio and Technology.

# SHEPHERD COLLEGE
### Shepherdstown, West Virginia

**Contact:** Office of Admissions, King Street, PO Box 3210, Shepherdstown, WV 25443-3210. *Phone:* toll-free 800-344-5231 Ext. 5212. *Fax:* 304-876-5165. *E-mail:* admoff@shepherd.wvnet.edu *Web site:* http://www.ufl.edu/ *Visit location:* Office of Admissions, McMurran Hall, King and German Streets.

## QUICK FACTS

Enrollment: 3,250; UG: 3,250. Entrance: moderately difficult. SAT>500: N/R; ACT>18: N/R. Resident

*Shepherd College (continued)*

tuition and fees: $2228. Nonresident tuition and fees: $5348. Room and board: $4139. Application deadline: 2/1.

### GENERAL

State-supported, 4-year, coed. Part of State College System of West Virginia. Awards associate and bachelor's degrees. Founded 1871. Setting: 320-acre small-town campus with easy access to Washington, DC. Faculty: 290 (114 full-time, 176 part-time); student-faculty ratio is 14:1. Most popular recent majors: business administration, elementary education, secondary education.

### CAMPUS VISITS

**College Calendar 1998–99:** *Regular classes:* Aug. 24–Dec. 14; Jan. 13–May 7. *Breaks:* Nov. 21–29; Mar. 20–28; Apr. 22–25. *Final exams:* Dec. 15–19; May 10–14. *Special campus days:* Commencement, May 22; Homecoming, Oct. 3.

### VISIT OPPORTUNITIES

|  | Appointments? | Who? |
| --- | --- | --- |
| **Campus Tour** | required | open to all |
| **Information Session** | required | open to all |
| **Admission Interview** | required | open to all |
| **Classroom Visit** | required | open to all |
| **Faculty Meeting** | required | open to all |

**Information Sessions:** Select Sat.; Mon. at 1:30 pm; Fri. at 1:30 pm; 45 minutes.

**Interviews:** M–F; 30 minutes.

**Campus Tours:** Conducted by students. M–F at 2:00 pm; select Sat.; 60 minutes.

**Class Visits:** Prospective students may attend a class in their area of interest.

### CAMPUS FACILITIES

**Science:** Robert Byrd/Snyder Science and Technology Center.

**Arts:** Frank Creative Arts Center.

**Athletic:** Butcher Athletic Center.

### LOCAL ATTRACTIONS

Harpers Ferry National Park; Antietam National Battlefield.

# WEST LIBERTY STATE COLLEGE
## West Liberty, West Virginia

**Contact:** Mr. Paul Milam, Director of Admissions, West Liberty State College, West Liberty, WV 26074. *Phone:* 304-336-8076 or toll-free 800-732-6204. *Fax:* 304-336-8285. *E-mail:* wladmsn1@vms. wlsc.wvnet.edu *Web site:* http://www.wlsc.wvnet.edu/ *Visit location:* Admissions, Shaw Hall, West Liberty State College.

### QUICK FACTS

Enrollment: 2,397; UG: 2,397. Entrance: minimally difficult. SAT>500: 35% V, 30% M; ACT>18: 68%. Resident tuition and fees: $2200. Nonresident tuition and fees: $5640. Room and board: $3200. Application deadline: 8/1.

### GENERAL

State-supported, 4-year, coed. Part of State College System of West Virginia. Awards associate and bachelor's degrees. Founded 1837. Setting: 290-acre rural campus with easy access to Pittsburgh. Faculty: 138 (120 full-time, 18 part-time); student-faculty ratio is 19:1. Most popular recent majors: business administration, education, criminal justice/law enforcement administration.

### CAMPUS VISITS

**College Calendar 1998–99:** *Regular classes:* Aug. 24–Dec. 14; Jan. 11–May 5. *Breaks:* Nov. 20–30; Mar. 12–22; Apr. 2–5. *Final exams:* Dec. 15–18; May 10–14. *Admission office closed:* Dec. 23–Jan. 2. *Special campus days:* Commencement, Dec. 19; Homecoming, Oct. 3; Parents Day/Open House, Nov. 14.

### VISIT OPPORTUNITIES

|  | Appointments? | Who? |
| --- | --- | --- |
| **Campus Tour** | required | applicants and parents |
| **Information Session** | recommended |  |
| **Admission Interview** | required |  |
| **Classroom Visit** | required |  |
| **Faculty Meeting** | recommended | applicants and parents |
| **Overnight Visit** | recommended |  |

**Information Sessions:** M–F 8:00 am–4:00 pm; telephone sessions available; 30 minutes.

**Interviews:** M–F; recruiters may conduct off-campus interviews; 30 minutes.

**Campus Tours:** Conducted by students and admission reps. M–F 8:00 am–4:00 pm; call for special arrangements; 60 minutes.

**Class Visits:** Classroom visits are determined by the visit schedule.

**Overnight Visits:** During the regular academic year and over the summer.

### CAMPUS FACILITIES

**Science:** Acreage maintained in natural setting; Appointment Required: Classrooms (Science Labs), Greenhouse.

**Arts:** Appointment Required: Art Labs, Gallery.

**Athletic:** Blatnik Hall, Bartell Field House; Appointment Required: Football Arena.

**Of Special Interest:** Elbin Library.

# WEST VIRGINIA UNIVERSITY
## Morgantown, West Virginia

**Contact:** Ms. Evie Brantmayer, Interim Director, Admissions and Records, PO Box 6009, Morgantown, WV 26506-6009. *Phone:* toll-free 800-344-9881. *Web site:* http://www.wvu.edu/ *Visit location:* Visitors Center, Communications Building, Patteson Drive, PO Box 6690.

### QUICK FACTS

Enrollment: 22,238; UG: 14,959. Entrance: moderately difficult. SAT>500: 59% V, 58% M; ACT>18: 92%. Resident tuition and fees: $2336. Nonresident tuition and fees: $7356. Room and board: $4832. Application deadline: rolling.

### GENERAL

State-supported, university, coed. Part of University of West Virginia System. Awards bachelor's, master's, doctoral, and first professional degrees. Founded 1867. Setting: 541-acre small-town campus with easy access to Pittsburgh. Undergraduate faculty: 1,575 (1,313 full-time, 262 part-time); student-faculty ratio is 18:1. Most popular recent majors: accounting, journalism.

### CAMPUS VISITS

**College Calendar 1998–99:** *Regular classes:* Aug. 25–Dec. 11; Jan. 11–Apr. 30. *Breaks:* Nov. 21–29; Mar. 27–Apr. 4. *Final exams:* Dec. 14–19; May 3–8. *Special campus days:* Graduates Convocation, Dec. 11; Graduation, May 16; Homecoming, Oct. 24; Moun-

taineer Day, Nov. 7; New Student Convocation, Aug. 24; Parents Weekend, Sept. 26; Weekend of Honors, Apr. 16.

### VISIT OPPORTUNITIES

|  | Appointments? |
| --- | --- |
| **Campus Tour** | recommended |
| **Information Session** | recommended |
| **Classroom Visit** | required |
| **Faculty Meeting** | required |

**Information Sessions:** M–F at 10:30 am, 2:00 pm; Sat. at 10:00 am; part of tour.

**Campus Tours:** Conducted by students and admission reps. M–F at 10:30 am, 2:00 pm; Sat. at 10:00 am; 120 minutes.

**Class Visits:** Certain predetermined classrooms are open to visitors.

**Video:** Free on request.

### CAMPUS FACILITIES

**Science:** Appointment Required: Chemistry, Biology, Geology, Physics, Computer Science.

**Arts:** Appointment Required: Theatre, Art, Music.

**Athletic:** Appointment Required: Football Stadium, Basketball Coliseum.

**Of Special Interest:** Appointment Required: Engineering Labs, Personal Rapid Transit, West Virginia University farms.

### LOCAL ATTRACTIONS

Coopers Rock State Forest; West Virginia University Forest; Cheat Lake.

# WEST VIRGINIA WESLEYAN COLLEGE
## Buckhannon, West Virginia

**Contact:** Beth Lampinen, Assistant Director of Admission, 59 College Avenue, Buckhannon, WV 26201. *Phone:* toll-free 800-722-9933 (out-of-state). *Fax:* 304-473-8108. *E-mail:* lampinen_b@wvwc.edu *Web site:* http://www.wvwc.edu/ *Visit location:* Office of Admission, Middleton Hall, Camden Avenue.

*West Virginia Wesleyan College (continued)*

## QUICK FACTS

Enrollment: 1,686; UG: 1,569. Entrance: moderately difficult. SAT>500: 50% V, 48% M; ACT>18: 83%. Tuition and fees: $16,750. Room and board: $4100. Application deadline: 8/1.

## GENERAL

Independent, comprehensive, coed, United Methodist Church. Awards bachelor's and master's degrees. Founded 1890. Setting: 80-acre small-town campus. Undergraduate faculty: 148 (72 full-time, 76 part-time); student-faculty ratio is 15:1. Most popular recent majors: psychology, education, political science.

## CAMPUS VISITS

**College Calendar 1998–99:** *Regular classes:* Sept. 1–Dec. 11; Jan. 4–22; Jan. 27–May 6. *Breaks:* Nov. 21–30; Mar. 27–Apr. 6. *Final exams:* Dec. 14–17; Jan. 22; May 8–13. *Admission office closed:* Dec. 21–Jan. 4. *Special campus days:* Homecoming, Oct. 10; Spring Weekend, Apr. 24–25.

## VISIT OPPORTUNITIES

|  | Appointments? | Who? |
|---|---|---|
| **Campus Tour** | recommended, not required | open to all |
| **Information Session** | recommended, not required | open to all |
| **Admission Interview** | required | open to all |
| **Classroom Visit** | required | open to all |
| **Faculty Meeting** | required | open to all |
| **Overnight Visit** | required | applicants only |

**Information Sessions:** M–F 8:00 am–4:30 pm; Sat. 10:00 am–1:00 pm.

**Interviews:** M–F, Sat.

**Campus Tours:** Conducted by students. M–F, Sat.; 60 minutes.

**Class Visits:** Prospective students may attend a class in their area of interest, classroom visits are determined by the visit schedule.

**Overnight Visits:** During the regular academic year, prospective applicants may spend an evening in a residence hall with a student host.

**Video:** Free on request.

## CAMPUS FACILITIES

**Science:** Planetarium, Greenhouse.

**Arts:** Sleeth Art Gallery.

**Athletic:** Rockefeller Physical Education Center, Cebe Ross Field.

**Of Special Interest:** Wesley Chapel, Benedum Campus Center.

## LOCAL ATTRACTIONS

Year round outdoor recreational activities.

# WISCONSIN

## BELOIT COLLEGE

### Beloit, Wisconsin

**Contact:** Admissions Office, 700 College Street, Beloit, WI 53511. *Phone:* toll-free 800-356-0751 (out-of-state). *Fax:* 608-363-2075. *E-mail:* admiss@ beloit.edu *Web site:* http://www.beloit.edu/ *Visit location:* Admissions Office, Middle College, 700 College Street.

## QUICK FACTS

Enrollment: 1,160; UG: 1,160. Entrance: very difficult. SAT>500: 96% V, 90% M; ACT>18: 100%. Tuition and fees: $19,050. Room and board: $4140. Application deadline: rolling.

## GENERAL

Independent, 4-year, coed. Awards bachelor's degrees. Founded 1846. Setting: 65-acre small-town campus with easy access to Chicago and Milwaukee. Faculty: 134 (95 full-time, 39 part-time); student-faculty ratio is 11:1. Most popular recent majors: anthropology, biology, English.

## CAMPUS VISITS

**College Calendar 1998–99:** *Regular classes:* Aug. 25–Dec. 9; Jan. 19–May 5. *Breaks:* Oct. 10–18; Mar. 6–14. *Final exams:* Dec. 10–15; May 6–11. *Special campus days:* Commencement, May 16; Homecoming Weekend, Sept. 25–27; Parents Weekend, Oct. 23–25; Spring Day, Apr. 21; Student Symposium Day, Apr. 15.

## VISIT OPPORTUNITIES

|  | Appointments? | Who? |
|---|---|---|
| **Campus Tour** | required | open to all |

VISIT OPPORTUNITIES—*continued*

| | Appointments? | Who? |
|---|---|---|
| **Information Session** | required | open to all |
| **Admission Interview** | required | open to all |
| **Classroom Visit** | required | open to all |
| **Faculty Meeting** | required | open to all |
| **Overnight Visit** | required | open to all |

**Interviews:** M–F; select Sat. during academic year; 60 minutes.

**Campus Tours:** Conducted by students. M–F at 9:00 am, 10:00 am, 11:00 am, 1:00 pm, 2:00 pm, 3:00 pm; Sat. at 9:00 am, 10:00 am, 11:00 am; 60 minutes.

**Class Visits:** Prospective students may attend a class in their area of interest.

**Overnight Visits:** During the regular academic year, prospective applicants may spend an evening in a residence hall with a student host.

**Video:** Free on request.

## CAMPUS FACILITIES

**Science:** Chamberlin Science Hall.

**Arts:** Wright Art Museum; Appointment Required: Neese Theatre.

**Athletic:** Appointment Required: Pohlman Field—Telfer Park, Strong Stadium.

**Of Special Interest:** Logan Museum of Anthropology.

## LOCAL ATTRACTIONS

Beloit Snappers, minor league baseball team; Riverside Park; nearby major metropolitan areas (Madison, Milwaukee, Chicago).

# CARTHAGE COLLEGE

### Kenosha, Wisconsin

**Contact:** Mr. Mark S. Kopenski, Assistant Vice President for Enrollment, 2001 Alford Park Drive, Kenosha, WI 53140. *Phone:* 414-551-6000 or toll-free 800-351-4058. *Fax:* 414-551-5762. *E-mail:* msk@carthage.edu *Web site:* http://www.carthage.edu/ *Visit location:* Office of Admissions, Lentz Hall, 2001 Alford Park Drive.

## QUICK FACTS

Enrollment: 1,917; UG: 1,873. Entrance: moderately difficult. SAT>500: 58% V, 59% M; ACT>18: 92%.

Tuition and fees: $15,365. Room and board: $4415. Application deadline: rolling.

## GENERAL

Independent, comprehensive, coed, Evangelical Lutheran Church in America. Awards bachelor's and master's degrees. Founded 1847. Setting: 72-acre suburban campus with easy access to Chicago and Milwaukee. Undergraduate faculty: 124 (94 full-time, 30 part-time); student-faculty ratio is 16:1. Most popular recent majors: business administration, education, social sciences.

## CAMPUS VISITS

**College Calendar 1998–99:** *Regular classes:* Sept. 9–Dec. 15; Jan. 4–27; Feb. 3–May 14. *Breaks:* Nov. 24–30; Mar. 12–22; Apr. 1–6. *Final exams:* Dec. 16–18; Jan. 28; May 17–19. *Special campus days:* Family Weekend/Honors Convocation, Apr. 23–25; Homecoming, Oct. 3; Parents Weekend, Oct. 24–25.

## VISIT OPPORTUNITIES

| | Appointments? | Who? |
|---|---|---|
| **Campus Tour** | required | open to all |
| **Information Session** | required | open to all |
| **Admission Interview** | required | open to all |
| **Classroom Visit** | required | open to all |
| **Faculty Meeting** | required | open to all |
| **Overnight Visit** | | admitted applicants only |

**Information Sessions:** Select Sat.; call or visit Web site for schedule; 60 minutes.

**Interviews:** M–F, Sat.; 30 minutes.

**Campus Tours:** Conducted by students. M–F at 9:00 am, 11:00 am, 1:00 pm, 3:00 pm; Sat. at 9:00 am, 10:00 am, 11:00 am, 12:00 pm; 60 minutes.

**Class Visits:** Prospective students may attend a class in their area of interest.

**Overnight Visits:** During the regular academic year.

## CAMPUS FACILITIES

**Science:** Appointment Required: Geography Information Systems Lab, Greenhouse, Mathematics Lab.

**Arts:** Appointment Required: Civil War Museum, Wartburg Auditorium.

**Athletic:** Physical Education Center; Appointment Required: Swimming Pool.

*Carthage College (continued)*

**Of Special Interest:** Library, Chapel; Appointment Required: Dormitories/Residence Halls.

# LAWRENCE UNIVERSITY
## Appleton, Wisconsin

**Contact:** Campus Visit Coordinator, PO Box 599, Appleton, WI 54912-0599. *Phone:* toll-free 800-448-3072. *Fax:* 920-832-6782. *E-mail:* excel@lawrence. edu *Web site:* http://www.lawrence.edu/ *Visit location:* Visit Coordinator/Receptionist, Wilson House-Admissions Office, 706 East College Avenue.

### QUICK FACTS
Enrollment: 1,127; UG: 1,127. Entrance: very difficult. SAT>500: 95% V, 95% M; ACT>18: 100%. Tuition and fees: $19,620. Room and board: $4575. Application deadline: 2/1.

### GENERAL
Independent, 4-year, coed. Awards bachelor's degrees. Founded 1847. Setting: 84-acre small-town campus. Faculty: 171 (115 full-time, 56 part-time); student-faculty ratio is 11:1. Most popular recent majors: biology, English, psychology.

### CAMPUS VISITS
**College Calendar 1998–99:** *Regular classes:* Sept. 23–Dec. 5; Jan. 4–Mar. 13; Mar. 29–June 4. *Breaks:* Dec. 15–Jan. 3; Mar. 22–28. *Final exams:* Dec. 8–11; Mar. 16–19; June 7–10. *Special campus days:* Celebrate!, May 8; Commencement, June 13; Homecoming, Oct. 17; Parents Weekend, Oct. 31–Nov. 1.

### VISIT OPPORTUNITIES

|  | Appointments? | Who? |
| --- | --- | --- |
| **Campus Tour** | recommended | open to all |
| **Admission Interview** | required | open to all |
| **Classroom Visit** | required | open to all |
| **Faculty Meeting** | required | open to all |
| **Overnight Visit** | required | open to all |

**Interviews:** M–F; Sat. except Jul.–Sept.; 45 minutes.
**Campus Tours:** Conducted by students. Mon., Wed., Fri. at 9:45 am, 11:10 am, 1:15 pm, 3:00 pm; Tue., Thu. at 11:00 am, 1:15 pm; Sat. at 9:45 am, 10:45 am; weekdays during academic year; Sat. unavailable Jul., Aug., and Sept.; 70 minutes.

**Class Visits:** Prospective students may request the subject area of interest.
**Overnight Visits:** During the regular academic year, prospective applicants may spend an evening in a residence hall with a student host.
**Video:** Free on request.

### CAMPUS FACILITIES
**Of Special Interest:** Seeley G. Mudd Library.

### LOCAL ATTRACTIONS
Experimental Aircraft Association, Oshkosh; Fox Cities Children's Museum, Appleton; Outagamie County Historical Museum, Appleton; Green Bay Packers Hall of Fame, Green Bay.

# MARQUETTE UNIVERSITY
## Milwaukee, Wisconsin

**Contact:** June Smith, Visit Coordinator, P.O. Box 1881, Milwaukee, WI 53201-1881. *Phone:* toll-free 800-222-6544. *Fax:* 414-288-3764. *Web site:* http://www.marquette.edu/ *Visit location:* Office of Undergraduate Admissions, Marquette Hall, Suite 106.

### QUICK FACTS
Enrollment: 10,374; UG: 7,063. Entrance: moderately difficult. SAT>500: 84% V, 83% M; ACT>18: 99%. Tuition and fees: $15,384. Room and board: $5530. Application deadline: rolling.

### GENERAL
Independent Roman Catholic (Jesuit), university, coed. Awards associate, bachelor's, master's, doctoral, and first professional degrees. Founded 1881. Setting: 80-acre urban campus. Undergraduate faculty: 1,035 (560 full-time, 475 part-time); student-faculty ratio is 14:1. Most popular recent majors: business administration, psychology, nursing.

### CAMPUS VISITS
**College Calendar 1998–99:** *Regular classes:* Aug. 31–Dec. 12; Jan. 19–May 8. *Breaks:* Dec. 20–Jan. 17; Mar. 7–14. *Final exams:* Dec. 14–19; May 10–15. *Admission office closed:* Nov. 27, Apr. 1–5. *Special campus days:* Baccalaureate and Commencement, May 22–23; Summer Session 1, May 24–July 3; Summer Session 2, July 6–Aug. 14.

## VISIT OPPORTUNITIES

| | Appointments? | Who? |
|---|---|---|
| **Campus Tour** | recommended | applicants and parents |
| **Admission Interview** | recommended | applicants and parents |
| **Classroom Visit** | required | applicants and parents |
| **Faculty Meeting** | required | applicants and parents |
| **Overnight Visit** | required | |

**Information Sessions:** M–F; 60 minutes.

**Interviews:** M–F, select Sat.; call for Sat. schedule; 50 minutes.

**Campus Tours:** Conducted by students. M–F, select Sat.; on the hour from 9:00 am to 3:00 pm; separate campus and 30 minute residence hall tours; 60 minutes.

**Class Visits:** Prospective students may attend a class in their area of interest, classroom visits are determined by the visit schedule.

**Overnight Visits:** During the regular academic year, prospective applicants may spend an evening in a residence hall with a student host.

## CAMPUS FACILITIES

**Arts:** Haggerty Museum of Art.

**Athletic:** Helfaer Recreation and Tennis Stadium.

**Of Special Interest:** St. Joan of Arc Chapel; Appointment Required: University Archives.

## LOCAL ATTRACTIONS

Milwaukee Public Museum, Miller Brewery, Milwaukee County Zoo, Milwaukee Art Museum, restaurants.

# ST. NORBERT COLLEGE
**De Pere, Wisconsin**

**Contact:** Jane Gunnlaugsson, Admissions, Office of Admissions 100 Grant Street, De Pere, WI 54115. *Phone:* 920-337-3005 or toll-free 800-236-4878. *Fax:* 920-403-4072. *E-mail:* admit@sncac.snc.edu *Web site:* http://www.snc.edu/ *Visit location:* Jane Gunnlaugsson, Office of Admissions, 100 Grant Street.

## QUICK FACTS

Enrollment: 2,000; UG: 1,926. Entrance: moderately difficult. SAT>500: N/R; ACT>18: 97%. Tuition and fees: $14,434. Room and board: $5120. Application deadline: rolling.

## GENERAL

Independent Roman Catholic, comprehensive, coed. Awards bachelor's and master's degrees. Founded 1898. Setting: 86-acre suburban campus. Undergraduate faculty: 170 (126 full-time, 44 part-time); student-faculty ratio is 14:1. Most popular recent majors: business administration, elementary education, mass communications.

## CAMPUS VISITS

**College Calendar 1998–99:** *Regular classes:* Aug. 31–Dec. 11; Jan. 19–May 7. *Breaks:* Oct. 9–13; Mar. 8–14; Apr. 2–5. *Final exams:* Dec. 14–19; May 10–14. *Admission office closed:* fall break; spring break. *Special campus days:* Family Weekend, Sept. 18–20; Homecoming, Oct. 23–24; Winter Fest, Feb. 20–21.

## VISIT OPPORTUNITIES

| | Appointments? | Who? |
|---|---|---|
| **Campus Tour** | | open to all |
| **Admission Interview** | required | open to all |
| **Classroom Visit** | required | open to all |
| **Faculty Meeting** | required | open to all |
| **Overnight Visit** | required | open to all |

**Interviews:** M–F, select Sat.; 45 minutes.

**Campus Tours:** Conducted by students. M–F; Sat.; 60 minutes.

**Class Visits:** Classroom visits are determined by the visit schedule.

**Overnight Visits:** During the regular academic year, prospective applicants may spend an evening in a residence hall with a student host.

**Video:** Available, fee charged.

## CAMPUS FACILITIES

**Of Special Interest:** Todd Wehr Library.

## LOCAL ATTRACTIONS

Packer Hall of Fame, Railroad Museum.

# UNIVERSITY OF WISCONSIN–LA CROSSE
## La Crosse, Wisconsin

**Contact:** Admissions Office, 115 Main Hall 1725 State Street, La Crosse, WI 54601. *Phone:* 608-785-8939. *Fax:* 608-785-6695. *E-mail:* admissions@uwlax.edu *Web site:* http://www.uwlax.edu/ *Visit location:* Admissions Office, 115 Main Hall, 1725 State Street.

### QUICK FACTS

Enrollment: 8,778; UG: 8,163. Entrance: moderately difficult. SAT>500: N/R; ACT>18: 99%. Resident tuition and fees: $2859. Nonresident tuition and fees: $8801. Room and board: $3060. Application deadline: rolling.

### GENERAL

State-supported, comprehensive, coed. Part of University of Wisconsin System. Awards associate, bachelor's, and master's degrees. Founded 1909. Setting: 119-acre suburban campus. Undergraduate faculty: 469 (354 full-time, 115 part-time); student-faculty ratio is 19:1. Most popular recent majors: biology, business administration, elementary education.

### CAMPUS VISITS

**College Calendar 1998–99:** *Regular classes:* Sept. 8–Dec. 16; Jan. 25–May 11. *Breaks:* Nov. 26–29; Mar. 13–21; Apr. 2–5. *Final exams:* Dec. 17–22; May 12–18. *Special campus days:* Campus Close-Up programs–visit day for prospective students and their parents, Oct. 16, Oct. 29, Nov. 13, Feb. 12, Oct. 30, Apr. 23; Commencement, Dec. 20, May 15; Family Weekend, Nov. 6–8; Homecoming, Oct. 16–18.

### VISIT OPPORTUNITIES

| | Appointments? | Who? |
|---|---|---|
| **Campus Tour** | recommended | applicants and parents |
| **Information Session** | required | |
| **Admission Interview** | required | applicants and parents |

**Information Sessions:** Select M–F during academic yea, Jul. and Aug.; call for schedule; 60 minutes.
**Interviews:** M–F; 45 minutes.
**Campus Tours:** Conducted by students. M–F at 11:00 am, 2:00 pm; during summer at 11:00 am; 60 minutes.

### CAMPUS FACILITIES
**Science:** Cowley Hall.
**Arts:** Center for the Arts.
**Athletic:** Mitchell Hall, Recreational Eagle Center.
**Of Special Interest:** Cartwright Center (Student Union), Residence Halls.

### LOCAL ATTRACTIONS
Grandad's Bluff, Riverside Park.

# UNIVERSITY OF WISCONSIN–RIVER FALLS
## River Falls, Wisconsin

**Contact:** Admissions Office, 410 South Third Street, 112 South Hall, River Falls, WI 54022. *Phone:* 715-425-3500. *Fax:* 715-425-0676. *E-mail:* admit@uwrf.edu *Web site:* http://www.uwrf.edu/ *Visit location:* Admissions Office, South Hall Room 112, 410 South Third Street.

### QUICK FACTS

Enrollment: 5,441; UG: 5,037. Entrance: moderately difficult. SAT>500: N/R; ACT>18: 97%. Resident tuition and fees: $2750. Nonresident tuition and fees: $8692. Room and board: $3036. Application deadline: 1/1.

### GENERAL

State-supported, comprehensive, coed. Part of University of Wisconsin System. Awards bachelor's and master's degrees. Founded 1874. Setting: 225-acre suburban campus with easy access to Minneapolis–St. Paul. Undergraduate faculty: 318 (305 full-time, 13 part-time); student-faculty ratio is 18:1. Most popular recent majors: business administration, animal sciences, elementary education.

### CAMPUS VISITS

**College Calendar 1998–99:** *Regular classes:* Sept. 2–Dec. 15; Jan. 19–May 14. *Breaks:* Dec. 22–Jan. 19; Mar. 27–Apr. 5. *Final exams:* Dec. 16–22; May 17–21. *Special campus days:* Commencement, Dec. 19, May 22; Thanksgiving, Nov. 26–29.

### VISIT OPPORTUNITIES

| | Appointments? | Who? |
|---|---|---|
| **Campus Tour** | required | applicants and parents |
| **Information Session** | required | |

VISIT OPPORTUNITIES— *continued*

| | Appointments? | Who? |
|---|---|---|
| Admission Interview | required | applicants and parents |
| Faculty Meeting | required | applicants and parents |

**Information Sessions:** M–F at 11:00 am, 1:00 pm; 45 minutes.

**Interviews:** M–F; 30 minutes.

**Campus Tours:** Conducted by students. M–F, select Sat. at 10:00 am, 12:00 pm, 2:00 pm; times change during College Visit Days scheduled on select Fri.; 60 minutes.

## CAMPUS FACILITIES

**Of Special Interest:** Davee Library.

# UNIVERSITY OF WISCONSIN–STEVENS POINT

## Stevens Point, Wisconsin

**Contact:** Office of Admissions, 102 Student Services Building, Stevens Point, WI 54481. *Phone:* 715-346-2441. *Fax:* 715-346-2558. *E-mail:* admiss@uwsp.edu *Web site:* http://www.uwsp.edu/ *Visit location:* Admissions Officer, Student Services Building, 1108 Fremont Street.

## QUICK FACTS

Enrollment: 8,446; UG: 8,122. Entrance: moderately difficult. SAT>500: N/App; ACT>18: 96%. Resident tuition and fees: $2790. Nonresident tuition and fees: $8732. Room and board: $3188. Application deadline: rolling.

## GENERAL

State-supported, comprehensive, coed. Part of University of Wisconsin System. Awards associate, bachelor's, and master's degrees. Founded 1894. Setting: 335-acre small-town campus. Undergraduate faculty: 435 (376 full-time, 59 part-time); student-faculty ratio is 19:1. Most popular recent majors: biology, elementary education, business administration.

## CAMPUS VISITS

**College Calendar 1998–99:** *Regular classes:* Sept. 2–Dec. 15; Jan. 19–May 7. *Breaks:* Nov. 25–29; Mar. 13–21. *Final exams:* Dec. 17–22; May 10–14. *Admis-*

*sion office closed:* Nov. 27, Dec. 24, Dec. 31, Jan. 18, May 31, July 5. *Special campus days:* Commencement, Dec. 20, May 16; Homecoming, Oct. 3; Winterim Session, Jan. 2–15.

## VISIT OPPORTUNITIES

| | Appointments? | Who? |
|---|---|---|
| Campus Tour | recommended | open to all |
| Information Session | recommended | open to all |
| Classroom Visit | required | open to all |
| Faculty Meeting | recommended | open to all |

**Information Sessions:** M–F at 10:30 am, 1:30 pm; Campus Preview Days–Oct. 10 and Nov. 7; Pointer Perspective Days–Oct. 16, Oct. 29, Oct. 30, Apr. 5, Apr. 30; call for summer schedule; 30 minutes.

**Campus Tours:** Conducted by students. M–F at 11:00 am, 2:00 pm; available with Campus Preview and Pointer Perspective programs; call for summer schedule; 75 minutes.

**Class Visits:** Prospective students may attend a class in their area of interest, classroom visits require departmental approval.

## CAMPUS FACILITIES

**Science:** College of Natural Resources—mosaic mural and nature displays, Museum of Natural History; Appointment Required: Planetarium and Observatory.

**Arts:** Carlsten Art Gallery.

**Athletic:** Health Enhancement Center, Cardio Fitness Center.

**Of Special Interest:** Schmeeckle Nature Reserve, Wisconsin Conservation Hall of Fame.

# UNIVERSITY OF WISCONSIN–SUPERIOR

## Superior, Wisconsin

**Contact:** Ms. Lorraine Washa, Program Assistant, 1800 Grand Avenue, Superior, WI 54880. *Phone:* 715-394-8230. *Fax:* 715-394-8407. *Web site:* http://www.uwsuper.edu/ *Visit location:* Admission Office, Old Main, 1800 Grand Avenue.

## QUICK FACTS

Enrollment: 2,574; UG: 2,253. Entrance: moderately difficult. SAT>500: N/App; ACT>18: 100%. Resi-

*University of Wisconsin–Superior (continued)*

dent tuition and fees: $2652. Nonresident tuition and fees: $8600. Room and board: $3200. Application deadline: rolling.

## GENERAL

State-supported, comprehensive, coed. Part of University of Wisconsin System. Awards associate, bachelor's, and master's degrees. Founded 1893. Setting: 230-acre small-town campus. Undergraduate faculty: 160 (110 full-time, 50 part-time); student-faculty ratio is 12:1. Most popular recent majors: business administration, education, social work.

## CAMPUS VISITS

**College Calendar 1998–99:** *Regular classes:* Sept. 2–Dec. 15; Jan. 22–May 15. *Breaks:* Nov. 26–30; Dec. 16–Jan. 21. *Final exams:* Dec. 16–22; May 10–15.

## VISIT OPPORTUNITIES

| | Appointments? | Who? |
|---|---|---|
| **Campus Tour** | recommended, not required | open to all |
| **Information Session** | recommended, not required | open to all |

## VISIT OPPORTUNITIES—*continued*

| | Appointments? | Who? |
|---|---|---|
| **Admission Interview** | required | open to all |
| **Classroom Visit** | required | open to all |
| **Faculty Meeting** | required | open to all |
| **Overnight Visit** | required | open to all |

**Information Sessions:** Call for available schedule; 60 minutes.

**Interviews:** M–F; Sat. by appointment; 60 minutes.

**Campus Tours:** Conducted by students and admission reps. M–F 9:00 am–3:00 pm; Sat. by appointments; 60 minutes.

**Class Visits:** Prospective students may attend a class in their area of interest, classroom visits are determined by the visit schedule.

**Overnight Visits:** During the regular academic year, prospective applicants may spend an evening in a residence hall.

**Video:** Free on request.

## CAMPUS FACILITIES
**Of Special Interest:** Jim Dan Hill Library.

# Index of Colleges and Universities

This index provides reference to profiles by institution name. The schools are listed in alphabetical order, with the page number of the school profile appearing to the right of the school name.

# Index of Colleges and Universities

# Index of Colleges and Universities

# NOTES

# NOTES

# NOTES

# NOTES

# NOTES

# GETTING INTO COLLEGE ISN'T AS HARD AS YOU THINK— AS LONG AS YOU THINK PETERSON'S!

## Get on line at petersons.com for a jump start on your college search.

- Search our college database
- Get financial aid tips
- Browse our bookstore

**And when you're ready to apply, you're ready for ApplyToCollege.com!**

ApplyToCollege.com is our **free** online college application service that lets you apply to *more colleges than anyone else on the Internet!*

**Why ApplyToCollege.com?**
- Fill out one application for nearly 1,000 colleges!
- Talk with admission deans!
- Keep track of your applications!
- IT'S FREE!

Peterson's is on your side with everything you need to get ready for college. And it's all just a mouse click away!

## P PETERSON'S
### Princeton, New Jersey
### www.petersons.com

## 1-800-338-3282

Wait! There's more!➡

# WHEN YOU THINK COLLEGE, THINK PETERSON'S!

### Guide to Four-Year Colleges 1999
The bestselling guide to over 2,000 colleges and universities in the U.S., Canada, and throughout the world.
ISBN 1-56079-987-0, with CD, $24.95 pb/$34.95 CAN/£17.99 UK, 29th ed., 1998

### Scholarships, Grants & Prizes 1999
Find all of the non-institutional sources of financial aid—over 2.5 billion in private aid.
ISBN 0-7689-0034-4, with CD, $26.95 pb/$37.95 CAN/£18.99 UK, 4th ed., 1998

### College Money Handbook 1999
Explore all of the college, state, and federal sources of financial aid to support your education through programs at over 1,700 colleges and universities.
ISBN 0-7689-0051-4, with CD, $26.95 pb/$37.95 CAN/£20.00 UK, 16th ed., 1998

### The Ultimate College Survival Guide
Get straight talk from college students on everything about college life.
ISBN 0-7689-0010-7, $14.95 pb/$20.95 CAN/£12.99 UK, 2nd ed., 1998

### SAT* Success 1999
Prepare to do your best on the SAT with no gimmicks!
ISBN 0-7689-0014-X, with CD, $14.95 pb/$20.95 CAN/£12.99 UK, 5th ed., 1998

*SAT is a registered trademark of the College Entrance Examination Board, which was not involved in the production of, and does not endorse, this book.

## At fine bookstores near you.

## To order: Call 800-338-3282
## Or fax: 609-243-9150.

## On line: http://www.petersons.com/ bookstore.

**PETERSON'S**
Princeton, New Jersey
www.petersons.com

← There's more in store!